Game Programming All in One

Bruno Miguel Teixeira de Sousa

PREMIER PRESS
GAME DEVELOPMENT

Premier Press

Publisher: Stacy L. Hiquet
Marketing Manager: Heather Buzzingham
Managing Editor: Sandy Doell
Acquisitions Editor: Mitzi Foster
Series Editor: André LaMothe
Project Editor: Heather Talbot
Technical Reviewer: André LaMothe
Copy Editor: Jenny Davidson
Interior Layout: Marian Hartsough
Cover Design: Mike Tanamachi
CD-ROM Producer: Keith Davenport
Indexer: Kelly Talbot
Proofreaders: Anne Owen, Fran Blauw, Linda Seifert

ISBN: 1-931841-23-3
Library of Congress Catalog Card Number: 2001096486
Printed in the United States of America

02 03 04 05 06 RI 10 9 8 7 6 5 4 3 2 1

De todas as coisas que quero,
és a única coisa que eu preciso.

Para ti, Ana.

Acknowledgments

Now is the time I should go up to the stage, get the Oscar, and recite a book-length script of all the people that helped make this book. However, the thank you would probably be as big as this book, so to prevent from forgetting anyone, I would like to thank everyone that directly or indirectly made this book possible.

On the technical side, I would like to thank the people at Premier Press for giving me the opportunity to write this book. I would also like to thank my editors, Emi Smith, Mitzi Foster, Heather Talbot, and Jenny Davidson for all their patience and all they had to put up with. (Yes, the usual delays and the incessant questions.) Please remember that what you are reading is not a book that I wrote myself, but one that comprises the work of many talented people who are usually forgotten.

I would also like to thank André LaMothe for reviewing the book.

On the personal side, I would like to thank my mom and dad for their support and love during my life, and of course, for paying those enormous Internet bills when I was still learning game programming.

I would also like to thank all of my friends and relatives for their support not only with the book, but also with my life. I would like to send a special thanks to Diana for always being there for me whenever I needed her.

Last, and probably most important, I would like to thank Ana for her love, support, patience, and just about everything. I love you from the bottom of my heart.

About the Author

Bruno Miguel Teixeira de Sousa began programming at age 11. Although he began his programming career at age 15 as a database programmer in Visual Basic, he never lost his passion for game development. Two years later, he began a full-time career performing general game programming for a UK-based company. He has been using C++ for more than 4 years and remains an avid game hobbyist.

Ronald Penton wrote Chapter 17. Ron started programming on his Tandy 1000TL way back in 1989, when he became interested in making games, rather than just playing them. Ever since then, he has been on a never-ending quest to learn more about computers and become more efficient at programming them. He started school at the Rochester Institute of Technology in 1998, and is currently finishing his bachelor's degree in computer science at The University of Buffalo.

Contents at a Glance

Introduction xxxvi

Part One
C++ Programming 1

Chapter 1 Introduction to C++ Programming 3

Chapter 2 Variables and Operators 25

Chapter 3 Functions and Program Flow 51

Chapter 4 Multiple Files and the Preprocessor 95

Chapter 5 Arrays, Pointers, and Strings 107

Chapter 6 Classes 153

Chapter 7 Developing Monster 197

Chapter 8 Streams 245

Chapter 9 Basic Software Architecture 279

Part Two
Windows Programming 297

Chapter 10 Designing Your Game Library: Mirus 299

Chapter 11 Beginning Windows Programming 317

Chapter 12 Introduction to DirectX 357

Chapter 13 DirectX Graphics 369

Chapter 14 DirectInput 521

Chapter 15 DirectSound 567

Part Three
Hardcore Game Programming 595

Chapter 16 Introduction to Game Design 597

Chapter 17 Data Structures and Algorithms 609

Chapter 18 The Mathematical Side of Games . . . 661

Chapter 19 Introduction to Artificial Intelligence 697

Chapter 20 Introduction to Physics Modeling . . . 723

Chapter 21 Building Breaking Through 791

Chapter 22 Publishing Your Game 851

Part Four
Appendixes 863

Appendix A What's on the CD-ROM 865

Appendix B Debugging Using Microsoft Visual C++ 870

Appendix C Binary, Hexadecimal, and Decimal System. 874

Appendix D A C Primer 877

Appendix E Answers to the Exercises 885

Appendix F C++ Keywords 893

Appendix G Useful Tables 895

Appendix H More Resources 902

Index 907

Contents

Letter from the Series Editor xxxiv

Introduction xxxvi

Part One
C++ Programming. 1

Chapter 1
Introduction to C++ Programming . . . 3

Why Use C++? 4
Setting Up Visual C++ 5
Creating a Workspace 5
Creating Projects. 6
Creating and Adding Files 8
Your First Program: "Hello all you happy people" 9
Structure of a C++ Program 12
Program Design Language 12
Program Source and Compiling 14
Objects and Linking 14
Executable 15
Commenting 16
Catching Errors 17
Warnings 20
Summary 21
Questions and Answers 21
Exercises. 23

Chapter 2
Variables and Operators 25

Variables and Memory 26
What Type of Variables Are There? 27
Using Variables in Your Programs 30
Declaring a Variable 30
Using Variables 31
Initializing Variables 32
Variable Modifiers 33
Const 33
Register 35
Variable Naming 36
Redefining Types 36
What Is an Operator? 37
Assignment Operator 37
Mathematical Operators 37
Unary Operators 38
Binary Operators 39
Compound Assignment Operators 41
Bitwise Shift Operators 41
Relational Operators 42
Conditional Operator 43
Logical Operators 44
Operator Precedence 45
Summary 47
Questions and Answers 48
Exercises 48

Chapter 3 Functions and Program Flow 51

Functions: What Are They and What Are They Used For? 52

Creating and Using Functions 54

Declaring the Prototype 55

Return Type 55

Name 55

Parameters 56

Function Body 56

Default Parameters 58

Variable Scope 60

Locals 61

Global 61

Static 62

Recursion 64

Things to Remember When Using Functions 66

Program Flow 66

Code Blocks and Statements 66

if, else if, else Statements 67

if 67

else 70

while, do ... while, and for Loops 70

while 70

do ... while 72

for 73

Breaking and Continuing 75

break 75

continue 76

Switching to switch 77

Randomizing 80

First Game: "Craps" 83

Objective 83

Rules 84

Design . . . 84
Implementation . . . 85
Summary . . . **92**
Questions and Answers . . . **93**
Exercises . . . **93**

Chapter 4
Multiple Files and the Preprocessor . . . 95

Differences between Source and Header Files . . . **96**
Handling Multiple Files . . . **97**
What Is the Preprocessor? . . . **99**
Avoiding Multiple Includes . . . **101**
Using #pragma . . . 101
Using #ifdef, #define, and #endif . . . 102
Macros . . . **104**
Other Preprocessor Directives . . . **104**
Summary . . . **106**
Exercises . . . **106**

Chapter 5
Arrays, Pointers, and Strings . . . 107

What Is an Array? . . . 108
Declaring and Using an Array . . . **109**
Declaration . . . 109
Using . . . 109
Initializing an Array . . . 112
Multi-Dimensional Arrays . . . **112**
Pointers to What? . . . **116**
Pointers and Variables . . . **117**
Declaring and Initializing . . . 117
Using Pointers . . . 117

Pointers and Arrays **119**
Relation of Pointers to Arrays 119
Passing Arrays to Functions 120
Declaring and Allocating Memory to a Pointer **122**
Allocating the Memory 123
Freeing the Memory 123
Pointer Operators **126**
Manipulating Memory **129**
memcpy 129
memset 130
Strings **131**
Strings and Arrays 131
Using Strings 132
Strings and Arrays 132
String Allocation at Compilation 132
Input and Output 132
String Operations 133
strcpy 133
strncpy 134
strlen 135
strcat 136
strncat 138
strcmp 138
strncmp 140
strchr 140
strstr 142
atoi 143
atof 145
atol 145
sprintf 145
strftime 147
Summary **150**
Questions and Answers **151**
Exercises **151**

Chapter 6 Classes 153

What Is a Class? **154**

New Types 155

Building Classes **155**

Design 155

Definition 156

Implementation 157

Using Classes **158**

Private, Protected, and Public Members **158**

private 159

public 159

protected 159

What Kind of Access Is Right? 160

Constructors and the Destructor **161**

Default Constructor 161

General Constructors 162

Copy Constructor and References 162

Destructor 163

Operator Overloading **164**

Putting It All Together—The String Class **166**

Basics of Inheritance and Polymorphism **172**

Inheritance 172

Deriving from a Class 173

Virtual Methods 174

Polymorphism 178

Casting 180

Enumerations **182**

Unions **183**

Static Members **185**

Useful Techniques Using Classes **186**

A Singleton Class 186

An Object Factory 190

Summary 195
Questions and Answers 195
Exercises 196

Chapter 7
Developing Monster 197

ConLib 198
Design 199
Implementation 202
Building Monster 215
Objective 215
Rules 215
Design 216
Game Description 216
Thinking in Classes 216
Implementation 221
Summary 244

Chapter 8
Streams 245

What Is a Stream? 246
Binary and Text Streams 246
Input and Output 247
istream 247
get 248
getline 249
ignore 250
Extraction Operator (>>) 251
ostream 251
put 251
flush 252
Insertion Operator (<<) 252

File Streams **253**
Opening and Closing Streams 253
open 254
close 255
is_open 256
Text 259
Binary 264
write 264
read 267
seekg 268
seekp 269
tellg 269
tellp 269
Modifying Monster to Save and Load Games **270**
Summary **277**
Questions and Answers **278**
Exercises **278**

Chapter 9
Basic Software Architecture . . . 279

The Importance of Software Design **280**
Design Approaches **281**
Top Down 281
Bottom Up 282
Top Down Versus Bottom Up 282
Some Basic Techniques **283**
Example 1: Assignment Instead of Equality Operator 283
Example 2: Statements Versus Blocks 284
Example 3: Macros Versus Inline Functions 284
Example 4: Private Versus Public, the First Case 285
Example 5: Private Versus Public, the Second Case 287

Modules and Multiple Files 288
Creating Modules with C++ 288
Why Make Something a Module? 288
Naming Conventions 289
Function Naming 289
Variable Names 290
Identification 290
Where Common Sense Beats Design 292
The Design Used in This Book 292
Summary 293
Questions and Answers 294
Exercises 295

Part Two Windows Programming 297

Chapter 10 Designing Your Game Library: Mirus 299

General Description 300
Mirus Components 301
Helper Component 301
Window Component 302
Graphics Component 302
mrScreen 303
mrRGBAImage 303
mrSurface 304
mrTexture 304
mrTemplateSet 304
mrAnimation 305
mrABO 305

Sound Component 306
mrSoundPlayer 306
mrCDPlayer 306
Input Component 307
mrKeyboard 307
mrMouse 307
mrJoystick 308
Building the Help Component 308
Declaring the Types 308
mrTimer 309
How to Create the Error File 315
How to Use Mirus 316
Summary 316
Questions and Answers 316

Chapter 11
Beginning Windows Programming . . 317

History of Windows 318
Introduction to Windows Programming 319
Windows 319
Multitasking 321
Windows Has Its Own API 322
Message Queues 322
Visual C++ and Windows Applications 322
Building the Windows Application 323
WinMain Versus Main 326
Creating the Window 328
The Window Class 328
Creating the Window 332
The Message Loop 334
The Message Handler 335

Creating a Real-Time Message Loop 336
Making a Reusable Window Class 342
Using the Mirus Window Framework 350
Some Common Window Functions 351
SetPosition 351
GetPosition 352
SetSize 354
GetSize 354
Show 355
Summary 355
Questions and Answers 355
Exercises 356

Chapter 12 Introduction to DirectX 357

What Is DirectX? 358
Brief History of DirectX 359
Why Use DirectX? 360
DirectX Components 361
How Does DirectX Work? 362
Hardware Abstraction Layer 362
The Component Object Model 363
Virtual Tables 365
COM and DirectX 365
How to Use DirectX with Visual C++ 366
Summary 367
Questions and Answers 367
Exercises 368

Chapter 13 DirectX Graphics 369

Interfaces You Will Be Using 370
Using Direct3D: The Basics 372
Surfaces, Buffers, and Swap Chains 387
Surfaces 387
Buffers 388
Swap Chains 388
Rendering Surfaces 389
Vertices, Polygons, and Textures 397
Vertices and Polygons 397
Textures 398
Texture Coordinates 399
From the Third Dimension to the Second 401
Rendering in 2D 401
Windows Bitmaps 411
Bitmap Structure 411
Loading a Bitmap 413
Full Screen and Other Bit Modes 414
Color Theory and Color Keying 416
Color Theory 416
Color Keying 419
Targa Files 420
Structure of a Targa File 420
Loading a Targa File 421
Animation and Template Sets 422
Animation 422
Template Sets 423
Collision Detection 424
Bounding Volumes 424
Bounding Circles 425
Bounding Rectangles 426

2D Image Manipulation **428**
Translation 428
Scaling 429
Rotation 430
2D Primitives Revealed **433**
Lines 433
Rectangles and Other Polygons 437
Circles 438
Developing Mirus **438**
mrScreen 439
mrRGBAImage 458
mrSurface 472
mrTexture 480
mrTemplateSet 488
mrAnimation 493
mrABO 501
Summary **519**
Questions and Answers **519**
Exercises **520**

Chapter 14 DirectInput **521**

Introduction to DirectInput **522**
Unbuffered Data 523
Buffered Data 523
mrInputManager **524**
mrKeyboard **527**
mrMouse **541**
mrJoystick **554**
Summary **565**
Questions and Answers **566**
Exercises **566**

Chapter 15
DirectSound 567

Sound Theory 568
DirectSound Basics 569
mrSoundPlayer 571
mrSound 575
Media Control Interface 586
mrCDPlayer 587
Summary 593
Questions and Answers 593
Exercises 594

Part Three
Hardcore Game Programming 595

Chapter 16
Introduction to Game Design 597

What Is Game Design? 598
The Dreadful Design Document 599
Why the "It's in My Head" Technique Isn't Good 600
The Two Types of Designs 600
Mini Design 601
Complete Design 601
A Fill In Design Document Template 602
General Overview 602
Target System and Requirements 602
Story 602
Theme: Graphics and Sound 603
Menus 603
Playing a Game 603
Characters and NPCs Description 603

Artificial Intelligence Overview 603
Conclusion 603
A Sample Game Design: Space Invaders. 604
General Overview 604
Target System and Requirements 604
Story 605
Theme: Graphics and Sound 605
Menus 605
Start New Game 605
Continue Previously Saved Game 605
See Table of High Scores 605
Options 606
Exit 606
Playing a Game 606
Characters and NPCs Description 606
Normal Ships 607
Bonus Ships 607
Artificial Intelligence Overview 607
Conclusion 607
Summary 607
Questions and Answers 608
Exercises 608

Chapter 17 Data Structures and Algorithms 609

The Importance of the Correct Data Structures and Algorithms 610
Lists 612
Basic Structure 613
Iterators 615
Inserting into a List 618
Appending Items to a List 619

Deleting a Node from a List 620
Doubly Linked Lists 621
Modifying the Algorithms for Doubly Linked Lists 622
Circular Lists 622
Advantages of Lists 623
Disadvantages of Lists 623
Trees. 624
General Trees 625
Constructing a General Tree 629
Traversing a General Tree 630
General Tree Destructor 632
Uses of General Trees 632
Binary Search Trees 633
A Primer on Binary Trees 633
What Is a Binary Search Tree? 634
Searching a Binary Search Tree. 635
Inserting into a Binary Search Tree 637
Removing a Value from a Binary Search Tree 638
Efficiency Considerations. 646
Uses of Binary Search Trees. 647
Sorting Data. 648
Bubble Sort 648
Swap Counter Optimization 649
Declining Inner Iterations 650
Combining the Optimizations 650
The Quick Sort 651
Another Optimization 653
Source Listing 653
Comparisons of the Sorts 655
Compression 656
RLE Compression 657
RLE Compression Code 658

Summary **659**
Questions and Answers **659**
Exercises **660**

Chapter 18 The Mathematical Side of Games

661

Trigonometry **662**
Visual Representation and Laws 662
Angle Relations 666
Vectors **667**
Addition and Subtraction 671
Scalar Multiplication and Division 673
Length 674
Normalization 674
Perpendicular Operation 675
Dot Product 676
Perp-dot Product 677
Matrices **678**
Addition and Subtraction 681
Scalar and Multiplication and Division 682
Special Matrices 684
Transpose 685
Matrix Concatenation 686
Vector Transformation 688
Probability **688**
Sets 689
Union 689
Intersection 690

Functions 691
Integration and Differentiation 692
Differentiation 693
Summary 694
Questions and Answers 694
Exercises 695

Chapter 19 Introduction to Artificial Intelligence 697

The Various Fields of Artificial Intelligence 698
Expert Systems 698
Fuzzy Logic 701
Genetic Algorithms 703
Neural Networks 706
Deterministic Algorithms 707
Random Motion 707
Tracking 709
Patterns 710
Finite State Machines 713
Fuzzy Logic 715
Fuzzy Logic Basics 715
Fuzzy Matrices 717
A Simple Method for Memory 719
Artificial Intelligence and Games 720
Summary 720
Questions and Answers 721
Exercises 721

Chapter 20 Introduction to Physics Modeling 723

Introduction to Physics 724
Building a Physics Engine 725
Why Make a Physics Engine? 725
Designing the Engine 725
mrEntity 726
Basic Physics Concepts 728
Mass 728
Time 729
Position 729
Velocity 731
Linear Velocity 731
Angular Velocity 732
Acceleration 732
Linear Acceleration 733
Angular Acceleration 733
Center of Mass 734
Forces 735
Linear Force 736
Torque 739
The Resulted Force 740
Gravitational Interaction 741
Law of Universal Gravitation 742
Gravity on Earth and Other Planets 743
Simulating Projectiles 745
Friction 748
Friction Concept 748
Decomposing Friction 749
The Normal Force 749

Static Friction 751
Kinetic Friction 752
Friction on a Sloped Surface 752
The Computer Method 753
Handling Collisions 755
Maintaining the Momentum 755
Conservation of Momentum 755
The Impulse Method 756
Simulating 761
Getting the Step 763
Particle Systems. 770
Particle Systems 101 770
Designing a Particle System 770
Particle Systems' Data Structures 770
Making It Work 775
Particle Demo 784
Summary 788
Questions and Answers 788
Exercises. 789

Chapter 21 Building Breaking Through 791

Designing Breaking Through 792
General Overview 792
Target System and Requirements 792
Story 793
Rules 793
Theme: Graphics 794
Menus 795
Playing a Game 796

Code Design 798
btBlock 798
btPaddle 798
btBall 798
btGame 799
BreakThroughWindow 799
Building Breaking Through 799
btBlock 800
btPaddle 804
btBall 809
btGame 817
BreakThroughWindow 848
Conclusion 850

Chapter 22
Publishing Your Game 851

Is Your Game Worth Publishing? 852
Whose Door to Knock On 853
Learn to Knock Correctly 854
Contracts 854
Non-disclosure Agreement 855
The Actual Publishing Contract 856
Milestones 856
Bug Report 856
Release Day 857
No Publisher, Now What? 857
Interviews 857
Niels Bauer: Niels Bauer Software Design 857
André LaMothe: Xtreme Games LLC 859
Summary 861
References 861
Conclusion 862

Part Four Appendixes 863

Appendix A What's on the CD-ROM 865

Source 867
Microsoft DirectX 8.0 SDK 867
Programs 867
Jasc Paint Shop Pro 7. 867
Syntrillium Cool Edit 2000. 868
Caligari TrueSpace 5. 868
Games 868
Gemdrop. 868
Smiley 869
Smugglers 2 869

Appendix B Debugging Using Microsoft Visual C++ 870

Breakpoints and Controlling Execution. 871
Breakpoints 871
Controlling the Execution 872
Modifying Variables During Runtime 872
Watching Variables. 873

Appendix C Binary, Hexadecimal, and Decimal System. 874

Binary. 875
Hexadecimal 875
Decimal 876

Appendix D
A C Primer 877
Standard Input and Output 878
File Input and Output 879
Structures: Say Bye-Bye to Classes 882
Dynamic Memory 882

Appendix E
Answers to the Exercises 885
Chapter 1 886
Chapter 2 886
Chapter 3 887
Chapter 4 887
Chapter 5 887
Chapter 6 888
Chapter 7 888
Chapter 8 888
Chapter 9 888
Chapter 10 889
Chapter 11 889
Chapter 12 889
Chapter 13 889
Chapter 14 889
Chapter 15 890
Chapter 16 890
Chapter 17 890
Chapter 18 891
Chapter 19 891
Chapter 20 891

Appendix F
C++ Keywords 893

Appendix G
Useful Tables 895

ASCII Table. 896

Integral Table 900

Derivatives Table 901

Inertia Equations Table 901

Appendix H
More Resources 902

Game Development and Programming. 903

News, Reviews, and Download Sites 904

Engines. 904

Independent Game Developers 904

Industry 905

Computer Humor 905

Books 906

Index 907

Letter from the Series Editor

Game programming has become serious business! With the introduction of the Microsoft Xbox, Sony PlayStation II, Nintendo GameCube, and Nintendo Game Boy Advance, we see that there is no slowing down of the gaming market in sight. Moreover, programming games on the PC and on consoles is becoming more and more a unified approach. The Xbox is nothing more than a really, really, really, ***REALLY***, fast PC! Hence, as a newbie game programmer interested in learning either PC or console game programming, a good place to start is the PC and move on from there. *Game Programming All in One* is an ambitious lead into game programming.

As the series editor, what I wanted was a book that started from ground zero and taught C++, Algorithms, Data Structures, Game Programming, and DirectX, culminating in something simple like an arcade or action game—that's the theme of this book. Granted it's literally impossible to cover all those topics in fewer than 3,000–5,000 pages in complete fashion, but we think that *Game Programming All in One* has definitely come close to being an all-in-one guide that a complete beginner can pick up to learn game programming.

So if you're a beginner interested in becoming a game programmer, or you just want to know what it's about but don't want to spend hundreds of dollars on books covering all the specific game programming topics then this is a great book for you to start with. Although having programming experience is a big plus, this book assumes you have none and teaches C++ along with Windows programming before getting into the game programming material. Once there, you're not going to learn 3D graphics and how to make **Quake** or **HALO**, but you will learn about the fundamental processes and techniques to create a solid 2D game; from there it's up to you if you want to keep on learning and move to ISOmetric 3D games, Multiplayer Games, or full 3D Games—the choice is yours, but with *Game Programming All in One* you will have a solid foundation to start from.

Additionally, the coding habits you will learn in this book are excellent. The author Bruno Sousa is one of the best coders I have seen; his code is clean, functional, and very object-oriented, thus you will begin learning good habits from day 1 rather than bad ones which can kill you when creating games that easily near the 1 million line mark these days.

So without further ado, get your compiler set up, open this book wide, and take your time reading and exploring for I really do envy the journey that you're about to go on. Learning game programming was probably one of the most interesting and exciting times of my life, and I can only expect you will have just as much fun or more—since when I learned I was getting excited with 4 colors and 8 × 8 bitmaps!!!

Sincerely,

André LaMothe
Series Editor
CEO@xgames3d.com

Introduction

I still remember my first trip to the arcades. I was four years old, and my father took me to a local fair where I played a racing game. I instantly fell in love with games. I wanted to play them; I wanted to design them.

At the age of eight I started programming my old ZX Spectrum with 64KB of memory and an old tape player, and I had fun like I never had before.

It wasn't until the age of 13 that I seriously started programming games. Reading anything I could get my hands on about programming, I managed to do some VGA (if you are young, you probably don't know what VGA is) games in Pascal and evolved from there.

When I first logged on to the Internet, in 1995, if I'm not mistaken, I found a whole new world. Among other things, it housed a collection of sites about game programming with enough information to last a lifetime. I was amazed.

Today, I do remote programming from Portugal (when will someone put some bucks on the table and start a game company here?) and work on tools for programmers. I've also decided to go to college to pursue a Mathematics and Computer Science degree at the Universidade do Minho here in Portugal. I hope I can finish it.

This book is a collection of my own experiments during these last years. I hope it will help you get started as a game programmer. But don't finish this book and stop there; there are loads of other good books and sites you should read to continue your career. This book is just the tip of the iceberg.

I've created an Internet site for this book where I include errata, updated source code, and more information regarding this book. You can visit it at **http://gpaione.kyuumu.com**.

Also, don't hesitate to e-mail me (**bsousa@kyuumu.com**) if you have any questions about the book, the source code on the CD, or just general questions about game development. Of course, if you just finished your game and want someone to play it, don't forget to send me an e-mail so I can try it.

Also, if you want a live chat, you can probably find me in GameDev's IRC channel (**http://www.gamedev.net/**). Just ask for Akura.

What You Are Going to Learn

This is an ambitious book; it covers all the elements to get you started in developing your own games, including:

- The basics of C++ programming
- C++ techniques and practices
- Windows programming
- The DirectX 8.0 API
- Game programming techniques

And a little more . . .

How This Book Is Organized

This book is divided into four parts. Each relies on the preceding part to explain the concepts. If you already know C++ programming, you can just skim through the first part and move to Parts 2 and 3, but if you are a beginner, I suggest you read this book linearly, from start to finish.

Part 1 covers C++ programming. You will learn the basics and the most important aspects of C++ programming, such as text input and output, file manipulation, and pointers. You will also develop two simple text games.

Part 2 explains Windows programming and DirectX. It covers the basics to get your Windows application running and covers in detail the three main components of DirectX: DirectXGraphics, DirectSound, and DirectInput. In this part, you will build Mirus, the game library you will be using in this book.

In Part 3, you will see many game programming related fields, such as mathematics, physics, and artificial intelligence. You finish this part by building a breakout type of game.

Part 4 contains the appendixes, where you can find information about using the CD-ROM, the debugging application, the chapter exercises' answers, and some references you may want to check while you read the book.

Don't forget to check out the CD; it contains loads of cool tools and all the source code included in the book (which should save you a lot of time). You will need your own copy of Microsoft Visual C++ to compile the source code from the CD-ROM.

PART ONE

C++ Programming

1 Introduction to C++ Programming

2 Variables and Operators

3 Functions and Program Flow

4 Multiple Files and the Preprocessor

5 Arrays, Pointers, and Strings

6 Classes

7 Developing Monster

8 Streams

9 Basic Software Architecture

CHAPTER 1

Introduction to C++ Programming

Welcome. This is the first chapter, so I hope you have a big, tasty cup of coffee. Got it? Good, let's get on with it.

Learning how to efficiently set up and use Visual C++, knowing how C++ programs work, and being able to deal with errors and warnings will save you a lot of trouble later, so let's go over all those things now.

Some of the code in this chapter may sound a little confusing at first because you don't have any C++ base. This is natural since it is impossible to learn the C++ language in just one chapter. If you are having trouble grasping the concepts, don't worry, they will be explained in much more detail in the following chapters.

Why Use C++?

I've chosen C++ for this book for several reasons. C++ is a popular programming language that is easy to work with on big projects and is used to build independent components and more. Let's go over some of these advantages to prove this choice.

As you may have heard, C++ is an object-oriented programming language, but what does this mean? Object-oriented programming (or OOP) is a programming paradigm that has proved to be very successful. The idea behind it is to think of modules as objects, it lets you incorporate the attributes and methods of things into working objects. OOP and other programming paradigms to aid your code construction are described in Chapter 9.

C++ is a low-level language—it works at a very low, or near, level with the computer. The lower level a language is, the faster it will perform, but the more cryptic it will become. At this time, Assembly (do not confuse with Assembler, which is the Assembly compiler) is the lowest language available. There is also C (the predecessor to C++), which is a bit lower level than C++ but higher level than Assembly; however, it isn't as OOP-friendly as C++. Various other higher languages are available, such as Pascal, Delphi, Visual Basic, and so on.

C++ is similar to its predecessor. Apart from offering more capabilities than C, like classes and polymorphism, it is compatible with C, which means that a C++ compiler can compile existing C code without any problem. You can also use C and C++ code in the same program.

Setting Up Visual C++

Before digging your head into programming, you need to set up the programming environment, in your case Visual C++. Visual C++ is the most popular compiler used in game programming and therefore the choice for the book.

If you run Visual C++, your screen should look like Figure 1.1. To compile programs in Visual C++ you need to create a project and the source files.

Creating a Workspace

I presume you are reading this book comfortably sitting in a chair, in front of a desk probably with other books and papers scattered around and with a computer. That is your workspace. In development, the equivalent to that workspace is the Visual C++ workspace, which holds everything you work with. The books and papers are the projects, the pages your source files.

You will be using one workspace in each chapter that contains all the projects and files related to that workspace.

To create a workspace, go to the File menu and select New. Doing this will display a dialog box with various tabs. Select the Workspaces tab and specify the name of the workspace. You can change the default location for your workspace. It is good to

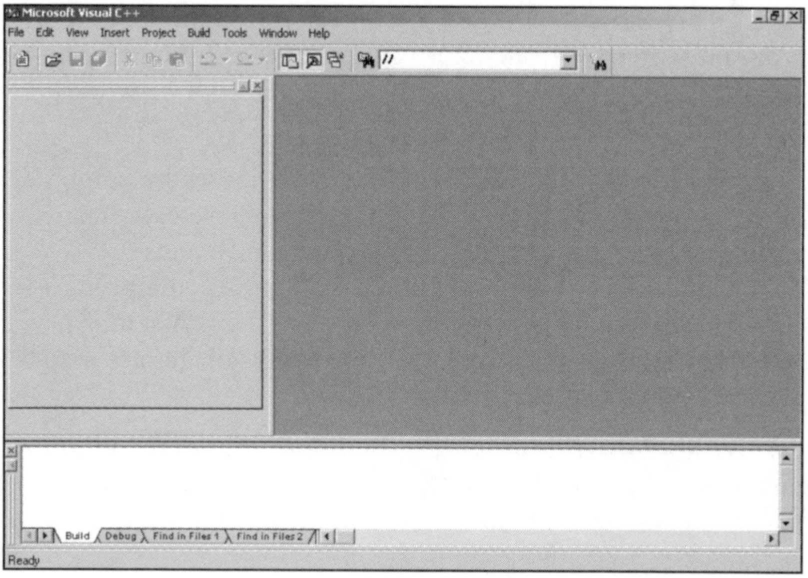

Figure 1.1

Microsoft Visual C++ appearance.

specify a base directory or hard drive for all your workspaces so that you can easily find them if you need to.

Create the workspace you can use later for your project. First, go to the File menu and select New. Now you need to name the workspace, go ahead and use what you prefer, but try to use a name that exemplifies what the workspace is for. I'll use `Chapter_01` for the workspace name since this workspace will contain all the projects of this chapter. The last thing you need to do is to set the base directory. You can use the default one or choose your own. Let's create the workspace in the root of drive C in the Book directory, to do this, just type `C:\Book`.

And that's it, you have the workspace ready for the project that you will create next.

Creating Projects

Visual C++ offers various types of projects, and during the course of the book you will use three of them, but for now you will use the Win32 Console Application project. A console application is a program that usually resembles the old DOS/UNIX text interface. This is the best application type in which to learn C++ because it doesn't need any type of window setup.

To create a Win32 Console Application, or any type of project, you need to click on the File menu and select New. A dialog box similar to the one shown in Figure 1.2 will appear.

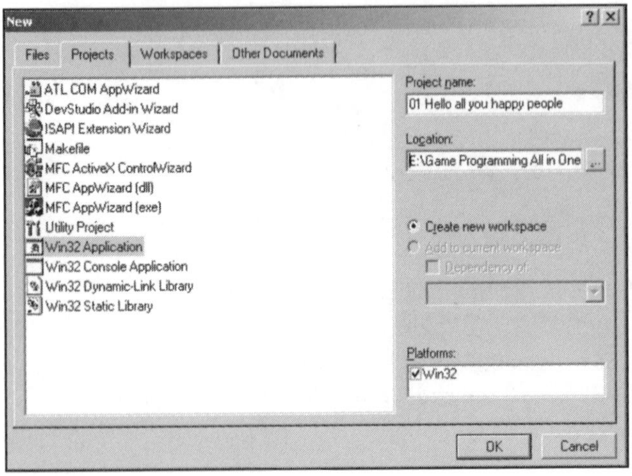

Figure 1.2

Creating a Win32 Console Application.

You need to select the Win32 Console Application type from the list of available project types. You can check Table 1.1 for a description of useful projects for game programming. After you have done this, you need to set up your project. Throughout the book, each project will be named with a program number and the description of the project, like `01 Hello all you happy people` for this project. You may see that there are a few other options in that dialog box: the directory selection and the workspace information. You can ignore the platform type because in Visual C++ you are only allowed to create Win32 applications. You can specify another directory for your project as you see fit, but let's leave it as it is since it will use the default workspace directory to create the project.

You are now ready to create the project. Click OK and you will see a new dialog named Win32 Console Application - Step 1 of 1. This dialog is where you set the

TABLE 1.1 Useful Visual C++ Project Types for Game Programming

Project Name	Description
MFC AppWizard (dll)	Creates a Microsoft Foundation Classes (MFC) dll.
MFC AppWizard (exe)	Creates a Microsoft Foundation Classes (MFC) executable. This project is extremely useful for tools.
Win32 Application	Creates a normal Win32 Application. This is the project type you will use later to develop Windows applications.
Win32 Console Application	Creates a DOS/UNIX-like application. You will use this project type to learn C++ programming.
Win32 Dynamic-Link Library	Creates a dynamic dll library. This project type is particularly useful when you want to create a collection of classes and functions that are included in the executable at runtime.
Win32 Static Library	Creates a static library. The same as a dynamic library but all the code is included at compile time.

initial attributes of the project. You will use an empty project for all the remaining projects you do. There are advantages to using some of the options given in this dialog but I leave that for you to find out.

The project is created and ready, what more do you need? Files. You need to create a source file in the project you just created.

Creating and Adding Files

Now that you have your project, you need to add new files to it. You can do this by selecting the menu Project, Add to Project, New. This will display a dialog similar to the one shown in Figure 1.3.

As you may have already figured out, you will be using a C++ source file from the available file types. There are two kinds of files you will be using during the course of the book—C++ source files and C++ header files. I will go over the differences between them later, for now let's use a C++ source file and specify its name; as with projects, you will use a terminology throughout the whole book to maintain some consistency. Source files will be identified by the program number and by the objective of the file with the file extension .cpp so that Visual C++ identifies the file as a valid C++ source file. Name your file `01 Main.cpp`, `01` from the program number, and `Main` because this is the main, and in this case, the only part of your program. As you progress, you will separate the functionality of your program in different files; for example, a part of the program that manages the game sound

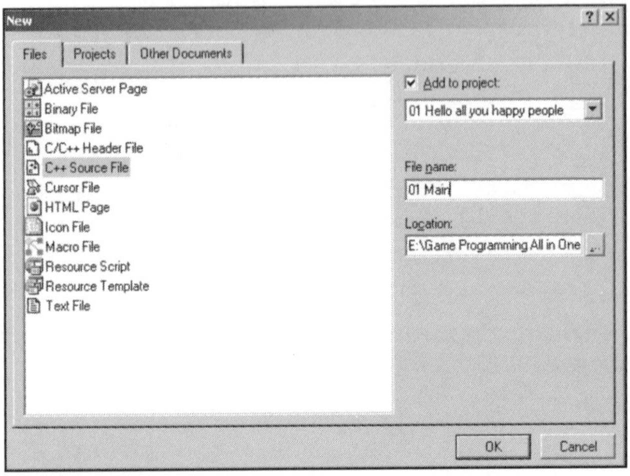

Figure 1.3

Creating a new source file inside a project.

system would probably be called `04 Sound.cpp`. More details on correct file naming are given in Chapter 9.

As you can see, you can also specify the location of the file like you could with the location of the project. For now, leave the default location chosen by Visual C++, which is usually the project directory.

Do you remember the talk about workspaces? Well, if you had various other projects in your workspace you could select to which project you would add the new file, but since you only have one, leave it like that.

You have your project and your source file. What is missing? Source! Coming right up sir!

Your First Program: "Hello all you happy people"

It is a general rule of thumb that when learning a programming language, one should start with a simple text message output. You will do the same by creating a program that outputs `"Hello all you happy people"` to the screen.

Making such a simple program helps you focus on how C++ programs work without dealing with all the language-specific keywords.

Make sure you have it all. First create a workspace for the projects, and then create a project for your program. After this is done, add a new source file to the project. Now you're ready to type in the listing.

Type the following code into the file you created earlier and then press Ctrl+F5 to run it. I will discuss running and compiling programs in a bit, but for now just do it.

```
 /* '01 Main.cpp' */

 /* Input output stream header file */
#include <iostream>

 /* Start */
main (void)
{
 std::cout << "Hello all you happy people" << std::endl;
 return 0;
}
```

If all went well, you should see that a DOS look-alike window opened with the message `"Hello all you happy people"`, as shown in Figure 1.4.

Let's analyze the code line by line to better understand what is happening.

> **CAUTION**
>
> **Header files usually have the .h extension. There are two `iostream` files, one with the .h and one without it. I use the one without the .h because it is the ANSI/ISO C++ standard. Using the `iostream` file instead of the `iostream.h` file makes your code compatible with the C++ standards, thus, supported by many different compilers.**

In line 4 of the program is `#include <iostream>`. The `#include` word is a preprocessor directive, on which you will dig the details later; for now, just think of it as a way to include code from another file in your own file, in this case, the code in `iostream`. You use < and > to encapsulate the header file, so you tell the compiler to look on the default include directory. If you use quotation marks instead of < and > it means that the compiler will use the project directory to look for the header files.

> **NOTE**
>
> **The default include directory is usually X:\VSDirectory\VC\Include where X is the drive and VSDirectory is the directory where you installed Visual C++. All the C++ built-in headers are in that directory.**

After including the `iostream` file, you have access to the functions, variables, classes, and namespaces in it. All this will be described later so for now assume they are pieces of code that enable you to do certain things. If you check, the `iostream` name can be divided into `io` and `stream`. `io` means

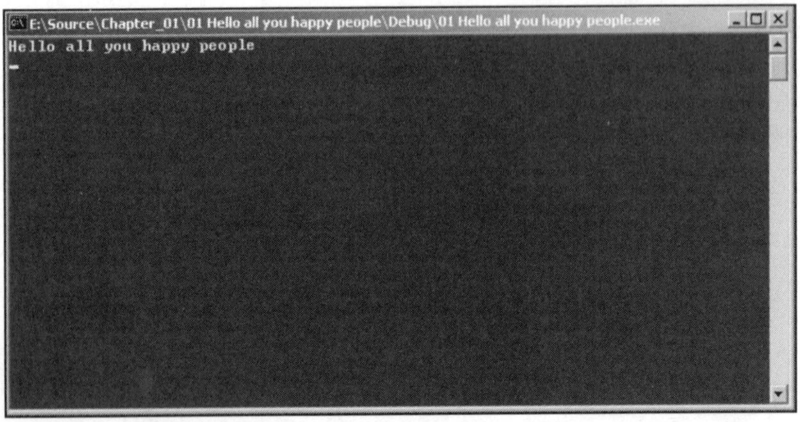

Figure 1.4

Output from your first C++ program.

Input/Output and a `stream` is the way you can communicate with the computer files, screen, keyboard, and more. Almost every file or function uses this type of abbreviation to tell you what they are for.

Now you need to create a function from where the program will start. All C++ (and C for that matter) programs start execution from the function `main` in line 7. When you try to run a console program, the operating system will call the `main` function. You are defining `main` in your program as accepting no arguments, or more correctly, no command-line arguments. You do this by enclosing `void`, which means there are no parameters, inside the parentheses following the `main` keyword. I will go over function creation, arguments, and more in the next couple of chapters.

If you look closely you will see that the code is between the curly braces in lines 8 and 11. The curly braces specify a code block. All functions, loops, and a couple of other C++ control keywords use code blocks to define their scope. All code included between the braces belongs to the `main` function. You can have nested code blocks, but you always must have a closing brace for each opening brace. I will explain code blocks when I deal with functions, so if you haven't understood it well, don't worry, it will all make sense later.

And you have reached the main part of the code, the actual message output. Let's go over line 9 slowly so you don't miss anything. The code line starts with `std::cout`; this is the standard console output stream, or in English, the screen. Again if you divide it you get `std` and `cout`. `std` for standard namespace and `cout` for (`c`)console (`out`)output. To be able to use any member or method of the `std` namespace you need to use the `::` token to specify that `cout` belongs to `std`. Any method or member that you will use from the `std` namespace will use `std::` and the member name. Before checking the `<<` operator, let's go over strings and C++. Strings in C++ can be used in three different ways—arrays, pointers, and hard coded—I will go over strings using arrays and pointers in Chapter 5, "Arrays, Pointers, and Strings"; that leaves you with hard coded strings now. Hard-coded strings are a set of characters defined in code. Strings must be enclosed in quotation marks like in line 9, in this case `"Hello all you happy people"`.

How do you show this string on the screen? Use the `<<` (insertion) operator. As the name says, it inserts whatever is on the right side of it, in your case, the string, into whatever is on the left side, `std::cout`.

You also inserted `std::endl` line to the output stream. This will create a new line. If you didn't want to use this, you could include the new string character `\n` to introduce a new line like:

```
std::cout << "Hello all you happy people\n";
```

Which would produce exactly the same effect as before.

You can see that at the end of line 9 is the semicolon token ;. This token tells the compiler that the line of code ended.

Each code line must end with the ; token. A code line defines one statement, but it doesn't mean that it is the entire text line. A single text line can have multiple code lines if you terminate each statement correctly, usually with the semicolon token.

> ***Token.*** **A token is the smallest language statement a C++ compiler recognizes. The tokens can be used for identifiers, keywords, operators, and other statements.**

To finish the program, you just need to return a value from your `main` function in line 10. You usually specify the return type of a function using the type keyword before the function name, for example, `int Function (void)`. This line of code would declare a function nicely named `Function` that returned an integer. In your `main` function you haven't specified the return type but by the ANSI/ISO C++ standard, the `main` function as it is needs to return an integer. To return a value or variable, you need to use the `return` keyword, followed by the value you want to return, in this case, `0` and ending the code line with the ; token.

So you have your first C++ program done, it wasn't very hard was it? You will learn how to do accomplish other tasks during the rest of the book, and many of the concepts briefly explained here are also covered more in-depth in the following chapters.

Structure of a C++ Program

When you use an integrated development environment (IDE), such as Visual C++, you see only two things: the source and the final executable. There are various steps to create a C++ program. From prototyping the program to the final executable you need to go over various development stages. The entire development process can be seen in Figure 1.5.

Let's go over each phase in detail before moving on to errors and warnings.

Program Design Language

The first step in development is design. To efficiently develop your code to do what you want, you should design or prototype it first. This step is the most important step of the development process. It is here that you test the logic of the program.

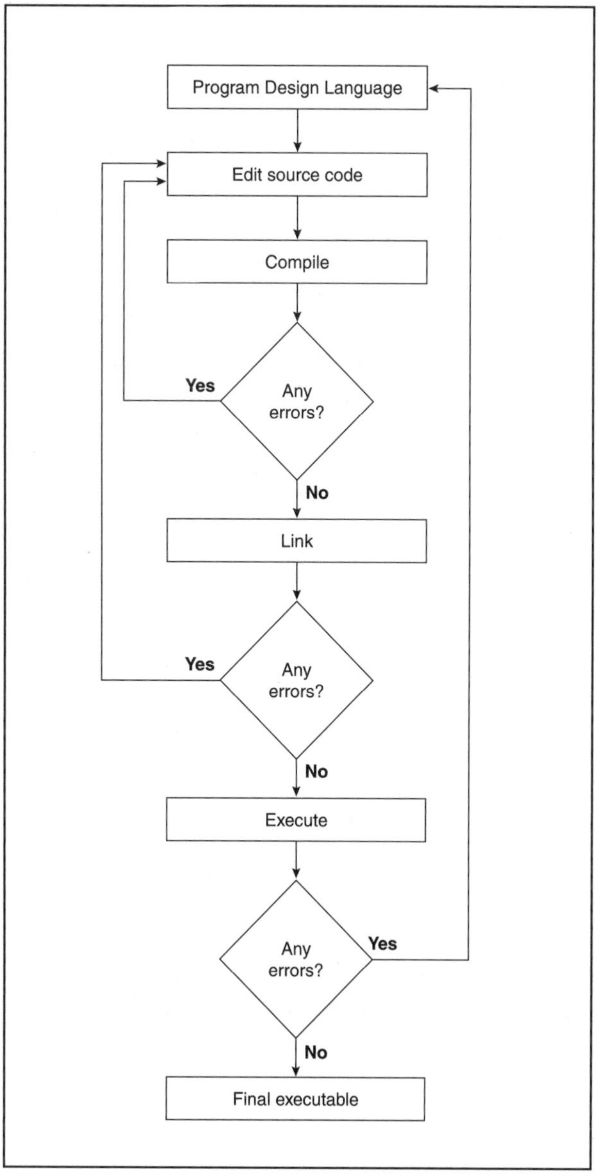

Figure 1.5

The development process.

I usually use something called Program Design Language (PDL) or, more traditionally, pseudo code. What you do is use limited (shorthand) English (or whatever language you are most comfortable with) to explain by steps how the code works.

Take a look at the pseudo code below to get the general idea.

```
for each RacingCar do
Begin
  Move car to next position
  Check for collision with other car
  Handle all physics reactions
  Draw car on screen
End
```

After checking the above pseudo code, you probably have a good idea of what that routine must do even if you don't know how to do it.

If you take that pseudo code to different programmers who use different programming languages, they can all implement the above routine using whatever programming language they prefer. If you had designed that routine in C++, only C++ programmers would be able to understand it.

Try to be specific and consistent in your pseudo code. Indent each line correctly and start with `begin` and `end` statements to differentiate things.

Program Source and Compiling

A simple program like the one earlier needs a single file, but this isn't always the case. Can you imagine a 100,000 line program in just one file? That would make the life of any programmer the living representation of hell. You will have various files that need to be compiled into objects by the compiler. You can compile individual files in Visual C++ by right-clicking in the left menu on the source filename and selecting `Compile XYZ.cpp`, where XYZ is the name of the file, from the drop-down menu. This will create a file, in case you haven't changed the project settings, in a sub-directory of the project `Debug`, named `XYZ.obj`. Again, XYZ is the name of the file. These object files are compiled code but can't be used just yet.

You can also compile individual files by using the Build menu or by pressing Ctrl+F7 if they are selected from the file list on the left.

For you to create a correct final executable, you should have an object file for each source file containing the latest code used.

Objects and Linking

So you have the objects. Now what? To create an executable, you need to link all the objects you created into an executable; this step is done by a *linker*. The linker takes all the objects created in the compiling phase and links them together, with a couple of more default C++ objects to create a final executable. This is a very simple step, and you can do this either by selecting Build XYZ.exe from the Build menu or by pressing F7 in Visual C++. This tells Visual C++ to build the executable by linking the objects. One nice thing about Visual C++ is that it identifies which source files were already compiled and which weren't and compiles the files needed for this operation to be successful. You will rarely compile individual files and then link them. You are using a very sophisticated piece of software, so Visual C++ gives many benefits to other compilers, and the build process can be used to both compile and link the files.

Executable

Two types of executables exist: debug and release. A debug executable is usually slower and bigger than a release executable because it contains a lot of debug information and extra calls. The debug executable is the best kind to test the program and debug it. Debugging is basically trying to find and fix all errors, even during runtime. More information on debugging using Visual C++ can be found in Appendix B, "Debugging Using Microsoft Visual C++."

To specify what type of executable you want to work with you need to go to the Build menu and select Set Active Configuration. This will show a dialog similar to the one in Figure 1.6.

You can run the executable for testing inside Visual C++ by either selecting Execute XYZ.exe from the Build menu or by pressing Ctrl+F5.

If all is working fine there and are no errors in any of these stages, you have your final executable.

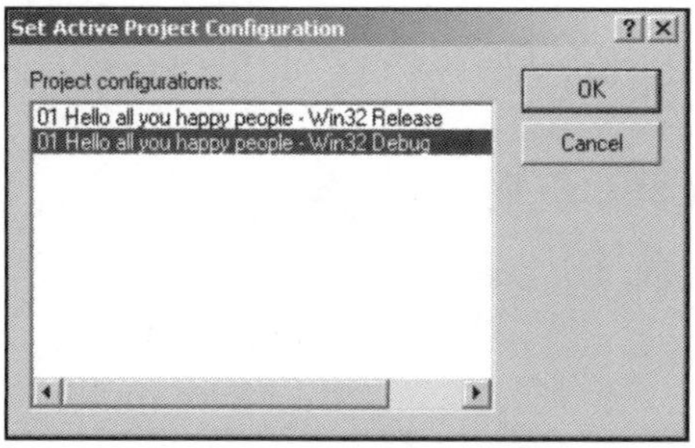

Figure 1.6

Selecting the executable type for the current project.

Commenting

A comment is a piece of text that the compiler will discard so that it has no effect on the code that is compiled. You have seen some comments even if you didn't know what they were.

A comment must be between /* and */. A comment can appear on part of a line, an entire line, or various lines, as shown in the following code:

```
/* Calculates Cosine (Single line) */
Vector = Vector / Vector_Length; /* Normalize Vector (Part of line) */
/*
Function name : PrintNames ()
Description : Prints the names of all players in server
(Multiple lines)
*/
```

Each comment must start with a /* and end with a */. Nested comments are not recommended because most compilers, including Visual C++, will generate an error, for example:

```
/*
/* Print names */
(Nested) */
```

would generate an error since `(Nested)` would be compiled (or at least try) generating an error and the compiler would also complain about an extra */ in the code.

Commenting

- Use comments to explain harder or somehow cryptic code.
- Use comments to enter notes about the code.
- Use comments to hide code you don't want to compile, but you don't want to delete either.
- Don't use comments to literally explain what each line of code does.
- Don't use cryptic or code language to explain concepts when making code notes or explanations.

Catching Errors

Before being programmers, we are humans, and as such, we are condemned to make mistakes. Therefore, learning to use Visual C++ to rapidly identify and fix the errors is crucial.

Type the following code into a new project and see what happens:

```
 /* '02 Main.cpp' */

 /* Input output stream header file */
#include <iostream>

 /* Start */
main (void)
{
 std::cout << "Hello all you happy people" << std::endl
 return 0;
```

If you try to run the program you will get two errors in the output window. Before going on, the *output window* is the window in Visual C++ that shows what is happening or happened while compiling and linking the program. You can see the output window for the program above in Figure 1.7.

The following is the complete output from the compile process:

```
--------------------Configuration: 02_Errors - Win32 Debug--------------------
Compiling...
02_Main.cpp
E:\...\Chapter_01\02 Errors\02 Main.cpp(10) : error C2143: syntax error : missing ;
before return
E:\...\Chapter_01\02 Errors\02 Main.cpp(11) : fatal error C1004: unexpected end of
file found
Error executing cl.exe.
02 Errors.exe - 2 error(s), 0 warning(s)
```

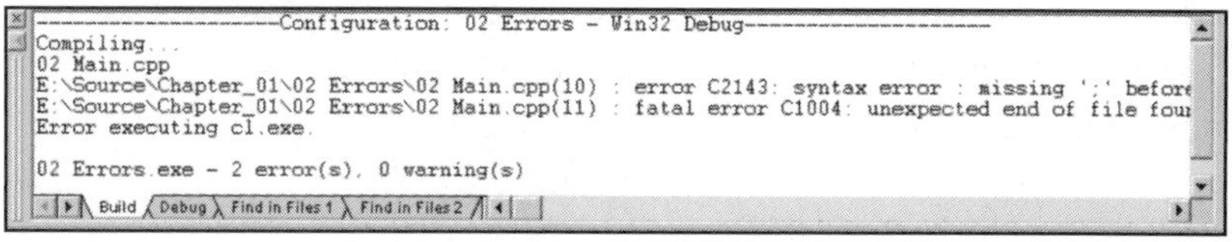
--------------------Configuration: 02 Errors - Win32 Debug--------------------
Compiling...
02 Main.cpp
E:\Source\Chapter_01\02 Errors\02 Main.cpp(10) : error C2143: syntax error : missing ';' before
E:\Source\Chapter_01\02 Errors\02 Main.cpp(11) : fatal error C1004: unexpected end of file four
Error executing cl.exe.
02 Errors.exe - 2 error(s), 0 warning(s)
Build
Debug
Find in Files 1
Find in Files 2

Figure 1.7

The output window showing the program errors.

If you check the output window carefully you will see valuable information. The first line tells you what project and executable type you are trying to create; in this case the second program of the chapter in debug mode. After that the output window shows you what is happening; in this case, trying to compile the `02_Main.cpp` file.

Now the errors, two of them to be exact, are clearly shown and a lot information on them is given. The first part of the error message is the file that contains the error, followed enclosed in parentheses by the line where the error occurred. You can double-click the error message and you will be automatically directed to the file and line where the error occurred. After that you have the error code, which you can look at for more information on the Microsoft Developers' Network (MSDN), which you will do in a bit. In the end, a small description of the error is given.

So, in relation to the code, what does this mean? For the first error it means you have missed a ; before `return`, or just after the `string` declaration. As you have seen before, each code line needs to end with a ;. You can see this because of the error description, or if you want more information you can try to find information on the error code in MSDN.

C2143 Error Code in MSDN

syntax error : missing token1 before token2

(...)

The compiler expects certain language elements to appear before or after other elements. For instance, an `if` statement requires that the first non-whitespace character following the word `if` must be an opening parenthesis. If anything else is used, the compiler cannot "understand" the statement.

(...)

You can see the error in the 02_Main.cpp file in line 9. Now you are asking, if a ; is missing before return 0, that is, after the message declaration, why does the error show line 10 instead of line 9? Well, since you are missing the ; token, you have never specified the end of the code line where you use cout, so the compiler treats both lines as just one code line. If you include the ; after "Hello all you happy people" you specify the end of the code line and eliminate the error.

The second error is similar to the first one. Remember that for each opening curly brace you need a closing one to define a code block? Well, that is exactly what is missing here, the closing curly brace. Visual C++ reports an unexpected end of file found error because the compiler was expecting the code block to end and it never did. You can span code through various files, but you can't span code blocks. Each code block must start and end before the end of the file or the declaration of another function. You will just add a } after return, or in a new line after return to make the code easier to read, to fix the error.

If you were paying attention, you may have noticed that those errors have different *grades*. The first is a normal error and the second is a fatal error, but what is the difference between them? Well, when you have a *normal error*, the compiler still tries to compile the rest of the file showing all the following errors. When you have a *fatal error*, the compiler is incapable of continuing the compile process because of the error.

There is just one more error type you should go through before ending all this discussion: linking errors. *Linking errors* are errors that occur during the linking phase and usually happen due to missing object files or duplicate declaration of functions. Take a look at the linking error that follows:

```
LINK : fatal error LNK1104: cannot open file "object.obj"
```

Visual C++ reports linking errors similarly to compiling errors, the main differences are that linking errors don't have file or line information, and that the error codes are identified by the LNK prefix. The rest is exactly the same, it reports it as an error and gives the error code and a small description of the error. In this case, it means that the compiler can't open, or find, the object.obj file. This file is one of the files needed to build the final executable, and since the compiler can't find it, it just stops the linking phase and shows the error.

Warnings

A warning is a way the compiler tells you something may be wrong. It doesn't mean it will cause an error or problem, but where there is smoke, there is fire! So, knowing this, warnings shouldn't be ignored. Type the following code in a new console project and I will go over the warning in a second.

```
 /* '03 Main.cpp' */

 /* Input output stream header file */
#include <iostream>

 /* Start */
main (void)
{
 std::cout << "Hello all you happy people" << std::endl;
}
```

This program will compile, link, and produce a final executable. You can even run it and you will not notice any difference, except on the output window. You can see that a warning is reported to the output window.

```
e:\...\chapter_01\03_warnings\03_main.cpp(5) : warning C4508: main : function
should return a value; void return type assumed
```

A warning report has the exact same structure as an error report. You have the file, the line, the warning code, and the warning description. In your case, your warning is because you aren't returning a value like you should. This warning will rarely cause you any trouble, but some others may. To solve this you need to add `return 0;` as you had it before.

What can cause a warning? Just about everything, using different type variables in operations, compiler options, forgetting a token or keyword, and so on.

What should you do when you come across a warning? Fix it as soon as possible to prevent problems like this from happening.

But what can you do when you can't get around warnings and you really don't want them to show in the output window? You must disable that warning by using a `pragma` directive. You should use the following code just after the `#include <iostream>` to disable the C4508 warning.

```
#pragma warning(disable:4508)
```

You use the `pragma` keyword preceding the pre-processor directive # to let the compiler know you will be using a pre-processor directive. Following, there is the type of `pragma` directive you want to use, in your case `warning` and then specifying the parameters for it, since you want to disable the warning C4508 you use `disable:4508` in parentheses.

NOTE

Pragma directives are compiler and operating system dependent and usually change between systems and compilers.

Summary

If you haven't skipped any of the pages, you should be confident on the choice of C++ as your programming language. You should also be confident about the power of the Visual C++ compiler and why it was chosen for this book. And you should know how to use the Visual C++ compiler well enough to create your own projects and source files.

You now know how a C++ program works and its structure; you should also be able to handle errors and warnings without much hassle.

NOTE

Whenever you are having trouble with Visual C++, try looking at the help. Visual C++ comes with a huge help system (part of MSDN) which can be used to your advantage.

This was a rather simple, but, at the same time, complicated chapter. I went over some basic concepts in-depth and some more advanced C++ concepts briefly. Make sure you understand how Visual C++ and C++ programs work so that you don't get lost in the next couple of chapters.

Questions and Answers

Q: If Assembly and C languages are faster than C++, why use C++ for game programming?

A: With modern compilers, C++ code can be as fast as C, and nearly as fast as Assembly. C++ offers some advanced capabilities, such as classes, polymorphism, and operator overloading to name a few, that offer you a better and easier way to build your programs and games.

Q: When I open the executable I created in Notepad, I only see a lot of gibberish. Why?

A: When you open an executable file, you don't see C++ source code, or even any human understandable code. What you see is code the operating system uses when using your program.

Q: What do I need to give a friend of mine so that he can run a program I wrote?

A: For a friend of yours to be able to use your program, you need to give him the executable generated by your compiler. More advanced programs may also need data from other files.

Q: Is it possible to make Visual C++ create executables for other systems, such as Linux?

A: No. Visual C++ outputs only executables for the Windows family of operating systems. There are a couple of different Windows executable types, but it can't be used to create executables to other operating systems.

Q: Can I completely disable warnings in Visual C++?

A: Yes, even if you shouldn't, you can disable warnings by going to the Project menu, selecting Settings, and selecting the C/C++ tab. There you can change the warning level to None from the drop-down combo box.

Q: Why do I need to create a project for each executable I want to build? Wouldn't it be easier to have a process of compiling a source file into an executable without projects?

A: Visual C++ forces you to build projects for one simple reason. If you had a source file, how would Visual C++ identify it as being a console application or a Windows application? This is why you need to create projects, so Visual C++ knows which type of application it should create.

Q: What are classes, polymorphism, operator overloading, and all that mumbo-jumbo you talked about?

A: Classes are a C++ way to encapsulate functions and variables to objects. Polymorphism and operator overloading are topics related to classes, which I will cover in detail in Chapter 6.

Exercises

1. How do you create a Win32 Console Application in the D:\Book\Hello directory?
2. What is the iostream file?
3. What is wrong with the following block of code?

```
#include <iostream>
int main (void)
{
 cout << "What is wrong with this ? << endl;
}
```

4. What will be the output of the following program?

```
#include <iostream.h>
int main (void)
{
 cout << "Line 1" << endl << "Line 2" << "Line 3" << endl;
}
```

5. What are the three different errors Visual C++ reports to you?
6. Fix the following code:

```
#include <iostream>
int main (void)
{
 cout < "What is wrong with this ?;
}
```

7. What type of header should C++ programs use, `iostream` or `iostream.h`? And why?
8. What is wrong with the following program?

```
#include <iostream
int main (void)
{
 cout << "What is wrong with this ?"
}
```

9. What is a linking error?
10. What happens after the compiling process?
11. What is a possible source for checking out compiler error codes?
12. Develop a Win32 Console Application that shows the "Welcome to my world" message and returns the integer 5.
13. Try to develop a program that asks for the user name and then shows it (tip: use `cin` to get input from the user).
14. Try to make the first program you develop include a new line before and after the message is shown on the screen (tip: use the `endl` manipulator).
15. Try to compile and link your first program without the use of the Visual C++ Integrated Development Enviroment (tip: use the executables in the BIN directory where you have installed Visual C++ to).

CHAPTER 2

Variables and Operators

Computer programs, especially computer games, need a way to store different types of data, from players' names, to scores, to lives. Programs also need a way to modify and operate on them. C++ enables you to do this with variables and operators. Throughout the rest of the book, you will use various types of variables and operators, each with its own uses.

On a simple definition, a *variable* is someplace where you can store information in memory. Let's go over how variables and memory interact.

Variables and Memory

Just in case you didn't know, a computer has two types of memory: random access memory (RAM) and read-only memory (ROM). ROM is the part of the memory that isn't *erased* when the computer is shut down. It is usually very small and is used for storing the BIOS.

> **NOTE**
> **The BIOS, or Basic Input Output System, is a system that allows the software communication with hardware. The BIOS has many functions, such as the Power-On self test and booting an operating system from a drive.**

The memory you are interested in is the RAM. RAM is located in chips usually called SIMMs (Single Inline Monolithic Memories) or DIMMs (Duel Inline Monolithic Memories), depending on the system, inside your computer. In these days, computers usually come with 64 megabytes (or more) of memory. Typically, development machines use a lot more than that.

> **NOTE**
> **1 megabyte (MB) is 1,024 kilobytes (KB), and 1 kilobyte is 1,024 bytes. So 1 megabyte is not 1,000,000 bytes like you would suppose but 1,048,576. Those 64MB of memory are actually 67,108,864 (1,048,576 * 64) bytes of memory.**

Information stored in RAM is easily erased and modified, and maintains its contents only while the power is on. If you shut down the computer, it will be completely erased.

I will talk about memory in terms of bytes now. A byte is the smallest memory unit you can store in a computer, and it can hold values that range from 0 to 255. I will talk about bytes, bits, and more on memory manipulation in Chapter 5, "Arrays, Pointers, and Strings."

RAM is organized sequentially, one byte after another. For a visual concept take a look at Figure 2.1.

As you can see in Figure 2.1, each byte of memory has an address assigned to it. Memory addresses are usually addressed in hexadecimal notation. If you don't know how decimal notation relates to hexadecimal, check out Appendix C.

Variables are stored in the computer RAM. Each variable type uses a different number of bytes, resulting in each holding bigger or smaller values.

You will be using variables for just about anything you want to store, and for each variable you use, you are using a little bit of memory. You will learn later how to allocate and de-allocate memory, but for now, you will let the compiler take care of that.

What Type of Variables Are There?

As you may know already, all the information in the computer is stored in binary form (for information on binaries, see Appendix C). A binary number is stored as lots of 1s and 0s called bits. As said earlier, a byte comprises 8 bits. Different variables need more or less memory, thus using the appropriate type for each kind of data is recommended so that you don't waste memory.

Some variables are more suited to hold small numbers, other letters, or even store floating-point numbers. Each of them has different uses, range, and memory requirements.

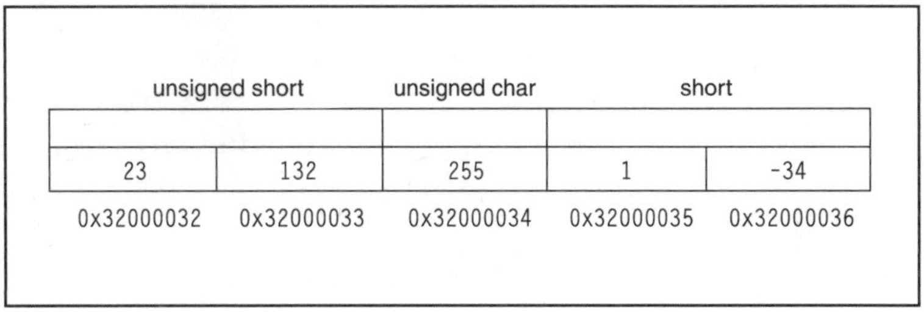

Figure 2.1

Memory organized sequentially.

You usually store three different types of numbers, and you also have various types of variables for each type of number, so you can hold various numbers with various ranges. You have characters or letters, which are also stored as numbers. You also have integers that are numbers that have no decimal part, and floating-point numbers that are numbers that have a decimal part and are stored as mantissa and exponent. You don't need to worry how the mantissa and exponent are stored in memory because C++ enables you to use the floating-point variables as if they were stored in the normal way.

NOTE

Any floating-point number can be represented by a mantissa and an exponent. For example, the number 12943234.3493 can be represented accurately by $1{,}29432343493*10^7$ or $1.2943*10^7$ approximately. This is often referred as scientific notation. This is the way C++ stores floating-point numbers, where the mantissa is the base of the number, in this case, 1.2943 and the exponent is 10^7.

Check Table 2.1 for the various C++ types, keywords, memory requirements, and their range.

All integer types come in two forms: `signed` or `unsigned`. `signed` variables can either be positive or negative and is the default when you create any variable. `unsigned` variables, on the other hand, are always positive and need to have the `unsigned` keyword preceding the variable type.

Let's go over some examples of data and see which variable types from Table 2.1 you would use for them.

The single letter A is represented as the decimal number 65 (you can check Appendix F for a table of symbols and the respective value). If you are just using the standard letters and symbols, like a, J, L, 4, 1, (numbers can be also be represented as letters) you only need to use values from 0 to 127. These values are part of the ANSI ASCII Standard and are the same for all systems and languages, so you can use only a `char`. If you want to use some extended characters and symbols that range from 127 to 255, you should use an `unsigned char`.

If you wanted to hold the players' lives you should use an `unsigned char`. You could use a `short` to hold the number of lives, but do you really need the extra byte? An `unsigned char` can hold values up to 255, which is more than needed in any game.

If you wanted to hold a year, you would use a `short`. You could just use an `unsigned char` and hold the last two elements of the year, but you have probably heard of the

TABLE 2.1 C++ Data Types

Variable Description	C++ Keyword	Memory Required (Bytes)	Range
Boolean	`bool`	1	0 or 1
Character	`char`	1	-128 to 127
Unsigned character	`unsigned char`	1	0 to 255
Short integer	`short`	2	-32,768 to 32,767
Unsigned short integer	`unsigned short`	2	0 to 65,535
Long integer	`long`	4	-2,147,483,648 to 2,147,483,647
Unsigned long integer	`unsigned long`	4	0 to 4,294,967,295
*Integer	`int`	4	-2,147,483,648 to 2,147,483,647
*Unsigned integer	`unsigned int`	4	0 to 4,294,967,295
Single-precision floating-point	`float`	4	3.4E +/- 38 (7-digit precision)
Double-precision floating-point	`double`	8	1.7E +/- 308 (15-digit precision)

*Integer and unsigned integers are 32-bit values in Windows 9X/ME/NT and they are the same as a long integer and an unsigned long integer.

Millennium Bug. Do you know what caused that? Exactly, holding just the last couple of digits of the year.

Now for a floating-point number, you should use a `float` or a `double` of course, but which of the two should you use? You want to store the number 3.141592, which is rather small and doesn't have a high precision so you will use a `float`.

> **NOTE**
>
> The millennium bug was caused by dates being stored using only the last two digits of the year. When you reached 2000, the computer clock would just go from 99 to 00, without updating the century (19); that is, the year would change from 1999 to 1900, which would be great for the real-estate market, but bad for computers!

You can check the size of any variable using the `sizeof` keyword. If you want to see Table 2.1 in code, check out the sample `02_Variable Sizes.cpp` program on the CD.

Using Variables in Your Programs

Well, all this mumbo-jumbo isn't worth a nickel if you can't use it in a program, right? Right! For using variables in your program you first need to declare them, and only then can you use them.

Declaring a Variable

In C++, you need to declare a variable before you can use it. The declaration will tell the compiler the name of the variable, the type, and that it has to reserve memory for it. The syntax to declare a variable is as follows:

```
VariableType            VariableName;
```

Where `VariableType` is one of the types you have seen before, and `VariableName` is the name of the variable. When you declare variables, you need to be aware of some rules, which you will see in a second.

If you want to declare a `long` integer for the time elapsed since the computer started and a floating-point number for the value of an angle, you would do it as follows:

```
long TimeElapsed;
float Angle;
```

You can also declare various variables of the same type on just one line of code separating each variable name with a comma:

```
short NumberOfEnemies, BoosterEnergy, WidthOfWorld;
unsigned char CharacterType, xLoop;
```

Using Variables

Having variables declared just isn't enough, is it? After you have them declared, you can use them as you wish. In a bit I will go over operators and the many things you can do by combining operators and variables, but for now, let's just see how you can use variables to communicate with the player.

A simple program showing how to use variables is provided here.

```
 1:  /* '01 Main.cpp' */
 2: #include <iostream>
 3:
 4: main (void)
 5: {
 6:   /* Variable declarations*/
 7:  unsigned char   Age;
 8:  long             StartEnergy;
 9:  char             CharacterType;
10:   /* Get the Information */
11:  std::cout << "What is your character's age?: ";
12:  std::cin >> Age;
13:  std::cout << "How much start energy?: ";
14:  std::cin >> StartEnergy;
15:  std::cout << "What is the character type?: ";
16:  std::cin >> CharacterType;
17:   /* Show the Information */
18:  std::cout << "Your character is " << Age << " years old." << std::endl;
19:  std::cout << "Has " << StartEnergy << " of starting energy." << std::endl;
20:  std::cout << "And its type is " << CharacterType << "." << std::endl;
21:  return 0;
22: }
```

There are a couple of new things in this program so let's go over each of them one step at a time. At first you declare three variables, an `unsigned char`, a `long`, and a `char`, respectively for the age, start energy, and the character type (lines 7–9). After

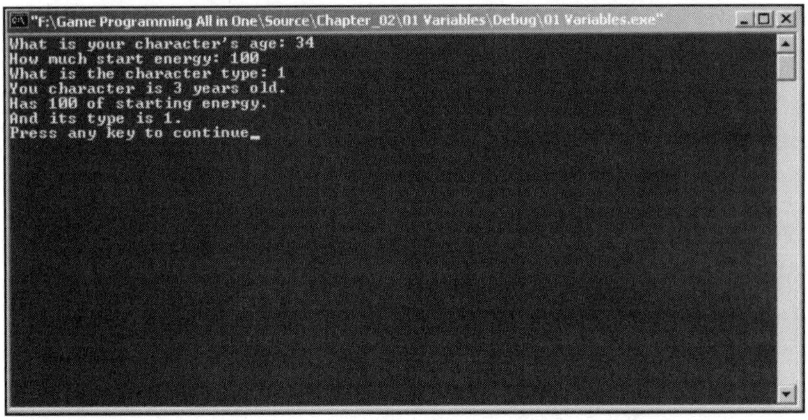

Figure 2.2

Using variables.

this is done you need to get the information from the user, you do can do this with the `std::cout` counterpart, `std::cin`. `std::cin` is similar to `std::cout` but used for input from the keyboard. You use the extraction (>>) operator to get data from the console input (lines 12, 14, and 16). After you do this for the three variables, you output the results using `std::cout` and the insertion operator (lines 18–20). So let's look at how `std::cin` and variables work together.

If you've run the program, you will see that you have to type the variable values in the keyboard for them to be stored, but how does this work? If you look at your program, you have the following line:

```
std::cin >> Age;
```

What are you doing here? In the simplest of terms, you are sending whatever was inserted in `std::cin` to the variable `Age` with the extraction operator >>. The extraction operator does exactly what its name suggests, it extracts something from what is on its left and inserts it in its right side. A good thing about the extraction operator and the insertion operator is that they are smart. They recognize which type of variables are being used and react accordingly. You will see how this really works later.

By using the extraction operator with `std::cin`, you can get all the information you want from the player.

Initializing Variables

When you declare a variable, the compiler sets a bit of memory aside for it. This memory may or may not already be used by other programs. The compiler just allocates memory to the variable and doesn't set any value to it, except when a variable is a global one, but I will talk about global and local variables when I talk about function and scope, so for now, just accept that variables aren't initialized.

And what if you don't want to leave your variables with the old values because it may interfere somewhere in your games? You can initialize the variables to some value. To do this, you will use the assignment operator just after the declaration of the variable. Take a look at the following examples.

```
short Age = 10;
float PI = 3.14159;
long ElapsedTime = 5559265;
```

This code will initialize the different variables to the values you want. This can be done with just about any variable type.

Don't worry about the assignment operator workings since I will cover it later in the chapter.

Variable Modifiers

You should know about some special variables. They offer different functionality and are sometimes advantageous to use over normal variables. Let's see what, how, and when they should be used.

Const

The first special variable type is constants. *Constants* are variables that must be initialized at declaration time and can't be changed during program execution.

Constants are useful for values that will be the same no matter what. Constants make it easier to read the code and also offer a way to change a value once and not care for the rest of its use. Imagine 10,000 lines of code where the value of the number of enemies is used about 200 times. Can you imagine the amount of work you would do in order to change all the references to that value to the new one? Wouldn't it be easier to define the value in a variable and use that variable everywhere? And if you had to change the number of enemies, you would just change the variable value.

In C++, the `const` keyword is used to specify that a value of a variable is a constant and by definition cannot be changed. You use `const` as a variable type modifier so that means you have to change a bit of your variable declaration to account for the modifier. The new declaration is as follows:

```
ModifierType    VariableType    VariableName;
```

You don't need to use `ModifierType` if you don't want to set any special attribute for the variable, but if you want to use a variable modifier, you set it where `ModifierType` is. So, how do you actually use this? Easy as pie. You just add the `const` keyword before your class declaration like this:

```
const unsigned char MaximumLives = 10;
const unsigned char MaxLives = 5;
```

And now you would use the variable names `MaximumLives` and `MaxLives` in your programs whenever you needed those values. If you ever need to change them during development, you just change the value in the declaration. Take a look at the following program to see the use of constants on a length converter.

```
/* '02 Main.cpp' */
#include <iostream>

main (void)
{
  /* Variable declarations */
 const float   FeetPerMeter = Value;
 float   Length1;
 float   Length2;
 float   Length3;
  /* Get the information from the user */
 std::cout << "Enter the first length in meters: ";
 std::cin >> Length1;
 std::cout << "Enter the second length in meters: ";
 std::cin >> Length2;
 std::cout << "Enter the third length in meters: ";
 std::cin >> Length3;
  /* Show the information */
 std::cout << "First length in feet is: " << Length1 * FeetPerMeter << std::endl;
 std::cout << "Second length in feet is: " << Length2 * FeetPerMeter << std::endl;
 std::cout << "Third length in feet is: " << Length3 * FeetPerMeter << std::endl;

 return 0;
}
```

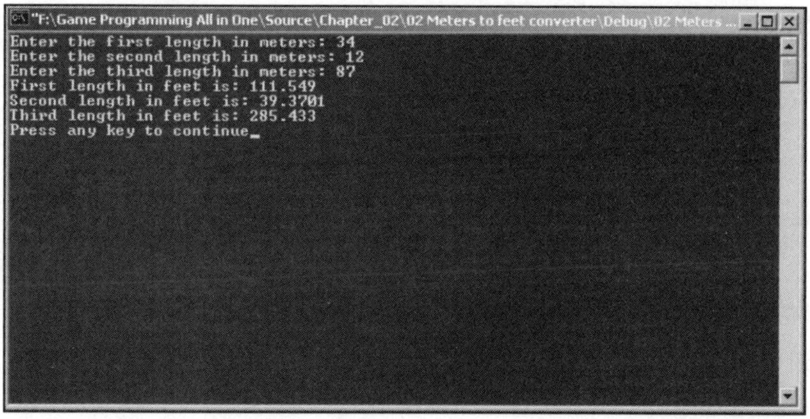

Figure 2.3

Converting values.

If, for some reason, you need to change the conversion value, you would just change it where you declared it rather than in various places.

Don't worry if you don't understand how the operators work, for now just focus on the constant use.

Register

The `register` modifier suggests that compiler put the variable in the processor register, not the normal memory. There are several advantages to doing this, but before that, let's see what the processor register is.

Your computer CPU contains a small bit of *memory* where the actual operations on data are done. To do any operation on the data, the CPU needs to pick the data from normal memory and put it in the registers, do the operations, and send back the data to memory. Moving data from one place to another takes time, not much but some. If a variable were always in the register processor, the operations done on it would be a lot faster because the data wouldn't need to be moved. By using the `register` modifier, you ask, and the key term here is *ask*, the compiler to put the variable in those registers.

Registers aren't always available, so you can't demand that the variables be stored there, but in case they aren't, you don't have to bother much since the compiler will treat this variable as a normal variable.

You define a register variable as:

```
register short iTemp;
register long xLoop;
```

Registers should be used when you know that the variable will be used many times like in loops of various calculations as you will see later.

Variable Naming

Variable names, as all things, have rules. You can't name your variable as you solely wish, but thankfully, C++ grants you a great deal of freedom when doing so.

C++ naming rules are as follows: The variable name can contain only letters, digits, and the underscore character _.

Variables are case sensitive, this is, `Apple` is different from `apple`.

C++ (and Visual C++) keywords can't be used as variable names.

The variable name must start either with a letter or the underscore character.

Redefining Types

There is a final subject about variables you should go through. Redefining the basic types.

As you will see later, redefining variables to other names more convenient to your projects is a good thing, and C++ enables you to do this with the `typedef` keyword. Its syntax is as follows:

```
typedef  BaseType  NewType
```

A few C++ examples follow:

```
typedef  float  Coordinate;
typedef  short  Number;
```

And now you could use `Coordinate` or `Number` in your code instead of `float` and `short`.

So, is this all there is about variables? Yes and no. You can use various operators or functions with variables to produce or change the variables themselves, but in the overall picture, this is how variables are used. I will go over a few more modifiers when I deal with functions and variable scope.

What Is an Operator?

An *operator* is a way to tell the compiler to perform some operation on the operand(s). The *operand* is what the operator operates on.

You should think of operators as exactly the same as mathematical symbols for additions, assignments, comparisons, and so on, and thankfully C++ lets you use operators exactly like you do in math and even offers you a few more things.

Assignment Operator

The first operator I will help you learn about is the *assignment operator.* It uses the equal (=) symbol and works exactly the same way the equal symbol does in math. It assigns, or copies, the value on the right to the left operand. The right operand can be a variable or a literal but it must be of the same type as the left operand or else the compiler will give you an error or warning. The usual way to use the assignment operator is as follows:

```
LeftOperand = RightOperand
```

The `LeftOperand` must always be a variable or value holder and the `RightOperand` can take the form of a variable, a literal, or a set of operators. In actual C++ code you have:

```
short Money;
Money = 12;
```

You can also do multiple assignments using the following code:

```
long  FirstWorldEnemies, SecondWorldEnemies;
FirstWorldEnemies = SecondWorldEnemies = 22;
```

Here the assignments are performed from the right to the left, assigning 22 to `FirstWorldEnemies` and then to `SecondWorldEnemies`.

Mathematical Operators

Several mathematical operators in C++ act just like the normal mathematical operators do. The first set of mathematical operators you will see are the unary operators.

Unary Operators

A *unary operator* takes only one operand and operates on it. There are two unary operators in C++. These are the increment and the decrement operators. They can be used as follows:

```
short A, B, C, D;
A = B = C = D = 10;
A++;
B--;
++C;
--D;
```

Look at what happens at each line. You first declare four `short` integers and set their initial values to 10. Now for `A`, you use the postfix increment operator (`A++`), meaning that the `A` variable will be used, and only then incremented by 1, leaving the value of `A` at 11 after using it. For `B`, you use the postfix decrement operator (`B--`), which will decrement `B` by 1, leaving it at 9 again after it is used. For `C`, you use the prefix increment operator that will increment `C` by 1 before it is used, and finally for `D`, you use the prefix decrement operator that will decrement `D` by 1 before it is used.

A simple example of the difference between postfix and prefix operators can be seen in the following code:

```
/* '03 Main.cpp' */
#include <iostream>

main (void)
{
  // Variable declarations
 short   A, B, C, D;
  // Variable initialization
 A = B = C = D = 10;
  // Show the operator use
 std::cout << "Using the operators " << std::endl;
 std::cout << "A = " << A++ << std::endl;
 std::cout << "B = " << B-- << std::endl;
 std::cout << "C = " << ++C << std::endl;
 std::cout << "D = " << --D << std::endl;
  // Show the final values
 std::cout << "After using the operators " << std::endl;
```

```
    std::cout << "A = " << A << std::endl;
    std::cout << "B = " << B << std::endl;
    std::cout << "C = " << C << std::endl;
    std::cout << "D = " << D << std::endl;

    return 0;
}
```

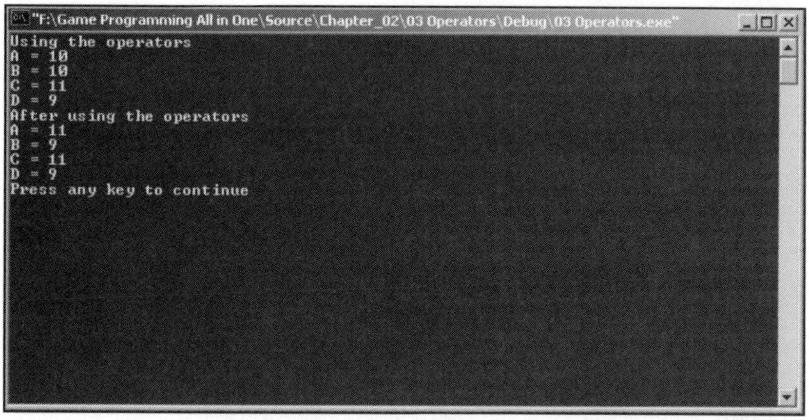

Figure 2.4

Unary operators.

This simple program displays how the unary operators work.

A quick note before progressing. You are probably wondering what `std::endl` is and what it does. The `std::endl` is a formatting manipulator that inserts a newline character to the stream. It basically creates a new line write on. You will see how manipulators work later when you deal with input and output.

Binary Operators

Binary operators work on two operands at the same time, returning one result. These binary operators do exactly the same as the mathematical operators so there isn't a need for a big explanation. Just take a look at Table 2.2 for the available operators and you will do a small test program after.

As you can see, C++ mathematical operators work exactly the same as the normal mathematical operators. Let's look at the following program that demonstrates all the operators in Table 2.2.

TABLE 2.2 C++ Binary Mathematical Operators

Operator	Symbol	Description
Addition	+	Adds two operands
Subtraction	-	Subtracts the right operand from the left operand
Multiplication	*	Multiplies two operands
Division	/	Divides the left operand by the right one
Modulus	%	Calculates the remainder of a division of the left operand by the right operand

You can see how this works with the following code:

```
#include <iostream>

main (void)
{
   // Show result of various operations
  std::cout << "3 + 5 = " << 3 + 5 << std::endl;
  std::cout << "17 - 7 = " << 17 - 7 << std::endl;
```

Figure 2.5
Mathematical operators.

```
    std::cout << "23 * 4 = " << 23 * 4 << std::endl;
    std::cout << "4 / 2 = " << 4 / 2 << std::endl;
    std::cout << "43 % 5 = " << 43 % 5 << std::endl;

    return 0;
}
```

Compound Assignment Operators

There is just one more set of operators before I can wrap up with this entire C++ operator math, the *compound assignment operators.* These operators work in a way similar to the earlier operators but have the peculiarity of an operand being used as a normal operator operand and also for storing the result of the operation.

Look at the following code:

```
short Exams = 5;
Exams = Exams + 10;
```

Because `Exams` is 5, the preceding operation would result in 15 (5 + 10). Using the compound assignment operator, you would have a shorter line, as follows:

```
short Exams = 5;
Exams += 10;
```

Which is exactly the same thing as the preceding code. The compound assignment operators pick the left operand and the right operand, perform the operation on them, and when finished, store the result on the left operand.

Any of the mathematical operators you just learned can be used as a compound assignment operator by adding the assignment operator before the actual operator.

Bitwise Shift Operators

One pair of operators is the shift operators. These two operators (left shift and right shift) shift all the bits of a variable to the left or right by a number of places. This will achieve the same effect as multiplication or division of a number by multiples of two.

For example, the number 23 can be represented in binary by:

```
00010111
```

If you shift all the bits two places to the left, you would get the following value:

```
01011100
```

Which is 92. If you noticed, it is the same as $23*2^2$. So shifting the values two places to the left is the same as multiplying the value by $23*2^2$. How about shifting it three places? You would get:

```
10111000
```

Which in decimal is 184, or $23*2^3$. You can see that the number of places you shift the bit to the left represents the same as multiplying the number by two elevated to the number of places. The same thing is true for division. If you shift the number three places to the right, it's the same as dividing by 2^3. If you want proof, just check it out with the above numbers.

Now, how to use shift operators in C++. Easy, the base syntax is:

```
Variable    (ShiftOperator)   PlacesToShift
```

Where the `ShiftOperator` can be either << for a left shift or >> for a right shift. The C++ code for the above examples is:

```
23 << 2 /* 92 */
23 << 3 /* 184 */
184 >> 3 /* 23 */
```

Relational Operators

The *relational operators* evaluate the relation of the two operands. They are used to compare the behavior of two operands. If the comparison results in a `true` statement, the operator returns 1, if it is `false`, the operand returns 0.

Relational operators are used the same way the math operators are. You can see them all in Table 2.3.

You use these operators with the following form:

```
LeftOperand Operator RightOperand
```

In C++, the relational operators return either 0 (`false`) or 1 (`true`) depending on the result. Any other number that is different from 0 is also considered `true` by C++. Any of the following numbers would result in `true`: -2, 34, -123, and 1.

Relational operators are mostly used in program control, as you will see in the next chapter.

TABLE 2.3 C++ Relational Operators

Operator	Symbol	Description
Equality	==	Evaluates whether operands are equal
Not equal	!=	Evaluates whether operands are different
Greater than	>	Evaluates whether the left operand is greater than the right operand
Greater than or equal to	>=	Evaluates whether the left operand is greater than or equal to the right operand
Less than	<	Evaluates whether the left operand is less than the right operand
Less than or equal to	<=	Evaluates whether the left operand is less than or equal to the right operand

Conditional Operator

The conditional is the only *ternary* operator in C++, which means that it takes three operands. This *conditional operator* is mostly used to return one of two values depending on the relation of two operands. The syntax for this operator is as follows:

```
TestOperand ? LeftOperand : RightOperand
```

The `TestOperand` can be anything, but it is usually the result of a relational operation. The `LeftOperand` and the `RightOperand` are the possible return types. If `TestOperand` is `true`, the value returned from this operator is the `LeftOperand`; if it is `false`, the result is the `RightOperand`.

Check out the following program that uses the conditional operator to check which of two variables is the greatest.

```
#include <iostream>

main (void)
{
```

```
 5:
 6:   short ValueA, ValueB, ValueResult;
 7:   ValueA = 5;
 8:   ValueB = 7;
 9:   ValueResult = (ValueA > ValueB) ? ValueA : ValueB;
10:   std::cout << "The greater value is: " << ValueResult << std::endl;
11:
12:   return 0;
13: }
```

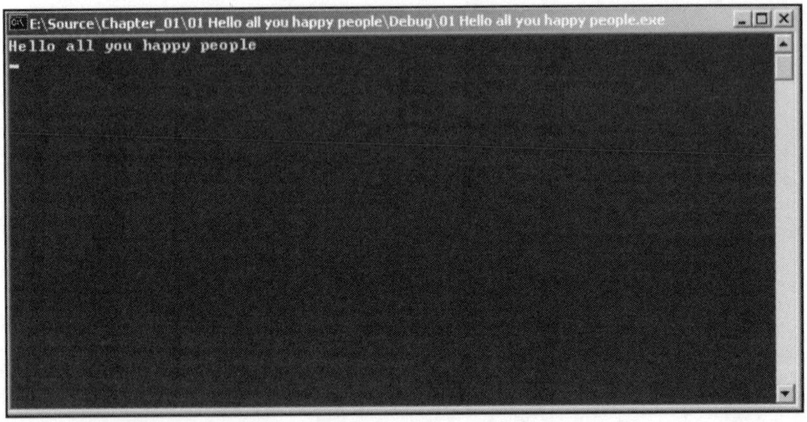

Figure 2.6

A conditional operator.

The program uses the conditional operator to determine whether `ValueA` is greater than `ValueB` (line 9). If it is, it assigns `ValueA` to `ValueResult` in line 10; if it isn't, it assigns `ValueB` to `ValueResult`.

Logical Operators

Logical operators are a way to combine various *relational operators.* There are three logical operators, each with its own separate use.

The next two logical operators follow this syntax:

```
LeftOperand     (LogicalOperator)     RightOperator
```

The AND operator (`&&`) returns `true` if both the operands are true or returns `false` if they are both false or one is false and the other is true. Look at the following code.

```
(5 > 2) && (0==0)
```

Because 5 is greater than 2 and 0 is equal to 0, this operation would return `true`.

The OR operator (`||`) returns `true` if any one of the operands is true or returns `false` if both the operands are false.

The following code would return `true` (1) because one of the relational operators is true.

```
(5=>2) || (0==1)
```

The NOT (`!`) operator returns `true` if the operand is false, or returns `false` if the operand is true.

The NOT operator is a unary operator and it is used like this:

```
(LogicalOperator)Operant
```

The following code would return `false` because the NOT operator returns false for any true operand.

```
!(5>2)
```

What happens in the preceding code is that the expression `5>2` is evaluated and returns `true`. Because the NOT operator returns `false` on any `true` value, it will in the end return `false`.

Operator Precedence

C++ operators act just like mathematical operators, and so, they have different precedence. Check Table 2.4 for all the operators you have seen before and a couple of new ones.

I haven't talked about some of the operators in Table 2.5 yet. They will be referred to in the next few chapters so don't worry about it.

There is only one thing I want to go into before finishing all this operator talk, parentheses. In C++, you can also change the order of the operations by giving them a higher priority with parentheses, for example:

```
1 + 4 * (2 + 3)
```

would do the `2 + 3` operation and then multiply the result by 4 and in the end add 1.

TABLE 2.4 Operator Precedence

Level	Operator Description	Operator
1	Scope resolution	::
2	Post-increment	++
	Post-decrement	--
	Function call	()
	Array Element	[]
	Pointer to member of	->
	Member of	.
3	Pre-increment	++
	Pre-decrement	--
	Logical NOT	|
	Bitwise NOT	~
	Unary minus	-
	Unary plus	+
	Address of	&
	Indirection of	*
	Size of	sizeof
	New allocation	new
	De-allocation	delete
	Typecast	(type)
4	Pointer to member object	.*
	Pointer to member pointer	->*
5	Multiplication	*
	Division	/
	Remainder	%
6	Addition	+
	Subtraction	-

TABLE 2.4 Operator Precedence *(continued)*

<table>
<tr><th>Level</th><th>Operator Description</th><th>Operator</th></tr>
<tr><td>7</td><td>Left shift</td><td><<</td></tr>
<tr><td></td><td>Right shift</td><td>>></td></tr>
<tr><td>8</td><td>Less than</td><td><</td></tr>
<tr><td></td><td>Less than or equal to</td><td><=</td></tr>
<tr><td></td><td>Greater than</td><td>></td></tr>
<tr><td></td><td>Greater than or equal to</td><td>>=</td></tr>
<tr><td>9</td><td>Equal to</td><td>=</td></tr>
<tr><td></td><td>Not equal to</td><td>!=</td></tr>
<tr><td>10</td><td>Bitwise AND</td><td>&</td></tr>
<tr><td>11</td><td>Bitwise exclusive OR</td><td>^</td></tr>
<tr><td>12</td><td>Bitwise inclusive OR</td><td>|</td></tr>
<tr><td>13</td><td>Logical AND</td><td>&&</td></tr>
<tr><td>14</td><td>Logical OR</td><td>||</td></tr>
<tr><td>15</td><td>Conditional</td><td>? :</td></tr>
<tr><td>16</td><td>Assignment</td><td>=</td></tr>
<tr><td>17</td><td>Compound assignment</td><td>+= /= %= += -= <<= >>= &= ^= |=</td></tr>
<tr><td>18</td><td>Comma</td><td>,</td></tr>
</table>

Summary

I covered a good bit of information in this chapter. You learned how to declare and use variables in your programs, how to use the various operators to modify your variables, and how to use them all together.

Most of the following chapters will use the information covered in this chapter to build more advanced programs, so make sure you understand the information covered here pretty well.

Questions and Answers

Q: If a byte is the smallest bit of memory you can use, why have bits?

A: A byte is made up of 8 bits. Each bit represents a value in the binary system. For more information about the binary system, see Appendix B.

Q: How does the compiler know how to convert the numbers I use in the decimal system to the binary system?

A: All data is represented in the computer as bits; the numbers you use in decimal are just representations of the binary form.

Q: What is `sizeof`?

A: `sizeof` is a C++ operator that returns the number of bytes a variable or type uses in memory.

Q: Shouldn't `true` be a positive number and `false` zero or a negative number?

A: No. Any number that is different from zero has at least one bit set. By trying to evaluate any number that isn't all zeros in binary form, the compiler can easily and quite quickly identify whether a value is `true`.

Exercises

1. How would the number 2321 be spanned through memory?
2. When is an `int` a 32-bit value and when is it a 16-bit value?
3. What is wrong with the following variable declaration?

```
Short   Variable;
```

4. What is wrong with the following variable declaration?

```
unsigned short  2PI;
```

5. What would be the value of `Result` after the following operations?

```
int Result, A, B;
A = 4;
B = 23;
Result = 9 + (A++ - --B) * B
```

6. Which of the following operators has higher PRECEDENCE: a post-fix operator or unary operator?
7. Why should you use the compound operators?
8. What is wrong with the following code?

```
int Result, A, B, C;
A = 4;
B = 1;
C = 23;
Result += B + A++ * (--C * B);
```

9. What would be the value of `Result` after the following operations?

```
int Result, A, B, C;
A = 9;
B = 1;
C = 2;
Result = C-- + (B++ - --B) * A + C
```

CHAPTER 3

Functions and Program Flow

One of the main advantages of structured programming is the ability to totally control the execution of your program.

Starting by going through simple functions and their uses in game programming and then talking about program flow, this chapter covers two of the most important subjects in C++ programming.

Functions: What Are They and What Are They Used For?

A function is a way to separate code blocks, or functionality if you prefer, in parts. Functions provide the programmer a way to efficiently develop programs without the need for listing thousands of lines in `main`. Functions also provide a nice way to reuse some of the code in many locations without having to actually type the code but rather by calling a function.

Even if you haven't noticed, you have already used a function in your programs. Remember `main`? Well, `main` is a function like the ones you will see here with just a different attribute. It is a required function to any C++ program and is called automatically by the operating system.

Functions have the objective to keep the code shorter, clear, and functional. They work by calling and executing specific code blocks without having to repeat them. Take a look at Figure 3.1 to see how it works.

Calling a function makes the computer execute a specific code block in the location where the function was called. It doesn't include the code, but rather calls it.

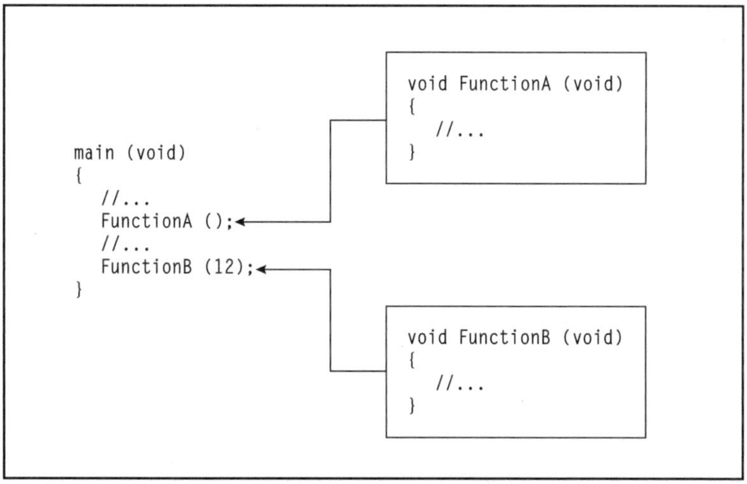

Figure 3.1

Functions call independent specific code blocks that are defined in different parts of the code.

You can see how functions work in the following program that computes the square of a number using a function.

```
 /* '01 Main.cpp' */

 /* Input output stream header*/
#include <iostream>

 // Function prototype */
double Square (double Value);

main ()
{
 double Number, SquaredNumber;

 Number = 5;

  /* Call the function */
 SquaredNumber = Square (Number);

 std::cout << SquaredNumber << std::endl;

 return 0;
```

```
}

 /* Function definition */
double Square (double Value)
{
  /* Function code */
 double SquareReturn;

 SquareReturn = Value * Value;

 return SquareReturn;
}
```

"F:\Game Programming All in One\Source\Chapter_03\01 Square Function\Debug\01 Square Function...
25
Press any key to continue

Figure 3.2

The square function.

Without getting into the specific functions, what you do here is to declare and define a function to find the square of a number, as shown in Figure 3.2. You ask the user for a number with `std::cin` and calculate the square of it by calling the function, showing it in the end.

Creating and Using Functions

Two steps are involved in creating functions: declaring and defining them. After this is done, the functions can be called in the code normally.

Declaring the Prototype

The first step to create a function is to declare the function prototype. You do this by defining the function header followed by a semicolon.

A function header defines a function with three parts: the return type, the function name, and the function parameters.

Return Type

The return type can be any variable type you have seen in the preceding chapter. It tells the compiler what kind of value the function returns to the calling section of the program.

You can also specify a function to return no value by specifying the return type as `void`. In the previous example, `Square` returns a `double` value, which was the square of the argument. You can assign that value to any variable, as shown.

Name

The function name (see Figure 3.3) is what identifies the function in the code. If you need to call the function, you do this by using this name, which should be clear, specify what the function does, and be neither too long nor too short. More advice on function naming is given later when I talk about software architecture.

The function name must follow the same rules as variable naming, which can be found in Chapter 2.

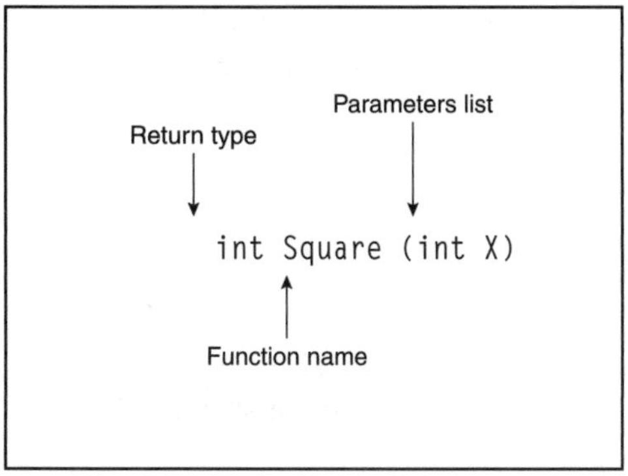

Figure 3.3

The function name identifies the function in the code.

Parameters

The last part of the function header is the parameters list. This is a list of parameters, or values, that are passed to the function. They must be enclosed in parentheses after the function name. This tells the compiler the number and the type of each parameter to expect.

If you don't want to pass any variables to the function, you should specify the parameter list as `void`. This isn't strictly necessary since you can just leave the parameter list empty, but it is a good programming practice to do so.

If you want to pass various parameters you need to separate them with commas.

A few examples of function prototypes are as follows:

```
double Square (double Value);
void ShowHelp (void);
double Area (double Width, double Height);
```

The `Area` function requires two values of type `double` that will be used as the rectangle width and height respectively, to calculate the area of the rectangle.

Function Body

The function body is the code that is actually executed; it is what the function does. This is done by declaring a function header without the final semicolon and then the code block. Inside the code block is the code that is called. From the example in the previous section a function body that calculates the area of a rectangle is the following:

```
double Area (double Width, double Height)
{
 double AreaReturn;

 AreaReturn = Width * Height;

 return AreaReturn;
}
```

This code declares a variable to hold the result, and then it multiplies the `Width` and `Height` parameters to get the area, and returns the result.

You can now use this function in your code by writing the function name followed by parentheses with the function arguments, thus calling the function, and in your example looks like: `Area (10, 20);`.

You have learned what a parameter is, but what is an argument? Arguments are the values you pass as parameters to the function that is used in its calculations. Confused? Don't be, just check Figure 3.4 and the following program:

```
/* '02 Main.cpp' */

/* Input output stream header*/
#include <iostream>

double Cube (double Value);

main ()
{
 double Number, CubeNumber;

 std::cout << "Enter a number: ";
 std::cin >> Number;

  /* Number is the function argument */
 CubeNumber = Cube (Number);

 std::cout << CubeNumber << std::endl;

 return 0;
}

/* Value is the function parameter */
double Cube (double Value)
{
 double CubeReturn;

 CubeReturn = Value * Value * Value;

 return CubeReturn;
}
```

Figure 3.4

The cube function

In this program, you pass the variable `Number` to the function `Cube`. In the `Cube` function prototype, you see it has one parameter, `Value`. `Number` is the argument you pass to the parameter `Value`.

Default Parameters

C++ offers a very nice feature in default parameters. *Default parameters* are a way to specify a common default value for a parameter so that when you call the function you don't have to specify the argument.

To specify a default parameter, you just assign a value to the parameter in the function prototype like this:

```
void CalculateIVA (long Money, double IVA = 0.17);
```

This way, you can call the function without specifying the `IVA` value. Check the following program to see how this works:

```
 /* '03 Main.cpp' */

 /* Input output stream header*/
#include <iostream>

 /* Use default parameter for IVA - 17% */
void CalculateIVA (long Money, double IVA = 0.17);

main ()
{
```

```
 std::cout << "Specifying the IVA value : $1000" << std::endl;
 CalculateIVA (1000, 0.12);

 std::cout << "Using the default IVA value : $1000" << std::endl;
 CalculateIVA (1000);

 return 0;
}

void CalculateIVA (long Money, double IVA)
{
 double MoneyWithIVA;

  /* Calculate IVA */
 MoneyWithIVA = Money * IVA;

 std::cout << "Money after IVA at " << IVA << " is " << MoneyWithIVA;
 std::cout << std::endl;
}
```

The preceding program calls the function `CalculateIVA` first specifying the `IVA` value, and then without specifying it. Try it and see the differences for yourself.

Default parameters must always be the last parameters in the list. This prevents the compiler from calling the incorrect function when using default parameters. See Figure 3.5

> **NOTE**
>
> **Functions with the same name can have different parameters lists. This is called function overloading, which you will deal with later.**

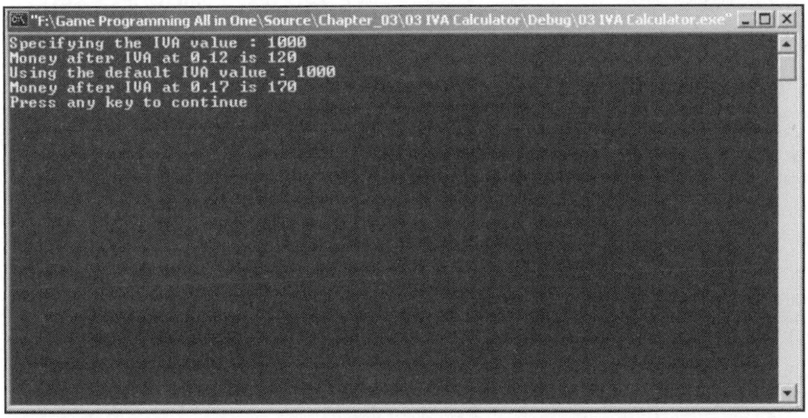

Figure 3.5

The default parameters are the last in the list.

Variable Scope

One of the nicest features of C++ is that you can declare functions as you go; they can be at the start of the program, in the middle, or inside other functions: you decide. But this comes at a cost. A variable you define inside a function can only be used inside that function. A variable you define in the third line of the program can't be used in line 2. This is called *variable scope.*

The scope of the variable is usually defined by the code block it is in. Take a look at the following example:

```
{
 short Age, ID;

 Age = 10;
 ID = 0;
 {
  short ID;
  long Energy;

  Age = 0;
  ID = 123;
  Energy = 12334;
 }

  Energy = 23;
}
```

There are a couple things to note about this code:

- This code doesn't work! The variable `Energy` before the last } is undeclared. This is because the variable `Energy`'s scope is only the second code block.
- You declare `ID` twice; it should give you an error since each variable must have a unique name, but it doesn't. This is because the second `ID` has different scope than the first, so it is treated as a completely different variable.
- Inside the second code block you have access to the variable `Age` declared in the first block.
- In the end of that code, the variable `Age` is `0` and the `ID` variable is also `0`. This happens because for the variable `Age`, the second code block has normal access to `Age` and can use it at will. The reason that `ID` has the initial value is

because in the second code block you specify another variable named `ID`, thus you lose any access to the first one.

Locals

Even if you don't know what local variables are, you have been using them all along.

Local variables are variables that are defined inside the scope of a function, that is, inside the function itself. They can only be accessed inside the function where they are declared. Examples of local variable declaration are in the functions you have been using for calculating the square or cube of a number.

Global

A global variable has the whole file as scope. They are declared usually after the `#include` directive and can be accessed during the rest of the file. Here is an example:

```
 /* '04 Main.cpp' */

 /* Input output stream header*/
#include <iostream>

short NumberOfPlayers;
long Energy;

main ()
{
 std::cout << "Before the variables are used" << std::endl;
 std::cout << "Number of players: " << NumberOfPlayers << std::endl;
 std::cout << "Energy: " << Energy << std::endl;
 std::cout << std::endl;

 NumberOfPlayers = 10;
 Energy = 438534;

 std::cout << "After the variables are used" << std::endl;
 std::cout << "Number of players: " << NumberOfPlayers << std::endl;
 std::cout << "Energy: " << Energy << std::endl;

 return 0;
}
```

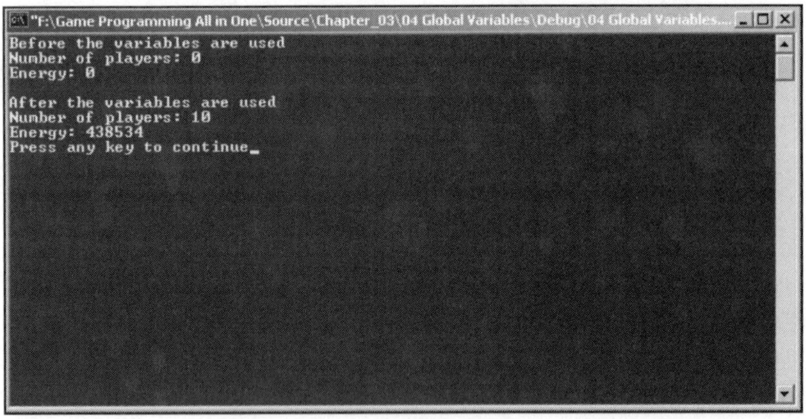

Figure 3.6

An example of global variables.

As you can see, you can use the variables that were defined after `#include` normally. The only difference between global and local variables is that global variables are always initialized to 0 whereas local variables aren't. See Figure 3.6.

You won't make much use of global variables since you don't want to be able to change variables where you shouldn't and to keep all the code modular and self-containing, which are topics I will discuss later.

Static

A static variable retains its value between function calls. If you modify a static variable inside a function, the next time you call that function, the static variable will have the value that it had the last time the function was called. See Figure 3.7.

You declare a static variable using the `static` modifier on a variable like the following:

```
static short Energy;
static unsigned char Players;
```

Check the following program to see this at work.

```
 /* '05 Main.cpp' */

 /* Input output stream header*/
#include <iostream>

void AddPrintEnergy (short EnergyToAdd);

main ()
```

```
{
 AddPrintEnergy (10);
 AddPrintEnergy (10);
 AddPrintEnergy (10);
 AddPrintEnergy (10);

 return 0;
}

void AddPrintEnergy (short EnergyToAdd)
{
 static short Energy = 0;

 Energy += EnergyToAdd;

 std::cout << Energy << std::endl;
}
```

As you can see, `Energy` isn't set to zero every time the function is called, just the first time. It holds its value during the four calls to `AddPrintEnergy`.

The main difference in technical terms of static variables and normal variables, or more accurately, automatic variables, is that automatic variables are created each time they are declared and static variables are created only the first time they are declared.

> **NOTE**
> **Automatic variables are the default when you create a variable without the `static` keyword. Optionally, you can specify the `auto` keyword before the variable type to define it as automatic.**

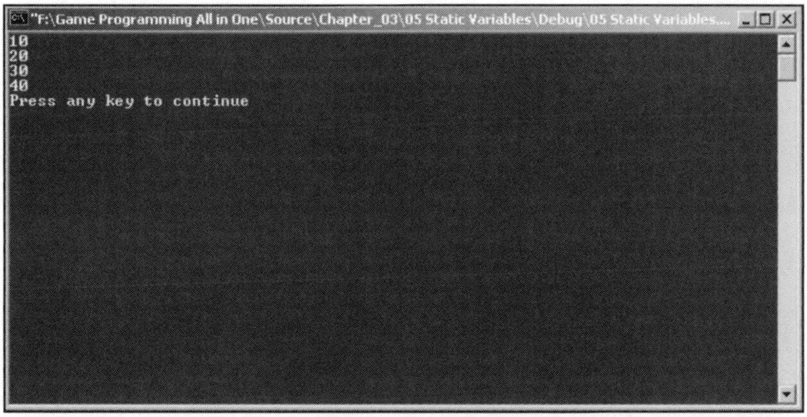

Figure 3.7

Static variables.

Recursion

The last topic on functions I should talk about is recursion. *Recursive functions* are functions that call themselves. Weird? Naaaaah.

If you want to calculate the value of a number to some exponent, you would do something like this:

```
4 ^ 5 = 4 * 4 * 4 * 4 * 4 = 1024
```

Using a linear function to calculate exponents of any number would be, to say the least, hard. Using a recursive function, you can easily do this and do it in a few lines. Don't believe me? Check out the following program:

```
 /* '06 Main.cpp' */

 /* Input output stream header*/
#include <iostream>

long Exponential (unsigned long Number, short Exponent);

main (void)
{
 long ExponentialValue;

 ExponentialValue = Exponential (4, 5);

 std::cout << ExponentialValue << std::endl;

 return 0;
}

long Exponential (unsigned long Number, short Exponent)
{
 static long OriginalNumber = Number;

  /* Performs the exponential operation */
 Number *= OriginalNumber;
  /* Verify that the exponent is valid */
 if (Exponent > 2)
 {
  return Exponential (Number, Exponent-1);
```

```
  }

  return Number;
}
```

The Exponential function calculates the exponential value of any `Number` raised to `Exponent` using a recursive function. It calls itself continuously while `Exponent` is greater than 2. Each time the function is called, it multiplies the `Number` by `OriginalNumber` (the base). You also decrease `Exponent` by one each time to correctly calculate the result. When `Exponent` is less than or equal to two, the function returns the result.

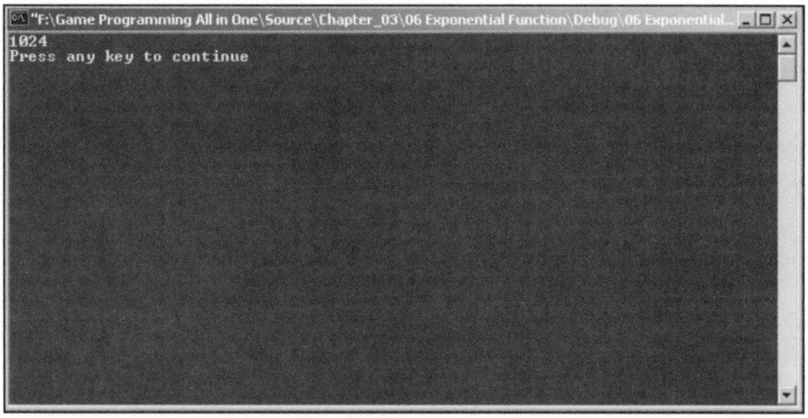

Figure 3.8

The exponential function.

You can see in Figure 3.9, the way the function is called on the left, and the values it returns on the right side.

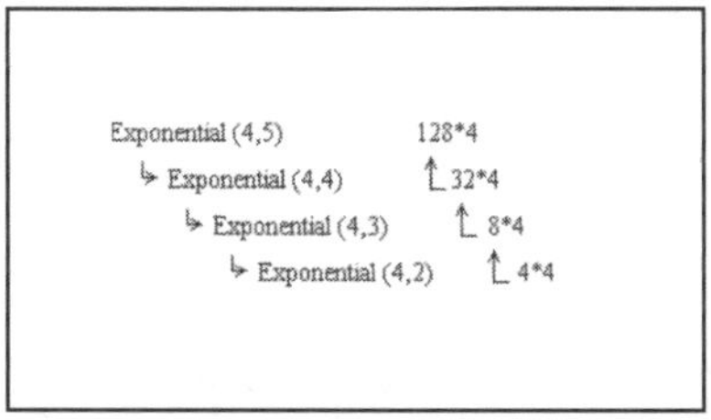

Figure 3.9

Don't worry about the `if` in the code; it is just a way to check whether the exponent is valid. I will go over it in just a second. Just know that if the expression after the `if` is `true`, the next code block is called; if it isn't, it is jumped.

Things to Remember When Using Functions

Here is a useful list of things to remember when dealing with functions:

- Function headers have three parts: the return type, the function name, and the parameters list.
- Function names must comply with the variable naming rules, and each function must have a unique name.
- Default parameters should be used when one or more arguments of the function are the same value when called.
- Default parameters must be the last parameters in the parameters list of the function.
- Variables have specific scope to the functions where they are created.
- Global functions should be avoided, or at least, not modified much in function code.
- Recursion should be used when the code actually benefits from it; take care to avoid its overuse.

Program Flow

The execution order of C++ is very linear; it starts with the first call after `main` and goes through every code line until the last one. If you couldn't control this, for even a small simple game, you would have to do many, many lines of code. C++ offers a couple of statements so that you can control how this flow is done. Instead of going the normal begin-end way, you can skip certain parts of code and execute certain code several times.

I will first go over the C++ relational operators to start explaining how the flow is processed, and when you are briefly familiar with them, I will go over loop statements.

Code Blocks and Statements

The control statements you will see next require a code block or statement after them. What is the difference between them? A code block, as you have seen, is a section of code enclosed in curly braces. Each of the code lines inside the block is a statement. For example:

```
{
 ShowHelp ();
}
```

Does exactly the same as:

```
ShowHelp ();
```

Whereas the first uses a code block with the statement, and the second one uses only the statement.

So, a statement is a code line, and a code block is a collection of statements. Why should you care? Well, the following statements require either a code block or a statement. If you use a code block, all the statements inside that block are called and then control returns to the calling statement; if you use just one statement, then that statement is executed and control returns to the calling statement.

Don't worry if you don't understand it; it will start to make sense when you see both in action.

if, else if, else Statements

These statements are used to check whether a certain code block should be called or not. If the expression to be evaluated with these statements is true, then the code block is called.

if

The `if` statement evaluates the expression that follows it and if it is true, it executes the code that follows; if it isn't true, it skips it. The form of the `if` statement is:

```
if (ExpressionToEvaluate)
{
 Statement1;
 Statement2;
 Statement..;
 StatementN;
}
```

If `ExpressionToEvaluate` is true, the following code is called; if it isn't true, then the program control just skips it and continues after it. See Figure 3.10.

The code block in the code above can also be just one statement followed by a semicolon.

Take a look at the following program that shows how the if statement is used with code blocks and statements.

```
/* '07 Main.cpp' */

/* Input output stream header*/
#include <iostream>

void ShowHelp (void);

main ()
{
 short Action;
  /* Ask the user what he wants to do */
 std::cout << "What do you want to do: ";
 std::cin >> Action;

  /* Check to see what the player wanted to do */
 if (Action == 1)
 {
  std::cout << "You have chosen to run away.";
  std::cout << std::endl;
 }
 if (Action == 2)
 {
  std::cout << "You have chosen to fight.";
  std::cout << std::endl;
 }
 if (Action == 3)
 {
  std::cout << "You did wrong, you die!";
  std::cout << std::endl;
 }
 if (Action == 4)
  ShowHelp ();

 return 0;
}
```

```

void ShowHelp (void)
{
  /* Show the help commands */
  std::cout << std::endl;
  std::cout << "1 - Run";
  std::cout << std::endl;
  std::cout << "2 - Fight";
  std::cout << std::endl;
  std::cout << "3 - Surprise action";
  std::cout << std::endl;
  std::cout << "4 - Shows this help screen";
  std::cout << std::endl;
}
```

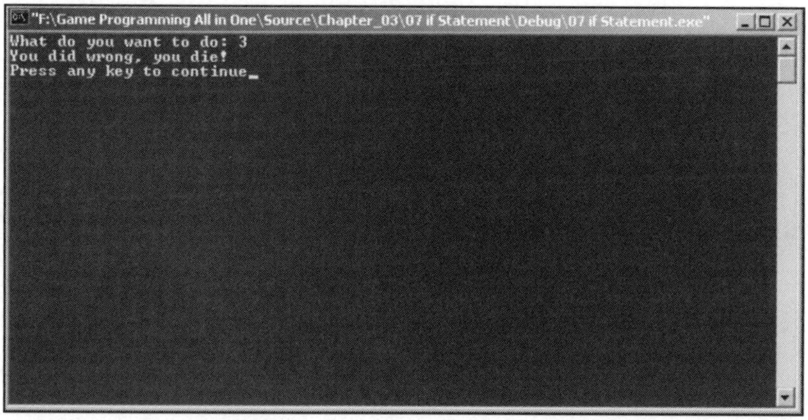

"F:\Game Programming All in One\Source\Chapter_03\07 if Statement\Debug\07 if Statement.exe"
What do you want to do: 3
You did wrong, you die!
Press any key to continue

Figure 3.10

An example of an if statement.

Even if this simple program is a little hard to work with, many of the old text MUDs were programmed this way. The code actually asks the player what he wants to do and then tests it against four numbers, each one defining an action: one for running away, two for fighting, three for a surprise, which actually kills the player, and four that shows the available actions. Depending on the choice, the program shows a string with the action description.

You can also see the `if` statement can be used with single expressions or code blocks.

else

You can add a little extra functionality to the if statement, with an else clause. The syntax for using the else is as follows:

```
if (ExpressionToEvaluate)
 Statement1
else
 Statement2
```

This evaluates whether ExpressionToEvaluate is true; if so, it performs Statement1; if it isn't, it performs Statement2 instead.

Modify the previous example by replacing if (Action == 4) with else and check the result.

You see that if Action is different from 1, 2, or 3, it will execute the ShowHelp () function. This is a nice way to deal with out-of-range problems that the user may cause.

The if ... else statements will prove very handy in the games you will be developing so make sure you understand this well.

while, do ... while, and for Loops

C++ offers you three different ways to create loops, each of them offering different functionalities but basically doing the same thing: processing the same code loop while an expression is true.

while

The while loop is probably the easiest of the loop structures. It executes the loop while the evaluation expression is true; its syntax is:

```
while (EvaluatingExpression)
{
 Statements
 ...
}
```

This code will execute the code block after the `while` line while `EvaluatingExpression` is true. The following program outputs all the square roots of numbers 1 through 20 using the `while` loop.

```
 /* '08 Main.cpp' */

 /* Input output stream header*/
#include <iostream>
 /* Math header*/
#include <math.h>

main ()
{
 short Number = 1;

 while (Number <= 20)
 {
  std::cout << "The square root of " << Number << " is: ";
  std::cout << sqrt (Number) << std::endl;
  Number ++;
 }

 return 0;
}
```

This code outputs the square root of all the numbers between 1 and 20 by repeating the output and calculation code while `Number` is less than or equal to 20. You also need to increment `Number` by one each loop iteration. See Figure 3.11.

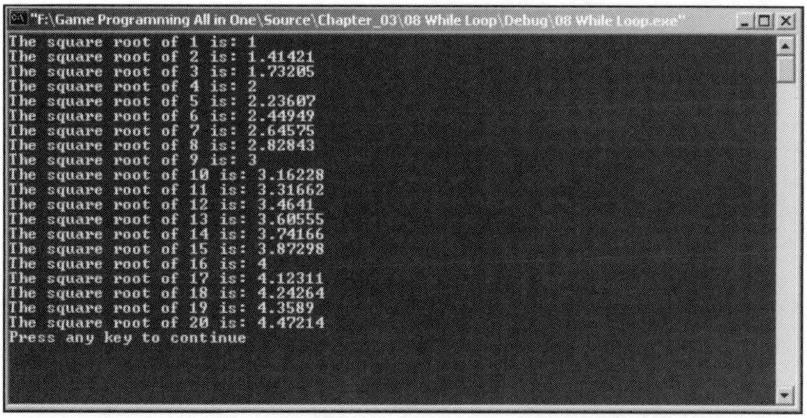

Figure 3.11

The `while` *loop.*

do ... while

The `do ... while` loop is very similar to the `while` loop, but the evaluation is only done at the end of the loop. This way, the code inside the loop is executed at least once. The syntax for the `do ... while` loop is as follows:

```
do
{
 Statements
 ..
}
while (EvaluatingExpression);
```

This will execute the code within the block while `EvaluatingExpression` is true. It will also execute the code block at least once if `EvaluatingExpression` is false.

The following example uses the `do ... while` loop to develop a menu.

```
 /* '09 Main.cpp' */

 /* Input output stream header*/
#include <iostream>

main ()
{
 short Action = 0;

 do
 {
  std::cout << "1 - Do exactly nothing.";
  std::cout << std::endl;
  std::cout << "2 - Try to do nothing.";
  std::cout << std::endl;
  std::cout << "3 - Exit.";
  std::cout << std::endl;
  std::cin >> Action;
 }
 while (Action != 3);

 return 0;
}
```

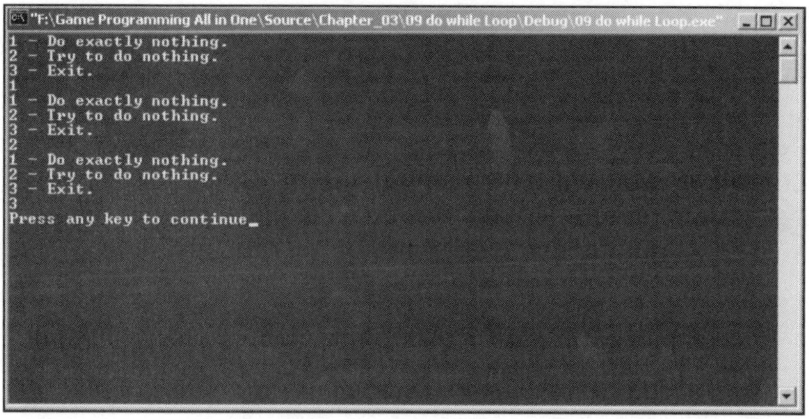

Figure 3.12

The `do...while` *loop.*

This is a very simple program that shows how loops, the `do ... while` loop in this case, can be used to create menus. It does nothing more than output the options to the player while `Action` is different from 3. See Figure 3.12.

for

The last loop you should learn about is the `for` loop. The `for` loop offers you a couple of more options than the `while` or `do ... while` loops.

The `for` loop is composed of three parts, usually used in this order: initialization, evaluation, modifying. See Figure 3.13. The actual syntax is as follows:

```
for (InitializeVariable; EvaluationExpression, ModifyVariable)
{
 Statements
 ...
}
```

I think an example would be easier to understand, so check out the following program that calculates the square of all the numbers between 1 and 20.

```
 /* '10 Main.cpp' */

 /* Input output stream header*/
#include <iostream>

main (void)
```

```
{
  short Number;

  for (Number = 1; Number <= 20; Number++)
  {
    std::cout << "The square of " << Number << " is: ";
    std::cout << Number * Number << std::endl;
  }

  return 0;
}
```

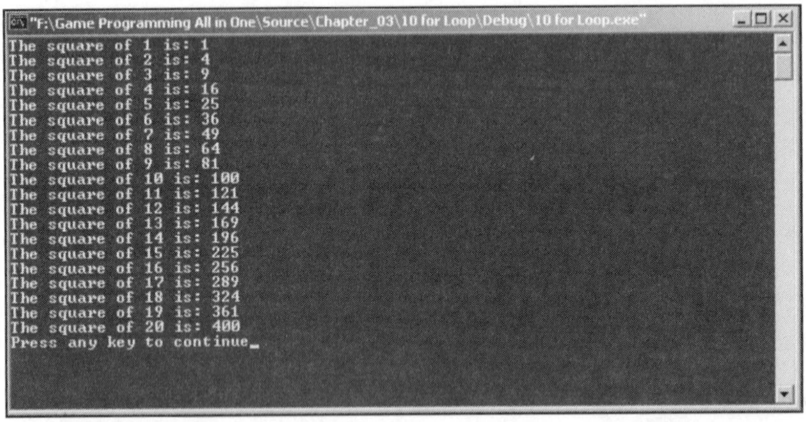
"F:\Game Programming All in One\Source\Chapter_03\10 for Loop\Debug\10 for Loop.exe"
The square of 1 is: 1
The square of 2 is: 4
The square of 3 is: 9
The square of 4 is: 16
The square of 5 is: 25
The square of 6 is: 36
The square of 7 is: 49
The square of 8 is: 64
The square of 9 is: 81
The square of 10 is: 100
The square of 11 is: 121
The square of 12 is: 144
The square of 13 is: 169
The square of 14 is: 196
The square of 15 is: 225
The square of 16 is: 256
The square of 17 is: 289
The square of 18 is: 324
The square of 19 is: 361
The square of 20 is: 400
Press any key to continue

Figure 3.13

The `for` *loop.*

This example uses the `for` statement to initialize `Number` to 1, evaluate the control expression, increment `Number`, and execute the loop code.

The first part of the `for` statement is used to initialize `Number` to 1. This part of the statement can be used to do anything or to do nothing at all, but it is mostly used for this.

The second part is the normal evaluation, in this case `Number <= 20`. While this expression evaluates to true, the loop code is called. The third and last part is where you increment `Number` by one. This section also accepts any statement, but it is commonly used to increment a value.

Additionally, you can slightly alter the syntax of the `for` loop and omit the `InitializeVariable` and `ModifyVariable`. For example:

```
short Number = 1;

 for ( ; Number <= 20 ; )
 {
  std::cout << "The square root of " << Number << " is: ";
  std::cout << sqrt (Number) << std::endl;
  Number ++;
 }
```

This code does exactly the same thing as the `while` loop shown earlier. You initialize `Number` outside the loop, then in the `for` statement you just use the evaluating part and ignore the other two.

Breaking and Continuing

When you enter a loop, you also need a way to get out of it or to bypass an iteration. This is accomplished with the `break` and `continue` keywords respectively.

break

The `break` statement enables you to get out of a loop when you want. Imagine you are inside the game loop but want to allow the player to get out of it if he presses the Esc key. You would use the `break` statement to get out of the loop. Check the following code:

```
while (GameIsRunning)
{
 // Do game stuff
 if (EscPressed)
 {
  break;
 }
}
```

This example will run the loop while `GameIsRunning` is true, different from zero. If the player presses the ESC key, making `EscPressed` true, you use the `break` statement to get out of the loop.

NOTE

You will see how to check whether certain keys are pressed when you deal with advanced input and output in the next chapter.

continue

The `continue` keyword enables you to skip a loop iteration. Suppose you are calculating the tangent of the values from 0 to 180; you know that the tangent of 90 is invalid so you would need to skip that value. The `continue` keyword enables you to do it. Try the following program that outputs the tangent of the values from 0 to 180 in intervals of 10.

```
 /* '11 Main.cpp' */

 /* Input output stream header*/
#include <iostream>
 /* Math header*/
#include <math.h>

double DegreeToRadian (double Angle);

main ()
{
 short Angle;

 for (Angle = 0; Angle < 180; Angle += 10)
 {
  if (Angle == 90)
  {
   std::cout << "The tangent of 90 is invalid."  << std::endl;
   continue;
  }
  std::cout << "The tangent of " << Angle << " is: ";
  std::cout << tan( DegreeToRadian(Angle) ) << std::endl;
 }

 return 0;
}

double DegreeToRadian (double Angle)
{
 double Radian;

 Radian = (Angle * 180) / 3.14159;

 return Radian;
}
```

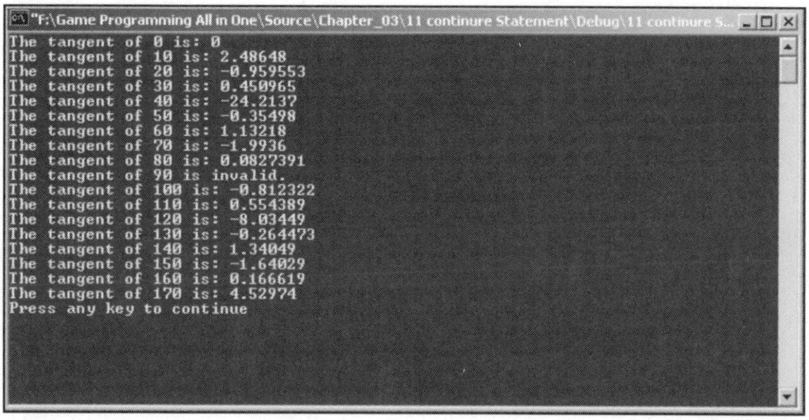

Figure 3.14

The `continue` *statement.*

This code uses a normal loop to calculate all the tangents of the numbers from 0 to 180 using intervals of ten. Nothing really new except when the angle is 90. You use an `if` statement to find when angle is 90, and when it is, you present an error message and skip the calculation of the tangent using the `continue` statement. See Figure 3.14.

> **NOTE**
>
> **Because all C++ math functions use radians as angles, you need a function to convert degrees to radians. This is explained later in the math chapter.**

> **NOTE**
>
> **The `tan` function is a math function defined in the `math.h` header file.**

Switching to switch

To finish the program control material there is just one more control statement to go over: the `switch` statement. (See Figure 3.15.) The `switch` statement enables you to check whether a variable is equal to any specific value, and if so, execute a statement. The syntax for the `switch` statement is as follows:

```
switch (Variable)
{
  case 1:
    Statement1
    break;
```

```
  case 2:
    Statement2
    break;
  default:
  Statement3
  Break;
}
```

Look at the following program. It does exactly the same thing as the program earlier but uses `switch` instead of several `if`s.

```
/* '12 Main.cpp' */

/* Input output stream header*/
#include <iostream>

void ShowHelp (void);

main ()
{
 short Action;
  /* Ask the user what he wants to do */
 std::cout << "What do you want to do: ";

 std::cin >> Action;

  /* Check to see what the player wanted to do */
 switch (Action)
 {
 case 1:
  std::cout << "You have chosen to run away.";
  std::cout << std::endl;
  break;

 case 2:
  std::cout << "You have chosen to fight.";
  std::cout << std::endl;
  break;

 case 3:
  std::cout << "You did wrong, you die!";
  std::cout << std::endl;
```

```
   break;

  default:
   ShowHelp ();
   break;
  }

 return 0;
}

void ShowHelp (void)
{
  /* Show the help commands */
 std::cout << std::endl;
 std::cout << "1 - Run";
 std::cout << std::endl;
 std::cout << "2 - Fight";
 std::cout << std::endl;
 std::cout << "3 - Surprise action";
 std::cout << std::endl;
 std::cout << "4 - Shows this help screen";
 std::cout << std::endl;
}
```

If you run the program, you will see that it does exactly the same as the previous one, but in code you see that you ditched all the `if` clauses and included a simple and cleaner way to work with this kind of problem. It accepts the action as the

Figure 3.15

The `switch` *statement.*

switch argument and then compares it with each case. If it matches with any of the cases, then it executes the code until the break. As seen before, the break statement gets you out of any program control statements, in this case, the switch. If you didn't include it, whenever a match was found, the program would execute that case and any case following until getting out of the switch block.

The default case works similarly to the else statement and is executed if none of the cases matches.

Randomizing

C++ also provides you with a way to get random numbers using the rand function.

rand returns a value between 0 and RAND_MAX, which is, by default, 32767. You rarely use the maximum value to get a random number, so what can you do? Well, if you read the previous chapter (you did, didn't you?), you certainly remember the remainder operator. If you divide any number by another number, you can only get as many different remainders as the dividend; that is, if you divide number 10 by 5, the only possible remainders are 0, 1, 2, 3, 4. Take a look at the following code that illustrates this.

```
/* '13 Main.cpp' */

/* Input output stream header*/
#include <iostream>

main ()
{
 short Value;
 short Dividend = 4;

  /* Calculate the remainder from 0 to 25 */
 for (Value = 0; Value < 25; Value++)
 {
   /* Show the remainder */
  std::cout << Value << "%" << Dividend << "=" << Value % Dividend;
  std::cout << std::endl;
 }

 return 0;
}
```

Figure 3.16

A sample of randomizing.

What you do here is loop from 0 to 25 using the `for` loop and calculate the remainder of each value. As you can see, all the remainders are 0, 1, 2, or 3. This theory applies to random numbers also. Try the little "Guess the number" game, as follows:

```
 /* '14 Main.cpp' */

 /* Input output stream header*/
#include <iostream>
 /* Standard library header*/
#include <stdlib.h>

main ()
{
 short Number;
 short Guess = 0;

  /* Get random number and add one to prevent it from being zero */
 Number = rand () % 100;
 Number++;

  /* Until player finds the number continue to loop */
 while (Guess != Number)
 {
  std::cout << "Enter a number between 1 and 100: ";
  std::cin >> Guess;

   /* If guess is higher, give hint */
```

```
    if (Guess < Number)
    {
     std::cout << "You are guessing low.";
     std::cout << std::endl;
    }
     /* If guess is lower, give hint */
    if (Guess > Number)
    {
     std::cout << "You are guessing high.";
     std::cout << std::endl;
    }
  }

   /* Show win message */
  std::cout << "You got it bud, the winning number is: " << Number;
  std::cout << std::endl;

  return 0;
}
```

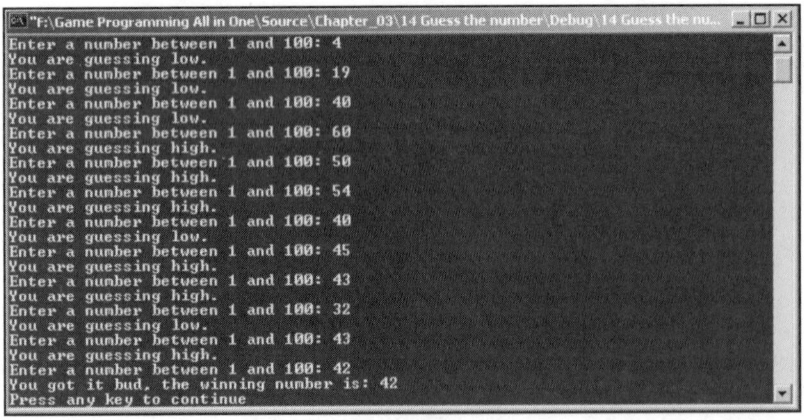
"F:\Game Programming All in One\Source\Chapter_03\14 Guess the number\Debug\14 Guess the nu...
Enter a number between 1 and 100: 4
You are guessing low.
Enter a number between 1 and 100: 19
You are guessing low.
Enter a number between 1 and 100: 40
You are guessing low.
Enter a number between 1 and 100: 60
You are guessing high.
Enter a number between 1 and 100: 50
You are guessing high.
Enter a number between 1 and 100: 54
You are guessing high.
Enter a number between 1 and 100: 40
You are guessing low.
Enter a number between 1 and 100: 45
You are guessing high.
Enter a number between 1 and 100: 43
You are guessing high.
Enter a number between 1 and 100: 32
You are guessing low.
Enter a number between 1 and 100: 43
You are guessing high.
Enter a number between 1 and 100: 42
You got it bud, the winning number is: 42
Press any key to continue

Figure 3.17

A "Guess the Number" game.

This is an easy game to program. You first get a random number between 1 and 100, which is done by using `rand () % 100` and then incrementing it since the remainder of a division by 100 is always in the 0 to 99 range. After that you should already know what is happening; you enter a `while` loop and only leave it when the user guesses the number. In the loop, the program asks for a guess and shows a hint depending on whether the guess is higher or lower than the number.

> **NOTE**
>
> The `rand`, `srand`, and `RAND_MAX` are part of the `stdlib.h` header file. The `time` function is part of `time.h`. To be able to use these functions, you need to include the `stdlib.h` and `time.h` header files in your project like you did with `iostream`.

If you run the game a couple of times you will notice something—the number is always the same. This is weird since you want a random number, right? Well, this is to the nature of the `rand` function itself since it uses a seed (number) for calculating the random number. You don't need to know the inner workings of `rand` but rather how to change that seed, and C++ provides you with a function to do this also: `srand`. `srand` takes an `unsigned int` as an argument and changes the `rand` seed with that number. To get a truly random number you can use a number that changes over time. The `time` function does just that! It takes a pointer to a long integer as argument and returns the time as a long integer.

In the preceding "Guess the number" game, add the following line

```
srand (time (NULL));
```

before `rand () % 100;` and run the game a couple of times. See the difference? Each time you start a new game, it generates a random number different from the last one.

First Game: "Craps"

Finally, you will develop your first game. If you haven't had much trouble grasping all the material until here, you will have no problem with this simple game.

Objective

The objective of the game is to get as much money as possible. This is accomplished by placing bets that make the player gain or lose money, depending on the amount put down and the type of bet, and obviously, the number of the dice, the player either wins or loses the money.

This game is a simple version of the normal casino craps, with simplified rules and bets. But, of course I wouldn't know since I never gamble! He-he-he.

Rules

The rules for this game are very simple. The player starts with $1,000. Before the dice are thrown, the player must place a bet on the outcome of the dice sum. There are three types of bets: 2 or 12, 4 or 10, and 6 or 8. If the sum of the dice value is any of these values, and the player had a bet on it, the money is multiplied as shown in Table 3.1.

If the sum of the dice is any value different from the one the player bet, all the money returns to the casino.

The minimum amount the player may bet is $10 and the maximum $100. The player loses the game when he runs out of money to go home.

TABLE 3.1 Bet Payouts

Bet	Payout
2 or 12	5:1
4 or 10	2.5:1
6 or 8	1.5:1

Design

At first, the player will be presented with a simple screen showing the rules of the game. The player is then taken to the betting menu. Here he can choose the type of bet and the amount he wants to bet. After this is done, the dice are thrown and depending on the result, the user will gain or lose his money. This small bet-roll dice procedure is repeated until the user has no money to gamble.

NOTE

This is a very simple design for this simple game. I will deal with game design in more depth when you get to Part 3, "Hardcore Game Programming."

This is shown in pseudo code, as follows:

```
Show intro screen
While player has money to play
Begin
  Ask player for kind of bet
  Ask player for amount to bet
  Roll dice
  Calculate gains
End
```

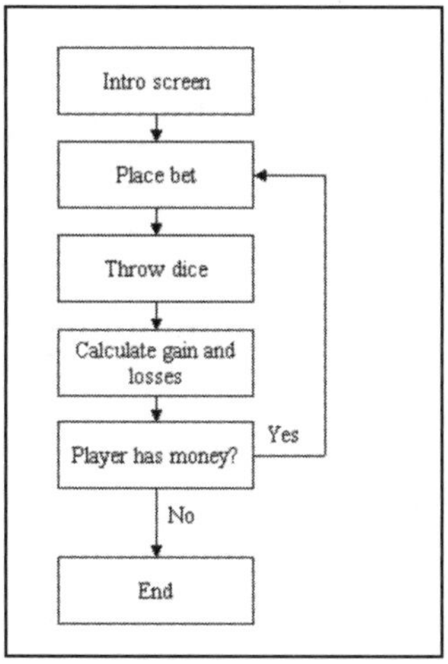

Figure 3.18

A flowchart of our code example.

Implementation

Before starting to code, let me explain how I am going to describe the program.

All the code for this game will be presented in this section, but in part. It will start with a small bit of code, then a brief explanation of it, then another bit of code, then explanation. This is repeated until the code is complete. If you want to try to program for yourself, you should copy only the code blocks to the source file in the order they are presented here or you can copy them from the CD. In the end you will have a complete game.

Ready to start? Good! Let's begin with including the header files you need and declaring the function prototypes.

```
1: #include <iostream>
2: #include <stdlib.h>
```

```
#include <time.h>

void ShowIntroScreen (void);
void ShowInformation (unsigned long Money);
short GetBet (void);
short DoDiceThrow (void);
unsigned short DoMoneyCalc (short Dice, short Bet, short BetMoney);
unsigned long GetAmount (void);
```

You include the `iostream` header to be able to do input and output, the `stdlib.h` header to use `srand`, `rand`, and the `time.h` header so you can truly randomize the numbers with `time`.

You then declare the function prototypes you will be using during the game. These will be explained with `time` when you start building their body.

You will now move to `main`:

```
main (void)
{
 unsigned long MoneyEarned;
 unsigned long Money;

 short DiceValue;
 short Bet;
 short BetMoney;
  /* Show intro and setup game
 ShowIntroScreen ();
 Money = 1000;

  /* Play while player has money
      Keep 100 dollars for the cab home */
do
{
  ShowInformation (Money);
   // Get bet information */
  Bet         = GetBet ();
  BetMoney    = GetAmount ();
  DiceValue   = DoDiceThrow ();
  MoneyEarned = DoMoneyCalc (DiceValue, Bet, BetMoney);

  Money -= BetMoney;
```

```

    /* Show the number */
   if (MoneyEarned == 0)
   {
    std::cout << "You lost. Number was: " << DiceValue;
    std::cout << std::endl << std::endl;
   }
   else
   {
    std::cout << "You won " << MoneyEarned  - BetMoney;
    std::cout << " dollars. Number was: " << DiceValue;
    std::cout << std::endl << std::endl;

    Money += MoneyEarned;
   }
  }
  while (Money > 100);
  std::cout << "Game Over. Keep $" << Money << " for the ride home";
  std::cout << std::endl;

  return 0;
}
```

The main function is the representation of the pseudo code in the previous section. You declare some variables you will be using and show the intro screen. You then set up the initial money and enter the main game loop.

In the game loop, you first show the money available to the player and then ask which type of bet he wants and how much he wants to bet. The bet amount is deducted from the player money. After this, the dice are thrown and the earnings (if any) calculated.

In the end of the game loop, it shows the dice result and, if the player won, shows how much he won.

This game loop continues until the player has fewer than $100; when this happens, a game over message is shown.

```
void ShowIntroScreen (void)
{
 std::cout << "      Welcome to Craps 1.0";
 std::cout << std::endl << std::endl;
```

```
 std::cout << "Here are the rules:";
 std::cout << std::endl << std::endl;

 std::cout << "You have 1000 dollars to start gambling. ";
 std::cout << std::endl << std::endl;

 std::cout << "You can do three different bets. You can bet on ";
 std::cout << "numbers 2 and 12 which will give";
 std::cout << "you a win ratio of ";
 std::cout << "5 to 1 if you win. You can also bet on the numbers 4 ";
 std::cout << "and 10  ";
 std::cout << "which will give you a win ratio of 2.5 to 1. ";
 std::cout << std::endl;
 std::cout << "The last kind of bet you can do is on the numbers 6 ";
 std::cout << "and 8 which will give you a win ratio of 1.5 to 1.";
 std::cout << std::endl << std::endl;

 std::cout << "The minimum amount to bet is 10 dollars and the ";
 std::cout << "maximum 100 dollars.";
 std::cout << std::endl << std::endl;

 std::cout << "Have fun playing.";
 std::cout << std::endl << std::endl  << std::endl;
}
```

This function is rather simple. It shows the rules to the Craps game. Nothing really new here.

```
void ShowInformation (unsigned long Money)
{
 std::cout << "You have : " << Money << " dollars.";
 std::cout << std::endl;
}
```

`ShowInformation` shows how much money the player still has. This would be the place to show other information like lives (if the game had lives), time played, and so on.

```
short GetBet (void)
{
 unsigned short BetType;

```

```
 /* Get bet */
std::cout << "Enter type of bet (1 = '6/8' 2 = '4/10' 3 = '2/12'): ";
std::cin >> BetType;

 /* If bet invalid bet on 6/8 */
if ((BetType == 1) || (BetType == 2) || (BetType == 3))
{
 return BetType;
}
else
{
 return 1;
}
}
```

And you have your first 'game' function. `GetBet` returns the kind of bet the player wants to do. It asks for the bet type using the normal `std::cin` like you saw before. The number 1 stands for 6 or 8, number 2 for 4 or 10, and number 3 for 2 or 12. If the player doesn't choose a valid bet, it will return by default 1, which is the 6 or 8 bet.

```
short DoDiceThrow (void)
{
 short DiceValue;

  /* Get dice value */
 srand (time (NULL));
 DiceValue = (rand () % 11) + 2;

  /* If 4/10 get another number, this will make this
     event more improbable so pay ratio is bigger */
 if ((DiceValue == 4) || (DiceValue == 10))
 {
  srand (time (NULL));
  DiceValue = (rand () % 12) + 1;
 }

  /* If 2/12 get another number, this will make this
     event more improbable so pay ratio is bigger */
 if ((DiceValue == 2) || (DiceValue == 12))
```

```
 {
  srand (time (NULL));
  DiceValue = (rand () % 12) + 1;

  if ((DiceValue == 2) || (DiceValue == 12))
  {
   srand (time (NULL));
   DiceValue = (rand () % 12) + 1;
  }
 }

 return DiceValue;
}
```

This function is the core of your game. `DoDiceThrow` returns the random dice value following some guidelines. It firsts get a random number between 2 and 12 using `rand () % 11 + 2`. Using `rand` like this, you know it will return a value between zero and ten. Since you want a value between 2 and 12, you add two to value returned by `rand () % 11`.

After you get the number, you check to see if the value is either 4 or 8. If it is, you will get another number. This is done to give lower chances to getting the number 4 or 8 since it pays more. You do the same if the number is 2 or 12 but three times since the pay is even bigger.

```
unsigned short DoMoneyCalc (short Dice, short Bet, short BetMoney)
{
 unsigned long MoneyEarned = 0;

  /* See which type of bet the player made */
 switch (Bet)
 {
  /* 6/8 - pay amount of 1.5:1 */
 case 1:
  if ((Dice == 6) || (Dice == 8))
  {
   MoneyEarned = BetMoney * 1.5;
  }
  break;  break;
  /* 4/10 - pay amount of 2.5:1 */
```

```
 case 2:
  if ((Dice == 10) || (Dice == 4))
  {
   MoneyEarned = BetMoney * 2.5;
  }
  break;  break;
  /* 2/12 - pay amount of 5:1 */
 case 3:
  if ((Dice == 2) || (Dice == 12))
  {
   MoneyEarned = BetMoney * 5;
  }
  break;
 default:
  MoneyEarned = 0;
  break;
 }

 return MoneyEarned;
}
```

`DoMoneyCalc` calculates the total earnings of the player. It uses a `switch` statement to check which kind of bet the player chose, and then checks to see if he won by checking whether the dice value is any of the numbers of the bet. If it is, it calculates the earnings depending on the win ratio and returns the result. This is where you want to add your cheating code!

```
unsigned long GetAmount (void)
{
 unsigned short BetAmount;

  /* Get bet amount */
 std::cout << "Enter amount to bet (min 10 - max 100): ";
 std::cin >> BetAmount;

  /* If bet out of range fix it */
 if (BetAmount < 10)
 {
  BetAmount = 10;
 }
```

```

  if (BetAmount > 100)
  {
    BetAmount = 100;
  }

  return BetAmount;
}
```

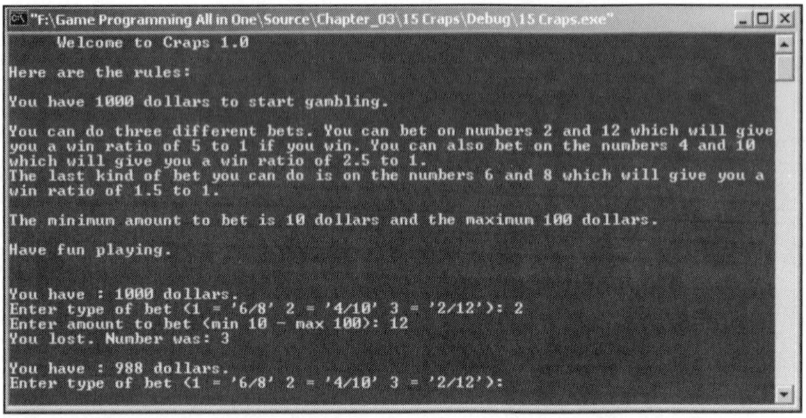

"F:\Game Programming All in One\Source\Chapter_03\15 Craps\Debug\15 Craps.exe"
Welcome to Craps 1.0
Here are the rules:
You have 1000 dollars to start gambling.
You can do three different bets. You can bet on numbers 2 and 12 which will give you a win ratio of 5 to 1 if you win. You can also bet on the numbers 4 and 10 which will give you a win ratio of 2.5 to 1.
The last kind of bet you can do is on the numbers 6 and 8 which will give you a win ratio of 1.5 to 1.
The minimum amount to bet is 10 dollars and the maximum 100 dollars.
Have fun playing.
You have : 1000 dollars.
Enter type of bet (1 = '6/8' 2 = '4/10' 3 = '2/12'): 2
Enter amount to bet (min 10 - max 100): 12
You lost. Number was: 3
You have : 988 dollars.
Enter type of bet (1 = '6/8' 2 = '4/10' 3 = '2/12'):

Figure 3.19

Rules of the craps game.

GetAmount returns the amount of money the player wants to bet. It also does a bounds check to see if the amount the player entered is valid, and if not, fixes it.

And this is your game. A rather simple game but showing the main principles of game programming.

Summary

You covered a lot of ground in this chapter. After reading it, you should be confident with C++ programming basics of program control and also be ready to do small text games on your own.

You also went through your first game, Craps. This game was rather easy to implement and to play, but even so, it teaches some game fundamentals, which will be used in more complicated games later.

Questions and Answers

Q: Why should I use functions?

A: Functions will make your code compact, modular, and easier to maintain.

Q: Don't default parameters limit the functionality of functions?

A: No, default parameters can be overridden if you don't want to use them.

Q: Why use a `do ... while` loop as opposed to the `while` loop?

A: In a `do ... while` loop, the code after the loop is executed at least once, whereas the `while` loop only runs if the evaluation expression is true.

Exercises

1. What are the parts of creating a function?
2. What is wrong with the following code?

```
void Function (void);
{
 // ...
}
```

3. What is the difference between a local and a global variable?
4. What is wrong with the following code?

```
int a,b;
a = 0;
b = 0;
while (a < 2)
{
 std::cout << b << std::endl;
}
```

5. Create a program that uses a `for` loop to print the square roots of all even numbers with a four number interval (ex: 2 6 10 14 ...) from 2 to 38.
6. For what are the three statements in the `for` loop usually used?

7. Create a program that uses a `while` loop to show all the even numbers from 1 to 15.
8. Modify the Craps game so the user can also bet on 3/9 with a winning ratio of 1.7:1.
9. Modify the Craps game so when the user presses an invalid key (letter) the program shows an error message.
10. Modify the Craps game to change the limit of money allowed to bet per round.

CHAPTER 4

Multiple Files and the Preprocessor

One of the most important characteristics of a programmer is being able to organize projects. By separating functionality into different files, you keep the code organized while maintaining the same overall functionality.

The C++ preprocessor is also an important tool to know because it provides some features that can aid your programs.

Differences between Source and Header Files

I will talk about two different files: header files and source files.

The main difference between the two is that header files are usually used for declaring function prototypes, defining types, and classes whereas source files are where you usually implement the functions and other code.

Table 4.1 shows a few suggestions of where things should be included.

TABLE 4.1 Headers and Source Files

Type	Location
Header includes	Header
Type definitions	Header
Class definitions	Header
Function prototypes	Header
Preprocessor directives	Header
Global variables	Source
Function implementation	Source

Handling Multiple Files

Let's go by the simple task of creating a header and source file pair containing a couple of functions and then use them in a normal program.

The first thing to do is to add a header file to your project. In case you don't remember from Chapter 1, to add a file to a project you select the menu Project, then Add to Project, and New. From the dialog box, select C/C++ Header File. You now have your header file included in the project. Let's add two prototypes to it:

```
 /* 01 Header.h */

double Square (double x);

double Cube (double x);
```

This will declare two functions that you already developed in earlier chapters. Now you need to add the function implementation to the source file. Add a new source file to the project and type:

```
 /* 01 Header.cpp */

 /* Include complement header file */
#include "Header.h"

 /* Function definition */
double Square (double Value)
{
  /* Function code */
 double SquareReturn;

 SquareReturn = Value * Value;

 return SquareReturn;
}

 /* Function definition */
double Cube (double Value)
{
  /* Function code */
 double CubeReturn;

```

```
23:   CubeReturn = Value * Value * Value;
24:
25:   return CubeReturn;
26: }
```

Except for line 4, this shouldn't be difficult to understand. You implement the functions you defined in the header file. Now, what about that `include` in line 4? Well, the compiler needs to know what files are related to each other. By including the header file in the source file, you will have access to anything that is defined inside the header file, in your case, the function prototypes. You may have also noticed that I don't use the normal <INCLUDE NAME> but rather quotation marks like this: "INCLUDE NAME". This tells the compiler to look for the file in the current directory as opposed to the default include header if you used <INCLUDE NAME>.

Now that you have this pair of files, you can use them in any project as long as you include them. To test them, add a source file to the project and let's do a small program to see whether it is working.

```
 /* 01 Main.cpp */

 /* Include header file */
#include "Header.h"

 /* Input/output stream header*/
#include <iostream>

main ()
{
 double Number;
 double SquaredNumber, CubedNumber;

 Number = 5;

  /* Call the function */
 SquaredNumber = Square (Number);
 CubedNumber = Cube (Number);

 std::cout << "Square of 5 = " << SquaredNumber << std::endl;
 std::cout << "Cube of 5 = " << CubedNumber << std::endl;

 return 0;
}
```

Figure 4.1

Multiple files.

This program is nothing new except you included the header you created so that you could use the functions implemented there. If you want to use those functions in other projects, you just need to copy `Header.h` and `Header.cpp` to the other project and include them with `#include "Header.h"`.

Figure 4.2 shows a common way various files are used together.

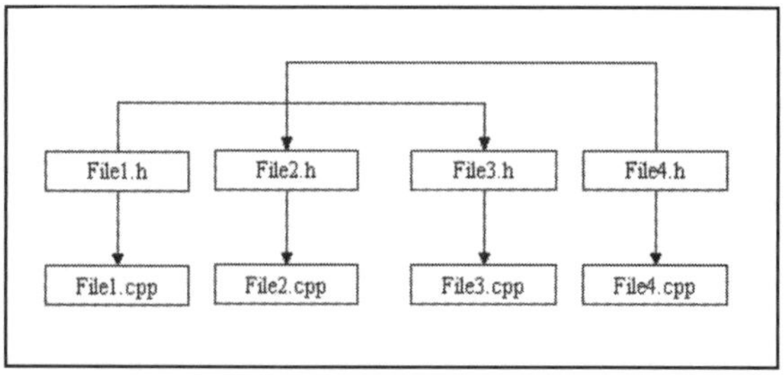

Figure 4.2

Using files together.

What Is the Preprocessor?

If this were a child's book, I could say that the preprocessor is a tiny elf with big pointy ears that reads your files and performs some magic on them before sending them to the master elf for compiling. But because you don't live in the fantasy world (to my sadness), let's get back to the real world. The objective of the preprocessor is to go through the files before compiling, and perform any changes when it reaches a preprocessor directive.

You have been using the preprocessor already with the `#include` directive.

What happens is, when the preprocessor finds a preprocessor instruction, it does the necessary changes to the text in the code. When you include the header files using `#include`, you are including all the text inside that file into your own files.

> **NOTE**
> All preprocessor directives start with a pound symbol (#) and should start at the beginning of the line.

By going through the files before compile time, you are able to do modifications to the code depending on the system, compiler options, and other things.

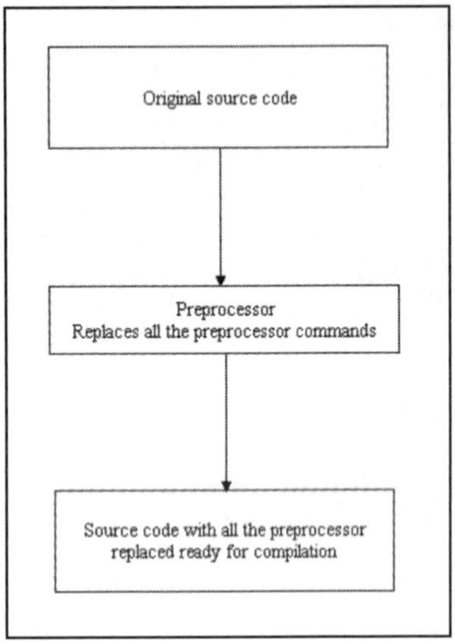

Figure 4.3

A flowchart demonstrating the progress of the source code.

One of the most used preprocessor directives is the define directive, `#define`. Its prototype is:

```
#define identifier token-string
```

This directive replaces all references to `identifier` by the `token-string`, for example:

```
#define PI 3.141592
```

Before preprocessor:

```
/* ... */
double AreaCircle;
AreaCircle = PI * Radius;
/* ... */
```

After preprocessor:

```
/* … */
double AreaCircle;
AreaCircle = 3.141592 * Radius;
/* … */
```

As you can see, after the preprocessor, `PI` was replaced with `3.141592` as desired. This directive can be expanded to just about everything from strings to normal code and back.

Here are some other examples:

```
#define MYNAME "Bruno Sousa"
#define E 2.718281
#define ESQUARED E*E
/* … */
```

As you can see, you can use definitions that have already been declared inside other definitions.

NOTE

By convention, preprocessor definitions have been made all uppercase. This is how most programmers make their definitions, so you will also, but please note they can be lowercase or upper- and lowercase mixed together.

Avoiding Multiple Includes

One of the best uses for preprocessor directives is to prevent the same file from being included various times. Suppose you are still working with the header file created earlier. If you wanted to use the functions implemented in `Header.cpp` in various files, you would have to include `Header.h` in those files. Doing this would create a linker error since it was trying to implement the functions in `Header.cpp` various times.

To prevent this from happening, you need to tell the compiler that the header is already processed and it doesn't need to be included again in any following files. This can be done in two ways using the preprocessor.

Using #pragma

The first and easier way to prevent multiple header includes is to include the following preprocessor directive in the header file where you define the functions prototype:

```
#pragma once
```

When the preprocessor reaches this line, it will know that this file should only be included (opened) once.

So, your original header file would then appear as follows:

```
 /* 02 Header.h */

 /* Include only once */
#pragma once

double Square (double x);

double Cube (double x);
```

This way, this file would be included once, preventing any linking errors.

Using #ifdef, #define, and #endif

The other method to prevent multiple includes is a bit more complicated but more common.

> **NOTE**
> Most programmers prefer to use this type of preventing multiple includes because some compilers don't support the `#pragma once` directive very well or at all.

Before going into the details of how to prevent multiple includes, let's go over what each directive does.

I have already described `#define`, so let's just focus on `#ifdef` and `#endif`. The `#ifdef` prototype is:

```
#ifdef identifier
```

This directive checks to see whether `identifier` is defined, and if so, includes the code following, and if not, it discards it.

Now for `#endif`. `#endif` simply ends any preprocessor if-line. For example:

```
#define HELP
 /* … */
#ifdef HELP
  /* … */
 std::cout << "Help me" << endl;
#endif
 /* … */
```

```
#ifdef DEBUG
  /* … */
 std::cout << "This is debug code." << endl;
#endif
/* … */
```

The preceding code line would include the code between `#ifdef HELP` and the first `#endif` since `HELP` is defined but wouldn't include the code between `# ifdef DEBUG` and `#endif` since `DEBUG` isn't defined.

Now, how can you use this to prevent multiple includes? Easy, if you put all the code of each header inside an `#ifdef` and `#endif` block, you could prevent it from being included in various files.

> **NOTE**
> if-line directives work similarly to the normal equivalents in code. The three if-line directives are `#if`, `#ifdef`, and `#ifndef`.

The first step is to test whether some definition was defined or not, and since you are interested that it isn't, you can use the `!` operator to include the code only if the definition doesn't exist. If you were including the header for the first time, then you would have to define the constant to prevent future use. At the end of the file you would just throw an `#endif` to end the first `#ifdef`. This process is shown in the following code snippet:

```
#ifdef ! _FILENAME_H_
#define _FILENAME_H_
 /* Header code here */
#endif
```

This would check to see whether `_FILENAME_H_` is defined, and if it is, it just skips the header; if it isn't, it defines it and includes the header code.

Your `Header.h` would end up being something like this:

```
 /* 03 Header.h */

 /* Include only once */
#pragma once

double Square (double x);

double Cube (double x);
```

And you wouldn't have to worry about the functions being defined multiple times. Nice, huh?

Macros

Another use for the preprocessor is macros. Macros can replace small functions without adding the function calling overhead.

What exactly is a macro? A macro is a way to create a definition that instead of replacing the identifier with a number replaces it with working code that executes a specific function.

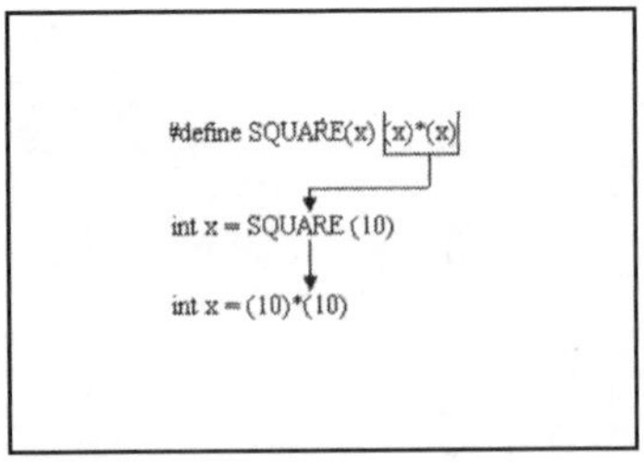

Figure 4.4

A macro.

Macros are defined using three main parts: the macro's name, the arguments, and the string-token, as follows:

```
#define MACRONAME(arguments) code
```

Taking the two examples from `Header.h`, you could use two macros to replace the functions, and thus, reduce the overhead of calling the function.

For example:

```
double Square (double Value)
{
 /* Function code */
double SquareReturn;

SquareReturn = Value * Value;

return SquareReturn;
}
```

Would be

```
#define SQUARE(X) (x)*(x)
```

Which would do the exact same thing. But how does it work then? Well, when you create a macro, the code for the macro actually replaces the macro call in your source code, thus it's a source level expansion. To define the macro you need to put an argument list after the macro identifier just like in functions, but you don't need to define the type. These arguments are then used in the code to be replaced. For example:

```
SquaredNumber = SQUARE (Number);
```

Would be transformed by the preprocessor to:

```
SquaredNumber = (Number)*(Number);
```

There are some disadvantages to using macros. One is the lack of type safe checking. That is, the compiler doesn't check the values passed to the macro, so if you pass a character to a macro when you were supposed to pass a floating-point value, it will probably cause a problem later.

I personally don't recommend the use of macros, but in the end, it is up to you to know what you should and what you shouldn't use.

Other Preprocessor Directives

There are some other preprocessor directives than the ones discussed here. Table 4.2 lists them and Table 4.3 explains the options the `#pragma` directive has.

TABLE 4.2 Other Preprocessor Directives

Directive	Description
`#error`	Produces a compiler error message
`#import`	Imports a file
`#elif`	Else if
`#else`	Else
`#ifndef`	If not defined
`#line`	Changes the internal line number
`#undef`	Undefines an identifier

Table 4.3 #pragma Options

Option	Description
comment	Puts a specific comment in the code
message	Produces a compiler message
warning	Produces a compiler warning message

Summary

This has been a small but important chapter. To be able to use multiple files in your programs is a requirement for good code.

From now on, you will start to separate functionality into separate files so you can reuse code without having to manually include it.

Exercises

1. Without doing multiple includes prevention, try to include `Header.h` in various files and see what error it produces.
2. Using the code from Chapter 3 for the game craps, try to separate game code in a separate header file.
3. What happens in the following line of code?

```
#ifndef _FILE_H
 /* Header code */
#endif
```

4. What is wrong with the following code?

```
#ifdef _FILE_H
 /* Header code */
#endif
```

5. On your own: Try to create a small header and source file containing functions to calculate the areas of a square, a rectangle, and a circle.
6. On your own: Try to produce a compiler error if `STRESS` identifier isn't defined.

CHAPTER 5

Arrays, Pointers, and Strings

This chapter goes over some very important aspects of C++, such as arrays, pointers, and strings. By learning to understand pointers and arrays you will be able to use advanced programming techniques that rely heavily on this material.

Additionally, a brief explanation of strings in C++ and their relationship to arrays and pointers is given at the end of the chapter.

What Is an Array?

An *array* is a collection of variables of the same type and name, ordered sequentially in memory. For example, if you have a set of values that represent a collection of numbers that are related to the same thing, such as the wake-up time of each day of the week, you could use an array of six (come on, no one wakes up early on Sundays) elements to keep each day's wake-up hour in each element. This would be ordered in memory sequentially, as shown in Figure 5.1.

Arrays are very useful for all sorts of things, from look-up tables to bitmaps; you will use arrays throughout your games.

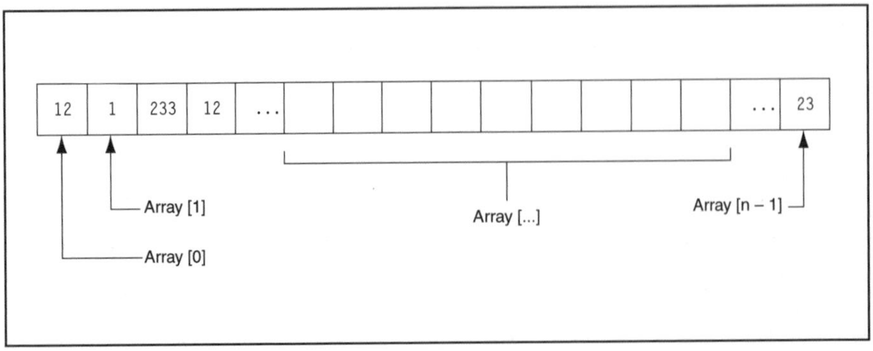

Figure 5.1

An array in memory.

Declaring and Using an Array

As with any variable, you need to first declare an array and then use it, and it isn't very different from normal variable use either.

Declaration

You declare the variable normally but after the variable's name, you use a number inside brackets—the subscript. The subscript is what defines the variable as an array and defines the number of array elements. So, to declare your wake-up schedule you would do:

```
short WakeUp [6];
```

Which would create an array of six elements of type `short`, named `WakeUp`. This is called a single-dimensional array, and the elements are indexed 0, 1, 2, 3, 4, 5.

> **NOTE**
>
> Like any other variable, when you declare an array, you allocate a bit of memory to it. Beware using large arrays because the system may not be able to allocate enough memory to it, leaving you with a nasty program crash right at the start.

Using

After you have your array declared, you can use it like any other variable. How? Simple, you just include the subscript and you can use it as the variable that it is.

Taking the previous wake-up schedule example, if you wanted to set Monday's alarm to nine o'clock, you would do:

```
WakeUp [0] = 9;
```

Which would set the first element, assuming 0 is Monday, in the array to 9.

In C++, all arrays are indexed starting with zero and ending at the array's size at declaration minus one. For example:

```
int Days [356];
```

Can only be used from 0 to 355:

```
Days [0] = 12; /* First element */
Days [65] = 292; /* Any element between 0 and 355 */
Days [355] = 232; /* Last element */
Days [356] = 67; /* Error, out of range */
```

Now for the normal useful program, the code below calculates the cosine of 50000000 (yes, that's a lot) random values using both a look-up table, which is calculated at the beginning of the program, and using the normal `cos` function during runtime (see Figure 5.2). This was (and still is for some speed intensity programs) one of the uses for arrays some time ago, before the new gazillion MHz computers.

```
 /* '01 Main.cpp' */

 /* Input output stream header file */
#include <iostream>
 /* C++ math header file */
#include <math.h>

 /* Start */
main (void)
{
  /* Declare look up table */
 double COSTable [360]; /* 360 elements for all angles between 0 and 359 */
 int Number;

  /* Calculate look up table */
 std::cout << "Calculating Cosine look up table..." << std::endl;

 for (Number = 0; Number < 360; Number++)
 {
  COSTable [Number] = cos (Number * 3.14159 / 180);
 }

  /* Calculate Cosine of 50000000 values using look up table
     and then using cos */
 std::cout << "Calculating cosine of 50000000 random values using look";
 std::cout << " up table..." << std::endl;
  /* Look up table */
 for (Number = 0; Number < 50000000; Number++)
 {
```

```
30:    COSTable [rand () % 360];
31:   }
32:
33:   std::cout << "Calculating cosine of 50000000 random values using cos";
34:   std::cout << " function..." << std::endl;
35:    /* cos function */
36:   for (Number = 0; Number < 50000000; Number++)
37:   {
38:    cos (rand () % 360);
39:   }
40:
41:
42:   return 0;
43: }
```

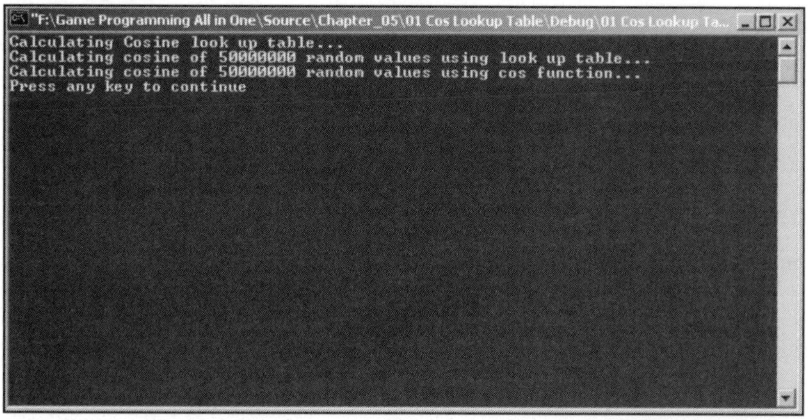

Figure 5.2

Cosine look-up table.

Type, compile, run, and check the difference! Great, isn't it?

You first declare a 360-element array in line 12 named `COSTable`. You calculate each of the table's elements by using a `for` loop (lines 18 through 21). The rest is just showing the time difference between using the look-up table (lines 28 through 31) and the normal `cos` function (lines 36 through 39) by using them both 50000000 times.

> **NOTE**
>
> **Don't forget that you need to convert the angles from degrees into radians, and you do this by multiplying the degree by π and dividing the result by 180. Check the math chapter for more information on degrees and radians.**

I'll leave it as homework to change the code to print each number calculated, so when your friends enter your room you can pretend you are a genius who is actually reading the number and taking notes.

Initializing an Array

You can also initialize the array elements at declaration time similarly to how you did with single variables. You declare all or part of the array only by following the declaration with the assignment operator and a set of values enclosed in braces and separated by commas. For example:

```
short WakeUp [6] = { 9, 8, 8, 9, 9, 12 };
```

This code would declare the `WakeUp` array but also initialize each of the array's elements to the values in the list. This would have the same effect as:

```
short WakeUp [6];
WakeUp [0] = 9;
WakeUp [1] = 8;
WakeUp [2] = 8;
WakeUp [3] = 9;
WakeUp [4] = 9;
WakeUp [5] = 12;
```

You can also initialize part of the array by supplying fewer elements than the array size.

The other way to declare an array is to leave the subscript empty but use the initialization to create the array, for example:

```
short WakeUp [] = { 9, 8, 8, 9, 9, 12 };
```

Would create the exact same array as before. When you don't supply the array's subscript, the compiler creates an array large enough to hold the number of elements you initialize it with.

Multi-Dimensional Arrays

The last topic I want to talk about before moving to pointers is multi-dimensional arrays. Multi-dimensional arrays have two or more (as the name states: multi) subscripts.

Imagine a game playfield that is made of a grid of squares, sort of like a checkers or chess board. The total size of the field is ten units wide and eight units tall. You can declare this playfield as:

```
short Playfield [10] [8];
```

Where you could use the array like:

```
Playfield [0] [0] = 0;
Playfield [1] [6] = 5;
Playfield [8] [2] = 1;
Playfield [9] [3] = 2;
Playfield [9] [7] = 6;
```

For storing the position of the players in the playfield.

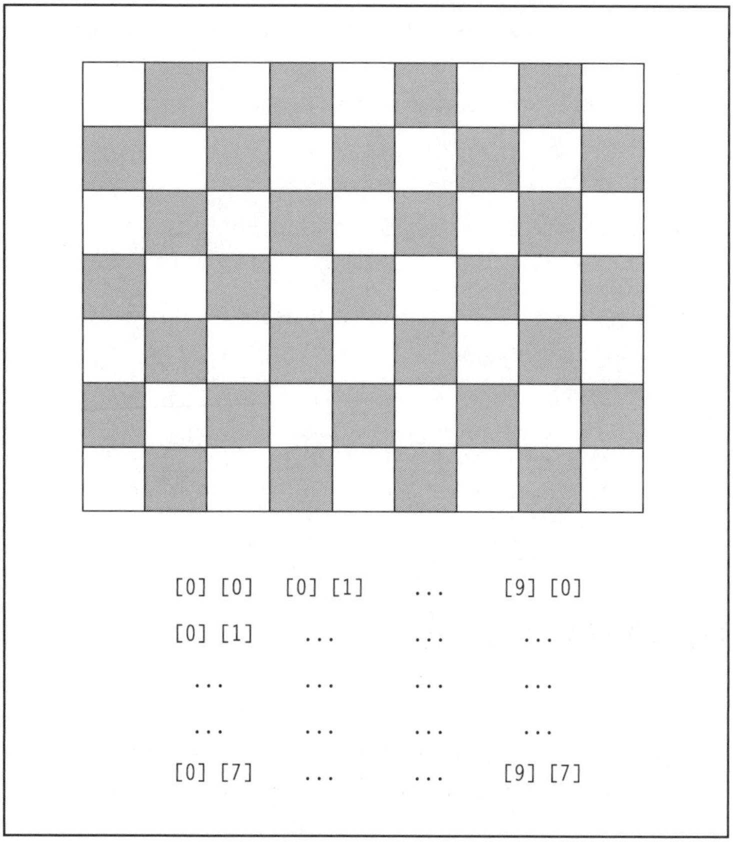

Figure 5.3

Playfield and arrays.

You can also initialize a multi-dimensional array using either:

```
short Square [2] [2] = {0, 1, 2, 3};
```

Or:

```
short Square [2] [2] = { {0, 1} , {2, 3} };
```

That would be the same as:

```
short Square [2] [2];
Square [0] [0] = 0;
Square [0] [1] = 1;
Square [1] [0] = 2;
Square [1] [1] = 3;
```

Both ways initialize the array equally, but the second is probably better because it enables you to separate each subscript array into braces making the code clear.

Picking up the cosine example, let's create a look-up table for the cosine, sine, and tangent of all the values between 0 and 359 using a multi-dimensional array. The first subscript value will specify the type of values the second subscript holds; for example, `Table [1] [32]` would refer to the sine of the angle 32 as can be seen next:

```
 /* '02 Main.cpp' */

 /* Input output stream header file */
#include <iostream>
 /* C++ math header file */
#include <math.h>

 /* Use definitions so you don't need to worry what value is which
    table */
#define COSTABLE 0
#define SINTABLE 1
#define TANTABLE 2

 /* Define PI */
#define PI 3.14159

```

```
  /* Start */
main (void)
{
  /* Declare look up table */
 double Table [3][360]; /* 360 elements for all angles between 0 and
                             359 times three for cosine, sine
                             and tangent */
 int Number;

  /* Calculate look up tables */
 std::cout << "Calculating look up tables..." << std::endl;

 for (Number = 0; Number < 360; Number++)
 {
  Table [COSTABLE] [Number] = cos (Number * PI / 180);
  Table [SINTABLE] [Number] = sin (Number * PI / 180);

   /* Check if number is different than 90 since tan (90) is not
      valid */
  if (Number != 90)
  {
   Table [TANTABLE] [Number] = tan (Number * PI / 180);
  }
 }

  /* Print cosine, sine and tangent of ten random values */
 for (Number = 0; Number < 10; Number++)
 {
  int TempNumber = rand () % 360;
  std::cout << "Number = " << TempNumber;
  std::cout << "  cos = " << Table [COSTABLE] [TempNumber];
  std::cout << "  sin = " << Table [SINTABLE] [TempNumber];
  std::cout << "  tan = " << Table [TANTABLE] [TempNumber]
  std::cout << std::endl;
 }
 return 0;
}
```

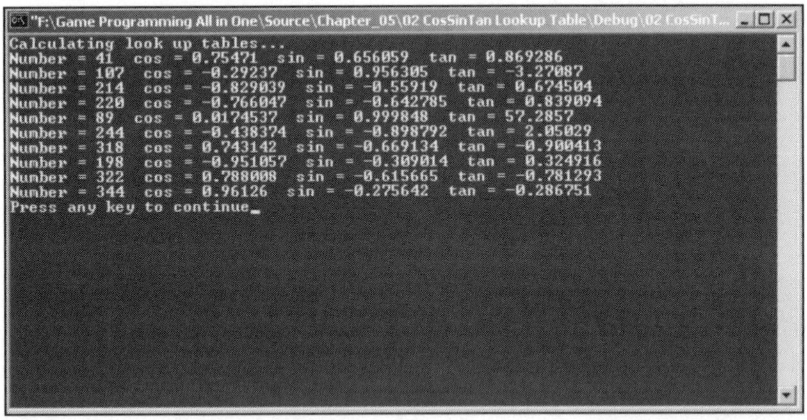

Figure 5.4

Cosine, sine, and tangent look-up table.

There isn't anything new here either. You declare a multi-dimensional array with three subscripts, each forming an array of 360 elements in line 21. You then calculate the look-up table for each trigonometric function (lines 29 through 40) and output the value of 10 random numbers between 0 and 355.

> **NOTE**
>
> **Note that if the `Number` is 90, you don't calculate the tangent for it because the tangent of 90 is invalid.**

Pointers to What?

As you have seen before, when you declare a variable, the compiler reserves a space in memory for it. That space has a location in the computer memory cleverly called *address* (no, it isn't a high-tech name). The address of a variable is the place it occupies in memory.

So, what is a pointer? Well. . . . A *pointer* is a variable that holds the address of another variable. Neat, huh? This may not make much sense but take a look at Figure 5.5.

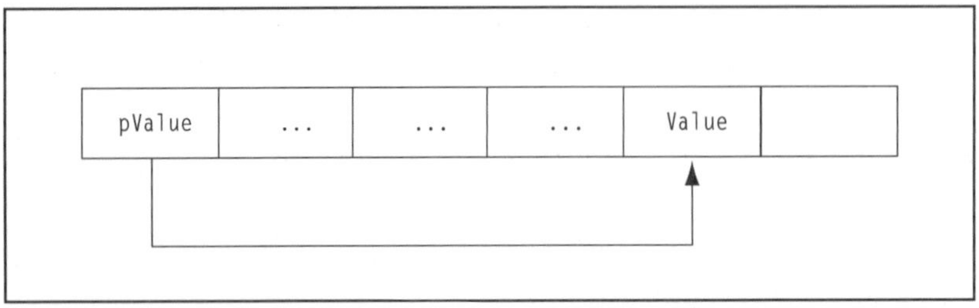

Figure 5.5

A pointer pointing to a variable.

The pointer `pValue` holds the value of the address of the `Value` variable.

It might not be clear why I use pointers, but you will see in a little while how they are useful, so stick around!

Pointers and Variables

Pointers are like normal variables but with a few more advantages and also some problems.

Declaring and Initializing

Declaring a pointer is similar to declaring normal variables, except that you place an asterisk before the variable name. For example:

```
short * Value;
unsigned long * Money;
```

Declares two pointers, one named `Value` that points to a variable of type `short`, and one named `Money` which points to a variable of type `unsigned long`. There isn't much to learn about declaring pointers, is there? I wish using them were as easy!

Initializing pointers is another story. Trying to guess a variable's address would be tough. What you need is an operator that tells you the address of a variable, hence the *address-of operator* (`&`). When placed before a variable, the address-of operator returns the address of a value instead of the value the variable holds. For example, the following piece of code would initialize `PointerValue` to the address of the variable `Value`, thus, making it point to the variable.

```
short * PointerValue;
short Value;
PointerValue = &Value;
```

Using Pointers

Using pointers isn't difficult either. You can use a pointer to change the value of the variable it points to with the *indirection operator* (`*`). You use the actual pointer if you want to deal with the address of the variable it points to, or you use the indirection operator and the pointer to use the value that the variable the pointer points to holds.

Here is a simple example that shows how to use pointers as normal variables:

```
 1:  /* '03 Main.cpp' */
 2:
 3:  /* Input output stream header file */
 4: #include <iostream>
 5:
 6:  /* Start */
 7: main (void)
 8: {
 9:   /* Declare a normal int and a pointer to an int */
10:  int Value;
11:  int * PointerValue;
12:
13:   /* Init Value to 23 and PointerValue to the address of Value */
14:  Value = 23;
15:  PointerValue = &Value;
16:
17:   /* Print value of Value using the variable and using the indirection
18:      operator in the pointer */
19:  std::cout << "Using Value = " << Value << std::endl;
20:  std::cout << "Using indirection operator = ";
21:  std::cout << *PointerValue << std::endl;
22:
23:   /* Print address of Value using the address-of operator and using the
24:      pointer value */
25:  std::cout << "Using address-of operator = " << &Value << std::endl;
26:  std::cout << "Using PointerValue = ";
27:  std::cout << PointerValue << std::endl;
28:
29:  return 0;
30: }
```

This program starts by declaring a variable and a pointer and then initializing the variable to 23 and the pointer to the address of the variable using the `address-of` operator (lines 10 through 15). Then you output the value of the variable using direct access (line 19) and indirect access (line 20) and the address of the variable using the `address-of` operator (line 25) and the pointer (line 27).

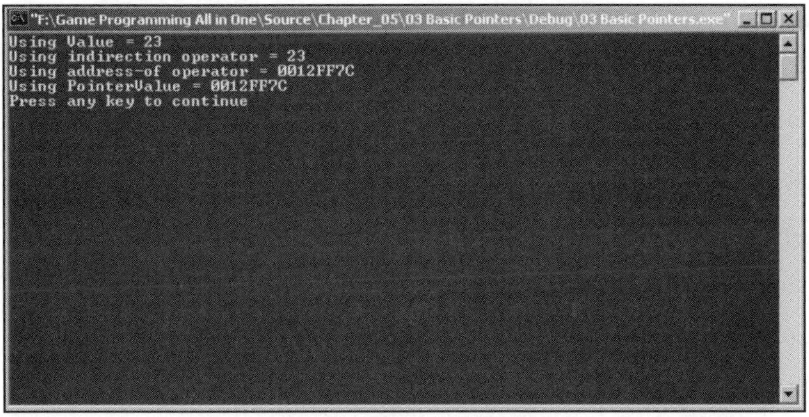

Figure 5.6

Basic pointers.

Pointers and Arrays

Up until now, using pointers wasn't anything that would benefit you. In this section you will learn how pointers and arrays are used to achieve some effects you couldn't normally receive.

Relation of Pointers to Arrays

When you access an array using the subscript, you are telling the computer to go to the n-th element of the array. As you know, an array is ordered sequentially, so you are advancing memory from the start of the array to the n-th element by the size of the array element. Now, if you don't supply any subscript to the array name, you are actually using a pointer.

How can this be? Well. . . . If you think that an array is a sequential block of memory, each array element has an address in memory. If you don't use the subscript when using the array, the value that the array returns isn't the *value* of the first element but the *address* of the first element. For example, in the following code:

```
int * Pointer;
int Array [10];
Pointer = &Array [0];
```

Pointer points to the first element of Array. This is the same as doing:

```
int * Pointer;
int Array [10];
Pointer = Array;
```

Meaning Pointer points to the first element of Array. This code is illustrated in Figure 5.7.

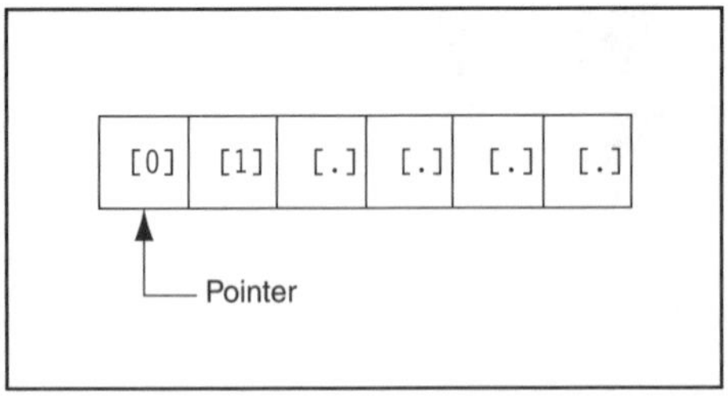

Figure 5.7

Arrays and pointers.

Passing Arrays to Functions

As you learned in Chapter 3, you can pass values to functions as arguments but unfortunately, you can only pass a single value to them.

The only way to pass an array to a function is using a pointer to the array as an argument. When passing a pointer to the function, you are letting the function know the address of the array, and as such, you can use it inside the function. There is one problem when passing arrays as pointers: the function only knows about the starting address of the array. It has no information on the size of the array whatsoever.

You can handle this problem one of two ways. The first, and easiest, is to make sure an array of the correct size is always passed to the function. This is the approach I will be using more later because it saves you the trouble of passing unnecessary

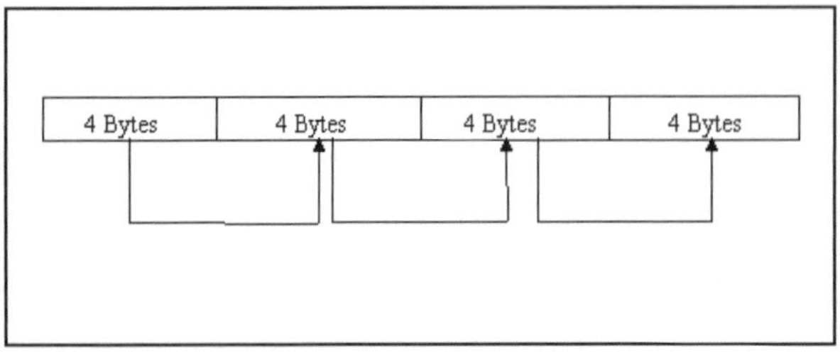

Figure 5.8

Passing arrays.

arguments to the function and additional tests inside the function. The other way to handle the problem is to pass an extra argument to the function holding the number of elements in the array, as shown in the following program that calculates the average of all the values inside an array:

```
 /* '04 Main.cpp' */

 /* Input output stream header file */
#include <iostream>

double Average (int * ListValues, int Elements);

 /* Start */
main (void)
{
 /* Declare a normal int and a pointer to an array of ints */
 int Values [5];
 int NumberValues;

  /* Get five values from user*/
 for (NumberValues = 0; NumberValues < 5; NumberValues ++)
 {
  std::cout << "Enter value " << NumberValues + 1 << " : ";
  std::cin >> Values [NumberValues];
 }

  /* Calculate average */
 double AverageValues;
 AverageValues = Average (Values, 5);

  /* Print average */
 std::cout << "The average of all the values is : " << AverageValues;
 std::cout << std::endl;

 return 0;
}

 /* Calculate average */
double Average (int * ListValues, int Elements)
{
 double Total = 0;
```

```
37:   int NumberElement;
38:
39:    /* Add all values to Total */
40:   for (NumberElement = 0; NumberElement < Elements; NumberElement ++)
41:   {
42:    Total += ListValues [NumberElement];
43:   }
44:    /* Calculate average and return it */
45:   return Total / Elements;
46: }
```

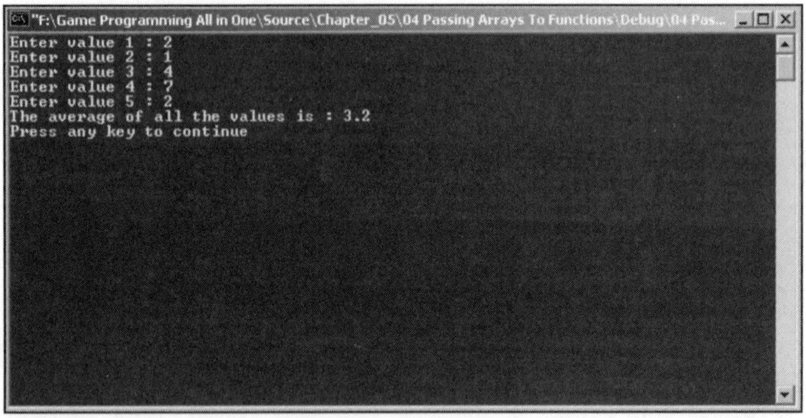
"F:\Game Programming All in One\Source\Chapter_05\04 Passing Arrays To Functions\Debug\04 Pas...
Enter value 1 : 2
Enter value 2 : 1
Enter value 3 : 4
Enter value 4 : 7
Enter value 5 : 2
The average of all the values is : 3.2
Press any key to continue

Figure 5.9

Passing arrays to functions.

If you have been paying attention, this code should be a snap to you. The entire program is basically a re-cap of all the material covered until here except the fact that I pass an array to a function (line 24) to calculate the average of the values and not use a loop inside the main code. I then use that array and the number of elements passed to `Average` to calculate the actual average of the array elements (lines 34 through 46).

Declaring and Allocating Memory to a Pointer

Having arrays is great, but it leaves you with a small problem. Their size needs to be decided when you compile the program. If you create an array of ten elements, you can't change it during program execution. This is where dynamic memory comes in.

Allocating the Memory

When you declare a pointer, the compiler only reserves memory for the pointer itself. You want to make that pointer point to a block of memory allocated by you. To do this, you need to use the operator `new`, as follows:

```
AddressOfMemory = new VariableType;
```

Or:

```
AddressOfMemory = new VariableType [NumberOfObjects];
```

`new` returns the address of the allocated memory object(s). You can work with `new` two ways. You either allocate memory for just one object, or you allocate memory for many, which makes the pointer work like an array.

Here are a few examples:

```
int *Age = new int;
short * WakeUp = new short [6];
float * Ratios = new float [7];
```

The preceding code dynamically allocates an `int` and points `Age` to it. It would also allocate six `short`s as an array and point `WakeUp` to the first element of the array. The last line would also point `Ratios` to the first element of a dynamically allocated array of `float`s.

NOTE

The amount of memory used when working with dynamic memory is the same as if you used a normal array plus a small amount that holds the information about the memory allocated for the operating system to track it.

You don't need to concern yourself about this unless you are writing your own memory manager.

Freeing the Memory

If you allocate memory in your programs, you also need to de-allocate it when it's no longer needed, which is done by calling the operator `delete`. The `delete` operator is called using the pointer storing the address of the allocated memory, such as:

```
delete PointerToObject;
```

Or:

```
delete [] PointerToObject;
```

In case you used the `new []` operator to allocate the memory.

NOTE

Each `new` call must be accompanied by a `delete` call, and each `new []` call must be accompanied by a `delete []` call. If you use the `[]` operator when allocating memory, you also need to use it when releasing the memory.

Use the example given previously and modify it to use a dynamic array of values chosen by the user:

```
 /* '05 Main.cpp' */

 /* Input output stream header file */
#include <iostream>

double Average (int * ListValues, int Elements);

 /* Start */
main (void)
{
  /* Declare a pointer to an int */
 int * Values;
 int NumberValues;
 int TotalValues;

  /* Get number of values */
 std::cout << "Enter number of values : ";
 std::cin >> TotalValues;

  /* Dynamically allocate the array */
 Values = new int [TotalValues];

  /* Get five values from user*/
 for (NumberValues = 0; NumberValues < TotalValues; NumberValues ++)
 {
  std::cout << "Enter value " << NumberValues + 1 << " : ";
  std::cin >> Values [NumberValues];
 }

```

```
  /* Calculate average */
 double AverageValues;
 AverageValues = Average (Values, TotalValues);

  /* Print average */
 std::cout << "The average of all the values is : " << AverageValues;
 std::cout << std::endl;

  /* Free the memory used by the array */
 delete [] Values;

 return 0;
}

 /* Calculate average */
double Average (int * ListValues, int Elements)
{
 double Total = 0;
 int NumberElement;

  /* Add all values to Total */
 for (NumberElement = 0; NumberElement < Elements; NumberElement ++)
 {
  Total += ListValues [NumberElement];
 }
  /* Calculate average and return it */
 return Total / Elements;
}
```

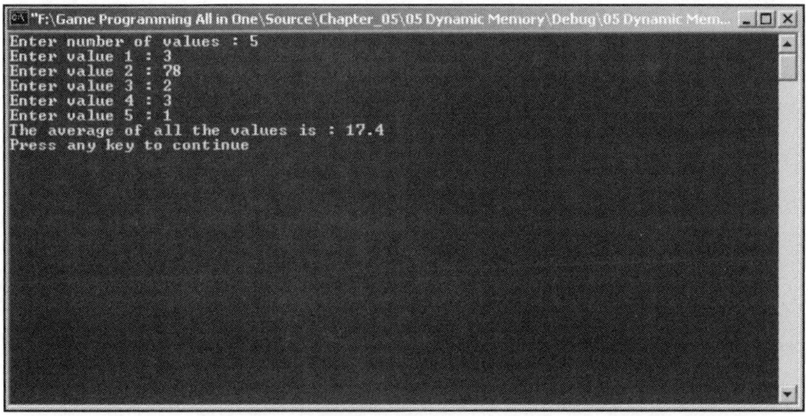

Figure 5.10

Dynamic memory.

This program does the same thing as before, but this time it asks the user how many values he wants to enter (line 18) and then allocates the memory needed using the `new []` operator (line 21).

In the end of `main`, you de-allocate the memory using the operator `delete []`.

Pointer Operators

Now that you know what pointers are, you should go over pointer operators. No, don't worry, it's not that bad. Pointer operators enable you to make some advanced use of pointers such as comparison or incrementing.

Only nine operators work with pointers, as shown in Table 5.1

Using pointer operators is pretty easy. The assignment, equality, and not equal operators work exactly as they do with the normal value variable operators. You already used the indirection and the address-of operators but just in case you're rusty, both these operators are used before the pointer name and the indirection

TABLE 5.1 Pointer Operators

Operation	Symbol	Description
Assignment	=	Assigns a value to the pointer
Equality	==	Evaluates whether operands are equal
Not equal	!=	Evaluates whether operands are different
Increment	++	Increments the pointer's address by one
Decrement	--	Decrements the pointer's address by one
Addition	+	Adds a value to the operator address
Subtraction	-	Subtracts a value from the operator address
Indirection	*	Returns the value the pointer points to
Address-of	&	Returns the address of a pointer

operator returns the value of the variable that the pointer points to, and the address-of operator returns the address of a variable or pointer.

Before moving to the last four operators let me explain something. When you work with arrays, the memory for each element is organized sequentially, but this doesn't mean that each element is only a byte away from the last one. As you saw in Chapter 2, each type of variable has a certain size. Take a look at Figure 5.11 to see what I mean.

As you can see, an array of `char`s is organized one byte after another, while an array of `float`s has a four-byte gap between each element. If you think of it, it makes sense. Because each variable needs four bytes, it's only reasonable that the next element needs four bytes also, so there is a four-byte space between them.

Okay, now that you have been through that, it's time to get back to the operators.

When you use the increment and decrement operators, you increment your pointer by the size of the variable it points to. Don't understand? Don't worry, just take a look at Figure 5.11. If `pAges` points to 0x0001AF02, or 110338 in decimal, and you want to increase `pAges`, you will increase it by one so that it points to 110339, right? Right, now pick the `pInterest` pointer. If you increase this pointer, you don't want to move just one byte, but four, so you can make `pInterest` point to the next element in the array. So the original address would be increased by four bytes, as shown in Figure 5.12.

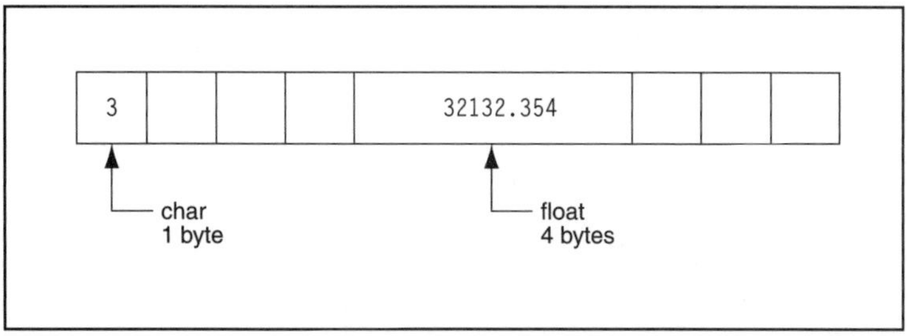

Figure 5.11

Each variable type uses a different amount of memory.

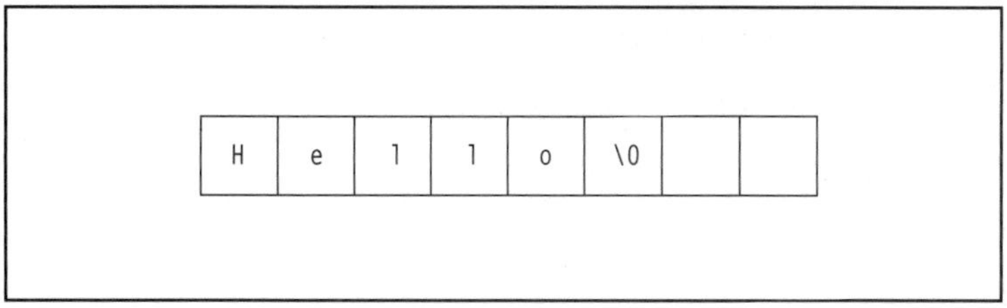

Figure 5.12

Increasing the pointer will make it jump four bytes.

This same concept is used in all the remaining operators. If you decrease the pointer, you decrease it by the size of the variable it points to. If you want to use the addition or subtraction operators, you can do the following:

```
pAge = pAge + 2;
pInterest = pInterest - 9;
```

Which would increase `pAge` by 2, and would decrease `pInterest` by 36 (`9 * sizeof (float)`), or 9 `floats`.

Take a look at the following program that fills an array with random values and uses pointer arithmetic to print the array's values.

```
 /* '06 Main.cpp' */

 /* Input output stream header file */
#include <iostream>

 /* Start */
main (void)
{
  /* Declare an array of ints */
 int Values [10];
 int * PointerValues;
 int NumberValues;

  /* Initialize the pointer to the first element of array */
 PointerValues = Values;

  /* Fill in array with random values */
 for (NumberValues = 0; NumberValues < 10; NumberValues ++)
 {
  Values [NumberValues] = rand () % 1000;
 }

  std::cout << "Array \tIndirection \tAddress" << std::endl;

  /* Print array using normal array accessing and pointer arithmetic */
 for (NumberValues = 0; NumberValues < 10; NumberValues ++)
 {
  std::cout << Values [NumberValues] << "\t";
  std::cout << *PointerValues << "\t\t";
  std::cout << PointerValues++ << std::endl;
```

```
31:   }
32:
33:   return 0;
34: }
```

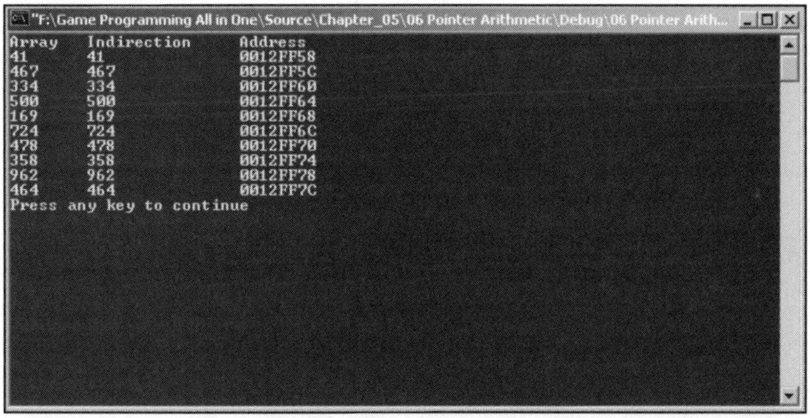

Figure 5.13

Pointer arithmetic.

The main part of this program is lines 28, 29, and 30. In line 28, you print the value of the array normally. In line 29, you print the value of the variable `PointerValues` points to, which is the first element of the array. In line 30, you print the value of `PointerValues`, which is the address it points to, and then increase the pointer. In the next iteration of the `for` loop, `PointerValues` will point to the second element of the array because you increased it, and so on.

Manipulating Memory

Sometimes it is useful to copy a partial or an entire array to another one or sometimes just set all the array elements to a specific value. The first thing you might think is "Let's use a loop." Although this is possible, if you are talking about a very big array, it may be a slow thing to do. For this, there are two nice functions you can use.

memcpy

The first function you should see is `mempcy`. `mempcy` enables you to copy a number of bytes from a buffer to another and its prototype is:

```
void * mempcy (void *dest, const void *src, size_t count);
```

Where the first parameter is a pointer to the destination buffer, the second parameter is a pointer to the source buffer, and the last parameter is the number of bytes to copy.

This function returns a pointer to the destination buffer.

If, for example, you have an array of `ints` of size 10, and you wanted to copy the first half of the array to the second half, you could do something like:

```
int Buffer [10];
 /* Buffer initialization */
memcpy (& (Buffer [5]), & (Buffer [0]), sizeof (int) * 5);
```

Which would take as the destination buffer a pointer to the sixth (remember that C++ arrays start at zero) element of the buffer, and would take as the source parameter the first element of the array, and copy five elements from the start to the middle.

You had to add the number of elements times the size of an `int` since `memcpy` works in bytes. Because you want to copy five `ints`, you need to copy five times the size of an `int` bytes. This is shown in Figure 5.14.

TIP

A *buffer* is simply a sequence of data, in this case, a sequence of bytes.

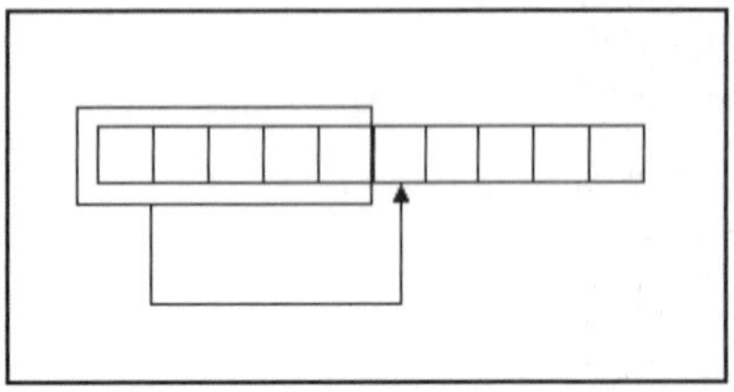

Figure 5.14

Copying the first half of the array to the second half.

memset

The second method I want to cover is `memset`. `memset` enables you to set a partial or an entire buffer to a specific value. It is defined as:

```
void * memset (void *dest, int c, size_t count);
```

Where the first parameter is the pointer to the buffer you want to set, the second is parameter of the value you want to set the buffer with, and the last parameter is the number of bytes you want to set. This function returns a pointer to the buffer.

If you wanted to clear an entire array to the value 0, you could do:

```
int Buffer [123];
memset (Buffer, 0, sizeof (int) * 123);
```

Which would set all the data in the buffer to 0.

Strings

One of the biggest complaints C++ programmers have (especially programmers with backgrounds in BASIC or Pascal) is the fact that C++ doesn't have a native string variable type.

NOTE

C++ Standard Template Library (STL) has a String type. STL is part of the C++ language; however, it's beyond the scope of this book because it's based on templates and advanced use of classes.

Strings and Arrays

Since C++ doesn't have a native string type, another method is used to hold strings. This is where arrays come in.

If you think of it, a `char` is a normal character like your letters; isn't it reasonable to say an array of `chars` is a string? I think so. Take a look at Figure 5.15.

So, an array of `chars` can be a string, but what is that funny `\0` at the end? `\0` is called the *NULL-terminating character*. It tells the system that the string ends there.

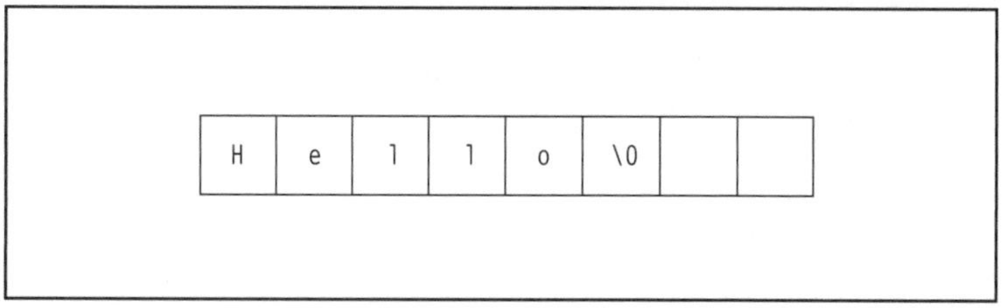

Figure 5.15

An array of characters.

Using Strings

Using strings isn't much different from using normal variables. You just need to pay some special attention to some cases.

Strings and Arrays

As you have already seen, strings are represented in C++ as arrays. If, for example, you wanted to create a string storing the phrase "C++ is great", you would type the following:

```
char Phrase [13] = "C++ is great";
```

Which would create an array storing 13 elements, namely the phrase. Now you may be asking, if the phrase "C++ is great" has only 12 characters, why do you allocate 13 elements? As said before, each string must be terminated with the NULL-terminating character. When you create a string using quotation marks, C++ automatically adds the NULL-terminating character to the string. So in your case, it would really be `"C++ is great\0"`.

String Allocation at Compilation

You can also create strings using pointers. For example:

char *Phrase = "C++ is great";

Would create the same string as before. The memory for these types of strings is allocated automatically by the compiler at load time.

How does this work? Well, when you run a program on your computer, the entire executable is usually loaded to memory. So every single byte of code of your programs is in memory, including `"C++ is great"`. The program makes the `Phrase` pointer point to that place in memory.

Input and Output

Using strings for input and output is basically the same as other variables. You use both the insertion and extraction operator like before, for example:

```
char Name [255];
std::cout << "What Is your first name?" << std::endl;
std::cin >> Name;
std::cout << "Your first name is " << Name << std::endl;
```

Would declare an array of 255 elements, since it is for a string, 254 characters plus the NULL-terminating character. It would then ask for the user to type his name, and would output it afterward.

String Operations

Apart from the basic string manipulation that C++ provides you, there are a few more string operations that are useful.

strcpy

The first error a programmer may incur when working with strings is trying to copy a string to another string using the assignment operator. Unfortunately, it isn't that simple. Strings are stored as arrays, so you need a way to copy the part of the array of interest, namely, all the elements up until the NULL-terminating character.

This can be done using `strcpy`. `strcpy` enables you to copy a string to another until the NULL-terminating character is found. Its prototype is:

```
char * strcpy (char * strDestination, const char * strSource);
```

This function takes two parameters. The first parameter is a pointer to the string to where you want to copy the original string. The second parameter is a pointer to the original string. `strcpy` also returns a pointer to the destination string.

Here is a small program that uses `strcpy` to copy a string to another:

```
 /* '07 Main.cpp' */

 /* Input output stream header file */
#include <iostream>

 /* Start */
main (void)
{
  /* Declare a string */
 char String [255];
 char Test [255];

  /* Get a string from the user and copy it to String */
 std::cout << "Type any string: ";
 std::cin >> Test;
```

```
16:
17:  strcpy (String, Test);
18:
19:   /* Output both strings */
20:  std::cout << "Test string: " << Test << std::endl;
21:  std::cout << "Input string: " << String << std::endl;
22:
23:  return 0;
24: }
```

"F:\Game Programming All in One\Source\Chapter_05\07 strcpy\Debug\07 strcpy.exe"
Type any string: Weeeeeeeee.....
Test string: Weeeeeeeee.....
Input string: Weeeeeeeee.....
Press any key to continue

Figure 5.16
strcpy.

The only thing to pay attention to is line 17 where you use strcpy to copy the input string to String array.

strncpy

strncpy works like strcpy with the difference that it enables you to specify the maximum number of characters to be copied. Here is the prototype:

```
char * strncpy (char * strDestination, const char * strSource, size_t count);
```

strncpy is similar to strcpy but has an extra parameter, count, which specifies the maximum number of characters to copy.

> **NOTE**
> size_t is defined in C++ as a normal int type variable. It is used in C++ functions usually to specify sizes of all types.

For example:

```
char * StringSource = "Hello World!";
char StringDest [9];
strncpy (StringDest, StringSource, 8);
```

Would copy only the first eight characters of StringSource to StringDest, leaving this one with the string "Hello Wo".

strlen

Sometimes it is pretty useful to know how many characters a string has. Don't confuse this with the size of the array. The string length is the character count until the NULL-terminating character is found. This can be done with strlen, the prototype is:

```
size_t strlen (const char * string);
```

This function takes as the only parameter a pointer to the string you want to know the length of, and returns the number of characters until the NULL-terminating character.

The following example takes a string as input from the user, and uses the string's length to create a dynamic array to hold the string. The dynamic array is more efficient than using a big array because it has the exact memory needed for the string:

```
 /* '08 Main.cpp' */

 /* Input output stream header file */
#include <iostream>

 /* Start */
main (void)
{
  /* Declare a string and a pointer to a char */
 char Test [255];
 char * String;

  /* Get a string from the user */
 std::cout << "Type any string: ";
 std::cin >> Test;

  /* Use length of string to allocate the new string */
 String = new char [strlen (Test) + 1];
 strcpy (String, Test);
```

```
20:
21:   /* Output both strings */
22:  std::cout << "Test string: " << Test << std::endl;
23:  std::cout << "Input string: " << String << std::endl;
24:  std::cout << "String length: " << strlen (Test) << std::endl;
25:  delete [] String;
26:
27:  return 0;
28: }
```

"F:\Game Programming All in One\Source\Chapter_05\08 strlen\Debug\08 strlen.exe"
Type any string: Hi!
Test string: Hi!
Input string: Hi!
String length: 3
Press any key to continue

Figure 5.17

`strlen`.

Nothing new here either except the fact that you use the string's length to create another dynamic string by first getting a string from the user in line 15 using the extraction operator. You then create a dynamic array in line 18 the size of the string's length plus one for the NULL-terminating character.

strcat

Another nice thing to know is how to concatenate two strings. This can be done using the function `strcat`:

```
char *strcat (char *strDestination, const char *strSource);
```

`strcat` takes two parameters, the destination string, which should already contain the original string and the source string, which will be concatenated to the destination string. `strcat` also returns a pointer to the destination string.

The following program gets two strings from the user and concatenates them:

```
/* '09 Main.cpp' */
```

```

/* Input output stream header file */
#include <iostream>

/* Start */
main (void)
{
  /* Declare three strings */
 char FirstString [255];
 char SecondString [255];
 char FinalString [255];

  /* Get two strings from the user */
 std::cout << "First string: ";
 std::cin >> FirstString;
 std::cout << "Second string: ";
 std::cin >> SecondString;

  /* Concatenate two strings */
 strcpy (FinalString, FirstString);
 strcat (FinalString, SecondString);

  /* Output final strings */
 std::cout << "Final string: " << FinalString << std::endl;

 return 0;
}
```

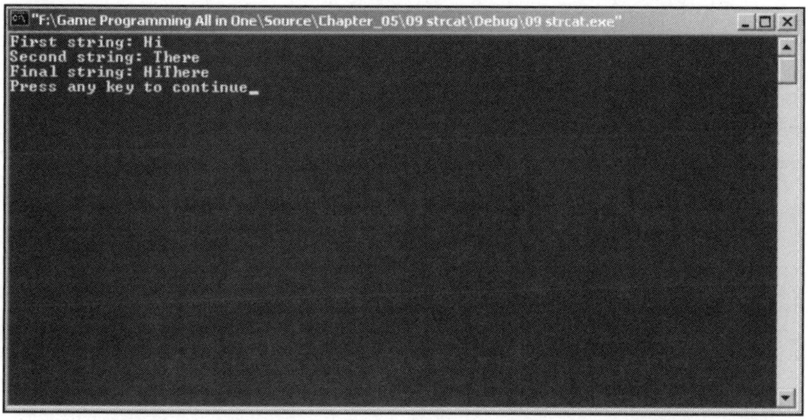

Figure 5.18
strcat.

The only thing to point out here is lines 21 and 22 where you first copy FirstString to FinalString and then concatenate SecondString to FinalString.

strncat

strncat works like strcat but specifies the maximum characters to append to the original string. Its prototype is:

```
char *strncat (char *strDest, const char *strSource, size_t count);
```

Which works similarly to strcat with the difference that it takes an extra parameter which is the number of characters to append.

For example:

```
char * StringA = "Hello World!";
char * StringB = "It's cold out here.";
char StringDest [255];
strcpy (StringDest, StringA);
strncat (StringDest, StringB, 9);
```

Would first copy StringA to the destination string, StringDest, and then use strncat to append nine characters from StringB to the destination string. In the end, StringDest would be "Hello World!It's cold" only.

strcmp

The strcmp C++ function enables you to compare two strings to determine whether they are exactly the same. It's defined as:

```
int strcmp (const char *string1, const char *string2);
```

Where the two parameters are pointers to the strings you want to compare. strcmp returns an int that specifies whether the strings are equal. If strcmp returns 0, the strings are equal. If strcmp returns a value less than 0, string1 is less than (first character that isn't equal has a lower ASCII value than the other) string2. If strcmp returns a value greater than 0, then string2 is greater than string1.

The following program asks the user for two strings and checks whether they are equal or not:

```
/* '10 Main.cpp' */

/* Input output stream header file */
#include <iostream>
```

```

 /* Start */
main (void)
{
  /* Declare two strings */
 char FirstString [255];
 char SecondString [255];

  /* Get two strings from the user */
 std::cout << "First string: ";
 std::cin >> FirstString;
 std::cout << "Second string: ";
 std::cin >> SecondString;

  /* Compare the two strings */
 if ( false == strcmp (FirstString, SecondString) )
 {
  std::cout << "Strings match!" << std::endl;
 }
 else
 {
  std::cout << "Strings don't match!" << std::endl;
 }

 return 0;
}
```

"F:\Game Programming All in One\Source\Chapter_05\10 strcmp\Debug\10 strcmp.exe"
First string: Bruno
Second string: Sousa
Strings don't match!
Press any key to continue

Figure 5.19

strcmp.

You are probably bored by now, but there isn't anything remarkably new here either. You just get two strings from the user (lines 15 and 17) and then use `strcmp` to see whether they are exactly the same (line 20).

strncmp

As before, there is a function to compare two strings using only a maximum number of characters: `strncmp`. Its prototype is:

```
int strncmp (const char *string1, const char *string2, size_t count);
```

Which works the same way as `strcmp` but taking the extra parameter to check how many characters it should compare.

For example:

```
char * StringA = "Hello Anna!";
char * StringB = "Hello John.";
int IsEqual;
IsEqual = strncmp (StringA, StringB, 5);
```

`IsEqual` would be zero since `strncmp` only compared the first five characters of both strings, and since they are equal, it returns 0.

strchr

`strchr` enables you to check whether a certain character exists in a given string. This can be extremely useful if you are doing games that use string commands for messages. `strchr` is defined as follows:

```
char *strchr (const char *string, int c);
```

Where the first parameter is a pointer to the string to check and the second parameter is the character to look for. `strchr` returns a pointer to the first occurrence of the character in the string.

The following example asks the user for a string and then a character and determines whether the character exists in the string:

```
/* '11 Main.cpp' */

/* Input output stream header file */
#include <iostream>

```

```
 /* Start */
main (void)
{
  /* Declare a string */
 char String [255];
 char Character;

  /* Get a string and a character from the user */
 std::cout << "String: ";
 std::cin >> String;
 std::cout << "Character: ";
 std::cin >> Character;

  /* Check to see if character exists on the strings */
 if ( 0 == strchr (String, Character) )
 {
  std::cout << "Character isn't part of the string!" << std::endl;
 }
 else
 {
  std::cout << "Character is part of the string!" << std::endl;
 }

 return 0;
}
```

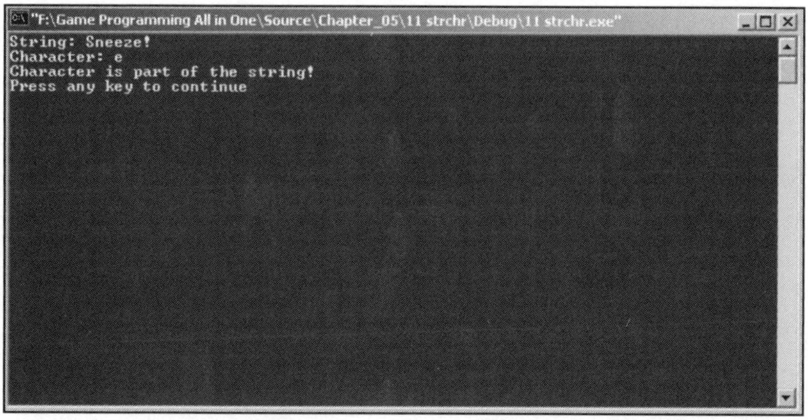

"F:\Game Programming All in One\Source\Chapter_05\11 strchr\Debug\11 strchr.exe"
String: Sneeze!
Character: e
Character is part of the string!
Press any key to continue

Figure 5.20

strchr.

Yes, another boring program. In this one you get a string and a character from the user (lines 15 and 17) and then use `strchr` (line 20) to see whether the character the user typed exists in the string.

strstr

`strstr` works similarly to `strchr` but instead of finding the first occurrence of a character in a string it finds the first occurrence of another string. It is sort of like `strcmp` but does partial comparison. The `strstr` prototype is:

```
char *strstr (const char * string, const char * strCharSet);
```

Where the first parameter is a pointer to the string to be searched and the second parameter is a pointer to the sub-string to look. `strstr` returns a pointer to the first occurrence of the sub-string inside the first string.

The following program asks for a string and a search sub-string from the user and checks whether the sub-string exists in the first one:

```
 1:  /* '12 Main.cpp' */
 2:
 3:  /* Input output stream header file */
 4: #include <iostream>
 5:
 6:  /* Start */
 7: main (void)
 8: {
 9:   /* Declare two strings */
10:  char FirstString [255];
11:  char SecondString [255];
12:
13:   /* Get two strings from the user */
14:  std::cout << "First string: ";
15:  std::cin >> FirstString;
16:  std::cout << "Search string: ";
17:  std::cin >> SecondString;
18:
19:   /* Check for second string occurrence */
20:  if ( false == strstr (FirstString, SecondString) )
21:  {
22:   std::cout << "Second string isn't part of the string!" << std::endl;
```

```
23:   }
24:   else
25:   {
26:    std::cout << "Second string is part of the string!" << std::endl;
27:   }
28:
29:   return 0;
30: }
```

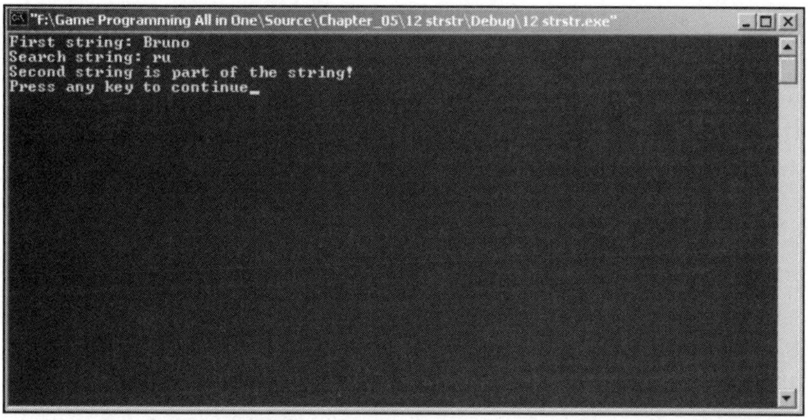
"F:\Game Programming All in One\Source\Chapter_05\12 strstr\Debug\12 strstr.exe"
First string: Bruno
Search string: ru
Second string is part of the string!
Press any key to continue

Figure 5.21

strstr.

Again, nothing new, you get two strings from the user (lines 15 and 17) and use `strstr` to see whether the second string exists in the first (line 20).

atoi

`atoi` enables you to convert a string into a numerical `int`. It is defined as:

```
int atoi (const char *string);
```

Which takes as the only parameter a pointer to the string and returns the converted `int`.

The following program gets a string from the user and converts it to an `int`.

```
/* '13 Main.cpp' */

/* Input output stream header file */
#include <iostream>
```

```
 5:
 6:  /* Start */
 7: main (void)
 8: {
 9:   /* Declare a string and an int */
10:  char String [255];
11:  int Number;
12:
13:   /* Get a string from the user */
14:  std::cout << "Enter a string: ";
15:  std::cin >> String;
16:
17:   /* Convert string to integer */
18:  Number = atoi (String);
19:
20:   /* To prove it is an int, calculate square of number */
21:  std::cout << "Square of Number is " << Number * Number << std::endl;
22:
23:  return 0;
24: }
```

Figure 5.22

atoi.

This program just gets a string from the user and converts it to an int using atoi (line 18).

atof

atof works like atoi but returns a floating-point number. Its prototype is:

```
double atof (const char *string);
```

Where the only parameter is a pointer to the string and it returns a converted double.

atol

Last you have atol, which is the same as atof or atoi but returns a long value. It is defined as:

```
long atol (const char *string);
```

Which takes again a pointer to the string as the only parameter and returns the converted long.

sprintf

sprintf enables you to create a string using various arguments. This enables you to format strings to your needs without having to output each element (text or variable), you can use sprintf to create a single string as you want.

sprintf's prototype is:

```
int sprintf (char *buffer, const char * format [, arguments] …);
```

Where the first parameter is a pointer to the destination buffer. The second parameter is a pointer to a string specifying the format. This format string specifies how the arguments are included in the string. Okay, pick a simple example:

```
sprintf (String, "%s %d %f", Name, Age, Height);
```

What happens here is, when sprintf finds a format specifier (the percent symbol and a character), it replaces it with the corresponding parameter. So in the preceding example, the format string "%s %d %f" would be replaced with the Name, Age, and Height variables, in order.

Table 5.2 shows some of the most frequent format specifiers.

> **NOTE**
>
> sprintf uses a little trick to achieve the capability of having a different number of parameters called variable-argument lists. This is a more advanced topic that I will not cover in the book. You can check any of the references or MSDN for more information on them.

TABLE 5.2 Format Specifiers

Format Specifier	Description
c	Character
d	Signed integer
u	Decimal integer
s	String
f	Floating point

strftime returns an int specifying the number of characters copied to the destination string.

The following program gets the user information separately and creates a formatted string with sprintf to present the information to the user.

```
 /* '14 Main.cpp' */

 /* Input output stream header file */
#include <iostream>

 /* Start */
main (void)
{
  /* Declare a string */
 char FinalString [255];

  /* Declare user's information variables */
 char Name [255];
 int Age;
 float Height;
 float Weight;

  /* Get all information from the user */
 std::cout << "What is your first name : ";
 std::cin >> Name;
```

```
21:  std::cout << "What is your age : ";
22:  std::cin >> Age;
23:  std::cout << "What is your height : ";
24:  std::cin >> Height;
25:  std::cout << "What is your weight : ";
26:  std::cin >> Weight;
27:
28:   /* Convert information to a single string */
29:  sprintf (FinalString, "Your first name is %s. You are %d years old\
30: and your height %f and weight %f.", Name, Age, Height, Weight);
31:
32:   /* Output final string */
33:  std::cout << FinalString << std::endl;
34:
35:  return 0;
36: }
```

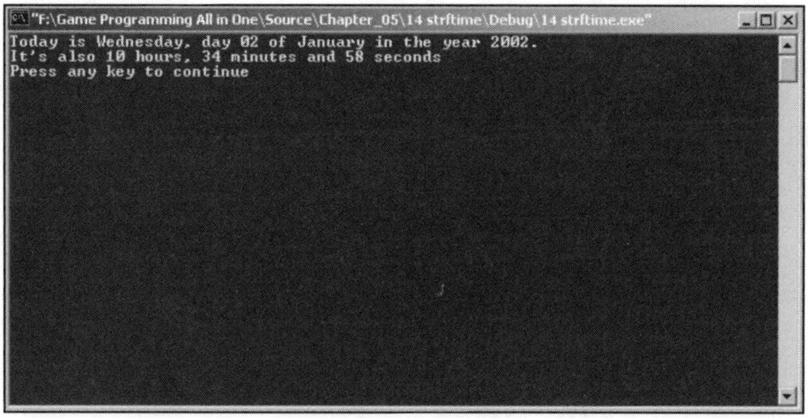

"F:\Game Programming All in One\Source\Chapter_05\14 strftime\Debug\14 strftime.exe"
Today is Wednesday, day 02 of January in the year 2002.
It's also 10 hours, 34 minutes and 58 seconds
Press any key to continue

Figure 5.23

sprintf.

Another boring program. It just gets some user information (lines 19 through 26) and formats them using `sprintf` in line 29.

strftime

The last string manipulation I will cover is `strftime`. Even if this isn't used much, it is a nice function to know, especially if you want to output the current time in your own format. Its prototype is:

```
size_t strftime (char * strDest, size_t maxsize, const char * format,
const struct tm * timeptr);
```

strftime has a few more parameters than what you are accustomed to, but as usual, the first parameter is a pointer to the destination string. The next parameter is the maximum number of characters to include in the destination string. The third parameter is how you want to format the string. This works similarly to the sprintf format parameter but has a specific set of format specifiers, as shown in Table 5.3.

The last parameter is a tm structure. The tm structure holds the current system date and time information and is defined as follows:

```
struct tm {
        int tm_sec;     /* seconds after the minute - [0,59] */
        int tm_min;     /* minutes after the hour - [0,59] */
        int tm_hour;    /* hours since midnight - [0,23] */
        int tm_mday;    /* day of the month - [1,31] */
        int tm_mon;     /* months since January - [0,11] */
```

Table 5.3 strftime Format Specifiers

Format Specifier	Description
a	Abbreviated weekday
A	Full weekday
d	Day of month as number
b	Abbreviated month name
B	Full month name
m	Month as number
Y	Year
H	Hour in 24-hour format
I	Hour in 12-hour format
P	AM/PM indicator
M	Minutes in number
S	Seconds in number

```
int tm_year;     /* years since 1900 */
int tm_wday;     /* days since Sunday - [0,6] */
int tm_yday;     /* days since January 1 - [0,365] */
int tm_isdst;    /* daylight savings time flag */
};
```

I believe the code speaks for itself.

`strftime` returns the number of characters placed in the destination string.

The following program shows the current date and time in a formatted and clean way:

```
 /* '15 Main.cpp' */

 /* Input output stream header file */
#include <iostream>
 /* Time header file */
#include <time.h>

 /* Start */
main (void)
{
  /* Declare a string and a time structure */
 char String [255];
 time_t Today;
 tm * Time;

  /* Get current time */
 time (&Today);
  /* Convert time to a structure*/
 Time = localtime (&Today);

  /* Convert time to our format */
 strftime (String, 255, "Today is %A, day %d of %B in the year %Y.\n\
It's also %H hours, %M minutes and %S seconds", Time);

  /* Output the time */
 std::cout << String << std::endl;

 return 0;
}
```

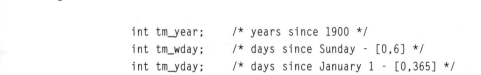

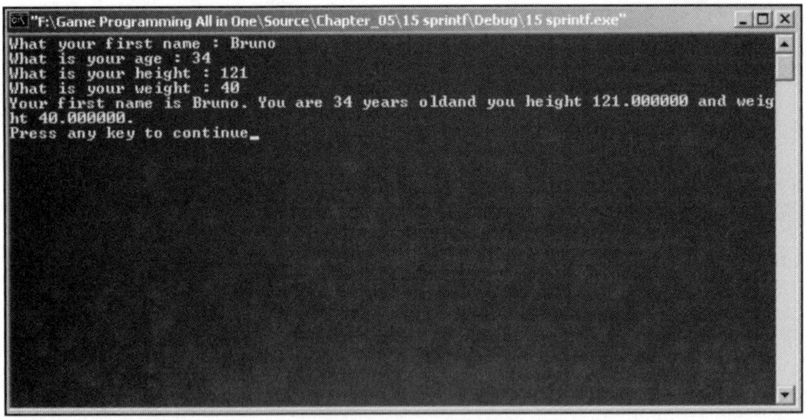

Figure 5.24
strftime.

Finally a little change! You declare a few variables, names `Today` and `Time`, which are respectively `time_t` and `tm` types (lines 13 and 14). `time_t` is used by many time-related functions while the `tm` type is mostly used to convert from `time_t` to a more readable format.

You then get the current time with the function `time` in line 17. You only need to pass the address of a `time_t` variable, in this case, `Today`. This function stores the current date and time to `Today`. Next you need to convert `Today` to a more readable format using `localtime` in line 19. This will return a pointer to `tm` type variable, which you will store in `Time`.

In lines 22 and 23, you format the string to output the time as you want, using `strftime`.

Summary

Whoa, complex chapter, no? You have learned about two of the most advanced subjects of C++—arrays and pointers. It is extremely important that you understand how arrays and pointers work because most of the advanced topics I will cover later will make use of them.

In this chapter you have also learned how to use strings in C++. Later you will create a string class that will make working with strings easy.

Questions and Answers

Q: Why use arrays to store multiple elements if you can simply use a number after the variable name to store indexes?

A: Arrays offer you a way to check each element by supplying a number to inside brackets; this can even be done with a variable. This is good when you want to check all elements for some value and you can use a `for` loop. If you did this in code, there would be a large number of lines just to check each element.

Q: What is the maximum size of an array?

A: This depends on the limits set by the compiler or the system. Some compilers don't allow arrays to be bigger than 640KB but allow bigger arrays if they are allocated using `new`.

Q: Why are pointers so important?

A: Most advanced programming techniques are almost impossible to accomplish without pointers. When I talk about advanced data structures later, you'll see how pointers make things easier.

Q: What is ASCII?

A: ASCII stands for American Standard Code for Information Interchange. It defines a standard format for text. All characters are represented with a numerical value; ASCII makes it possible to expect that a specific set of characters will always have the same numerical value.

Q: Why does the extraction operator only get the first word in a string?

A: The extraction operator stops as soon as it finds either the NULL-terminating string, `\0`, or the new line character `\n` and a space.

Exercises

1. What is an array?
2. What is wrong with the following code:

```
int Test [123];
int i;
for (i=0, I <= 123; i++)
{
 Test [i] = rand () % 100;
}
```

3. What does the following line of code do:

```
int Array [] = { 10, 23, 123, 3433, 43 };
```

4. What is a pointer?
5. What is the function of new?
6. What is wrong with the following code?

```
char * Bills;
Bills = new char [10];
 /* … */
delete Bills;
```

7. To which array element will the following pointer point in the end of the code:

```
int BigArray [100];
int * PointerArray;
PointerArray = BigArray;
PointerArray = PointerArray + 5;
PointerArray --;
PointerArray = PointerArray + 3;
PointerArray --;
PointerArray = PointerArray -1;
```

8. What is the meaning of \0?
9. What will teststring contain in the end of the following code:

```
char TestString [255];
char String1 [255] = "Hello you all.";
char String2 [255] = "I'm sad.";
char String3 [255] = "Happy birthday!";
strncat (String1, String2, 5);
strncat (String3, String1, 1);
strncpy (TestString, String3, 10);
strncat (TestString, String1, 10);
```

CHAPTER 6

Classes

These last few chapters have taught you the basics of programming. Even if you have learned the syntax to C++ functions and variables, the concepts I've covered are shared among just about every programming language in existence. It is now time to learn about one of the features that distinguishes C++ from other languages: classes.

In this chapter you will learn some of these important concepts about C++ classes:

- What a class is
- Different class access
- Constructors and destructors
- Operator overloading
- Unions and enumerations
- Inheritance and polymorphism

Hang on to your seat, because this will be a bumpy ride.

What Is a Class?

A *class* is a collection of both data and functions in a single type, which work together to create a programming representation of objects. See Figure 6.1.

Now I will expand the concepts of classes to a real game object, the typical street fighter enemy you come across in many games. You need to define two distinctive parts: what he can do and his attributes. Because this is a relatively simple enemy, you probably only want to keep the enemy's vital energy, the type of sprite (image

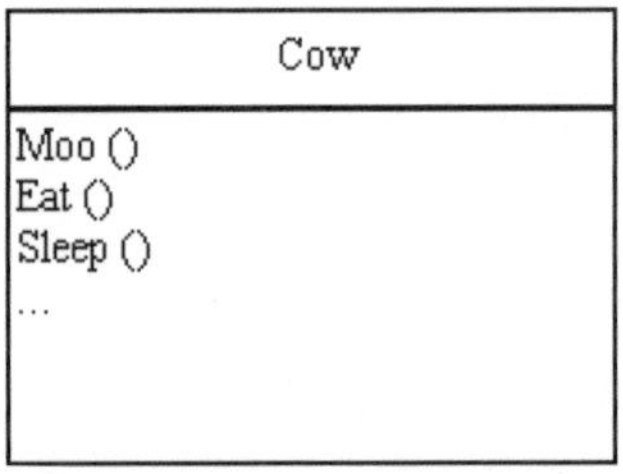

Figure 6.1

A sample class.

of itself), and his strength. Also, you want him to be able to kick, punch, jump, and move around.

Because you know what the object is and what it can do, you could create a class to represent it in code, as you will do in a minute.

New Types

Why create new, structured types, if you can just use some kind of array or naming scheme to store all your data? The first reason is explicit in the last phrase, it is a structured way to keep data, all the information relative to an object type in a single namespace, which can be accessed easily.

Second, creating new data types enables you to keep your code clear, smaller, more functional. It also enables you to have specific parts of code isolated from others, making the code easier to update, and that can be reused over time.

Building Classes

As with building programs, building classes also come in two phases: design and implementation. Designing a robust and efficient class is hard work, thus, spending a few extra minutes, to a couple of days to design a class (depending on the size of your project, of course) will probably be beneficial in the end.

Design

Designing a class isn't difficult, but it isn't easy either. Being able to create a class that works correctly and efficiently with other classes and other code, while keeping information hidden is a stressful task, because you need to imagine almost every possible environment.

The first thing to do when designing something is to think of what it should do. The objective of the class should be explicit and coherent. The class should have one purpose, but do it well. If you are battling yourself with naming a class, because to describe the class you need some name like `GamesAndPlayers` or `BunnyDog`, you would probably benefit from creating two or more different classes so they can be kept simple and objective.

After you have the class purpose, you should try to identify all the class data members, because that enables you to know how the class is described, making it easier to know how it works.

The next step, probably the more important one when designing a class, is to know how the class works with other classes. If you have a class that has no way to communicate with other classes or functions, even if the class is more than 10,000 lines long with enough functions to make NASA cry, it will still be worth nothing, since it doesn't work correctly in concrete programs.

The final thing to do is to define the functions, usually called methods. All the functions should define what the class can do.

To aid in class design, some drawings were created to visually represent class functionality and relation to other classes. Some of the most common symbols are shown in Figure 6.2.

Definition

After you have your class designed, you need to define it. You do this by typing the `class` keyword, followed by the class name and a code block with all the class members. When you used code blocks (code between `{` and `}`), you usually didn't need a semicolon at the end, but when declaring a class, you need to supply the semicolon in the end. This allows the compiler to know where the class definition ends. For your enemy class you saw earlier, an empty class definition would be:

```
class Enemy
{
 /* ... */
};
```

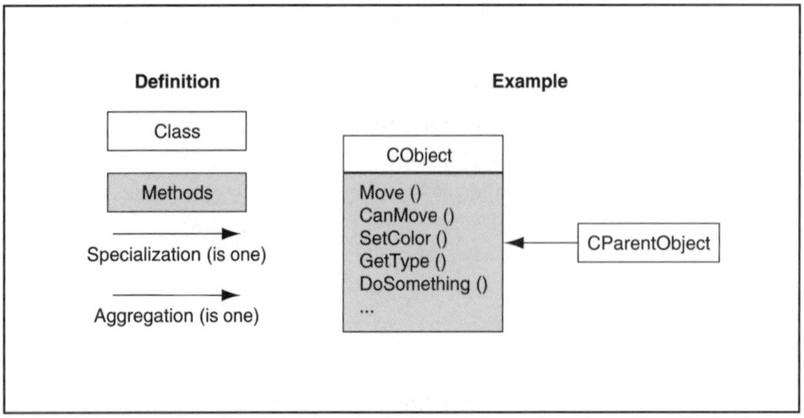

Figure 6.2

Class design symbols.

Now, you need to declare the class members. This is done exactly like before, but instead of declaring the variables and functions in the global scope, you define it within the class scope (inside the code block). Your enemy class, with the functionality you defined earlier, would be something like:

```
class Enemy
{
public:
 int Energy;
 int SpriteType;
 int Strength;

 void Kick (void);
 void Punch (void);
 void Jump (void);
 void Move (int Direction);
};
```

> **NOTE**
> Don't worry about that `public:` in the code, which will be fully explained in a little while.

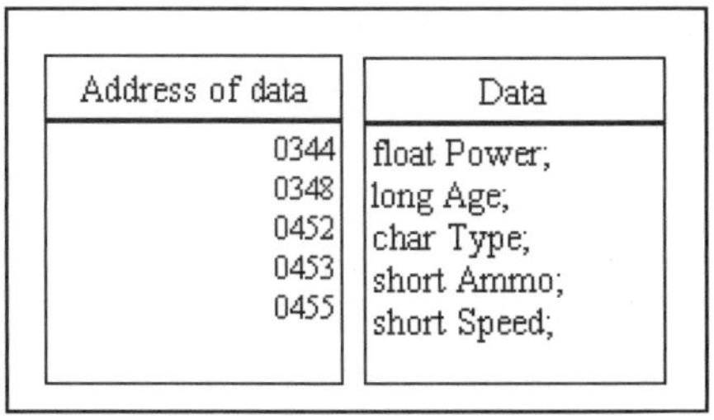

Figure 6.3

How a class is organized in memory.

Implementation

The final step when developing a class is obviously the actual class methods implementation. This isn't very different from before except that you need to specify the scope of the function. Remember when you used `std::cout`? The `::` resolved the scope, meaning that `cout` is a part of `std`. So, to specify that you are implementing the `Enemy` methods, you need to implement the function adding the class name and the scope resolution operator before the class name like:

```
void Enemy::Punch (void)
{
 /* Punch code */
}
```

Which would tell the compiler that you are defining `Punch` in `Enemy`'s scope.

Using Classes

Using a class isn't much different from using a normal function or variable. You use the class's object, followed by either `member of` or `pointer to member of` operators, and then the according function or variable. For example:

```
Enemy  BadGuy;
Enemy * PointerBadGuy;
PointerBadGuy = &BadGuy;
BadGuy.Kick ();
PointerBadGuy->Energy = 100;
```

Using a class is as easy as that.

Private, Protected, and Public Members

Classes have different access modes for their members: private, protected, and public. Each of these modes has advantages and disadvantages, but used wisely, they will make your class very robust.

Any method inside the class can use all the other class members, but sometimes you don't want functions outside the class to be able to modify the class data. You will use access modes to protect the data.

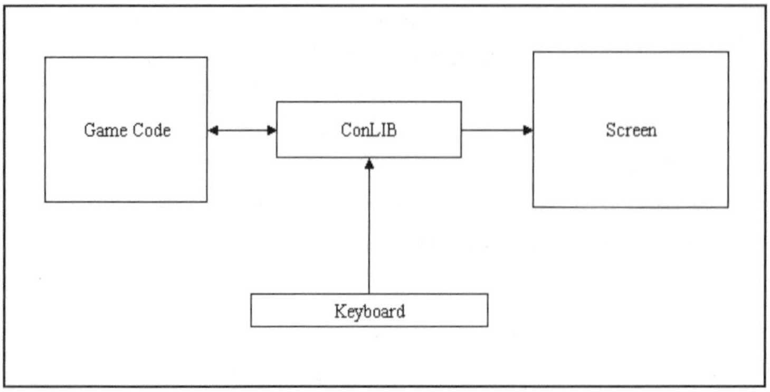

Figure 6.4

Class protection levels.

private

By default, all class members are private. Private members can only be accessed inside the class. Inside the class functions, you can use any member that is defined as private, but outside the class scope, you can't. When you define the class access to private, all the following members declared after you stated the private keyword are also private until a new access method is found.

public

Public class access is exactly that, public. All class members are ready to be used, inside the class or not.

By allowing all members to be public, you can access all the information within it from anywhere, but this has a disadvantage, if you are working with other people, or planning to distribute your code, leaving all methods public provides a way for people to break your class by supplying invalid data to class members.

Here's an example where leaving the data members public is bad:

```
class SomeClass
{
public:
int NumberLives;
}
 /* … */
SomeClass Game;
Game.NumberLives = -59;
```

As you can see, by leaving the member public, you enable anyone to change the data without verifying it, and I think it's pretty bad to have –59 lives, don't you?

protected

The protected access level is tricky. It works exactly like the private access level but members who have protected level can be accessed by a derived class, while private members can't.

The following example illustrates this point (if you change `protected` to `private`, it will result in the same error since they both protect outside access to the class):

```
class SomeClass
{
protected:
int Score
public:
int NumberLives;
}
 /* … */
SomeClass Game;
Game.Score = 0; /* Error */
Game.NumberLives = 5;
```

Although you can change the `NumberLives` member since it is public, the compiler will give you an error when you try to use the `Score` member, because it is protected.

NOTE

You will see what a derived class is later in the chapter, so don't worry about it right now.

What Kind of Access Is Right?

So, what kind of access should you use? All of them—a class can have all of the three access levels for different members.

Public members should be mostly functions to allow control over the class. Of course you can make your data public, but this goes against the object-oriented programming (OOP) practice, as you will se in Chapter 9, "Basic Software Architecture."

Private members should be used mostly for data that isn't shared with derived classes and that the user shouldn't mess with alone. Private functions should probably be functions that are specific to the class and that should only be called from within the class itself.

Protected members should be mostly data that shouldn't be available to the end user, but should be available for derived classes. This includes mostly data-like attributes.

As with your enemy class earlier, a good way to separate the access levels would be to make all the data protected (because you might want to derive the class to create different enemies) and the functions public:

```
class Enemy
{
protected:
```

```
 int Energy;
 int SpriteType;
 int Strength;

public:
 void Kick (void);
 void Punch (void);
 void Jump (void);
 void Move (int Direction);
};
```

Making the class with this access level enables you to control the enemy while not caring how the enemy is stored. Of course, a few more methods would be needed to make the preceding class totally functional, but that's a different story.

When designing a class, pay special attention to the access level members have. Try to imagine all the circumstances under which your class can be used, and see which members benefit from each access level.

Constructors and the Destructor

Do you remember that when a variable was created, it was either initialized to 0, if it was in the global namespace, or not initialized at all if it was inside some function scope? Well, class members aren't initialized, but sometimes you wish they were. When a class is declared, a special function inside the class is called, named *constructor*. When a class is deleted, a special function is also called, named *destructor*.

Default Constructor

When the class is declared, and if you don't explicitly call a constructor, the default constructor will be called. This function is usually responsible for initializing the class members, but can be used for just about everything.

You declare a default constructor by creating a function with no return type, with the name of the class, and no arguments. If you don't do this, the compiler will create a blank constructor for you, but it is always better for you to create the constructor yourself. The compiler should always create a blank constructor, but just in case, better to be safe than sorry.

Your Enemy class with a constructor with arguments would be something like:

```
class Enemy
{
protected:
 /* … */
public:
 Enemy (void);
 /* … */
};
```

General Constructors

A good thing about constructors is that they can have parameters similarly as normal functions. This way you can initialize a class with the values you want when you declare it.

Creating constructors that accept parameters is like creating normal functions, except that you don't supply a return type and the name must match the class name, such as:

```
class Enemy
{
protected:
 /* … */
public:
 Enemy (int OtherEnergy, int OtherSpriteType, int OtherStrength);
 /* … */
};
```

You would then implement this constructor to initialize each class member to the given arguments.

Copy Constructor and References

The copy constructor is like a normal constructor but has gained this name because it is used to copy all the data from one class to another. Copy constructors have only one parameter, which is a reference to a class of the same type.

If you remember from Chapter 3, "Functions and Program Flow," when you pass a variable to a function, the function will have a copy of that same variable. Passing a variable by reference, the function will have the exact object, not a copy. Briefly, when you pass a class by reference, you pass the exact same class to the function, and the function can modify the class, sort of like passing a pointer that you can modify.

To pass a class as reference, you need to include the reference operator `&` between the type and the variable name.

Your `Enemy` class with a copy constructor would be the following:

```
class Enemy
{
protected:
 /* … */
public:
 Enemy (Enemy & OtherEnemy);
 /* … */
};
 /* … */
Enemy::Enemy (Enemy & OtherEnemy)
{
 /* Copy all the members of OtherEnemy to this class */
}
```

Now you could safely create one class and set it up, and use that class to create new classes like:

```
Enemy EnemyOne;
 /* Set EnemyOne properties and other */
Enemy EnemyTwo (EnemyOne); /* Use copy constructor */
Enemy EnemyThree (EnemyOne); /* Use copy constructor */
```

And you would create two more enemies that were exactly like `EnemyOne` (thus the name *copy constructor*).

Destructor

If a function is called when a class is created, it is only fair that a function is called when the class is destroyed, right? For that, you have the destructor. There can be only one destructor per class (kind of like the Highlander), and it must be declared the same way as the default constructor but with a ~ symbol before the name.

The compiler also takes care of creating this function if you don't, but as before, it is better that you create it so that you know exactly what is happening.

With all the constructors and the destructor, your `Enemy` class would now look like:

```
class Enemy
{
protected:
 int Energy;
 int SpriteType;
 int Strength;
 int * Name;

public:
 Enemy (void);
 Enemy (int OtherEnergy, int OtherSpriteType, int OtherStrength);
 Enemy (Enemy & OtherEnemy);
 ~Enemy (void); void Kick (void);
 void Punch (void);
 void Jump (void);
 void Move (int Direction);
};
 /* … */
Enemy::Enemy (void)
{
 Name = new char [100];
}
Enemy::~Enemy (void)
{
 if (Name != NULL)
 {
  delete [] Name;
 }
}
```

Creating a destructor like this would ensure that any memory allocated by the class would be deallocated when the destructor is called, which is when the class object is destroyed.

Operator Overloading

I have already talked about operators for the simple types you have been working with, now it is time to learn how to create and use operators with your own classes.

Creating operators for your classes is called *operator overloading* and works similarly to creating class methods, with a few limitations, of course.

The first difference when creating operators from normal functions is that you no longer specify a function name but use the `operator` keyword followed by the operator itself. For example, if you wanted to create a postfix-increment operator, you would declare the operator inside the class like:

```
operator ++ (void);
```

Or if you wanted to implement a multiplication operator that accepts an `int` and returns an `int`, you would do:

```
int operator * (int OtherNumber);
```

There is a caveat when using operator overloading, the declaration syntax has to follow the operator's syntax. For example, the array element operator (`[]`) must take only one parameter of type `int`, while the postfix-increment operator (++) doesn't have any parameters.

> **TIP**
>
> **It is common to prefix a class name with a capital `C` like `CSomeClass` and prefix class member data with `m_` like `m_Data`.**

Here is a simple example of an addition operator for a vector class:

```
class Vector
{
public:
 int x, y;
  /* Constructor / destructor / Other methods */
 Vector operator + (Vector & OtherVector);
 Vector & operator += (Vector & OtherVector);
}
 /* … */
Vector Vector::operator + (Vector & OtherVector)
{
 Vector TempVector;
 TempVector.x = x + OtherVector.x;
 TempVector.y = y + OtherVector.y;
 return TempVector;
}
 Vector & Vector::operator += (Vector & OtherVector)
```

```
{
 x += OtherVector.x;
 y += OtherVector.y;
 return * this;
}
 /* ... */
Vector VectorOne;
Vector VectorTwo;
Vector VectorThree;
 /* Do something with vectors */
VectorOne = VectorTwo + VectorThree;
VectorThree += VectorOne;
```

This class would have an addition operator that returns another vector as can be seen in the operator body, and an assignment addition operator that uses the first vector to store the final vector. When you use assignment type operators you usually return a `this` value.

The `this` pointer is a class member that is only accessible inside a class function that always points to the class you are using; in this case, it would be pointing to the class you were using to store the final result. In the code, it would be `VectorThree`.

Putting It All Together— The String Class

You will develop a small string class that aids in the use of general classes to demonstrate all the concepts covered up until now.

You need to first include the normal header files, `iostream` and `string.h`, and then declare your string.

```
 /* '01 Main.cpp' */

 /* Input output stream header */
#include <iostream>
 /* String manipulation header */
#include <string.h>

 /* Our class */
class CString
{
```

```
11: private:
12:   char                m_aString [1024];
13: public:
14:    /* Constructors */
15:   CString (void);
16:   CString (CString & rString);
17:   CString (char * pString);
18:    /* Destructor */
19:   ~CString (void);
20:
21:    /* Operators */
22:   CString & operator = (CString & rString);
23:   CString & operator = (char * pString);
24:   bool operator == (CString & rString);
25:   bool operator == (char * pString);
26:   bool operator != (CString & rString);
27:   bool operator != (char * pString);
28:
29:    /* Other functions */
30:   char * GetString (void);
31:   int GetLength (void);
32: };
```

You first declare your class: `CString`. The first thing you have to do is declare an array of characters to hold the actual string, which is done in line 12. After that you declare all the constructors: default, copy, and the normal one, and the destructor.

Next you declare the operators. You declare two types of uses in each operator, using a `CString` by reference and a pointer to a string. This enables you to use the operators like:

```
CString Text;
Text = "Hello";
```

Which is very helpful when you hardcode some strings. In the end, you declare two functions to return a pointer to the actual string that is sometimes needed by some functions and the string's length.

Next you have the constructors:

```
34:  /* Constructors */
35: CString::CString (void)
36: {
37:  m_aString [0] = '\0';
```

```
}

CString::CString (CString & rString)
{
  if (rString.GetLength () > 0)
  {
    strcpy (m_aString, rString.GetString ());
  }
  else
  {
    m_aString [0] = '\0';
  }
}

CString::CString (char * pString)
{
  if (pString)
  {
    strcpy (m_aString, pString);
  }
  else
  {
  m_aString [0] = '\0';
  }
}
```

The default constructor does nothing more than make the first element of the string the NULL-terminating character, which enables you to later check whether the string is used or not. The second constructor takes a pointer to a string (C style), and if the length of the string is greater than 0, it copies the string to the current one. The last constructor, the copy constructor, copies the string to the current one.

The next destructor does nothing more than set the first element of the string to the NULL-terminating character.

```
  /* Destructor */
CString::~CString (void)
{
  m_aString [0] = '\0';
}
```

The next two operators, the assignment operators, copy a string to the current one; they work very similarly to the constructors:

```
 /* Operators */
CString & CString::operator = (CString & rString)
{
 if (rString.GetLength () > 0)
 {
  strcpy (m_aString, rString.GetString ());
 }
 else
 {
 m_aString [0] = '\0';
 }

 return *this;
}

CString & CString::operator = (char * pString)
{
 if (pString)
 {
  strcpy (m_aString, pString);
 }
 else
 {
 m_aString [0] = '\0';
 }

 return *this;
}
```

The next four operators are to test whether the string is equal to or different from another. Remember, strcmp returns 0 if the strings are equal:

```
bool CString::operator == (CString & rString)
{
 if (strcmp (rString.GetString (), m_aString) != 0)
 {
  return false;
 }
```

```
 else
 {
  return true;
 }
}

bool CString::operator == (char * pString)
{
 if (strcmp (pString, m_aString) != 0)
 {
  return false;
 }
 else
 {
  return true;
 }
}

bool CString::operator != (CString & rString)
{
 if (strcmp (rString.GetString (), m_aString) == 0)
 {
  return false;
 }
 else
 {
  return true;
 }
}

bool CString::operator != (char * pString)
{
 if (strcmp (pString, m_aString) == 0)
 {
  return false;
 }
 else
 {
  return true;
 }
}
```

The next two functions return a pointer to the actual string and the string's length:

```
  /* Other functions */
char * CString::GetString (void)
{
 return m_aString;
}

int CString::GetLength (void)
{
 return strlen (m_aString);
}
```

The following program uses the class you created to make it easier to work with strings:

```
 /* Start */
int main ()
{
  /* Use constructor */
 CString Test ("This is just a test!");
 CString Welcome;

  /* Use assignment operator */
 Welcome = "Welcome to the world!";

  /* Use strings */
 std::cout << Welcome.GetString () << std::endl;
 std::cout << Test.GetString () << std::endl;
 std::cout << "Welcome length: " << Welcome.GetLength () << std::endl;

  /* Use comparison operator */
 if (Welcome != Test)
 {
  std::cout << "'Welcome' is different than 'Test'." << std::endl;
 }
 else
 {
  std::cout << "'Welcome' is equal to 'Test'." << std::endl;
 }

 return 0;
}
```

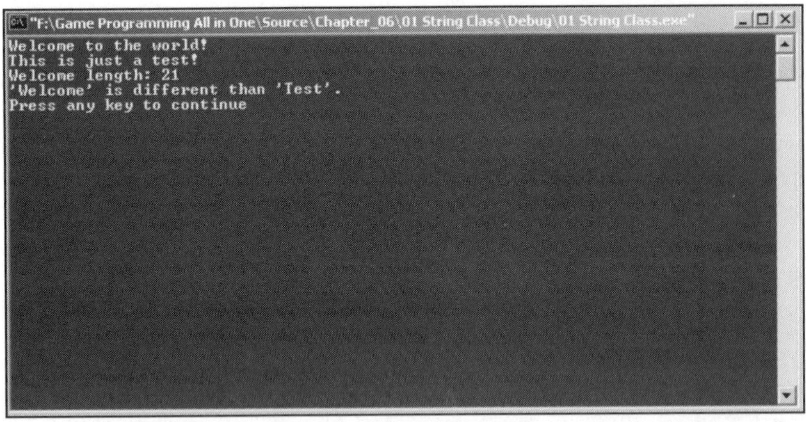

Figure 6.5

String class.

In line 162 you create a string using a constructor to specify the string value, in this case—"`This is just a test!`". In line 166 you use the assignment operator to create a string as if it were just like any other class. In lines 169, 170, and 171 you use both `GetString` and `GetLength` methods with the `std::cout` stream to output the string's text and string's length, respectively, to the user. Lastly, in line 176 you use the `different than` operator to see whether both the strings are equal.

What you did here was to create a full-featured string class that allows strings to be created using various constructors (supplying an already existing string class or by supplying a real string), and you also implemented some operators to make it easier to work with strings. Now you can use strings just like any other variables, copying each other with the assignment operators.

Basics of Inheritance and Polymorphism

Now that you have the basic knowledge of classes, let's dig into two of the advanced features of C++: inheritance and polymorphism.

Inheritance

The best way to explain what inheritance is is with an example. Suppose you are creating some kind of animal game where you have mammals, birds, fishes, and so on. In each type of animal you have various species like dogs, cats, cows, for mammals, and eagles and vultures for birds. Then inside each species you would have subspecies or specializations like a Sheppard dog, a Saint Bernard, and so on.

The first thing the marketing guy would tell the programmer would be: "Hey, we need one hundred animals in this game; you better start making some animal classes" (that is, if the marketing guy is smart enough to know what a class is). Creating one hundred classes to describe each animal wouldn't only be tiring, but a pain to work with.

The programmer would probably do it another way, using inheritance.

By using inheritance the programmer can create a base class for a mammal, with all the necessary data and functions, and then derive from that class to create mammal species. By deriving from a base class, the derived class will have all the data and functions that are defined by having either a public or a protected access level in the base class, automatically declared and defined in the derived class.

Take a look at Figure 6.6 to see how a cat and a cow class would end if they were derived from a mammal class.

Deriving from a Class

Deriving a class from another class isn't difficult. After you have defined the class name and before the start of the code block, you include a colon followed by the

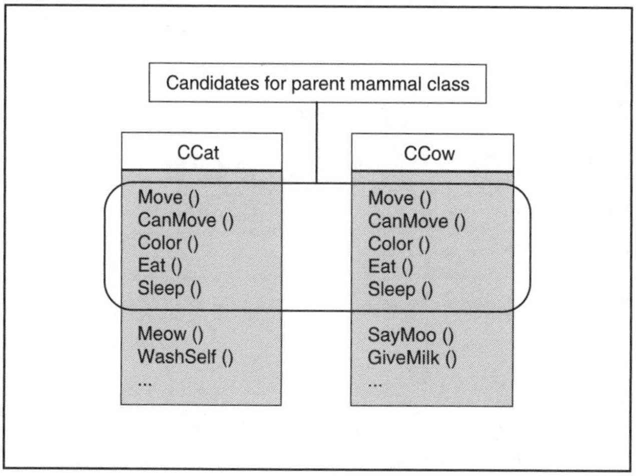

Figure 6.6

Both a cat and a cow share the same data because they are mammals, but they have extra methods because they are of different species.

type of level access and the base (parent) class name. If you want to derive from multiple classes (multi-inheritance) you precede each extra parent class with a comma:

```
class Derived : public BaseA, protected BaseB
{
 /* … */
};
```

Defining a class like this would create a class, `Derived`, which has all the elements defined in `BaseA` and in `BaseB`.

> **NOTE**
>
> If you don't supply any access level when deriving from a class, the default access level is public.

Virtual Methods

When you derive from a parent class, you can only add methods to that class. If you try to overwrite already defined functions, you get errors. This is where virtual methods come into play. If you define a class function as virtual, a derived class can implement its own version of that method, but if you don't, the derived class will not be able to override some functions. See Figure 6.7.

Making a class function a virtual function is pretty easy. You only need to insert the `virtual` keyword before the return type of the function like:

```
virtual Return_Type FunctionName (Parameters_List);
```

I chose the animal example to show these concepts. The following example will use a base animal class from where a dog and a cat class are derived. Using virtual

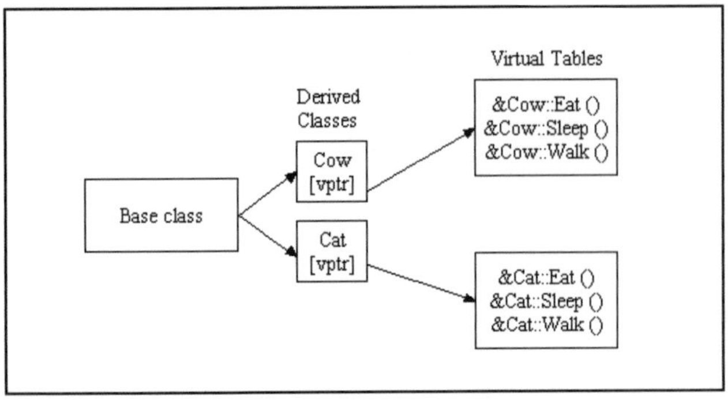

Figure 6.7

Virtual methods and the class virtual table.

methods, you will be able to call different implementations of a class method (`Talk`).

```
/* '02 Main.cpp' */

/* Input output stream header */
#include <iostream>

/* Base animal class */
class CAnimal
{
public:
 int    m_MaxAge;
 int    m_Age;

 CAnimal ();
 virtual ~CAnimal ();

 virtual void Talk (void);
};
```

Your animal class isn't complicated, you just defined a maximum age, an age, the constructor, the destructor, and a virtual method `Talk`. This is the method you will override. Following are the constructors which `init` the class members to 0:

```
CAnimal::CAnimal ()
{
 m_MaxAge = 0;
 m_Age    = 0;
}

CAnimal::~CAnimal ()
{
}

void CAnimal::Talk (void)
{
 std::cout << "Base animal doesn't talk!";
}
```

Next you have your dog class derived from CAnimal. You don't need to declare the class data because it was already done in CAnimal, so you simply need to take care of the constructors and the functions you want, in this case, just Talk.

```
 /* Derived dog class */
class CDog : public CAnimal
{
public:
  CDog ();
  virtual ~CDog ();

  virtual void Talk (void);
};
```

Next are the CDog constructor and destructor. The constructor initializes the maximum age member, m_MaxAge, to 9, which is a typical life for a dog, and the destructor does nothing.

```
CDog::CDog ()
{
  m_MaxAge = 9;
  m_Age    = 0;
}

CDog::~CDog ()
{
}
```

You finally get to your virtual method. You implement a virtual method like any normal class method; in this case, it will just check whether the dog is still alive, and if so, bark and add a year to his life.

```
void CDog::Talk (void)
{
  if (m_Age < m_MaxAge)
  {
    std::cout << "Bark..." << std::endl;
    m_Age ++;
  }
}
```

The same logic as for the CDog class is used in the CCat class, except that the normal life for a cat is around five years and instead of barking, the cat meows.

```
 /* Derived cat class */
class CCat : public CAnimal
{
public:
 CCat ();
 virtual ~CCat ();

 virtual void Talk (void);
};

CCat::CCat ()
{
 m_MaxAge = 5;
 m_Age    = 0;
}

CCat::~CCat ()
{
}

void CCat::Talk (void)
{
 if (m_Age < m_MaxAge)
 {
  std::cout << "Meow..." << std::endl;
  m_Age ++;
 }
}
```

The main program creates a cat and a dog and calls each Talk method 10 times. This will show that the cat meows five times while the dog barks nine.

```
 /* Start */
int main ()
{
 CDog Dog;
```

```
 CCat Cat;
 int Loop;

 for (Loop = 0; Loop < 10; Loop ++)
 {
  Dog.Talk ();
  Cat.Talk ();
 }

 return 0;
}
```

Figure 6.8
Animal farm.

Inheritance is pretty useful when you deal with large projects where many objects share the same proprieties and functions as others or when some kind of pluggable interface is required. Inheritance's advantages are even more useful when used with some kind of polymorphism, as you will see next.

Polymorphism

Polymorphism is a feature supported by C++, which in its most basic sense, allows you to change class types.

By allowing various classes to derive from a single one, you can morph any of the derived classes to the base one, thus allowing you to store various class types in a class base that is shared by all the derived classes.

If you use the previous animals example, you know that both the CDog and CCat classes derived from CAnimal. If you wanted to store both the animals in pointers, you would need to create at least two different pointers, which isn't very bad, but suppose you are simulating an entire zoo?! It would have hundreds of animal classes, and storing all of them in each type pointers would be harsh.

Polymorphism solves this problem. Because each animal will derive from CAnimal, each animal-derived class can be cast (we will see this next) to the base type CAnimal and stored in a CAnimal pointer. After this is done, you can call each of the animals' derived methods (the ones you get from deriving from CAnimal) or you can cast the animals to their own type and use their specific method. Cool, isn't it?

Check out Figure 6.9 which shows a sample class hierarchy and I will discuss how you can use polymorphism to change class types.

If you have a class of type CWindow, but you need a way to convert it to a CControl or CObject, which may be required for several reasons like making store lists of objects and/or passing different types of classes to the same function.

Casting enables you to travel the hierarchy tree and convert each derived class to a type of parent class.

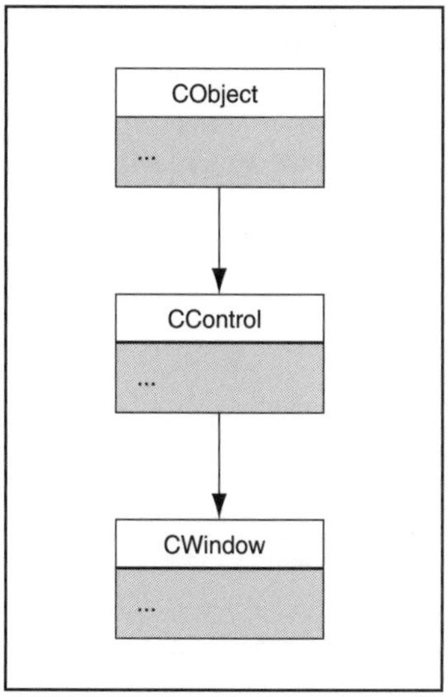

Figure 6.9

A sample window class hierarchy.

Casting

One of the fundamentals of polymorphism is casting. Casting is how C++ converts types from one to another whether they be classes or simple data types.

There are four kinds of casts: `static_cast`, `dynamic_cast`, `const_cast`, and `reinterpret_cast`. I will only cover the first two, but feel free to check MSDN or other C++ books for more information on the latter two.

static_cast

The `static_cast` expression enables you to convert a type to a type id based exclusively on the expression and no verification is performed to ensure the validity of the conversion.

Its syntax is as follows:

```
static_cast <type-id> expression
```

For example:

```
int Number = 74;
char Letter;
float Energy = 54.4;
Letter = static_cast <char> Number;
Number = static_cast <int> Energy;
```

This enables you to convert from type to type. The end result would be `Letter` holding the character '`J`' (ASCII value for 74), `Number` holding 54, and `Energy` 54.4.

This works the same for classes:

```
class Base
{
 /* … */
};
class Derived : public Base
{
 /* … */
};
/* … */
Base    * BaseClass;
Derived * DerivedClass;
 /* … */
```

```
13: BaseClass = static_cast <Base *> (DerivedClass);
14: DerivedClass = static_cast <Derived *> (BaseClass);
```

This piece of code first does an upcast from Derived to Base (line 13). It is called an upcast because it moves up within the class hierarchy. Next, you do a downcast in line 14 by converting a Base type class to a Derived type. See Figure 6.10. By the way, this was your first example of polymorphism!

dynamic_cast

dynamic_cast works similarly to static_cast but does a type check to prevent unsafe casts.

Its syntax is as follows:

```
dynamic_cast <type-id> expression
```

By ensuring type checking, unsafe casts will result in a null pointer, which can be detected and handled gracefully. If there is no checking, an unsafe cast could lead to an access violation error that isn't very nice.

If you tried the static_cast class example using dynamic_cast, it would not work since the downcast from Base to Derived would not be possible.

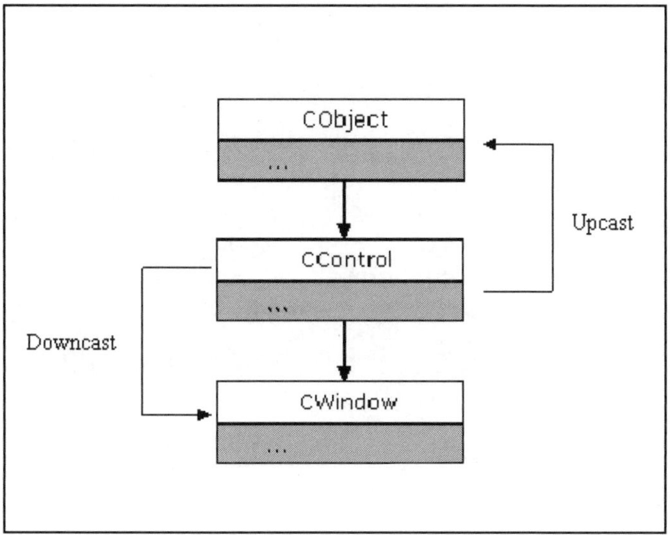

Figure 6.10

Casting objects up and down.

Enumerations

An enumeration is a simple topic that resembles sets of constants. Enumerations enable you to define a set of constants relative to a topic in a single structured way. You use it like:

```
enum EnumName
{
 ConstantName = Value,
 /* … */
};
```

By creating an enumeration type, you can specify a set of constants that can be used through the program. A simple example would be the difficulty of a game. By creating an enumeration with the different game difficulties, you can use the constants through the game instead of magic numbers:

```
enum GameDifficulty
{
 Easy = 1,
 Medium,
 Hard,
 Nightmare
};
```

One of the advantages of enumerations is the fact that the next constant will have a value equal to the previous constant plus one. In your example, `Medium` would be two, `Hard` would be three, and `Nightmare` would be four. If you don't supply any value, the first constant will have the value 0. You can also specify the values to all or just a few of the constants if you want.

> **NOTE**
>
> Magic numbers are numbers that are usually found in programs and games that are used to tweak the program but have no accurate real value, just look good, or are used to define stuff that an outsider wouldn't understand.

Take note that all constants except the last one need a comma at the end.

An example of this would be to use enumerations in a game to define game difficulty:

```
enum GameDifficultyConstants
{
```

```
 Easy = 0;
 Intermediate = 1;
 Hard = 2;
 AreYouNuts = 3;
};
 /* … */
switch (GameDifficulty)
{
 case Easy:  /* 0 */
  Lives = 5;
 break;
case Intermediate:  /* 1 */
  Lives = 3;
 break;
case Hard:  /* 2 */
  Lives = 2;
 break;
case AreYouNuts:  /* 3 */
  Lives = 1;
 break;
}
```

This way, you wouldn't have to use real numbers, but constants to specify game stuff. While it doesn't bring any advantages code-wise, it helps code readability. Try to use numbers instead of constants like this for your game, rest for a week, and then come back to programming. I assure you that you won't remember what the values mean. This way, you will always know!

Unions

Unions are funny! Really they are. A union is a way to create one variable (more like a structure) that can hold different types (`floats`, `ints`). Think of a box that can hold only one object at a time, but that object can be a doll, a toy car, or an apple. The box, of course, is as big as the biggest object it holds. The box can be thought of as being a union.

A union is created in the same way as a class. It starts with the keyword `union`, followed by the union name, and then the block with all the elements. For example:

```
union PixelType
{
```

```
 unsigned char EightBit;
 unsigned short SixteenBit;
 unsigned long ThirtyTwoBit;
};
```

This union is made of three elements that can be used exclusively (only one of them contains a valid value) depending on the type of pixel type you want to use. This union would be as big as the biggest element, in this case, an `unsigned long`.

`PixelType` could be used as follows:

```
 /* … */
PixelType Color;
If (ScreenType == 8)
{
 Color. EightBit = OtherColor8;
}
if (ScreenType == 16)
{
 Color. SixteenBit = OtherColor16;
}
if (ScreenType == 32)
{
 Color. ThirtyTwoBit = OtherColor32;
}
```

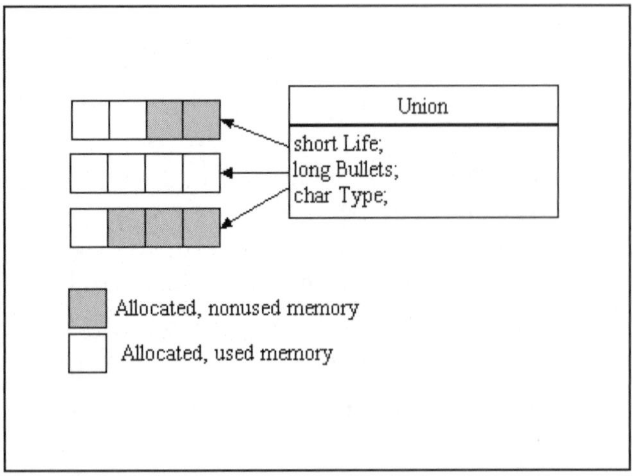

Figure 6.11

Memory alignment for `unions`*.*

Static Members

Static class member is a C++ feature that may come in handy when you need global access to the class. Static members enable you to create a generic singleton class, which will let you create classes that exist only once in your program. A useful technique that you will be using extensively for the screen manager, sound manager, enemy manager, and other classes (mostly managers) later.

I have already talked about global scope functions and variables, it's time to talk about static functions and variables.

A static member (be it either a variable or function) is a member that can be accessed without the use of a real instance of the class. Also, static variables are shared between every instance of that class type. This means that a class type with a static variable will hold the same value for every instance of the class. So, if you create ten classes and change the value of a static variable of one of them, it will also change the value of the static variable in the others.

Static members are created using the `static` keyword before the `return` type (for functions), or the `variable` type (for variables), in the class definition, like so:

```
class StaticExample
{
 public:
static int m_NumberOfClasses;
static void PrintNumberOfClasses (void);
};
int StaticExample::m_NumberOfClasses;
```

You can utilize class static members by using the class type followed by the scope resolution operator (`::`) and the static member name, like so:

```
StaticExample::m_NumberOfClasses ++;
StaticExample::PrintNumberOfClasses ();
```

> **NOTE**
>
> **Static data members must also be declared in the global namespace using the class namespace before the static member variable as shown in the previous examples with `int StaticExample::m_NumberOfClasses;`.**

Useful Techniques Using Classes

Knowing how to use classes is an important aspect when using C++. Classes enable you to have a more structured way to work and manage your data, but there are some other special uses for classes that have been used more recently to aid in the implementation of software, these are singletons and object factories.

A Singleton Class

A *singleton* is an object that has only one valid instance at any time. This means you can have only one singleton class at one time while running a program. If you try to create another instance of a singleton, the program will generate an error if it is in debug mode.

Singleton classes are useful for classes like enemies or a sound manager. They provide access to a class all over your programs using static members.

Singletons are based on static pointers to classes. By keeping a static pointer of the current instance of the object, and by having a static class function to return that pointer, you can at any time know whether there is an active instance of the object, and if so, use it.

A basic singleton example is the following:

```
 /* '03 Main.cpp' */

 /* Input output stream header */
#include <iostream>
 /* Assertion header */
#include <assert.h>

 /* Singleton class */
class CSingletonExample
{
private:
 static CSingletonExample * m_Singleton;

public:

```

```
 CSingletonExample ();
 virtual ~CSingletonExample ();

 static CSingletonExample * GetSingleton (void);
};

CSingletonExample * CSingletonExample::m_Singleton;
```

The first thing you probably noticed that hasn't been done before is the inclusion of `assert.h`. This header file is included so you can use the `assert` function to produce a debug-only error as you will see later.

Next, you have the class definition with the normal constructor and destructor. The two things to note are the static pointer to a `CSingletonExample` class (same type as the class itself) and the static function `GetSingleton` that also returns a pointer to a `CSingletonExample` class. These two class members are used to create the actual class singleton.

Don't forget to include the static pointer declaration in the global namespace.

```
CSingletonExample::CSingletonExample ()
{
 assert (!m_Singleton);

 m_Singleton = this;
}
```

Your constructor isn't very complicated, but first, a word about `assert`. The `assert` function is used to create a breakpoint in debug mode when its argument is `false` (`0`). This is a handy function when you aren't sure of some behavior of your program. Or when you want to make sure everything is 100 percent right and that some code should never be executed, you use assertions. Assertions have the advantages of generating a breakpoint that leads the debugger to the line where `assert` has been called, making it easier to diagnose and fix the problem.

Knowing how `assert` works, let's see what it does for you. When you use the syntax `!m_Singleton`, you are determining whether `m_Singleton` isn't valid, because if it is, it will return `false` (remember, `!true` is `false`). Since `m_Singleton` is a static member, it will have the same value for any instance of the class that exists. If you are creating a second instance of the class, then `m_Singleton` is a valid class, thus, `!m_Singleton` returns `false` and assertion exists.

After this check is done to ensure that there isn't any valid instance of the class, you initialize m_Singleton by pointing it to the class you are declaring by using the this pointer.

```
CSingletonExample::~CSingletonExample ()
{
  assert (m_Singleton);

  m_Singleton = NULL;
}
```

Next you have the destructor, which does the exact opposite of the constructor. It checks to see whether m_Singleton is valid (if it is being destroyed, then there has to be one valid instance of the class) and resets the m_Singleton member to NULL to enable you to create another instance of the class later.

```
CSingletonExample * CSingletonExample::GetSingleton ()
{
  assert (m_Singleton);

  return m_Singleton;
}
```

Finally, you have the static class function that returns a pointer to the valid singleton. You first check whether the m_Singleton member is valid, and if so, you return it. This allows you to access the only instance of the class.

Now, using the singleton class is easy, you just declare one instance of the class, and whenever you want to use it, you call the static member GetSingleton:

```
int main ()
{
 CSingletonExample Singleton;
 CSingletonExample *PointerSingleton;

 PointerSingleton = CSingletonExample::GetSingleton ();

 return 0;
}
```

This sample program would create one instance of CSingletonExample in the first line, and then a pointer to a CSingletonExample (a pointer that isn't initialized isn't a valid instance of a class). You would then use the static function GetSingleton to make PointerSingleton point to the actual singleton class, which you could then use as you wish.

The following is an example of bad use of the singleton class:

```
int main ()
{
 CSingletonExample Singleton;
 CSingletonExample *PointerSingleton;

 PointerSingleton = CSingletonExample::GetSingleton ();

 CSingletonExample SecondSingleton;

 return 0;
}
```

With the preceding code, you would get an error message and if you were in debug mode, the program would launch the debugger when you declare the second instance of CSingletonExample. This would happen because there is an instance of a CSingletonExample already.

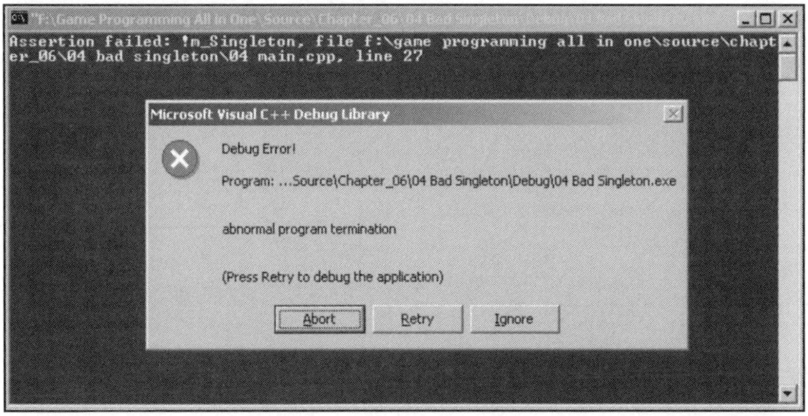

Figure 6.12
Bad singleton.

Singletons are used mostly for managers of some kind; for example, if you have a class that will manage all the enemies, this class would be better done with a singleton assigned to it, which would avoid passing classes to various functions, and you would still have access to it. If you think about it, there are many other uses like memory managers, image managers, and so on.

An Object Factory

You may be wondering what the heck an object factory is. . . . Well, I'm going to start by saying it is an extremely useful tool for games. It enables you to create classes in runtime with little info on them. You can, for example, load a file from the hard drive and create the necessary classes in runtime depending on the file. This is extremely useful when loading levels or generating enemies.

An object factory is based mostly on polymorphism, so make sure you have understood that part well before advancing.

An object factory's workings aren't very complicated (well, at least the ones I will cover in this book, since there are many different and more complicated object factories out there). They are based on a function or static class that returns a pointer to a certain class, depending on the type of parameters you supply. By creating a base class and deriving all the possible classes that you want to use with the object factory from that class, you are able to create just one function that returns various class pointers that are returned as a base class pointer which can later be cast.

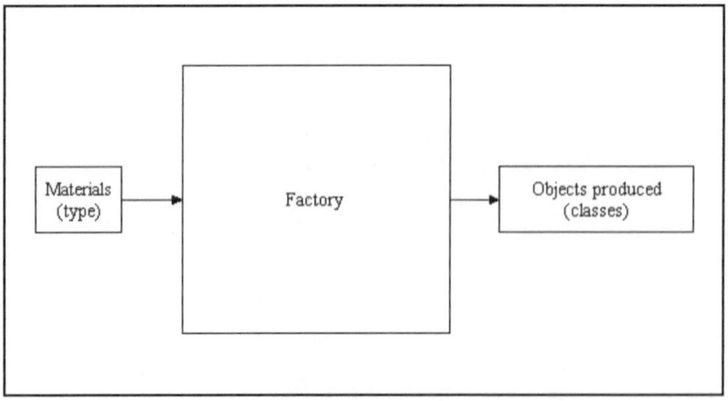

Figure 6.13

A factory in action.

You will be using the same classes from the polymorphism program:

```
/* '06 Main.cpp' */

/* Input output stream header */
#include <iostream>
/* Assertion header */
#include <assert.h>

```

```
 /* Object types */
enum ObjectTypes
{
 DogType,
 CatType
};

class CAnimal
{
public:
 int   m_MaxAge;
 int   m_Age;

 CAnimal ();
 virtual ~CAnimal ();

 virtual void Talk (void);
};

CAnimal::CAnimal ()
{
 m_MaxAge = 0;
 m_Age    = 0;
}

CAnimal::~CAnimal ()
{
}

void CAnimal::Talk (void)
{
 std::cout << "Base animal doesn't talk!";
}

 /* Derived dog class */
class CDog : public CAnimal
{
public:
 CDog ();
 virtual ~CDog ();

```

```
 virtual void Talk (void);
};

CDog::CDog ()
{
 m_MaxAge = 9;
 m_Age    = 0;
}

CDog::~CDog ()
{
}

void CDog::Talk (void)
{
 if (m_Age < m_MaxAge)
 {
  std::cout << "Bark..." << std::endl;
  m_Age ++;
 }
}

 /* Derived cat class */
class CCat : public CAnimal
{
public:
 CCat ();
 virtual ~CCat ();

 virtual void Talk (void);
};

CCat::CCat ()
{
 m_MaxAge = 5;
 m_Age    = 0;
}

CCat::~CCat ()
{
}
```

```
 90:
 91: void CCat::Talk (void)
 92: {
 93:  if (m_Age < m_MaxAge)
 94:  {
 95:   std::cout << "Meow..." << std::endl;
 96:   m_Age ++;
 97:  }
 98: }
 99:
100:  /* Object factory class */
101: class CObjectFactory
102: {
103: public:
104:  static CAnimal * GetType (int Type);
105: };
```

The first thing to note is that you declare an enumeration in line 9 containing the type of objects that the factory can return, nothing new. You then declare the already covered polymorphic classes and your object factory class. I decided to keep the object factory a class even if it has only one member to allow it to be upgraded as required, making code changes minimal. `GetType` returns a pointer to the `CAnimal` class, but take note that the actual pointer is usually a pointer to a class that derived from `CAnimal` that is cast to `CAnimal`.

```
107: CAnimal * CObjectFactory::GetType (int Type)
108: {
109:  switch (Type)
110:  {
111:  case DogType:
112:   return new CDog ();
113:  break;
114:  case CatType:
115:   return new CCat ();
116:  break;
117:
118:  default:
119:   assert (0);
120:  }
121:  return NULL;
122: }
```

This function is the real meat of the object factory. It uses a `switch` clause to check which type of class you want to create, and according to the `Type` argument, it returns a pointer to a new class of the asked type. If a class outside the available range is specified, it generates an error with `assert` and returns `NULL`.

```
 /* Start */
int main ()
{

 CAnimal * Dog;
 CAnimal * Cat;

 Dog = CObjectFactory::GetType (DogType);
 Cat = CObjectFactory::GetType (CatType);

 Dog->Talk ();
 Cat->Talk ();

 delete Dog;
 delete Cat;

 return 0;
}
```

Figure 6.14
Object factory.

The program to use the object factory isn't complicated either. You first create two `CAnimal` types (base classes), and then use the object factory to create two animals, first a dog and then a cat. Since `CObjectFactory::GetType` returns an already cast type, you can use a `CAnimal` class with it. If you preferred to declare `Dog` and `Cat` as `CDog` and `CCat`, you would need to cast the return pointer from `CObjectFactory::GetType` to their types (which would be safer). You then call `Dog`'s and `Cat`'s `Talk` method to ensure the exact objects were created.

> **NOTE**
> A good use for a singleton class is an object factory; try it.

Don't forget to delete the pointers when you don't need them.

Summary

In this chapter you have been introduced to one of the features that distinguish it from other programming languages: classes.

In C++, classes are one of the basics of object-oriented programming, making it easy and accessible to represent concepts as objects, or more accurately, classes.

Also, two of the most advanced features of C++, inheritance and polymorphism, were briefly covered so that you can use them in your game.

In the end, you were presented with two design patterns that were built upon the knowledge learned in this chapter and may prove useful later.

Questions and Answers

Q: Why are classes so important in object-oriented programming?

A: In C++, the simplest way to describe an object is by a collection of data and methods. By allowing the data and methods to be connected to some structured type is very beneficial. These structured types, the classes in C++, can be thought of as the representation of the object.

Q: Why use inheritance if you can just retype the code?

A: Even if inheritance isn't necessary (even though it is helpful, especially when you deal with polymorphism), it has the advantage of code reuse, which is what you are looking for.

Exercises

1. What is a class?
2. What are the three different access levels a class member can have?
3. What is the difference between protected and private access levels?
4. What is wrong with the following code?

```
class SomeObject
{
 private:
 int iData;
 /* ... */
}
```

5. What is inheritance?
6. What is wrong with the following code?

```
Class Base
{
 int Data;
};
Class Derived : public Base
{
 int MoreData;
}
/* ... */
Derived NewClass;
NewClass.Data = 0;
NewClass.MoreData = 0;
```

7. What is polymorphism?
8. Describe two possible uses for unions.
9. Provide two possible uses for a singleton class.

CHAPTER 7

Developing Monster

I know the last few chapters were a little boring for you, so now I have to present you with something to make up for them. How about a full-featured game? In this chapter, I will focus only on developing a small library to create text-based games and a complete game called Monster. This entire chapter will be based on the knowledge covered earlier, so you shouldn't have a problem with it.

ConLib

Unfortunately, one of C++'s biggest caveats is its lack of support for advanced text output. Unless you use an external library of functions that are compiler specific, you don't have much control over the way you can output your text.

Fortunately, Microsoft has a set of console functions that enable you to do some advanced text output.

> **NOTE**
>
> **A console is what you have been using until now. It's the text-only window where you have been working.**

To make it easier to work with consoles, you will develop a small console library named ConLib, which will be able to clear the background to a specific color, output text to any place in the console, and also have a better input method.

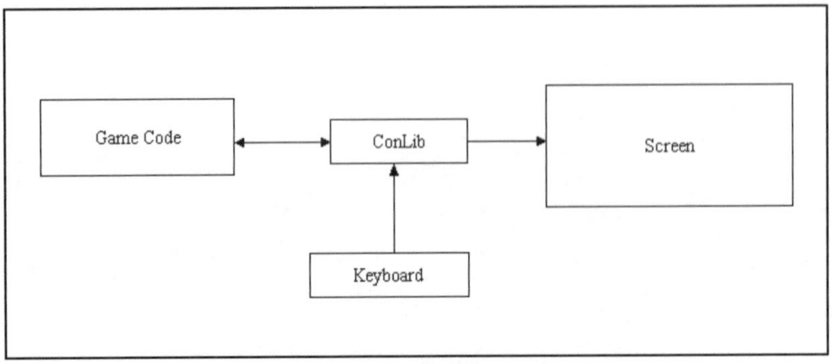

Figure 7.1

ConLib at work.

Design

ConLib is a small library to handle console input and output. Its objective is to be simple to use yet allowing you to have the control you need to develop a text game. The base features are:

- Specifying both background and text color
- Ability to clear the entire console
- Outputting text at any position
- Reading text from the keyboard
- Handling keystrokes from the keyboard

It may seem pretty small but ConLib can handle just about anything needed to develop a text game.

ConLib is made up of a single class named `ConLib`. Imaginative, no? From this class you can access any of the methods you need to handle the screen or keyboard. The header including the class definition is as follows:

```
 /* 'ConLib.h' */

 /* Avoid redefinition */
#pragma once

 /* Windows standard header file */
#include <windows.h>

 /* ConLib color codes */
enum ConColor
{
 ConRed    = 1,
 ConGreen  = 2,
 ConBlue   = 4
};

 /* ConLib control class */
class ConLib
{
  /* Screen and keyboard handles */
 HANDLE m_Screen;
```

```
22:  HANDLE m_Keyboard;
23:
24:   /* Color attributes */
25:  WORD   m_TextColor;
26:  WORD   m_BackgroundColor;
27:
28: public:
29:
30:   /* Constructor / destructor */
31:  ConLib ();
32:  ~ConLib ();
33:
34:   /* Set attributes */
35:  void SetBackgroundColor (WORD Color);
36:  void SetTextColor (WORD Color);
37:  void SetTitle (char * Title);
38:  void SetPosition (COORD Position);
39:
40:   /* Output methods */
41:  void Clear (void);
42:  void OutputString (char * String);
43:
44:   /* Input methods */
45:  void Read (char * Buffer, DWORD BufferSize);
46:  int GetKey (void);
47: };
```

You see a few new things here, but before I discuss that, check out Table 7.1 for a description of each of the important methods.

Now that you know what each method does, it's time to check all the new stuff. And as you may notice, the first is in the `windows.h` header file in line 7. As said before, C++ doesn't have a good set of functions for text output, so you need to use Microsoft's own code to do it. This code is included in the `windows.h` header file. This will all be explained when you deal with Windows programming but for now, just remember that `windows.h` contains all the Windows functions you need to operate with the console.

The next things to check are lines 21 and 22, namely:

```
HANDLE m_Screen;
HANDLE m_Keyboard;
```

Table 7.1 ConLib Methods

Method	Description
`SetBackgroundColor`	Sets the color of the background when text is typed or the screen is cleared
`SetTextColor`	Sets the color of the text
`SetTitle`	Sets the window console title
`SetPosition`	Sets the cursor position from where text will be written
`Clear`	Clears the entire console
`OutputString`	Outputs a string to the current cursor position
`Read`	Reads a string from the keyboard
`GetKey`	Returns if a key is pressed and if so, which key it was

A Windows handle is a way to communicate with something. In this case, you are going to communicate with the screen, which is the output, and the keyboard, which is the input. There are many types of handles that you will look at later. Handles are a major part of Windows programming, but they aren't a big deal to work with. They basically offer a way to communicate with an object. It's like a wire connecting the computer to your keyboard—you have the keyboard, which is the object, and you have the computer, which is sort of like the functions you will use. The wire is the handle that allows the communication between them.

> A *handle* is a variable that identifies an object or an operating system resource. Handles come in all forms and sizes, from hardware handles to image and sound handles. A handle is the way you communicate with operating system resources, and since operating system resources can be moved to other places in memory, it's always advisable to get the handle after releasing it since there is no assurance that a previously retrieved handle will be stored in the same place forever.

These two members will be initialized in the constructor, as you will see later. Keeping them as class members allows you to use them at various times during your games without having to get the handle to the device each time.

You will also keep the current background and text color inside the class. Even if this isn't a necessity, it will make programming easier.

Implementation

By now, you probably have a good understanding of what ConLib is and how it works so it is time to start programming it. First, include the `ConLib.h` header file so that you have the class definition in the source file. Next, code your constructor and destructor as follows:

```
 /* 'ConLib.cpp' */

 /* ConLib complement header file */
#include "ConLib.h"

 /* Get standard screen and keyboard handles */
ConLib::ConLib ()
{
 m_Screen = GetStdHandle (STD_OUTPUT_HANDLE);
 m_Keyboard = GetStdHandle (STD_INPUT_HANDLE);

 SetTextColor (ConRed | ConGreen | ConBlue);
 SetBackgroundColor (0);
}
```

Your constructor does two separate things. First it gets a handle to the standard input device, usually the keyboard, and a handle to the standard output device, usually the monitor. It does this using the function `GetStdHandle`, which is defined as:

```
HANDLE GetStdHandle (DWORD nStdHandle);
```

This function takes only one parameter that specifies the device for which to return the handler; the available devices are shown in Table 7.2.

And returns a handle to the specified device. If the function fails, this `GetStdHandle` returns `INVALID_HANDLE_VALUE`.

The last thing the constructor does is set the background color to black and the text color to white.

TABLE 7.2 GetStdHandle Devices

Device	Description
STD_INPUT_HANDLE	Standard input device
STD_OUTPUT_HANDLE	Standard output device
STD_ERROR_HANDLE	Standard error device

Now, how does the color combination work? As shown with `ConLib.h`, you created an enumerator `ConColor` with three constants, each one with a value that for each constant is a multiple of two. If you are wondering why you did this, take a look at the numbers that follow:

```
0^0 = 0 = 00000000
2^0 = 1 = 00000001
2^1 = 2 = 00000010
2^2 = 4 = 00000100
2^3 = 8 = 00001000
```

As you can see, each multiple of two has a bit set. Depending on the number, the corresponding bit is set. So how can this help you? In the constructor, you used the bitwise-inclusive-OR (`|`) operator to set the color. The bitwise-inclusive-OR takes two numbers and compares each bit of the two. If either bit is set (`1`), the resulting number will also have the bit set, for example:

```
11010001 |
01001011
--------
11011011
```

If a bit of either number is set, the resulting number will have that bit set. So in your color case, the combination `ConRed | ConGreen | ConBlue` would generate the number `00000111`, which will let you know later what colors are passed to the function. If you, for example, wanted the color purple, you had to mix red and blue like `ConRed | ConBlue`, which would generate `00000101`. If you pass zero as the color, the number will be 00000000 which means that none of the color bits is set, meaning, lack of any color: black.

> **NOTE**
>
> **If you need to brush up on your binary to decimal base systems knowledge, try Appendix C, "Binary, Hexadecimal, and Decimal Notation."**

The following method, SetBackgroundColor, uses the argument Color to set the specified console background color:

```

 /* Does nothing */
ConLib::~ConLib ()
{

}

 /* Sets background color */
void ConLib::SetBackgroundColor (WORD Color)
{
 m_BackgroundColor = 0;

  /* Use bit manipulation to get the color combinations */
 if (Color & ConRed)
 {
  m_BackgroundColor |= BACKGROUND_RED;
 }
 if (Color & ConGreen)
 {
  m_BackgroundColor |= BACKGROUND_GREEN;
 }
 if (Color & ConBlue)
 {
  m_BackgroundColor |= BACKGROUND_BLUE;
 }

  /* Set the color using combinations from above */
 SetConsoleTextAttribute (m_Screen, m_TextColor | m_BackgroundColor);
}
```

The first thing to do is set the background color to black (0). This enables you to perform bit manipulation without worrying about previous colors. To better understand why you use all the ifs and bit stuff, let's take a look at SetConsoleTextAttribute first, which is defined as:

> **NOTE**
> A WORD is the same as an unsigned short in Windows.

```
BOOL SetConsoleTextAttribute (HANDLE hConsoleOutput, WORD wAttributes);
```

Where hConsoleOutput is a handle to the console output, and if you remember correctly, in your case m_Screen. The second parameter is what matters; the combination of colors passed to it will be used to set the console colors. The only way to pass a color combination to it is like before, using the bitwise-inclusive-OR operator with a combination of flags that specify what colors you want to use. These flags are described in Table 7.3.

By specifying a combination of the flags in Table 7.3, you can create various color combinations like:

```
FOREGROUND_RED | FOREGROUND_BLUE | BACKGROUND_GREEN
```

Would make the text have a purple color (red and blue) on a green background. SetConsoleTextAttribute returns zero in case of error, and any other value if successful.

TABLE 7.3 SetConsoleTextAttribute Devices

Device	Description
FOREGROUND_RED	Red text
FOREGROUND_GREEN	Green text
FOREGROUND_BLUE	Blue text
BACKGROUND_RED	Red background
BACKGROUND_GREEN	Green background
BACKGROUND_BLUE	Blue background

So, how do you convert from your ConLib color flags to `SetConsoleTextAttribute` background flags? Again, you use bit manipulation, this time using the bitwise-AND (`&`) operator. The operator compares all the bits in two numbers, and if both bits are set (1), the returning bit will also be set. If any other combination is used (both bits not set or one is set and the other is not set), the end bit will be `0`. For example:

```
11010001 &
01001011
--------
01000001
```

So, if you were using flags to set the colors, for example, the purple color (`00000101`), and if you wanted to know which bits were set, you would have to compare each bit with a bitwise logical AND. Confusing? It's pretty simple actually. For example:

```
00000101 & /* Color */
00000100 /* ConRed */
--------
00000100
```

Would return the number four (00000100 in binary) since the only bit that is true in both operands is the 4 bit. Moreover, in C++ any nonzero value is true, thus if you did:

```
if (Color & ConRed)
{
 /* Do something */
}
```

Would evaluate to `true` since the end result would be four. If you wanted to check whether the green flag was set, you would replace `ConRed` with `ConGreen`, like so:

```
00000101 & /* Color */
00000010 /* ConGreen */
--------
00000010
```

Which would return zero, thus, evaluating any `if` expression to `false`.

Let's do a quick recap: using numbers that are powers of two, you in essence have numbers which only have a single bit set, creating a mutually exclusive collection of bit flags. If you want to set any bit of a number, you use the | operator with the correct bit flag (which is a power of two), and if you want to check whether a certain bit of a number is set, you use the `&` operator with the correct power of two, which would return `true` if the bit was set and `false` if it wasn't.

Back to your code, you check Color for what bits are set using ConLib flags, and depending on the ones that are, you set them in m_BackGround using the BACKGROUND_ Windows flags.

Now that you have your background color combination, you need to use it with SetConsoleTextAttribute. You also need to OR the current text color because SetConsoleTextAttribute is used for both the text and background color. To combine both the background color and the text color, you use the OR operator, like so:

```
m_TextColor | m_BackgroundColor
```

And you finally have your SetBackgroundColor done. Flag manipulation is pretty handy in game programming and it is widely used in Windows programming to set windows attributes and other flags.

The next function, SetTextColor, works exactly like SetBackgroundColor, but instead of doing the bit manipulation and setting the BACKGROUND_ flags, it sets the FOREGROUND_ flags, like so:

```
 /* Sets text color */
void ConLib::SetTextColor (WORD Color)
{
 m_TextColor = 0;

  /* Use bit manipulation to get the color combinations */
 if (Color & ConRed)
 {
  m_TextColor |= FOREGROUND_RED;
 }
 if (Color & ConGreen)
 {
  m_TextColor |= FOREGROUND_GREEN;
 }
 if (Color & ConBlue)
 {
  m_TextColor |= FOREGROUND_BLUE;
 }

  /* Set the color using combinations from above */
 SetConsoleTextAttribute (m_Screen, m_TextColor | m_BackgroundColor);
}
```

The next method, `SetTitle` changes the title of the current console window:

```
 /* Sets window title */
void ConLib::SetTitle (char * Title)
{
 SetConsoleTitle (Title);
}
```

This function is only a container for `SetConsoleTitle`. `SetConsoleTitle` is used to set the window name, the top bar text, of the current console window, that is, the window you are using. It is defined as:

```
BOOL SetConsoleTitle (LPCTSTR lpConsoleTitle);
```

The only parameter of the function is the new console title. If the function isn't successful, it returns zero; if it is successful, it returns any nonzero value.

Now you have the `Clear` function. This function clears the screen using the current background color.

```
 /* Clears the screen */
void ConLib::Clear (void)
{
 COORD Start;
 DWORD Written;

 Start.X = 0;
 Start.Y = 0;

 FillConsoleOutputAttribute (m_Screen, m_TextColor | m_BackgroundColor,
                             80*25, Start, &Written);
 FillConsoleOutputCharacter (m_Screen, ' ',
                             80*25, Start, &Written);
 SetConsoleCursorPosition (m_Screen, Start);
}
```

The first thing you do is declare two variables, one of type `COORD` and one of type `DWORD`. `DWORD` is simply a type definition and is the same as an `unsigned long` in Windows. `COORD`, on the other hand, is a structure that holds two variables, `X` and `Y`, which define a 2D coordinate on the screen.

```
typedef struct _COORD {
SHORT X;
SHORT Y;
} COORD;
```

There isn't much to explain here. `X` holds the horizontal coordinate and `Y` holds the vertical coordinate. Easy!

Because you want to clear the console from the beginning, you set both `X` and `Y` of `Start` to zero. After this is done, there are two things to do: set the attributes like color and the fill the console with a space character to actually clear the console. This is done with `FillConsoleOutputAttribute` and `FillConsoleOutputCharacter`.

`FillConsoleOutputAttribute` is used to fill the attributes of all the specified positions of the console, or as MSDN calls them, character cells. Its prototype is:

```
BOOL FillConsoleOutputAttribute (
  HANDLE hConsoleOutput,
  WORD wAttribute,
  DWORD nLength,
  COORD dwWriteCoord,
  LPDWORD lpNumberOfAttrsWritten
);
```

There are a few parameters, but nothing too difficult. The first parameter is the handle to the console you want to fill; in your case `m_Screen`. Next you have the attribute, which is filled with the background and text color information, `m_TextColor | m_BackgroundColor` like before. Then you have a new parameter, this is the number of character cells to write, and you use 80*25 since it is the common size of a console window—80 characters wide and 25 characters tall. After that is the starting coordinate, which you already set to the beginning of the console earlier—`Start`. Finally, a pointer to a `DWORD` to where the number of character cells will be stored, here `&Written`. This is more of a formality and has almost no value to you. See Figure 7.2.

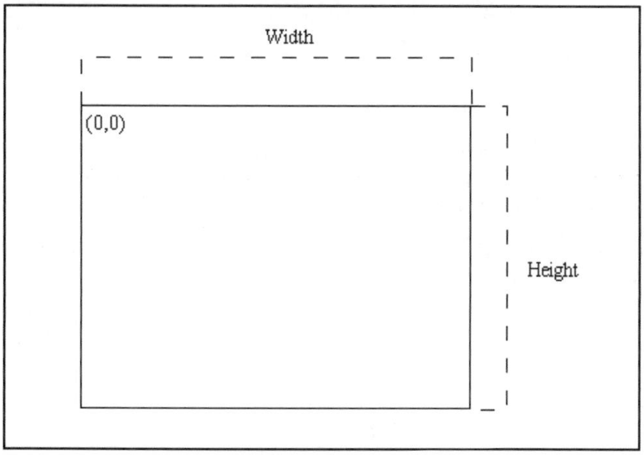

Figure 7.2

Screen anatomy.

FillConsoleOutputAttribute returns a BOOL like before, which returns zero if the function was not successful and a nonzero value if it was successful.

> **TIP**
>
> **From now on, every function that returns a BOOL where no description of the return value is given can be considered a standard return type that means zero for unsuccessful and nonzero for successful.**

Now that you have the attributes of the character cells, you need to fill them with something. You can fill them with any character, but to make the background all of the same color you use a space instead of a letter; that way, the cells will only have the background color. This is done with FillConsoleOutputCharacter, which writes a character to the console with the current attributes. Its prototype is as follows:

```
BOOL FillConsoleOutputCharacter (
  HANDLE hConsoleOutput,
  TCHAR cCharacter,
  DWORD nLength,
  COORD dwWriteCoord,
  LPDWORD lpNumberOfCharsWritten
);
```

Which work similarly to FillConsoleOutputAttribute with the only changes being that instead of passing an attribute, you pass a char, in your case space ' ', and instead of storing the number of attributes written, it stores the number of characters written.

> **NOTE**
>
> When you enclose a single character inside the single quotes ' ', you tell the compiler to convert that character to its ASCII code, a char. For example 'A' would convert to 64.

The last thing you do is set the cursor position to the beginning of the console. This prevents the console from being scrolled in some Windows versions. You just need to pass a COORD type as a parameter to SetPosition that specifies the position to move to.

And talking about SetPosition, let's check it out:

```
/* Sets the cursor position */
void ConLib::SetPosition (COORD Position)
{
```

```
SetConsoleCursorPosition (m_Screen, Position);
}
```

SetPosition is just a wrapper method for the real function, SetConsoleCursorPosition that is defined as:

```
BOOL SetConsoleCursorPosition (
  HANDLE hConsoleOutput,
  COORD dwCursorPosition
);
```

Where the first parameter is a handle to the console where you want to set the cursor position and the last parameter is the position of the cursor.

Next there is the OutputString method. This method enables you to output a string to the current cursor position:

```
 /* Sends a string to the screen */
void ConLib::OutputString (char * String)
{
 DWORD Written;

 WriteConsole (m_Screen, String, strlen (String), &Written, NULL);
}
```

Another wrapper method, this time for WriteConsole that is defined as:

```
BOOL WriteConsole (
  HANDLE hConsoleOutput,
  CONST VOID *lpBuffer,
  DWORD nNumberOfCharsToWrite,
  LPDWORD lpNumberOfCharsWritten,
  LPVOID lpReserved
);
```

WriteConsole takes, as usual, a handle to the console you want to use with the function as the first parameter. Next, there is a pointer to a buffer, the actual string to output—in your case, the string passed to OutputString, String. Then there is the number of characters to write, and you will use the length of String as parameter. Next you have a pointer to the number of characters written, where you pass the address of Written, as before, you don't use this but you pass it to ensure it works properly. Windows reserves the last parameter so you just need to pass NULL to it.

If you can output to the console, it's only fair that you can also read from it. You use Read to do this:

```
 /* Reads a string from the keyboard */
void ConLib::Read (char * Buffer, DWORD BufferSize)
{
 DWORD Read;

 ReadConsole (m_Keyboard, Buffer, BufferSize, &Read, NULL);
}
```

Read works similarly to OutputString, it is a wrapper for ReadConsole, which also works similarly to WriteConsole, which is defined as:

```
BOOL ReadConsole (
  HANDLE hConsoleOutput,
  CONST VOID *lpBuffer,
  DWORD nNumberOfCharsToRead,
  LPDWORD lpNumberOfCharsRead,
  LPVOID lpReserved
);
```

These function parameters work exactly like the ones for WriteConsole, with the difference that the second parameter is used to store the input and not the string to output.

The last method of ConLib, GetKey enables you to know whether a certain key is pressed down. If it is, it will return the key virtual key code, or if no key is pressed, it returns zero.

```
 /* Gets a key from the keyboard */
int ConLib::GetKey (void)
{
 DWORD Read;
 INPUT_RECORD Event;

  /* Get console input */
 ReadConsoleInput (m_Keyboard, &Event, 1, &Read);

  /* If input event is a key event see if there is any key pressed
     and return its virtual-key code */
 if (Event.EventType == KEY_EVENT)
 {
```

```
    if (Event.Event.KeyEvent.bKeyDown)
    {
      return Event.Event.KeyEvent.wVirtualKeyCode;
    }
  }

  return 0;
}
```

There are two important parts of this function: getting the input event from the console and checking whether it is a key down event. You get the input using `ReadConsoleInput`:

```
BOOL ReadConsoleInput (
  HANDLE hConsoleInput,
  PINPUT_RECORD lpBuffer,
  DWORD nLength,
  LPDWORD lpNumberOfEventsRead
);
```

The first parameter, as always, is the handle to the console you are working with. Next you have a pointer to a `PINPUT_RECORD` structure that will hold the event. This is a standard input record structure to console applications and is defined as follows:

```
typedef struct INPUT_RECORD {
  WORD EventType;
  union {
    KEY_EVENT_RECORD KeyEvent;
    MOUSE_EVENT_RECORD MouseEvent;
    WINDOW_BUFFER_SIZE_RECORD WindowBufferSizeEvent;
    MENU_EVENT_RECORD MenuEvent;
    FOCUS_EVENT_RECORD FocusEvent;
  } Event;
} INPUT_RECORD;
```

The first member of the structure, `EventType`, tells you what kind of event originated. Table 7.4 shows the possible event macros.

How does this work? Well, the value of `EventType` tells you the event type, and depending on the type, the union will contain a structure corresponding to the event. So if `EventType` is `KEY_EVENT`, then the `Event` structure would contain a `KEY_EVENT_RECORD`, and since you are only interested in keyboard events, you will only be checking for `KEY_EVENT`. If this is the event, then you need to check

Table 7.4 INPUT_RECORD Event Type Macros

Macro	Description
KEY_EVENT	Event member contains a KEY_EVENT_RECORD structure.
MOUSE_EVENT	Event member contains a MOUSE_EVENT_RECORD structure.
WINDOW_BUFFER_ SIZE_EVENT	Event member contains a WINDOW_BUFFER_SIZE _RECORD structure.
MENU_EVENT	Event member contains a MENU_EVENT_RECORD structure.
FOCUS_EVENT	Event member contains a FOCUS_EVENT_RECORD structure.

what happened using the Event member as a KEY_EVENT_RECORD, which is defined as follows:

```
typedef struct KEY_EVENT_RECORD {
  BOOL bKeyDown;
  WORD wRepeatCount;
  WORD wVirtualKeyCode;
  WORD wVirtualScanCode;
  union {
    WCHAR UnicodeChar;
    CHAR AsciiChar;
  } uChar;
  DWORD dwControlKeyState;
} KEY_EVENT_RECORD;
```

There is a lot of information in this structure, but you'll only be using two: bKeyDown, which if set to true, means that a key is down, and wVirtualKeyCode which holds the virtual key-code of the key pressed.

If bKeyDown is true, you then return wVirtualKeyCode in ReadKey, but if bKeyDown is false, meaning that no key is pressed, then you return zero to let the calling function know there isn't any key pressed.

> **NOTE**
>
> **A *virtual key-code* is an identifier that specifies a certain key in a device-independent manner.**

Even if it isn't the most complete console library, it offers enough functionality to create almost any text game, and to prove this, you will use ConLib to develop the game Monster next.

Also, Windows offers a few more functions to handle console applications that I encourage you to check out on MSDN.

Building Monster

You probably have heard of the game Monster, but for those who haven't, Monster is a puzzle game that was pretty popular a long time ago. The game was usually completed using only basic text routines.

In the following pages, you will develop your own version of Monster with various difficulty levels, lives, and some color.

Objective

The objective of Monster is simple: destroy all the monsters in the arena while not getting yourself killed.

The game can end three different ways. The first, and the desired way, is by destroying all the monsters. The second way is by losing all the lives, and lastly by the user giving up.

Rules

Monster is a simple game with few rules, which are described as follows:

- The game starts with the monsters and the player randomly placed in the arena. An extra effort is expended to ensure the player isn't placed in a cell (x-y coordinate inside the arena) already used by a monster.
- The player can move in any of eight possible directions (North, North-East, East, South-East, South, South-West, West, North-West).
- Each monster can move in any of the eight possible directions but always makes the move that makes it near the player.
- The player can leap to a random place in the arena. There is no assurance the player will not land in a cell with a monster, thus losing a life.
- Neither the player nor the monsters can move outside the arena.
- When two monsters share the same cell, both monsters are killed.

- When a monster and the player share the same cell, the monster is killed and the player loses a life.
- When all monsters are dead, the game ends with the player winning.
- When the player loses all the lives, the game ends with the player losing.

Design

There are two parts of the game that can be separated: the game itself and the menus and information screens.

Game Description

The game starts with the normal splash screen showing information about the game. After the player presses a key, the main menu appears where the player can choose to either start the game in one of the three difficulties, as shown in Table 7.5, or exit the game.

When the user starts the game, he is taken to the main game area, which shows the arena and the game information in gray/white, the player in green, and the monsters in red.

Thinking in Classes

You will be using two main classes to develop Monster: `CGame` and `CPlayer`. `CGame` will hold all the information about the game such as the monsters, the arena size, and one instance of the player. `CPlayer` will hold the player position, the number of lives and leaps left, and the player's score.

TABLE 7.5 Difficulty Settings

Difficulty	Description
Easy	Monsters = 10, Arena size = 25*15, Lives = 4, Leaps = 3
Medium	Monsters = 20, Arena size = 35*18, Lives = 3, Leaps = 2
Hard	Monsters = 30, Arena size = 50*23, Lives = 2, Leaps = 1

NOTE

Both the arena and the monsters could be classes of their own. This would make it easier if you planned to add custom arenas with special items or different designs or create various types of monsters. I've decided not to make them classes since for this version of the game they are unnecessary because the arena is always a rectangular field, making it only necessary to hold the size, and the monsters are described only by a position.

The CPlayer class is defined as:

```
 /* '02 Player.h' */

 /* Windows standard header file */
#include <windows.h>
 /* Time header file */
#include <time.h>

 /* Player class */
class CPlayer
{
private:

  /* Player attributes */
 COORD   m_Position;
 short   m_Lives;
 int     m_Score;
 int     m_Leaps;

public:

  /* Constructor / destructor */
 CPlayer ();
 ~CPlayer ();

  /* Move player */
 void Move (COORD Direction);
```

```
 void RandomLeap (COORD ArenaSize);

  /* Maintenance methods */
 void GetPosition (COORD * Position);

 void SetLives (short Lives);
 short GetLives (void);

 void SetScore (int Score);
 int GetScore (void);

 void SetLeaps (int Leaps);
 int GetLeaps (void);
};
```

As stated before, `CPlayer` holds the position, the score, the number of available leaps, and the score of the player. Most of the methods are simple and don't need explanation. They are used to set or get the member you want. The only two methods that actually are of importance are `Move` and `RandomLeap`. `Move`, obviously, moves the player by a certain coordinate and `RandomLeap` makes the player move to a random place inside the arena. I will discuss the implementation of these methods in a bit.

The next class, `CGame`, is the heart of your game. It contains all the information such as the monsters' positions, the arena size, the player, the last key pressed, and so on. The file '02 Game.h' also contains some enumerated types that you use to make your code more readable. Both the types and the class are defined, as follows:

```
 /* '02 Game.h' */

 /* Windows standard header file */
#include <windows.h>
 /* Standard input/output header file */
#include <stdio.h>

 /* ConLib header file */
#include "ConLib.h"
 /* CPlayer header file */
#include "02 Player.h"

 /* Game status enumerator */
enum GameStatus
```

```
{
 GameMainMenu     = 1,
 GameRunning      = 2,
 GamePaused       = 3,
 GameWon          = 4,
 GameLostLife     = 5,
 GameLost         = 6,
 GameExit         = 7,
 GameSplashScreen = 8
};

 /* Game difficulty enumerator */
enum GameDifficulty
{
 GameEasy         = 1,
 GameMedium       = 2,
 GameDifficult    = 3,
};

 /* Game base class */
class CGame
{
private:

  /* Input/output information */
 ConLib *    m_Console;
 int         m_LastAction;

  /* Game information */
 int         m_GameStatus;
 COORD       m_Arena;
 CPlayer     m_Player;
 COORD *     m_Monsters;
 int         m_MonstersNumber;

public:

  /* Constructors / destructor */
 CGame ();
 CGame (ConLib * Console);
 ~CGame ();
```

```

    /* Shows the relative information depending on game status */
  void ShowSplash (void);
  void ShowMenu (void);
  void ShowGame (void);
  void ShowWon (void);
  void ShowLostLife (void);
  void ShowLost (void);
  void ShowExit (void);
  void Show (void);

    /* Process the turn depending on game status */
  void ProcessSplash (void);
  void ProcessMenu (void);
  void ProcessGame (void);
  void ProcessWon (void);
  void ProcessLostLife (void);
  void ProcessLost (void);
  void ProcessExit (void);
  void ProcessTurn (void);

    /* Set console information */
  void SetConsole (ConLib * Console);

    /* Game methods */
  void StartNewGame (int Difficulty);
  void EndGame (void);
  void CheckCollisions ();
  int GetAction (void);
  int GetStatus (void);
  void MoveMonsters (void);
};
```

Okay, let's go over a quick examination of the code. First include the header files as normal. Then create two enumerated types, GameStatus and GameDifficulty. You create these types to make code more readable later.

You then have your CGame class that has several members. m_Console is a pointer to your ConLib library and m_LastAction is the last key pressed. You keep it to let you know whether there was any action, as you will see later. You then have the m_GameStatus which holds the game status, the arena size, m_Arena which is defined as a COORD to make it easier to work with, an instance of the player, and m_Player which is the type of the class you defined earlier. Last, you have the monster's pointer to a COORD, m_Monsters, and the monster's number, m_MonstersNumber.

You store the monsters as a COORD because each monster is defined as a coordinate with values between one and m_Arena - 1. When a monster has a coordinate equal to zero, it means that it is dead, thus saving a bit of memory.

You then have your constructors and destructor—nothing new. The next set of methods, ShowXXXX, just shows the screen according to the method. For example, ShowMenu shows the menu screen. The Show method is responsible for calling the correct function depending on the game status.

The next set of methods works exactly the same, but the methods are used to process (do the logic of) the current game status. They are named ProcessXXXX, and the function responsible for calling the correct method is Process.

The next method, SetConsole, enables you to set the console you are using. This function exists in case you want to change the console later.

NOTE

I've chosen to have various methods for Show and Process to make it easier to separate functionality. In Chapter 9, you will see why this was done.

StartNewGame and EndGame are responsible for setting up a game and destroying it, respectively. These methods create dynamic arrays, set up initial values, and free memory used by the game. The next function, CheckCollisions, checks for collisions between monsters and the player. GetAction and GetStatus have the task of returning the last key pressed and the current game status, respectively. The last method, MoveMonsters, moves the monsters to the player. It is basically the artificial intelligence of the game.

Implementation

In the next pages, you will see how Monster is implemented. Additionally, I will refrain from complex descriptions of the code from here on. However, where needed to help you understand, I will discuss the code in complex areas.

Let's start with CPlayer, which is the class that has fewer dependencies.

```
/* '02 Player.cpp' */

/* CPlayer complement header file */
```

```
#include "02 Player.h"

 /* Does nothing */
CPlayer::CPlayer ()
{

}

 /* Does nothing */
CPlayer::~CPlayer ()
{

}

 /* Moves player */
void CPlayer::Move (COORD Direction)
{
 m_Position.X += Direction.X;
 m_Position.Y += Direction.Y;
}

 /* Makes leap to random position */
void CPlayer::RandomLeap (COORD ArenaSize)
{
 srand (time (NULL));

 m_Position.X = (rand () % (ArenaSize.X - 1)) + 1;
 m_Position.Y = (rand () % (ArenaSize.Y - 1)) + 1;
}
```

Both the constructor and destructor do nothing. They aren't needed since the initialization of the class members is performed in `CGame`. You have `Move`, which moves the player position, and `RandomLeap`, which takes the size of the arena and moves the player randomly to a place inside the arena, but why are the `-1` and `+1` there? You use these offsets to get a number inside the arena, but preventing it from overflowing numerically to one of the borders. So, if an arena is of size 40, you can use `rand () % (ArenaSize.X - 1)` to get a number between 0 and 39, and then add one to make sure the numbers are between 1 and 40. This way, the position is always inside the arena.

The next set of methods are just to set or get a function, they shouldn't need any explanation.

```
 /* Gets player position */
void CPlayer::GetPosition (COORD * Position)
{
 memcpy (Position, &m_Position, sizeof (COORD));
}

 /* Sets player lives */
void CPlayer::SetLives (short Lives)
{
 m_Lives = Lives;
}

 /* Gets player lives */
short CPlayer::GetLives (void)
{
 return m_Lives;
}

 /* Sets player score */
void CPlayer::SetScore (int Score)
{
 m_Score = Score;
}

 /* Gets player score */
int CPlayer::GetScore (void)
{
 return m_Score;
}

 /* Sets player available leaps */
void CPlayer::SetLeaps (int Leaps)
{
 m_Leaps = Leaps;
}

```

```
 /* Gets player available leaps */
int CPlayer::GetLeaps (void)
{
 return m_Leaps;
}
```

And the implementation of CPlayer is complete. Nothing fancy or hard, right? Let's move to CGame then.

```
 /* '02 Game.cpp' */

 /* CGame complement header file */
#include "02 Game.h"

 /* Init members to initial status */
CGame::CGame ()
{
 m_Console    = NULL;
 m_GameStatus = GameSplashScreen;
 m_LastAction = 0;
 m_Monsters   = NULL;
}

 /* Init members to initial status with console information */
CGame::CGame (ConLib * Console)
{
 m_Console    = Console;
 m_GameStatus = GameSplashScreen;
 m_LastAction = 0;
 m_Monsters   = NULL;
}

 /* Default destructor */
CGame::~CGame ()
{
 m_Console    = NULL;
 m_GameStatus = GameSplashScreen;
 m_LastAction = 0;
 m_Monsters   = NULL;
}

 /* Sets a pointer to the console */
```

```
void CGame::SetConsole (ConLib * Console)
{
 m_Console     = Console;
}

 /* Returns the game status */
int CGame::GetStatus (void)
{
 return m_GameStatus;
}
```

The constructors and destructors are simple, they initialize the class members. The next two methods are merely for setting the console and returning the game status.

The following set of functions displays the splash screen and main menu. There is nothing new here for the most part:

```
 /* Shows the splash screen with playing instructions */
void CGame::ShowSplash (void)
{
 m_Console->Clear ();
 m_Console->OutputString ("\tWelcome to Monster 1.0 \n\n");
 m_Console->OutputString ("Playing Monster is very easy. \n\n");

 m_Console->OutputString ("The objective of the game is to destroy \n");
 m_Console->OutputString ("all the monsters. Two or more monsters \n");
 m_Console->OutputString ("are destroyed when they move to the \n");
 m_Console->OutputString ("same cell in the field. You also lose a \n");
 m_Console->OutputString ("life if you move to a cell where a \n");
 m_Console->OutputString ("monster is. You move the player with the \n");
 m_Console->OutputString ("numerical keypad in the eight possible \n");
 m_Console->OutputString ("directions. You can also press Insert \n");
 m_Console->OutputString ("which will make you leap to a random \n");
 m_Console->OutputString ("place in the field.\n\n");

 m_Console->SetTextColor (ConRed);
 m_Console->OutputString ("NOTE: Make sure NumLock is turned off.\n\n");
 m_Console->SetTextColor (ConRed | ConGreen | ConBlue);

 m_Console->OutputString ("There are three difficulties available:\n\n");
 m_Console->OutputString (" Easy :     Monsters = 10    Arena = 25*15\n");
 m_Console->OutputString ("            Lives    = 4     Leaps = 3\n");
```

```
 m_Console->OutputString (" Medium :  Monsters = 20   Arena = 35*18\n");
 m_Console->OutputString ("           Lives    = 3    Leaps = 2\n");
 m_Console->OutputString (" Hard :    Monsters = 30   Arena = 50*23\n");
 m_Console->OutputString ("           Lives    = 2    Leaps = 1\n");
}

 /* Shows the main menu */
void CGame::ShowMenu (void)
{
 COORD Position;

 m_Console->SetBackgroundColor (0);
 m_Console->SetTextColor (ConRed);
 m_Console->Clear ();

 m_Console->SetBackgroundColor (ConRed | ConGreen | ConBlue);

 m_Console->OutputString ("                                        \n");
 m_Console->OutputString ("         Monster - version 1.0          \n");
 m_Console->OutputString ("                                        ");

 m_Console->SetBackgroundColor (0);
 m_Console->SetTextColor (ConRed | ConGreen | ConBlue);

 Position.X = 1;
 Position.Y = 4;
 m_Console->SetPosition (Position);
 m_Console->OutputString ("What do you want to do? ");

 Position.X = 3;
 Position.Y = 6;
 m_Console->SetPosition (Position);
 m_Console->OutputString ("1 - Start new game - Easy");
 Position.Y = 7;
 m_Console->SetPosition (Position);
 m_Console->OutputString ("2 - Start new game - Medium");
 Position.Y = 8;
 m_Console->SetPosition (Position);
 m_Console->OutputString ("3 - Start new game - Hard");

 Position.Y = 10;
```

```
  m_Console->SetPosition (Position);
  m_Console->OutputString ("Q - Exit game");
}
```

You use ConLib class to make your splash screen and menus, nothing hard. Next you have `ShowGame`. This method shows the current status of the game. There are a few lines that I need to explain, so take a look at the code:

```
 /* Shows the actual game */
void CGame::ShowGame (void)
{
 COORD Position;
 int Monster;

  /* Draw player position */
 m_Console->SetBackgroundColor (0);
 m_Console->SetTextColor (ConGreen);

 m_Player.GetPosition (&Position);

 m_Console->SetPosition (Position);
 m_Console->OutputString ("P");

  /* Draw field */
 int FieldX, FieldY;
 m_Console->SetBackgroundColor (ConRed | ConGreen | ConBlue);
 m_Console->SetTextColor (ConRed | ConGreen | ConBlue);

 for (FieldY = 0; FieldY <= m_Arena.Y; FieldY++)
 {
  if ( (FieldY == 0) || (FieldY == m_Arena.Y) )
  {
   for (FieldX = 0; FieldX <= m_Arena.X; FieldX++)
   {
    Position.X = FieldX;
    Position.Y = FieldY;
    m_Console->SetPosition (Position);
    m_Console->OutputString ("#");
   }
  }
  else
  {
```

```
      Position.X = 0;
      Position.Y = FieldY;
      m_Console->SetPosition (Position);
      m_Console->OutputString ("#");
      Position.X = m_Arena.X;
      Position.Y = FieldY;
      m_Console->SetPosition (Position);
      m_Console->OutputString ("#");
    }
  }

  /* Draw monsters */
  m_Console->SetBackgroundColor (0);
  m_Console->SetTextColor (ConRed);
  for (Monster = 0; Monster < m_MonstersNumber; Monster++)
  {
   if (m_Monsters [Monster].X != 0)
   {
    m_Console->SetPosition (m_Monsters [Monster]);
    m_Console->OutputString ("M");
   }
  }

  /* Show lives and score */
  char Buffer [100];

  sprintf (Buffer, "  Lives: %d \t\t Score: %d \t Leaps: %d",
           m_Player.GetLives () - 1, m_Player.GetScore (),
           m_Player.GetLeaps ());
  Position.X = 5;
  Position.Y = 24;
  m_Console->SetPosition (Position);
  m_Console->SetTextColor (ConRed | ConGreen);
  m_Console->OutputString (Buffer);
}
```

The first thing you do is draw the player; next you draw the field by using two `for` loops. The first loop draws each horizontal line. If `FieldY` is zero or equal to `m_Arena.Y` (the borders), you draw a horizontal line using another `for` loop. If it isn't, then it means that the current horizontal line only needs to be drawn at the beginning and the end of the current line. This piece of code draws the border of a rectangle of `m_Arena` dimensions.

The next three methods display a message box explaining that the player lost a life, lost the game, or won the game:

```
 /* Shows game won box */
void CGame::ShowWon (void)
{
 ShowGame ();

 COORD Position;

 Position.X = 20;
 Position.Y = 11;
 m_Console->SetPosition (Position);

 m_Console->SetBackgroundColor (ConGreen);
 m_Console->SetTextColor (ConRed);

 m_Console->OutputString ("########################################");
 Position.Y = 12;
 m_Console->SetPosition (Position);
 m_Console->OutputString ("#            Congratulations!             #");
 Position.Y = 13;
 m_Console->SetPosition (Position);
 m_Console->OutputString ("#  You have killed all the monsters.   #");
 Position.Y = 14;
 m_Console->SetPosition (Position);
 m_Console->OutputString ("########################################");
}

 /* Shows life lost box */
void CGame::ShowLostLife (void)
{
 ShowGame ();

 COORD Position;

 Position.X = 20;
 Position.Y = 11;
 m_Console->SetPosition (Position);

 m_Console->SetBackgroundColor (ConGreen);
```

```
 m_Console->SetTextColor (ConRed);

 m_Console->OutputString ("########################################");
 Position.Y = 12;
 m_Console->SetPosition (Position);
 m_Console->OutputString ("#          You have lost a life         #");
 Position.Y = 13;
 m_Console->SetPosition (Position);
 m_Console->OutputString ("########################################");
}

 /* Shows game lost box */
void CGame::ShowLost (void)
{
 ShowGame ();

 COORD Position;

 Position.X = 20;
 Position.Y = 11;
 m_Console->SetPosition (Position);

 m_Console->SetBackgroundColor (ConGreen);
 m_Console->SetTextColor (ConRed);

 m_Console->OutputString ("########################################");
 Position.Y = 12;
 m_Console->SetPosition (Position);
 m_Console->OutputString ("#              Tough luck!             #");
 Position.Y = 13;
 m_Console->SetPosition (Position);
 m_Console->OutputString ("#     You have lost all your lives.    #");
 Position.Y = 14;
 m_Console->SetPosition (Position);
 m_Console->OutputString ("########################################");
}
```

To finalize the ShowXXXX methods, you have the goodbye message:

```
 /* Shows exit text */
void CGame::ShowExit (void)
{
```

```
 m_Console->SetBackgroundColor (0);
 m_Console->SetTextColor (ConRed | ConGreen | ConBlue);
 m_Console->Clear ();
 m_Console->OutputString ("\n   Monster 1.0 \n\n\n");
 m_Console->OutputString (" by: Bruno Sousa (bsousa@fireworks");
 m_Console->OutputString ("-interactive.com)\n\n\n\n");
 m_Console->OutputString ("Thanks for playing!\n\n\n");
 m_Console->OutputString ("And remember, stay away from drugs.\n\n");
}
```

The next method, Show, is responsible for calling the appropriate ShowXXXX method depending on the game status:

```
 /* Shows the correct screen depending on the status */
void CGame::Show (void)
{
 m_Console->SetBackgroundColor (0);
 m_Console->SetTextColor (ConRed | ConGreen | ConBlue);
 m_Console->Clear ();

 switch (m_GameStatus)
 {
 case GameMainMenu:
  ShowMenu ();
 break;

 case GameRunning:
  ShowGame ();
  break;

 case GameWon:
  ShowWon ();
  break;

 case GameLostLife:
  ShowLostLife ();
  break;

 case GameLost:
  ShowLost ();
  break;

```

```
 case GameExit:
  ShowExit ();
  break;

 case GameSplashScreen:
  ShowSplash ();
  break;

 default:
  break;
 }
}
```

Next you have StartNewGame:

```
 /* Starts a new game */
void CGame::StartNewGame (int Difficulty)
{
 int Monster;

 COORD Position;

 m_GameStatus = GameRunning;

  /* Set game difficulty */
 switch (Difficulty)
 {
 case GameEasy:
  m_MonstersNumber = 10;
  m_Player.SetLives (4);
  m_Player.SetLeaps (3);
  m_Arena.X = 25;
  m_Arena.Y = 15;
  break;
 case GameMedium:
  m_MonstersNumber = 25;
  m_Player.SetLives (3);
  m_Player.SetLeaps (2);
  m_Arena.X = 35;
  m_Arena.Y = 18;
  break;
 case GameDifficult:
```

```
    m_MonstersNumber = 35;
    m_Player.SetLives (2);
    m_Player.SetLeaps (1);
    m_Arena.X = 50;
    m_Arena.Y = 23;
    break;
  }

  /* Create player */
  m_Player.RandomLeap (m_Arena);
  m_Player.GetPosition (&Position);
  m_Player.SetScore (0);

  /* Create monsters */
  m_Monsters = new COORD [m_MonstersNumber];
  srand (time (NULL));

  /* Calculate random positions for monsters */
  for (Monster = 0; Monster < m_MonstersNumber; Monster++)
  {
    /* Make sure position is different than player's position */
    do
    {
      m_Monsters [Monster].X = (rand () % (m_Arena.X - 1)) + 1;
      m_Monsters [Monster].Y = (rand () % (m_Arena.Y - 1)) + 1;
    }
    while ( (m_Monsters [Monster].X == Position.X) &&
            (m_Monsters [Monster].Y == Position.Y) );
  }
}
```

The first thing you do is check the difficulty parameter and based on it, set the game variables. Next you make the player take a random leap inside the arena. Then you create a dynamic array of COORDs that are the monsters, and initialize all the monsters to a random position in the arena. This method also compares each monster position to the player's position to make sure they are not the same.

The next method returns the current game status:

```
/* Get player action */
int CGame::GetAction (void)
{
```

```
  /* Get input from user */
 m_LastAction = m_Console->GetKey ();

 return m_LastAction;
}
```

Now a more robust method, `MoveMonsters`. This is where the artificial intelligence comes into play. This method moves the monsters to the player:

```
 /* Move monsters according to player position */
void CGame::MoveMonsters (void)
{
 COORD Distance, Position;
 int Monster;

 m_Player.GetPosition (&Position);

 for (Monster = 0; Monster < m_MonstersNumber; Monster++)
 {
  /* Check if monster is dead */
  if (m_Monsters [Monster].X != 0)
  {
   Distance.X = Position.X - m_Monsters [Monster].X;
   Distance.Y = Position.Y - m_Monsters [Monster].Y;

    /* Make sure movement is unitary */
   if (Distance.X > 0)
   {
    Distance.X = 1;
   }
   if (Distance.X < 0)
   {
    Distance.X = -1;
   }
   if (Distance.Y > 0)
   {
    Distance.Y = 1;
   }
   if (Distance.Y < 0)
   {
    Distance.Y = -1;
   }
```

```

      /* Move monsters */
     m_Monsters [Monster].X += Distance.X;
     m_Monsters [Monster].Y += Distance.Y;
    }
  }
}
```

MoveMonsters iterates through every monster that is alive (coordinates must be different from zero) and subtracts its position from the position of the player. This is the way you get a coordinate that indicates the distance from the monster to the player (this is actually a vector subtraction, which you will see later in the book). The next step is to make sure the monster never moves more than a unit cell; that is, it only moves one cell. This is done by checking whether any of the elements of Distance is greater than one (absolute value), and if it is, truncating it to one.

ProcessSplash waits for a key press, and when one key is pressed, the game moves to the main menu:

```
 /* Process splash screen */
void CGame::ProcessSplash (void)
{
  /* If user pressed key, just move to main menu */
 if (m_LastAction)
 {
  m_GameStatus = GameMainMenu;
 }
}
```

Next you have ProcessMenu. which waits for a key press and reacts accordingly based on the key pressed:

```
 /* Gets menu option and either quit or start new game */
void CGame::ProcessMenu (void)
{
 switch (m_LastAction)
 {
  /* Quit game */
 case VK_ESCAPE:
 case 'Q':
 case 'q':
  m_GameStatus = GameExit;
  break;
```

```

    /* Start new game */
   case '1':
    StartNewGame (GameEasy);
    m_GameStatus = GameRunning;
    break;
   case '2':
    StartNewGame (GameMedium);
    m_GameStatus = GameRunning;
    break;
   case '3':
    StartNewGame (GameDifficult);
    m_GameStatus = GameRunning;
    break;

   default:
    break;
   }
 }
```

The next two methods are probably the most important of the entire game and will be explained fully. `ProcessGame` handles the game specifics like moving the player, calling other functions, or checking for movement against the arena bounds:

```
  /* Moves player and monsters */
void CGame::ProcessGame (void)
{
 COORD Movement;
 int Monster, MonstersAlive;

 Movement.X = 0;
 Movement.Y = 0;

  /* Move player */
 switch (m_LastAction)
 {
 case VK_UP:
  Movement.Y = -1;
  break;
 case VK_DOWN:
  Movement.Y = 1;
```

```
     break;
    case VK_LEFT:
     Movement.X = -1;
     break;
    case VK_RIGHT:
     Movement.X = 1;
     break;

    case VK_HOME:
     Movement.X = -1;
     Movement.Y = -1;
     break;
    case VK_PRIOR:
     Movement.X = 1;
     Movement.Y = -1;
     break;
    case VK_END:
     Movement.X = -1;
     Movement.Y = 1;
     break;
    case VK_NEXT:
     Movement.X = 1;
     Movement.Y = 1;
     break;
    case VK_INSERT:
     if (m_Player.GetLeaps () > 0)
     {
      m_Player.RandomLeap (m_Arena);
      m_Player.SetLeaps (m_Player.GetLeaps () - 1);
     }
     break;
    case VK_ESCAPE:
     EndGame ();
     m_GameStatus = GameMainMenu;
     break;
    }

     /* There was movement */
    if ( (Movement.X != 0) || (Movement.Y != 0) )
    {
     COORD PlayerPosition;
```

```
  m_Player.GetPosition (&PlayerPosition);

   /* If inside bounds move */
  if ( (Movement.X + PlayerPosition.X > 0) &&
       (Movement.Y + PlayerPosition.Y > 0) &&
       (Movement.X + PlayerPosition.X < m_Arena.X) &&
       (Movement.Y + PlayerPosition.Y < m_Arena.Y) )
  {
   m_Player.Move (Movement);
  }

   /* Do monster AI and check for any collision */
  MoveMonsters ();
  CheckCollisions ();

   /* Check to see if any monster is alive */
  MonstersAlive = 0;
  for (Monster = 0; Monster < m_MonstersNumber; Monster ++)
  {
    /* Check if monster is dead */
   if (m_Monsters [Monster].X != 0)
   {
    MonstersAlive = 1;
    break;
   }
  }
  if (MonstersAlive == 0)
  {
   m_GameStatus = GameWon;
  }
 }
}
```

The first thing you do in `ProcessGame` is check which key the user pressed. If it was any of the keypad keys, it moves the player accordingly, and if the user presses Insert, it makes the user take a random leap. The user can also press Esc and the player is taken to the main menu.

Next, you call `MoveMonsters` and `CheckCollisions`, which of course, moves the monsters and checks collisions. Finally, you just go through every monster and see whether there is any monster alive; if there is, the game continues; if there isn't, the game's status changes to `GameWon`.

```
 /* Check for collisions between monsters and player */
void CGame::CheckCollisions ()
{
 COORD Position;
 int MonsterA, MonsterB;

 m_Player.GetPosition (&Position);

 for (MonsterA = 0; MonsterA < m_MonstersNumber; MonsterA ++)
 {
   /* Check if monster is dead */
  if (m_Monsters [MonsterA].X != 0)
  {
    /* Check for collision with player */
   if ( (m_Monsters [MonsterA].X == Position.X) &&
        (m_Monsters [MonsterA].Y == Position.Y) )
   {
    m_Monsters [MonsterA].X = 0;
    m_Monsters [MonsterA].Y = 0;

     /* Set to see if player has any remaining lives */
    if (m_Player.GetLives () - 1 <= 0)
    {
     m_GameStatus = GameLost;
    }
    else
    {
     m_GameStatus = GameLostLife;
    }
    return;
   }
    /* Check for collisions with other monsters */
   for (MonsterB = MonsterA+1; MonsterB < m_MonstersNumber; MonsterB++)
   {
     /* Check if monster is dead */
    if (m_Monsters [MonsterB].X != 0)
    {
      /* Check for collision with monsters */
     if ( (m_Monsters [MonsterA].X == m_Monsters [MonsterB].X) &&
          (m_Monsters [MonsterA].Y == m_Monsters [MonsterB].Y) )
```

```
        {
         m_Monsters [MonsterA].X = m_Monsters [MonsterB].X = 0;
         m_Monsters [MonsterA].Y = m_Monsters [MonsterB].Y = 0;
         m_Player.SetScore (m_Player.GetScore () + 15);
        }
       }
      }
    }
  }
}
```

CheckCollisions goes through every monster and checks for collisions between the player and the active monster and with other monsters. If there is a collision between the player and the monster, it changes the game to GameLostLife and if there is a collision between two monsters, they are both killed.

The next method waits for a key press and changes the game status (state) to GameMainMenu and calls EndGame.

```
 /* End game and return to main menu */
void CGame::ProcessWon (void)
{
  /* If user pressed key, just move to main menu */
 if (m_LastAction)
 {
  m_GameStatus = GameMainMenu;
 }

 EndGame ();
}
```

The next method frees all the memory used by the monsters:

```
 /* Finish the game */
void CGame::EndGame (void)
{
 if (m_Monsters != NULL)
 {
  delete [] m_Monsters;
 }
 m_Monsters = NULL;
}
```

`ProcessLostLife` subtracts a life from the player, and if the player runs out of lives, it ends the game, If, however, the player still has lives, the method moves the player to a random position, but makes sure the player isn't in a cell with a monster.

```
 /* Removes a life from the player */
void CGame::ProcessLostLife (void)
{
 int IsValid = 0;
 int Monster;
 COORD Position;

  /* Remove a life from player, if ran out of lives, end game */
 m_Player.SetLives (m_Player.GetLives () - 1);
 if (m_Player.GetLives () - 1 <= -1)
 {
  m_GameStatus = GameLost;
 }
 else
 {
  m_GameStatus = GameRunning;
  IsValid = 0;
   /* Calculate random position for Player */
  do
  {
   m_Player.RandomLeap (m_Arena);
   m_Player.GetPosition (&Position);

    /* Make sure position is different than other monsters position */
   for (Monster = 0; Monster < m_MonstersNumber; Monster++)
   {
     /* Check if monster is dead */
    if (m_Monsters [Monster].X != 0)
    {
     if ( (m_Monsters [Monster].X != Position.X) &&
          (m_Monsters [Monster].Y != Position.Y) )
     {
      IsValid = 1;
     }
     else
     {
```

```
        IsValid = 0;
       }
      }
    }
   }
  while ( IsValid == 0 );
 }
}
```

ProcessLost waits for a key press and moves the player to the main menu:

```
 /* End game and return to main menu */
void CGame::ProcessLost (void)
{
  /* If user pressed key, just move to main menu */
 if (m_LastAction)
 {
  m_GameStatus = GameMainMenu;
 }

 EndGame ();
 Show ();
}
```

Process has the job of calling the appropriate ProcessXXXX method depending on the game status:

```
 /* General function that does all tasks for this turn */
void CGame::Process (void)
{
  /* Since the splash screen must be shown when we begin, we must
     force it to be shown because there is no action pending */
 if (m_GameStatus == GameSplashScreen)
 {
  Show ();
 }

  /* If user presses a key, act accordingly */
 if (GetAction ())
 {
  switch (m_GameStatus)
  {
  case GameMainMenu:
```

```
     ProcessMenu ();
     break;

    case GameRunning:
     ProcessGame ();
     break;

    case GameWon:
     ProcessWon ();
     break;

    case GameLostLife:
     ProcessLostLife ();
     break;

    case GameLost:
     ProcessLost ();
     break;

    case GameSplashScreen:
     ProcessSplash ();
     break;

    default:
     break;
    }
    Show ();
  }
}
```

And that ends your CGame class. It wasn't that hard, was it? Hope not! To end this game you need to code your main function, which is pretty simple:

```
  /* '02 Main.cpp' */

  /* ConLib header file */
#include "ConLib.h"
  /* CGame header file */
#include "02 Game.h"

  /* Start */
void main ()
```

```
{
ConLib          Console;
CGame           Game (&Console);

  /* Set window title */
Console.SetTitle ("Monster");

  /* Start and run game */
while (Game.GetStatus () != GameExit)
{
  Game.Process ();
}
}
```

You do the basic stuff like declaring a game and a console and then while the game status is different from `GameExit`, you call the process, which will do all the necessary game stuff.

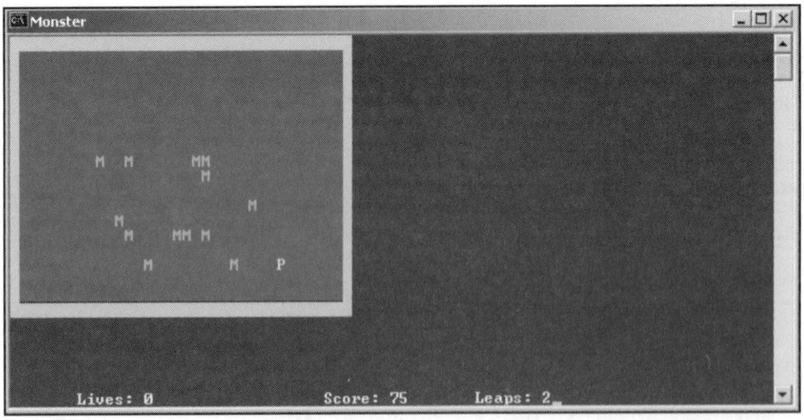

Figure 7.3

Your Monster game.

Summary

And you have your Monster game completed. If you understood the concepts of the game well, you should have no problems doing some small games on your own. And in case you are thinking this is such a trivial game that couldn't even be considered a game by your friends, a version of Monster simpler than the one that you developed was sold as shareware a few years ago with much success.

CHAPTER 8

STREAMS

In this chapter, you will review some of the basic concepts of streams and get a better understanding how they relate to the hardware devices in your computer.

You will also learn how to load and save data from and to files, and in the end you will see how you can upgrade the Monster game that you developed in the preceding chapter to allow game saving and loading.

What Is a Stream?

A *stream*, as the name indicates, is a sequence of bytes of data. Streams allow an abstract way to communicate with any hardware supported both for input and output. The same functions or classes work both for file output or text output in the screen. They are called *device independent.*

Streams that receive data from the hardware (either by reading from a file or getting keyboard input) are called *input streams.* Streams that pass data to the hardware (saving to a file or outputting text to the screen) are called *output streams.*

> **NOTE**
>
> During the rest of the chapter, the word *stream* will be used for both normal streams and files. Sometimes, referring to files as streams is more convenient for logical reasons.

Streams will be replaced with DirectX later on for both input and output.

Binary and Text Streams

Streams come in two different packages. They are either binary or text. A text stream consists of bytes that represent a character, number, or symbol. Text streams can be as big as 255 characters and are usually terminated with a new end of line character. See Figure 8.1.

Binary streams, on the other hand, consist of bytes of data that represent the data as it is, like in memory. They are manipulated as they would be manipulated in memory.

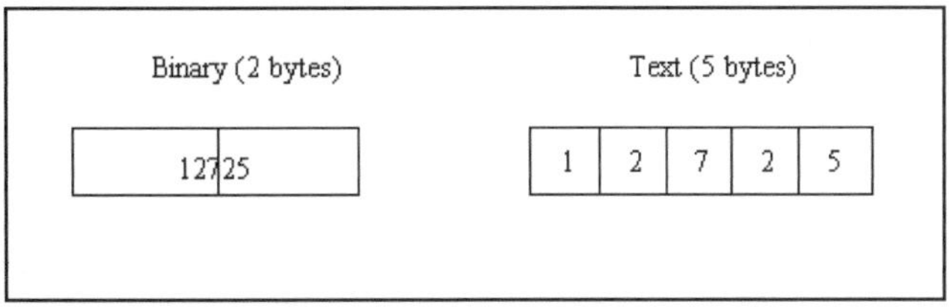

Figure 8.1

Binary versus text.

Whereas text streams are used for disk files, screen output, keyboard input, and other uses, binary streams are usually used for disk files only. Binary streams are typically smaller than text streams due to the way the data is stored. (For example, the number 23,454,344 can be stored in four bytes using binary mode because a 32-bit number can hold roughly plus or minus 2 billion, whereas if you used text mode you would have to save each number as an ASCII text character using eight bytes of memory.)

> **NOTE**
>
> Due to the nature of the stream classes in C++, some methods are defined in parent classes that are available to the child classes, and in these cases, the prototype shown will use the child class as namespace so it is easier to understand. If a method isn't explicitly defined in the child class and is in the parent class, it will be treated as if it were defined in the child class. This causes no problem to your programming.

Input and Output

Input and output in C++ is performed using streams. To make the job easier for the programmers, C++ contains some abstract and generic stream classes that can be used for just about any input and output device. They are `istream` and `ostream`.

istream

The `istream` class is a generic input class that serves as the base for other derived classes for input. `istream` is also derived from another class which is, in turn, derived from another base class, which honestly, doesn't interest you a bit.

By focusing on the workings of the `istream`, you can learn how to use streams to get input from almost any device. To make things easier, you will use `std::cin` because it is automatically supplied to you.

get

One of the advantages (or disadvantages, depending on what ground you stand on when you deal with default parameters) is that the same class function can be used for various purposes, or, at least, in different ways. get is no exception because it has eight different forms, but I will only be focusing on two of them.

NOTE

MSDN contains all the possible arguments that each function can use and has the different uses for them. Give it a try.

The first method gets only one character from the input buffer:

```
int istream::get (void);
```

This function will extract a character from the beginning of the stream and return it.

The second way to use get is like this:

```
istream & istream::get (char * pch, int nCount, char delim = '\n');
```

This extracts all the characters from the stream until the character delim is found or nCount is reached. This method is usually used to get strings.

Don't worry about the weird return type because you won't use it. (It is simply a reference to the stream.)

```
 /* '01 Main.cpp' */

 /* Input Output stream header file */
#include <iostream>

 /* Start */
main (void)
{
 int TypedLetter;

 std::cout << "Press q to quit...";

  /* Wait until user pressed 'q' or 'Q' */
 TypedLetter = std::cin.get ();
 while ((TypedLetter != 'q') || (TypedLetter != 'Q'))
 {
```

```
17:     TypedLetter = std::cin.get ();
18:   }
19:
20:   return 0;
21: }
```

In this program, you first ask for a letter from the user (line 11) and try to acquire it using the `get` method of `std::cin` (line 14).

You then enter a loop that will keep acquiring the letter from the user until he or she presses the letter Q (lines 15 through 18).

When the user finally presses the letter Q, the program exits.

getline

A very similar function to `get` is `getline`. `getline` works the same way as `get` except that it removes the delimiter character from the stream whereas `get` doesn't.

`getline` can be used in three different ways, with the following being the most used:

```
istream & istream::getline (char * pch, int nCount, char delim = '\n');
```

The parameters and return type are exactly the same as `get`, so there's no need to go over them.

```
 /* '02 Main.cpp' */

 /* Input Output stream header file */
#include <iostream>

 /* Start */
main (void)
{
 char TypedString [256];

 std::cout << "Type any text: ";

  /* Get a string from the user */
 std::cin.getline (TypedString, 256);

 std::cout << "You typed: " << TypedString;

 return 0;
}
```

Another simple program asks the user for any text (line 11) and then tries to acquire an entire string from the user using the `getLine` method (line 14) and outputs it to the screen (line 16).

ignore

As the name states, `ignore` is used to ignore bytes from the stream. This method is useful, for example, when you are waiting for input from the user, and you simply want to retrieve a certain number of letters and ignore the rest.

Its prototype is as follows:

```
istream & istream::ignore (int nCount = 1, int delim = EOF);
```

`nCount` is the number of bytes to ignore and `delim` is the delimiter when you should stop ignoring bytes. If `ignore` reaches the `delim` character, it doesn't ignore any more characters.

> **NOTE**
>
> **`EOF` is a special character that stands for End Of File, or in your case end of stream.**

```
 1:  /* '02 Main.cpp' */
 2:
 3:  /* Input Output stream header file */
 4: #include <iostream>
 5:
 6:  /* Start */
 7: main (void)
 8: {
 9:  int TypedLetter;
10:
11:   /* Ignore first two letters */
12:  std::cin.ignore (2);
13:  TypedLetter = std::cin.get ();
14:
15:  std::cout << TypedLetter;
16:
17:  return 0;
18: }
```

This program starts by ignoring the first two bytes in `std::cin` using the method `ignore` (line 12). It then gets the next (third) byte in `std::cin` with `get` (line 13) and outputs it to the screen (line 15).

Extraction Operator (>>)

The extraction operator is a handy operator, which you have been using up to now, that enables you to retrieve any type of value from a stream without using any special function to do it. You can call it a "smart" operator if you want.

The inner logic of this operator is that it's defined various times in each stream using a different data type to extract. That is, you can use the >> operators with the base C++ types, such as chars, ints, and so on, relieving the programmer from the task of calling each appropriate function for each type.

ostream

`ostream` is the opposite of `istream`. It is used only for output and is where most output streams are derived.

Using `std::cout` as an example, you can focus more on what each function does than the actual stream.

put

In output terms, `put` is sort of the equivalent of `get` in input terms, with the disadvantage that `put` works only with characters, not strings. `put` can be used to output a character to a stream and is defined as follows:

```
ostream & ostream::put (char ch);
```

`ch` is the character you want to output. As with the `istream` return types, you don't need to worry about this either.

```
 /* '04 Main.cpp' */

 /* Input Output stream header file */
#include <iostream>

 /* Start */
main (void)
{
 unsigned char ASCIIValue = 0;

 while (ASCIIValue < 256)
 {
```

```
13:     /* Output ASCII character */
14:    std::cout.put (ASCIIValue);
15:    ASCIIValue ++;
16:   }
17:
18:   return 0;
19: }
```

This program starts by entering a `while` loop while `ASCIIValue` is less than 256 (line 11). This will ensure that every value in the ASCII table (0 through 255) will be output.

Inside the `while` loop, the program outputs the character representation of `ASCIIValue` (line 14) and increases it (line 15).

flush

No, I'm not talking about bathrooms. `flush` is an output method that enables you to synchronize the stream buffer with the actual stream. What does this mean? Well, when you send data to the stream, depending on what method you use, it may or may not be written at the same time. Generally, there is a buffer associated with the stream that holds a collection of bytes, which in due time sends to the stream.

To better exemplify this concept, think of a bucket of water. You don't put in a little bit of water, wash a bit of the floor, then put more water in the bucket, and wash another bit of the floor, do you? No, you fill the bucket with the necessary amount of water and then wash the floor. If the floor is too big, you simply empty and refill the bucket. This is exactly what happens with streams; you first need to fill the buffer, and only when it is full do you send it to the actual stream.

The `flush` method forces the buffer to be sent to the stream even if it isn't full. It is defined as follows:

```
ostream & ostream::flush (void);
```

This is fairly simple to understand.

Insertion Operator (<<)

The insertion operator is basically the same as the extraction operator except that it is used for output instead of input.

As with the extraction operator, the insertion operator can be used with a variety of types without any trouble.

File Streams

A special type of stream is a file stream. File streams are nothing more than a logical connection to a file in the hard drive or other media available.

One of the main differences of file streams compared to other streams is that file streams must be opened and closed. File streams can also be opened in either text or binary mode.

File streams are of type `ifstream` for input only, `ofstream` for output only, and `fstream` for input or output, depending on the way the file is opened. Figure 8.2 illustrates this concept.

Opening and Closing Streams

Before being able to read from or write to a file, you first need to open it. This will create a link from the stream and the file. After you are done with it, you need to close the file.

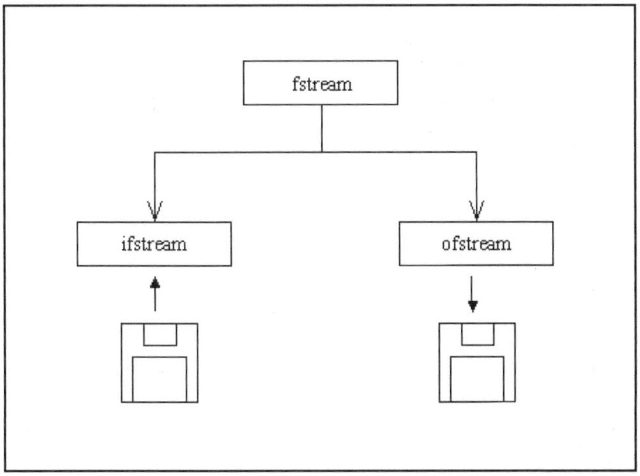

Figure 8.2

Input and output file streams.

open

You can open a file two ways in C++: You can explicitly call the method open of fstream, or you can use a constructor with the same parameters as the open method. You will be focusing on the open method that is defined as:

```
void fstream::open (const char * szName, int nMode, int nProt = filebuf::openprot);
```

szName is the actual file name you want to open, and nMode is the way you want to open the file. Table 8.1 shows all the possible flags when opening files.

The flags in Table 8.1 can be combined with the operator or (||) to open the file exactly like you want; for example, the following combination of flags:

```
ios::out | ios::ate | ios::binary
```

Would mean that the file should be opened for output only and the file marker be moved to the end of the file and opened in binary mode?

The last parameter is nProt, which is the file protection you want to open the file with. This is the protection, or access level, you want to allow other programs to the file you are opening. The access modes flags are described in Table 8.2.

> **NOTE**
> If you don't supply the ios::binary flag when opening a file, the file will be opened in text mode.

Table 8.1 File Open Modes

Flag	Description
ios::in	Opens the file for input
ios::out	Opens the file for output
ios::app	Moves the file marker at the end of the file and prevents any data from the original file from being overwritten
ios::ate	Moves the file marker at the end of the file
ios::nocreate	If the file doesn't exist, open fails
ios::noreplace	If the file already exists, open fails
ios::binary	Opens the file in binary mode

TABLE 8.2 File Open Protection Modes

Flag	Description
`filebuf::sh_compat`	Compatibility share mode
`filebuf::sh_none`	No sharing
`filebuf::sh_read`	Read sharing
`filebuf::sh_write`	Write sharing

`filebuf::sh_read` and `filebuf::sh_write` can be used together with the operator or (||)

The default mode for opening is `filebuf::openprot`, which is the equivalent to the operating system default mode.

You will be using the default mode in your programs, so you don't need to supply any value to the function.

close

`open`'s archenemy is `close`. When you open a file, you have to close it, because if you don't, you will not release the file for other programs, and if it is opened for output, it may end up corrupted. `close` is defined as follows:

```
void fstream::close (void);
```

This closes the file.

```
 /* '05 Main.cpp' */

 /* File stream header file */
#include <fstream.h>
 /* Input Output stream header file */
#include <iostream>

 /* Start */
```

```
 9: main (void)
10: {
11:   /* File streams */
12:  fstream   FileOne;
13:  fstream   FileTwo;
14:  fstream   FileThree;
15:
16:   /* Open the file for output in text mode */
17:  FileOne.open ("Data.txt", ios::out);
18:   /* Open the file for output in binary mode */
19:  FileTwo.open ("Data.bin", ios::out | ios::binary);
20:   /* Open the file for output in appending and text mode */
21:  FileThree.open ("Data2.txt", ios::out | ios::app);
22:
23:
24:   /* Close files */
25:  FileOne.close ();
26:  FileTwo.close ();
27:  FileThree.close ();
28:
29:  return 0;
30: }
```

Like the previous example, this example is pretty simple. It starts by declaring three file streams (lines 12 through 14) and then opens them each in their own mode, using the method `open`.

In line 17, `FileOne` is opened for output in text mode. Next, in line 19, `FileTwo` is opened for output in binary more, and finally in line 21, `FileThree` is opened for output in appending mode.

In the end, you just close the files using the `close` method (lines 25 through 27).

is_open

The last method I should go over about opening and closing files is the `is_open` method. This method enables you to check whether a certain stream is opened, so you can work with it without errors. It is defined as follows:

```
int fstream::is_open (void) const;
```

This method returns zero if the disk file isn't opened, or any nonzero if it is opened.

The following program tries to open and close various files using different flags and shows whether it was successful:

```
 /* '06 Main.cpp' */

 /* File stream header file */
#include <fstream.h>
 /* Input Output stream header file */
#include <iostream>

 /* Start */
main (void)
{
  /* File stream */
 fstream   File;

 std::cout << "Trying to open Data.txt for output..." << std::endl;
  /* Open the file normally */
 File.open ("Data.txt", ios::out);
 if (File.is_open ())
 {
  std::cout << "File opened successfully..." << std::endl;
 }
 else
 {
  std::cout << "File not opened..." << std::endl;
 }
 File.close ();

  /* Open the file without replacing */
 std::cout << "Trying to open Data.txt with ";
 std::cout << "ios::noreplace..." << std::endl;

 File.open ("Data.txt", ios::out | ios::noreplace);
 if (File.is_open ())
 {
  std::cout << "File opened successfully..." << std::endl;
 }
 else
 {
```

```
38:    std::cout << "File not opened..." << std::endl;
39:   }
40:   File.close ();
41:
42:    /* Open the file without creating */
43:   std::cout << "Trying to open Data2.txt with ";
44:   std::cout << "ios::nocreate..." << std::endl;
45:
46:   File.open ("Data2.txt", ios::out | ios::nocreate);
47:   if (File.is_open ())
48:   {
49:    std::cout << "File opened successfully..." << std::endl;
50:   }
51:   else
52:   {
53:    std::cout << "File not opened..." << std::endl;
54:   }
55:   File.close ();
56:
57:   return 0;
58: }
```

This program tries to open three files in three different ways and depending on whether they were successful or not, shows the corresponding message.

It starts by declaring a file stream (line 12) and then tries to open it for output only (line 16) as Data.txt. Next, you use the `is_open` method (line 17) to determine whether the file was opened successfully, and if so, tell the user that the file was opened (line 19), and if not, tell the user that the file wasn't opened (line 23).

You then close the file (line 25) and try to reopen the file, this time for output without replacing an existing file as Data.txt (line 31). Then depending on whether it is opened or not (line 32), show the appropriate message (lines 33 through 39), and close the file (line 40).

Finally, you try to open the file for output without creating a file as Data2.txt (line 46). Then, again, depending on whether it is opened or not (line 47), show the appropriate message (lines 48 through 54), and close the file (line 55).

Only the first try to open the file should be successful, because the second try attempts to open the file Data.txt without replacing it, and because it already exists, it should fail. The third attempt tries to open Data2.txt that doesn't exist without creating it, and so, should fail also.

Text

Because you already went through the process of generic text input and output, I will not go over much more than a few examples. In the end of this section, you will create a small program that counts the number of lines in a file and outputs files that resemble the code listings in this book.

To be able to read something from a file, you first need to have a file with data. You could pick one random file from your Windows directory and try to read from it, but it would be more than likely that you wouldn't get any useful data. Because of this, you will first create a program that outputs a sequence of data to a file and then another program that reads and displays that data.

Your first program should ask the user for his or her first name, last name, age, and whether he or she is married, and then store all the data in a file:

```
 /* '07 Main.cpp' */

 /* File stream header file */
#include <fstream.h>
 /* Input Output stream header file */
#include <iostream>

 /* Start */
main (void)
{
  /* File stream */
 fstream   File;
  /* Program data */
 char FirstName [256];
 char LastName [256];
 int  Age;
 char IsMarriedReturn;
 bool IsMarried;

  /* Open the file for output */
 File.open ("Data.txt", ios::out);

  /* If file was opened successfully continue */
 if (File.is_open ())
 {
  std::cout << "What is your first name: ";
```

```
27:     std::cin >> FirstName;
28:     std::cout << "What is your last name: ";
29:     std::cin >> LastName;
30:     std::cout << "What is your age: ";
31:     std::cin >> Age;
32:
33:     std::cout << "Are you married (y for yes, anything else for no): ";
34:     std::cin >> IsMarriedReturn;
35:
36:     if ((IsMarriedReturn == 'y' || IsMarriedReturn == 'Y'))
37:     {
38:      IsMarried = true;
39:     }
40:     else
41:     {
42:      IsMarried = false;
43:     }
44:
45:      /* Write data to file */
46:     File << FirstName << " " << LastName << " " << Age << " " << IsMarried;
47:    }
48:
49:    /* Close file */
50:   File.close ();
51:
52:   return 0;
53: }
```

This program starts by declaring a file stream and a few variables (lines 12 through 18) and opening it for output in text mode (line 21). After that, it checks to see whether the file was opened successfully (line 24) and if so, gets the information from the user (lines 25 through 43).

Just in case you haven't noticed, you used a `char` to see whether the user was married (line 34). You did this because `std::cin` doesn't have any input method that retrieves a `bool`. So, you use a `char` and see whether it was the letter Y the user pressed (line 36), and if so, set the value of `IsMarried` accordingly (lines 37 through 43).

After all data is gathered, the program uses the insertion operator (line 46) to save the data to the file and finally closes the file (line 50).

Now that you have your data, you need a program that reads the data from the file and outputs it to the screen:

```
 /* '08 Main.cpp' */

 /* File stream header file */
#include <fstream.h>
 /* Input Output stream header file */
#include <iostream>

 /* Start */
main (void)
{
  /* File stream */
 fstream   File;
  /* Program data */
 char FirstName [256];
 char LastName [256];
 int  Age;
 int  IsMarried;

  /* Open the file for input */
 File.open ("Data.txt", ios::in);

  /* If file was opened successfully continue */
 if (File.is_open ())
 {
   /* Read data from file */
  File >> FirstName >> LastName >> Age >> IsMarried;

  std::cout << "Your name is " << FirstName << " " << LastName;
  std::cout << " and you are " << Age << " years old." << std::endl;

  if (IsMarried == 1)
  {
   std::cout << "Good luck on your marriage!" << std::endl;
  }
  else
  {
   std::cout << "Good luck finding someone!" << std::endl;
```

```
38:     }
39:   }
40:
41:     /* Close file */
42:   File.close ();
43:
44:   return 0;
45: }
```

Here you do the opposite of the preceding program and read the information from the file and output it to the screen.

You start by declaring some needed variables (lines 12 through 17) and opening the file for input in text mode (line 20). If the file was opened successfully (line 23), you retrieve the information from the file using the extraction operator (line 26). After that you output the information to the screen (lines 28 through 39) and close the file (line 42).

Because you are probably bored to death right now, it's time to bring in a little program that has some actual use. It is the line counter, which is very similar to the one I used to do the code listings:

```
  /* '09 Main.cpp' */

  /* File stream header file */
#include <fstream.h>
  /* Input Output stream header file */
#include <iostream>

  /* Start */
main (void)
{
    /* File streams */
  fstream   InputFile;
  fstream   OutputFile;

    /* Program data */
  char  InputFileName [256];
  char  OutputFileName [256];
  char  TempInLine [256];
  char  TempOutLine [256];

  long  CurrentLine = 0;
```

```

  /* Get file names */
 std::cout << "Input file name: ";
 std::cin >> InputFileName;
 std::cout << "Output file name: ";
 std::cin >> OutputFileName;

  /* Open files */
 InputFile.open (InputFileName, ios::in);

 if (InputFile.is_open ())
 {
  OutputFile.open (OutputFileName, ios::out);

  if (OutputFile.is_open ())
  {
   while (1)
   {
     /* Increase line count */
    if (EOF == InputFile.peek ())
    {
     break;
    }

     /* Get the line and increase line count */
    CurrentLine ++;
    InputFile.getline (TempInLine, 256);

     /* Format the line with the line number and write to the file */
    sprintf (TempOutLine, "%ld: %s\n", CurrentLine, TempInLine);
    OutputFile << TempOutLine;
   }

   OutputFile.close ();
  }
  InputFile.close ();
 }

 return 0;
}
```

The first thing you do is declare two file streams (lines 12 and 13), four strings—two for the file names and another two for file lines (lines 16 through 19)—and a counter for the total of lines (line 21).

Next, you get the input and output file names from the user (lines 24 through 27) and try to open first the input file (line 30), and then the output file (line 34). If both files were opened successfully (lines 32 and 36), continue with the program.

Next, you enter a `while` loop (line 38) which will only end when you reach the end of the file (lines 41 through 44). In the loop, you increase the total number of lines (line 47) and get the appropriate line from the input file (line 48). You then format the string adding the line number before it (line 51) and output it to the file (line 52).

In the end, you close both files (lines 55 and 57).

Binary

I already talked about the differences between text and binary streams, but you might still be wondering why is it more common to use binary files than text files, which are easier to understand. One of the already mentioned reasons is that binary files are typically smaller than text files. It's easier for humans to read the number 3482234 like this, but for the computer, it is ten times easier to read it like this: 1101010010001001111010. Yes, it is the binary representation of 3482234. Most of the files in your hard drives are binary: executables, dlls, and many others.

Working with binary files isn't as hard as you may think; actually, it's fairly easy as you will see next.

write

As you probably have imagined, `write` is used to write to a file. Writing in binary mode is a little different than writing in text mode. Whereas in text mode you had various methods to output the data, in binary mode, you have `write` that writes a certain number of bytes to the files. `write` is defined as follows:

```
fstream & fstream::write (const char * pch, int nCount);
```

`pch` is a pointer to the buffer which holds the data you want to write, and `nCount` is the number of bytes you want to write.

Before I continue with an example, let's go over one simple thing. `pch` must be a pointer to a `char`, although you may want to write to the file an `int` or even a `class`.

This is done because a `char` is the smallest variable type existing in C++ (one byte). The obvious solution would be to cast the type to a `char` using C++ casts, but you won't do this. You will use C casting to convert any pointer to a `char` pointer. This can be done like so:

```
(char *) &A_Class;
```

The preceding line of code would cast the address of `A_Class` to a pointer of type `char`. You could then use this in the `write` functions like this:

```
File.write ((char *) &A_Class, sizeof (A_Class_Type));
```

This writes `A_Class` (which implicitly is of type `A_Class_Type`) to the file.

C casting follows this form:

```
(Type_To_Cast) OriginalVariable;
```

This casts `OriginalVariable`, whichever the type is, to a variable of `Type_To_Cast`.

NOTE

When you want to write various elements, like an entire array, you would make `pch` point to the first element of the array, and `nCount` being the number of elements to write times the size of the element like this:

```
SomeClass    Data [10];
/* … */
File.write ((char *) Data, 10 * sizeof (SomeClass);
```

So, for your example you will use the same code from the text output example and make it save the data as binary:

```
 /* '10 Main.cpp' */

 /* File stream header file */
#include <fstream.h>
 /* Input Output stream header file */
#include <iostream>

 /* Start */
```

```
main (void)
{
  /* File stream */
 fstream   File;
  /* Program data */
 char FirstName [256];
 char LastName [256];
 int  Age;
 char IsMarriedReturn;
 bool IsMarried;

  /* Open the file for output */
 File.open ("Data.bin", ios::out | ios::binary);

  /* If file was opened successfully continue */
 if (File.is_open ())
 {
  std::cout << "What is your first name: ";
  std::cin >> FirstName;
  std::cout << "What is your last name: ";
  std::cin >> LastName;
  std::cout << "What is your age: ";
  std::cin >> Age;

  std::cout << "Are you married (y for yes, anything else for no): ";
  std::cin >> IsMarriedReturn;

  if ((IsMarriedReturn == 'y' || IsMarriedReturn == 'Y'))
  {
   IsMarried = true;
  }
  else
  {
   IsMarried = false;
  }

   /* Write data to file */
  File.write ((char *) &FirstName, sizeof (char) * 256);
  File.write ((char *) &LastName, sizeof (char) * 256);
  File.write ((char *) &Age, sizeof (int)  );
  File.write ((char *) &IsMarried, sizeof (bool) );
```

```
50:  }
51:
52:   /* Close file */
53:  File.close ();
54:
55:  return 0;
56: }
```

This program does exactly the same thing as the text version of it except that instead of opening the file in text mode, it opens it in binary mode (line 21) and uses the method `write` to save the information to a file (lines 46 through 49).

read

`read` is your first binary reading function. It is used to read a sequence of bytes in binary mode from a stream. `read` is also defined various times using different types. The most used definition is as follows:

```
fstream & fstream::read (char * pch, int nCount);
```

`pch` is a pointer to the buffer where the bytes will be stored, and `nCount` is the number of bytes to read.

```
 /* '11 Main.cpp' */

 /* File stream header file */
#include <fstream.h>
 /* Input Output stream header file */
#include <iostream>

 /* Start */
main (void)
{
  /* File stream */
 fstream   File;
  /* Program data */
 char FirstName [256];
 char LastName [256];
 int  Age;
 int  IsMarried;

  /* Open the file for input */
 File.open ("Data.bin", ios::in | ios::binary);
```

```
21:
22:    /* If file was opened successfully continue */
23:  if (File.is_open ())
24:  {
25:     /* Read data from file */
26:   File.read ((char *) &FirstName, sizeof (char) * 256);
27:   File.read ((char *) &LastName, sizeof (char) * 256);
28:   File.read ((char *) &Age, sizeof (int)  );
29:   File.read ((char *) &IsMarried, sizeof (bool) );
30:
31:   std::cout << "Your name is " << FirstName << " " << LastName;
32:   std::cout << " and you are " << Age << " years old." << std::endl;
33:
34:   if (IsMarried == 1)
35:   {
36:    std::cout << "Good luck on your marriage!" << std::endl;
37:   }
38:   else
39:   {
40:    std::cout << "Good luck finding someone!" << std::endl;
41:   }
42:  }
43:
44:    /* Close file */
45:  File.close ();
46:
47:  return 0;
48: }
```

Again, this program does the same thing as the text version but in binary mode by opening the file in binary mode (line 20) and using the `read` method to get the information from the file (lines 26 through 29).

seekg

A few more functions that you should be aware of are used to move and retrieve the position marker in the stream. For example, if you want to ignore the first ten bytes of data, you use a function that moves you ten bytes forward to the beginning of the stream.

The function to move the `get` marker (for input) is `seekg`, which is defined as follows:

```
fstream & fstream::seekg (streamoff off, ios::seek_dir dir);
```

off is the offset to move the get marker, and dir is the direction. The possible types for dir are shown in Table 8.3.

seekp

The equivalent for output of seekg is seekp, which moves the put marker and is defined as follows:

```
fstream & fstream::seekp (streamoff off, ios::seek_dir dir);
```

The parameters are equivalent to seekg.

tellg

tellg is the opposite of seekg. It is used to get the position of the get marker and is defined as follows:

```
streampos fstream::tellg (void);
```

This returns the position of the get marker.

tellp

As with seekg, you also have a method to return the position of the put marker: tellp, which is defined as follows:

```
streampos fstream::tellp (void);
```

This returns the position of the put marker.

> **NOTE**
> Both streamoff and streampos correspond to long types.

TABLE 8.3 Seek Direction Types

Flag	Description
ios::beg	Seek from the beginning of the stream
ios::cur	Seek from the current position of the stream
ios::end	Seek from the end of the stream

When using ios::end, off must be a negative value.

Modifying Monster to Save and Load Games

Modifying your previous game Monster to save and load games isn't difficult. You add a couple of functions to `CGame` and one to `CPlayer`, and modify three existing functions to allow the user to press either the S key to save or the L key to load the game. You will first see how to modify the functions from the following code. Figure 8.3 also illustrates this concept.

```
void CGame::ShowMenu (void)
/* … */
  m_Console->SetPosition (Position);
  m_Console->OutputString ("3 - Start new game - Hard");
  Position.Y = 10;
  m_Console->SetPosition (Position);
  m_Console->OutputString ("L - Load game");

  Position.Y = 12;
  m_Console->SetPosition (Position);
  m_Console->OutputString ("Q - Exit game");
}
/* … */
```

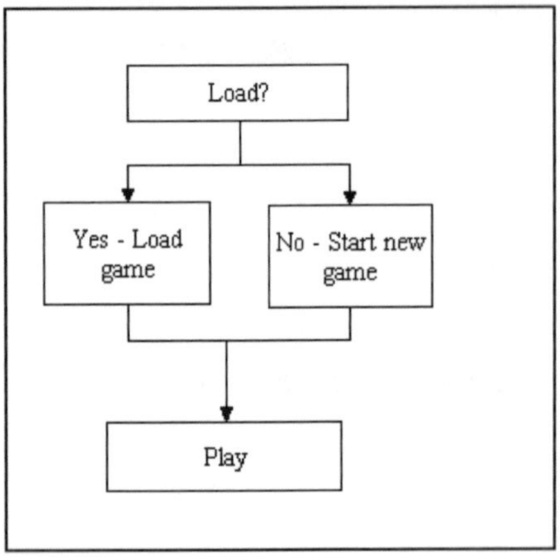

Figure 8.3

Changing Monster to allow saving.

You have modified this method to let the user know that he or she can load a previously saved game by showing "`L - Load game`" as an option in the menu (lines 110 through 112).

```
120: void CGame::ShowGame (void)
/* … */
177:  char Buffer [100];
178:
179:  sprintf (Buffer, "Lives: %d   Score: %d   Leaps: %d   S - Save Game",
180:            m_Player.GetLives () - 1, m_Player.GetScore (),
181:            m_Player.GetLeaps ());
182:  Position.X = 0;
/* … */
```

Again, you have just modified this function to let the user know he can save the game by pressing S (line 179).

```
440: void CGame::ProcessMenu (void)
/* … */
460:  case '3':
461:   StartNewGame (GameDifficult);
462:   m_GameStatus = GameRunning;
463:   break;
464:  case 'L':
465:  case 'l':
466:   StartNewGame (GameEasy);
467:   Load ();
468:   m_GameStatus = GameRunning;
469:   break;
470:
471:  default:
472:   break;
473:  }
/* … */
```

You have changed this function so that if the user presses the L key in the main menu, the game is loaded (lines 464 through 468).

Now you should add a few methods to the classes, which aren't many. To avoid confusion, let's see the entire classes redefined:

```
 /* '12 Player.h' */
/* ... */
 /* Player class */
class CPlayer
{
private:

  /* Player attributes */
 COORD   m_Position;
 short   m_Lives;
 int     m_Score;
 int     m_Leaps;

public:

  /* Constructor / destructor */
 CPlayer ();
 ~CPlayer ();

  /* Move player */
 void Move (COORD Direction);
 void RandomLeap (COORD ArenaSize);

  /* Maintenance methods */
 void GetPosition (COORD * Position);

 void SetLives (short Lives);
 short GetLives (void);

 void SetScore (int Score);
 int GetScore (void);

 void SetLeaps (int Leaps);
 int GetLeaps (void);

 void SetPosition (COORD * Position); /* Print */
};
```

In the CPlayer class you added a SetPosition method to enable you to set the saved player position when loading a file.

```
/* '12 Game.cpp' */
/* … */
/* Game base class */
class CGame
{
private:

  /* Input/output information */
 ConLib *   m_Console;
 int        m_LastAction;

  /* Game information */
 int        m_GameStatus;
 COORD      m_Arena;
 CPlayer    m_Player;
 COORD *    m_Monsters;
 int        m_MonstersNumber;

public:

  /* Constructors / destructor */
 CGame ();
 CGame (ConLib * Console);
 ~CGame ();

  /* Shows the relative information depending on game status */
 void ShowSplash (void);
 void ShowMenu (void);
 void ShowGame (void);
 void ShowWon (void);
 void ShowLostLife (void);
 void ShowLost (void);
 void ShowExit (void);
 void Show (void);

  /* Process the turn depending on game status */
 void ProcessSplash (void);
 void ProcessMenu (void);
```

```
void ProcessGame (void);
void ProcessWon (void);
void ProcessLostLife (void);
void ProcessLost (void);
void ProcessExit (void);
void Process (void);

 /* Set console information */
void SetConsole (ConLib * Console);

 /* Game methods */
void StartNewGame (int Difficulty);
void EndGame (void);
void CheckCollisions ();
int GetAction (void);
int GetStatus (void);
void MoveMonsters (void);

 /* Load / Save methods */
void Load (void);
void Save (void);
};
```

In CGame, you added two methods, Load and Save, which are the basis for loading and saving the game.

```
/* '12 Player.cpp' */
/* ...*/
/* Sets player position */
void CPlayer::SetPosition (COORD * Position)
{
 m_Position.X = Position->X;
 m_Position.Y = Position->Y;
}
```

This is a relatively easy method, isn't it? You use a COORD type to set the new player position in the arena.

```
/* '12 Game.cpp' */
/* ... */
/* Loads a previously saved game */
void CGame::Load (void)
{
```

```
752:  fstream  File;
753:
754:  File.open ("Monster.sav", ios::in | ios::binary);
755:
756:  if (File.is_open ())
757:  {
758:   COORD PlayerPosition;
759:   short PlayerLives;
760:   int   PlayerScore;
761:   int   PlayerLeaps;
762:
763:    /* Load the game from the file */
764:   File.read ((char *) &m_Arena, sizeof (COORD));
765:   File.read ((char *) &PlayerPosition, sizeof (COORD));
766:   File.read ((char *) &PlayerLives, sizeof (short));
767:   File.read ((char *) &PlayerScore, sizeof (int));
768:   File.read ((char *) &PlayerLeaps, sizeof (int));
769:   File.read ((char *) &m_MonstersNumber, sizeof (int));
770:   if (m_Monsters != NULL)
771:   {
772:    delete [] m_Monsters;
773:   }
774:   m_Monsters = new COORD [m_MonstersNumber];
775:   File.read ((char *) m_Monsters, sizeof (COORD) * m_MonstersNumber);
776:
777:    /* Set information from player class */
778:   m_Player.SetPosition (&PlayerPosition);
779:   m_Player.SetLives (PlayerLives);
780:   m_Player.SetLeaps (PlayerLeaps);
781:   m_Player.SetScore (PlayerScore);
782:  }
783:
784:  File.close ();
785: }
```

Now, there is one very important method: `CGame::Load`. This method is responsible for loading a previously saved game. It opens a file for input in binary mode (line 754) and declares a few temporary variables (lines 758 through 761) for storing the player information. It then uses the `read` method to get both the game and player data from the file (lines 764 through 775) and sets the `m_Player` data accordingly (lines 778 through 781).

NOTE

A quick note before proceeding: you probably have noticed that you delete the current monsters (lines 770 through 773) and allocate a new array for the loaded game (line 775). This is done because the current game and the saved game may have a different number of monsters, and as such, need different array sizes.

```
787:  /* Saves the current game */
788: void CGame::Save (void)
789: {
790:  fstream  File;
791:
792:  File.open ("Monster.sav", ios::out | ios::binary);
793:
794:  if (File.is_open ())
795:  {
796:   COORD PlayerPosition;
797:   short PlayerLives;
798:   int   PlayerScore;
799:   int   PlayerLeaps;
800:
801:    /* Get information from player class */
802:   m_Player.GetPosition (&PlayerPosition);
803:   PlayerLives = m_Player.GetLives ();
804:   PlayerLeaps = m_Player.GetLeaps ();
805:   PlayerScore = m_Player.GetScore ();
806:
807:    /* Save the game to the file */
808:   File.write ((char *) &m_Arena, sizeof (COORD));
809:   File.write ((char *) &PlayerPosition, sizeof (COORD));
810:   File.write ((char *) &PlayerLives, sizeof (short));
811:   File.write ((char *) &PlayerScore, sizeof (int));
812:   File.write ((char *) &PlayerLeaps, sizeof (int));
813:   File.write ((char *) &m_MonstersNumber, sizeof (int));
```

```
814:     File.write ((char *) m_Monsters, sizeof (COORD) * m_MonstersNumber);
815:   }
816:
817:   File.close ();
818: }
```

You have now reached the last function: `CGame::Save`. Here you will do the opposite of `CGame::Load` and save the game.

You first open the file for output in binary mode (line 792) and by declaring a few temporary variables (lines 796 through 799). You then get the player information from `m_Player` (lines 802 through 805) and use the `write` method to save the game to the file (lines 808 through 814). Figure 8.4 illustrates this concept.

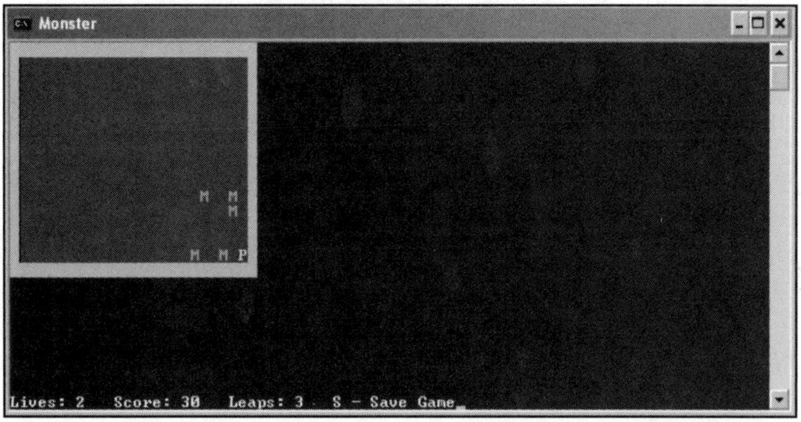

Figure 8.4

You finish the function by closing the file (line 818).

Summary

In this chapter, you have browsed a very important aspect of programming—working with files.

Knowing how to read and write information to files is critical because it allows you to use external files for data for your program, thus keeping the code separate from the data.

You also learned the advantages of developing games with classes by means of upgrading Monster to save and load games without much hassle.

Questions and Answers

Q: How can a stream be used to communicate with files and the monitor and keyboard?

A: Streams are just sequences of bytes that are associated with a device. Although the operating system takes care of the communication with the hardware, C++ offers an easy-to-use interface for streams and also specific methods and classes for each stream.

Q: Why do binary files use less space than text files?

A: Because numbers in text files are stored as characters, the number 132 is stored as the string "132", which uses three bytes. In binary, the number is stored like that but in binary form, so it will only use one byte. Although this number doesn't prove this, a `float` like 23923.3242343 will use 13 bytes in text mode but only four in binary.

Q: Why do you need to cast to `char` when using `Write or Read` methods of the `fstream` family of streams?

A: In C++, the `char` type is the smallest variable possible (using one byte). C++ uses the `char` type, so it will ensure that the correct number of bytes is written or read.

Exercises

1. What is a stream?
2. What is the difference between a normal stream and a file stream?
3. Modify the line counter program to make room for empty before the numbers (like the ones in the book) to allow a correct alignment of the code.
4. What is wrong with the following code?

   ```
   fstream File;
   File.open ("Data.bin", ios::in | ios::binary);
   File.open ("Data.bin", ios::out | ios::binary);
   File.close ();
   ```

5. On your own, try to make the Monster game ask for a file name before saving and loading.

CHAPTER 9

Basic Software Architecture

Now that you have a fairly good understanding of the C++ language, you need to learn how to make your code reusable, clean, and easy to use.

In this chapter, you will learn basic techniques to develop better code. You will also be exposed to two of the most common approaches to software design, the fundamentals of working with modules, a few function and variable naming techniques, and the design that will be used in the upcoming chapters.

The Importance of Software Design

When you build a house, either you build it right, or you build it wrong, in which case, it will eventually fall. The same is true when building a piece of software. If you try to build a program with no techniques or plan, the result is a broken piece of software, a few months of your life wasted, not to mention that you're broke (in case you took your kids' college money to fund your project). To prevent this (and you want to prevent this, don't you?), you will use some basic techniques that will probably be lifesavers in the long run.

Until a few years ago, software design and architecture was almost a forbidden topic among game developers. Programmers thought of themselves as a revolutionary and genius who didn't need to follow any rules. Of course, this industry (and game development is an industry) has grown considerably in the past few years, from the players to the makers. This growth introduced a few rules that many game companies now follow and love. Here are some of those rules, but there are a million more, and as you gain more experience, you will probably develop your own rules.

Through this chapter, you will see some standard and not so standard techniques that will be used throughout the rest of the book when you start developing your game library.

Design Approaches

When developing software, there are usually two approaches: top down and bottom up. They have both proven successful and choosing which to use will be based more on the type of project and personal taste than anything else.

Top Down

One of the approaches you will analyze is the top down approach. This works by defining a higher-level objective, and by slowly dividing each objective into smaller ones until the basic levels have been achieved. Usually start with `main` and gradually develop all the routines and classes needed. This system is particularly beneficiary for systems layout in a hierarchical fashion, as can be seen in Figure 9.1.

An advantage of this system is its easiness. Dividing each section into smaller sections makes it easier for people to understand and work with it.

One of the main disadvantages is usually the identification of the top routine, which only gets worse if you have several top routines or objectives of similar importance.

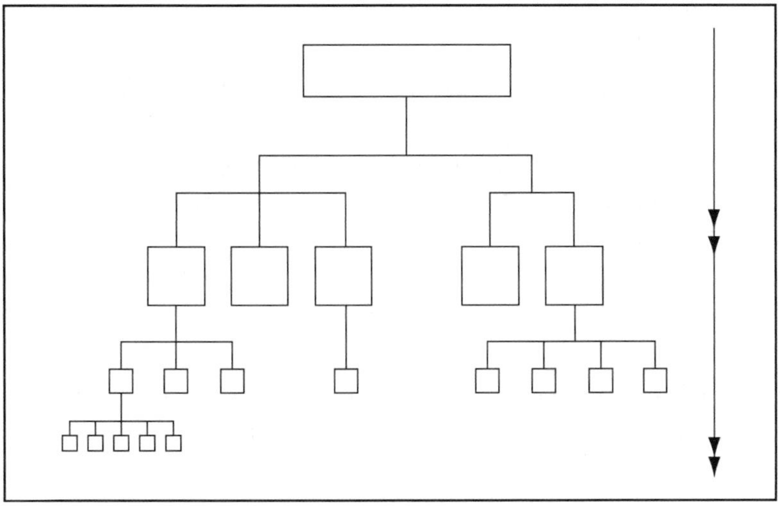

Figure 9.1

In a top down approach, the system is decomposed in sections, and those sections are developed to produce the final software.

Bottom Up

The other approach I will explain is the bottom up approach. In this system you start by defining all the low-level details of your software or module and gradually combining them into something bigger. This method is described in Figure 9.2.

The bottom up approach is good for developing modules where you can define their functionality in text or in a list and then convert them to a working module by defining each low-level component and joining them as if they were a puzzle.

The main disadvantage of this technique is that it is usually too abstract to be used exclusively. If you don't know what kind of house you want to build, you don't know which materials you will need, do you?

Top Down Versus Bottom Up

Probably the best approach to take is to merge the preceding two, using the best of each.

Use the top down approach to specify the main objectives and the design of the system. Use the bottom up approach to define each of the system components. Then join both to produce the final design. This method is beneficial because you rule out most of the disadvantages of each approach.

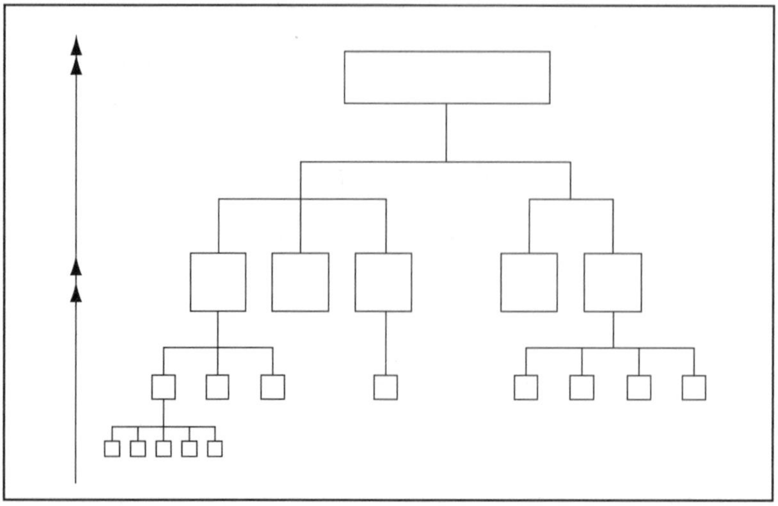

Figure 9.2

In a bottom up approach, the system is composed by producing low-level sections combined to build the final software.

Some Basic Techniques

There a few basic techniques, that if used properly, can really help you avoid errors and help improve development time. All these techniques are presented here through good and bad code examples.

Example 1: Assignment Instead of Equality Operator

```
/* Example 1 - Bad */
if (Pointer = NULL)
{
 /* Code here */
}
```

If you are paying attention, you have probably noticed that this code, even if it compiles correctly, isn't what you want. Instead of testing whether `Pointer` is `NULL`, you are actually assigning it to `NULL`. This is a common error to commit, because it is usually a typing error, but still a tough one to spot. The corrected version would be the following:

```
 /* Example 1 - Correct */
if (Pointer == NULL)
{
 /* Code here  */
}
```

This is the correct code you wanted. What can you do to help prevent this error? When using the equality operator to check variables against constants, a nice trick to use is to switch their order like so:

```
 /* Example 1 - Good */
if (NULL == Pointer)
{
 // Code here
}
```

Because `NULL` is a defined constant, even if you had used the assignment operator, the compiler would give you an error. Using this method, you know that you will never use an assignment operator where you wanted to use the equality operator.

Example 2: Statements Versus Blocks

```
 /* Example 2 - Correct */
if (NULL == Pointer)
 Alloc (Pointer);
```

Even if this example is correct, it is tricky. If you want to add another statement to be executed, you would probably put it below `Alloc (Pointer);` like so:

```
/* Example 2 - Bad */
if (NULL == Pointer)
 Alloc (Pointer);
 Init (Pointer);
```

As you can see, `Init (Pointer);` would always be called whatever the value of `Pointer`. A safe way to prevent this error is to always use code blocks, even if you only want to call one statement, when situations like this exist:

```
 /* Example 2 - Good */
if (NULL == Pointer)
{
 Alloc (Pointer);
 Init (Pointer);
}
```

This way, if you want to add more code, you would automatically add it to the code block, like it should be.

Example 3: Macros Versus Inline Functions

One of the more debated arguments among C++ programmers is when to use macros and when to use inline functions. Here I present a case where the use of a macro should be avoided.

```
 /* Example 3 - Bad */
#define MAX(a,b) (a > b) ? a : b
/* ... */
short A, B, Bigger;
A = B = 0;
Bigger = MAX (A, B++);
```

The first thing to notice is that B will be increased before using it, but it should only be incremented after using it. The second thing to note is that in the end, B will be two instead of one. This is because b is used twice in the macro, because you define b as B++, it is incremented twice.

You could fix this code by using the post-increment operator after the macro, but this would be limiting to use, and a less experienced programmer may forget and before the bug is found it will be too late. A better way to fix this would be to actually use an inline function like so:

```
 /* Example 3 - Good */
inline long MAX (short a, short b)
{
 return (a > b) ? a : b;
}
/* … */
short A, B, Bigger;
A = B = 0;
Bigger = MAX (A, B++);
```

This way, B is only incremented in the end, and only once.

Example 4: Private Versus Public, the First Case

A good example of when class members should be private is for class state holders. The following example allows uncontrolled use of the class variables:

```
 /* Example 4 - Bad */
class Data
{
public:
 short * m_pData;
 short m_sMaxData;
 /* … */
}
```

This code allows access to any of the members of Data. If m_pData was allocated using, for example, the following:

```
Data::Data ()
{
```

```
 m_pData = new short [10];
 m_sMaxData = 10;
}
```

The programmer could commit the error of doing:

```
Data Values;
Values.m_pData [11] = 23;
```

Which would go out of bounds on the `m_pData` array and thus generate an error. A better way would be the following:

```
/* Example 4 - Good */
class Data
{
private:
 short * m_pData;
 short m_sMaxData;
public:
 Data (void);
 GetMember (unsigned long dwElement);
 /* … */
}
Data::Data (void)
{
 m_pData = new short [10];
 m_sMaxData = 10;
}
short * GetMember (unsigned long dwElement)
{
 if (dwElement <= m_sMaxData)
 {
  return &m_pData [dwElement];
 }
 else
 {
  return NULL;
 }
}
```

This way, the programmer would always have to go through `Data::GetMember()` to get access to `m_pData`, thus preventing out of bounds errors.

Example 5: Private Versus Public, the Second Case

The second case of the private versus public debate is that some encapsulation classes should have their members' public.

```
/* Example 5 - Bad */
class Vector3
{
private:
 float X;
 float Y;
 float Z;

  /* … */
 void SetX (float X);
 void SetY (float Y);
 void SetZ (float Z);
 float GetX (void);
 float GetY (void);
 float GetZ (void);
};
```

As you can imagine, this vector class will be a bit difficult to use since every time you want to change one of its members (and you usually change them a lot), you need to add the overhead of using a function for it. A better solution would be to make the members public like so:

```
/* Example 5 - Good */
class Vector3
{
public:
 float X;
 float Y;
 float Z;

private:

  /* … */
};
```

This way, you could access any vector member by using the name of the vector and access member like so:

```
Vector2 Velocity;
Velocity.X = 10.0;
```

Modules and Multiple Files

Being able to construct reusable modules is one of the hardest, but most rewarding tasks in software development.

A module is usually a collection of routines, classes, variables, interfaces, structures, and so on that relate to some part of the program. Modules come in all shapes and sizes, it may be an image module or a sound module. Producing good and solid modules makes them able to be reused in other projects, which will save you development time, and they are easy to work with and independent.

Creating Modules with C++

One of the main advantages of C++ is its object-oriented programming methodology, which makes it easy to create modules. If you remember from earlier, C++ provides a way to use various files in one project. You will use this functionality and Visual C++ to create independent, reusable modules.

The first thing to do when creating a module is to define its functionality. When this is done, you should divide the module in sections, which will be converted to final usable classes. The conjunction of all these classes will be the module you want.

Why Make Something a Module?

The main objective, as far as you are concerned, is to make code that is reusable. There are a few other things such information hiding, modularity, or code cohesion that makes modules a good programming technique. I will focus mainly on the reusable proprieties of modules.

When you have a section of your code dedicated entirely to something, like graphics, which you know you can use in other projects, you should make a module out of it. In Parts II and III, you will be building modules for just about everything you do: graphics, sound, input, math. If you are unsure whether you should take the little extra effort and develop a module for anything you are developing, try the following checklist:

- Can the code you are developing be used in other projects?
- Is the code independent?
- Will other people use your code?
- Can you say that the code you are developing a functional description can be stated in a single phrase?
- Is the code cohesive?
- Does the code provide a set of complete operations to work with?
- Does the code provide information hiding?

If you have answered yes to at least two of the preceding questions, then you should think of creating a module out of your code.

Naming Conventions

Properly naming your variables and functions is a very important step if you plan to let others use your code, or even if you don't, it is still a good skill to gain. If you develop a routine with cryptic variable names, and then look at it six months later, you will have a hard job trying to figure out what each variable is used for.

Function Naming

Function names should be clear, to the point (neither too long nor too short), and explain what the functions do.

A quick way to know whether you are using correct function names is to check the following list:

- Is the name of the function clear?
- Does it explain what the function does?
- Is it easy to read?
- Is it the correct length (not too short or too long)?
- Does it use natural language to describe what it does?

If you have answered no to just one of the questions, then you should revise why you aren't doing the suggested.

Here is a list of examples of bad naming/good naming:

```
FormatSavePrintGameData / ProcessGameData
DoStuff / RenderObject
SvGmDt / SaveGameData
```

NOTE

The first example presents another aspect when building functions. Each function should do *one* significant thing. In the first example, you should have three functions that formatted, saved, and printed the game data, respectively, and then another function that would call the main three functions. This makes the code clear, consistent, and modular.

Variable Names

Variable naming should follow the same rules as function naming. Clear, descriptive, and average in size.

If you want to know whether you are naming your variables correctly, check the following list, to which your answers should be yes:

- Is the name of the variable clear?
- Does it explain what data it holds?
- Is it descriptive?
- Does it indicated what type of data it holds?
- Is it in natural language?

Here are some bad name/good name examples:

```
i / IDLoop
x / xPosition
temp / tempName
```

Identification

When dealing with big routines and modules, knowing which type the variables are is a must.

You don't want to get caught in line 3423 and have to return to the first line of the file to identify the variable as a short or a float, do you?

A while ago, a man named Charles Simonyi, developed a naming scheme for variables to be used in Microsoft. This system was named Hungarian notation due to the author being, of course, Hungarian.

Table 9.1 shows the Hungarian notation, which has been used by many companies and as base to many other in-house created ones.

TABLE 9.1 Hungarian Notation

Prefix	Description	Type	Example
b	Boolean	bool	bRunning
by	Byte	unsigned char	byLives
s	Short integer	short	sVelocity
w	Word	unsigned short	bMoney
l	Long integer	long	lFlags
dw	Double word	unsigned long	dwHighScore
f	Single precision floating point	float	fPI
d	Double precision floating point	double	dCosPi
p	Pointer	type *	pImage
sz	Null terminated string	char */ char []	szTitle
c	Constant	const	cWeightToPounds
h	Handle	HWND	hMainWindow
I	Interface	Interface	IDirectInput8
C	Class	Class	CWindow
m_	Member of	type	m_bGameRunning

Only the most used notations are shown.

Where Common Sense Beats Design

Sometimes, good common sense beats the rules. A good example of this is notation. If you have a variable that is declared as `float fData` and is used hundreds of times during the program, if for some reason you need to change it to a `double`, you would have to change all the references to `fData` to `dData`.

In the end, you should decide what works better for you, if it is the predefined rules, use them; if it isn't, use your own rules. The power to decide is yours.

The Design Used in This Book

During the rest of the book, you will use a hybrid mix of all the techniques shown before and a few of your own.

The first thing to define is the design approach. You will use a mix of both top down and bottom up to produce a feasibly way to design your code.

By using a bottom up approach to define the modules, and then develop the modules top down, you can use the best of both approaches.

All the code that follows this chapter for your Mirus library will be presented in a class definition, and then each of the relevant methods will be developed, as in the following example:

```
 /* BaseVector.h */
class BaseVector
{
 float   m_afComponents;
public:
 BaseVector (void);
/* … */
 void Normalize (void);
 /* … */
};
```

> **NOTE**
>
> **This class uses `math.h` header file.**

This would tell you to create a file named `BaseVector.h` (or if it already existed, to add to it) that includes the `math.h` header file and that class.

If there isn't any explanation on constructors or destructors or any accessing methods like in the `Get/Set` family, it would mean that they are only used to initialize all the members to zero or `NULL` or retrieve/set the values, and they should be implemented by you, which isn't hard.

After this, each method that needs explanation is presented as follows:

```
/* BaseVector.cpp */
void BaseVector::Normalize (void)
{
 /* Normalize vector here */
 /* … */
}
```

This would tell you to create a source file (or add to the existing one) with the function definition. Each source file should include the corresponding header file, in this case `BaseVector.h`.

Also, after every module or method is shown, it contains an explanation on what is happening.

Last, I will specify the code notation. You will use a hybrid of Hungarian notation and your own. See Table 9.2 for a complete description.

Summary

Even if this was a small chapter, a lot of important information was covered. Software design and architecture are very important topics to learn, and you will gradually learn to love them.

The concepts here are just a tip of the iceberg. You should have enough information to write clear and solid code, but you should always be on the look out for new techniques, rules, and notations that arise and check whether your code can benefit from them.

The remainder of the chapters use most of the techniques described here to produce the final modules or software, so make sure you understood what is happening before proceeding.

TABLE 9.2 Your Code Notation

Prefix	Description	Type	Example
b	Boolean	bool	bRunning
i	Any integer	int, short, long	iTime
ui	Any unsigned integer	unsigned short, unsigned long	uiEnergy
f	Any floating point	float/double	fPI
p	Pointer	type *	pImage
a	Array	type []	aComponents
sz	Null terminated string	char */ char [ ]	szTitle
c	character (letter)	char	cLetter
h	Handle	HWND	hMainWindow
t	Template type	template	tVectorComponent
I	Interface	Interface	IDirectInput8
C	Class	Class	CWindow
k	Class type	Class	m_kWindow
r	Reference	type &	rkVector
m_	Member of	type	m_bGameRunning

Questions and Answers

Q: Why shouldn't you write code without a plan?

A: Like building a house, if you don't have a plan and just start building what you think you want, you end up with a post modern house which is either good or safe. Developing software is done the same way, either you plan it or it will eventually fall.

Q: Should I always play by the rules?

A: Some rules were made with a specific job in mind, and even if they have suited some projects very well, they can be disastrous to your own. You should always see if your code would benefit from using any of the rules you try to use.

Exercises

1. Define the top down approach.
2. Define the bottom up approach.
3. Why should you create a module?
4. Try to name the following variables according to Hungarian notation:

```
int Time;
char * Name;
LPVOID Pointer;
MSG WindowMessage;
HINSTANCE App;
```

PART TWO

Windows Programming

10 Designing Your Game Library: Mirus

11 Beginning Windows Programming

12 Introduction to DirectX

13 DirectX Graphics

14 DirectInput

15 DirectSound

CHAPTER 10

Designing Your Game Library: Mirus

To have a game library that is easy to use but complete and powerful, you first need to design it correctly.

In this chapter you will design the library that you develop during the remainder of this part of the book. Figure 10.1 shows the Mirus library.

General Description

Mirus is a game library specifically designed to use with Windows and DirectX. It uses various wrapper classes for DirectX to make developing games easier, and it adds functionality to the base of DirectX.

Mirus was created for the following reasons:

- To relieve the programmer from having to deal with the inner workings of DirectX, making the game code lighter and more understandable.
- To be reused in various projects.
- To be both easy to understand and modify.

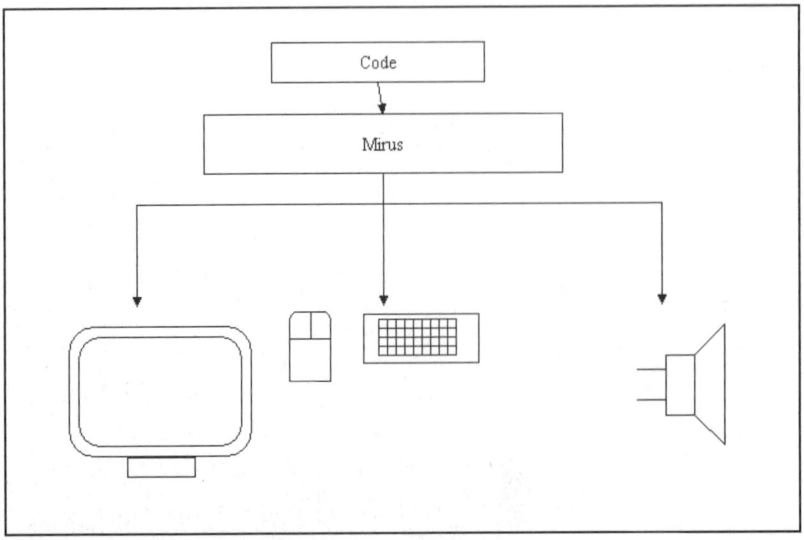

Figure 10.1

Mirus overview.

Mirus Components

Mirus is divided into five separate components that can be used interchangeably.

The following is a list of the components:

- **Helper Component.** Contains helper classes for the other components to use.
- **Window Component.** Deals with the creation and maintenance of the windowing part of the game.
- **Graphics Component.** Deals with DirectX Graphics and all graphics-related functionality.
- **Sound Component.** Deals with DirectX Audio and all sound-related functionality.
- **Input Component.** Deals with DirectInput and all input-related functionality.

Except for the Helper Component, all the other components can be used separately, but the Mirus works best when they are all used together.

Helper Component

The Helper Component has only a few variable type definitions and a class, `mrTimer`, that is used to perform time calculations in Mirus.

You will use the `mrError.h` file for all your error definitions, but this will be developed as the library is developed.

You use a few variable type definitions to enable you to know the exact size of each variable you are declaring and to make it easier to port to another system.

> **NOTE**
> One of the most problematic aspects of programming is that sometimes what looks very good in design, doesn't look right in code. You have specified a list of methods of the class, but at any time there may be some changes, such as adding or removing methods to make the code easier and simpler.

`mrTimer` can get the current date and time, and also measures intervals of time with the minimum amount of error possible (which is accomplished by the hardware timer as you will see later).

The important methods of this class are `Update` and `GetDelta`.

Window Component

The Window component is made of a single class, with the option to improve it later, which will encapsulate all the window management of Mirus.

mrWindow can create a window and manage it the simplest way possible. A desired scenario would be something like the following:

```
mrWindow Window;
Window.Create ();
Window.Run ();
```

All the necessary workings of the Win32 API for window management will be handled by this class, but leaving the option of returning a window handle to enable the user to do whatever he likes with the window.

Here are the most important methods of mrWindow:

```
Create
WndProc
Run
MessageHandler
Frame
```

Graphics Component

This is probably the component that more people are interested in. The Graphics component includes many features, such as setting the display mode, displaying textures, showing objects, and so on.

Several classes are in this component, such as these:

- mrScreen, which is responsible for setting the screen modes and maintenance functions, such as clearing the screen or presenting the information to the screen.
- mrRGBAImage, which is an arbitrary software 32-bit image that is used to provide a simple interface for mrSurface and mrTexture and image files.
- mrSurface, which is an arbitrary hardware-accelerated variant bit image that can be copied to the screen.
- mrTexture, which is a power of two sized hardware-accelerated variant bit image that can me mapped to polygons.

- `mrSprite`, which is a static image made of two polygons (quad) that is textured using an `mrTexture`.

Except for `mrRGBAImage`, all the other classes rely on DirectX Graphics for hardware acceleration.

You will see a few more graphics-related classes when you read about 2D images later in the book.

mrScreen

The `mrScreen` class is responsible for dealing with all screen-related operations, such as clearing the screen to a certain color or presenting the image in the back buffer.

It encapsulates all the needed DirectX Graphics functionality, so it resembles the DirectX Graphics object (which I will talk about later). When you need to create a surface or texture you use this class to return a valid pointer to a surface or texture that you can then use.

`mrScreen` is a singleton class. This will make it easier to get access of the Direct3D objects when you need to create surfaces (`mrSurface`) and textures (`mrTexture`). Destruction of those is left to the user.

Following is a list of the class methods:

```
Init
SetModeClear
StartFrame (void);
EndFrame (void);
DrawLine
DrawRectangle
DrawCircle
IsModeSupported
ShowCursor
```

mrRGBAImage

Being one of the core components of Mirus, `mrRGBAImage` is the most basic form of representing an image in Mirus.

Instead of creating methods in each class that needs a basic image, an independent class is created, which the other classes use to store the raw image. Keeping this design will lead to code efficiency and a smaller code base.

The class methods are the following:

```
operator =
LoadFromBitmap
LoadFromTarga
void SetColorKey
```

mrSurface

An mrSurface object is a hardware-accelerated image, which can reside either in video or system memory of any size (depending on system support), and can be copied to the screen without much problem, but unfortunately for 2D programmers, it can't have color keying or alpha.

A surface class was created to be used with large still images, like background images, to avoid the need for tiling that textures have.

mrSurface methods are as follows:

```
Create
Update
Render
```

mrTexture

The mrTexture is a class that can't be copied to the screen directly but must be mapped to polygons that can be rendered, as you will see in the next chapter.

The mrTexture image has two limitations from an mrSurface image, such as its size must be a power of two (2, 4, 8, 16, 32, 64, 128, and so on) and must be squared (even though this is mostly a hardware limitation and some hardware can render irregular-sized textures).

The texture class methods are the following:

```
Create
Update
```

mrTemplateSet

A template set is nothing more than a collection of images in a texture. You will be using template sets for animation later. For now, think of a template set as a grid, with each grid cell containing an image.

mrTemplateSet methods are the following:

```
Create
GetUV
SetActiveTexture
```

mrAnimation

The mrAnimation is a set of coordinates inside a template set that define an animation. The most important methods are the following:

```
Create
Update
Render
```

mrABO

mrABO is a set of animations of type mrAnimation with both size, position and direction. It is the representation of animated objects in the screen.

mrABO should be as easy to load and render as possible. A desired scenario would be as follows:

```
mrABO Abo;
Abo.LoadFromFile ("Abo.txt");
Abo.SetPosition (10,10);
Abo.SetSize (25,25);
Abo.Render ()
```

mrAbo methods are as follows:

```
Create
Update
Render
LoadFromFile
Rotate
Collide
ContainsPoint
```

Sound Component

The sound component isn't difficult to develop or use. Divided into two separate components, one for playing files and the other for playing music CDs, it features two simple classes of direct use.

mrSoundPlayer

The `mrSoundPlayer` is based on DirectX Audio components and encapsulates all the necessary methods to play wave or midi (or any other supported types) files. It should be easily initialized.

This class is a singleton, so it is easier to access anywhere in the game, such as in game objects or the main menu.

A desired usage would be the following:

```
 /* Initialization */
mrSoundPlayer Player;
Player->LoadSound ("Sound.wav");
 /* Somewhere in the game */
Player::GetSingleton->PlaySound ("Sound.wav")
```

Of course, other methods that are useful are as follows:

```
LoadFromFile
SetVolume
Play
Stop
```

mrCDPlayer

The `mrCDPlayer` is a simple CD player that enables you to play any track of a CD that is inserted using the Windows API.

This class will use the MCI API to play the CDs. MCI is a Windows API that enables you to use the default codecs (software that reads or writes files of certain types, usually multimedia files) to play the video or audio files.

This class is also a singleton that allows the use of the same instance of the class in the menus or the game itself without the need to keep unnecessary instances created.

The necessary methods are as follows:

```
Eject
Play
Stop
Update
```

Input Component

The input will be a little more complicated than the previous components and will be made of two distinctive types of classes, the devices classes (keyboard, mouse, and joystick) and an action mapper class that will make working with the input devices easier. The input component's only method is `init`.

mrKeyboard

The `mrKeyboard` class is responsible for handling and reporting all the keyboard events to you and also enables you to query the keyboard state at any time.

Its methods are as follows:

```
Init
Update
IsButtonDown
IsButtonUp
```

mrMouse

The `mrMouse`, similar to the `mrKeyboard` class handles and reports all the mouse events to you and enables you to query the mouse state at any time.

Its methods are as follows:

```
Init
Update
IsButtonDown
IsButtonUp
GetXAxis
GetYAxis
Clear
```

mrJoystick

mrJoystick is similar to the other device classes and is responsible for handling and reporting all the joystick events to you and enabling you to query its state at any time

Its methods are as follows:

```
Init
Update
IsButtonDown
IsButtonUp
GetXAxis
GetYAxis
```

Building the Help Component

The help component is made of the types file, the mrTimer, and the error file.

Declaring the Types

The first thing you will create is the data types file, mrDataTypes.h. Look at the following code:

```
 /* 'mrDatatypes.h' */

 /* Include this file only once */
#pragma once

 /* Basic type definitions */
typedef   char                 mrInt8;
typedef   unsigned char       mrUInt8;
typedef   short                mrInt16;
typedef   unsigned short      mrUInt16;
typedef   long                 mrInt32;
typedef   unsigned long       mrUInt32;
typedef   int                  mrInt;
typedef   unsigned int        mrUInt;
```

You first declare all the nonfloating-point types. These are just the basic C++ types but typedefed to tell you whether they are unsigned or not, and their sizes in bits.

Next you have the floating-point types:

```
typedef    float                 mrReal32;
typedef    double                mrReal64;
```

These are nothing more that the C++ floating-point types `typedef`ed to know the size of them.

```
 /* Composed definitions */
enum mrBool32
{
 mrFalse                    = 0,
 mrTrue                     = 1,

 mrBool32_Force32          = 0xFFFFFFFF
};
```

This one is a little bit trickier. `mrBool32` is an enumeration that defines `mrFalse` as zero (0) and `mrTrue` as one (1). You have done this to make sure that your Boolean type always returns either zero or one.

The `mrBool32_Force32` ensures that the `mrBool32` is a 32-bit type, as you declare it as `0xFFFFFFFF`, which is the higher value you can have for a 32-bit value.

This header file will be included in just about every Mirus file from now on.

mrTimer

The `mrTimer` class is defined as:

```
 /* 'mrDatatypes.h' */

 /* Mirus base types header */
#include "mrDatatypes.h"
 /* Windows header file */
#include <windows.h>
 /* Time header file */
#include <time.h>

 /* Include this file only once */
#pragma once

 /* Mirus timer class */
class mrTimer
```

```
{
protected:
  /* Hardware timer variables */
 LARGE_INTEGER   m_iFrequency;
 LARGE_INTEGER   m_iLastQuery;
 LARGE_INTEGER   m_iDelta;

  /* Time and date variables */
 tm *             m_pkTime;

public:
  /* Constructor / Destructor */
 mrTimer (void);
 ~mrTimer (void);

  /* Update the time variables */
 void Update (void);

  /* Return the timer information */
 mrReal32 GetDelta (void);
 mrUInt32 GetSeconds (void);
 mrUInt32 GetMinutes (void);
 mrUInt32 GetHours (void);
 mrUInt32 GetDay (void);
 mrUInt32 GetMonth (void);
 mrUInt32 GetYear (void);
};
```

Before proceeding to the explanation of this class, let me introduce to you the type LARGE_INTEGER.

LARGE_INTEGER is a Visual C++ type (not C++) that is defined as:

```
typedef union _LARGE_INTEGER
{
 struct
 {
  DWORD LowPart;
  LONG HighPart;
 }
 LONGLONG QuadPart;
}
LARGE_INTEGER;
```

This union can be accessed by using the structure with the low part (last 32 bits from left to right) or the high part (first 32 bits from left to right) of the number, or by using the LONGLONG type, which is a Visual C++ specific type of 64 bits. You will be using the QuadPart member because Visual C++ enables you to use a LONGLONG type like any other normal integer.

> **NOTE**
>
> In Visual C++, DWORD is the same as unsigned long, and LONG is the same as long.

Now for your class, you first declare three LARGE_INTEGERs (lines 18 through 20). The first one, m_iFrequency, is the frequency (number of counts per second) of the hardware timer; the next one, m_iLastQuery, is the value of the counter when the last call to Update has occurred; and m_iDelta is the difference between the last call to Update and the current call to Update.

Next you declare a pointer to a structure of type tm, m_pkTime. You will keep the system time and date here.

Then you have the default constructor and destructor (nothing new). You also have the Update methods, which will update both the hardware timer and the time/date structure.

Finally you have methods to return the difference of time in seconds of the hardware timer, GetDelta, and various functions to return the system time and date.

In the source file, the first thing you need to do is to include the mrTimer.h header file:

```
 /* 'mrWindows.cpp' */

 /* Complement header file */
#include "mrTimer.h"

 /* Default constructor */
mrTimer::mrTimer (void)
{
  /* Get the hardware clock frequency and current count */
 QueryPerformanceFrequency (&m_iFrequency);
 Update ();
}
```

Your constructor calls QueryPerformanceFrequency that returns the hardware timer count frequency and calls the class method Update.

QueryPerformanceFrequency is used to return the number of counts that the hardware timer does per second—that is, the number of "ticks" that the timer evaluates per second. QueryPerformanceFrequency is defined as follows:

```
BOOL QueryPerformanceFrequency (
 LARGE_INTEGER * lpFrequency
);
```

This takes as argument a pointer to a type LARGE_INTEGER union, which will hold the frequency of the timer.

If no hardware timer is installed, QueryPerformanceFrequency returns zero; otherwise, it returns any nonzero value.

```
 /* Default destructor */
mrTimer::~mrTimer (void)
{
 m_iFrequency.QuadPart = 0;
 m_iLastQuery.QuadPart = 0;
}
```

NOTE

BOOL in Visual C++ is the same as bool.

In the destructor you just set the hardware counters to zero.

Next you have the Update function, which is the core of your timer.

```
 /* Update timer */
void mrTimer::Update (void)
{
 LARGE_INTEGER  kTempTimer;
 time_t         iTempTimeDate;

  /* Get current timer information and calculate difference */
 QueryPerformanceCounter (&kTempTimer);
 m_iDelta.QuadPart = kTempTimer.QuadPart - m_iLastQuery.QuadPart;

  /* Save current timer information */
 m_iLastQuery.QuadPart = kTempTimer.QuadPart;

  /* Get current time and date */
 time (&iTempTimeDate);
 m_pkTime = localtime (&iTempTimeDate);
}
```

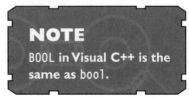

You start by declaring two temporary variables (lines 24 and 25). You then use `QueryPerformanceCounter` (line 28) to get the count number of the hardware timer. `QueryPerformanceCounter` is defined as:

```
BOOL QueryPerformanceCounter (
 LARGE_INTEGER * lpPerformanceCount
);
```

This takes as parameter a pointer to a `LARGE_INTEGER` that will store the current hardware timer count. This function also returns zero if the hardware timer isn't available.

After you have the current timer count, you calculate the difference between the last call to `Update` and this one (line 29), and you save the current timer count (line 32).

After that, you call the `time` function to get the current system time and date and convert it to a `tm` structure using `localtime`.

And there you have it; the `Update` function is all done. Now you just need to develop the `Get` methods

```
39:  /* Get delta time from last update */
40: mrReal32 mrTimer::GetDelta (void)
41: {
42:   /* Convert to float and calculate delta in seconds */
43:  return (mrReal32)(m_iDelta.QuadPart) /
44:         (mrReal32)(m_iFrequency.QuadPart);
45: }
```

The `GetDelta` method isn't hard, but there is a catch": You need to convert the `QuadParts` of the `m_iDelta` and `m_iFrequency` values to get the elapsed time in seconds. You do this using C-style casting.

You divide the `m_iDelta` by `m_iFrequency` to get the difference in seconds; as an example think of the following problem:

If there are 23,454 timer counts per second (frequency), how many seconds is 429 timer counts (delta)? The solution is obvious, 429/23454, which is 0.18291. This is what you do when you divide `m_iDelta` by `m_iFrequency`.

> **NOTE**
>
> Even if this timer is very accurate, there is still a little incoherency in the values because it takes time to call the functions (namely function overload time), which can change the values returned by the timer. You don't need to worry, however, because they are usually in the 0.00001 seconds or less range.

The next set of functions returns the system time and date members of `m_pkDate` so there is no need for explanation:

```
 /* Get system seconds */
mrUInt32 mrTimer::GetSeconds (void)
{
 return m_pkTime->tm_sec;
}

 /* Get system minutes */
mrUInt32 mrTimer::GetMinutes (void)
{
 return m_pkTime->tm_min;
}

 /* Get system hours */
mrUInt32 mrTimer::GetHours (void)
{
 return m_pkTime->tm_hour;
}

 /* Get system day */
mrUInt32 mrTimer::GetDay (void)
{
 return m_pkTime->tm_mday;
}

 /* Get system month */
mrUInt32 mrTimer::GetMonth (void)
{
 return m_pkTime->tm_mon;
}

 /* Get system year */
mrUInt32 mrTimer::GetYear (void)
{
 return m_pkTime->tm_year;
}
```

And that is it! You have now a hardware timer class ready to be used in your games.

NOTE

Almost every recent (and not so recent) computer has a built-in hardware timer. `mrTimer` was created with the assumption that the target computer has one. To have a reliable timer class, you should include a check to `QueryPerformanceCounter` in the constructor, and if it fails, create a timer of your own using normal Win32 API functions.

How to Create the Error File

Creating the error file, mrError.h isn't hard. The very basic file is as follows:

```
 /* mrError.h' */

 /* Include this file only once */
#pragma once

 /* Error codes */
enum mrError32
{
 mrNoError                    = 0,

 mrError32_Force32            = 0xFFFFFFFF
};
```

This is basically enumeration mrError32 with mrNoError (0) defined. When a function succeeds, the constant mrNoError is returned.

Here's how to construct the rest of the error codes. Whenever you see some function having a return type mrError32, and within the code there is a line like this:

```
return mrErrorSomething;
```

Where Something is usually a word or a small abbreviated phrase, it means an error occurred and that you should add the mrErrorSomething code to your enumeration next to the last error you added, or if it is the first time, after mrNoError like this:

```
enum mrError32
{
 mrNoError                    = 0,
 mrErrorSomething1,
 mrErrorSomething2,
  /* …*/
 mrError32_Force32            = 0xFFFFFFFF
};
```

Easy, no?

How to Use Mirus

To use Mirus in other projects, you need to copy all the Mirus files to the project's directory and include only the header files you want.

At the end of the book, you should create a file, probably named `Mirus.h`, which has all the needed headers for Mirus to work efficiently by only including that header in the main project.

Even though there are better methods to use Mirus, such as creating a static library for linking, this step is left for you to implement.

Summary

In this chapter you have completed one of the most important aspects of Mirus development—its design.

By having the library briefly designed, it will be easier to keep focus on what is important and what isn't, and how the components work, which will save you a lot of time when you are doing the development.

You have also created the most accurate timer using the hardware timer to calculate the time it takes to draw a frame so you can use it in your games.

Questions and Answers

Q: Why should I make some of the components singletons?

A: When you create a game, sometimes you need to create a Mirus object (like `mrABO`) from a class, which has no access to the manager (for example, `mrScreen`). By making these classes singletons, you can access them anywhere in your code.

Q: Why should I create a `mrRGBAImage` and not implement the loading routines inside the `mrSurface` and `mrTexture` classes?

A: By creating an independent class, you can modify the code for loading the files as you wish in only one place (like adding support for other file formats), and you don't need to worry about the other classes.

CHAPTER 11

Beginning Windows Programming

Windows is here, and is here to stay. Knowing how to create and show windows and know the basics of window use is crucial to any DirectX developer.

In this chapter, I will explain the basics of window creation and manipulation and take a look at some of the more popular functions related to Windows programming. In the end, you will build a reusable window framework to use in the rest of your games.

History of Windows

Windows has come a long way since its first release. From Windows 1.0 to the more recent Windows XP, Windows has grown from a simple user interface with drop-down menus to one of the most complex pieces of software ever created.

The first incarnations of Windows were as hard to program as they were to work with. The entire development structure was modified in Windows 3.1, which was a blessing to all Windows programmers.

In 1995, Microsoft released its 32-bit system, Windows 95. This was when Microsoft really conquered the market (and the world for that matter). Microsoft created a system that was user friendly, developer friendly, powerful, and nice to look at. At this time, Microsoft had the operating system for most applications, but it was not very friendly for games. About a year later, Microsoft introduced the Game SDK (later renamed DirectX) to try to get developers to make games for this new system.

With the arrival of Windows 98 (and a much better version of DirectX), Microsoft developed the perfect solution both for applications and games. Being a true 32-bit system, it guaranteed a fast, reliable system for games. It still looked and felt like Windows 95, but under the hood, Windows 98 was very different from its predecessor.

Alongside Windows 95 and 98, Microsoft also developed Windows NT (currently in its fifth incarnation named Windows 2000), which was a reliable system for networks and applications, but very poor in terms of performance for games. It wasn't until Windows NT 5 that Microsoft put a real effort in making a game friendly NT system.

Windows Millennium Edition (Me) has great support for both games and normal applications. It is user friendly and compatible with just about any hardware that exists. Microsoft has recently released Windows XP, which has the stability of Windows 2000 and the easy use of Windows 98.

Overall, Windows started by being a simple user interface system to a complete operating system, which is considered one of the most complex systems ever created.

Introduction to Windows Programming

I will focus compatibility with Windows 98 and newer versions mainly because of its true 32-bit capabilities, but that doesn't mean that the code here doesn't work with Windows 95. Windows 95 had a lot of 16-bit legacy code that made it unstable and buggy, and Windows 98 doesn't have those problems. Also, code that works in Windows 98 should work perfectly with newer releases of Windows because Microsoft made an effort to ensure compatibility with programs released in previous systems.

> **NOTE**
>
> This type of support for older versions of systems is called *legacy support*. It means that applications or code developed for older systems will work in newer ones.

You should take a few things into account when developing games (or any kind of software) for Windows. Some you really don't need to worry about and others you do.

Windows

Windows applications usually work with windows (try to make sense out of that). Windows (not the operating system but the windowed applications) are made of several components. Take a look at Figure 11.1 for the most common parts of a window.

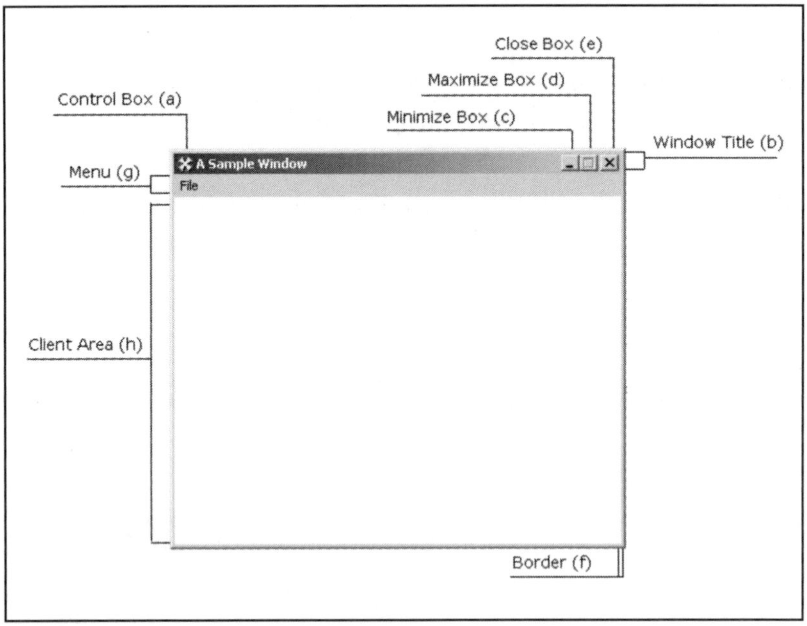

Figure 11.1

A typical window has several different components.

Figure 11.1 shows a typical window using the most commonly needed components but this doesn't mean you need them all. Here's a brief description of each:

a) This icon, when clicked, shows a system menu with the common window functions, such as Move, Size, Minimize, and so on.

b) This bar shows the window title.

c) This box minimizes the window to the taskbar.

d) This box maximizes the window to the size of the screen (when possible).

e) This box closes/exits the application.

f) This border is used for resizing and to show a visible division between the window and other windows or the desktop.

g) The menu is usually used to give some extra commands to the user in the form of a collection of menus and submenus.

h) This is what you are interested in—the client area. Here is where you will draw what you need.

Multitasking

Windows is a multitasking system. It can run several applications at the same time. Windows supports two types of multitasking, process-based and thread-based. Figure 11.2 shows an example of multitasking.

Even if you don't need to deal with this issue yourself, you should ensure that your games will not have exclusive access to the CPU. You can't expect to have 100% processing power from the system and should expect that from the user's system.

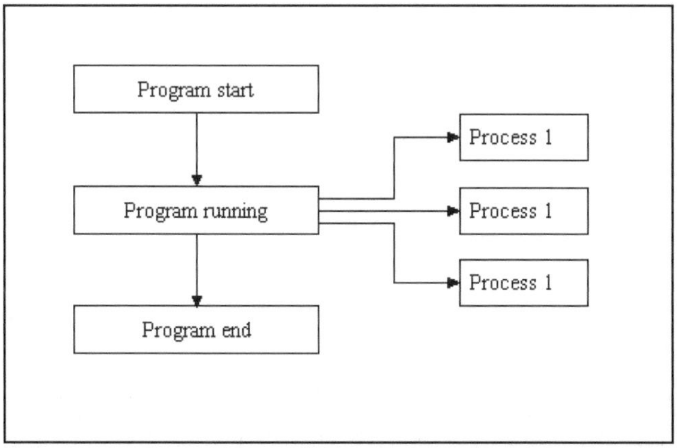

Figure 11.2

Multitasking in a single program.

NOTE

Unless a computer has multiple processors, a system can't truly do two things at the same time. Windows, however, emulates multitasking by running each application code a bit at a time, giving the impression that different things are happening at the same time because a computer is so fast. For example, if you have a program that does ten calculations each cycle, and another that does ten calculations also, Windows manages to do a calculation in one application, one in another, and then another calculation in the first application, and so on until all calculations of both applications have been completed.

Windows Has Its Own API

Unlike the console programs you have been developing, you don't have any direct control over how your Windows applications work. You have an Application Programming Interface (API) that provides you control on how windows are shown, manipulated, twisted, and cooked. (Fried windows, anyone?)

You will be using the Win32 API, which is the 32-bit version of the Windows API. The old API used to develop 16-bit applications is the Win16 API. The newer API has hundreds of functions you can use to get control over your application.

You will use this API exclusively to develop all the code during the rest of this chapter and a few others.

Message Queues

Windows has another big difference from the console applications you have been developing: messages, or input queues. All things that happen in your program (such as the mouse moving, the user pressing a key, aliens landing) are reported to your application by a message.

In each cycle dedicated to your application, you will see whether there is a message in the queue. You will either chose to handle it or ignore it, as you will see when you learn more about the message handler.

> **NOTE**
>
> **A *queue* is a list of events, data, and anything that works in "first in, first out (FIFO)" priority. The first data to get in the list is the first to get out.**

Visual C++ and Windows Applications

When developing Windows applications, you don't use the Win32 Console project anymore. To be able to develop Windows applications, you now need to use the Win32 Application project.

You should already know how to create a new project, but just in case, you need to go to File, New, and select the Projects tab. Then choose the Win32 Application and give the project a name.

If you remember console applications, then you know that when you created a new console project, you could define a couple of prestarter options to aid in creating the project. Win32 Application project also has a few options to help you do this. I'll leave it up to you to play with those options.

Now add a C++ source file to the project, and you are ready to start.

Building the Windows Application

Developing a Windows has four main steps. These steps are illustrated in Figure 11.3.

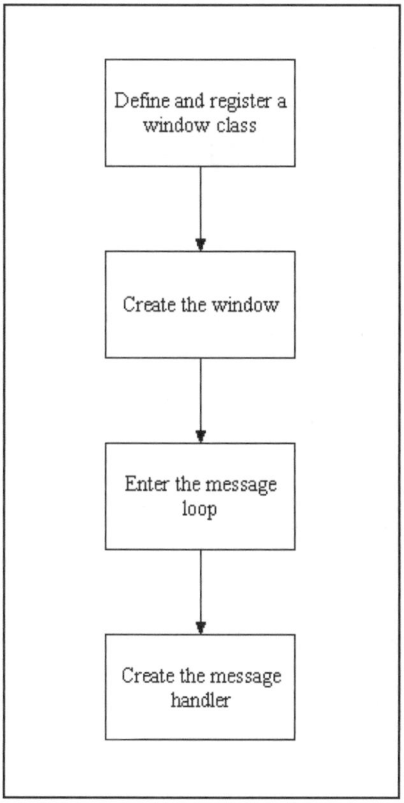

Figure 11.3

Building a Windows application.

I believe it is better to start by seeing the complete code for a Windows application and then dissect it by relevant parts, so here it is:

```
 /* '01 Main.cpp' */
#include <windows.h>

 /* Message handler prototype */
LRESULT CALLBACK WndProc (HWND hWindow, UINT iMessage,
                          WPARAM wParam, LPARAM lParam);

 /* "WinMain Vs. main" */
int WINAPI WinMain (HINSTANCE hInstance, HINSTANCE hPrevInst,
                    LPSTR lpCmdLine, int nShowCmd)
{
  /* "The Window Class" */
 WNDCLASS  kWndClass;

  /* 'Visual' properties */
 kWndClass.hCursor       = LoadCursor (NULL, IDC_ARROW);
 kWndClass.hIcon         = LoadIcon (NULL, IDI_APPLICATION);
 kWndClass.hbrBackground = (HBRUSH) GetStockObject (WHITE_BRUSH);

  /* System properties */
 kWndClass.hInstance     = hInstance;
 kWndClass.lpfnWndProc   = WndProc;
 kWndClass.lpszClassName = "01 Basic Window";

  /* Extra properties */
 kWndClass.lpszMenuName  = NULL;

 kWndClass.cbClsExtra = NULL;
 kWndClass.cbWndExtra = NULL;
 kWndClass.style      = NULL;

  /* Try to register class */
 if (!RegisterClass (&kWndClass))
 {
  return -1;
 }

```

```
  /* "The Window" */
 HWND hWindow;
  /* Create the window */
 hWindow = CreateWindow ("01 Basic Window", "A Blank Window",
                           WS_OVERLAPPEDWINDOW | WS_VISIBLE, CW_USEDEFAULT,
                           CW_USEDEFAULT, CW_USEDEFAULT, CW_USEDEFAULT,
                           NULL, NULL, hInstance, NULL);

  /* "The Message Loop" */
 MSG kMessage;
  /* Enter the message loop and deal with all messages sent to our
     window */
 while (GetMessage (&kMessage, hWindow, 0, 0))
 {
  TranslateMessage (&kMessage);
  DispatchMessage (&kMessage);
 }

return 0;
}

/* "The Message Handler" */
LRESULT CALLBACK WndProc (HWND hWindow, UINT iMessage,
                            WPARAM wParam, LPARAM lParam)
{
 switch (iMessage)
 {
 /* Close window */
 case WM_CLOSE:
  PostQuitMessage (0);
 break;

 default:
  return DefWindowProc (hWindow, iMessage, wParam, lParam);
 }
 return 0;
}
```

If all went well, you should see a window similar to the one in Figure 11.4.

Figure 11.4

Your created window.

The first thing you do is include the `windows.h` header file (line 2). This header file contains almost all the Win32API functions, structures, constants, and so on that you will need to create Windows applications. After this is done, you declare your message handler prototype `WndProc` (lines 5 and6). Don't worry about this function now because I discuss it later.

WinMain Versus Main

`WinMain` (line 9) is the Windows equivalent to `main` for console applications. It uses a different structure than `main`. First, the return type is an `int`. This doesn't mean you are forced to use an `int`, but you should. The second thing you have probably noticed is that it looks like it returns two types, which isn't true. `WINAPI` is a calling convention, such as `static` or `inline`, as you have seen before but specific to Windows applications.

Then there are the parameters. The first parameter, `HINSTANCE hInstance`, is the instance of the program. Think of it as the ID of your application to the operating system. The second parameter isn't used in the 32-bit versions of Windows and will always be `NULL`.

> **NOTE**
>
> A *handle* is a pointer to a pointer, meaning that it points to an address inside a list. These are needed because Windows memory manager moves objects as it most suits it, so you cannot access the memory normally without external help.

The third parameter, `LPSTR lpCmdLine`, is a string with the command-line arguments. This works a bit differently from the console version. If you try to run a program like this:

```
Executable.exe First Second
```

`lpCmdLine` will be a string like this:

```
"First Second"
```

So if you want to parse the command-line arguments, you do it the same way you parse a normal string. The last parameter is how the window should be shown. This parameter can take any of the following values shown in Table 11.1, which you will be using later.

TABLE 11.1 Window State Passed to WinMain

Value	Description
SW_HIDE	Hides the window
SW_MINIMIZE	Minimizes the window
SW_RESTORE	Activates and displays the window in its original size and position if it is minimized or maximized
SW_SHOW	Activates and displays a window
SW_SHOWMAXIMIZED	Activates and displays a window maximized
SW_SHOWMINIMIZED	Activates and displays a window minimized
SW_SHOWMINNOACTIVE	Activates and displays a window minimized and active
SW_SHOWNA	Activates and displays a window active
SW_SHOWNOACTIVATE	Activates and displays a window
SW_SHOWNORMAL	Activates and displays the window in its original size and position if it is minimized or maximized

Creating the Window

Creating the window can also be divided into two sections: defining a window class and actually creating the window.

The Window Class

The first step to defining the window class is declaring the variable like so:

```
WNDCLASS kWndClass;
```

This creates a variable you will use to specify the windows attributes. The WNDCLASS structure has several members that you will use and it is defined as so:

```
typedef struct _WNDCLASS {
 UINT style;
 WNDPROC lpfnWndProc;
 int cbClsExtra;
 int cbWndExtra;
 HANDLE hInstance;
 HICON hIcon;
 HCURSOR hCursor;
 HBRUSH hbrBackground;
 LPCTSTR lpszMenuName;
 LPCTSTR lpszClassName;
} WNDCLASS;
```

By order of appearance, here is an explanation of each of the structure fields.

style specifies the window class style. You won't use it now, so set it to NULL. Then there is lpfnWndProc, which is a pointer to the window message handler that the window will call. Remember you declared a function prototype earlier? Well, this is where you use it, so you assign it to this field.

After the window procedure comes two fields, cbClsExtra and cbWndExtra, which are used to specify the number of extra bytes to allocate after the window class structure and the window structure, respectively. You won't use them, so set them to zero.

Next, you have the instance field—hInstance. This is the instance of the application where you create the window. You will use the hInstance parameter of WinMain for this.

The next field is the icon handle—`hIcon`. This field will specify the icon shown in the title bar. You use the API function `LoadIcon` to load the icon, which is declared like this:

```
HICON LoadIcon (HINSTANCE hInstance, LPCSTR lpIconName);
```

This function, if successful, returns a handle to an icon, which you use in the window class field. Its parameters are the instance from where you want to load the icon. Here you use `NULL` because you don't have any icons in your application. By using `NULL` as an instance, you can use a predefined icon. The second parameter is a null terminated string specifying the name of the icon to load. You are using the `IDI_APPLICATION` predefined icon in this case. Table 11.2 lists a few more icons you can use.

Next is the cursor information—`hCursor`, which is the handle to the cursor you want your window to have. You use the `LoadCursor` function similarly to how you used `LoadIcon`.

```
HCURSOR LoadCursor (HINSTANCE hInstance, LPCTSTR lpCursorName);
```

The first parameter is also the instance of your program, or `NULL` if you want to use any of the predefined cursors, which you do. The second parameter is the cursor name or a predefined icon value. You use `IDC_ARROW`, which is the normal arrow you see all around Windows. Table 11.3 contains the predefined cursors you can use.

TABLE 11.2 Predefined Icons

Value	Description
IDI_APPLICATION	Default application icon
IDI_ERROR	Error icon
IDI_INFORMATION	Information icon
IDI_WARNING	Warning icon
IDI_QUESTION	Question icon
IDI_WINLOGO	Windows logo icon

Table 11.3 Predefined Cursors

Value	Description
IDC_APPSTARTING	Standard arrow with small hourglass
IDC_ARROW	Standard arrow
IDC_CROSS	Crosshair
IDC_HELP	Arrow and question mark
IDC_IBEAM	I-Beam
IDC_NO	Slashed circle (prohibition)
IDC_SIZEALL	Four-pointed arrow
IDC_SIZENESW	Double-pointed arrow pointing northeast and southwest
IDC_SIZENS	Double-pointed arrow pointing north and south
IDC_SIZENWSE	Double-pointed arrow pointing northwest and southeast
IDC_SIZEWE	Double-pointed arrow pointing west and east
IDC_UPARROW	Vertical arrow
IDC_WAIT	Hourglass

Now there are only three more. The next one is the background style—`hbrBackGround`. Here is where you specify the kind of background brush you want your window to have. By using `GetStockObject`, you can use a predefined stock object, or brush. It is defined as so:

```
HGDIOBJ GetStockObject (int fnObject);
```

This returns a handle to the object and takes as parameter the object type. Table 11.4 provides a complete list of brush objects you can use.

And your next field is the menu name—`lpszMenuName`. You won't use a menu for this window, so set it to `NULL`.

Table 11.4 Predefined Brushes

Value	Description
BLACK_BRUSH	Black brush
DKGRAY_BRUSH	Dark gray brush
GRAY_BRUSH	Gray brush
HOLLOW_BRUSH	Hollow brush (transparent)
WHITE_BRUSH	White brush

Last, but not least, the class name—`lpszClassName`. This is the name Windows will use to refer to the class. When you create the window, you need to know it, and for this example you use `01 Basic Window`.

And you have your window class setup for registering. Now what? Register!!

In line 33 you try to register the class by using the function `RegisterClass`, which is defined as so:

```
ATOM RegisterClass (CONST WNDCLASS *lpWndClass);
```

This function returns, if successful, an `ATOM`, which identifies the window class, or zero if it failed. You won't use the return type except for checking whether it was successful, so you really don't need to worry about it. Its only parameter is a pointer to a window class, in your case `&kWndClass`. This function will register your class for later use.

You also check whether you registered the window class correctly, and if not, just quit the program, returning `-1`.

With this you finish the declaring and registering part of your window creation process. If all was successful, you are ready to move to the actual creation of the window.

Creating the Window

> **NOTE**
>
> Just in case your memory is failing, a handle is an address of a resource in Windows. Windows manages the handle itself so you don't need to worry how they are stored. Just remember it will point to the resource you want—in this case, the window.

You have now reached the point where you create the actual window. The first step (okay, maybe not a real step) to creating a window is to declare a window handle, as follows:

```
HWND hWindow;
```

After this is done, you can create your window as shown in lines 41 through 44 using the following code:

```
hWindow = CreateWindow ("01 Basic Window", "A Blank Window",
                        WS_OVERLAPPEDWINDOW | WS_VISIBLE, CW_USEDEFAULT,
                        CW_USEDEFAULT, CW_USEDEFAULT, CW_USEDEFAULT,
                        NULL, NULL, hInstance, NULL);
```

`CreateWindow` has a lot parameters, so start by looking at the function definition and then go over the parameters one by one.

```
HWND CreateWindow (LPCTSTR lpClassName,
                   LPCTSTR lpWindowName,
                   WORD dwStyle,
                   int x,
                   int y,
                   int nWidth,
                   int nHeight,
                   HWND hWndParent,
                   HMENU hMenu,
                   HANDLE hInstance,
                   LPVOID lpParam);
```

`CreateWindow` returns a handle to the created window if it was successful or `NULL` if it wasn't. The returned window handle will be used in almost any operation you try to perform with the window.

So I'll go over the parameters. The first one is the class name—`lpClassName`—from where the window will take its properties. This name must be the name of a class registered in your program. You use `01 Basic Window` because it was the name of the window class you registered.

The second parameter is the window title—lpWindowName. This is the text that will be shown, by default, in the window title bar (in your example, A Blank Window.)

You then have the window's style—dwStyle. This parameter specifies how the window is shown. You are using WS_OVERLAPPEDWINDOW to create a normal window with all the normal window components (except the menu) (refer to Figure 11.1). You also use WS_VISIBLE to force the window to be visible on creation. You combine both the styles using the OR operator. Table 11.5 shows some of the common window styles.

Most of the values in Table 11.5 and other windows style values can be used together with the OR operator.

The next two parameters—x and y—are the position of the window in the screen. You use CW_USEDEFAULT to allow Windows to choose the position.

In resemblance to the previous parameters, you have the width and height of the window next—nWidth and nHeight. You also let Windows decide what values to use by passing CW_USEDEFAULT.

Next, you have the window parent handle—hWndParent. You don't make use of it, but specify NULL, which tells Windows that the parent of your window will be the desktop.

You then have the menu handle parameter—hMenu. This menu handle works similarly to the window class one, but you will go over this in the next chapter, so for now, set it to NULL.

Table 11.5 Window Styles

Value	Description
WS_CHILDWINDOW	Creates a child window
WS_HSCROLL	Creates a window with a scrollbar
WS_OVERLAPPEDWINDOW	Creates a window with the normal window components
WS_POPUP	Creates a pop-up window
WS_VISIBLE	Creates a window initially visible
WS_VSCROLL	Creates a window with a vertical scrollbar

You have the instance of the application—`hInstance`. This isn't new to you, and like before, you will use the `hInstance` parameter of `WinMain`.

Finally, you have the custom data sent to the window creation message—`WM_NCCREATE`. This parameter will be used later in the chapter when you build a reusable window class so I'll discuss it there.

Now that you have your window created, you will use `ShowWindow` to show the window in accordance with the `WinMain nCmdShow` parameter. This isn't a necessary step but you should leave it there so that Windows can manipulate your window.

And you're done. You have the window created and on the screen. Next, I'll go over the message loop and handler to finish your first Windows application.

The Message Loop

Now that you have created your window, you need to create a message loop. The message loop is part of almost every windows program. (There are some advanced techniques that actually allow you to skip this.) When an application is running, it continually receives messages sent by Windows. These messages are then sent to your application message queue. When your application is ready to process the next message, it will call the function `GetMessage` that will store the message into a `MSG` structure and then translate to and process it by your message handler. Because you want to let your application continually run and process all the messages, you use a loop to repeat all these steps until the user quits the application. This entire step is shown from lines 47 through 54.

You first declare a `MSG` structure and create the message loop as so:

```
MSG kMessage;
while (GetMessage (&kMessage, hWindow, 0, 0))
```

This creates a message loop that will continue executing until the user exits the application.

The `GetMessage` function is used to retrieve a message from the application message queue and store it in a `MSG` structure. Its prototype is as follows:

```
BOOL GetMessage(LPMSG lpMsg,
                HWND hWnd,
                UINT wMsgFilterMin,
                UINT wMsgFilterMax);
```

This function returns zero when the user exits the application, or more accurately, the application receives a `WM_QUIT` message. The first parameter to this function is a pointer to a `MSG` structure. This is where the information about the message will be stored.

The second parameter is the handle to the window where you retrieve the message. You will use `hWindow` because it's the handle to the window you created.

The last two parameters are the filter values that enable you to filter some messages out. You won't use them, so set them both as zero.

Inside the loop, you have to translate all virtual key codes into character messages. This isn't a necessary or an important step but you should do it to guarantee total keyboard integration with your program. You achieve this by calling `TranslateMessage` with the address of your message as the parameter.

When this is done, you just need to send the message to your message handler with `DispatchMessage`. To do this, call `DispatchMessage` with the address of your message as parameter.

The last line in `WinMain` is just the return value of the application, zero.

The Message Handler

You are in the final part of your first Windows application with just the message handler missing. The message handler is the function that handles all the messages sent to your window. You have already defined its prototype in the beginning of the file, so focus on the function itself.

When the user presses a key or moves the mouse, a message is sent to your application. When this happens, you have the choice of processing it or letting Windows do it. You usually process only a few messages from more than hundreds available. In this program, you only take in account the `WM_CLOSE` message, which is sent to your application whenever the user tries to quit the application. When this message is sent, you handle it by sending a quit message using the `PostQuitMessage` function.

> **NOTE**
>
> **You refer to the message handler as handler. Windows and some documents refer to this message handler as the window procedure. Both of these names stand for the same thing.**

So, back to the code! Four parameters are in your message handler function `WndProc`. The first one—`hWindow`—is the handle of the window that received the message. The second parameter—`iMessage`—is the actual message code that is sent to your window. The third and fourth parameters—`wParam` and `lParam` respectively—are just the message parameters. I will explain them when I deal with other messages.

Inside the function you use a `switch` statement to check what message was sent and then handle it. In this simple program, you are only interested in the `WM_CLOSE` message so it will be the only one you will handle. Tell Windows to quit your application with the following code:

```
PostQuitMessage (0);
```

The `PostQuitMessage` is defined like this:

```
void PostQuitMessage(int nExitCode);
```

This function has only one parameter—the exit code that will be sent to the `WM_QUIT` message.

Now that you have your message handled, you need to add a `default` case to your switch to allow Windows to handle the messages that you didn't. In the `default` case, you simply send it back to Windows for processing using the `DefWindowProc` function using the same parameters that your message handler accepts, like this:

```
return DefWindowProc (hWindow, iMessage, wParam, lParam);
```

You also return the result of this function to let Windows know what happened when you dealt with the message. You don't need to worry about the inner workings of this because Windows does it all automatically.

You are done with your first Windows application. It wasn't that bad, was it? Well, now comes the fun part: making a real-time message loop and encapsulating all this into a working class.

Creating a Real-Time Message Loop

Even if the window you created is okay for normal applications like Word or Notepad, it isn't for games. You need a loop that can execute your code each time the application has no messages. This is called a real-time loop.

The pseudocode behind the loop is as follows:

```
While Game is running
Begin
 If there is any message in the window message queue
 Begin
  If it is quit message
  Begin
   Quit
  End
  If it is a normal message
  Begin
   Process message
  End
 End
 If there is no message
 Begin
  Do game code
 End
End
```

So, how does this translate to code? The first thing you do is remove your old message loop to give space for the new one. Done? Okay, continue then. From the preceding pseudocode, you can see that you will be running the loop until you wish to quit, so the first step is to create an infinite loop using something like the following:

```
while (1) {
```

Now that you are inside the loop, you need to determine whether there are any messages in your window queue. This is achieved with a call to `PeekMessage`. The `PeekMessage` function works similarly to the `GetMessage` function but returns true if there is any message pending and returns false if there isn't. Here is its definition:

```
BOOL PeekMessage (LPMSG lpMsg,
                  HWND hWnd,
                  UINT wMsgFilterMin,
                  UINT wMsgFilterMax,
                  UINT nRemove);
```

`PeekMessage` returns true if there are any message in the window message queue and false if there isn't. You will be using that return value shortly but first I'll go over the parameter list. As you can see, the first four parameters in the list are equal to the GetMessage parameters, and they do exactly the same thing they did in GetMessage, so I won't go over them now. The big news is the last parameter—nRemove. This parameter specifies how the message should be handled. If you want to remove the message you are *peeking* from the message queue, then you would specify PM_REMOVE as argument, and if you want to let the message remain in the message queue you use PM_NOREMOVE as argument. Because you don't want to leave the message in the queue, you will remove it, which leads you to the following code:

```
if (PeekMessage (&kMessage, hWindow, 0, 0, PM_REMOVE)) {
```

This will check to see whether there are any messages in the queue; if there are, copy the one that was sent first to kMessage and remove it.

Next, check whether the message was WM_QUIT. As the name suggests, it is the message sent to quit the application. Do this by checking the message member of kMessage. Take a look how MSG (which is kMessage type) is defined:

```
typedef struct tagMSG {
    HWND   hwnd;
    UINT   message;
    WPARAM wParam;
    LPARAM lParam;
    DWORD  time;
    POINT  pt;
} MSG;
```

The first four members are used for the same thing as the parameters in your message handler function. Respectively, they store the handle to the window to which the message was sent, the actual message code, and the message parameters. The fifth member—time—is the time when the message was sent to your application, and the last member—pt—specifies the cursor position when the message was sent. You won't make direct use of these parameters except for the message code, so you can ignore them.

So, you were checking whether the message was WM_QUIT, which is done like this:

```
if (WM_QUIT == kMessage.message) {
```

Now, what do you do if the message is equal to WM_QUIT? You need to quit your while loop using a break statement like you normally do:

```
break; }
```

And what should you do if you have a message but it isn't `WM_QUIT`? You need to send it to your message handler normally with `TranslateMessage` and `DispatchMessage` like this:

```
else
{
 TranslateMessage (&kMessage);
 DispatchMessage (&kMessage);
}
}
```

And you are done with the handle message code. Now you simply need to add a bit of code to do whatever you want when there are no messages. How do you do this? You add an `else` clause to `if (PeekMessage (…))`, which will be executed when `PeekMessage` returns false (you have no messages).

> **NOTE**
>
> **The last closing brace (`}`) finishes the `if (PeekMessage (…)) if` statement.**

```
else
{
 /* Do something */
}
```

And you have a real-time message loop. It wasn't that hard, was it? The following is the complete code listing for a real-time application:

```
 /* '02 Main.cpp' */
#include <windows.h>

 /* Message handler prototype */
LRESULT CALLBACK WndProc (HWND hWindow, UINT iMessage,
                         WPARAM wParam, LPARAM lParam);

 /* "WinMain Vs. main" */
int WINAPI WinMain (HINSTANCE hInstance, HINSTANCE hPrevInst,
                    LPSTR lpCmdLine, int nShowCmd)
{
  /* "The Window Class" */
 WNDCLASS  kWndClass;

  /* 'Visual' properties */
```

```
kWndClass.hCursor        = LoadCursor (NULL, IDC_ARROW);
kWndClass.hIcon          = LoadIcon (NULL, IDI_APPLICATION);
kWndClass.hbrBackground = (HBRUSH) GetStockObject (WHITE_BRUSH);

 /* System properties */
kWndClass.hInstance     = hInstance;
kWndClass.lpfnWndProc   = WndProc;
kWndClass.lpszClassName = "02 Real time message loop";

 /* Extra properties */
kWndClass.lpszMenuName  = NULL;

kWndClass.cbClsExtra = NULL;
kWndClass.cbWndExtra = NULL;
kWndClass.style      = NULL;

 /* Try to register class */
if (!RegisterClass (&kWndClass))
{
 return -1;
}

 /* "The Window" */
HWND hWindow;
 /* Create the window */
hWindow = CreateWindow ("02 Real time message loop",
                        "02 Real time message loop",
                        WS_OVERLAPPEDWINDOW | WS_VISIBLE, CW_USEDEFAULT,
                        CW_USEDEFAULT, CW_USEDEFAULT, CW_USEDEFAULT,
                        NULL, NULL, hInstance, NULL);
ShowWindow (hWindow, nShowCmd);

 /* "The Message Loop" */
MSG kMessage;
 /* Enter the real time message loop */
while (1)
{
  /* Query to see if there is any message in the queue */
 if (PeekMessage (&kMessage, hWindow, 0, 0, PM_REMOVE))
```

```
  {
   /* If it is the WM_QUIT message, quit the loop */
   if (WM_QUIT == kMessage.message)
   {
    break;
   }
   /* Process the message normally */
   else
   {
    TranslateMessage (&kMessage);
    DispatchMessage (&kMessage);
   }
 }
  /* No message, do whatever we want */
  else
  {
   /* Do idle ... */
  }
}

return 0L;
}

/* "The Message Handler" */
LRESULT CALLBACK WndProc (HWND hWindow, UINT iMessage,
                          WPARAM wParam, LPARAM lParam)
{
 switch (iMessage)
 {
 /* Close window */
 case WM_CLOSE:
  PostQuitMessage (0);
 break;

 default:
  return DefWindowProc (hWindow, iMessage, wParam, lParam);
 }
 return 0;
}
```

Making a Reusable Window Class

Now that you know how to create a general window, and because this is code you will reuse in every Windows application you will develop, you should create your own reusable class for it, no? Yes!

The following is the class header definition:

```
 /* 'mrWindow.h' */

 /* Mirus base types header */
#include "mrDatatypes.h"
/* Windows header file */
#include <windows.h>

 /* Include this file only once */
#pragma once

 /* Mirus window framework */
class mrWindow
{
protected:
 WNDCLASS  m_kWndClass;
 HWND      m_hWindow;
 MSG       m_kMessage;

public:
  /* Constructor / Destructor */
 mrWindow (void);
 ~mrWindow (void);

  /* Window manipulation functions */
 mrError32 Create (HINSTANCE hInstance, LPSTR szTitle,
                   mrInt iWidth = CW_USEDEFAULT,
                   mrInt iHeight = CW_USEDEFAULT,
                   mrUInt32 iStyle = WS_OVERLAPPEDWINDOW | WS_VISIBLE);
 static LRESULT CALLBACK WndProc (HWND hWindow, UINT iMessage,
```

```
                             WPARAM wParam, LPARAM lParam);
 void Run (void);

  /* Custom functions */
 virtual mrBool32 MessageHandler (UINT iMessage, WPARAM wParam,
                                          LPARAM lParam);
 virtual mrBool32 Frame (void) = 0;
};
```

The design of this class is pretty simple. You have a function to create the window (`Create`), and a function to enter the real-time message loop (`Run`). You also have a static message handler (`WndProc`), which will direct the messages to your own message handler (`MessageHandler`). You also have a pure virtual function `Frame` that is called each frame when there are no messages waiting and must be implemented in the derived class.

You use default parameters in `Create` to simplify the use of the class. They are `CW_USEDEFAULT` for `iWidth` and `iHeight` and `WS_OVERLAPPEDWINDOW | WS_VISIBLE` for `iFlags` that will create a normal visible window later.

> **NOTE**
>
> `mrWindow` is a pure virtual class. It needs to be derived in order to be able to use it.

```
 /* 'mrWindow.cpp' */

 /* Complement header file */
#include "mrWindow.h"

 /* Default constructor */
mrWindow::mrWindow (void)
{
 /* Do nothing */
}

 /* Default destructor */
mrWindow::~mrWindow (void)
{
 /* Do nothing */
}

```

The first thing you do is include the complement header file `mrWindow.h`. After this is done, you create an empty constructor and destructor. Nothing out of this world here.

```
 /* Create the window */
mrError32 mrWindow::Create (HINSTANCE hInstance, LPSTR szTitle, mrInt iWidth,
                            mrInt iHeight, mrUInt32 iStyle)
{
  /* 'Visual' properties */
 m_kWndClass.hCursor       = LoadCursor (NULL, IDC_ARROW);
 m_kWndClass.hIcon         = LoadIcon (NULL, IDI_APPLICATION);
 m_kWndClass.hbrBackground = (HBRUSH) GetStockObject (WHITE_BRUSH);

  /* System properties */
 m_kWndClass.hInstance     = hInstance;
 m_kWndClass.lpfnWndProc   = WndProc;
 m_kWndClass.lpszClassName = "Mirus Window";

  /* Extra properties */
 m_kWndClass.lpszMenuName  = NULL;

 m_kWndClass.cbClsExtra = NULL;
 m_kWndClass.cbWndExtra = NULL;
 m_kWndClass.style      = NULL;

  /* Try to register class */
 if (!RegisterClass (&m_kWndClass))
 {
  return mrErrorRegisterClass;
 }

  /* Create the window */
 m_hWindow = CreateWindow ("Mirus Window", szTitle, iStyle, CW_USEDEFAULT,
                           CW_USEDEFAULT, iWidth, iHeight,
                           NULL, NULL, hInstance, (void *) this);
 SetWindowText (m_hWindow, szTitle);

 return mrNoError;
}
```

The code in Create is almost the same as the previous windows applications. You fill the window class with all the relevant information, register the class, and create the window. There are just a few changes I will go over now.

First, the window class name will always be Mirus Window. This enables you to have only one window for your application (like you should).

The second thing to note is in line 48, where you pass the last parameter (void *) this to CreateWindow instead of the usual NULL. Do you still remember what the last parameter in CreateWindow was for? If not, it was used to send custom data to the window WM_NCCREATE message. You will use this in the message handler. For now, just remember that you passed the address of your window to it.

The last modification is that you don't use ShowWindow anymore, but use SetWindowText instead. You don't use ShowWindow because you are forcing your window to be visible and have the size you want and are not using nShowCmd from WinMain anymore.

The SetWindowText is an API function that sets the title of your window. For some strange reason, CreateWindow has some problems with setting the window title when this is done in classes, even if this isn't constant, it is a problem. This issue should be fixed if you install Service Pack 2 or above but you never know.

NOTE

You now store all the window variables (kWndClass, hWindow, and kMessage as window members namely m_kWndClass, m_hWindow, and m_kMessage.

NOTE

You can have various windows running your application, but for optimal performance, you should have only one window using Direct3D and divide that window to other windows on your own.

NOTE

WM_NCCREATE is the message sent to the window immediately before the control from CreateWindow returns to your program. It is sent a tiny moment before the window is actually created.

NOTE

You can download the latest Service Pack for Visual C++ from Microsoft, free of charge at http://msdn.microsoft.com/visualc.

The first argument of SetWindowText is the handle to the window you want to change the title of, and the second argument is a string that holds the window title.

```
/* Normal message handler - direct messages to our own*/
LRESULT CALLBACK mrWindow::WndProc (HWND hWindow, UINT iMessage,
                                        WPARAM wParam, LPARAM lParam)
{
 mrWindow * pkWindow    = NULL;
 mrBool32   bProcessed = mrFalse;

 switch (iMessage)
 {
  /* Window is creating - set custom information */
 case WM_NCCREATE:
  SetWindowLong (hWindow, GWL_USERDATA,
                 (long)((LPCREATESTRUCT(lParam))->lpCreateParams));
  break;
  /* Window message - Let our handler process it */
 default:
   pkWindow = (mrWindow *) GetWindowLong (hWindow, GWL_USERDATA);
   if (NULL != pkWindow)
   {
    bProcessed = pkWindow->MessageHandler (iMessage, wParam, lParam);
   }
  break;
 }
   /* Message not processed - let windows handle it */
 if (mrFalse == bProcessed)
 {
  return DefWindowProc (hWindow, iMessage, wParam, lParam);
 }
 return 0;
}
```

Now, this one is tricky, no? Even if this is a message handler, you handle only one message here. Why? Well, the message handler must be a static function, and as you know, a static function can't access any of the class members. In this case, your message handler can't access any of your window's members, which is bad. Because of this, you will have to use a little trick with the window class to direct all messages to your custom handler—MessageHandler.

This first thing to note is the `WM_NCCREATE` message. This message is sent when the window is being created and fortunately for you, one of the parameters of the message—`lParam`—has the custom data you passed to `CreateWindow`. (You remember—you passed the address of your class to it.)

What do you do exactly in lines 65 and 66? You use `SetWindowLong` to store the address of your window class. `SetWindowLong` is defined like this:

```
LONG SetWindowLong (HWND hWnd,
                    int nIndex,
                    LONG dwNewLong);
```

This function is used to store custom data related to the window. The first parameter is the window where you want to store the information, which in this case is `m_hWindow`. The second parameter is the type of data you want to store, in this case, user data—`GWL_USERDATA`. And the last parameter is the data you want to store, in this case the window class's address. But how do you get it from `lParam`?

The first step is to type cast `lParam` to an `LPCREATESTRUCT` structure. This enables you to access the structure field that holds the address you passed in `CreateWindow` and then you need to typecast that data into a `long`. You do this as follows:

```
(long)((LPCREATESTRUCT(lParam))->lpCreateParams)
```

So, you now know that the `lpCreateParams` field of `LPCREATESTRUCT` holds the custom data passed to `WindowCreate` and can be accessed with a typecast of `lParam`. But what does this do for you? Well, you will be storing your window class's address in the window handle, which you can later use anywhere the handle to the window is known, as you will do next.

This message handler is called every time a message is sent to your window, so you need a way to redirect the message to your window handler, but how? You use the address of your window class to point a pointer to your class.

Every time a message is sent, and it isn't `WM_NCCREATE`, you let your message handler handle it. You first get the address of your window class using `GetWindowLong`, which is the opposite of `SetWindowLong`. It returns the data you stored with `SetWindowLong`. `GetWindowLong` is defined like this:

```
LONG GetWindowLong (HWND hWnd,
                    int nIndex);
```

This function returns the data stored and has two parameters: the handle to the window where the data is stored, and the type of data, in this case—`GWL_USERDATA`. By using `GetWindowLong`, you can get the address of your window class and create a pointer to it, as shown in line 70:

```
pkWindow = (mrWindow *) GetWindowLong (hWindow, GWL_USERDATA);
```

`pkWindow` is a pointer to `mrWindow`, as declared in line 58.

After this is done, you can redirect the message to your custom message handler `MessageHandler` method.

You also check to see whether `MessageHandler` processed the message. If it didn't, it should have returned `mrFalse`, and so you let Windows take the message like this:

> **NOTE**
>
> **Both `SetWindowLong` and `GetWindowLong` accept a handle to the window. This handle is the handle passed to the message handler, which is the handle of the window you created.**

```
return DefWindowProc (hWindow, iMessage, wParam, lParam);
 85:  /* Real time message loop */
 86: void mrWindow::Run (void)
 87: {
 88:  while (1)
 89:  {
 90:    /* Query to see if there is any message in the queue */
 91:   if (PeekMessage (&m_kMessage, m_hWindow, 0, 0, PM_REMOVE))
 92:   {
 93:     /* If it is the WM_QUIT message, quit the loop */
 94:    if (WM_QUIT == m_kMessage.message)
 95:    {
 96:     break;
 97:    }
 98:     /* Process the message normally */
 99:    else
100:    {
101:     TranslateMessage (&m_kMessage);
102:     DispatchMessage (&m_kMessage);
103:    }
```

```
   }
     /* No message, do frame */
   else
   {
    Frame ();
   }
  }
}
```

This message loop is exactly the same as the real-time message loop in example two except this time you call a function (Frame) when there are no messages. You check to see whether there are any messages pending, and if there are, you handle them. If the message is WM_QUIT, you quit the loop. If there aren't any messages, you call Frame, which is usually the code that is executed each frame.

```
 /* Our message handler */
mrBool32 mrWindow::MessageHandler (UINT iMessage, WPARAM wParam,
                                   LPARAM lParam)
{
 switch (iMessage)
 {
  /* Close window */
 case WM_CLOSE:
  PostQuitMessage (0);
  return mrTrue;
 break;
  /* Not handled - let Windows handle */
 default:
  return mrFalse;
 break;
 }
}
```

And finally, your custom message handler that works in a similar way to the message handler you used in examples one and two. You handle the messages normally, but this time you return a value telling the static message handler whether you handled the message or not.

And you have a reusable window framework. It is very simple to use and to add functionality, as you will see next.

Using the Mirus Window Framework

You have your window framework done, but what is its use if you don't know how to use it? None, right? So I'll go over how to make use of the newly created class.

Take a look at the following code that shows how simple and fast it is to use your window framework:

```
 /* '03 Main.cpp' */

 /* Mirus window framework header */
#include "Mirus.h"

 /* Custom derived class */
class CustomWindow : public mrWindow
{
public:
  /* Constructor / Destructor */
 CustomWindow (void) { };
 ~CustomWindow (void) { };

  /* Window manipulation functions */
 mrBool32 Frame (void) {return mrTrue;} ;
};

 /* "WinMain Vs. main" */
int WINAPI WinMain (HINSTANCE hInstance, HINSTANCE hPrevInst,
                   LPSTR lpCmdLine, int nShowCmd)
{
  /* Our window */
 CustomWindow     kWindow;

  /* Create window */
 kWindow.Create (hInstance, "03 Mirus Example");
  /* Enter message loop */
 kWindow.Run ();
}
```

As you can see, you created a window and entered the message loop in 29 lines of code (actually it was only 7 lines).

The first thing you do is include the Mirus header file—`Mirus.h`—which holds all the classes and function of Mirus. When this is done, you can define a class—`CustomWindow`—that is derived from `mrWindow`, which gives you all the methods you need to get your window on the road.

You need to define `Frame` because, if you remember, it is a pure virtual function that is called each frame when there are no messages. You simply make it return `mrTrue`, as shown in line 14.

After this class is defined, you can start worrying about `WinMain`. The first thing you do is declare a `CustomWindow` class, as shown in line 23. Now that you have done this, you can use `Create` to create your window with `03 Mirus Example` as title and `Run` to enter the message loop. This is shown in Figure 11.5

Some Common Window Functions

Now that you have a basic window done, you can add more features to it. In this section is a small set of functions that will greatly improve functionality.

SetPosition

The first method you will implement is setting the window position. Its prototype is as follows:

```
void SetPosition (mrInt iX, mrInt iY)
```

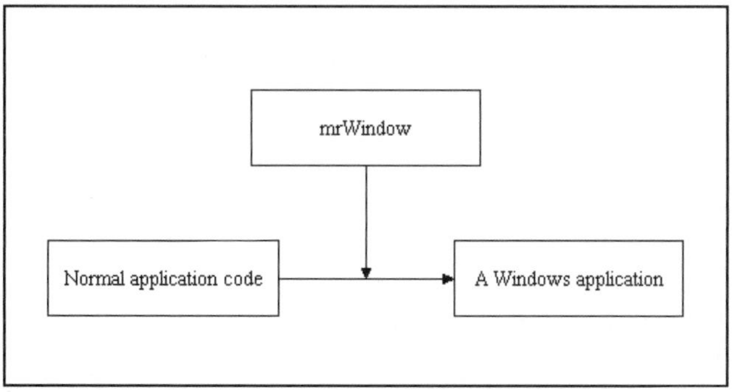

Figure 11.5

`mrWindow` at work.

It accepts two parameters, the x and y positions of the window. This method is defined as this:

```
SetWindowPos(m_hWindow, HWND_TOP, iX, iY, 0, 0, SWP_NOSIZE);
```

`SetWindowPos` enables you to change the window size and position, depending on the parameters. Its prototype is defined as follows:

```
BOOL SetWindowPos(HWND hWnd,
                  HWND hWndInsertAfter,
                  int X,
                  int Y,
                  int cx,
                  int cy,
                  UINT uFlags);
```

This function has seven parameters. The first one is the window handle of which you are setting the size.

The second parameter is the handle to the way the window should be inserted in the Z buffer, that is, show in the back or in the front. You use `HWND_TOP` because you want to bring the window to the top so it is visible.

The next four parameters are respectively the x and y coordinates and the width and height of the window. The last parameter is the flags parameter—`uFlags`—that tells `SetWindowPos` how to operate. In your case, you just want to move the window, so you set it to `SWP_NOSIZE`, which tells it to not resize the window, and it ignores the size parameters.

> **NOTE**
>
> **Remember you have to define the prototype normally inside the class definition and then build the function specifying the scope as `void mrWindow::SetPosition (mrInt iX, mrInt iY)`.**

GetPosition

The `GetPosition` function returns a `POINT` structure containing the x and y coordinates of the window; its prototype is:

```
void GetPosition (POINT * pkPosition);
```

`POINT` is defined as:

```
typedef struct tagPOINT {
    LONG x;
    LONG y;
} POINT;
```

Its fields are the x coordinate and the y coordinate. The function body is as follows:

```
{
 RECT  rcWindow;
 POINT pPosition;
  /* Get window position */
 GetWindowRect (m_hWindow, &rcWindow);

 pPosition.x = rcWindow.left;
 pPosition.y = rcWindow.top;

 memcpy (pkPosition, &pPosition, sizeof (POINT));
}
```

This gets the window left, top, right, and bottom positions and stores them in a `RECT` like this:

```
GetWindowRect (m_hWindow, &rcWindow)
```

`GetWindowRect` usually takes the window handle as the first parameter and an address to a `RECT` structure to hold the values which is defined as this:

```
typedef struct _RECT {
    LONG left;
    LONG top;
    LONG right;
    LONG bottom;
} RECT;
```

This holds, respectively, the `left`, `top`, `right`, and `bottom` coordinates of a rectangle.

The `left` and the `top` fields of the structure hold the x and y coordinates of the window, respectively.

NOTE

Pass a pointer to a `POINT` structure to hold the position, because if you return the position, you can't assign it to any variable because `POINT` doesn't have an assignment operator.

SetSize

This function takes the width and height of the window as parameters and resizes the window. Its prototype is:

```
void SetSize (mrInt iWidth, mrInt iHeight)
```

And you set the window size using SetWindowPos as follows:

```
SetWindowPos(m_hWindow, HWND_TOP, 0, 0, iWidth, iHeight, SWP_NOMOVE);
```

This time you use SWP_NOMOVE as an argument to flags to tell SetWindowPos to resize the window and ignore the position parameters.

GetSize

This function returns a POINT structure with the width and height of the window. The prototype is as follows:

```
void GetSize (POINT * pkSize);
```

The x field of POINT holds the width of the window, and the y field holds the height of the window.

```
{
 RECT  rcWindow;
 POINT pSize;
  /* Get window position */
 GetWindowRect (m_hWindow, &rcWindow);

 pSize.x = rcWindow.right  - rcWindow.left;
 pSize.y = rcWindow.bottom - rcWindow.top;

 memcpy (pkSize, &pSize, sizeof (POINT)); }
```

You use GetWindowRect again to get the window position and size.

To get the width of the window, you subtract the left coordinate from the right coordinate, and to get the height you subtract the top coordinate from the bottom coordinate.

Show

The Show function is a function that hides ShowWindow. It takes the show state of the window and sets it. The function prototype is as follows:

```
void Show (mrInt iShow)
```

And the body is the following:

```
{
  /* Change window visibility */
 ShowWindow (m_hWindow, iShow);
}
```

Summary

Whoa! A crash course in Windows programming in one chapter was stressful, no? Fortunately, after you get the hang of it, Windows programming is easy because you usually work with the same code or very similar code.

Creating your first reusable class—mrWindow—enables you to create a basic window framework, which can be used in any project with just a few lines of code.

Questions and Answers

Q: What's the main difference between a 32-bit console application and a 32-bit windowed application?

A: A console application uses a text-only interface similar to UNIX and DOS systems. A windowed application has all the functionality of windows, menus, buttons, and so on.

Q: Why do you need a virtual class?

A: You use a virtual class to force the user to define a derived class and write his or her own Frame method. This ensures that everything works and all methods are implemented.

Q: Why should you use complicated code for the message handler instead of using a couple of global variables or functions?

A: As you learned in Chapter 9, global variables or functions shouldn't be used because they don't provide information hiding or namespace identification, and any function can wrongly change a global variable.

Exercises

1. What is the purpose of `PostQuitMessage`?
2. What is the logic behind making a real-time message loop?
3. What is the difference between `PeekMessage` and `GetMessage`?
4. Why should you create both a static and a nonstatic message handler in your window class?
5. Add an option to quit the program if `Frame` returns `mrFalse`.
6. Add the code necessary to the windows framework that maximizes the window when a `WM_CCREATE` message is received.
7. Add the code necessary to the windows framework so the user cannot resize the window.
8. Add the code necessary to the windows framework to prevent the window from being maximized or minimized.
9. Add the code necessary to the windows framework to make the user also select the background color.

CHAPTER 12

Introduction to DirectX

By now you should have a nice understanding of C++ programming, so I think you can move on to more cool stuff. If you have played a game the past couple of years, you probably have heard of DirectX, and now it's time to learn how to use it from a programmer's perspective.

For instructions on how to install the DirectX SDK, take a look at Appendix A, "What's on the CD."

What Is DirectX?

When Windows 95 was released, there was a saying among game programmers: "DOS until hell freezes over." What they meant was that, even if Windows 95 was a very good operating system for applications, it still wasn't too friendly for games, mostly because it lacked the control to use the hardware to its full capabilities.

Microsoft wanted to make its Windows operating system the predominant (which is today installed in about 90 percent of the computers in the world) operating system for all kinds of uses, from databases to the bleeding-edge 3D games. Microsoft realized that even if its new Windows was good, it could be made better. That was why they decided to develop DirectX.

DirectX is a set of interfaces (I will get back to this in a bit) which enable you to communicate with the available hardware in the computer without dealing with each specific card or input device in existence.

Each hardware manufacturer develops drivers for its hardware that are compatible with DirectX, relieving you of the trouble of worrying about specific hardware. Think of all hardware as a big black box that you don't need to know what is inside, only how to make it work from the outside (you don't need to know how an automobile motor works to be able to press the pedals and make it move, do you?).

Brief History of DirectX

DirectX has come a long way from where it started. At the time of writing, you are currently at the eighth incarnation of DirectX.

First released in 1995 with the name DirectX, Microsoft made it possible to create games that actually ran fast enough to be fun in Windows. This version was, in my opinion, more of a test bed than an actual SDK.

In 1996 Microsoft released version two of DirectX, now called, obviously, DirectX 2.0. The main change in the SDK was the inclusion of Direct3D, the 3D component of DirectX.

With the release of DirectX 3.0, Microsoft finally conquered the game market as well by finally creating an API that was fast, abstract, and not hard to use.

Microsoft released DirectX 5.0 later (no, you read it right, Microsoft never released DirectX 4.0) that was wonderful to work with. Most hardware manufacturers were developing drivers for their hardware that were compatible with DirectX, the API was stable and consistent, and the games looked pretty good.

In DirectX 6.0, Microsoft dropped the Direct3D Retained Mode, and it started to use Direct3D Immediate Mode exclusively.

> **NOTE**
>
> **Direct3D Immediate Mode enables you to control your application to the lowest level possible. On the other end was Direct3D Retained Mode which was a higher level API that made it easier to work with Direct3D but didn't offer the control programmers demanded.**

In DirectX 7.0, the new generation of Transformation and Lighting cards was supported and the Direct3DX utility library was included.

There weren't many big modifications in each new release of DirectX until the release of DirectX 8.0. Microsoft really put its bodies and minds to work to develop such a perfect API. Some components were blended to take more advantage of the hardware, the whole API was made simpler, and there are so many new cool things that it would be impossible to name them all.

And do you know what is the best thing of all? Even if you develop a game using DirectX 5.0 or 6.0, if the player has a version of DirectX that is the same or more recent than the one your game requires, the game will still work since DirectX is backward-compatible.

Why Use DirectX?

There are many advantages to using DirectX over using the other available APIs. DirectX is fast, stable, abstract, easy, and . . . did I mentioned fast?

Table 12.1 displays a comparison of DirectX, OpenGL/OpenAL/OpenIL, and the Windows API.

Table 12.1 DirectX, Open Libraries, and the Windows API Features

Feature	DirectX	OpenXX	Windows API
3D	Supported	[OpenGL]Supported	Not available
2D	Supported	[OpenGL]Supported but not designed for 2D	Supported
Audio	Supported	[OpenAL]Supported but not many hardware devices have drivers	Supported
Input	Supported	[OpenIL]Supported but not many hardware devices have drivers	Supported
Networking	Supported	Not available	Supported, but hard to work with
Compatibility	Almost all hardware	Some manufacturers are neglecting OpenGL support	Almost all hardware
Portability	Windows OS family	Almost every operating system	Windows OS only and Xbox only
Difficult to use	Easy	Easy	Intermediate
Documentation	Very well documented	Well documented	Well documented
Speed	Fast	Fast	Slow

In case you don't know, OpenGL, OpenAL and OpenIL are libraries that are available in various platforms for graphics (Open Graphics Library), audio (Open Audio Library), and input (Open Input Library).

After checking out Table 12.1 you probably have a good idea why using DirectX is the best choice. You have access to all the hardware components you need to create a game (3D, 2D, Input, Audio, Networking) in the same API.

Another possibility is to use OpenGL, OpenAL, and OpenIL or even mix OpenGL with the input part of DirectX (as shown in Figure 12.1), but I will focus only on DirectX programming.

DirectX Components

DirectX 8.0 is divided into six individual components. Microsoft tried to make each component as independent as possible. This made it possible to use any combination of them you want. I will not deal with DirectPlay, DirectShow, or DirectSetup, but I encourage you to try them out on your own.

Here's a small description of each component:

- **Microsoft DirectX Graphics.** This component was introduced in DirectX 8.0 merging both DirectDraw (2D) and Direct3D (3D) into one single API for any graphics programming. This blend was done to simplify the library and make the memory footprint lower. This also includes the Direct3DX utility library that offers help when doing 3D programming. The DirectX Graphics component will be used exclusively to develop your graphics library later.

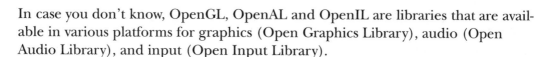

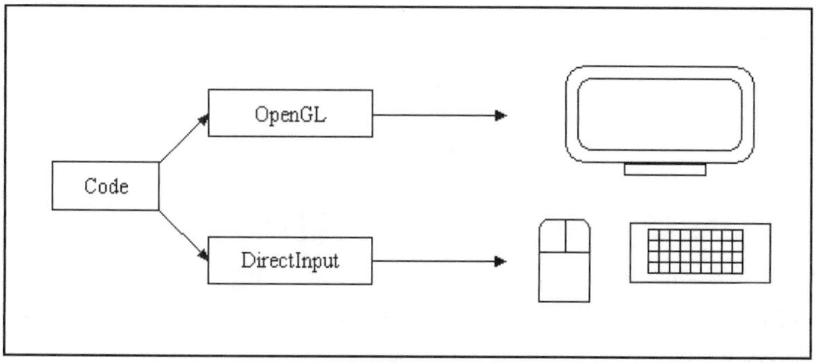

Figure 12.1

Mixing OpenGL and DirectInput.

- **Microsoft DirectX Audio.** This component was also introduced in DirectX 8.0 that was also a blend of two of the former components into a single API, DirectSound and DirectMusic. It enables you to play normal sounds, 3D sounds, music, and just about everything your sound card can handle.
- **Microsoft DirectInput.** This is the input component of DirectX. It handles all communication with the input hardware such as the mouse, keyboard, joystick, and other input devices like steering wheels, pedals, and force feedback devices.
- **Microsoft DirectPlay.** This is the networking component of DirectX. This part of DirectX was completely revamped with new interfaces and features. It enables you to create peer-to-peer and client/server games easily.
- **Microsoft DirectShow.** This component features support for playing and capturing multimedia streams. This component was derived from the old DirectX Media, which was a separate component from old versions of the DirectX SDK.
- **Microsoft DirectSetup.** This small component enables you to check for the version of DirectX installed and to install another version. There isn't much of interest to you unless you are developing install programs for your games.

How Does DirectX Work?

DirectX is made of a set of Dynamic Link Libraries (DLLs) and compatible drivers made by hardware manufacturers that allows almost direct communication with the hardware. To do this, Microsoft had to create an abstraction layer to allow programmers to work with DirectX as a big black box and let the core of DirectX send or receive the information from the hardware, as shown in Figure 12.2.

To be able to support a black box architecture and backward-compatibility, Microsoft used the Component Object Model (COM) to make DirectX work.

Hardware Abstraction Layer

DirectX Graphics provides hardware abstraction (the black box model) using a Hardware Abstraction Layer, or HAL. The hardware manufacturer develops the device interface that DirectX Graphics uses to display the graphics.

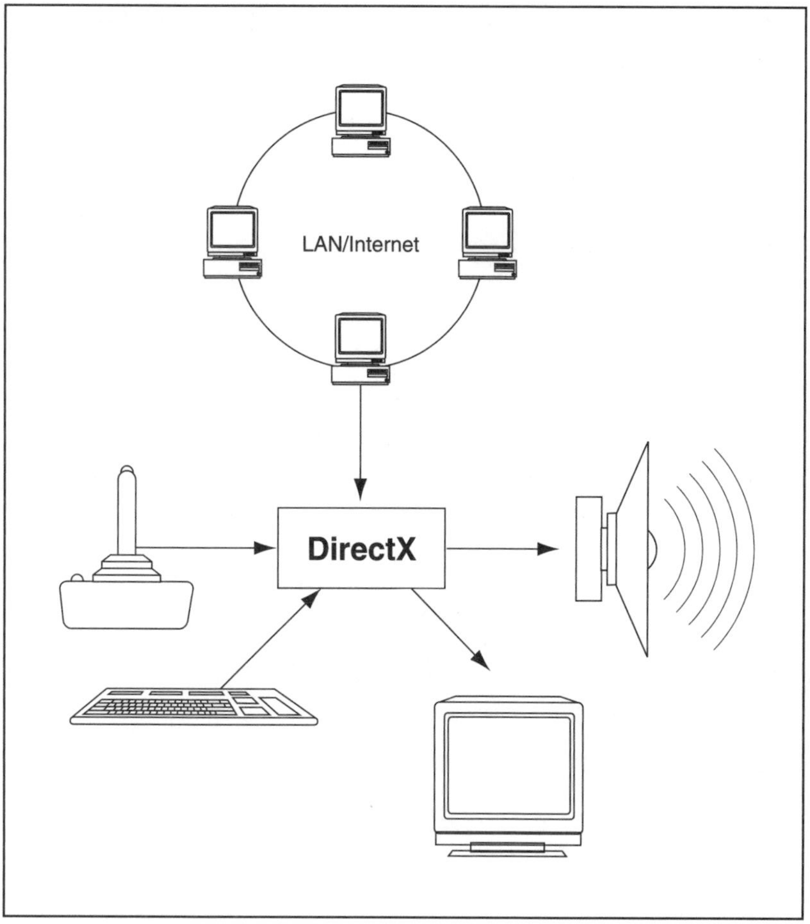

Figure 12.2

Overview of DirectX at work.

The programmer communicates with the HAL using a set of interfaces created by DirectX Graphics that are common to all hardware. Figure 12.3 shows how the same objective is performed by two different hardware devices but with the same code.

The Component Object Model

The Component Object Model, or COM, is a software design paradigm that, if implemented correctly, allows you to make software components that are reusable, independent, large, and easy to work with.

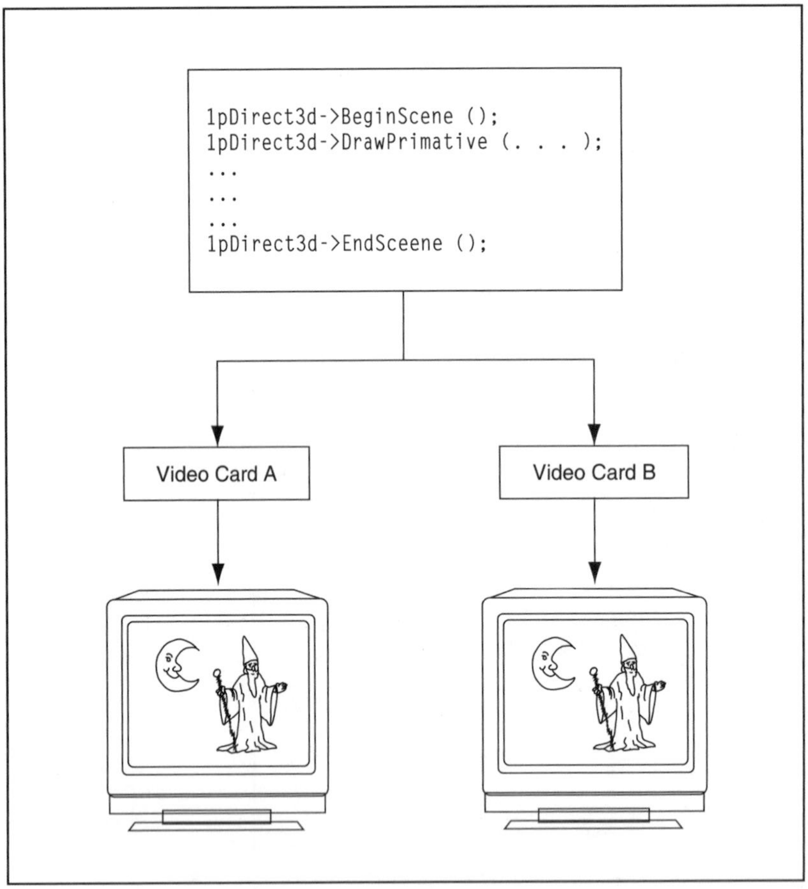

Figure 12.3

Same code, two hardware devices, same result.

> **NOTE**
>
> Creating a COM object that agrees with all specifications is a hard and complicated job. I will not go over the process of creating one, but if you feel adventurous and you have your OOP under your belt, check out the references section on links and books on how to create your own COM objects.

A COM object is a set of classes that implement a specific set of interfaces. Those classes, or interfaces, are used to work with the COM object itself.

There are many advantages when working with COM objects:

- COM interfaces can't be changed, so you don't need to worry about future updates.
- COM interfaces are always backward-compatible.
- COM is language-independent, which means if you develop a COM object in C++, you can access it from any language that supports COM.
- COM objects are normally stored in a DLL that can be easily upgraded.

Virtual Tables

When you call a COM object method, you call the method by using a Virtual Table, or v-table as it is commonly called. For example:

```
SomeInterface->lpVtbl->SomeMethod ();
```

Will call `SomeMethod` of the `SomeInterface` COM object by means of a virtual table, `lpVtbl`. Thankfully, if you are using a C++ compiler you can discard the `lpVtbl` referencing because COM objects and C++ classes are binary-compatible, so the C++ compiler automatically dereferences the virtual table which allows you to do the same thing as above using only the following:

```
SomeInterface->SomeMethod ();
```

Most COM object calls are done like the preceding line of code.

COM and DirectX

All DirectX objects are COM objects. I will not get too deep on the specifics of using them since they work as normal COM objects but I will discuss what is needed to work with them.

Each DirectX object is defined in a header file and implemented in a library file. A library file is a compiled file with implementations of code that can be reused and distributed without having to use the source code.

Usually, DirectX objects have the headers and library files names resembling the names of the objects. The following is a list of the ones you will be using:

d3d8.lib/d3d8.h

dsound.lib/dsound.h

dinput8.lib/dinput.h

dxguid.lib

While d3d8, dsound, and dinput8 are normal DirectX files, there is dxguid.lib that also has to be included in the project when you use DirectX. This file contains the globally unique identifiers (GUIDs) for DirectX interfaces.

How to Use DirectX with Visual C++

Because DirectX is a Microsoft product, making it work with Visual C++ is as easy as saying "yabba-dabba-do."

When you install the DirectX 8.0 SDK, at the end of installation, the setup program usually asks whether you want to automatically set up Visual C++ to use with DirectX 8.0 SDK. If this dialog box appears, answer yes and you can skip the rest of this section; if the dialog does not appear, read on.

To use DirectX in Visual C++, you need to set two paths where Visual C++ will look for DirectX. To do this go to Tools and then Options. A dialog box named Options will appear. You need to select the Directories tab. This should look like Figure 12.4.

In the Show Directories For: combo box, first select Include Files. If you haven't messed with Visual C+ much, three entries should be available in the listbox. You will need to create a new entry for the DirectX headers. To do this, click the tiny dotted square with a sort of yellow star on the corner. A textbox will appear in the list, either type the correct path for the DirectX header files (usually DirectXSDKDirectory\Include) or click the button on the right to find the directory.

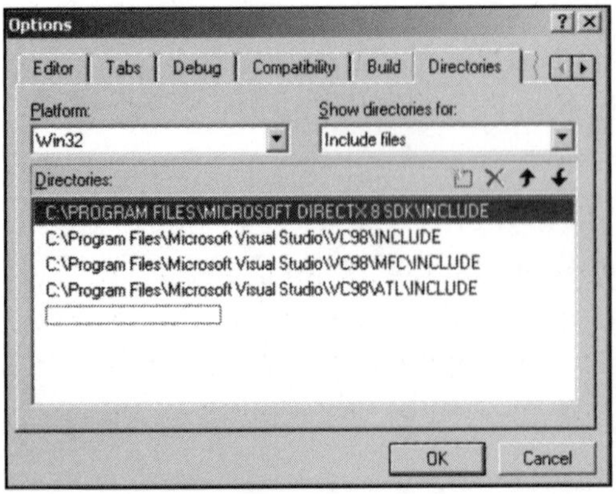

Figure 12.4

Directories options.

Now select Library Files from the Show Directories For: combo box and do the same as before but now for the library files (usually DirectXSDKDirectory\Lib).

Don't forget to move both the directories to the top of the list. This is needed because if you don't, Visual C++ will use the first headers or library files that it can find, and because Visual C++ ships with DirectX 3.0 SDK, you would end up using the old DirectX 3.0 files.

Next, include the libraries in the project. This will tell the compiler to link them to the final executable. To do this you go to the Project menu, select Settings, and when the Project Settings dialog box appears select the Link tab. In the Object/library Modules: textbox, type the name of the library files you will be using in the project; for example, if you will be using only DirectX Audio type dsound.lib, and you're ready to go. If you want to use any other component, you have to use the appropriate library files.

Summary

I know, I know, it was a rather small and sort of boring chapter. No code, no designs, but knowing how things work will help you understand the following chapters' code, and it will make you sound cool when you start shouting COM programming jargon in an IRC chat.

Questions and Answers

Q: OpenGL is supported in many systems; why not use OpenGL instead of DirectX?

A: While OpenGL is widely supported, many of the new features in hardware cards can only be accessed by using OpenGL extensions, which make programming more complicated. Also, DirectX is frequently updated whereas OpenGL has remained in version 1.2 for a long while.

Q: If COM is so good, why not use it for everything you develop?

A: COM is a good programming paradigm but not suitable for all projects. For example, the overhead in time when developing a small library for graphics would be too high in comparison to the actual library development. COM is good for large systems that feature a lot of code and have many other developers use the libraries.

Exercises

1. Name three reasons to use DirectX over the other APIs.
2. What is the basis of DirectX?
3. What is the v-table?
4. Name two advantages of using COM objects in programming.

CHAPTER 13

DirectX Graphics

Finally you will be creating some graphics. In this chapter you will learn the inner workings of DirectX Graphics, and I will go over the basics of animation.

At the end of the chapter you will be presented with some 2D techniques, some of which require a little math knowledge. Nothing fancy, mostly high school algebra and trigonometry. Just in case you are really rusty, take a look at Chapter 18, "The Mathematical Side of Games," in Part 3 whenever you run into trouble.

Interfaces You Will Be Using

As you saw in the preceding chapter, all DirectX components are COM components. They are based on interfaces (they are very similar to classes) to enable communication between the hardware and the code. DirectX Graphics is no exception; it is solely based on interfaces to be able to work.

There are various interfaces you will be using during the development of your library, such as the following:

```
IDirect3D8
IDirect3DDevice8
IDirect3DSurface8
IDirect3DTexture8
```

Each of these interfaces has its own purpose in Direct3D (I will refer to DirectX Graphics as Direct3D from now on).

For example, `IDirect3D8` is the main interface object for Direct3D. This object will be created so you can start using Direct3D and creating Direct3D devices. You will be using this interface to create the main device you will use for your games and also to get information on the available video modes. Also, various monitors and cards are supported in Windows 98 and above, and Direct3D enables you to use the ones you want, but for the sake of simplicity (and believe me when I say it is for your own good) you will assume that there is only one video card and monitor installed, this is basically using the default card the user has installed.

`IDirect3DDevice8` is your main concern when working with Direct3D. After you create this device using an `IDirect3D` interface, you will control what is displayed to the screen using this device. IDirect3DDevice8 has many methods, but you will only be using a few of them because most of them are used mainly in 3D programming.

IDirect3DSurface8 is the simplest Direct3D representation of an image that resembles old DirectX 7.0 and earlier DirectDraw surfaces. This kind of surface can be copied to the screen at any position but with many limitations, which you will see in a few moments.

The IDirect3DTexture8 is more of a 3D interface than 2D. In 3D terms, a texture is an image (or part of one) that is applied to a polygon. If you think about it, it is basically what happens in reality. Each object has one or several textures associated with it, which is what you use to visually differentiate materials.

There is another interface you won't be using, but it is important to know. IDirect3DVertexBuffer8 is an interface that is used to store a polygon, but before proceeding, take a look at how a polygon is stored in 3D, as shown in Figure 13.1.

A polygon is a collection of points that define a closed area. Those points are commonly called vertices (or vertexes). Each vertex is a 3D point in the world. An IDirect3DVertexBuffer8 is just a container for all the vertices you want. You will use a 4D vector (yes, four elements, but you will see that in a bit) to create a 2D polygon that is always facing the screen.

Using vertex buffers is probably the fastest way to output images to the screen, but also the most complicated because you need to update the buffer every time you want to draw a new image. For this reason you will use a function Direct3D supplies—DrawPrimitiveUP—which will use an array of vertices to draw the images. If you are looking for the very best performance possible, you should look at the DirectX documentation about vertex buffers. See Figure 13.2 for an example.

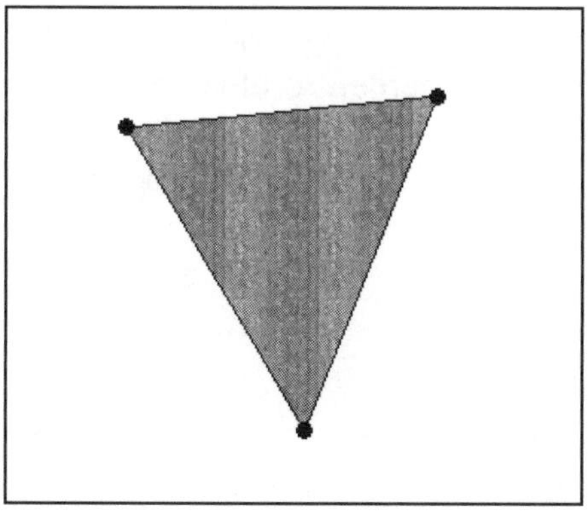

Figure 13.1

A polygon in 3D.

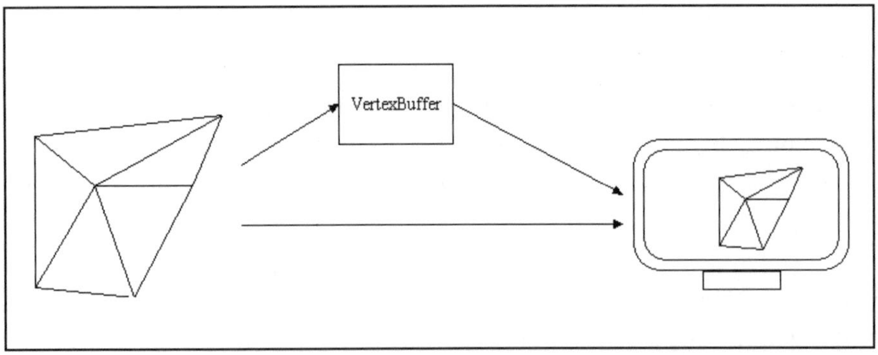

Figure 13.2

Vertex buffers versus direct output.

Using Direct3D: The Basics

Using Direct3D isn't difficult, but there are a few steps that must be completed before being able to put a simple image on the screen.

Later you will develop the graphics part of Mirus which will take care of almost every step mentioned here, but for now, let's see what you need to do, and how to do it:

1. Create an `IDirect3D8` object to be able to use Direct3D.
2. Create an `IDirect3DDevice8` interface from the `IDirect3D8` object created previously.
3. Set the screen display mode and resolution.
4. Create a texture or a surface.
5. Copy the texture or surface to the screen using `IDirect3DDevice8` and repeat until quitting the program.
6. Clean up every object by releasing them.

The following program initializes Direct3D and clears the screen to blue every frame (you won't do any drawing for now). Figure 13.3 illustrates this application.

```
 /* '01 Main.cpp' */

 /* Mirus window framework header */
#include "mrWindow.h"
 /* Direct3D header */
#include <d3d8.h>
```

```

 /* Custom derived class */
class D3DWindow : public mrWindow
{
  /* Direct3D interfaces */
 LPDIRECT3D8              m_pD3D;
 LPDIRECT3DDEVICE8        m_pD3DDevice;
public:
  /* Constructor / Destructor */
 D3DWindow (void) {};
 ~D3DWindow (void) {};

  /* Setup and shutdown Direct3D */
 HRESULT SetupDirect3D (void);
 HRESULT KillDirect3D (void);

  /* Window manipulation functions */
 mrBool32 Frame (void);
};

 /* Initializes Direct3D */
HRESULT D3DWindow::SetupDirect3D (void)
{
  /* Create the Direct3D object */
 if (NULL == (m_pD3D = Direct3DCreate8 (D3D_SDK_VERSION) ) )
 {
  return E_FAIL;
 }

  /* Get the current display mode so we can know what bitdepth
     we are */
 D3DDISPLAYMODE d3ddm;
 if (FAILED (m_pD3D->GetAdapterDisplayMode (D3DADAPTER_DEFAULT,
                                             &d3ddm) ) )
 {
  return E_FAIL;
 }

  /* Fill in the present parameters */
 D3DPRESENT_PARAMETERS d3dpp;
```

```
 ZeroMemory( &d3dpp, sizeof(d3dpp) );
  /* We want windowed mode */
 d3dpp.Windowed    = TRUE;
  /* Discard this */
 d3dpp.SwapEffect = D3DSWAPEFFECT_DISCARD;
  /* Same format as the current format
     (we got this from g_pD3D->GetAdapterDisplayMode)  */
 d3dpp.BackBufferFormat = d3ddm.Format;

  /* Create the device */
 if (FAILED(m_pD3D->CreateDevice(D3DADAPTER_DEFAULT,D3DDEVTYPE_HAL,
                                  m_hWindow,
                                  D3DCREATE_SOFTWARE_VERTEXPROCESSING,
                                  &d3dpp,
                                  &m_pD3DDevice ) ) )
 {
  return E_FAIL;
 }

 return D3D_OK;
}

 /* Shutdowns Direct3D */
HRESULT D3DWindow::KillDirect3D (void)
{
   /* If any of the Direct3D objects exist, release them */
 if (NULL != m_pD3D)
 {
  m_pD3D->Release ();
 }
 if (NULL != m_pD3DDevice)
 {
  m_pD3DDevice->Release ();
 }

 return D3D_OK;

}

```

```
/* Clears the screen to blue */
mrBool32 D3DWindow::Frame (void)
{
  /* Clear the window to blue */
 m_pD3DDevice->Clear (0, NULL, D3DCLEAR_TARGET,
                      D3DCOLOR_XRGB (0,0,255), 1.0f, 0);

  /* Start rendering */
 m_pD3DDevice->BeginScene();
 m_pD3DDevice->EndScene();

  /* Present the rendered scene to the screen */
 m_pD3DDevice->Present (NULL, NULL, NULL, NULL);

 return mrTrue;
}

/* "WinMain Vs. main" */
int WINAPI WinMain (HINSTANCE hInstance, HINSTANCE hPrevInst,
                    LPSTR lpCmdLine, int nShowCmd)
{
  /* Our window */
 D3DWindow  kWindow;

  /* Create window */
 kWindow.Create (hInstance, "D3D Demo");

  /* Setup Direct3D */
 kWindow.SetupDirect3D ();

  /* Enter message loop */
 kWindow.Run ();

  /* Shutdown Direct3D */
 kWindow.KillDirect3D ();

 return 0;
}
```

Figure 13.3

Your Direct3D application.

The first obvious difference between this class and the previous chapter window class is the declaration of two data members. These are the Direct3D (line 12) object and the Direct3D Device (line 13) object.

NOTE

The preceding program uses the previously developed Mirus window framework.

NOTE

You never use an interface directly but by using a pointer to it. DirectX has all its interfaces defined as pointers. You can get any definition for the interface by removing the I before the interface name and adding LP, and typing the name in uppercase.

TIP

For this program to compile fully you have to link d3d8.lib to it. For the program to run you need to have DirectX 8.0 installed.

You have also added two new methods to it:

```
HRESULT SetupDirect3D (void);
HRESULT KillDirect3D (void);
```

These will be the methods you will use to set up and shut down Direct3D. You will be reusing these methods during the rest of the chapter, so pay attention to how they work.

Apart from those two new methods, you haven't changed the class much from before except that you have implemented the method `Frame` differently to work with Direct3D as you will see.

Before digging into `SetupDirect3D`, let me just go over one thing. Almost every function in Direct3D (or DirectX for that matter) returns a type `HRESULT`. This type is a 32-bit simple value, but there is no guarantee that it won't change in future versions of DirectX.

So, how does error-checking work in DirectX? If each function returns an `HRESULT` value, then there are two ways to check whether a function was successful. You will use two macros provided by Microsoft to see whether a function was successful: `SUCCEEDED` and `FAILED`.

The first macro returns `true` if the function was executed correctly, and the second returns `true` if there was some error when executing the function. So, there are two ways to do the error checking; the first is by using `SUCCEEDED`:

```
if (SUCCEEDED (SomeDirectXFunction))
{
 /* Continue to run */
}
else
{
 /* Something wrong happened, handle error */
}
```

Which will run the code block following the `if` statement after the call to `SomeDirectXFunction` was successful or the code block next to `else` if it wasn't.

Using `FAILED`, you can do it like so:

```
if (FAILED (SomeDirectXFunction))
{
 /* Something wrong happened, handle error */
}
/* Continue to run */
```

Which will execute the code block next to the if statement if SomeDirectXFunction wasn't successful, and would continue to run the program.

Both ways have their uses, but you will use FAILED most of the time because it is more intuitive.

So, let's start by going over SetupDirect3D. You have already verified that it returns an HRESULT type and that it doesn't take any parameters. You use HRESULT as return type mostly for convenience, when you develop Mirus, you will use your own error code.

The first thing you do in SetupDirect3D is create a Direct3D object, which is done using the function Direct3DCreate8 (line 31), which is defined as:

```
IDirect3D8 * Direct3DCreate8 (UINT SDKVersion);
```

Which returns a pointer to an IDirect3D8 (LPDIRECT3D8) interface. If this pointer is NULL, then the function Direct3DCreate8 failed; otherwise, it points to a valid IDirect3D8 interface.

Its only parameter is the version of the SDK you are using. You should always use D3D_SDK_VERSION to ensure that you use the correct header files. D3D_SDK_VERSION is defined by DirectX.

So, in the code you assign the returned interface from Direct3DCreate8 to m_pD3D, and check whether it is NULL. If it is, you will return E_FAIL, which is also defined by Direct3D to describe an undetermined error. You will use it to symbolize that something went wrong.

As you may or may not know, when you are running Windows, you have your video card/monitor set to a certain resolution. There are various possible combinations of resolutions and modes, but the more common are 16-bit and 32-bit resolution using 640×480, 800×600, or 1024×768.

The sizes represent the number of pixels visible on the monitor, and the higher the resolution, the smaller the pixels, the smoother objects look. Old games used to use a resolution of 320×200 or 320×240, which was pretty low compared to today's standards.

What about those 16-bit and 32-bit numbers? Well, they are usually called the bit depth or color depth and represent the number bits that describe the color of the pixel which in turn dictates the number of possible colors that the monitor can display. Colors are stored in the computer as combinations of red, green, and blue (and sometimes alpha) that can form various colors.

So, what is the difference between the two? Well, a 16-bit mode can only assign a significant number of bits to a color, as shown in Figure 13.4.

Figure 13.4

Different 16-bit modes and memory alignment.

As you can see, you have five bits for red, six for green, and five for blue (called 565). This 16 bits can form 65,536 different colors.

> **NOTE**
>
> **There is an extra bit for green since your eyes are more sensitive to green light than red or blue. If you feel a little sadistic, try going to the local library and picking up a color theory book to better understand how color works.**

Then you have 32-bit mode. In this mode, each color component (alpha, red, green and blue) has eight bits for around sixteen million colors (called *ARGB*). This is more than what your eyes can differentiate. See Figure 13.5.

The problem with this is that even if theoretically this all works fine, practically it doesn't. Some video cards have different formats for 16-bit and 32-bit colors such as 555 mode for 16-bit, which discards the highest byte, or XRGB for 32-bit mode, which discards the highest eight bytes (the alpha component).

Don't worry about other bit depths because they are being more and more neglected in games nowadays.

So, what does this all have to do with Direct3D? Well, if you want to use Direct3D you have two choices: use it in windowed mode (like the previous program) where

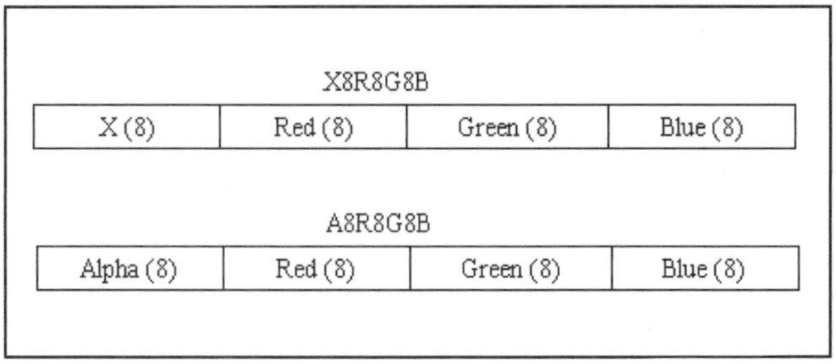

Figure 13.5

Different 32-bit modes and memory alignment.

you need to know the current resolution so you can create your device accordingly, or use it in full screen mode where you need to tell Direct3D which is the exact resolution you want.

Setting both types is practically the same except that when you use windowed mode you need to use the current Windows resolution, and if you are in full screen mode you need to set the exact resolution (which type of resolution, 565, 555, XRGB).

NOTE

You will use 32-bit modes throughout the rest of this section. This is possibly the best way to work because almost every card nowadays supports 32-bit mode and uses the ARGB format.

When there are significant differences between 16-bit and 32-bit mode, you will pay special attention to them.

Okay, back to your program. You need to get the current Windows display mode to get the bit depth information. You will do this with `IDirect3D::GetAdapterDisplayMode` that is defined as:

```
HRESULT IDirect3D8::GetAdapterDisplayMode (
 UINT Adapter,
 D3DDISPLAYMODE * pMode);
```

That returns an `HRESULT` that you should test for errors, and takes as the first parameter the adapter (video card) you want to query. You will use `D3DADAPTER_DEFAULT` that means that you will use the primary (default) adapter.

The second parameter is a pointer to a `D3DDISPLAYMODE` that will hold the current display mode. `D3DDISPLAYMODE` is defined as:

```
typedef struct _D3DDISPLAYMODE {
 UINT Width;
 UINT Height;
 UINT RefreshRate;
 D3DFORMAT Format;
} D3DDISPLAYMODE;
```

Where the first two members are the width and height of the current mode. The third member is the refresh rate of the monitor; that is, how many times per second the screen is updated. The last parameter is the mode format (bit depth). This is an enumerated type, which describes just about every possible mode Windows and Direct3D can support. You will only care for the more common generic ones (since there are modes specific to textures and surfaces), which are described in Table 13.1.

TABLE 13.1 Direct3D Commonly Used Formats

Enumerated Type	Description
D3DFMT_R5G6B5	16-bit format using five bits for red, six bits for green, and five bits for blue
D3DFMT_X1R5G5B5	16-bit format using five bits for red, five bits for green, and five bits for blue
D3DFMT_A1R5G5B5	16-bit format using one bit for alpha, five bits for red, five bits for green, and five bits for blue
D3DFMT_A8R8G8B8	32-bit format using eight bits for alpha, eight bits for red, eight bits for green, and eight bits for blue
D3DFMT_X8R8G8B8	32-bit format using eight bits for red, eight bits for green, and eight bits for blue

Now that you have this information, it is time to start filling a D3DPRESENT_PARAMETERS structure with them. This structure is used to create the device and holds all the information about the mode you are trying to set.

D3DPRESENT_PARAMETERS is defined as:

```
typedef struct _D3DPRESENT_PARAMETERS_ {
 UINT BackBufferWidth;
 UINT BackBufferHeight;
 D3DFORMAT BackBufferFormat;
 UINT BackBufferCount;

 D3DMULTISAMPLE_TYPE MultiSampleType;

 D3DSWAPEFFECT SwapEffect;
 HWND hDeviceWindow;
 BOOL Windowed;
 BOOL EnableAutoDepthStencil;
 D3DFORMAT AutoDepthStencilFormat;
 DWORD Flags;
```

```
 UINT FullScreen_RefreshRateInHz;
 UINT FullScreen_PresentationInterval;
} D3DPRESENT_PARAMETERS;
```

You don't need to care for all the elements in this structure for windowed mode, but even so, let's see the ones you use in the code for now and you will see the rest later. So, before you start setting elements let's clear the structure with `ZeroMemory` (line 47).

`ZeroMemory` fills a buffer with zeros and is defined as:

```
VOID ZeroMemory (
 PVOID Destination,
 DWORD Length);
```

Where `Destination` is a pointer to a buffer of any type and `Length` is the number of bytes to set to zero.

The first element you use if `Windowed`. This `BOOL` defines whether the mode you will be using is windowed or not (full screen). Since you are using windowed you will set it to `TRUE` (line 49).

Next you have `SwapEffect`, which is the way the information will be copied to the screen. There are various methods but you will supply `D3DSWAPEFFECT_DISCARD` (line 51), which allows Direct3D to choose the best method to do the copy.

Finally, you set the back buffer mode with the information you got from `GetAdapterDisplayMode` previously (line 54).

Even though you could specify a couple of more members of the structure, you won't since they are mostly used for other coding (3D and special effects) that you won't use during the rest of the book.

You are now ready to create your device. Exciting, huh? You do this by calling `IDirect3DDevice8::CreateDevice` which is defined as:

```
HRESULT IDirect3DDevice8::CreateDevice (
 UINT Adapter,
 D3DDEVTYPE DeviceType,
 HWND hFocusWindow,
 DWORD BehaviorFlags,
 D3DPRESENT_PARAMETERS * pPresentationParameters,
 IDirect3DDevice8 ** ppReturnedDeviceInterface);
```

The first parameter of CreateDevice is the adapter you will be using. Since you are interested only in the primary adapter you will use D3DADAPTER_DEFAULT.

Next you have the type of device you want to create. Here you have two choices: create a hardware device (D3DDEVTYPE_HAL) or a software device (D3DDEVTYPE_REF). So what is the difference? While a hardware device is faster than a software device, it may not support all the functionality you want; in other words, a software device is slower but supports everything in Direct3D. You will use a hardware device for the rest of the chapter, in case you are having problems with the programs, try using a software device.

Next you have a handle to the focus window, which is the window Direct3D will control, in your case, m_hWindow.

Next you have the behavior of the device, this is, how you know that Direct3D works, you will be using D3DCREATE_SOFTWARE_VERTEXPROCESSING, which will make Direct3D use a software vertex processing method. Other possibilities for this member are described in Table 13.2.

TABLE 13.2 Direct3D Device Behavior

Flag	Description
D3DCREATE_FPU_PRESERVE	Specifies that the application needs double precision FPU or FPU exceptions enabled.
D3DCREATE_HARDWARE_VERTEXPROCESSING	Specifies a hardware vertex processing.
D3DCREATE_MIXED_VERTEXPROCESSING	Specifies a mixed (both software and hardware) vertex processing.
D3DCREATE_MULTITHREADED	Requests that Direct3D be multithread safe.
D3DCREATE_PUREDEVICE	Specifies that Direct3D should not emulate any service for vertex processing.

Next you have a pointer to a D3DPRESENT_PARAMETERS that will specify how the information is presented to the screen, you will use the structure you filled previously.

Finally you have a pointer to a pointer to an IDirect3DDevice8 interface. This will be the created device.

And you have the device created. If you were creating a full screen program, at this time the screen resolution had already been changed, but since you are using a windowed Direct3D program you don't see much difference.

NOTE

From now on, for any Direct3D function that returns HRESULT, it will not be explicitly explained and it will be assumed that it returns an HRESULT type that should be tested for success with either FAILED or SUCCEEDED.

Next you will analyze KillDirect3D. This function is responsible for cleaning up your DirectX Graphics mess. What it does is check whether either the IDirect3D object and the IDirect3DDevice object are valid, and if so, releases them (lines 73 through 80).

Next you have Frame. If you remember from the previous chapter, this function is called every frame. This is where you will develop your rendering (rendering is the same as drawing but it's a more 3D term). You will use it due to the 3D nature of Direct3D code.

There are four important steps here, which are:

1. Clearing the screen to a certain color.
2. Start rendering process.
3. End rendering process.
4. Present the rendered scene to the screen.

The first step is done by IDirect3DDevice8::Clear that clears the screen and is defined as:

```
HRESULT IDirect3DDevice8::Clear (
 DWORD Count,
 CONST D3DRECT * pRects,
 DWORD Flags,
 D3DCOLOR Color,
 float Z,
 DWORD Stencil);
```

Where the first parameter is the number of rectangles you want to clear, and the second parameter the rectangles. Since you want to clear the entire screen, you use zero for the first parameter and `NULL` for the second.

Next is the `Flags` parameter. This parameter defines which surfaces will be cleared. Since you are doing basic 2D, you will only clear the render target. If you ever start learning 3D you will be able to use this function to clear different surfaces.

Next is the color you want to clear the back buffer to, it is of type `D3DCOLOR` which is the same as a `DWORD`.

NOTE

A `D3DCOLOR` type in Direct3D is defined as each component having eight bits and being in this order: alpha, red, green, blue.

The next two parameters you don't need to worry about because they are for 3D use only.

Next you have to start rendering. This informs Direct3D you will be sending information down the pipeline and you do this with `IDirect3DDevice8::BeginScene` that is defined as:

```
HRESULT IDirect3DDevice8::BeginScene (void);
```

Which is very simple since it has no parameters.

It will be here that you will do the rendering, in this case, you don't do anything so you just leave it like this.

Next you need to inform Direct3D you will end rendering using `Direct3DDevice8::EndScene` which is defined as:

```
HRESULT IDirect3DDevice8::EndScene (void);
```

Which again is very simple.

Finally you need to present what you rendered to the screen, which is done with `IDirect3DDevice8::Present`. This method is responsible for getting all the things you rendered presented to the screen and is defined as:

```
HRESULT IDirect3DDevice8::Present (
 CONST RECT * pSourceRect,
 CONST RECT * pDestRect,
 HWND hDestWindowOverride,
 CONST RGNDATA * pDirtyRegion);
```

Where the first parameter is the rectangle of the back buffer (you will see what this is in a bit) you want to copy to the screen, and since you want to copy the whole thing, you use NULL. Next is the destination rectangle, which is the rectangle in the screen you want to copy to, since you want to use the entire screen, you use NULL again. If you only want to copy to a certain rectangle in the screen, you would specify the rectangle here. Figure 13.6 shows a possible situation for it.

Next is the target window where Direct3D should copy the buffer, since you want to use the same window you created the device with, you use NULL.

Finally, the last parameter is not used and must be NULL. You also need to clean up after Direct3D, so in KillDirect3D you need to check whether the objects were created (by checking if they point to something valid), and if they were, you need to release them.

Releasing Direct3D objects is always done the same way. Use some example code for an arbitrary object, and then you can just use it anywhere you want to release an object without having to be specific about the type:

```
if (Direct3DObject != NULL)
{
 Direct3DObject->Release ();
 Direct3DObject = NULL;
}
```

Figure 13.6

One screen multiplayer.

Which will release the Direct3D object and then point that object to `NULL` (you don't need to do this if you know that the object will not be used again during the rest of the program).

In `WinMain` you also need to call `SetupDirect3D` before `mrWindow::Run` (line 114) and `KillDirect3D` just after (line 120).

See, your first Direct3D program. Sure it doesn't do much, but it is the starting point to all the other Direct3D code.

You will use the code developed in the next few chapters by only adding the new features to it without modifying the base code; this allows you to play with Direct3D without having to worry about Direct3D setup and shutdown.

Surfaces, Buffers, and Swap Chains

Direct3D offers you many advanced features, but some aspects of it are still common to other APIs and graphics theory in general. These are surfaces (or images), buffers (screen images), and chains (order of chains to be displayed).

Surfaces

A *surface* is the most basic image you can store using Direct3D. These images can be copied to the screen but unfortunately don't support many things such as alpha blending, rotating, color keying, sizing (you will see what these techniques are in a bit), and other stuff.

In Direct3D, surfaces are mostly used to show big images, such as splash or intro images, to the screen. Surfaces have the advantage that they can be of any size (as long as the computer can handle them), which makes using a 640×480 image very easy.

> **NOTE**
>
> **Until DirectX 8.0, a surface was one of the most important aspects of graphics programming. Surfaces were used for just about everything, especially in 2D programming where they were the only means to put stuff on the screen.**
>
> **Microsoft has decided that in DirectX 8.0, surfaces played almost no part in development (mostly due to their limitations) and almost made surfaces nonexistent.**

A surface can also be used to access the front and back buffer, as you will see next.

> **NOTE**
> In DirectX 8.0, surfaces can only exist in system memory.

Buffers

In Direct3D, there are two types of buffers, the front buffer and back buffers. While an application can have various back buffers, there can only be one front buffer.

The differences between the front and back buffer aren't much. They share the same properties, size, and format. What makes them different is the fact that the front buffer is the buffer that you see (what is on the screen) while the back buffer is the buffer you draw to.

While both buffers are Direct3D surfaces, you can only get access to the back buffer. Accessing the front buffer is unnecessary and, as such, Direct3D only allows you to retrieve a copy of the front buffer, not the buffer itself. The reason for this is that if you write directly to the front buffer, there will be flickering.

> **NOTE**
> *Flickering* is the term used when you are seeing the screen being drawn (not changing, but actually drawn).

You may be asking, how can it be? If you only see the front buffer, and you draw to the back buffer, what is going on? I will explain this next.

Swap Chains

Now that you know what a front and a back buffer are, let's see how they relate to swap chains.

As stated before, when you want to draw something on the screen, you do it by drawing it to the back buffer and then presenting it to the front buffer (remember `IDirect3DDevice8::Present`). What happens is that when you finish drawing to the back buffer, you swap the front and back buffers, making the back buffer the front buffer and vice versa. This makes the back buffer visible, and you will have access to the old front buffer (which is now the back buffer).

To make it a little easier, let's go over a completely ridiculous example that shares the same logic.

It's more than probable that you have seen one of those cartoons where for some reason a train is running on only two small tracks. The train is on one segment of the track, and when it leaves the last segment, the segment is moved to the front of the other segment (usually by some cartoon that for some reason runs faster than the train) so the train can continue, and then the back one is moved to the front again, and the back to the front until someone reaches the destination. Consider each segment of track a buffer. Each track is used, and when it isn't needed, it is sent to the back of the chain.

Figure 13.7 shows a possible example of a swap chain with two back buffers. While Direct3D supports various back buffers, most applications only use one or two of them. During the rest of the book you will only use one.

Rendering Surfaces

Now that the beautiful truth about surfaces has been uncovered, let's make a small demo that shows a surface in the screen using Direct3D.

TIP

To make the code smaller, there aren't as many error checks to Direct3D functions as there should be. Almost every function of Direct3D should be tested with the `FAILED` macro and if any error occurred, it should be handled correctly. From now on you will only check critical functions for failure.

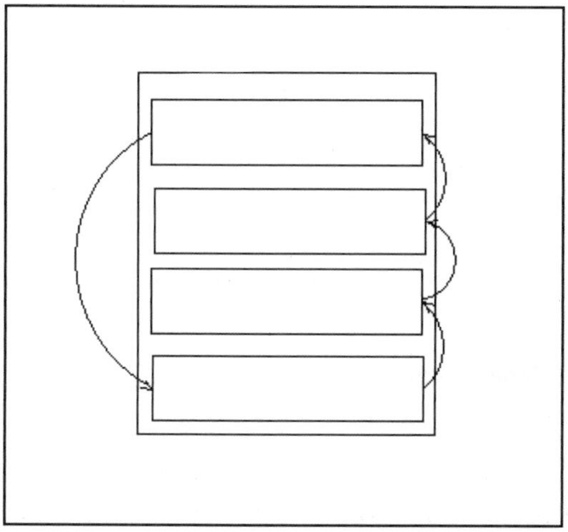

Figure 13.7

Direct3D swap chain.

Using the last demo framework code, you will change only the class definition (to add a surface interface) and change the Direct3D-only related functions to be able to render a simple surface to the screen:

```
/* ... */
 10:  /* Custom derived class */
 11: class D3DWindow : public mrWindow
 12: {
 13:   /* Direct3D interfaces */
 14:  LPDIRECT3D8              m_pD3D;
 15:  LPDIRECT3DDEVICE8        m_pD3DDevice;
 16:
 17:   /* Direct3D surface interface */
 18:  LPDIRECT3DSURFACE8       m_pD3DSurface;
 19:   /* Direct3D current format */
 20:  mrUInt32                 m_iD3DFormat;
 21:
 22: public:
 23:   /* Constructor / Destructor */
 24:  D3DWindow (void) {};
 25:  ~D3DWindow (void) {};
 26:
 27:   /* Setup and shutdown Direct3D */
 28:  HRESULT SetupDirect3D (void);
 29:  HRESULT KillDirect3D (void);
 30:
 31:   /* Window manipulation functions */
 32:  mrBool32 Frame (void);
 33: };
```

Here you have only added the surface interface to the class (line 18). This is the object you will be using to show something to the screen.

```
 35:  /* Initializes Direct3D */
 36: HRESULT D3DWindow::SetupDirect3D (void)
 37: {
/* ... */
 76:   /* Create the surface */
 77:  if (FAILED (m_pD3DDevice->CreateImageSurface (256, 256,
 78:                                               (D3DFORMAT) m_iD3DFormat,
 79:                                               &m_pD3DSurface ) ) )
 80:
```

```
{
 return E_FAIL;
}
```

After you have initialized Direct3D, you need to create the surface object, which is done using `IDirect3DDevice8::CreateImageSurface` that is defined as:

```
HRESULT IDirect3DDevice8::CreateImageSurface (
 UINT Width,
 UINT Height,
 D3DFORMAT Format,
 IDirect3DSurface8 ** ppSurface);
```

Where the first two parameters are the surface size. The next parameter is the surface format, which is the way the format will be stored. See Table 13.1 for a list of the common Direct3D formats. The last parameter is a pointer to a pointer of type `IDirect3DSurface8`, which is the address of `m_pD3DSurface` that is also a pointer.

Before proceeding, let me explain a little thing first. A surface, while it looks and behaves like a 2D array, isn't stored like that. To be able to write or read from it like an array, you need to lock the surface, so Direct3D returns a pointer to an array, which can be accessed. This is what you do next:

```
 /* Lock surface */
D3DLOCKED_RECT kLockedRect;
m_pD3DSurface->LockRect (&kLockedRect, NULL, 0);

 /* Cast a pointer to point to the first pixel */
DWORD * piSurfaceBuffer = (DWORD *) kLockedRect.pBits;
```

To lock a surface you just need to call the `LockRect` method of the surface. `LockRect` will lock the surface and if successful will return a structure with the information on the locked surface. `LockRect` is defined as:

```
HRESULT IDirect3DSurface8::LockRect (
 D3DLOCKED_RECT * pLockedRect,
 CONST RECT * pRect,
 DWORD Flags)
```

The first parameter of `LockRect` is a pointer to a `D3DLOCKED_RECT` structure that defines the locked surface, as you will see in a bit. Next, you have a pointer to a `RECT` structure, this defines the area you want to lock in the surface, since you want to lock the entire surface you will use `NULL`. The last parameter is the flags, as you want to lock the rectangle. The possible flags you can use are in Table 13.3.

TABLE 13.3 IDirect3DSurface8::LockRect Flags

Flag	Description
D3DLOCK_NO_DIRTY_UPDATE	Don't add a dirty region to the surface. Dirty regions are the parts of the surface that are copied when a copy operation takes place.
D3DLOCK_NOSYSLOCK	Don't hold a system-wide critical section. Enables the system to perform other duties for the duration of the lock.
D3DLOCK_READONLY	Surface is locked to read only operations.

The first parameter, as stated, is a structure containing the information about the locked surface (or rectangle if you have used a RECT structure as the second parameter). It is defined as:

```
typedef struct _D3DLOCKED_RECT
{
 INT Pitch;
 void * pBits;
} D3DLOCKED_RECT;
```

The first parameter is the pitch of the locked rectangle. What is the pitch you ask? Well, the *pitch* is the difference in bytes from the start of a line to the next one. The pitch is easily confused with the width of the locked rectangle, but they are two different things. While the width is the exact width of all the pixels in the rectangle, the pitch is the width of the entire locked rectangle. Take a look at Figure 13.8.

As you can see, in Direct3D when you lock the surface you get a pointer to the first pixel of the surface, but the array you get may not correspond to only the image buffer, actually most of the time it doesn't. What you get is an array that starts at the first pixel but has some extra information after each line. So, how do you know when the new line of the image starts? You use a little arithmetic. From Figure 13.6, you know that to get any pixel of the first line of the bitmap, you use the x location

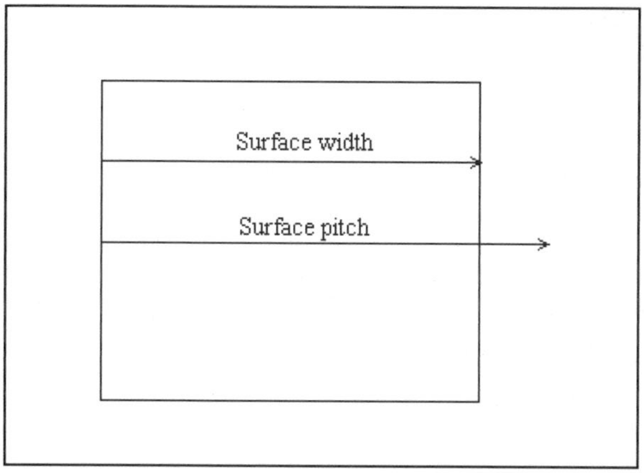

Figure 13.8

Differences between surface width and surface pitch.

as the element of the array. To get to the second line, you use the x location plus the pitch of the surface. To get to the third line, you use the x location plus the pitch times two. From this you can reach the formula:

```
LocationOnLockedImage [xPosition + (yPosition * Pitch)]
```

But before using this, there is a caveat with `Pitch`, it is expressed in bytes. Using the pitch directly is only useful if you are working in 8-bit mode (one byte). Since you are interested in 16- or 32-bit mode you need to divide the pitch by the number of bytes (not bits) the surface is in, so your formula would be:

```
LocationOnLockedImage [xPosition + (yPosition * (Pitch / SurfaceBytes)]
```

In your example, you would need to divide it by four, since 32-bits are four bytes.

> **NOTE**
>
> **When you deal with images, due to the nature of C++ arrays that start at zero, you start at (Zero, Zero) and end at (Width-1, Height-1).**

Next you have `pBits`, which is a pointer to `void`. This is the first pixel of the surface you have locked. In line 90, you declare a pointer to a `DWORD` (`unsigned long`), which you will also make point to the first pixel by casting the pointer `pBits` to a `DWORD`. You need to cast it to a `DWORD` (4 bytes or 32 bits) because you are using a 32-bit mode. If you were using a 16-bit mode you would need to cast it to a `WORD` (unsigned short which is 2 bytes or 16 bits).

Now that you have a correct pointer to the surface, you can begin to fill it with color:

```
 92:   /* Fill surface */
 93:  int iX, iY;
 94:  for (iY=0; iY<256; iY++)
 95:  {
 96:   for (iX=0; iX<256; iX++)
 97:   {
 98:     /* Form a pattern */
 99:    int iPower = (int)(sin (iY * iX) * 128 + cos (iY * -iX) * 128);
100:   piSurfaceBuffer [iX + iY* (kLockedRect.Pitch >> 2)] =
101:                          D3DCOLOR_XRGB (iPower, iPower, iPower);
102:   }
103:  }
104:
105:   /* Unlock */
106:  m_pD3DSurface->UnlockRect ();
107:
108:  return D3D_OK;
109: }
```

What you did here was to fill every pixel in the surface with a color (in this case, shades of gray) using two `for` loops. You have used a simple equation (line 99) that will form a floor-like pattern on the surface. You then used the location equation you developed earlier to fill the surface.

You have also used the `D3DCOLOR_XRGB` macro to form a color, and what this does is create a Direct3D color (a `DWORD`) with the red, green, and blue components and ignoring the alpha component. This macro works only for 32-bit modes and is defined as:

```
D3DCOLOR_XRGB (r,g,b) D3DCOLOR_ARGB (0xff, r, g, b)
```

And the `D3DCOLOR_ARGB` macro creates a Direct3D color like the `D3DCOLOR_XRGB` macro but using the alpha component and is defined as:

```
D3DCOLOR_XRGB (r,g,b)
((D3DCOLOR) ((((a)&0xff)<<24|(((r)&0xff)<<16|(((g)&0xff)<<8)|((b))&0xff)))
```

This macro creates a color where all the components use eight bits (values between 0 and 255) and are ordered in ARGB order.

If you were using a 16-bit mode, you couldn't use the `D3DCOLOR_XRGB` macro because this only produces valid colors for 32 bits. You will see how to work with other modes later. In the end, you unlock the surface (line 106) using `IDirect3DSurface8::UnlockRect` which is defined as:

```
HRESULT IDirect3DSurface8::UnlockRect (void);
```

Which is pretty easy to understand!

> **NOTE**
>
> **Remember that `Number >> n` is the same as `Number /` 2^n and `Number << n` is the same as `Number *` 2^n.**

The only difference you make to `KillDirect3D` is to also release your surface object:

```
111:  /* Shutdowns Direct3D */
112: HRESULT D3DWindow::KillDirect3D (void)
113: {
/* ... */
124:  if (NULL != m_pD3DSurface)
125:  {
126:   m_pD3DSurface->Release ();
127:  }
/* ... */
131: }
```

Next you have the `Frame` method. This is where you will draw the surface to the screen:

```
133:  /* Draw the surface */
134: mrBool32 D3DWindow::Frame (void)
135: {
/* ... */
140:   /* Get back buffer */
141:  LPDIRECT3DSURFACE8 pBackBuffer;
142:  m_pD3DDevice->GetBackBuffer(0, D3DBACKBUFFER_TYPE_MONO, &pBackBuffer);
143:
144:   /* Start rendering */
145:  m_pD3DDevice->BeginScene();
146:   /* Copy the surface to the screen */
147:  m_pD3DDevice->CopyRects (m_pD3DSurface, NULL, 0, pBackBuffer, NULL);
148:   /* End rendering */
149:  m_pD3DDevice->EndScene();
150:
151:   /* Release back buffer */
152:  pBackBuffer->Release ();
/* ... */
158: }
```

This method is the cream of your program showing the surface in the screen. To do this you first need to get access to the back buffer (so you can copy your surface to it), which is done with `IDirect3DDevice8::GetBackBuffer` that is defined as:

```
HRESULT IDirect3DDevice8::GetBackBuffer (
 UINT BackBuffer,
 D3DBACKBUFFER_TYPE Type,
 IDirect3DSurface8 ** ppBackBuffer);
```

Where the first parameter is the number of the back buffer you want to get from the chain, in your case `0` since you only have one (remember that in C++, most identifications start at zero). Next you have the back buffer type, which for some strange reason, can only be `D3DBACKBUFFER_TYPE_MONO` (still don't know why Microsoft forced you to supply this parameter and not just default it since it is the only thing you can do). And the last parameter is a pointer to a pointer to the surface where you will keep the back buffer.

After you have the back buffer, you need to copy your surface to it. This is done using `IDirect3DDevice8::CopyRects`, which copies one surface to another and is defined as:

```
HRESULT IDirect3DDevice8::CopyRects (
 IDirect3DSurface8 * pSourceSurface,
 CONST RECT* pSourceRectsArray,
 UINT cRects,
 IDirect3DSurface8 * pDestinationSurface,
 CONST POINT * pDestPointsArray);
```

The first parameter of `CopyRects` is a pointer to the source surface interface. Next you have an array of `RECT`s, these are the rectangles of the source surface you want to copy, or `NULL` in case you want to copy the entire surface, and following is the number of rectangles.

The fourth parameter is a pointer to the destination surface interface and following is an array of `POINT`s that define the destination position of each rectangle, supplying `NULL` to it makes it copy to the same location as the source rectangle top and left positions, or in case of `NULL` rectangles, to position (0, 0) of the surface.

Then you just need to release the back buffer (line 152) to release any resources allocated by it. The rest of the code is the same as before so no need to kill unnecessary trees. Figure 13.9 shows the final program running.

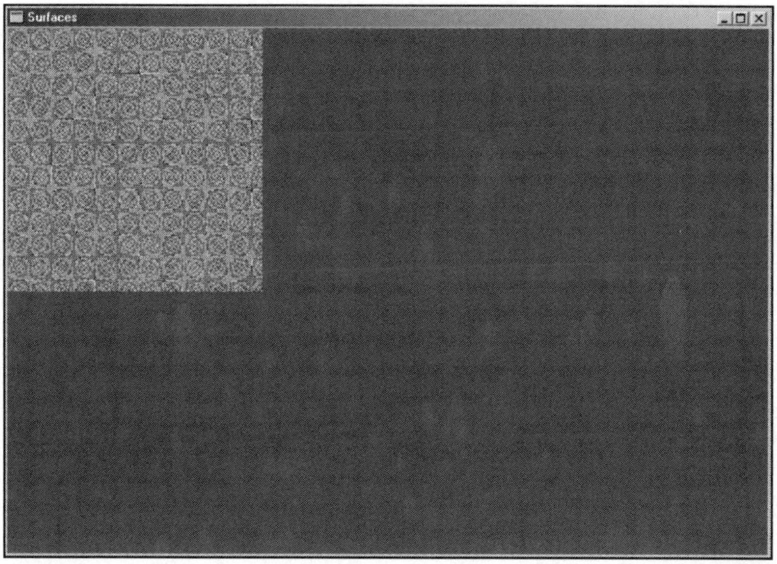

Figure 13.9

Rendering surfaces.

Vertices, Polygons, and Textures

The core of 3D programming is vertices, polygons, and textures. To make use of Direct3D, you will need to use some of the 3D concepts applied to 2D. The concepts being vertices, polygons, and textures.

Vertices and Polygons

In 3D, the most basic way to store something is as a polygon. A polygon is a collection of vertices that define an area, but what is a vertex? A vertex is the simplest way to store a position in the world.

So, how do polygons and vertices work? Easy, if you define three vertices with x- and y-coordinates, you can connect them using a single line to form a polygon, as shown in Figure 13.10.

This kind of polygon is usually called a triangle or tri. The most basic polygon you can render with Direct3D is a triangle, and this is what you will use to form your images.

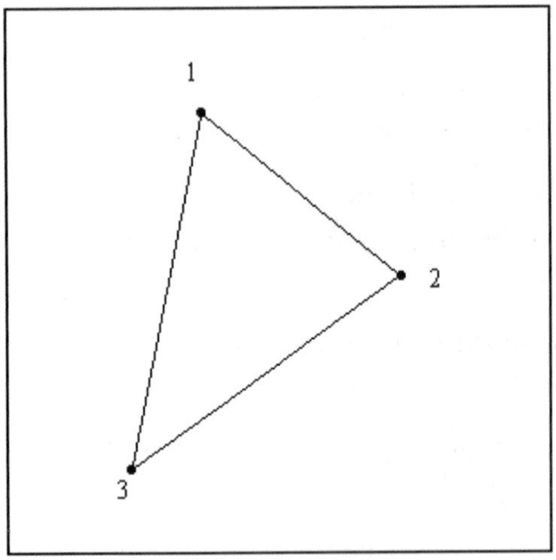

Figure 13.10

Connected vertices make a polygon.

Textures

Unlike the real meaning of texture, which describes the object's color, pattern, and surface roughness, a texture in computer terms is nothing more than a 2D image that can be mapped onto a polygon.

Using a polygon, you can map the texture to it in various ways (reversed, rotated, cropped, and so on), and thankfully, Direct3D does all these computations for you, you only need to supply the texture and various other parameters (I will talk about this in a bit).

Figure 13.11 shows a sample numbered texture. You will map this texture to a rectangular polygon in various ways to see the difference of each.

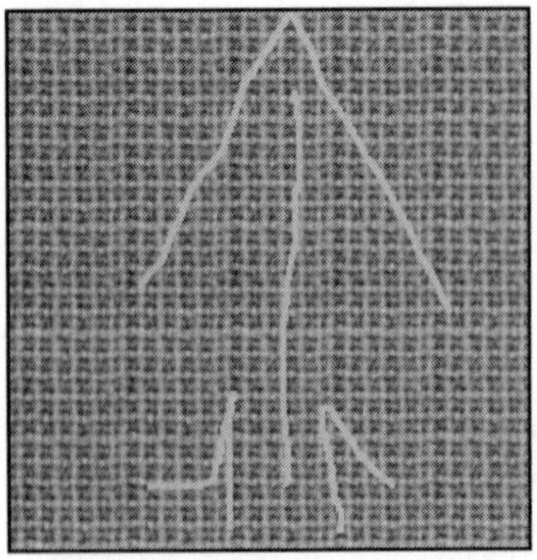

Figure 13.11

Sample texture.

Texture Coordinates

In Direct3D you just don't say "put texture A on polygon Z." You also need to say where and from where the texture is put. These are the texture coordinates.

Texture coordinates range from zero to one, where zero is the first pixel and one is the last pixel in the texture and are stored as two floating-point numbers (for horizontal position, or U, and for vertical position, or V).

So a texture coordinate with U=0.5 and V=0.5 would mean the exact center of the image.

Texture coordinates are stored in each vertex (along with the position and color) of the polygon, as shown in Figure 13.12.

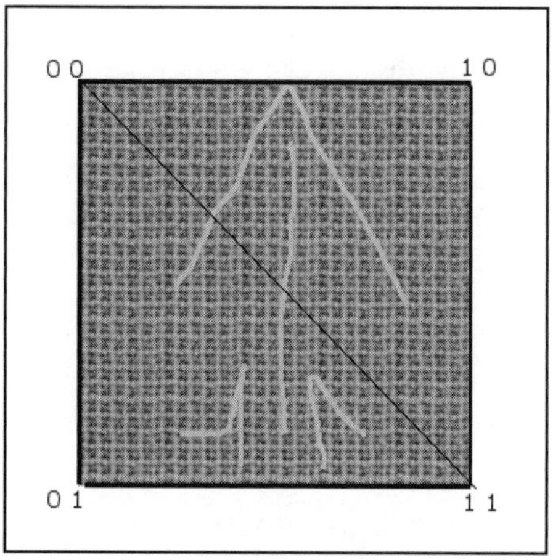

Figure 13.12

Normal texture mapping.

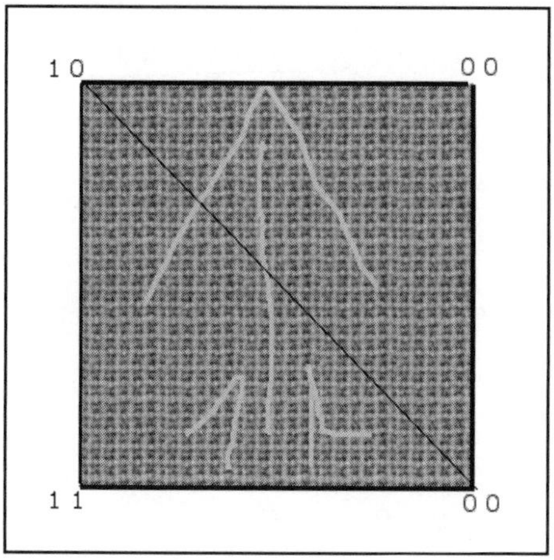

Figure 13.13

Mirrored texture mapping.

Texture coordinates also allow you to make some nice effects such as mirrored textures if you supply the U coordinates flipped, as shown in Figure 13.13.

Or flipped upside-down by flipping the vertical texture coordinates, as shown in Figure 13.14.

And you can also crop the figure to just a section by giving values between zero and one, as shown in Figure 13.15.

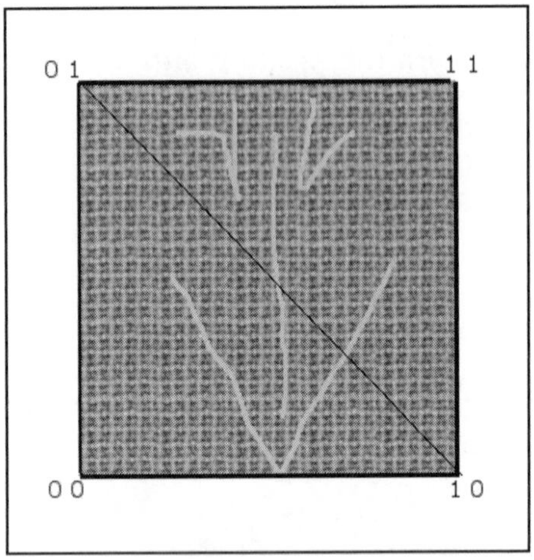

Figure 13.14

Flipped texture mapping.

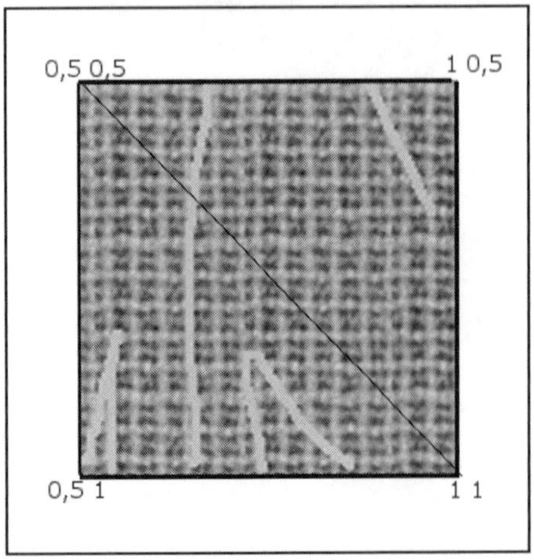

Figure 13.15

Cropped texture mapping.

From the Third Dimension to the Second

The last thing you need to know about polygons before the example is how to you store the position of the vertices. Unfortunately, in Direct3D you can't store vertices as x and y components. You need to store them as either x, y, and z, or x, y, z, and rhw components. The first type is for untransformed vertices (3D vertices), which will be transformed by Direct3D, which you don't need to care about. The second method is used for already transformed vertices, which is your situation.

By supplying a value of one to the rhw component, you specify that the x- and y-coordinates will already be transformed and should be used for displaying the polygons without any change. What this means is that you can then use the x and y component to specify the position of the vertex in the screen.

You can ignore the z coordinate since you are working in 2D.

Rendering in 2D

For your example, you will basically do what you have done previously, but this time by using a texture and a polygon:

```
 /* Our custom vertex structure */
class CustomVertex
{
public:
  /* Transformed position */
 FLOAT x, y, z, rhw;
  /* Color */
 DWORD Color;
  /* Texture coordinates */
 FLOAT tU, tV;
};

 /* Our custom vertex type */
#define D3DFVF_CUSTOMVERTEX (D3DFVF_XYZRHW|D3DFVF_DIFFUSE|D3DFVF_TEX1)
```

The first big difference from the previous examples is the fact that you have to specify a vertex structure and type. Your structure is pretty simple. You have the x, y, z, and rhw components of the vertex, then a normal color as a DWORD and the texture coordinates as FLOATs.

Next you have to define a Direct3D custom vertex specifying what you use in the vertex information. In your case you want to use a vertex that is already transformed (D3DFVF_XYZRHW), has a color component (D3DFVF_DIFFUSE), and has one set of texture coordinates (D3DFVF_TEX1). This type will tell Direct3D what to use to define the vertex and what Direct3D should do with it.

Next you have the class definition:

```
 /* Custom derived class */
class D3DWindow : public mrWindow
{
  /* Direct3D interfaces */
 LPDIRECT3D8              m_pD3D;
 LPDIRECT3DDEVICE8       m_pD3DDevice;

  /* Direct3D texture interface */
 LPDIRECT3DTEXTURE8      m_pD3DTexture;
  /* Direct3D current format */
 mrUInt32                 m_iD3DFormat;

  /* Vertices */
 CustomVertex            m_kVertices [4];

public:
  /* Constructor / Destructor */
 D3DWindow (void) {};
 ~D3DWindow (void) {};

  /* Setup and shutdown Direct3D */
 HRESULT SetupDirect3D (void);
 HRESULT KillDirect3D (void);

  /* Window manipulation functions */
 mrBool32 Frame (void);
};
```

Where the only differences are that you have an IDirect3DTexture8 interface to store your texture and an array of four elements of type CustomVertex to store the vertices of the polygon.

Next you need to change SetupDirect3D to create your texture:

```
 /* Initializes Direct3D */
HRESULT D3DWindow::SetupDirect3D (void)
{
/* ... */
  /* Create the texture */
 if (FAILED (m_pD3DDevice->CreateTexture (128, 128, 0, 0,
                                    (D3DFORMAT) m_iD3DFormat,
                                    D3DPOOL_MANAGED,
                                    &m_pD3DTexture ) ) )

 {
  return E_FAIL;
 }
```

You use the method IDirect3DDevice8::CreateTexture to create your texture, which is defined as:

```
HRESULT IDirect3DDevice8::CreateTexture (
 UINT Width,
 UINT Height,
 UINT Levels,
 DWORD Usage,
 D3DFORMAT Format,
 D3DPOOL Pool,
 IDirect3DTexture8 ** ppTexture);
```

Where the first two parameters are the texture size. Next you have the number of levels of the texture. This is for 3D use so you won't worry about it and set it to zero. Next you have the Usage parameter, which you won't use either, so set it to zero. Next is the format of the texture and then the Pool where the texture will be placed. The valid values for it are described in Table 13.4.

> **NOTE**
>
> Remember that texture sizes must be in power of two dimensions (2^2, 2^3, 2^4).

Table 13.4 Direct3D Pool Types

Value	Description
D3DPOOL_DEFAULT	Texture is put in the most appropriate location for it.
D3DPOOL_MANAGED	Direct3D manages the texture, usually by keeping a copy of it in system memory.
D3DPOOL_SYSTEMMEM	Texture is created in system memory.

In the end you have a pointer to a pointer to an `IDirect3DTexture8` interface where the texture will be stored.

Next you lock the texture and fill it with the same floor-type pattern and unlock it after as in the surface example.

```
  /* Lock texture */
 D3DLOCKED_RECT kLockedRect;
 m_pD3DTexture->LockRect (0, &kLockedRect, NULL, 0);

  /* Cast a pointer to point to the first pixel */
 DWORD * piTextureBuffer = (DWORD *) kLockedRect.pBits;

  /* Fill texture */
 int iX, iY;
 for (iY=0; iY<128; iY++)
 {
  for (iX=0; iX<128; iX++)
  {
    /* Form pattern */
   int iPower = (int)(sin (iY * iX) * 128 + cos (iY * -iX) * 128);
   piSurfaceBuffer [iX + iY* (kLockedRect.Pitch >> 2)] =
                         D3DCOLOR_XRGB (iPower, iPower, iPower);
  }
```

```
}

  /* Unlock */
m_pD3DTexture->UnlockRect (0);
```

Next you need to set up the vertices for your polygon:

```
  /* Setup a temporary vertices information */
CustomVertex kVertices [] =
{  /* x, y, z, w, color, texture coordinates (u,v) */
  {0.0f,  0.0f,  0.5f, 1.0f, D3DCOLOR_ARGB (255, 255, 255, 255), 0, 0},
  {50.0f, 0.0f,  0.5f, 1.0f, D3DCOLOR_ARGB (255, 255, 255, 255), 1, 0},
  {50.0f, 50.0f, 0.5f, 1.0f, D3DCOLOR_ARGB (255, 255, 255, 255), 1, 1},
  {0.0f,  50.0f, 0.5f, 1.0f, D3DCOLOR_ARGB (255, 255, 255, 255), 0, 1},
};

  /* Copy the vertices information to the vertex buffer */
memcpy (m_kVertices, kVertices, sizeof (CustomVertex) * 4);
```

You start by creating an array of vertices, which you will fill with four vertices like shown in Table 13.5.

And you finish it by copying this class to your class structure so you can use it later.

TABLE 13.5 Your Polygon Vertices

Vertex	X	Y	Z	W	Color	U	V
1	0.0	0.0	0.5	1.0	(255, 255, 255, 255)	0	0
2	50.0	0.0	0.5	1.0	(255, 255, 255, 255)	1	0
3	50.0	50.0	0.5	1.0	(255, 255, 255, 255)	1	1
4	0.0	50.0	0.5	1.0	(255, 255, 255, 255)	0	1

It is now time to set render states:

```
144:   /* Don't cull polygons */
145:  m_pD3DDevice->SetRenderState (D3DRS_CULLMODE, D3DCULL_NONE);
146:
147:   /* Don't use lighting */
148:  m_pD3DDevice->SetRenderState (D3DRS_LIGHTING, FALSE);
149:
150:   /* Set texture states */
151:  m_pD3DDevice->SetTextureStageState (0, D3DTSS_COLOROP,   D3DTOP_MODULATE);
152:  return D3D_OK;
153: }
```

Before proceeding, a render state is something Direct3D will use (or not) to produce the final image. There are many render states such as lighting, alpha blending, shading, and so on. I recommend that you enable only the render states you need since the more states enabled, the more processing that must be done by Direct3D to produce the final image.

So, to set a render state you use the `IDirect3DDevice8::SetRenderState` that is defined as:

```
HRESULT IDirect3DDevice8::SetRenderState (
 D3DRENDERSTATETYPE State,
 DWORD Value);
```

Where the first parameter is the state you want to set, and the second parameter is the value you want to set the state with.

So, in your example, since you don't want to cull (remove) any polygons, you set the `D3DRS_CULLMODE` state to `D3DCULL_NONE`. You don't want any lighting either (hey, it is 2D so lighting wouldn't make anything prettier) so you set the `D3DRS_LIGHTING` state to `FALSE`.

There are many other states, but thankfully for you, you need just a few, as you will see later.

You also need to set a texture state (line 151). Texture states are a little complicated but in a very simple description, you can say that they are the way textures are copied to the screen, and are set with `IDirect3DDevice8::SetTextureState` which is defined as:

```
HRESULT IDirect3DDevice8::SetTextureState (
 DWORD State
```

```
D3DTEXTURESTAGESTATETYPE State,
DWORD Value);
```

Where the first parameter is the identifier of the texture, since you will only use one texture, this member is zero. The next parameter is the state you want to set, while there are various texture stage states, you will use only D3DTSS_COLOROP for now but if you want, you can try some of the states in Table 13.6. The last parameter is the value you want to set the state to, in your case D3DTOP_MODULATE, which will multiply the color components of the textures.

Now you need to add the cleanup of the texture to KillDirect3D:

```
 /* Shutdowns Direct3D */
HRESULT D3DWindow::KillDirect3D (void)
{
/* ... */
 if (NULL != m_pD3DTexture)
 {
  m_pD3DTexture->Release ();
 }

 return D3D_OK;
}
```

TABLE 13.6 Texture Render States

Value	Description
D3DTSS_COLOROP	Texture stage state is a texture blending operation
D3DTSS_COLORARG1	Texture stage state is the first color argument for the stage
D3DTSS_COLORARG2	Texture stage state is the second color argument for the stage
D3DTSS_ÃLPHAOP	Texture stage state is a texture alpha blending operation
D3DTSS_ÃLPHAARG1	Texture stage state is the first alpha argument for the stage
D3DTSS_ÃLPHAARG2	Texture stage state is the second alpha argument for the stage

Finally, some rendering! What you need to do is set the texture you created as the active texture and then render the polygon(s) using that texture.

```
174:  /* Draw the entire frame */
175: mrBool32 D3DWindow::Frame (void)
176: {
177:   /* Clear the window to blue */
178:  m_pD3DDevice->Clear (0, NULL, D3DCLEAR_TARGET,
179:                         D3DCOLOR_XRGB (0,0,255), 1.0f, 0);
180:
181:   /* Start rendering */
182:  m_pD3DDevice->BeginScene();
183:
184:   /* Set texture source */
185:  m_pD3DDevice->SetTexture (0, m_pD3DTexture);
186:
187:   /* Set vertex source */
188:  m_pD3DDevice->SetVertexShader (D3DFVF_CUSTOMVERTEX) ;
189:  m_pD3DDevice->DrawPrimitiveUP (D3DPT_TRIANGLEFAN, 2, m_kVertices,
190:                                  sizeof (CustomVertex));
```

The first thing to do is set as the active texture your texture (line 185), this is done using the `SetTexture` of `IDirect3DDevice8` interface, which is defined as:

```
HRESULT IDirect3DDevice8::SetTexture (
 DWORD Stage,
 IDirect3DBaseTexture * pTexture);
```

Where the first parameter is the texture's stage. Again, something you won't use so you use zero to set as the first state. The last parameter is a pointer to an `IDirect3DBaseTexture` interface. You will use your `IDirect3DTexture` since it derives from `IDirect3DBaseTexture`, meaning it can be cast to `IDirect3DBaseTexture`.

Finally, you draw the polygons with `IDirect3DDevice8::DrawPrimitiveUP` that is defined as:

```
HRESULT IDirect3DDevice8::DrawPrimitiveUP (
 D3DPRIMITIVETYPE PrimitiveType,
 UINT PrimitiveCount,
 CONST void * pVertexStreamZeroData,
 UINT VertexStreamZeroStride);
```

Where the first parameter is the primitive (or polygon) type. Valid values for primitives are in Table 13.7. Next you have the primitive count, which is the number of polygons you will use. Following is a pointer to the vertices array, and last is the index of the first vertex in the array, or in your case zero since you want to start with the beginning of the array.

You are probably wondering what the differences are between a list, a strip, and a fan. Well, let's see, shall we?

A *list* is a collection of vertices that independently define a primitive, so if you have six vertices, you would have two triangles defined by the six vertices (the first three would form a triangle and the last three another).

A *strip* is also a collection of vertices that define a primitive, but this time it uses the last two vertices and a new one to form a new triangle, as shown in Figure 13.16.

Last, a *fan* is, you guessed it, a collection of vertices that define a primitive, and it uses the last and the first vertex to form a new triangle, as shown in Figure 13.17.

TABLE 13.7 Primitive Types

Value	Description
D3DPT_POINTLIST	Render vertices as individual points
D3DPT_LINELIST	Render vertices as individual lines
D3DPT_LINESTRIP	Render vertices as line strips
D3DPT_TRIANGLELIST	Render vertices as triangle list
D3DPT_ TRIANGLESTRIP	Render vertices as triangle strips
D3DPT_ TRIANGLEFAN	Render vertices as triangle fans

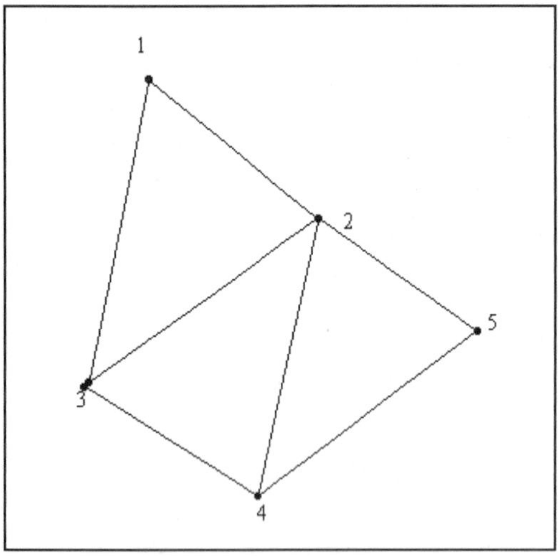

Figure 13.16

Triangle strip.

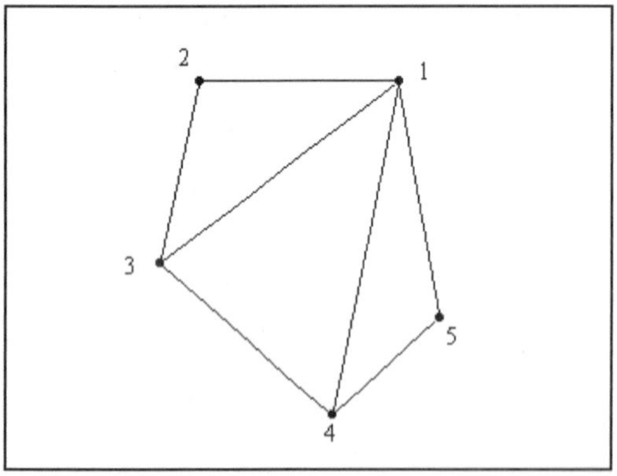

Figure 13.17

Triangle fan.

And you finish rendering by calling `IDirect3DDevice8::EndScene` and `IDirect3DDevice8::Present`.

```
 /* End rendering */
m_pD3DDevice->EndScene();

 /* Present the rendered scene to the screen */
m_pD3DDevice->Present (NULL, NULL, NULL, NULL);

return mrTrue;

```

Figure 13.18 shows your program running.

Figure 13.18

Rendering textures.

Windows Bitmaps

While creating the texture is fine, most of the time you prefer to have an artist do all the art in an external paint program and save it to files and make the game load those files.

Since almost every paint program in existence supports the Windows Bitmap type (.bmp) you will create a bitmap loader for your purposes.

Bitmap Structure

So, how is a bitmap stored? Well, it starts with a couple of headers, followed by palette information, and then the image data like shown in Figure 13.19.

As you can see, a bitmap starts with a header that stores some basic information about the bitmap. The detailed information can be found in Table 13.8.

The only information you want from this first structure is the Type and Offset. The type must be 0x4D42. This is how you identify whether this is a bitmap. The Offset field lets you know where the exact bitmap data starts.

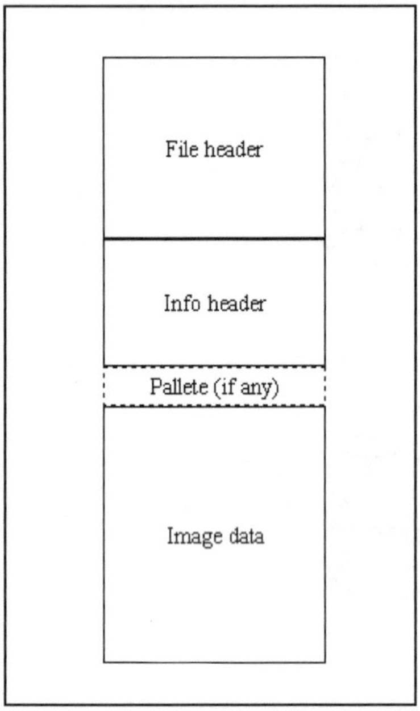

Figure 13.19
Windows bitmap structure.

Table 13.8 Bitmap File Header

Field	Size (Bytes)	Description
Type	2	Specifies the file type
Size	4	Specifies the size of the file
Reserved	4	Reserved, must be zero
Offset	4	Offset in bytes from the bitmap file header to the bitmap image data

Next there is the bitmap info header, which is described in Table 13.9.

Where you are only interested in the Width and Height, which are the image dimensions, the BitCount (the color depth, which must be 24), and the Compression field. You want to get the Compression field so you can check if the

TABLE 13.9 Bitmap Info Header

Field	Size (Bytes)	Description
Size	4	Size of this structure
Width	4	Width of bitmap
Height	4	Height of bitmap
Planes	2	Number of color planes
BitCount	2	Number of bits per pixel
Compression	4	Type of compression
ImageSize	4	Size of image data
XPelsPerMeter	4	Horizontal resolution
YPelsPerMeter	4	Vertical resolution
ClrUsed	4	Number of colors used by the bitmap
ClrImportant	4	Number of colors important to the bitmap

bitmap isn't compressed. You won't see how to load a compressed bitmap, so this flag must be `BI_RGB`.

So, next you only need to move the file pointer to the position described by offset, and read each pixel of the image. Each pixel is made of three bytes, describing the blue, green, and red components of the image (take note, not red, green, and blue like you were used to, but blue, green, and red).

Also, if the Height field is negative, you need to flip (swap the lines) of your bitmap. Almost every graphics application exports bitmaps flipped, so don't forget to check for this.

Loading a Bitmap

Since you will include a bitmap loading routine in Mirus, instead of going over the exact code to load a bitmap, let's just go over the pseudocode, and it will be up to you to implement the loader. If you are having trouble, just check the mrRGBAImage::LoadFromBitmap method in the next chapter.

```
If open Bitmap file
 Read two bytes (type) and if different than 0x4D42 stop
 Ignore eight bytes
 Read four bytes (start of image data)
 Ignore four bytes
 Read four bytes (width of bitmap)
 Read four bytes (height of bitmap)
 Ignore two bytes
 Read two bytes (bit count of bitmap) and if different than 24 stop
 Read four bytes (compression of bitmap) and if different than BI_RGB stop
 Move to start of image data
 Allocate memory for image data (3(one byte for red, other for
                   green other for blue) * ImageWidth * ImageHeight)
 Read (3 * ImageWidth * ImageHeight) bytes from file to buffer
 Swap the red and blue components of buffer
 If ImageHeight is negative
  Flip the buffer lines
 End if
Close file
```

If you pay close attention and compare this pseudocode with the previous two tables, what you do is read the data you want, and ignore (by skipping) the data you don't want.

Full Screen and Other Bit Modes

Windowed mode is pretty cool to develop, but most gamers prefer to have the game fullscreen. If you ever worked with previous versions of DirectX, making full-screen applications was easier than making windowed ones. In DirectX 8.0, it is a little more difficult to create full-screen applications because there are a few more parameters you need to set.

Remember CreateDevice? Well, if you don't I'll refresh your memory. CreateDevice was used to create the actual rendering device. This function had a parameter (D3DPRESENT_PARAMETERS) that defined how the scenes would be presented to the screen. Up until now you have filled in the necessary information on this structure with the current display settings. To use a full-screen mode you need to set most of them manually.

Let's go over each element you need to set to use full-screen mode:

```
BOOL Windowed;
```

You need to set this member to `false` to indicate you are using full-screen mode.

```
UINT BackBufferWidth;
```

This member will hold the back buffer width. Unlike in windowed mode, this value must be one of the normal resolutions (such as 640, 800, 1024 . . .) so it can work.

```
UINT BackBufferHeight;
```

This member will hold the back buffer height. Unlike in windowed mode, this value must be one of the normal resolutions (such as 480, 600, 768 . . .) so it can work.

```
UINT BackBufferCount;
```

This member is the back buffer count. You can use just about as many back buffers as the hardware can handle.

```
D3DSWAPEFFECT SwapEffect;
```

The swap effect member specifies how the back buffer and the swap chains should be handled, this works exactly the same way as in windowed mode.

```
UINT FullScreen_RefreshRateInHz;
```

This member will define the refresh rate of the screen, which is the rate at which the screen is updated. You will use `D3DPRESENT_RATE_DEFAULT` to use the default refresh rate.

```
UINT FullScreen_PresentationInterval;
```

This member will define the rate for which the swap chains are swapped. You will use `D3DPRESENT_INTERVAL_DEFAULT` so you don't need to worry about which card can handle what.

```
D3DFORMAT BackBufferFormat;
```

The back buffer format is probably the hardest member to set when using full-screen mode. The problem is that there are various formats, some of them supported by the some video cards, and other formats supported by other video cards. Programming an application so it works on all cards is hard.

To solve this problem, depending on the bit depth (16 or 32 bits), you will try to create the device with each format, and if one fails, you will try another, and again until you have no more devices. In pseudocode:

```
If BitDepth == 16
{
 If Failed (CreateDevice (..., D3DFMT_R5G6B5, ...)
 {
  If Failed (CreateDevice (..., D3DFMT_X1R5G5B5, ...)
  {
   /* ... */
  }
 }
}
```

You would still need to check a few more formats (the 32-bit ones) but you will do this when you start developing Mirus. And that's about it. Working with full-screen modes is exactly the same thing as working with windowed modes. You create the device, and use the surfaces, vertices, and textures normally.

Color Theory and Color Keying

When you use non-alpha textures or surfaces, you don't need to care much about transparency, mostly because there is none (at least without external routines). But using alpha textures and surfaces has many advantages, from nice effects to color keying.

Color Theory

Until now, you have been neglecting the pixel's alpha component and using pure colors. Well, from now on you will start using alpha to produce cooler images.

But what exactly is alpha? Well, *alpha* is the amount of color a pixel has. For example, a pixel with zero alpha will have no amount of color, so, it wouldn't be drawn. On the other hand, a pixel with an alpha value of 255 would have all the color possible and would be drawn fully.

In a mathematical way, the final pixel color would be something like:

```
InvAlpha = Alpha / 255;
FinalColor = (InvAlpha * Red, InvAlpha * Green, InvAlpha * Blue);
```

Which for `Alpha` values of 0, 100, and 255 would give the following values after you perform the math:

```
FinalPixelOne = (0, 0, 0);
/* (Alpha / 255 * ColorComponent) */
/* ((100 / 255) * 255, (100 / 255) * 255, (100 / 255) * 255) */
FinalPixelTwo = (100, 100, 100);
FinalPixelThree = (255, 255, 255);
```

But even if this produces the final pixel, it only takes into account the source pixel. If a pixel is half transparent, then the pixel that is already at the screen will also take part of the final color, so you need to change the equation to something like:

```
InvAlphaSrc = Alpha / 255;
InvAlphaDest = (255 - Alpha) / 255;
FinalColor =
(InvAlphaSrc * SrcRed, InvAlphaSrc * SrcGreen, InvAlphaSrc * SrcBlue) +
(InvAlphaDest * DestRed, InvAlphaDest * DestGreen, InvAlphaDest * DestBlue)
```

Which now blends the two pixels together. Now, a value of 0 for alpha would mean that the final pixel would be the same as the destination pixel, while a value of 255 would produce a final pixel the same as the source.

To enable this kind of effect in Direct3D you must first enable alpha blending, and then set the type of blending. The preceeding formula is the most common type of alpha blending, but there are other types to produce various effects.

So, the first effect is to enable alpha blending, right? You do it by calling `IDirect3DDevice8::SetRenderState` to tell Direct3D to use alpha blending as:

```
Direct3DDevice->SetRenderState (D3DRS_ALPHABLENDENABLE, TRUE);
```

Or you could use it with `FALSE` as the last parameter to disable alpha blending. Next you need to set the type of blending. Since you want to use the previous formula, you need to set the render states as:

```
Direct3DDevice ->SetRenderState (D3DRS_SRCBLEND, D3DBLEND_SRCALPHA);
Direct3DDevice ->SetRenderState (D3DRS_DESTBLEND, D3DBLEND_INVSRCALPHA);
```

Where the first line would set the source pixel to be multiplied by the source alpha and the second line would set the destination pixel to be multiplied by the inverse source alpha. For other blend factors check out Table 13.10.

What the Factor in Table 13.10 describes is the value that is used to multiply the color with; for example, for source pixel color only, and using D3DBLEND_SRCCOLOR as the blending factor, a color in the form (R, G, B, A) would end up being:

```
Rfinal = R * (A/255)
Gfinal = G * (A/255)
Bfinal = B * (A/255)
Afinal = A * (A/255)
```

TABLE 13.10 Direct3D Blend Factors

Flag	Description
D3DBLEND_ZERO	Factor is (0,0,0,0)
D3DBLEND_ONE	Factor is (1,1,1,1)
D3DBLEND_SRCCOLOR	Factor is (Rs, Gs, Bs, As)
D3DBLEND_INVSRCOLOR	Factor is (1-Rs,1-Gs,1-Bs,1-As)
D3DBLEND_SRCALPHA	Factor is (As, As, As, As)
D3DBLEND_INVSRCALPHA	Factor is (1-As,1-As,1-As,1-As)
D3DBLEND_DESTCOLOR	Factor is (Rd, Gd, Bd, Ad)
D3DBLEND_INVDESTCOLOR	Factor is (1-Rd,1-Gd,1-Bd,1-Ad)
D3DBLEND_DESTALPHA	Factor is (Ad, Ad, Ad, Ad)
D3DBLEND_INVDESTALPHA	Factor is (1-Ad,1-Ad,1-Ad,1-Ad)
D3DBLEND_SRCALPHASAT	Factor is (f, f, f, 1) where f = minimum (As, 1-Ad)

Rs, Gs, Bs, As, stand respectively for red source, green source, blue source, and alpha source.

Rd, Gd, Bd, Ad, stand respectively for red destination, green destination, blue destination, and alpha destination.

NOTE

Although in the table there is no indication of the division by 255, it is present since Direct3D uses color components in the range of 0 to 1.0. So, by dividing a color component (range from 0 to 255) by 255, you can get the color in the 0, 1 range. This is handled by Direct3D and you don't need to divide anything yourself.

Color Keying

If you know what a spectrum machine is (and not because you saw it at your local museum), you probably have played a game that could have benefited from color keying, but to better demonstrate what it is, take a look at Figure 13.20.

If your games would look like this, well, let's just say they wouldn't be the Mona Lisa of games. Direct3D gives you the option of copying images to the screen, but they are most of the time either squared or rectangular copying more than desired. To overcome this problem, programmers use color keying to only copy parts of the image that aren't of a color, usually a bright pink or some rarely used color. What this means is that every pixel of the image that doesn't match the color key is copied, and the ones that match, aren't.

For older versions of DirectX, color key was a built-in functionality. You would just tell Direct3D what was the color key and Direct3D would automatically discard that

Figure 13.20

No color key when copying an image to the screen.

color when copying. Direct3D 8.0 doesn't offer this feature anymore. For you to use color keying, you will need to set the alpha component of the image to 0. You do this by checking every pixel of the texture, and if the red, green, and blue components match the color you want to use as the color key, you will set the alpha value of that pixel to 0, thus making Direct3D not copy that pixel.

You will do this in the next chapter when you develop a generic image class.

Targa Files

Now that you know how to use alpha blending in your games, possibly the best thing to do is to also be able to load files that contain alpha. There are several file formats available that allow saving the alpha channel (the image alpha data) but since targa is the most widely known, and probably simpler, I will stick to it.

Structure of a Targa File

Fortunately for you, a targa file is very simple, well, actually not really, but you will restrict your loader to 32-bit images (has red, green, blue, and alpha components) without using any compression scheme. This makes loading a targa file as easy as baking an upside-down cake (please don't tell me you are one of those programmers who only know how to fry an egg). Table 13.11 shows the Targa file description.

While Table 13.11 looks a little complicated, it really isn't. Many of the fields can be easily ignored (since you are restricting the image to be uncompressed and 32-bit). Knowing this, you only need the following fields:

```
IDFieldSize
ImageCode
MapLength
XOrigin
YOrigin
Width
Height
PixelSize
ImageDesc
```

You will see how to use these fields when you are loading the targa file next.

Table 13.11 Targa File Description

Field	Size	Description
`IDFieldSize`	1	Number of bytes used by identification field
`ColorMapType`	1	Color map type
`ImageTypeCode`	1	Image type code (should always be two)
`ColorMapOrigin`	2	Color map origin
`ColorMapLength`	2	Color map length
`ColorMapSize`	1	Color map entry size
`XOrigin`	2	X origin of image
`YOrigin`	2	Y origin of image
`Width`	2	Width of image
`Height`	2	Height of image
`PixelSize`	1	Image pixel size
`ImageDescription`	1	Image description byte (bit 5 – screen origin)
`ImageIdentification`	IDFieldSize	Image identification field
`ColorMap`	ColorMapLength * 4	Color map data
`ImageData`	Width * Height * 4	Image data

Loading a Targa File

As with the bitmap loading, you will only use pseudocode to show the targa loading routine. You will develop a method for loading targa files in Mirus, so no need to repeat the same code.

```
If open Targa file
 Read one byte (IDFieldSize)
 Ignore one byte
```

```
 Read one byte (ImageCode) and if different than 2 stop
 Ignore two bytes
 Read two bytes (MapLength)
 Ignore one byte
 Read two bytes (XOrigin)
 Read two bytes (YOrigin)
 Read two bytes (Width)
 Read two bytes (Height)
 Read one byte (PixelSize) and if different than 32 quit
 Read one byte (ImageDesc)
 Ignore IDFieldSize bytes (Field description)
 Ignore MapLength * 4 bytes (Color map)
 Allocate memory for image data (4(one byte for red, other for
                 green, other for blue and other for alpha) *
                 ImageWidth * ImageHeight)
 Read (4 * ImageWidth * ImageHeight) bytes from file to buffer
 Convert from ARGB to RGBA
 If bit five of ImageDesc is zero
  Flip the buffer lines
 End if
Close file
```

And that's it, you will see the real C++ code later so don't worry if you are having trouble with this pseudocode.

Animation and Template Sets

Static games aren't much fun, are they? What good is a guy going side to side, if he seems to be sliding instead of running? Nothing really! That's why I will be talking about animation next.

Animation

At some point in your life, you have seen a cartoon. It doesn't matter if it was *Pocahontas* or *Transformers*; what matters is that you have seen it, and hopefully, remember a bit about it. Well, you have seen cartoons, and you probably know what happens behind the scenes, right? But just in case, let me summarize it.

A sequence of about 10 seconds takes approximately 250 drawings to produce. The sequence starts by showing the first drawing (or frame), and then changing to the second frame, and so on until the last frame. Since there are about 25 frames per second (depends on your place in the world, but it is basically around 25), there are 250 frames for a 10-second sequence; now imagine for a full-length movie!

That's basically what happens in computers! You have a sequence of frames, each of which you loop through to produce the effect of a cartoon, or the guy moving! It's really simple.

Template Sets

While a template set isn't something worth considering as a programming technique, I find them useful when developing small games. Think of a template set as a group of frames correctly ordered.

Imagine that you have a game with 1,000 frames, each 8×8 in size! Keeping 1,000 files for each frame will be madness, not just to use, but to organize also. Using template sets, you would only need two or three (depending on the template size) to keep all the images.

Take a look at Figure 13.21.

By using templates it makes it easier to organize your animations.

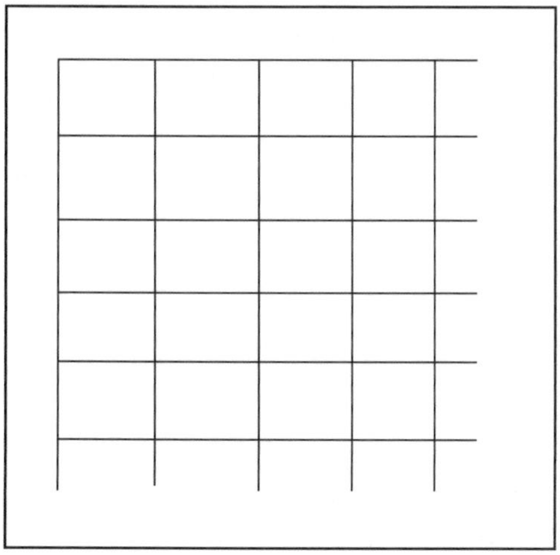

Figure 13.21

A sample template.

In Mirus, you will be able to use animations by loading them from a file as you will see.

Collision Detection

Having objects that go through each other isn't very fun. In this section, I will cover two methods to check for collisions of objects.

Bounding Volumes

While it is possible to do accurate collision checking on objects, most of the time it is unnecessary and time-consuming.

Bounding volumes is a technique to encapsulate the object into a bounding volume, usually a square or circle, which makes collision detection faster, since you don't need to test each pixel for the image, but there are disadvantages, too, and the worst is probably the fact that bounding volumes collision detection is erroneous; that is, sometimes there aren't collisions and the collision detection algorithm reports one.

As you can see from Figure 13.22, even if the two objects aren't really touching, the bounding volumes are, and the collision detection algorithm would return that a collision had occurred.

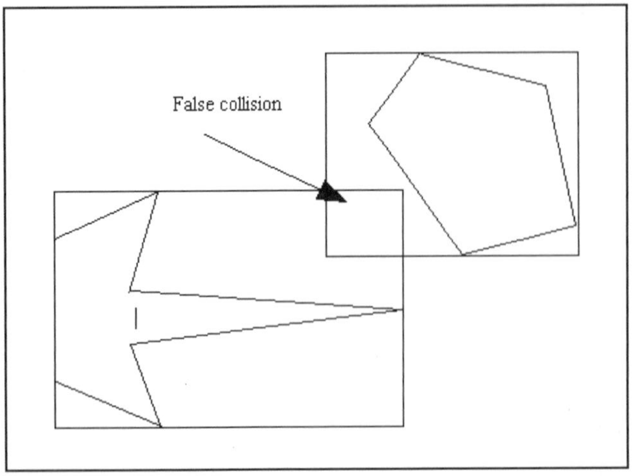

Figure 13.22

Bounding volume errors.

Most of the time, these errors don't affect the gameplay and are better than having to check for each pixel of each object every frame.

Bounding Circles

The first collision detection technique I will be covering are bounding circles. Bounding circles are easy to check for collisions because all the points of the circle are the same distance to the center.

You start by calculating the distance of two objects, and then compare it with the sum of the two circles' radii. If the distance is bigger than the sum of the radii, then there was no collision; if it was smaller, then a collision occurred, as shown in Figure 13.23.

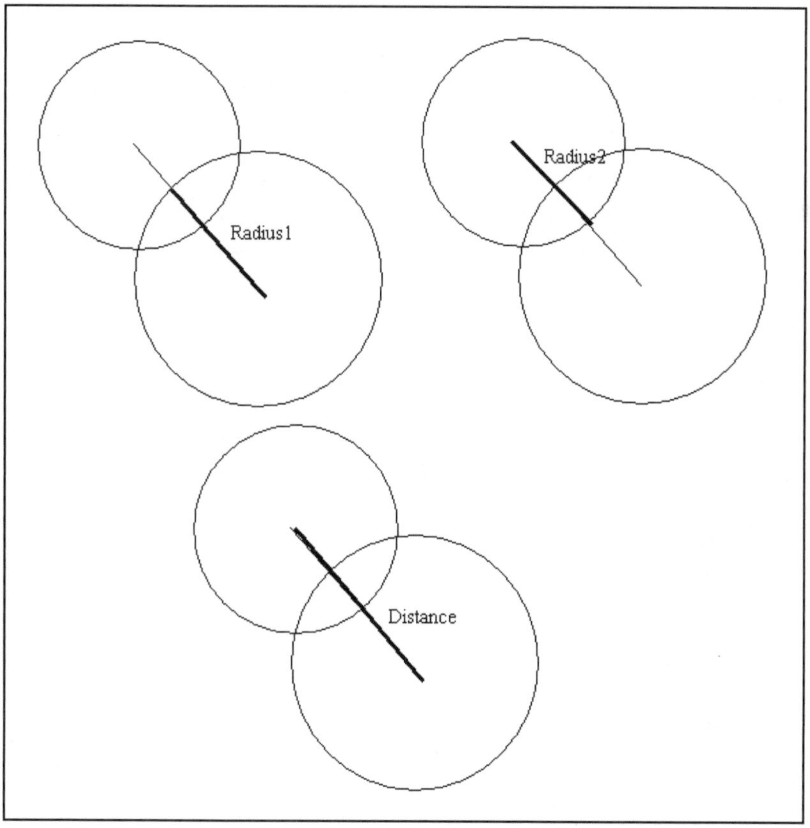

Figure 13.23

Bounding circles.

The code for this algorithm would be:

```
if (DistanceFromAtoB >= RadiusA+RadiusB)
{
 return NoCollision;
}
else
{
 return Collision;
}
```

Pretty simple, eh? You will add this code to Mirus later.

Bounding Rectangles

The second and last technique I should cover is bounding rectangles. Bounding rectangles are more accurate than bounding circles, but also a little complicated and slower.

As you can see in Figure 13.24, if any of the vertices of a rectangle is inside the area of the other rectangle, a collision was detected.

There are two functions or steps you should perform to see whether there is a collision between the objects. The first is to see if a point is inside a rectangle, and then to check whether each of the vertices of one rectangle is contained in the other.

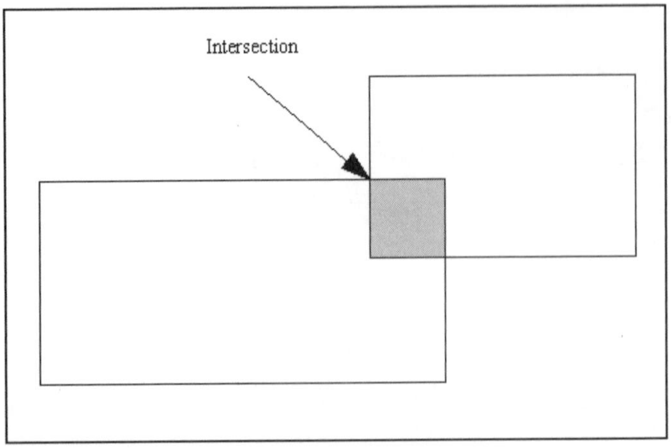

Figure 13.24

Bounding rectangles.

First things first, point containment. For a point to be inside a rectangle, the x component of the point must be larger than the minimal rectangle x and smaller than the maximum rectangle x, and the same for the y component. In code:

```
if ((x > rectangle.x1) && (x < rectangle.x2) &&
    (y > rectangle.y1) && (y < rectangle.y2) )


{
 return IsInside;
}
else
{
 return IsOutside;
}
```

Pretty simple, isn't it? Now you have to test for one rectangle's vertices for containment in the other rectangle, like so:

```
 /* Check all the vertices for containment */
if (RectangleA.ContainsPoint (RectangleB.iX1, RectangleB.iY1))
{
 return Collision;
}
if (RectangleA.ContainsPoint (RectangleB.iX1, RectangleB.iY2))
{
 return Collision;
}
if (RectangleA.ContainsPoint (RectangleB.iX2, RectangleB.iY2))
{
 return Collision;
}
if (RectangleA.ContainsPoint (RectangleB.iX2, RectangleB.iY1))
{
 return Collision;
}
else
{
 return NoCollision;
}
```

And that's it. You have a bounding rectangle collision detection algorithm ready!

2D Image Manipulation

While Direct3D handles just about everything for you, it also does some image manipulation on its own. But one of the disadvantages of letting Direct3D do everything for you is that you don't learn how to do some of the stuff you would kill to have if you didn't have Direct3D working for you. For this reason, knowing the basics of image manipulation is a priority (hey, suppose you are hired to develop to the Game Boy, don't expect that all you have to do is tell it to rotate a bitmap or draw a line, you need to tell it how to do it).

Translation

The simplest transformation is translation. Translating a polygon is as simple as moving it from the position it holds to a new one by either giving it the new position (absolute translation) or by moving x and y units from their current position (relative translation). This is usually done by adding the relative translation to all the vertices.

So, to move from the current position to a new position that is two pixels to the right and five pixels down, you would type the following:

```
Xposition += 2;
Yposition += -5;
```

This is the same as vector addition. Check Figure 13.25 for a visual representation of what happened above.

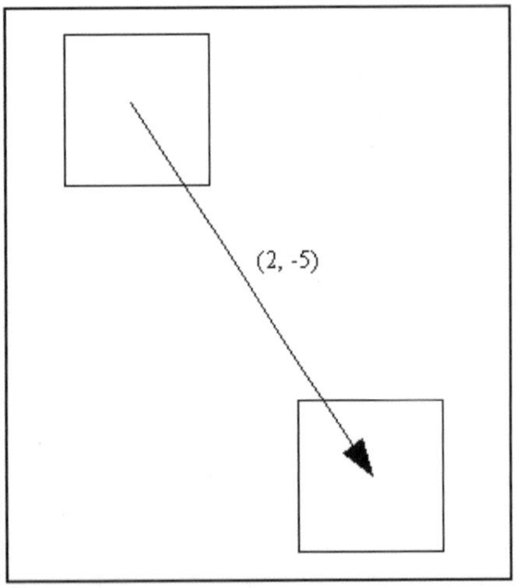

Figure 13.25

Relative translation of an object by (2, –5).

You have added a negative number so you can use that formula any time, independently of the direction you want to move, for example:

```
1 += 2; /* Move right - Result 3 - Right */
1 += -2; /* Move left - Result -1 - Right */
1 -= 2; /* Move right - Result -1 - Wrong */
1 -= -2; /* Move left - Result 3 - Wrong */
```

Would only hold correct results for the first two equations. Of course, you are talking about right-handed coordinate systems (right is positive, left is negative, up is positive, down is negative). You could use a left-handed or flipped system, you could even create one totally unusable and name it after your last name (come on, even if it useless, it is your coordinate system).

Scaling

The next transformation I should cover is scaling—another very basic transformation. The objective is to have a polygon and multiply each of the vertices by the scaling factor.

If, for example, you wanted to scale the polygon to make it twice as large, you would need to multiply each of the polygon's vertices by 2 to achieve the end result.

This operation is demonstrated in Figure 13.26.

While if you wanted to reduce the polygon's size to half, you would divide all the vertices by 2, or more accurately, you would multiply all the vertices by one-half. It is better to use multiplication so you can have a function to do all scaling operations instead of one for making the polygon smaller and another for making the polygon bigger.

Figure 13.27 shows how a division by two, or multiplication by one-half results in the same final polygon.

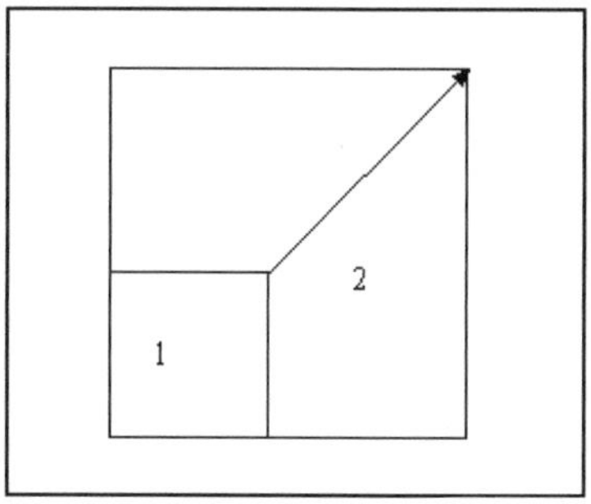

Figure 13.26

Scaling an object by two.

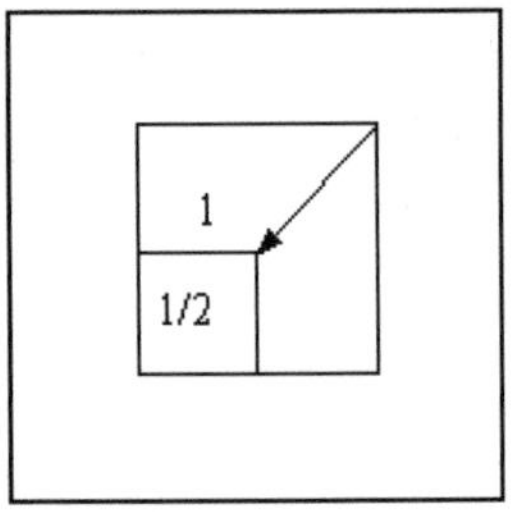

Figure 13.27
Scaling an object by one-half.

If you are having trouble finding which number you should multiply the vertices by, if you want to make the object smaller, the easier way is to think how many times you would like to make the object smaller, like two for one-half, four for one-quarter, ten for one-tenth, and divide one by the number and you get your factor.

Rotation

Rotation is one of the most troublesome tasks when doing 2D programming. The objective is to pick an image and rotate each pixel correctly by a given angle. Unfortunately, due to the fact that pixels' locations are not floating-point, most of the time, rotating each single pixel displayed an incorrect image with some gaps in it.

To fix this problem, people started to only rotate the images' vertices, and then map the image to the resulting vertex (you will let Direct3D handle the mapping).

A word of warning, if you don't have your trigonometry up to date, you may want to check the mathematics chapter before proceeding.

As you can see by Figure 13.28, if you want to rotate a point around the center of the circle, you just need to follow Equations 13.1 and 13.2.

Equation 13.1

$$X = \text{cosine}\ (\theta)\ *\ \text{Radius}$$

Equation 13.2

$$Y = \text{sine}\ (\theta)\ *\ \text{Radius}$$

These equations would work wonderfully if you wanted to rotate a point around the circle if the point is always in the x-axis (y component is 0). Unfortunately, you want something more (and more trouble).

What you want to do is to rotate the point by α. To do this, you need to rotate the point by $\theta + \alpha$, giving you Equations 13.3 and 13.4.

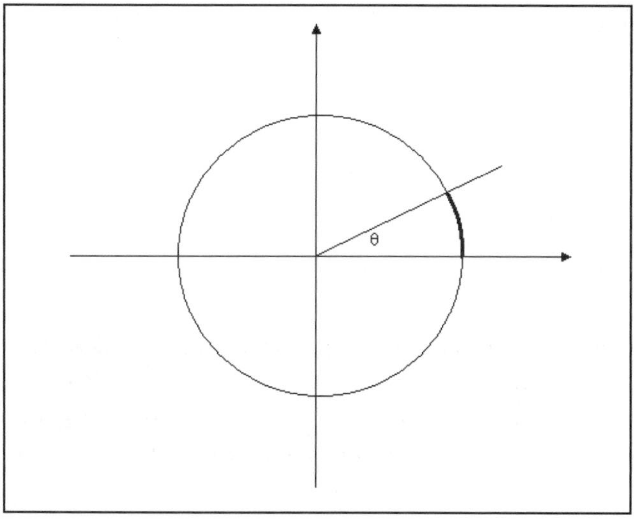

Figure 13.28

The trigonometric circle, axis rotation.

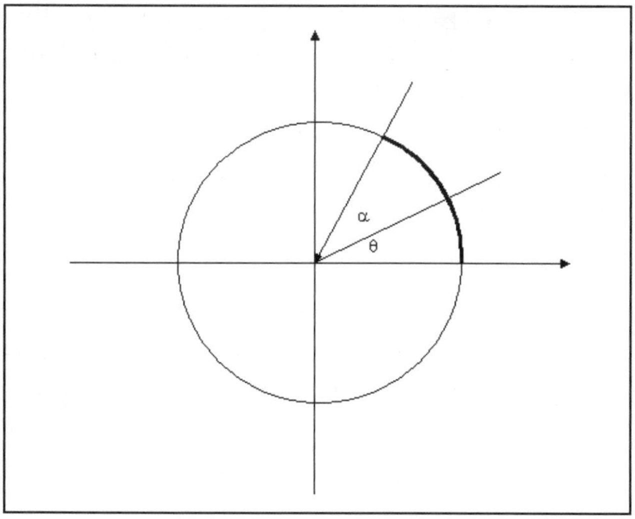

Figure 13.29

The trigonometric circle, arbitrary rotation.

Equation 13.3

$$FinalX = cosine\ (\theta + \alpha)\ *\ Radius$$

Equation 13.4

$$FinalY = sine\ (\theta + \alpha)\ *\ Radius$$

And if you consider that α is the angle you want to rotate around the axis, rotated by θ, you get Equations 13.5 and 13.6.

Equation 13.5

$$X = \text{cosine } (\alpha) * \text{Radius}$$

Equation 13.6

$$Y = \text{sine } (\alpha) * \text{Radius}$$

The main problem with this is that you don't know θ originally, so you can't use this formula directly, what you do is use the trigonometric identities to expand the equation to Equations 13.7 and 13.8.

> **NOTE**
>
> Just in case you are a little confused, what you do is rotate the main axis by θ, so you can then rotate the point by [A], because if you rotate the axis by θ, you can use Equations 13.1 and 13.2 to rotate the point.

Equation 13.7

$$\text{FinalX} = \text{cosine } (\theta) * \text{cosine } (\alpha) * \text{Radius} - \text{sine } (\theta) * \text{sine } (\alpha) * \text{Radius}$$

Equation 13.8

$$\text{FinalY} = \text{sine } (\theta) * \text{cosine } (\alpha) * \text{Radius} + \text{cosine } (\theta) * \text{sine } (\alpha) * \text{Radius}$$

In case you have forgotten, the trigonometric addition identity for cosine and sine are shown in Equations 13.9 and 13.10.

Equation 13.9

$$\text{cosine } (\theta + \alpha) = \text{cosine } (\theta) * \text{cosine } (\alpha) - \text{sine } (\theta) * \text{sine } (\alpha)$$

Equation 13.10

$$\text{sine } (\theta + \alpha) = \text{sine } (\theta) * \text{cosine } (\alpha) + \text{cosine } (\theta) * \text{sine } (\alpha)$$

So, now you know how to rotate a point around the circle, but the problem is that you don't know the radius of the circle, but you do know from Equations 13.5 and 13.6, that:

$$\text{Radius} = Y / \text{sine } (\alpha)$$

$$\text{Radius} = X / \text{cosine } (\alpha)$$

So you can replace in Equations 13.9 and 13.10 to make Equations 13.11 and 13.12.

Equation 13.11

$$\text{FinalX} = \text{cosine}\ (\theta)\ *\ X - \text{sine}\ (\theta)\ *\ Y$$

Equation 13.12

$$\text{FinalY} = \text{sine}\ (\theta)\ *\ X + \text{cosine}\ (\theta)\ *\ Y$$

And you have the equations to rotate a point around an angle, whatever the location of the point.

Now, you just have to use that equation in each vertex of your polygon, and the image will be rotated.

> **NOTE**
>
> Don't forget that if you are implementing these equations, both the `sin` and `cos` functions receive as arguments the angles as radians, if you want to convert degrees to radians you have to multiply the degrees by π / 180

2D Primitives Revealed

While drawing basic 2D primitives with Direct3D is as easy as making pie, doing it in software takes a little more work. I will start by teaching you how to draw lines, since any primitive is usually drawn as a collection of lines.

Lines

While there are several algorithms to draw lines on a computer (sometimes called *rasterization*), almost all evolve from the mathematical representation of a line.

In mathematical terms, a line can be represented simply by Equation 13.13.

Equation 13.13

$$y = mx + b$$

What Equation 13.13 means is that by giving the value of the slope of the line (the m) and the y coordinate where it intersects the vertical axis (when x is 0), you can get any value of y, given an x.

> **NOTE**
>
> The slope of the line is the change of vertical movement divided by the horizontal movement, or rise over run.

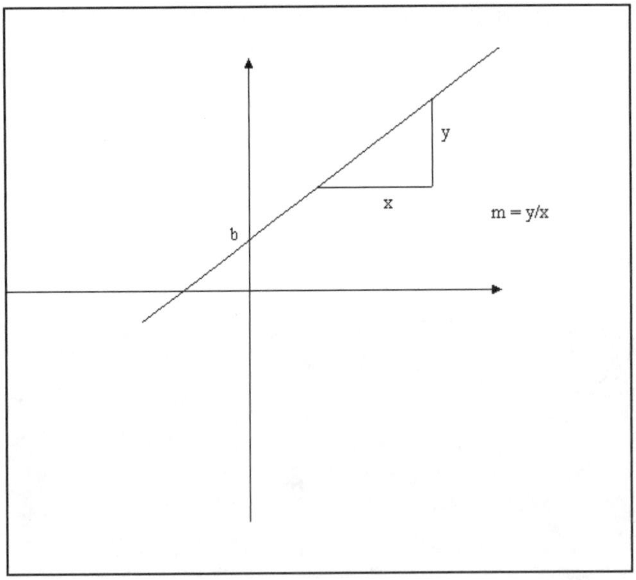

Figure 13.30

y = mx + b: A simple line.

As you can see in Figure 13.30, b is the exact y coordinate of the intersection, and m can be calculated by two values of x (x1 and x2) and divide the difference between the y components of those values by the difference of the x components. See Equation 13.14.

Equation 13.14

$$m = (y2 - y1)\ /\ (x2 - x1)$$

Now, you could just try to put this equation to work, but it wouldn't do you any good. Why? Well, try using a large value for m (like 4 or 5) and increment x by one each time. You will see various gaps between the plotted pixels. You could easily fix this problem by connecting the pixels, right? Well . . . You could, but how, if you are trying to draw a line by drawing another line? This would then cause gaps on the second line that was originally used to fix the gaps on the first, and you would have to eventually draw various lines to fill the gaps of the others to draw just one line. Another solution could be to increment x by smaller values (like one-tenth or smaller) but unfortunately, screen coordinates are integer values, so using floating-point variables would result in errors also.

Because of this problem, several algorithms have appeared to draw a correct line on a screen. This technique is usually called *rasterization.*

I will only be covering one algorithm, which is pretty standard in the industry, which is the Bresenham's line algorithm, named after its creator.

Bresenham's algorithm uses error tracking to know how to move in the y component. Take a look at Figure 13.31 to better understand what is going on:

Bresenham's algorithm starts by plotting a pixel at the first coordinate of the line (x0, y0), and to x+1, it takes the difference of the y component of the line to the two possible y coordinates, and uses the y coordinate where the error is the smaller, and repeats this for every pixel.

The last particularity about the algorithm is that it keeps the error for the next pixel. This allows for the next pixel to draw the most accurate to the real line possible, but also avoids making any gaps between two points. It prevents the line to have any gaps and also makes the line the most accurate possible to the theoretical line (the one that would cause gaps).

Now, this algorithm only works for the first quadrant of the plane (the Cartesian plane), fixing this is just a matter of rotating by 90 degrees (usually called the reflection, since it only involves switching some signs) the line for each following quadrant.

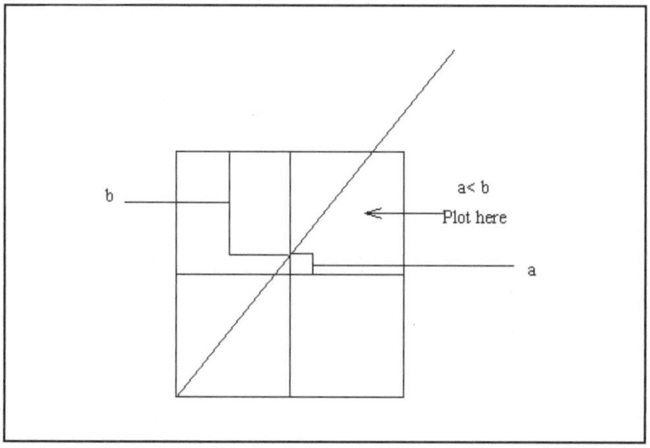

Figure 13.31

Decision of Bresenham's algorithm.

Okay, since Direct3D offers this algorithm in hardware (well, if the video card supports it of course), you will only cover the pseudocode for drawing the line:

```
Calculate X (x1 - x0) and Y (y1 - y0) deltas
Initialize error to zero
If Xdelta >= 0 then
 Xincrement = 1
Else
 Xincrement = -1
 Xdelta = - Xdelta
End if
If Ydelta >= 0
 Yincrement = 1;
Else
 Yincrement = -1
 Ydelta = -Ydelta
End if
If Xdelta > Ydelta
 For every x in Xdelta
  PlotPixel (X, Y)
  If Error >= 0
   Error = Error - Xdelta / 2
   Increase Y by one
  End if
  Error = Error + Ydelta / 2
  Increase X by Xincrement
 End for
else
For every y in Ydelta
  PlotPixel (X, Y)
  If Error >= 0
   Error = Error - Ydelta / 2
   Increase X by one
  End if
  Error = Error + Xdelta / 2
  Increase Y by Yincrement
 End for
End If
```

You start by calculating the deltas, and depending on whether the Xdelta is bigger than the Ydelta, set the appropriate signs (this means that it will do the rotation from the first quadrant to the corresponding quadrant of the line).

Next, depending on which of the deltas is larger, you draw the correct line (if Xdelta is larger, you draw it by using a vertical error tracking, or if Ydelta is larger you draw the line by using a horizontal error tracking).

Later you will use Direct3D to draw lines as fast as lightning, really!

Rectangles and Other Polygons

Now that you know how to draw a line, drawing just about any polygon is easy. Polygons are simply a collection of ordered vertices which need to be connected by lines. This works for any polygon, you have n vertices, and you connect each vertex to another like:

```
For every vertex
 Connect from last vertex to this one with a line
End for
If convex polygon
 Connect last vertex in polygon to first with a line
End if
```

> **NOTE**
> A convex polygon is a completely closed polygon (like a rectangle, a triangle, or a hexagon).

Of course, you don't connect the first vertex to the last, since there is no last vertex.

Drawing rectangles is the same thing as before, but with a slight difference. You can just have two vertices that define the rectangle, as shown in Figure 13.32.

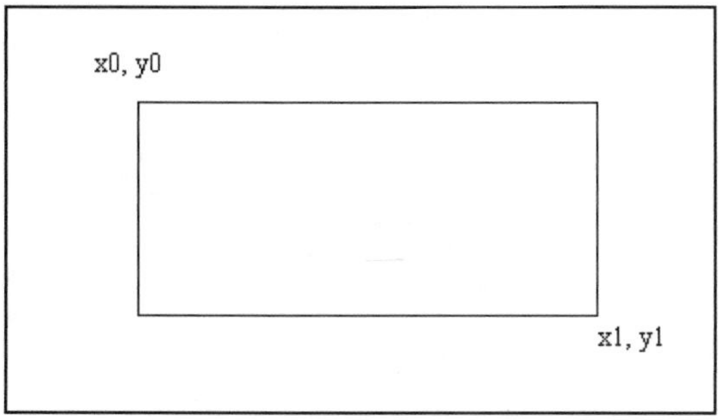

Figure 13.32

A rectangle defined by two vertices.

So, to draw a rectangle this way you just need to do this:

```
Connect (x0, y0) to (x0,y1) with a line
Connect (x0, y1) to (x1,y1) with a line
Connect (x1, y1) to (x1,y0) with a line
Connect (x1, y0) to (x0,y0) with a line
```

And that's about it. The order that you connect them doesn't have to be exactly like this, but remember that the vertices' connections must.

Circles

The final primitive you will see is the circle. Drawing a circle is easier than it seems. If you remember from Figure 13.23, you can rotate any point that has the y component set to 0 around the center of a circle. If you think about it, the x component is the radius of the circle. Now it's the time when your head goes: BING! I know how to draw a circle. And you're right, what you will do is connect several points that have been rotated with Equations 13.1 and 13.2. By incrementing a little bit of the angle in each iteration of the drawing routine, you get a perfect circle drawn.

```
For every Angle until 360
 X = XCircleCenter + Radius * cosine (Angle)
 Y = YCircleCenter + Radius * sine (Angle)
 Connect from last position to X and Y with a line
End for
```

And that's about it. You calculate the x and y coordinate of each point of the circle by increasing the angle by one, and connect the previous point with the current and you have your circle.

> **NOTE**
> In the preceding routine, you have incremented the angle by one degree. For circles with a big radius, this will create a circle that doesn't look very smooth. To fix this problem, increment the angle by a smaller number. And remember, C++ trigonometric functions work with radians.

Developing Mirus

Finally you will be developing some working code. Developing Mirus will let you reuse the same code for various projects without having to worry about the inner workings of DirectX, as illustrated in Figure 13.33.

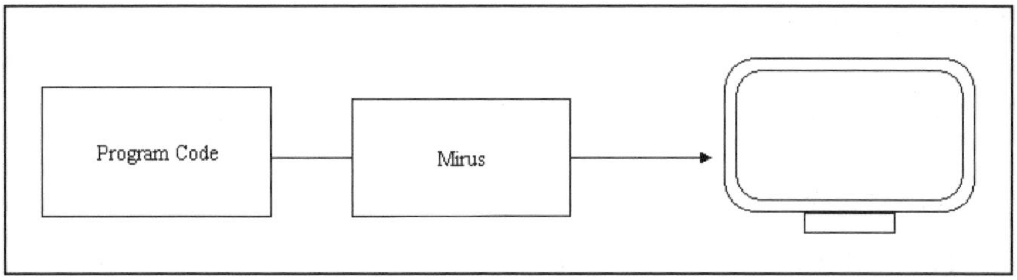

Figure 13.33
Mirus graphics at work.

As you saw in Chapter 10, the graphical part of Mirus works with several related classes. You will see each of them in detail next.

mrScreen

The first class you will develop is `mrScreen`. This class is responsible for setting up DirectX and some support methods to enable you to do some neat stuff. So you can work with `mrScreen`, you need to have a support class for storing your vertices, `mrVertex` which is just a container class. Both `mrScreen` and `mrVertex` are shown next:

```
 /* 'mrScreen.h' */

 /* Mirus base types header */
#include "mrDatatypes.h"
 /* Mirus error definitions header */
#include "mrTimer.h"
 /* Mirus error definitions header */
#include "mrError.h"
 /* Windows header file */
#include <windows.h>
 /* DirectX Graphics header file */
#include <d3d8.h>
 /* C++ math  header file */
#include <math.h>
 /* Assert header file */
#include <assert.h>

 /* Include this file only once */
#pragma once

 /* Mirus custom vertex structure */
class mrVertex
```

```
{
public:
  /* Transformed position */
 FLOAT m_fX, m_fY, m_fZ, m_fRHW;
  /* Color */
 DWORD m_iColor;
  /* Texture coordinates */
 FLOAT m_ftU, m_ftV;
};

 /* Mirus custom vertex type */
#define D3DFVF_MIRUSVERTEX (D3DFVF_XYZRHW|D3DFVF_DIFFUSE|D3DFVF_TEX1)
```

Before checking `mrScreen`, let me just say that you will use vertices which have an already transformed position, that are lit, and use one set of texture coordinates. You will use this kind of vertex from now on.

Continuing . . .

```
 /* Mirus screen class */
class mrScreen
{
protected:
 LPDIRECT3D8         m_pkD3D;
 LPDIRECT3DDEVICE8   m_pkD3DDevice;

 mrUInt32            m_iFPS;
 HWND                m_hWindow;

 mrTimer             m_kTimer;

 mrUInt32            m_iFormat;

  /* Singleton */
 static mrScreen *  m_pkSingleton;

public:
  /* Constructors / Destructor */
 mrScreen (void);
 mrScreen (HWND hWindow);

 ~mrScreen (void);

```

```
  /* Screen manipulation routines */
 mrError32 Init (HWND hWindow);
 mrError32 SetMode (mrUInt32 iFullscreen, mrUInt16 iWidth,
                    mrUInt16 iHeight, mrUInt16 iDepth,
                    bool bHardware);

  /* Render routines */
 mrError32 Clear (mrUInt8 iRed, mrUInt8 iGreen, mrUInt8 iBlue,
                  mrUInt8 iAlpha);
 mrError32 StartFrame (void);
 mrError32 EndFrame (void);

  /* Draw routines */
 mrError32 DrawLine (mrReal32 fX1, mrReal32 fY1,
                     mrReal32 fX2, mrReal32 fY2,
                     mrUInt8 iRed, mrUInt8 iGreen,
                     mrUInt8 iBlue, mrUInt8 iAlpha);
 mrError32 DrawRectangle (mrReal32 fX1, mrReal32 fY1,
                          mrReal32 fX2, mrReal32 fY2,
                          mrUInt8 iRed, mrUInt8 iGreen,
                          mrUInt8 iBlue, mrUInt8 iAlpha);
 mrError32 DrawCircle (mrReal32 fCenterX, mrReal32 fCenterY,
                       mrReal32 iRadius, mrUInt8 iRed,
                       mrUInt8 iGreen, mrUInt8 iBlue, mrUInt8 iAlpha,
                       mrUInt32 iVertices);

  /* Miscellaneous routines */
 mrBool32 IsModeSupported (mrUInt16 iWidth, mrUInt16 iHeight,
                           mrUInt16 iDepth);
 void ShowCursor (mrUInt32 iShowCursor);

  /* Maintenance methods */
 LPDIRECT3DDEVICE8 GetDevice (void);
 mrUInt32 GetFPS (void);
 mrUInt32 GetFormat (void);

 mrUInt32 GetBitdepth (void);

  /* Singleton */
 static mrScreen * GetSingleton (void);
};
```

You will see each of these methods with their explanation and purpose individually. Starting with the default constructor:

```
 /* 'mrScreen.cpp' */

 /* Complement header file */
#include "mrScreen.h"

 /* Singleton object */
mrScreen * mrScreen::m_pkSingleton = NULL;

 /* Default constructor */
mrScreen::mrScreen (void)
{
 m_pkD3D        = NULL;
 m_pkD3DDevice = NULL;
 m_hWindow      = NULL;
 m_iFPS         = 0;

 assert (!m_pkSingleton);
 m_pkSingleton = this;
}
```

In the constructor you just set the class members to zero or NULL and make initialize the singleton. You have also declared the singleton static variable.

In case the user wants to initialize Direct3D at the same time he wants to declare its variable, you have created the following assignment constructor:

```
 /* Assignment constructor */
mrScreen::mrScreen (HWND hWindow)
{
 m_pkD3D        = NULL;
 m_pkD3DDevice = NULL;
 m_iFPS         = 0;
 m_hWindow      = hWindow;

 assert (!m_pkSingleton);
 m_pkSingleton = this;

 Init (hWindow);
}
```

Where you initialize most of the members to NULL and the m_hWindow to the window handle that was passed to the constructor. After you initialize the singleton you call Init, which will initialize Direct3D as you will see.

You will also need to define your destructor, which will shut down Direct3D:

```
 /* Default destructor */
mrScreen::~mrScreen (void)
{
 if (NULL != m_pkD3DDevice)
 {
  m_pkD3DDevice->Release ();
  m_pkD3DDevice = NULL;
 }
 if (NULL != m_pkD3D)
 {
  m_pkD3D->Release ();
  m_pkD3D = NULL;
 }
 m_iFPS         = 0;

 assert (m_pkSingleton);
 m_pkSingleton = NULL;
}
```

As you learned before, each Direct3D object must be released, which is done in the destructor if any of them is valid. After that you just set up the singleton and that's it.

You now need to create the Direct3D main object, which is done in Init.

```
 /* Initialize Direct3D */
mrError32 mrScreen::Init (HWND hWindow)
{
  /* Create Direct3D object */
 m_pkD3D = Direct3DCreate8 (D3D_SDK_VERSION);
 m_hWindow     = hWindow;

 if (NULL == m_pkD3D)
 {
  return mrErrorInitDirect3D;
 }
 return mrNoError;
}
```

Here you just use Direct3DCreate8 (line 58) to create the object as you saw before, and determine whether it was successful by checking if the returned object is valid (line 61).

Next is probably the most complicated method of mrScreen. SetMode allows you to set the display mode to either full-screen or windowed and the screen properties. This is kind of a long method so I will cover it in parts:

```
68:  /* Sets the display mode / create the Direct3D device */
69: mrError32 mrScreen::SetMode (mrUInt32 iFullscreen, mrUInt16 iWidth,
70:                              mrUInt16 iHeight, mrUInt16 iDepth,
71:                              bool bHardware)
72: {
73:  D3DPRESENT_PARAMETERS kPresentParams;
74:  mrUInt32             iDeviceType;
75:
76:   /* Set type of device to create (hardware or software */
77:  if (!bHardware)
78:  {
79:   iDeviceType = D3DDEVTYPE_REF;
80:  }
81:  else
82:  {
83:   iDeviceType = D3DDEVTYPE_HAL;
84:  }
85:
86:   /* Reset present parameters and set swap effect */
87:  ZeroMemory (&kPresentParams, sizeof (D3DPRESENT_PARAMETERS) );
88:  kPresentParams.SwapEffect = D3DSWAPEFFECT_DISCARD;
```

Start by deciding whether you want to create a hardware- or software-only device (lines 77 through 84) and depending on which, set iDeviceType with the appropriate value. Next you just clear the kPresentParams and set the SwapEffect to D3DSWAPEFFECT_DISCARD. You do this here since all of this is the same either for windowed or full-screen mode.

Next you need to either set up windowed mode or full-screen mode. You will first see windowed mode:

```
90:   /* If windowed mode */
91:  if (!iFullscreen)
92:  {
93:   D3DDISPLAYMODE kCurrentMode;
94:
```

```
 95:     /* Get current mode information */
 96:    if (FAILED (m_pkD3D->GetAdapterDisplayMode (D3DADAPTER_DEFAULT,
 97:                &kCurrentMode) ))
 98:    {
 99:     return mrErrorGetAdapterDisplayMode;
100:    }
101:
102:     /* Set windowed mode and backbuffer format compatible with
103:        current format */
104:    kPresentParams.Windowed          = true;
105:    kPresentParams.BackBufferCount   = 1;
106:    kPresentParams.BackBufferFormat  = kCurrentMode.Format;
107:
108:     /* Try to create device */
109:    if (FAILED (m_pkD3D->CreateDevice (D3DADAPTER_DEFAULT,
110:                                 (D3DDEVTYPE) iDeviceType,
111:                                 m_hWindow,
112:                                 D3DCREATE_SOFTWARE_VERTEXPROCESSING,
113:                                 &kPresentParams, &m_pkD3DDevice ) ))
114:    {
115:     return mrErrorCreateDevice;
116:    }
117:   }
```

You don't do anything that you haven't done before. You start by getting the current display mode (lines 96 and 97) and set up the kPresentParams structure (lines 104 through 106) accordingly. You then try to create the device using these parameters (lines 109 through 113).

Next you need to set up full screen mode:

```
118:   else
119:   {
120:     /* Set full screen mode and full screen information */
121:    kPresentParams.Windowed          = false;
122:    kPresentParams.BackBufferCount   = 1;
123:    kPresentParams.BackBufferWidth   = iWidth;
124:    kPresentParams.BackBufferHeight  = iHeight;
125:
126:    kPresentParams.FullScreen_RefreshRateInHz =
127:                                  D3DPRESENT_RATE_DEFAULT;
128:    kPresentParams.FullScreen_PresentationInterval =
129:                                  D3DPRESENT_INTERVAL_DEFAULT;
```

Let's stop here for a moment. What you did in the previous lines was set up the structure to create a full-screen device. It isn't complicated, but the following lines of code might be:

```
  /* If 16 bit, try to create the device using different 16 bit pixel
     color formats */
 if (iDepth == 16)
 {
  kPresentParams.BackBufferFormat = D3DFMT_R5G6B5;
  if (FAILED (m_pkD3D->CreateDevice (D3DADAPTER_DEFAULT,
                                     (D3DDEVTYPE) iDeviceType,
                                     m_hWindow,
                                     D3DCREATE_SOFTWARE_VERTEXPROCESSING,
                                     &kPresentParams, &m_pkD3DDevice ) ))
  {
   kPresentParams.BackBufferFormat = D3DFMT_X1R5G5B5;
   if (FAILED (m_pkD3D->CreateDevice (D3DADAPTER_DEFAULT,
                                      (D3DDEVTYPE) iDeviceType,
                                      m_hWindow,
                                      D3DCREATE_SOFTWARE_VERTEXPROCESSING,
                                      &kPresentParams, &m_pkD3DDevice ) ))
   {
    kPresentParams.BackBufferFormat = D3DFMT_A1R5G5B5;
    if (FAILED (m_pkD3D->CreateDevice (D3DADAPTER_DEFAULT,
                                       (D3DDEVTYPE) iDeviceType,
                                       m_hWindow,
                                       D3DCREATE_SOFTWARE_VERTEXPROCESSING,
                                       &kPresentParams, &m_pkD3DDevice ) ))
    {
     return mrErrorCreateDevice;
    }
   }
  }
 }
  /* If 32 bit, try to create the device using different pixel 32
     color formats */
 else
 {
  kPresentParams.BackBufferFormat = D3DFMT_A8R8G8B8;
  if (FAILED (m_pkD3D->CreateDevice (D3DADAPTER_DEFAULT,
                                     (D3DDEVTYPE) iDeviceType,
```

```
                                           m_hWindow,
                                           D3DCREATE_SOFTWARE_VERTEXPROCESSING,
                                           &kPresentParams, &m_pkD3DDevice ) ))
     {
      kPresentParams.BackBufferFormat = D3DFMT_X8R8G8B8;
      if (FAILED (m_pkD3D->CreateDevice (D3DADAPTER_DEFAULT,
                                            (D3DDEVTYPE) iDeviceType,
                                            m_hWindow,
                                            D3DCREATE_SOFTWARE_VERTEXPROCESSING,
                                            &kPresentParams, &m_pkD3DDevice ) ))
      {
       return mrErrorCreateDevice;
      }
     }
    }

  }
  m_iFormat = kPresentParams.BackBufferFormat;
```

What you did here was to, depending on the bitdepth desired, try to create the device with a specific format, and if that failed, try to create it using another format that uses the same bitdepth, and so on until either one succeeds, or you run out of formats. You do this both for 16- and 32-bit modes.

If you already used Direct3D you may be wondering why I'm trying to create a backbuffer with alpha support since almost none (at least I don't know any) support them. The reason I'm doing this is that you don't know which video cards are coming, and if any support them, you may want to do some cool stuff with alpha windows. For now it has no use, but it was left that way for future use.

In the end, you just store the backbuffer format to your `mrScreen` class.

Next, you need to set the appropriate render states:

```
   /* Set render states */
  m_pkD3DDevice->SetRenderState (D3DRS_CULLMODE, D3DCULL_NONE);
  m_pkD3DDevice->SetRenderState (D3DRS_LIGHTING, FALSE);
  m_pkD3DDevice->SetRenderState (D3DRS_ALPHABLENDENABLE, TRUE);
  m_pkD3DDevice->SetRenderState (D3DRS_SRCBLEND, D3DBLEND_SRCALPHA);
  m_pkD3DDevice->SetRenderState (D3DRS_DESTBLEND, D3DBLEND_INVSRCALPHA);

   /* Set texture color states */
  m_pkD3DDevice->SetTextureStageState (0, D3DTSS_COLOROP, D3DTOP_MODULATE);
```

```
196:   m_pkD3DDevice->SetTextureStageState (0, D3DTSS_ALPHAOP, D3DTOP_MODULATE);
197:
198:   return mrNoError;
199: }
```

Nothing too hard, is it? You can now initialize Direct3D in any mode that the video card supports with just a single call to a method; nice, eh? But don't stop here, there are lots of cool things to come:

You also need a method that allows you to clear the backbuffer:

```
201:   /* Clear the window to color */
202: mrError32 mrScreen::Clear (mrUInt8 iRed, mrUInt8 iGreen, mrUInt8 iBlue,
203:                            mrUInt8 iAlpha)
204: {
205:   mrUInt32 iColor;
206:   iColor = D3DCOLOR_RGBA (iRed, iGreen, iBlue, iAlpha);
207:
208:    /* Clear the screen to certain color */
209:   if (FAILED (m_pkD3DDevice->Clear (0, NULL, D3DCLEAR_TARGET, iColor,
210:               0, 0) ))
211:   {
212:    return mrErrorClear;
213:   }
214:   return mrNoError;
215: }
```

In this method you choose the four-color components and use the D3DCOLOR_RGBA macro to create a Direct3D color (line 206) and then clear the device to that color (line 209).

To ensure that the mrScreen class works correctly and returns the correct number of frames, you need to let mrScreen know when you will start and end a frame.

One of the functions is StartFrame:

```
217:   /* Start rendering */
218: mrError32 mrScreen::StartFrame (void)
219: {
220:   m_kTimer.Update ();
221:
222:    /* Start rendering */
223:   if (FAILED (m_pkD3DDevice->BeginScene () ))
```

```
224:   {
225:    return mrErrorBeginScene;
226:   }
227:   return mrNoError;
228: }
```

Here you just update the class timer and tell Direct3D that you will start rendering.

You also need to let Direct3D know that you will stop rendering, which is done with EndFrame:

```
230:   /* End rendering */
231: mrError32 mrScreen::EndFrame (void)
232: {
233:    /* End rendering */
234:   if (FAILED (m_pkD3DDevice->EndScene () ))
235:   {
236:    return mrErrorEndScene;
237:   }
238:
239:    /* Present data to the screen */
240:   if (FAILED (m_pkD3DDevice->Present (NULL, NULL, NULL, NULL) ))
241:   {
242:    return mrErrorPresent;
243:   }
244:
245:    /* Calculate frames per second */
246:   m_kTimer.Update ();
247:   m_iFPS = (mrUInt32) (1 / m_kTimer.GetDelta ());
248:
249:   return mrNoError;
250: }
```

In this method you do a few things to terminate rendering. You first let Direct3D know that you won't send more data to the video card (line 234), and then you present what you rendered to the screen (line 240).

In the end, you update the class timer to calculate the frames per second. Getting the frames per second is easy, you start by getting the time it took to render the frame, which is done with `m_kTimer.GetDelta ()`, and since you know that it took that time to render one frame, you need to check how many frames could be rendered in a second. This is done by dividing one by the time to render one frame.

It's now time to create the primitive drawing methods. Let's start with DrawLine:

```
253: mrError32 mrScreen::DrawLine (mrReal32 fX1, mrReal32 fY1,
254:                              mrReal32 fX2, mrReal32 fY2,
255:                              mrUInt8 iRed, mrUInt8 iGreen,
256:                              mrUInt8 iBlue, mrUInt8 iAlpha)
257: {
258:  mrUInt32 iColor;
259:  iColor = D3DCOLOR_RGBA (iRed, iGreen, iBlue, iAlpha);
260:
261:   /* Create rectangle vertices */
262:  mrVertex kVertices [] =
263:  {  /* x, y, z, w, color, texture coordinates (u,v) */
264:   {fX1, fY1, 0, 1.0f, iColor, 0, 0},
265:   {fX2, fY2, 0, 1.0f, iColor, 0, 0},
266:  };
267:
268:   /* Draw the line */
269:  mrScreen::GetSingleton ()->GetDevice ()->SetVertexShader (
270:                                          D3DFVF_MIRUSVERTEX);
271:  if (FAILED (mrScreen::GetSingleton ()->GetDevice ()->DrawPrimitiveUP (
272:                                          D3DPT_LINELIST, 2, kVertices,
273:                                          sizeof (mrVertex))) )
274:  {
275:   return mrErrorDrawPrimitive;
276:  }
277:
278:  return mrNoError;
279: }
```

Remember that hard code for drawing a line? Well, you will forget all of that and use Direct3D built-in methods to draw lines, with the advantages of being much simpler to code and also faster, since it is hardware accelerated.

So, to draw a line you need to set up two vertices (one for each point of the line) with the appropriate color and position (lines 262 through 266). After that, you need a call to DrawPrimitiveUP but using D3DPT_LINELIST as the primitive type (lines 271 through 273). And that's it, pretty simple, right?

Next you will use the `DrawRectangle` method:

```
281: mrError32 mrScreen::DrawRectangle (mrReal32 fX1, mrReal32 fY1,
282:                                     mrReal32 fX2, mrReal32 fY2,
283:                                     mrUInt8 iRed, mrUInt8 iGreen,
284:                                     mrUInt8 iBlue, mrUInt8 iAlpha)
285: {
286:  mrUInt32 iColor;
287:  iColor = D3DCOLOR_RGBA (iRed, iGreen, iBlue, iAlpha);
288:
289:   /* Create rectangle vertices */
290:  mrVertex kVertices [] =
291:  {  /* x, y, z, w, color, texture coordinates (u,v) */
292:   {fX1, fY1, 0, 1.0f, iColor, 0, 0},
293:   {fX2, fY1, 0, 1.0f, iColor, 0, 0},
294:   {fX2, fY2, 0, 1.0f, iColor, 0, 0},
295:   {fX1, fY2, 0, 1.0f, iColor, 0, 0},
296:   {fX1, fY1, 0, 1.0f, iColor, 0, 0},
297:  };
298:
299:   /* Draw the line */
300:  mrScreen::GetSingleton ()->GetDevice ()->SetVertexShader (
301:                                       D3DFVF_MIRUSVERTEX);
302:  if (FAILED (mrScreen::GetSingleton ()->GetDevice ()->DrawPrimitiveUP (
303:                                       D3DPT_LINESTRIP, 4, kVertices,
304:                                       sizeof (mrVertex))) )
305:  {
306:   return mrErrorDrawPrimitive;
307:  }
308:
309:  return mrNoError;
310: }
```

This method is pretty simple, too. You set up five vertices (each line is made of two vertices, because you use the last vertex as the start of the next line, you need to define five vertices to draw four lines) to hold the complete rectangle (lines 290 through 297).

You can then finish up by drawing the rectangle using a call to `DrawPrimitiveUP` drawing four primitives (lines 302 through 304), the side of the rectangles.

The last primitive drawing method I will cover is `DrawCircle`:

```
312: mrError32 mrScreen::DrawCircle (mrReal32 iCenterX, mrReal32 iCenterY,
313:                                  mrReal32 iRadius, mrUInt8 iRed,
314:                                  mrUInt8 iGreen, mrUInt8 iBlue,
315:                                  mrUInt8 iAlpha, mrUInt32 iVertices)
316: {
317:  mrUInt32 iColor;
318:  iColor = D3DCOLOR_RGBA (iRed, iGreen, iBlue, iAlpha);
319:
320:  mrVertex * pkVertices;
321:   /* Allocate needed vertices */
322:  pkVertices = new mrVertex [iVertices + 1];
323:
324:  mrReal32 fAngle = 0;
325:  mrReal32 fComplete;
326:
327:  mrUInt32 iVertex;
328:
329:   /* Calculate each vertex position */
330:  for (iVertex = 0; iVertex < iVertices; iVertex ++)
331:  {
332:    /* Percentage of circle already drawn */
333:   fComplete = (mrReal32)iVertex / (mrReal32)iVertices;
334:   pkVertices [iVertex].m_fX = (mrReal32) ((mrReal32)iCenterX +
335:               ((mrReal32)iRadius * cos (6.2831f*fComplete)));
336:   pkVertices [iVertex].m_fY = (mrReal32) ((mrReal32)iCenterY +
337:               ((mrReal32)iRadius * sin (6.2831f*fComplete)));
338:
339:   pkVertices [iVertex].m_fZ      = 0;
340:   pkVertices [iVertex].m_fRHW    = 1.0f;
341:   pkVertices [iVertex].m_iColor = iColor;
342:   pkVertices [iVertex].m_ftU     = 0;
343:   pkVertices [iVertex].m_ftV     = 0;
344:  }
```

What you do up to here is set up all the vertices by starting to allocate enough memory to hold the number of vertices plus one (the closing vertex). You then set up the vertex's position which is done by going through all the vertices and depending on the percentage complete, you calculate the position of that vertex by using the trigonometric functions sine and cosine to get the position of that vertex in the circle. You end up by adding the center position of the circle to each vertex to be able to put the circle anywhere in the screen.

Next you need to close and render the circle:

```
346:   /* Close the circle */
347:  pkVertices [iVertex].m_fX = pkVertices [0].m_fX;
348:  pkVertices [iVertex].m_fY = pkVertices [0].m_fY;
349:
350:  pkVertices [iVertex].m_fZ      = 0;
351:  pkVertices [iVertex].m_fRHW    = 1.0f;
352:  pkVertices [iVertex].m_iColor = iColor;
353:  pkVertices [iVertex].m_ftU     = 0;
354:  pkVertices [iVertex].m_ftV     = 0;
355:
356:   /* Draw the circle */
357:  mrScreen::GetSingleton ()->GetDevice ()->SetVertexShader (
358:                                          D3DFVF_MIRUSVERTEX);
359:  if (FAILED (mrScreen::GetSingleton ()->GetDevice ()->DrawPrimitiveUP (
360:                                          D3DPT_LINESTRIP, iVertices,
361:                                          pkVertices, sizeof (mrVertex))) )
362:  {
363:   return mrErrorDrawPrimitive;
364:  }
365:  delete [] pkVertices;
366:  return mrNoError;
367: }
```

What you do here is set up the closing vertex to be exactly like the first vertex to make it possible to correctly close the circle (lines 347 and 348). You finish the method by drawing the circle using `DrawPrimitiveUP` as lines (lines 359 through 361) and release any memory you used for the vertices.

The next method you will develop allows you to see whether a determined full-screen mode is supported by the current video card. Since there are various new functions here, I will dissect this method and explain it to you in separate parts:

```
 /* Check if mode is supported */
mrBool32 mrScreen::IsModeSupported (mrUInt16 iWidth, mrUInt16 iHeight,
                                    mrUInt16 iDepth)
{
 mrUInt32       iNumberOfModes;
 mrUInt32       iMode;
 D3DDISPLAYMODE kMode;

  /* Get number of available modes */
 iNumberOfModes = m_pkD3D->GetAdapterModeCount (D3DADAPTER_DEFAULT);
```

Here is a new method, `GetAdapterModeCount`. This method allows you to know how many different full-screen modes one adapter can work with. It is defined as:

```
UINT IDirect3D8::GetAdapterModeCount (UINT Adapter);
```

Which returns the number of modes the adapter can support. A computer can have more than one adapter (multi-card support) but since you are only interested in the primary one, you will use `D3DADAPTER_DEFAULT` so Direct3D returns the number of modes the primary card can display.

Next you have to check whether any of the supported modes is equal to the one you want:

```
  /* For each mode check if mode is equal */
 for (iMode = 0; iMode < iNumberOfModes; iMode ++)
 {
   /* Get mode information */
  m_pkD3D->EnumAdapterModes (D3DADAPTER_DEFAULT, iMode, &kMode);
```

What you do here is loop through every available mode and get the mode information with `EnumAdapterModes`. `EnumAdapterModes` allows you to get information on a specific mode and is defined as:

```
HRESULT IDirect3D8::EnumAdapterModes(
 UINT Adapter,
 UINT Mode,
 D3DDISPLAYMODE * pMode);
```

Where the first parameter is the adapter you want to query. In this case, you want to use the default so you use D3DADAPTER_DEFAULT again. Next you have the mode you want to use, you will use the current loop variable to get the associated mode, and the last parameter is a pointer to a D3DDISPLAYMODE structure that will hold the mode information.

Next you need to compare the structure members with the mode to test:

```
    /* Compare dimensions */
   if ((iWidth == kMode.Width) && (iHeight == kMode.Height))
   {
     /* Compare bit depth */
    if (iDepth == 16)
    {
     if ((kMode.Format == D3DFMT_R5G6B5) ||
         (kMode.Format == D3DFMT_X1R5G5B5) ||
         (kMode.Format == D3DFMT_A1R5G5B5) )
     {
      return mrTrue;
     }
    }
    else
    {
     if ((kMode.Format == D3DFMT_A8R8G8B8) ||
         (kMode.Format == D3DFMT_X8R8G8B8))
     {
      return mrTrue;
     }
    }
   }
  }

  return mrFalse;
}
```

What you do is check whether the width and height of the mode match the exact mode you want, and if so, you then test to see if it supports any of the backbuffer formats for each bitdepth; if they all match, then the mode is supported and you can return mrTrue, if not, you will test to go through all the modes until either one matches or you run out of modes. In the case of the second result, you then know that the mode is not supported and you return mrFalse.

The last method that is directly related with Direct3D is ShowCursor. ShowCursor will either hide or show the cursor for your application:

```
 /* Shows or hides the cursor */
void mrScreen::ShowCursor (mrUInt32 iShowCursor)
{
 m_pkD3DDevice->ShowCursor (iShowCursor);
}
```

Which uses the ShowCursor of IDirect3DDevice8 to show or hide the cursor. ShowCursor is defined as:

```
BOOL IDirect3DDevice8::ShowCursor (BOOL bShow);
```

This function returns the previous state of the cursor, which is TRUE if it was visible and FALSE if it wasn't, and accepts as the only parameter a BOOL which defines whether the cursor should be visible, TRUE, or not, FALSE.

Following are the access methods. There is nothing difficult about these, but there is one I want to go over in particular:

```
 /* Returns the Direct3D device */
LPDIRECT3DDEVICE8 mrScreen::GetDevice (void)
{
 return m_pkD3DDevice;
}

 /* Returns the frames per second */
mrUInt32 mrScreen::GetFPS (void)
{
 return m_iFPS;
}

 /* Returns the backbuffer format */
mrUInt32 mrScreen::GetFormat (void)
{
 return m_iFormat;
}
```

The next method will be used to return the bitdepth, not the format of the back-buffer. You need to know for later:

```
 /* Returns the backbuffer depth */
mrUInt32 mrScreen::GetBitdepth (void)
```

```
{
 mrUInt32 iBitdepth;

 switch (m_iFormat)
 {
 case D3DFMT_R5G6B5:
 case D3DFMT_X1R5G5B5:
 case D3DFMT_A1R5G5B5:
  iBitdepth = 16;
  break;
 case D3DFMT_A8R8G8B8:
 case D3DFMT_X8R8G8B8:
  iBitdepth = 32;
  break;
 }

 return iBitdepth;
}
```

What you do is check the backbuffer format, and if it matches any of the 16-bit formats, then you return the bitdepth as 16, and if it matches any of the 32-bit formats, you obviously return the bitdepth as 32. There are various reasons you may want to know the bitdepth, such as presenting it to the user (its usually isn't a good idea to ask the user to chose a format, but it is a good idea to ask the user to chose a bitdepth) and also so you can lock the surfaces and texture later.

Next is just the singleton access method:

```
 /* Returns the mrScreen singleton */
mrScreen * mrScreen::GetSingleton (void)
{
 assert (m_pkSingleton);
 return m_pkSingleton;
}
```

And you are done. That wasn't so hard, was it? It required some little tricks to make it possible to use this with any mode, but it was worth it since now you can use the same code to set up any mode.

Here is how you can set up Direct3D with just three simple lines of code:

```
mrScreen Screen;
Screen.Init (hWindowHandle);
Screen.SetMode (true, 640, 480, 16, true);
```

Which would set up Direct3D to use a fullscreen, 640×480 resolution, 16 bitdepth, and hardware accelerated device. Of course, if you wanted to use windowed mode or any other full-screen mode you would just need to change a few parameters to `SetMode`.

Now, for each frame you would need to do the following:

```
Screen.Clear (255, 255, 255, 255);
Screen.BeginFrame ();
Screen.DrawLine (10, 10, 60, 34, 255, 0, 0, 255);
 /* Other drawing methods here */
Screen.EndFrame ();
```

Which would clear the back buffer to bright white and draw a red line from position 10, 10 to 60, 34. If you think this is easy, just wait until you develop some classes for animated objects, after that, making games will be a cinch.

mrRGBAImage

The `mrRGBAImage` class is the most basic representation of an image in Mirus. It is a sequence of bytes, actually, four bytes, that represent colors in the image. By using an image class that isn't specifically oriented to be used for something (like a surface or texture), you can add or change the image as you wish without worrying about other problems (like surface locking, and so on).

As you can see from the name of the class, `mrRGBAImage` stores the colors in the RGBA format—eight bytes for red, eight bytes for green, eight bytes for blue, and eight bytes for alpha.

`mrRGBAImage` is declared as:

```
 /* 'mrRGBAImage.h' */

 /* Mirus base types header */
#include "mrDatatypes.h"
 /* Mirus error definitions header */
#include "mrError.h"
 /* Windows header file */
#include <windows.h>
 /* File stream header file */
#include <fstream.h>
 /* DirectX Graphics header file */
#include <d3d8.h>

```

```
/* Include this file only once */
#pragma once

/* Mirus RGBA image class */
class mrRGBAImage
{
protected:
  /* Image size */
 mrUInt32        m_iWidth;
 mrUInt32        m_iHeight;

  /* Image buffer */
 mrUInt32 *      m_piImageBuffer;

public:
  /* Constructor / Destructor */
 mrRGBAImage (void);
 ~mrRGBAImage (void);

  /* Operators */
 mrRGBAImage & operator = (mrRGBAImage & rkImage);

  /* Load image from Windows bitmap */
 mrError32 LoadFromBitmap (LPSTR lpszFilename);
 mrError32 LoadFromTarga (LPSTR lpszFilename);

  /* Image manipulation */
 void SetColorKey (mrUInt8 iRed, mrUInt8 iGreen, mrUInt8 iBlue);

 void SetWidth (mrUInt32);
 void SetHeight (mrUInt32);
 void SetColor (mrUInt32 iX, mrUInt32 iY, mrUInt8 iRed,
                mrUInt8 iGreen, mrUInt8 iBlue,
                mrUInt8 iAlpha);
 void SetImageBuffer (mrUInt32 * pImage);

 mrUInt32 GetWidth (void);
 mrUInt32 GetHeight (void);
 mrUInt32 GetColor (mrUInt32 iX, mrUInt32 iY);
 mrUInt32 * GetImageBuffer (void);
};
```

All of the preceding methods should already ring a bell on your head. As usual, you will start by checking the constructor and the destructor:

```
 1:  /* 'mrRGBAImage.cpp' */
 2:
 3:  /* Complement header file */
 4: #include "mrRGBAImage.h"
 5:
 6:  /* Default constructor */
 7: mrRGBAImage::mrRGBAImage (void)
 8: {
 9:  m_iWidth         = 0;
10:  m_iHeight        = 0;
11:  m_piImageBuffer = NULL;
12: }
13:
14:  /* Default destructor */
15: mrRGBAImage::~mrRGBAImage (void)
16: {
17:  m_iWidth         = 0;
18:  m_iHeight        = 0;
19:
20:   /* If memory was allocated, release it */
21:  if (NULL != m_piImageBuffer)
22:  {
23:   delete [] m_piImageBuffer;
24:   m_piImageBuffer = NULL;
25:  }
26: }
```

Both of these methods are very simple. In the constructor, you initialize all the class members to zero or `NULL`, and in the destructor you take care of releasing the memory used by the class by checking whether the `m_ piImageBuffer` is valid and if so, delete it (lines 21 through 24).

Next is the assignment operator:

```
28:  /* Copy this image to another */
29: mrRGBAImage & mrRGBAImage::operator = (mrRGBAImage & rkImage)
30: {
31:  m_iWidth  = rkImage.GetWidth ();
32:  m_iHeight = rkImage.GetHeight ();
```

```
33:  SetImageBuffer (rkImage.GetImageBuffer ());
34:
35:   /* Return an instance of this class */
36:  return * this;
37: }
```

What you do here is copy the other image size to the other one (lines 31 and 32) and then you set the image buffer with `SetImageBuffer` (line 33).

Next are the two image-loading methods. Don't worry, I will go over them slowly to make sure everything is explained. I recommend that you keep the bitmap and targa loading pages marked so you can check them if you don't understand something:

```
39:  /* Load image from a windows bitmap file */
40: mrError32 mrRGBAImage::LoadFromBitmap (LPSTR lpszFilename)
41: {
42:  fstream       kBitmap;
43:
44:  kBitmap.open (lpszFilename, ios::binary | ios::in);
45:
46:  if (kBitmap.is_open ())
47:  {
48:   mrUInt16      iType;
49:   kBitmap.read ((char *) &iType, sizeof (mrUInt16));
50:
51:    /* Get bitmap type */
52:   if (0x4D42 != iType)
53:   {
54:    return mrErrorNotBitmapFile;
55:   }
```

Up to here what you do is open the file (line 46) and read two bytes (`mrUInt16` is two bytes) which is the bitmap type. If the type isn't `0x4D42` (lines 52 through 55), then this isn't a valid bitmap file and you should abort the loading process.

Next you will read the necessary data that describes the bitmap:

```
57:    /* Ignore eight bytes */
58:   kBitmap.seekg (8, ios::cur);
59:
60:    /* Get the position of the start of the bitmap buffer */
61:   mrUInt32      iStartBuffer;
```

```
62:  kBitmap.read ((char *) &iStartBuffer, sizeof (mrUInt32));
63:
64:   /* Ignore four bytes */
65:  kBitmap.seekg (4, ios::cur);
66:
67:   /* Get width and height of bitmap */
68:  kBitmap.read ((char *) &m_iWidth, sizeof (mrUInt32));
69:  kBitmap.read ((char *) &m_iHeight, sizeof (mrUInt32));
70:
71:   /* Ignore two bytes */
72:  kBitmap.seekg (2, ios::cur);
73:
74:   /* Get bit count */
75:  mrUInt16     iBitCount;
76:  kBitmap.read ((char *) &iBitCount, sizeof (mrUInt16));
77:
78:   /* If not 24 mode not supported, return error */
79:  if (iBitCount != 24)
80:  {
81:   return mrErrorBitmapNotSupported;
82:  }
83:   /* Get compression */
84:  mrUInt32     iCompression;
85:  kBitmap.read ((char *) &iCompression, sizeof (mrUInt32));
86:
87:   /* If compressed not supported, return error */
88:  if (iCompression != BI_RGB)
89:  {
90:   return mrErrorBitmapNotSupported;
91:  }
```

You start by ignoring eight bytes of data, which is information that you don't use (line 58). You then read the position of the start of the buffer (line 62). Again you ignore a few more bytes, this time four (line 65). You then read the width and height of the bitmap (lines 68 and 69) to only ignore another two bytes (line 72). Next you need to read the bit count (line 76) and if it is different from 24, you need to abort the loading operation since you only support 24-bit bitmaps (lines 79 through 82). In the end, you just read the compression member, and if it isn't `BI_RGB`, you also quit the loading routine since the bitmap is compressed, which you don't support.

Now you need to read the actual bitmap image:

```
93:  /* Move to bitmap buffer */
94: kBitmap.seekg (iStartBuffer, ios::beg);
95:
96:  /* Read image buffer from file */
97: mrUInt8 * piBuffer = new mrUInt8 [m_iWidth * m_iHeight * 3];
98: kBitmap.read ((char *) piBuffer, m_iWidth * m_iHeight * 3 *
99:              sizeof (mrUInt8));
```

You start by moving the file pointer to the start of the buffer by using the `iStartBuffer` variable you read before (line 94). After this is done, you need to allocate an array of bytes of size `m_iWidth * m_iHeight * 3` that means that you are allocating an array for the image, having each pixel three components (line 97) and you finally read the the same number of bytes you allocated to get the image bits information (lines 98 and 99).

Now you need to copy the information you read to your own class buffer:

```
 /* Allocate memory for image buffer */
if (NULL != m_piImageBuffer)
{
 delete [] m_piImageBuffer;
}
m_piImageBuffer = new mrUInt32 [m_iWidth * m_iHeight];

 /* Get each pixel color components and fill image buffer */
mrUInt32 iX, iY;

for (iY = 0; iY < m_iHeight; iY++)
{
 for (iX = 0; iX < m_iWidth; iX++)
 {
   /* Needs to be flipped */
  if (m_iHeight > 0)
  {
    m_piImageBuffer [iX + (m_iHeight - 1 - iY) * (m_iWidth)] = 255 |
          (piBuffer [(iX + iY * (m_iWidth)) * 3 + 0] << 8) |
          (piBuffer [(iX + iY * (m_iWidth)) * 3 + 1] << 16) |
          (piBuffer [(iX + iY * (m_iWidth)) * 3 + 2] << 24);
  }
   /* Doesn't need to be flipped */
```

```
124:       else
125:       {
126:        m_piImageBuffer [iX + (iY * m_iWidth)] =  255 |
127:                (piBuffer [iX + (iY * m_iWidth) * 3 + 0] << 8) |
128:                (piBuffer [iX + (iY * m_iWidth) * 3 + 1] << 16) |
129:                (piBuffer [iX + (iY * m_iWidth) * 3 + 2] << 24);
130:       }
131:     }
132:   }
```

Sounds like more than just a simple copy, right? Well, if you remember from earlier, a bitmap is stored in BGR order, and if the height of the bitmap is positive, then the image is up-side-down and you need to flip it, but before this, you need to first make sure to delete your image buffer if there is one (lines 102 through 104) and then allocate one that is big enough to hold this image (line 106). After that you need to check whether the height is positive (line 116), and if so, flip the image; if not, just copy each pixel to your buffer by using the correct order, BGR to RGBA (lines 126 through 129).

To flip an image you need to change every line of the image with its equivalent, if you assumed the image started at the bottom. So, the first line would be the last one, the second line would be the last one minus one, and all the others following the formula:

```
NewPositionLineY = Height - PositionLineY
```

And the horizontal position of the pixel remains the same. What you do then is for each pixel of the image you flip it with the correspondent, and also convert from BGR to RGBA (lines 118 through 121). You may have noticed that you didn't use the above equation correctly, you subtracted one from it. This is needed because, as you know, C++ arrays start at zero, so `Height` in the array corresponds to `Height - 1`.

> **NOTE**
>
> Remember that the temporary buffer was to store a color only in BGR mode, so it required only three bytes to store the color. By multiplying the position by three, you get the corresponding position of the first color component of each pixel, blue. To get the other components you need to add one to the position for the green component, and add two to the position for the red component.

After this you just need to clean up the mess you created:

```
134:     /* Close file, release memory and return no error */
135:    if (NULL != piBuffer)
136:    {
137:     delete [] piBuffer;
138:    }
139:
140:    kBitmap.close ();
141:   }
142:
143:   return mrNoError;
144: }
```

Where you first delete the temporary buffer where you stored the image (lines 135 through 137) and close the file (line 140).

To keep the talk about image loading, it's time to implement the targa loader. It's not much different from the bitmap loader, you read the file and image information from the file, and then you read the image data. Then you flip the image, if needed and convert the ARGB pixel format to RGBA:

```
 /* Load image from TARGA file */
mrError32 mrRGBAImage::LoadFromTarga (LPSTR lpszFilename)
{
 fstream       kTarga;

 kTarga.open (lpszFilename, ios::binary | ios::in);

 if (kTarga.is_open ())
 {
   /* Read field description size */
  mrUInt8       iFieldDescSize;
  kTarga.read ((char *) &iFieldDescSize, sizeof (mrUInt8));

   /* Ignore one byte */
  kTarga.seekg (1, ios::cur);

   /* Read image color code */
  mrUInt8       iImageCode;
  kTarga.read ((char *) &iImageCode, sizeof (mrUInt8));

  if (2 != iImageCode)
```

```
{
 return mrErrorTargaNotSupported;
}

 /* Ignore two bytes */
kTarga.seekg (2, ios::cur);

 /* Read color map */
mrUInt16      iMapLength;
kTarga.read ((char *) &iMapLength, sizeof (mrUInt16));

 /* Ignore one byte */
kTarga.seekg (1, ios::cur);

 /* Read image start positions */
mrUInt16      iXStart;
kTarga.read ((char *) &iXStart, sizeof (mrUInt16));
mrUInt16      iYStart;
kTarga.read ((char *) &iYStart, sizeof (mrUInt16));

 /* Read image size */
mrUInt16      iWidth;
kTarga.read ((char *) &iWidth, sizeof (mrUInt16));
mrUInt16      iHeight;
kTarga.read ((char *) &iHeight, sizeof (mrUInt16));

m_iWidth  = iWidth;
m_iHeight = iHeight;

 /* Read image bit depth */
mrUInt8      iImageBits;

kTarga.read ((char *) &iImageBits, sizeof (mrUInt8));
if (32 != iImageBits)
{
 return mrErrorTargaNotSupported;
}

 /* Read image description */
mrUInt8      iImageDesc;
kTarga.read ((char *) &iImageDesc, sizeof (mrUInt8));
```

Up to here it doesn't need much explanation, you just read the information you find important and skip the stuff that isn't. Next you will need to find the start of image data:

```
209:    /* Ignore field description */
210:   kTarga.seekg (iFieldDescSize, ios::cur);
211:    /* Ignore color map */
212:   kTarga.seekg (iMapLength * 4, ios::cur);
```

Unlike the bitmap format, the targa format doesn't directly tell you where the image data starts. So you can find the start of the image you need to, after you read the header, skip the field description and color map. You retrieved the size of each when you read the information from the targa, so you just need to skip them using `seekg`. In the color map you need to skip the size of the color map times four since the color map information just gives you the number of colors, not the size (the correct way to get the color map would be to get the color map entry size and multiply it by the map length, but since you restricted the targa to be only 32-bit images, you can safely assume each entry is four bytes).

Next you need to read the image data from the file:

```
214:    /* Read image buffer from file */
215:   mrUInt32 * piBuffer = new mrUInt32 [m_iWidth * m_iHeight];
216:   kTarga.read ((char *) piBuffer, m_iWidth * m_iHeight * 4 *
217:                    sizeof (mrUInt8));
218:
219:    /* Allocate memory for image buffer */
220:   if (NULL != m_piImageBuffer)
221:   {
222:    delete [] m_piImageBuffer;
223:   }
224:   m_piImageBuffer = new mrUInt32 [m_iWidth * m_iHeight];
```

You have created an array big enough to hold the image data (line 215) and then read the image data from the file (lines 216 and 217). You also need to clear out the buffer if it was being used and allocate a new one (lines 220 through 224).

You now need to copy the image data to your buffer:

```
226:   mrUInt8  iRed, iGreen, iBlue, iAlpha;
227:   mrUInt32 iColor;
228:
229:    /* Get each pixel color components and fill image buffer */
230:   mrUInt32 iX, iY;
```

```

  for (iY = 0; iY < m_iHeight; iY++)
  {
   for (iX = 0; iX < m_iWidth; iX++)
   {
     /* Doens't need to be flipped */
    if ((iImageDesc & 1) << 4)
    {
      /* Get color components */
     iColor = piBuffer [iX + (iY * m_iWidth)];

     iAlpha = (mrUInt8)((iColor & 0xFF000000) >> 24);
     iRed   = (mrUInt8)((iColor & 0x00FF0000) >> 16);
     iGreen = (mrUInt8)((iColor & 0x0000FF00) >> 8);
     iBlue  = (mrUInt8)((iColor & 0x000000FF));

      /* Copy flipped position */
     m_piImageBuffer [iX + (iY * m_iWidth)] =
            iAlpha << 0 | iBlue << 8 | iGreen << 16 | iRed << 24;
    }
     /* Needs to be flipped */
    else
    {
      /* Get color components */
     iColor = piBuffer [iX + (iY * m_iWidth)];

     iAlpha = (mrUInt8)((iColor & 0xFF000000) >> 24);
     iRed   = (mrUInt8)((iColor & 0x00FF0000) >> 16);
     iGreen = (mrUInt8)((iColor & 0x0000FF00) >> 8);
     iBlue  = (mrUInt8)((iColor & 0x000000FF));

      /* Copy position */
     m_piImageBuffer [iX + (m_iHeight - 1 - iY) * (m_iWidth)] =
            iAlpha << 0 | iBlue << 8 | iGreen << 16 | iRed << 24;
    }
   }
  }
```

If you refer to the pseudocode to load a targa file, you will see that while it doesn't look like it, this code block is pretty simple.

What you need to do is go through every pixel of the temporary buffer and if needed, flip it and convert it from ARGB to RGBA. This is done by first getting each of the color components for the current pixel (lines 240 and 255). After this is done, you need to convert the format from ARGB to RGBA, and depending on whether it needs to be flipped or not, copy it to the appropriate position (lines 248 to 249 and 264 to 265).

You just need to clean up again:

```
269:    /* Close file, release memory and return no error */
270:   if (NULL != piBuffer)
271:   {
272:    delete [] piBuffer;
273:   }
274:
275:   kTarga.close ();
276:   }
277:
278:  return mrNoError;
279:
280: }
```

Where you first delete the temporary buffer where you stored the image (lines 270 through 273), as you did with the bitmap loader, and close the file (line 275).

The next method sets the color key of an image. This is done here instead of being done directly on a texture so you don't deal with different pixel formats:

```
283:  /* Set image color key for rendering */
284: void mrRGBAImage::SetColorKey (mrUInt8 iRed, mrUInt8 iGreen,
285:                                mrUInt8 iBlue)
286: {
287:   /* Get each pixel color components and set color key */
288:  mrUInt32 iX, iY;
289:  mrUInt8 iOriRed, iOriGreen, iOriBlue;
290:
291:  for (iY = 0; iY < m_iHeight; iY++)
292:  {
293:   for (iX = 0; iX < m_iWidth; iX++)
294:   {
295:    iOriRed    = (mrUInt8)((m_piImageBuffer [iX + (iY * m_iWidth)]
296:                           & 0xFF000000) >> 24);
```

```
    iOriGreen = (mrUInt8)((m_piImageBuffer [iX + (iY * m_iWidth)]
                               & 0x00FF0000) >> 16);
    iOriBlue  = (mrUInt8)((m_piImageBuffer [iX + (iY * m_iWidth)]
                               & 0x0000FF00) >> 8);
```

You need to go through each pixel and get its color components, which is done in the preceding code. Since you aren't interested in the alpha component, you just retrieve the red, green, and blue ones.

Next you have to determine whether the colors match:

```
     /* If color matches, set alpha to 0 */
    if ( (iOriRed == iRed) && (iOriGreen == iGreen) && (iOriBlue == iBlue))
    {
     m_piImageBuffer [iX + (iY * m_iWidth)] = iOriRed   << 24 |
                                              iOriGreen << 16 |
                                              iOriBlue  << 8  |
                                              0;
    }
   }
  }
}
```

If the color does match with the desired color key, then you need to set the alpha of that pixel to zero. This will prevent this pixel from being copied.

After a color key is set, there is no turning back, that is, that color will not be visible for the image again until you reload it from disk.

Next are the access methods, you should already know what each one of them does, so they are here just for reference:

```
 /* Set image width */
void mrRGBAImage::SetWidth (mrUInt32 iWidth)
{
 m_iWidth = iWidth;
}

 /* Set image height */
void mrRGBAImage::SetHeight (mrUInt32 iHeight)
{
 m_iHeight = iHeight;
}

```

```
 /* Set color at given position */
void mrRGBAImage::SetColor (mrUInt32 iX, mrUInt32 iY, mrUInt8 iRed,
                              mrUInt8 iGreen, mrUInt8 iBlue,
                              mrUInt8 iAlpha)
{
 mrUInt32 iColor;
 iColor = D3DCOLOR_RGBA (iRed, iGreen, iBlue, iAlpha);

 m_piImageBuffer [iX + (iY * m_iWidth - 1)] = iColor;
}

 /* Set the image buffer */
void mrRGBAImage::SetImageBuffer (mrUInt32 * pImage)
{
 if (NULL != m_piImageBuffer)
 {
  delete [] m_piImageBuffer;
 }
 m_piImageBuffer = new mrUInt32 [m_iWidth * m_iHeight];

 memcpy (m_piImageBuffer, pImage,
         sizeof (mrUInt32) * m_iWidth * m_iHeight);
}

 /* Returns image width */
mrUInt32 mrRGBAImage::GetWidth (void)
{
 return m_iWidth;
}

 /* Returns image height */
mrUInt32 mrRGBAImage::GetHeight (void)
{
 return m_iHeight;
}

 /* Returns image color at a point */
mrUInt32 mrRGBAImage::GetColor (mrUInt32 iX, mrUInt32 iY)
{
 return m_piImageBuffer [iX + iY * m_iWidth];
}
```

```
 /* Returns image buffer */
mrUInt32 * mrRGBAImage::GetImageBuffer (void)
{
 return m_piImageBuffer;
}
```

And that's about it. You have a generic image class that can be used to load images or for direct manipulation without worrying about different pixel formats. You will convert pixel formats from RGBA to the appropriate formats in the `mrTexture` and `mrSurface` classes when needed.

mrSurface

The first available class to actually show images on the screen is `mrSurface`. `mrSurface` is very limited (mostly due to Direct3D since it limits the `IDirectSurface8` object).

The `mrSurface` can only be copied to the screen at a given position and can't be stretched, rotated, or clipped. A tip though, if you are rendering a surface normally and for some reason it doesn't appear in the screen, check whether the entire surface is inside the screen. If any of the vertices of the surface are outside the screen bounds, the entire surface won't be rendered.

Take a look at the class definition:

```
 /* 'mrSurface.h' */

 /* Mirus base types header */
#include "mrDatatypes.h"
 /* Mirus error definitions header */
#include "mrError.h"
 /* Mirus RGBA image header */
#include "mrRGBAImage.h"
 /* Mirus screen header */
#include "mrScreen.h"
/* DirectX Graphics header file */
#include <d3d8.h>

 /* Include this file only once */
#pragma once

 /* Mirus surface class */
class mrSurface
```

```
{
protected:
  /* Direct3D surface */
 LPDIRECT3DSURFACE8 m_pkD3DSurface;
 mrRGBAImage *      m_pkRawImage;

public:
  /* Constructors / Destructor */
 mrSurface (void);
 ~mrSurface (void);

  /* Surface manipulation routines */
 mrError32 Create (mrRGBAImage * pkRawImage);
 mrError32 Update (void);
 mrError32 Render (POINT * pkDestPoint, RECT * pkSourceRect = NULL);

  /* Surface maintenance methods */
 void SetRawImage (mrRGBAImage * pkRawImage);
 mrRGBAImage * GetRawImage (void);
};
```

This class has three main methods, `Create`, `Update`, and `Render`, which will be used to create and render the surface. You will see these in more detail. But first, the constructor and the destructor:

```
 /* 'mrSurface.cpp' */

 /* Complement header file */
#include "mrSurface.h"

 /* Default constructor */
mrSurface::mrSurface (void)
{
 m_pkD3DSurface = NULL;
 m_pkRawImage   = NULL;
}

 /* Default destructor */
mrSurface::~mrSurface (void)
{
 if (m_pkD3DSurface != NULL)
 {
  m_pkD3DSurface->Release ();
```

```
19:     m_pkD3DSurface = NULL;
20:   }
21:   if (m_pkRawImage != NULL)
22:   {
23:     delete m_pkRawImage;
24:     m_pkRawImage    = NULL;
25:   }
26: }
```

The sole purpose of the constructor is to initialize both class members to NULL (lines 9 and 10) while the destructor checks if the m_pkD3DSurface and m_pkRawImage pointers are valid, and if so, releases the surface object (lines 16 through 20) and frees the memory used by the raw image (lines 21 through 25).

The next method allows you to create a surface object with a single call:

```
28:   /* Creates the surface */
29: mrError32 mrSurface::Create (mrRGBAImage * pkRawImage)
30: {
31:    /* Set the surface raw image and update the Direct3D surface */
32:   SetRawImage (pkRawImage);
33:
34:   return Update ();
35: }
```

This method starts by setting the raw image (line 32) and then updating the surface (line 34).

You will see SetRawImage is pretty simple, it just copies a buffer to another, as you will see later, but the Update method is a little more complicated:

```
37:   /* Updates the Direct3D surface */
38: mrError32 mrSurface::Update (void)
39: {
40:   if (m_pkD3DSurface != NULL)
41:   {
42:     m_pkD3DSurface->Release ();
43:     m_pkD3DSurface = NULL;
44:   }
45:
46:   if (m_pkRawImage == NULL)
47:   {
48:     return mrErrorInvalidRawImage;
49:   }
```

This method starts by releasing the surface if it is being used (lines 40 through 44). If the raw image of this surface isn't valid, it returns an error (line 48).

Next you have to create and lock the Direct3D surface:

```
51:   /* Create the surface */
52:  if (FAILED(mrScreen::GetSingleton ()->GetDevice ()->CreateImageSurface(
53:                      m_pkRawImage->GetWidth (),
54:                      m_pkRawImage->GetHeight (),
55:                      (D3DFORMAT) mrScreen::GetSingleton ()->GetFormat (),
56:                      &m_pkD3DSurface ) ) )
57:
58:  {
59:   m_pkD3DSurface = NULL;
60:   return mrErrorCreateImageSurface;
61:  }
62:
63:   /* Lock surface */
64:  D3DLOCKED_RECT kLockedRect;
65:  m_pkD3DSurface->LockRect (&kLockedRect, NULL, 0);
```

The preceding code is nothing you haven't seen before. You start by creating the surface by using the raw image width and height, and the current back buffer format (lines 52 through 56).

You then lock the surface with `LockRect` (line 65). The only problem now is that you don't know whether the surface format is a 16- or 32-bit image. Because of this you need to do a little trick to get the appropriate pointer to the locked surface:

```
67:   /* Pointers to locked surface */
68:  WORD * pi16SurfaceBuffer;
69:  DWORD * pi32SurfaceBuffer;
70:
71:   /* Use correct pointer depending on depth */
72:  if (mrScreen::GetSingleton ()->GetBitdepth () == 16)
73:  {
74:    /* Cast a pointer to point to the first pixel */
75:   pi16SurfaceBuffer = (WORD *) kLockedRect.pBits;
76:  }
77:  else
78:  {
79:    /* Cast a pointer to point to the first pixel */
80:   pi32SurfaceBuffer = (DWORD *) kLockedRect.pBits;
81:  }
```

What you do here is declare two pointers, one a 16-bit pointer and another a 32-bit pointer (lines 68 and 69). After this, you get the bitdepth (not format) from the `mrScreen` class and depending on the bitdepth, point the correct pointer to the locked surface (lines 72 through 81).

Now you just need to feel the surface:

```
 83:    /* Fill surface */
 84:   mrUInt32 iX, iY;
 85:   mrUInt32 iDepth;
 86:
 87:    /* Get depth in bytes and calculate pitch */
 88:   iDepth = mrScreen::GetSingleton ()->GetBitdepth () / 8;
 89:   mrUInt32 iPitch = kLockedRect.Pitch / iDepth;
 90:
 91:   mrUInt8  iRed, iGreen, iBlue, iAlpha;
 92:   mrUInt32 iColor;
 93:
 94:   for (iY=0; iY < m_pkRawImage->GetHeight (); iY++)
 95:   {
 96:    for (iX=0; iX < m_pkRawImage->GetWidth (); iX++)
 97:    {
 98:      /* Get color components */
 99:     iColor = m_pkRawImage->GetColor (iX, iY);
100:
101:     iRed   = (mrUInt8)((iColor & 0xFF000000) >> 24);
102:     iGreen = (mrUInt8)((iColor & 0x00FF0000) >> 16);
103:     iBlue  = (mrUInt8)((iColor & 0x0000FF00) >> 8);
104:     iAlpha = (mrUInt8)((iColor & 0x000000FF));
105:
106:      /* Write color to surface buffer according to mode*/
107:     if (mrScreen::GetSingleton ()->GetBitdepth () == 16)
108:     {
109:      if (mrScreen::GetSingleton ()->GetFormat () == D3DFMT_R5G6B5)
110:      {
111:       pi16SurfaceBuffer [iX + iY * iPitch] =
112:                (mrUInt16)( (iRed * ((1 << 5) -1) / 255 << 11) |
113:                    (iGreen * ((1 << 6) -1) / 255 << 5) |
114:                    (iBlue  * ((1 << 5) -1) / 255));
115:      }
116:      if (mrScreen::GetSingleton ()->GetFormat () == D3DFMT_X1R5G5B5)
117:      {
```

```
118:       pi16SurfaceBuffer [iX + iY * iPitch] =
119:        (mrUInt16)((iRed   * ((1 << 5) -1) / 255 << 10) |
120:                   (iGreen * ((1 << 5) -1) / 25 << 5) |
121:                   (iBlue  * ((1 << 5) -1) / 255));
122:      }
123:      if (mrScreen::GetSingleton ()->GetFormat () == D3DFMT_A1R5G5B5)
124:      {
125:       pi16SurfaceBuffer [iX + iY * iPitch] =
126:        (mrUInt16)(((iAlpha > 0) ? 1 : 0 << 15) |
127:                   (iRed   * ((1 << 5) -1) / 255 << 10) |
128:                   (iGreen * ((1 << 5) -1) / 255 << 5) |
129:                   (iBlue  * ((1 << 5) -1) / 255));
130:      }
131:     }
132:     else
133:     {
134:      pi32SurfaceBuffer [iX + iY * iPitch] =
135:       D3DCOLOR_ARGB (iAlpha, iRed, iGreen, iBlue);
136:     }
137:    }
138:   }
```

Looks complicated but it isn't, really! You start by getting the appropriate pitch for the surface. This is done by dividing the bitdepth by eight to get the bitdepth in bytes. Then you divide the `iPitch` returned by `Lock` by the bitdepth in bytes to get the surface pitch (lines 88 and 89). Next, depending on the bitdepth and surface format, you convert the pixel from RGBA to the surface format (lines 107 through 138).

> **NOTE**
>
> **You multiply each pixel component by `((1 << 5) -1) / 255` or `((1 << 6) -1) / 255` so you can convert a value in the range of 0 to 255 to a value ranging from 0 to (1<<6) -1 (63) and (1<<5)-1 (31), the number of bits of each color.**

And you finish the method by unlocking the surface:

```
140:   /* Unlock */
141:  m_pkD3DSurface->UnlockRect ();
142:
143:  return mrNoError;
144: }
```

Next you will see how to implement Render, which isn't much different from the code you used in your surface demo:

```
146:  /* Draw the surface */
147: mrError32 mrSurface::Render (POINT * pkDestPoint, RECT * pkSourceRect)
148: {
149:   /* Get back buffer */
150:  if (m_pkD3DSurface != NULL)
151:  {
152:   LPDIRECT3DSURFACE8 pBackBuffer;
153:   mrScreen::GetSingleton ()->GetDevice ()->GetBackBuffer (
154:                                            0, D3DBACKBUFFER_TYPE_MONO,
155:                                            &pBackBuffer);
156:    /* Copy the surface to the screen */
157:   if (pkSourceRect != NULL)
158:   {
159:    mrScreen::GetSingleton ()->GetDevice ()->CopyRects (
160:       m_pkD3DSurface, pkSourceRect, 1, pBackBuffer, pkDestPoint);
161:   }
162:   else
163:   {
164:    RECT kImageRect;
165:     /* Use entire image */
166:    kImageRect.left   = 0;
167:    kImageRect.top    = 0;
168:    kImageRect.right  = m_pkRawImage->GetWidth () - 1;
169:    kImageRect.bottom = m_pkRawImage->GetHeight () - 1;
170:
171:    mrScreen::GetSingleton ()->GetDevice ()->CopyRects (
172:       m_pkD3DSurface, &kImageRect, 1, pBackBuffer, pkDestPoint);
173:   }
174:    /* Release back buffer */
175:   pBackBuffer->Release ();
176:  }
177:  return mrNoError;
178: }
```

You start by getting the back buffer with GetBackBuffer (lines 153 through 155). After that you see whether the source rectangle was passed to the function, if it was, you use it in the call to CopyRects (lines 157 through 161), but if it wasn't, you will use the entire image so you need to set the origin of the rectangle to (0, 0) and the width and height to the size of the image (lines 165 through 169) and then copy it to the backbuffer using `CopyRects` (line 171). In the end you release the backbuffer (line 175).

As usual, the access methods are shown:

```
 /* Set the surface raw image */
void mrSurface::SetRawImage (mrRGBAImage * pkRawImage)
{
 if (m_pkRawImage == NULL)
 {
  m_pkRawImage = new mrRGBAImage ();
 }

 m_pkRawImage->SetWidth (pkRawImage->GetWidth ());
 m_pkRawImage->SetHeight (pkRawImage->GetHeight ());
 m_pkRawImage->SetImageBuffer (pkRawImage->GetImageBuffer ());
}

 /* Returns the surface raw image */
mrRGBAImage * mrSurface::GetRawImage (void)
{
 return m_pkRawImage;
}
```

Using `mrSurface` is pretty simple also, take a look at the following example which also uses `mrRGBAImage`:

```
mrRGBAImage  kImage;
mrSurface  kSurface;
kImage.LoadFromTarga ("image.tga");
kSurface.Create (&kImage);
 /* ...*/
 /* Next call must be done between mrScreen::BeginFrame and
    mrScreen::EndFrame */
POINT kPosition = {100, 100};
kSurface.Render (&kPosition);
```

And you would render the contents of `kSurface` (which were loaded from image.tga to the screen at position 100, 100).

mrTexture

The next class you will develop is `mrTexture`. While `mrTexture` won't be used exclusively (it needs to be used with `mrTemplateSet`, and in turn, `mrTemplateSet` must be used with `mrAnimation` to be rendered) it is one of the fundamental classes of Mirus.

Here is the class definition:

```
 /* 'mrTexture.h' */

 /* Mirus base types header */
#include "mrDatatypes.h"
 /* Mirus error definitions header */
#include "mrError.h"
 /* Mirus RGBA image header */
#include "mrRGBAImage.h"
 /* Mirus screen header */
#include "mrScreen.h"
/* DirectX Graphics header file */
#include <d3d8.h>

 /* Include this file only once */
#pragma once

 /* Mirus texture class */
class mrTexture
{
protected:
  /* Direct3D surface */
 LPDIRECT3DTEXTURE8 m_pkD3DTexture;
 mrRGBAImage *      m_pkRawImage;

 mrUInt32           m_iID;
 mrBool32           m_iHasAlpha;

  /* Maintenance members */
 static mrUInt32    m_iActiveTexture;
 static mrUInt32    m_iCurrentID;

public:
  /* Constructors / Destructor */
 mrTexture (void);
```

```
~mrTexture (void);

 /* Texture manipulation routines */
mrError32 Create (mrRGBAImage * pkRawImage);
mrError32 Update (void);

void SetRawImage (mrRGBAImage * pkRawImage);
mrRGBAImage * GetRawImage (void);

 /* Texture maintenance methods */
void SetActiveTexture (void);
mrUInt32 GetID (void);

static mrUInt32 GetActiveTexture (void);
};
```

This class looks a lot like mrSurface with the addition that you keep some static members for the texture identification. While this looks a little wasteful, it is very important because you will need to keep the information on how many textures exist and which texture is active, so Mirus can take care of setting the correct active texture, releasing the user of Mirus of it, basically, relieving you of more trouble later.

Let's take a look at the constructor and the destructor:

```
 /* 'mrTexture.cpp' */

 /* Complement header file */
#include "mrTexture.h"

 /* Static texture members */
mrUInt32    mrTexture::m_iActiveTexture  = -1;
mrUInt32    mrTexture::m_iCurrentID      = 0;

 /* Default constructor */
mrTexture::mrTexture (void)
{
 m_pkD3DTexture = NULL;
 m_pkRawImage   = NULL;

 m_iHasAlpha    = mrFalse;
 m_iID          = 0;
}
```

```
19:
20:  /* Default destructor */
21: mrTexture::~mrTexture (void)
22: {
23:  if (m_pkD3DTexture != NULL)
24:  {
25:   m_pkD3DTexture->Release ();
26:   m_pkD3DTexture = NULL;
27:  }
28:  if (m_pkRawImage != NULL)
29:  {
30:   delete m_pkRawImage;
31:   m_pkRawImage    = NULL;
32:  }
33: }
```

You start by declaring the static members and initializing them. You initialize m_iActiveTexture to force Mirus to set the current texture when you create the first texture.

The constructor sets the members to NULL, zero, and mrFalse, and the destructor releases the texture and deletes the raw image if they are valid.

The next method to look at is Create:

```
34:
35:  /* Creates the texture */
36: mrError32 mrTexture::Create (mrRGBAImage * pkRawImage)
37: {
38:   /* Update methods */
39:  m_iID = m_iCurrentID;
40:  m_iCurrentID ++;
41:
42:   /* Set the texture raw image and update the Direct3D texture */
43:  SetRawImage (pkRawImage);
44:
45:  return Update ();
46: }
```

Which works exactly the same way as the Create method of mrSurface but sets the m_iID of the texture to the m_iCurrentID and increases it (lines 39 and 40). This will ensure that every texture will have a different ID from another (unless you reach

2^{32} surfaces, which is very unlikely!). Next you set the raw image and update the texture (lines 43 and 45).

Next you have Update which will synchronize the raw image and the texture:

```
48:  /* Updates the Direct3D texture */
49: mrError32 mrTexture::Update (void)
50: {
51:  if (m_pkRawImage == NULL)
52:  {
53:   return mrErrorInvalidRawImage;
54:  }
55:
56:  if (m_pkD3DTexture != NULL)
57:  {
58:   m_pkD3DTexture->Release ();
59:   m_pkD3DTexture = NULL;
60:  }
61:
62:  m_iHasAlpha = mrTrue;
63:   /* We are in 32 bit mode */
64:  if (32 == mrScreen::GetSingleton ()->GetBitdepth ())
65:  {
66:    /* Try to create alpha texture */
67:   if (FAILED (mrScreen::GetSingleton ()->GetDevice ()->CreateTexture (
68:                     m_pkRawImage->GetWidth (),
69:                     m_pkRawImage->GetHeight (),
70:                     0, 0,
71:                     D3DFMT_A8R8G8B8,
72:                     D3DPOOL_MANAGED,
73:                     &m_pkD3DTexture)) )
74:   {
75:     /* If failed, use back buffer format for texture */
76:    if (FAILED (mrScreen::GetSingleton ()->GetDevice ()->CreateTexture (
77:                      m_pkRawImage->GetWidth (),
78:                      m_pkRawImage->GetHeight (),
79:                      0, 0,
80:                      (D3DFORMAT) mrScreen::GetSingleton ()->GetFormat (),
81:                      D3DPOOL_MANAGED,
82:                      &m_pkD3DTexture)) )
```

```
  {
   m_pkD3DTexture = NULL;
   m_iHasAlpha = mrFalse;
   return mrErrorCreateTexture;
  }
 }
}
 /* We are in 16 bit mode */
if (16 == mrScreen::GetSingleton ()->GetBitdepth ())
{
  /* Try to create alpha texture */
 if (FAILED (mrScreen::GetSingleton ()->GetDevice ()->CreateTexture (
                    m_pkRawImage->GetWidth (),
                    m_pkRawImage->GetHeight (),
                    0, 0,
                    D3DFMT_A4R4G4B4,
                    D3DPOOL_MANAGED,
                    &m_pkD3DTexture)) )
 {
  m_iHasAlpha = mrFalse;
   /* If failed, use back buffer format for texture */
  if (FAILED (mrScreen::GetSingleton ()->GetDevice ()->CreateTexture (
                     m_pkRawImage->GetWidth (),
                     m_pkRawImage->GetHeight (),
                     0, 0,
                     (D3DFORMAT) mrScreen::GetSingleton ()->GetFormat (),
                     D3DPOOL_MANAGED,
                     &m_pkD3DTexture)) )
  {
   m_pkD3DTexture = NULL;
   return mrErrorCreateTexture;
  }
 }
}

 /* Lock Texture */
D3DLOCKED_RECT kLockedRect;
m_pkD3DTexture->LockRect (0, &kLockedRect, NULL, 0);

 /* Pointers to locked texture */
WORD * pi16TextureBuffer;
```

```
DWORD * pi32TextureBuffer;

 /* Use correct pointer depending on depth */
if (mrScreen::GetSingleton ()->GetBitdepth () == 16)
{
  /* Cast a 16-bit pointer to point to the first pixel */
 pi16TextureBuffer = (WORD *) kLockedRect.pBits;
}
else
{
  /* Cast a 32-bit pointer to point to the first pixel */
 pi32TextureBuffer = (DWORD *) kLockedRect.pBits;
}

 /* Fill the surface */
mrUInt32 iX, iY;
mrUInt32 iDepth;

 /* Get depth in bytes and calculate pitch */
iDepth = mrScreen::GetSingleton ()->GetBitdepth () / 8;
mrUInt32 iPitch = kLockedRect.Pitch / iDepth;

mrUInt8  iRed, iGreen, iBlue, iAlpha;
mrUInt32 iColor;

for (iY=0; iY < m_pkRawImage->GetHeight (); iY++)
{
 for (iX=0; iX < m_pkRawImage->GetWidth (); iX++)
 {
   /* Get color components */
  iColor = m_pkRawImage->GetColor (iX, iY);

  iRed   = (mrUInt8)((iColor & 0xFF000000) >> 24);
  iGreen = (mrUInt8)((iColor & 0x00FF0000) >> 16);
  iBlue  = (mrUInt8)((iColor & 0x0000FF00) >> 8);
  iAlpha = (mrUInt8)((iColor & 0x000000FF));

   /* Write color to surface buffer according to mode*/
  if (mrScreen::GetSingleton ()->GetBitdepth () == 16)
  {
   if (mrTrue == m_iHasAlpha)
```

```
    {
     pi16TextureBuffer [iX + iY * iPitch] =
      (mrUInt16)((iAlpha * (1 << 4) / 256 << 12) |
                 (iRed   * (1 << 4) / 256 << 8) |
                 (iGreen * (1 << 4) / 256 << 4) |
                 (iBlue  * (1 << 4) / 256 ));
    }
    else
    {
     if (mrScreen::GetSingleton ()->GetFormat () == D3DFMT_R5G6B5)
     {
      pi16TextureBuffer [iX + iY * iPitch] =
       (mrUInt16)((iRed   * (1 << 5) / 256 << 11) |
                  (iGreen * (1 << 6) / 256 << 5) |
                  (iBlue  * (1 << 5) / 256 ));
     }
     if (mrScreen::GetSingleton ()->GetFormat () == D3DFMT_X1R5G5B5)
     {
      pi16TextureBuffer [iX + iY * iPitch] =
       (mrUInt16)((iRed   * (1 << 5) / 256  << 10) |
                  (iGreen * (1 << 5) / 256  << 5) |
                  (iBlue  * (1 << 5) / 256 ));
     }
     if (mrScreen::GetSingleton ()->GetFormat () == D3DFMT_A1R5G5B5)
     {
      pi16TextureBuffer [iX + iY * iPitch] =
       (mrUInt16)(((iAlpha > 0) ? 1 : 0 << 15) |
                   (iRed   * (1 << 5) / 256  << 10) |
                   (iGreen * (1 << 5) / 256  << 5) |
                   (iBlue  * (1 << 5) / 256 ));
     }
    }
   }
   else
   {
    pi32TextureBuffer [iX + iY * iPitch] =
                 D3DCOLOR_ARGB (iAlpha, iRed, iGreen, iBlue);
   }
  }
 }

```

```
  /* Unlock */
 m_pkD3DTexture->UnlockRect (0);

 return mrNoError;
}
```

Because this method is just like the one in `mrSurface` with the difference that it uses a texture object instead of a surface object, just skip it.

NOTE

You also added two formats to the method that uses the alpha component. Because a surface can't be alpha blended, you didn't use it before, but the concept is the same as the other formats. After you get the pixel components, you just need to convert them to the appropriate format.

As usual, the access methods are presented next:

```
 /* Set the surface raw image */
void mrTexture::SetRawImage (mrRGBAImage * pkRawImage)
{
 if (m_pkRawImage == NULL)
 {
  m_pkRawImage = new mrRGBAImage ();
 }

 m_pkRawImage->SetWidth (pkRawImage->GetWidth ());
 m_pkRawImage->SetHeight (pkRawImage->GetHeight ());
 m_pkRawImage->SetImageBuffer (pkRawImage->GetImageBuffer ());
}

 /* Returns the surface raw image */
mrRGBAImage * mrTexture::GetRawImage (void)
{
 return m_pkRawImage;
}

 /* Set Direct3D active texture */
void mrTexture::SetActiveTexture (void)
{
 if (m_iActiveTexture != m_iID)
 {
  mrScreen::GetSingleton ()->GetDevice ()->SetTexture (0, m_pkD3DTexture);
  m_iActiveTexture = m_iID;
 }
}
```

Just a little interlude before proceeding. The `SetActiveTexture` method will set the Direct3D active texture (the one that is used). This method starts by checking whether the active texture isn't already this one (line 234) to prevent unnecessary calls to `SetTexture` and if it isn't, it will set this texture as the active one (lines 236 and 237).

```
241:  /* Returns texture ID */
242: mrUInt32 mrTexture::GetID (void)
243: {
244:  return m_iID;
245: }
246:
247:  /* Returns Direct3D active texture */
248: mrUInt32 mrTexture::GetActiveTexture (void)
249: {
250:  return m_iActiveTexture;
251: }
```

You won't do any concrete example of this class because it wouldn't do you much good since you can't render textures just yet. While creation of the texture is done just like the surface, you will see how you can render it in a while.

mrTemplateSet

I briefly talked about template sets earlier so this class will need a little more work. As you see, a template set is a collection of images organized in a grid for easier access. Working with templates is pretty simple, take a look at the class definition:

```
 /* 'mrTemplateSet.h' */

 /* Mirus base types header */
#include "mrDatatypes.h"
 /* Mirus error definitions header */
#include "mrError.h"
 /* Mirus RGBA image header */
#include "mrRGBAImage.h"
 /* Mirus screen header */
#include "mrScreen.h"
 /* Mirus texture header */
#include "mrTexture.h"

 /* Include this file only once */
```

```
#pragma once

 /* Mirus texture rectangle class */
class mrRectText
{
public:
 mrReal32          m_fLeft;
 mrReal32          m_fTop;
 mrReal32          m_fRight;
 mrReal32          m_fBottom;
};
```

This class is a container class, which describes a rectangle as texture coordinates. You will use this class to return the texture coordinates rectangle for a cell.

```
 /* Mirus template set cell id class */
class mrCellID
{
public:
 mrUInt32      m_iX;
 mrUInt32      m_iY;
};
```

This class is another container class that stores a position of a cell within a template set. You will use this class to specify the cell you are working with.

```
 /* Mirus template set class */
class mrTemplateSet
{
protected:
  /* Texture information */
 mrTexture *         m_pkTexture;
 mrUInt32            m_iTextureWidth;
 mrUInt32            m_iTextureHeight;

  /* Cell information */
 mrUInt32            m_iCellWidth;
 mrUInt32            m_iCellHeight;

public:
  /* Constructors / Destructor */
 mrTemplateSet (void);
 ~mrTemplateSet (void);
```

```

  /* Template manipulation routines */
 void Create (mrTexture * pkTexture, mrUInt32 iTextureWidth,
              mrUInt32 iTextureHeight, mrUInt32 iCellWidth,
              mrUInt32 iCellHeight);

 void GetUV (mrCellID kPosition, mrRectText * pkUVRect);

  /* Texture maintenance routines */
 void SetActiveTexture (void);

 mrUInt32 GetTextureWidth (void);
 mrUInt32 GetTextureHeight (void);
 mrUInt32 GetCellWidth (void);
 mrUInt32 GetCellHeight (void);
};
```

Apart from the texture, this class also stores the texture size and the cell size. You will need to know this to be able to return the correct texture coordinates for each cell. The other members you will check as you implement them.

For now, the constructor and the destructor:

```
 /* 'mrTemplateSet.cpp' */

 /* Complement header file */
#include "mrTemplateSet.h"

 /* Default constructor */
mrTemplateSet::mrTemplateSet (void)
{
 m_pkTexture        = NULL;
 m_iTextureWidth    = 0;
 m_iTextureHeight   = 0;
 m_iCellWidth       = 0;
 m_iCellHeight      = 0;
}

 /* Default destructor */
mrTemplateSet::~mrTemplateSet (void)
{
 m_iTextureWidth    = 0;
 m_iTextureHeight   = 0;
```

```
 m_iCellWidth       = 0;
 m_iCellHeight      = 0;
 m_pkTexture        = NULL;
}
```

Since this class won't allocate any memory or create any object, in both the constructor and the destructor you will set its members to either 0 or NULL. If a program passes a texture to a template set, it is the responsibility of the program to delete the texture safely.

Creating a template set is pretty easy:

```
 /* Create the template set */
void mrTemplateSet::Create (mrTexture * pkTexture,
                            mrUInt32 iTextureWidth,
                            mrUInt32 iTextureHeight,
                            mrUInt32 iCellWidth,
                            mrUInt32 iCellHeight)
{
 m_iTextureWidth  = iTextureWidth;
 m_iTextureHeight = iTextureHeight;
 m_iCellWidth     = iCellWidth;
 m_iCellHeight    = iCellHeight;

 m_pkTexture      = pkTexture;
}
```

Here you set the appropriate members to the wanted values to create the template set. Since you don't create any objects, you don't need anything more than this.

Next you need to know how to get the texture coordinate rectangle for a cell:

```
 /* Returns the texture UV rect for a given cell */
void mrTemplateSet::GetUV (mrCellID kPosition, mrRectText * pkUVRect)
{
 pkUVRect->m_fLeft   = (mrReal32)(1 + ((1 + m_iCellWidth)
  * kPosition.m_iX)) / m_iTextureWidth;
 pkUVRect->m_fRight  = (mrReal32)(1 + ((1 + m_iCellWidth)
  * kPosition.m_iX) + m_iCellWidth) / m_iTextureWidth;
 pkUVRect->m_fTop    = (mrReal32)(1 + ((1 + m_iCellHeight)
  * kPosition.m_iY)) / m_iTextureHeight;
 pkUVRect->m_fBottom = (mrReal32)(1 + ((1 + m_iCellHeight)
  * kPosition.m_iY) + m_iCellHeight) / m_iTextureHeight;
}
```

In a template, there are some borders you need to pay special attention to.

Each cell has a border of one pixel (this isn't really necessary, but it's easier to construct the template with the border, so Mirus will assume that there is one).

To get the starting coordinate of the first cell, you will have to add one to the origin. Since the origin is (0, 0), the starting position of the first cell is (1, 1). Now, what if you want the starting position of the second cell (suppose the second cell is at the right of the first cell)? If you think about it, you know that each cell is 32 pixels wide, and it is surrounded with a border of one, the obvious choice would be to multiply the width of the cell plus the borders with the cell position, right? Wrong. The thing is, the borders are shared, so you will multiply the width of the cell plus one of the borders and add one to it. The final one comes from the first border (the left-most border).

To find the final position, take the start position and add the cell size.

If you think about it, this assumes that the cell only has a border on the left, but the first cell starts at position one, which is in part true.

To get the vertical position you do the same thing, but this time using the vertical position of the cell.

So in code, you start by adding the border to the cell width (and height) and then add one. You then multiply this by the desired cell horizontal position to get the start position of the cell. Now, remember from before that texture coordinates must be in a range of 0 to 1, so you need to convert the pixel position in the image to a texture coordinate, which is done by dividing the position by the texture size.

To get the final position you add the cell start position to the cell size and divide by the texture size and you have it.

This is what you do to get the texture coordinates of the cell rectangle.

> **NOTE**
>
> There is just one problem with this, floating-point accuracy! Even if it is pretty rare, sometimes the floating-point error causes a cell to be mapped incorrectly. Unfortunately, unless you use double precision (and even using it sometimes allows this error to happen), you can't do much about it. If you see that something is wrong, try to tweak the cell size until it looks correct.

Following are the access methods:

```
 /* Set as active texture */
void mrTemplateSet::SetActiveTexture (void)
{
 m_pkTexture->SetActiveTexture ();
}

 /* Returns texture width */
mrUInt32 mrTemplateSet::GetTextureWidth (void)
{
 return m_iTextureWidth;
}

 /* Returns texture height */
mrUInt32 mrTemplateSet::GetTextureHeight (void)
{
 return m_iTextureHeight;
}

 /* Returns cell width */
mrUInt32 mrTemplateSet::GetCellWidth (void)
{
 return m_iCellWidth;
}

 /* Returns cell height */
mrUInt32 mrTemplateSet::GetCellHeight (void)
{
 return m_iCellHeight;
}
```

You won't do any example since there isn't much to it. Later on you will see how this works with other classes.

mrAnimation

The `mrAnimation` class contains all the information about a single animation. This class enables you to work with animations very easily after it is set up.

Let's start as always with the class definition:

```
 /* 'mrAnimation.h' */

 /* Mirus base types header */
#include "mrDatatypes.h"
 /* Mirus error definitions header */
#include "mrError.h"
 /* Mirus template set header */
#include "mrTemplateSet.h"
 /* Mirus screen header */
#include "mrScreen.h"
/* DirectX Graphics header file */
#include <d3d8.h>

 /* Include this file only once */
#pragma once

 /* Mirus Animation class */
class mrAnimation
{
protected:
 mrTemplateSet    m_kTemplateSet;
 mrUInt32          m_iFrames;
 mrUInt32          m_iCurrentFrame;

 mrCellID *        m_pkFramesID;

public:
  /* Constructors / Destructor */
 mrAnimation (void);
 ~mrAnimation (void);

  /* Animation manipulation methods */
 void Create (mrTemplateSet * pkTemplateSet, mrUInt32 iFrames,
               mrCellID * pkPosition);
 void Update (void);
 mrError32 Render (RECT kDestRect, mrUInt32 iColor, mrReal32 fAngle);

  /* Animation maintenance methods */
```

```
  void SetCurrentFrame (mrUInt32 iFrame);
  mrUInt32 GetCurrentFrame (void);
};
```

Again, this class looks like the ones you have been developing before, at least, the method names, but their inner workings are very different.

Let's start with the constructor and the destructor:

```
 /* 'mrAnimation.cpp' */

 /* Complement header file */
#include "mrAnimation.h"

 /* Default constructor */
mrAnimation::mrAnimation (void)
{
 m_pkFramesID    = NULL;
 m_iFrames       = 0;
 m_iCurrentFrame = 0;
}

 /* Default destructor */
mrAnimation::~mrAnimation (void)
{
 m_iFrames       = 0;
 m_iCurrentFrame = 0;

 if (NULL != m_pkFramesID)
 {
  delete [] m_pkFramesID;
 m_pkFramesID    = NULL;
 }
}
```

As usual, in the constructor you have initialized all the members to either `NULL` or 0 and in the destructor you do the same thing, but deleting `m_pkFramesID` if you need to.

```
 /* Create animation */
void mrAnimation::Create (mrTemplateSet * pkTemplateSet,
                          mrUInt32 iFrames, mrCellID * pkFramesID)
```

```
30: {
31:   m_iFrames        = iFrames;
32:   m_iCurrentFrame = 0;
33:
34:   m_pkFramesID = new mrCellID [iFrames];
35:
36:   memcpy (&m_kTemplateSet, pkTemplateSet, sizeof (mrTemplateSet));
37:   memcpy (m_pkFramesID, pkFramesID, sizeof (mrCellID) * iFrames);
38: }
```

In this method, you start by setting the number of frames this animation stores (line 31) and set the current frame to 0, the first frame (line 32). Next you need to allocate enough memory to hold the position of each frame in the template set (line 34). This will allow you to get the frame image by using the `GetUV` method of `mrTemplateSet`. In the end you use `memcpy` to copy both the template set to the `mrAnimation` class template set (line 36) and the array describing the frames position to the one you allocated (line 37).

The next method is `Update`:

```
40:  /* Update the animation (moves frame) */
41: void mrAnimation::Update (void)
42: {
43:   m_iCurrentFrame ++;
44:   if (m_iCurrentFrame >= m_iFrames)
45:   {
46:    m_iCurrentFrame = 0;
47:   }
48: }
```

This method is pretty simple also, you start by increasing the current frame (line 43) and if it is equal to or greater than the number of total frames, you make the animation start all over again by setting the current frame to the first one (lines 44 through 47).

Now you will see the `Render` function. This is a complicated method so pay close attention to what is happening. This method is divided into three distinct parts, you first must rotate each vertex of the polygon, then translate them to world position and finally render them.

Before checking the `Render` method, let me just explain the first parameter of `Render`, `kDestRect`. `kDestRect` will hold both the position and the size of the polygon.

This way you only need to pass one structure to the method. The `left` and `top` members of the `RECT` hold the polygon position and the `right` and `bottom` members hold the size of the polygon.

With this known, take a look at the code:

```
 /* Render the animation */
mrError32 mrAnimation::Render (RECT kDestRect, mrUInt32 iColor,
                                  mrReal32 fAngle)
{
 mrRectText kTextCoord;

 mrReal32 fX1;
 mrReal32 fY1;
 mrReal32 fX2;
 mrReal32 fY2;
 mrReal32 fX3;
 mrReal32 fY3;
 mrReal32 fX4;
 mrReal32 fY4;
```

Okay, up to here it's only the declaration of temporary variables that you will use to store the polygon information. Next you will rotate the polygon before you translate it to get the correct rotated image:

```
 if (fAngle != 0)
 {
  /* Convert degrees to radians */
 fAngle *= 0.0174f;

  /* Create relative rectangle */
 RECT         kRotRect;
 kRotRect.left    = - (kDestRect.right >> 1);
 kRotRect.top     = - (kDestRect.bottom >> 1);
 kRotRect.right   =   (kDestRect.right >> 1);
 kRotRect.bottom  =   (kDestRect.bottom >> 1);
```

What you do here is, if `fAngle` is different than 0, then it needs to be rotated, and if so, you need to convert the angle from degrees to radians by multiplying it by `0.0174f` (which is `180/PI`). After this is done, you will create a rectangle describing the polygon, but this time centered around (0, 0). To do this, take a look at Figure 13.34.

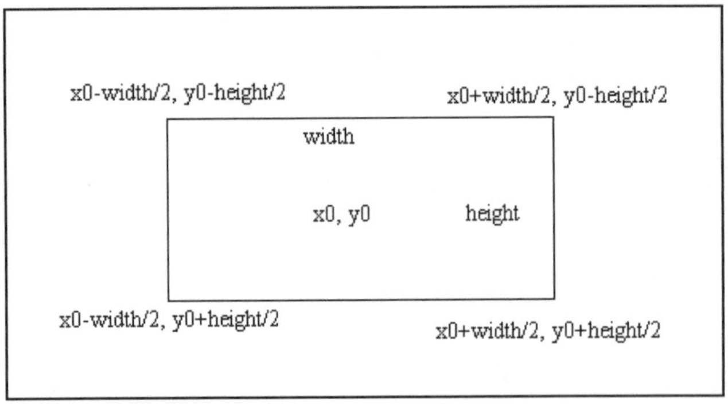

Figure 13.34

Creating a relative rectangle out of a polygon size.

As you can see from Figure 13.34, to convert from the size to a relative rectangle, you need to divide the width and height of the rectangle by 2, and then setting the appropriate values for the coordinates. Since the left and top coordinates will be positioned before the (0, 0) coordinate, you need to get the divided width and height from before and multiply it by –1, or negate it. You can use the divided width and height for the right and bottom coordinates.

You need to do this conversion so you can rotate the polygon relatively to its center, not any of its vertices.

You will then rotate the vertices:

```
   /* Rotate all the vertices */
  fX1 = (mrReal32)(kRotRect.left * cos (fAngle) +
                                  kRotRect.top * sin (fAngle));
  fY1 = (mrReal32)(kRotRect.left * sin (fAngle) -
                         kRotRect.top * cos (fAngle));

  fX2 = (mrReal32)(kRotRect.right * cos (fAngle) +
                                  kRotRect.top * sin (fAngle));
  fY2 = (mrReal32)(kRotRect.right * sin (fAngle) -
                         kRotRect.top * cos (fAngle));

  fX3 = (mrReal32)(kRotRect.left * cos (fAngle) +
                         kRotRect.bottom * sin (fAngle));
  fY3 = (mrReal32)(kRotRect.left * sin (fAngle) -
                                  kRotRect.bottom * cos (fAngle));

  fX4 = (mrReal32)(kRotRect.right * cos (fAngle) +
                         kRotRect.bottom * sin (fAngle));
```

```
 fY4 = (mrReal32)(kRotRect.right * sin (fAngle) -
                       kRotRect.bottom * cos (fAngle));
}
```

The preceding code uses the previous known formula for rotating in each vertex of the rectangle. In case you have forgotten, the equations to rotate a point around the origin are:

```
FinalX = cosine (θ) * X - sine (θ) * Y
FinalY = sine (θ) * X + cosine (θ) * Y
```

And that's it, you have the polygon rotated around the origin. Now you need to set up the coordinates of the relative rectangle if you don't rotate it. It isn't a wise choice to have a rotation of 0 angles to save time when coding, it is best to do two separate blocks, one for rotating and the other without rotating, since the trigonometric functions are time-consuming, so the best way to prevent this is to avoid them:

```
  /* Don't rotate */
else
{
  fX1 = (mrReal32) -(kDestRect.right >> 1);
  fY1 = (mrReal32)  (kDestRect.bottom >> 1);
  fX2 = (mrReal32)  (kDestRect.right >> 1);
  fY2 = (mrReal32)  (kDestRect.bottom >> 1);
  fX3 = (mrReal32) -(kDestRect.right >> 1);
  fY3 = (mrReal32) -(kDestRect.bottom >> 1);
  fX4 = (mrReal32)  (kDestRect.right >> 1);
  fY4 = (mrReal32) -(kDestRect.bottom >> 1);
}
```

You follow the previous logic to create the relative rectangle.

Next you need to move the relative rectangle from (0, 0) to the desired position which was passed to the `Render` method as the `left` and `top` members of `kDestRect`:

```
  /* Translate to absolute coordinates */
fX1 += kDestRect.left;
fY1 += kDestRect.top;
fX2 += kDestRect.left;
fY2 += kDestRect.top;
fX3 += kDestRect.left;
fY3 += kDestRect.top;
fX4 += kDestRect.left;
fY4 += kDestRect.top;
```

If you remember from earlier, to translate an object you just need to add the position of the object and the displacement, in this case, since the relative position of the rectangle is (0, 0), you need to add the destination position passed to Render and each of the vertex's positions to get the final position.

Next you need to render the polygon:

```
121:   /* Get UV rectangle from template set */
122:  m_kTemplateSet.GetUV (m_pkFramesID [m_iCurrentFrame], &kTextCoord);
123:
124:   /* Create rectangle vertices */
125:  mrVertex kVertices [] =
126:  {  /* x, y, z, w, color, texture coordinates (u,v) */
127:   {fX3, fY3, 0, 1.0f, iColor, kTextCoord.m_fLeft, kTextCoord.m_fTop},
128:   {fX4, fY4, 0, 1.0f, iColor, kTextCoord.m_fRight, kTextCoord.m_fTop},
129:   {fX2, fY2, 0, 1.0f, iColor, kTextCoord.m_fRight, kTextCoord.m_fBottom},
130:   {fX1, fY1, 0, 1.0f, iColor, kTextCoord.m_fLeft, kTextCoord.m_fBottom},
131:  };
132:
133:   /* Set as active texture */
134:  m_kTemplateSet.SetActiveTexture ();
135:
136:   /* Draw the rotated rectangle */
137:  mrScreen::GetSingleton ()->GetDevice ()->SetVertexShader (
138:                                            D3DFVF_MIRUSVERTEX);
139:  if (FAILED (mrScreen::GetSingleton ()->GetDevice ()->DrawPrimitiveUP (
140:                                            D3DPT_TRIANGLEFAN, 2, kVertices,
141:                                            sizeof (mrVertex))) )
142:  {
143:   return mrErrorDrawPrimitive;
144:  }
145:
146:  return mrNoError;
147: }
```

The first thing to do here is to get the texture coordinate rectangle of the template set for the current frame (line 122). Next you need to create a temporary vertex array to hold each of the polygon's vertex's position, texture coordinate, and color (lines 126 through 131). The order of the vertices could be any other, it just needs to follow the same logic to form two triangles describing a rectangle. Next you need to set the template set of this animation as the active one (line 134) and then render it (lines 137 through 141).

And that's it. It was long, but rendering the animation is easy. You will see how you can render it in the mrABO class.

There are only two access methods for this class:

```
 /* Sets the current frame */
void mrAnimation::SetCurrentFrame (mrUInt32 iFrame)
{
 m_iCurrentFrame = iFrame;
}

 /* Returns the current frame */
mrUInt32 mrAnimation::GetCurrentFrame (void)
{
 return m_iCurrentFrame;
}
```

And you are done. These last few classes haven't been put to much use but next you will develop mrABO, which will use directly, or indirectly, all of the classes you developed until now.

mrABO

Finally, you will be finishing this component. mrABO uses all the previous classes in the chapter to create a very simple to use class for animated objects.

mrABO allows you to control the size, color, and animations. And mrABO lets you do collision detection and render and load the animations from disc with simple to use functions.

Take a look at the class definition:

```
 /* 'mrABO.h' */

 /* Mirus base types header */
#include "mrDatatypes.h"
 /* Mirus error definitions header */
#include "mrError.h"
 /* Mirus texture header */
#include "mrTexture.h"
 /* Mirus animation header */
#include "mrAnimation.h"
/* DirectX Graphics header file */
#include <d3d8.h>
```

```

 /* Include this file only once */
#pragma once

 /* Mirus Animated Blittable Object (ABO) class */
class mrABO
{
protected:
 mrAnimation *    m_pkAnimations;
 mrUInt32          m_iCurrentAnimation;

 mrUInt32          m_iColor;

 mrUInt32          m_iXPosition;
 mrUInt32          m_iYPosition;

 mrUInt32          m_iWidth;
 mrUInt32          m_iHeight;

 mrReal32          m_fAngle;
 mrReal32          m_fRadius;

  /* Only if loading from file */
 mrTexture *      m_pkTexture;

public:
  /* Constructors / Destructor */
 mrABO (void);
 ~mrABO (void);

  /* ABO manipulation methods */
 void Create (mrUInt32 iAnimations, mrAnimation * pkAnimations);
 void Update (void);

 void SetAnimation (mrUInt32 iAnimation, mrAnimation * pkAnimation);
 void LoadFromFile (LPSTR lpszFilename);

 mrError32 Render (void);

 void Rotate (mrReal32 fAngle, mrUInt32 iAccumulate);

```

```
 mrBool32 Collide (mrABO & rkABO, mrUInt32 iUseSphere);
 mrBool32 ContainsPoint (mrInt32 iX, mrInt32 iY);

  /* ABO maintenance methods*/
 void SetCurrentAnimation (mrUInt32 iAnimation);
 mrUInt32 GetCurrentAnimation (void);

 void SetPosition (mrUInt32 iX, mrUInt32 iY);
 void SetSize (mrUInt32 iWidth, mrUInt32 iHeight);
 void SetColor (mrUInt8 iAlpha, mrUInt8 iRed, mrUInt8 iGreen,
                 mrUInt8 iBlue);
 void SetRadius (mrReal32 fRadius);

 mrUInt32 GetXPosition (void);
 mrUInt32 GetYPosition (void);
 mrUInt32 GetHeight (void);
 mrUInt32 GetWidth (void);
 mrUInt32 GetColor (void);
 mrReal32 GetDirection (void);
 mrReal32 GetRadius (void);
};
```

There are a lot of methods and members in this class, but the whole class isn't too complicated, really! Let's take a look at the constructor and destructor first:

```
 /* 'mrABO.cpp' */

 /* Complement header file */
#include "mrABO.h"

 /* Default constructor */
mrABO::mrABO (void)
{
 m_pkAnimations      = NULL;
 m_pkTexture         = NULL;
 m_iCurrentAnimation = 0;
 m_iXPosition        = 0;
 m_iYPosition        = 0;
 m_iWidth            = 0;
 m_iHeight           = 0;
 m_fAngle            = 0;
 m_fRadius           = 0;
```

```
18: }
19:
20:  /* Default destructor */
21: mrABO::~mrABO (void)
22: {
23:  if (NULL != m_pkAnimations)
24:  {
25:   delete [] m_pkAnimations;
26:   m_pkAnimations      = NULL;
27:  }
28:  if (NULL != m_pkTexture)
29:  {
30:   delete m_pkTexture;
31:   m_pkTexture         = NULL;
32:  }
33:  m_iCurrentAnimation = 0;
34:  m_iXPosition        = 0;
35:  m_iYPosition        = 0;
36:  m_iWidth            = 0;
37:  m_iHeight           = 0;
38:  m_fAngle            = 0;
39:  m_fRadius           = 0;
40: }
```

As usual, the constructor sets all the class members to 0 and NULL, and the destructor does the same thing but freeing any memory used by the members (lines 23 through 32).

The next function creates the ABO by supplying the number of animations and an array of animations:

```
 /* Create ABO */
void mrABO::Create (mrUInt32 iAnimations, mrAnimation * pkAnimations)
{
 m_pkAnimations = new mrAnimation [iAnimations];

 mrUInt32 iAnimation;

 for (iAnimation = 0; iAnimation < iAnimations; iAnimation ++)
 {
  SetAnimation (iAnimation, &pkAnimations [iAnimation]);
 }
}
```

What you do here is first allocate the memory required for the animations (line 45) and then go through each of the animations and copy each animation in the array to the one you allocated (lines 49 through 52) with SetAnimation, like so:

```
55:  /* Set ABO animation */
56: void mrABO::SetAnimation (mrUInt32 iAnimation, mrAnimation * pkAnimation)
57: {
58:  memcpy (&m_pkAnimations [iAnimation], pkAnimation, sizeof (mrAnimation));
59:  m_pkAnimations [iAnimation].SetCurrentFrame (0);
60: }
```

In this method, you copy the contents of the animation to your array, to the specified position (line 58), and set the animation current frame to the first one (line 59).

Now, you have all the methods and classes developed to create an ABO. What you need to do would be to create an mrRGBAImage, and from this create an mrTexture, and from this create an mrTemplateSet, and from this create an mrAnimation, and repeat this for every animation.

Okay, you have jumped from your chair just now. Well, there is another way. To create one single function that will load all the information about the ABO from a file, and create all the necessary classes and data to set up the ABO defined on the file. What do you prefer? Create all the classes by hand each time you need to use an ABO, or make a text file describing the ABO (you will see the format in a bit) and call just one function? Obviously you are now yelling "THE SECOND," so you will implement it also.

Now that you decided to create an ABO loader, you need to specify the ABO file format. Since you won't be using any known format, you need to create your own. So, let's first take a look at what in an ABO you need to define that will not change during the lifetime of the ABO (such attributes as size, color, and position should be defined by the application since the same ABO can be used for various objects, such as trees, which can be of different sizes or colors).

The unchangeable properties of the ABO are the following:

- Template image
- Color key
- Cell size
- Number of animations
- The number of frames of each animation
- The position on the template of each frame of the animation

So these are the properties you need to keep on file to store an ABO. But the file format like this may not sound too feasible to play. First, the template image may be a targa or a Windows bitmap file (or other if you have implemented any other loader), so you also need something to identify the template image format. The other problem with this description is how each animation is stored. Is it better to store all the number of frames for all the animations in a sequence and all the positions for each animation in another sequence? Or would it be better to store each animation in a sequence, with each animation composed by the number of frames, and the position of each frame? Or simply discard storing the information and use your birthday to store the number of frames? Except for the last idea, there are several things to consider when deciding on a file format. You will keep the second format.

So, you can now describe your ABO file format like:

```
FileName FileType
ColorKeyRed ColorKeyGreen ColorKeyBlue
CellWidth CellHeight
NumberOfAnimations
Animation[0]
Animation[1]
...
Animation[NumberOfAnimations-1]
```

And `Animation` can be defined as:

```
NumberOfFrames
FramePosition[0]
FramePosition[1]
...
FramePosition [NumberOfFrames-1]
```

While I made the properties to be aligned like this in the file, you can have each element on its own line, the only reason I put them like this is to be easier to edit.

There is just one thing I haven't discussed yet! How will each member be stored? You will only use strings and numbers (how original) to store each of the members. Except for the `FileName`, all the other members are numbers. You will be using a text file to store the ABO so the `FileName` member can't have any white spaces in it. Also, you need to specify how you will treat the `FileFormat` member. This member will tell you the format of the image file. For this case, I've chosen a value of one to represent a Windows bitmap and a value of two for a targa file; if you have implemented any other formats in `mrRGBAImage` you should decide which numbers represent what. The rest of the members are all numbers that hold the data relative to it. For example, the color key members can hold values from 0 to 255, and the other methods can hold the supported values for them. So, if you have a template that is only four cells wide, if you use a cell position of five while the ABO loads, when you try to use it the program will crash because you will be accessing a nonexistent part of the template.

Let's check one file example for the ABO:

```
Image.bmp 1
255 0 255
30 30
2
2
0 0
1 0
1
0 1
```

You can see from the preceding file description that the template set is stored in `IMAGE.BMP` and is of type bitmap (the 1 after the filename).

The next three elements represent the color key for this ABO, which is in this case purple (red is 255, green is 0, and blue is 255).

The next two elements are the cell size, which are both the width and height of the cell 30 (the first element is the width and the second the height).

Next you have the number of animations (two) and the two animations. The first animation has two frames, and the first frame position in the template set is (0, 0) and the second frame is (1, 0). The second animation only has one frame and it is positioned at location (0, 1).

One last consideration before checking out the code for the `LoadFromFile`, the ABOs are stored in text mode, this means that the text must be correctly formatted. If you include spaces where they shouldn't be, or include letters where numbers should be, there is no assurance the ABO will be loaded.

Okay, enough of theory let's check the code:

```
 /* Load ABO from file */
void mrABO::LoadFromFile (LPSTR lpszFilename)
{
 fstream      kABO;

```

```
67:  kABO.open (lpszFilename, ios::in);
68:
69:  if (kABO.is_open ())
70:  {
71:     /* Get texture name and type */
72:   mrInt8 aTextureName [256];
73:   kABO >> aTextureName;
74:   mrUInt32 iTextureType;
75:   kABO >> iTextureType;
76:
77:     /* Load the texture image */
78:   mrRGBAImage kTempImage;
79:
80:   if (1 == iTextureType)
81:   {
82:    kTempImage.LoadFromBitmap (aTextureName);
83:   }
84:   if (2 == iTextureType)
85:   {
86:    kTempImage.LoadFromTarga (aTextureName);
87:   }
```

What you have done up to here is open the file for reading in text mode (line 67) and read the filename and file type (lines 72 through 75). Then, depending on the file type, you load the image with the appropriate methods (lines 80 through 87).

Next you need to read the color key and create the texture:

```
89:     /* Read color key information */
90:   mrUInt32 iRed;
91:   mrUInt32 iGreen;
92:   mrUInt32 iBlue;
93:   kABO >> iRed;
94:   kABO >> iGreen;
95:   kABO >> iBlue;
96:
97:   kTempImage.SetColorKey ((mrUInt8)iRed, (mrUInt8)iGreen,
98:                           (mrUInt8)iBlue);
99:
100:    /* Create the texture */
101:  m_pkTexture = new mrTexture ();
102:  m_pkTexture->Create (&kTempImage);
```

The first thing you do is read the three color keys from the file (lines 93 through 95) and then set the color key of the image with `SetColorKey` (line 97). In the end, you allocate a new texture and create it (lines 101 and 102). Since you are loading the entire ABO without any interference from outside, you need to allocate the texture. If you were creating the ABO like before, one class at a time, you wouldn't need to allocate the texture since it would only point to a valid texture.

Next you have to create your template set:

```
104:    /* Read template set information */
105:   mrUInt32 iCellWidth;
106:   mrUInt32 iCellHeight;
107:   kABO >> iCellWidth;
108:   kABO >> iCellHeight;
109:
110:    /* Create the template */
111:   mrTemplateSet kTempTemplateSet;
112:   kTempTemplateSet.Create (m_pkTexture, kTempImage.GetWidth (),
113:                                  kTempImage.GetHeight (), iCellWidth,
114:                                  iCellHeight);
```

You start by reading the cell size from the file (lines 107 and 108) and then create a template set using the texture created before, the texture width and height (which are automatically read from the image file) and the cell width and height read from the file (lines 112 through 114).

Now you need to read and store the animations:

```
116:    /* Read number of animations */
117:   mrUInt32 iNumberOfAnimations;
118:   kABO >> iNumberOfAnimations;
119:
120:   mrAnimation * pkTempAnimations;
121:   pkTempAnimations = new mrAnimation [iNumberOfAnimations];
```

You start by reading the number of animations from the file (line 118) and then allocating a big enough array of animations for the ABO (line 121).

After this, you need to go through each animation and read its information:

```
123:   mrUInt32 iAnimation;
124:
125:    /* For each animation, read the number of frames */
126:   for (iAnimation = 0; iAnimation < iNumberOfAnimations; iAnimation++)
```

```
127:   {
128:    mrUInt32 iNumberOfFrames;
129:    kABO >> iNumberOfFrames;
130:
131:    mrCellID * pkFramePosition;
132:    pkFramePosition = new mrCellID [iNumberOfFrames];
133:    mrUInt32 iPosition;
134:
135:     /* For each frame, read the frames animation */
136:    for (iPosition = 0; iPosition < iNumberOfFrames; iPosition++)
137:    {
138:     kABO >> pkFramePosition [iPosition].m_iX;
139:     kABO >> pkFramePosition [iPosition].m_iY;
140:    }
141:
142:     /* Create the animation */
143:    pkTempAnimations [iAnimation].Create (&kTempTemplateSet ,
144:                                          iNumberOfFrames,
145:                                          pkFramePosition);
146:    delete [] pkFramePosition;
147:   }
```

What you do is go through each animation on the file (line 126) and read the number of frames of each animation (line 129) and allocate a big enough array of cell positions to hold the positions of each frame of the animation (line 132).

After that you loop through each position and read the X and Y positions of the current frame (lines 136 through 140).

Finally, you create the animation with the number of frames and the frames' position with the `Create` method of `mrAnimation` (lines 143 through 145) and you can't forget to release the memory you allocated (line 146).

Next you need to create the ABO with the animations you loaded:

```
    /* Create the ABO */
   Create (iNumberOfAnimations, pkTempAnimations);

   delete [] pkTempAnimations;

   kABO.close ();
  }
 }
```

which is done calling the Create method you did earlier and supplying the loaded data (line 151). You also need to release the memory allocated (line 153) and close the file (line 155).

And you are done. If you supply a correct ABO file to this function, the ABO will be completely loaded with just a single step.

The next method you see is Render:

```
159:  /* Render ABO */
160: mrError32 mrABO::Render (void)
161: {
162:  RECT kRect;
163:
164:   /* Send position and width as a rectangle */
165:  kRect.left    = m_iXPosition;
166:  kRect.top     = m_iYPosition;
167:  kRect.right   = m_iWidth;
168:  kRect.bottom = m_iHeight;
169:
170:  return m_pkAnimations [m_iCurrentAnimation].Render (kRect, m_iColor,
171:                                                             m_fAngle);
172: }
```

Which starts by creating a RECT structure and filling it up with the ABO position to the left and top members, and the ABO size to the right and bottom members (remember this is the way you did it in the Render method of mrAnimation (lines 165 through 168). You finish by calling the Render method of the current animation with the rectangle you created and the ABO color and size (lines 170 and 171).

Now, the next three methods are pretty simple, so they don't need much explanation:

```
174:  /* Update ABO animation */
175: void mrABO::Update (void)
176: {
177:  m_pkAnimations [m_iCurrentAnimation].Update ();
178: }
179:
180: void mrABO::SetCurrentAnimation (mrUInt32 iAnimation)
181: {
182:  m_iCurrentAnimation = iAnimation;
183: }
184:
```

```
185:  /* Returns ABO current animation */
186: mrUInt32 mrABO::GetCurrentAnimation (void)
187: {
188:  return m_iCurrentAnimation;
189: }
```

Now you just need to create a method to see if the ABOs collide, `Collide`:

```
191:  /* See if two ABOs collide */
192: mrBool32 mrABO::Collide (mrABO & rkABO, mrUInt32 iUseSphere)
193: {
194:   /* Use bounding sphere method */
195:  if (iUseSphere)
196:  {
197:    /* Get distance from one ABO to other */
198:   mrReal32 fXDelta = (mrReal32)m_iXPosition -
199:                       (mrReal32)rkABO.GetXPosition ();
200:   mrReal32 fYDelta = (mrReal32)m_iYPosition -
201:                       (mrReal32)rkABO.GetYPosition ();
202:
203:   mrReal32 fDistance;
204:   fDistance = (mrReal32) sqrt (fXDelta * fXDelta + fYDelta * fYDelta);
```

You will be using two different collision methods—bounding circles and bounding rectangles. For now, let's concentrate on the bounding circle method.

You start by checking which type of collision method you want to use. So, if the collision method is bounding circles (line 195), you will continue. You start by getting the distance of the two ABOs (lines 198 through 204). What you do is get the distance of each component and then you calculate its magnitude by calculating the square root of the sum of the squared sides:

```
Hypotenuse^2 = CatetA^2 + CatetB^2
```

This is called the vector magnitude, but you will see this later.

Now that you have the distance you need to get the radius of each ABO:

```
204:   mrReal32 fRadius1, fRadius2;
205:
206:     /* Get radius of each ABO */
207:   if (m_fRadius != 0)
208:   {
```

```
209:     fRadius1 = m_fRadius;
210:    }
211:    else
212:    {
213:     fRadius1 = (mrReal32) sqrt ( ((m_iWidth / 2) * (m_iWidth / 2)) +
214:                                  ((m_iHeight / 2) * (m_iHeight / 2)));
215:    }
216:    if (rkABO.GetRadius () != 0)
217:    {
218:     fRadius2 = rkABO.GetRadius ();
219:    }
220:    else
221:    {
222:     fRadius2 = (mrReal32) sqrt (
223:                  ((rkABO.GetWidth () / 2) * (rkABO.GetWidth () / 2)) +
224:                  ((rkABO.GetHeight () / 2) * (rkABO.GetHeight () / 2)));
225:    }
```

Here you check whether any of the ABOs has a bounding circle radius defined (lines 207 and 216). This is done because the user may want to use his own radius, which is usually more accurate than the smallest encapsulating radius which you calculate if there isn't any available radius (lines 213 and 214 and lines 222 through 224).

What you do to get the smallest encapsulating radius is get the distance of the center of the ABO to one of the vertices (since all the vertices in a rectangle have the same distance to the center) using the same formula as before to get the magnitude of the distance.

Now you just need to check whether or not the circles collide:

```
227:     /* If distance is smaller than the sum of the radius, return false */
228:    if (fDistance > (fRadius1 + fRadius2))
229:    {
230:     return mrFalse;
231:    }
232:    else
233:    {
234:     return mrTrue;
235:    }
236:   }
```

If you paid attention earlier, you will know that two circles intersect if the distance between the two is smaller than the sum of their radius (line 228). If it is, then you return `mrTrue` (line 234) and if it isn't, you return `mrFalse` (line 230).

If the user decided not to use bounding circles, then you must check for the collision using a bounding rectangle method:

```
237:  else
238:  {
239:    /* Bounding rectangle */
240:   mrInt32 iX0;
241:   mrInt32 iY0;
242:   mrInt32 iX1;
243:   mrInt32 iY1;
244:
245:   iX0 = m_iXPosition - m_iWidth / 2;
246:   iY0 = m_iYPosition - m_iHeight / 2;
247:   iX1 = m_iXPosition + m_iWidth / 2;
248:   iY1 = m_iYPosition + m_iHeight / 2;
```

You start by getting the position of the two diagonal vertices of the rectangle (lines 245 through 248). These two vertices represent any rectangle from which you can get any of the vertices of the rectangle.

Now you just need to check whether any of the rectangle vertices is contained in the other ABO bounding rectangle:

```
250:    /* Check all the vertices for containment */
251:   if (rkABO.ContainsPoint (iX0, iY0))
252:   {
253:    return mrTrue;
254:   }
255:   if (rkABO.ContainsPoint (iX0, iY1))
256:   {
257:    return mrTrue;
258:   }
259:   if (rkABO.ContainsPoint (iX1, iY1))
260:   {
261:    return mrTrue;
262:   }
263:   if (rkABO.ContainsPoint (iX1, iY0))
264:   {
265:    return mrTrue;
```

```
266:    }
267:
268:     /* If no point was inside return false */
269:    return mrFalse;
270:   }
271: }
```

You need to check each of the rectangle's vertices for containment in the other ABO rectangle, which is done with a call to `ContainsPoint` with the rectangle vertex. You do this for all the vertices. If any of them is contained in the other ABO, then there was a collision and you return `mrTrue`. If none of them is contained, then there wasn't any collision and you can return `mrFalse`.

Now you just need to create `ContainsPoint`:

```
273:  /* Checks if a point is within the area */
274: mrBool32 mrABO::ContainsPoint (mrInt32 iX, mrInt32 iY)
275: {
276:    /* Bounding rectangle */
277:   mrInt32 iX0;
278:   mrInt32 iY0;
279:   mrInt32 iX1;
280:   mrInt32 iY1;
281:
282:   iX0 = m_iXPosition - m_iWidth / 2;
283:   iY0 = m_iYPosition - m_iHeight / 2;
284:   iX1 = m_iXPosition + m_iWidth / 2;
285:   iY1 = m_iYPosition + m_iHeight / 2;
```

As before, you start by getting the position of the two diagonal vertices of the rectangle (lines 282 through 285). As soon as you have them, you can check whether the point is inside of this rectangle:

```
287:    /* See if point is inside the rectangle */
288:   if ((iX >= iX0) && (iX <= iX1))
289:   {
290:    if ((iY >= iY0) && (iY <= iY1))
291:    {
292:     return mrTrue;
293:    }
294:   }
295:   return mrFalse;
296: }
```

If you remember from before, a point is inside a rectangle if its horizontal position is between the vertical edges and if its vertical position is between the horizontal edges. You do this by checking if the horizontal component of the point is larger than or equal to the first vertex horizontal position (first vertical edge) and is smaller than or equal to the second vertex horizontal position (second vertical edge) (line 88). If it is, then you do the same thing but for the vertical position of the point (line 290), if this holds true, then the point is inside the rectangle and you return `mrTrue` (line 292), if any of the above conditions fail, then the point isn't inside the rectangle and you return `mrFalse` (line 295).

The next methods are the access methods so take a look at them:

```
298:  /* Sets ABO position */
299: void mrABO::SetPosition (mrUInt32 iX, mrUInt32 iY)
300: {
301:  m_iXPosition = iX;
302:  m_iYPosition = iY;
303: }
304:
305:  /* Sets ABO size */
306: void mrABO::SetSize (mrUInt32 iWidth, mrUInt32 iHeight)
307: {
308:  m_iWidth  = iWidth;
309:  m_iHeight = iHeight;
310: }
311:
312:  /* Sets ABO color */
313: void mrABO::SetColor (mrUInt8 iAlpha, mrUInt8 iRed, mrUInt8 iGreen,
314:                       mrUInt8 iBlue)
315: {
316:  m_iColor = D3DCOLOR_ARGB (iAlpha, iRed, iGreen, iBlue);
317: }
318:
319:  /* Sets ABO color */
320: void mrABO::SetRadius (mrReal32 fRadius)
321: {
322:  m_fRadius = fRadius;
323: }
324:
325:  /* Rotate ABO */
```

```
326: void mrABO::Rotate (mrReal32 fAngle, mrUInt32 iAccumulate)
327: {
328:  if (iAccumulate)
329:  {
330:   m_fAngle += fAngle;
331:  }
332:  else
333:  {
334:   m_fAngle = fAngle;
335:  }
336: }
```

What you do here is see whether you want to accumulate the rotation (relative rotation) (lines 328 through 331) where you add the angle to the existing angle or set the rotation (absolute rotation) (lines 333 through 335) where you just assign the angle to the ABO angle.

```
338:  /* Returns ABO horizontal position */
339: mrUInt32 mrABO::GetXPosition (void)
340: {
341:  return m_iXPosition;
342: }
343:
344:  /* Returns ABO vertical position */
345: mrUInt32 mrABO::GetYPosition (void)
346: {
347:  return m_iYPosition;
348: }
349:
350:  /* Returns ABO height */
351: mrUInt32 mrABO::GetHeight (void)
352: {
353:  return m_iHeight;
354: }
355:
356:  /* Returns ABO width */
357: mrUInt32 mrABO::GetWidth (void)
358: {
359:  return m_iWidth;
360: }
```

```

 /* Returns ABO color */
mrUInt32 mrABO::GetColor (void)
{
 return m_iColor;
}

 /* Returns ABO direction */
mrReal32 mrABO::GetDirection (void)
{
 return m_fAngle;
}

 /* Returns ABO collision radius */
mrReal32 mrABO::GetRadius (void)
{
 return m_fRadius;
}
```

And that's about it. To work with the mrABO class is pretty simple, you just load the ABO from a file, set the needed properties and each frame you render, and update it:

```
MrABO kABO;
kABO.LoadFromFile ("Abo.txt");
kAbo.SetColor (255, 255, 255, 255);
kABO.SetSize (100, 100);
kABO.SetPosition (200, 43);
 /* Each frame, between mrScreen::StartFrame and mrScreen::EndFrame */
kAbo.Render ();
 /* We may or may not update the ABO. We usually do */
kAbo.Update ();
```

And you have an ABO created from the file ABO.TXT using the normal colors (if you wanted it to be only shades of blue, you would set the red and green components to 0, or if you wanted the ABO semitransparent, you would set the alpha to 126 in SetColor) and a size of 100, 100 pixels. The ABO would be in position (200, 43).

Then each frame you would render the ABO and update it (you may not want to update the ABO if not enough time has passed since the last update).

And you are done with this graphical stuff. Of course, there are many other cool things Direct3D and 2D graphics, but these are more than enough to create some nice games.

> **NOTE**
> For this component to work, you will need to include the dxguid.lib and d3d8.lib libraries in your projects.

Summary

Umph . . . long chapter. With what you learned here you are now ready to start making some crazy games, really you are!

You started by covering the basics of Direct3D and advancing to some topics like alpha blending and windows bitmaps.

You have also created the Mirus graphics component, which you will be using to develop your final game.

Oh, by the way, if you read the entire chapter you can pat yourself on the back, you deserve it.

Questions and Answers

Q: What is a transformed vertex?

A: A transformed vertex is a vertex that was manually transformed from 3D (x, y, z) to 2D (x, y).

Q: Why do you need to test for various backbuffer formats when you use full-screen modes?

A: Unfortunately, Direct3D forces you to set the exact backbuffer format. Since there are various formats, even if you use only one that is mainstream, there will still be users who won't be able to play the game.

Q: What brand of coffee do you take?

A: I don't drink coffee, but Red Bull is a very good replacement for the caffeine.

Exercises

1. What is the advantage of using textures and polygons over surfaces?
2. What is the resulting color for red: 255, green: 230, blue: 110 in R5G6B5 format?
3. What effect would the following texture coordinates produce: (0.5, 0.5), (1, 0.5), (0.5, 1), (1, 1)?
4. What is a template set?
5. Why do you always include an extra vertex for the rectangle and circle drawing?

CHAPTER 14

DirectInput

Now that you know how to put some graphics on the screen, you need to know how to use the input devices (keyboard, mouse, and joystick) to control the game. Without them, you can forget about interactivity.

In this chapter, you will develop the input component of Mirus.

From now on, you will adopt a different method! You will be introduced to some of the basics (in this chapter is DirectInput), and then you will develop the necessary components to your library. While you create Mirus, you will see what happens and why.

Introduction to DirectInput

DirectInput, shown in Figure 14.1, enables you to work with any DirectInput device in an intuitive way. While working with the mouse is a little different from working with the joystick or the keyboard, they all share the same interfaces, which makes them easy to work with.

You will use only two interfaces while working with DirectInput, which are `IDirectInput8` and `IDirectInputDevice8`.

While you will focus only on input from the devices, some devices (for example, force feedback joysticks) enable you to send information to them. Using force feedback in your games isn't hard but introduces you to some new concepts, which you aren't really ready to grasp. If you feel adventurous, check out the DirectX SDK documentation on force feedback.

> **NOTE**
>
> **DirectInput8 needs both the `dinput8.h` and `dinput8.lib` files.**

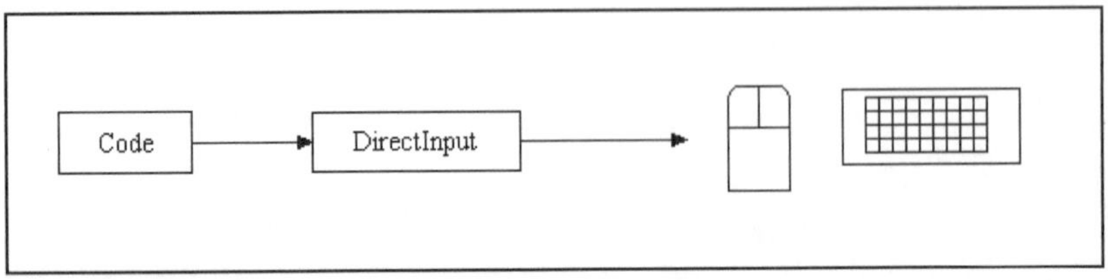

Figure 14.1

Introduction to DirectInput.

Setting up DirectInput isn't difficult either, you just need to create the DirectInput base object, create the devices you want, and set some information. Something like the following:

- Create the `IDirectInput8` object.
- Create the appropriate device (mouse, keyboard, or joystick).
- Set device data format.
- Set the cooperative level for the created device.
- Set device properties (if any).
- Acquire the device.

And you are ready to use your devices for input.

There are two ways to use DirectInput devices—unbuffered data or buffered data. I will explain the differences next.

Unbuffered Data

Using unbuffered data with your devices enables you to get only one state of the device. What this means is that when you try to get the device state, you can only get the actual state of the device. It doesn't matter if a key was pressed two milliseconds ago, if when you try to get the state the button isn't still held down, the device will return that the button isn't pressed.

This type of data is usually used in keyboards and joysticks, because you are usually only interested in retrieving the current state of the device.

Getting unbuffered data is as simple as getting the current device state with a single call, as you will see in a bit.

Buffered Data

On the other hand, buffered data enables you to get a specific number of states of the device. This enables you to get a sequence of actions between states to get the smoothest trail possible.

You usually use this kind of data when you are working with the mouse. Mouse movement is usually jerky because you usually move it quickly, or various times during a single frame. By using buffered data, you can get the actual movement of the mouse.

Getting buffered data is a little more complicated than getting unbuffered data. When you create a device, you need to set the length of the buffer. So, after you create the device with a specific buffer length, you need to loop through all the elements of the buffer and get the corresponding state. It looks more complicated than it really is, so don't worry, you will see how this is done when you work with the mouse.

mrInputManager

So, the basics are covered, time to develop Mirus and see the inner workings of DirectInput. Start by looking at the `mrInputManager` class definition:

```
 /* 'mrInputManager.h' */

 /* Mirus base types header */
#include "mrDatatypes.h"
 /* Mirus error definitions header */
#include "mrError.h"
 /* Windows header file */
#include <windows.h>
 /* Direct Input header file */
#include <dinput.h>
/* Assert header file */
#include <assert.h>

 /* Include this file only once */
#pragma once

 /* Mirus Input Manager class */
class mrInputManager
{
protected:
  /* DirectInput objects */
 LPDIRECTINPUT8          m_lpkDInput;

  /* Singleton */
 static mrInputManager * m_pkSingleton;

public:
  /* Constructors / Destructor */
```

```
  mrInputManager (void);
  ~mrInputManager (void);

   /* Input devices manipulation routines */
  mrError32 Init (HINSTANCE hInstance);
  LPDIRECTINPUT8 GetInput (void);

   /* Singleton */
  static mrInputManager * GetSingleton (void);
};
```

Fortunately for you, this class doesn't do much except initialize `DirectInput8` so you can start creating the devices.

You will see how this is done later, but for now, let's see the implementation of the constructor:

```
 6:  /* Singleton object */
 7: mrInputManager * mrInputManager::m_pkSingleton = NULL;
 8:
 9:  /* Default constructor */
10: mrInputManager::mrInputManager (void)
11: {
12:  m_lpkDInput = NULL;
13:
14:  assert (!m_pkSingleton);
15:  m_pkSingleton = this;
16: }
```

Nothing new here. You first need to declare the static Singleton member (line 7) and in the constructor, you initialize the `m_lpkDInput` to `NULL` and initialize the Singleton.

As with Direct3D, for each object you create, you need to release it, this is done in the destructor:

```
 /* Default destructor */
mrInputManager::~mrInputManager (void)
{
 if (NULL != m_lpkDInput)
 {
  m_lpkDInput->Release ();
  m_lpkDInput = NULL;
 }
```

```

  assert (m_pkSingleton);
  m_pkSingleton = NULL;
}
```

Here you release the lpkDInput member if it is different from NULL. This will ensure that you are releasing a valid object. You also verify the Singleton to see whether everything is okay.

Now, you need to know how to create the DirectInput object, which is done in Init:

```
 /* Initializes the input manager */
mrError32 mrInputManager::Init (HINSTANCE hInstance)
{
  /* Create Direct Input object */
 if (FAILED (DirectInput8Create (hInstance, DIRECTINPUT_VERSION,
                                 IID_IDirectInput8,
                                 (void**) &m_lpkDInput, NULL)))
 {
  return mrErrorDInputCreate;
 }
 return mrNoError;
}
```

As you can see, you use DirectInput8Create to create your object. DirectInput8Create is defined as:

```
HRESULT WINAPI DirectInput8Create (
 HINSTANCE hinst,
 DWORD dwVersion,
 REFIID riidltf,
 LPVOID * ppvOut,
 LPUNKNOWN punkOuter);
```

Where the first parameter is a handle to the application instance, and the second parameter is the DirectInput version you want to use, you should use DIRECTINPUT_VERSION to use the latest version available (the current SDK version).

Next you have the identifier of the interface you want to create. This can be either IID_IDirectInput8A which will create an ANSI-compatible interface or IID_IDirectInput8W which will create a UNICODE-compatible interface. Passing only IID_IDirectInput8 will create an interface depending on the compile flags or defines. You will use IID_IDirectInput8 for Mirus.

Following you have a pointer to a pointer to an `IDirectInput8` interface you want to create. In the end is a COM-specific value and you can use `NULL`.

Just to be sure, let's see the `GetSingleton` method:

```
 /* Returns the mrInputManager singleton */
mrInputManager * mrInputManager::GetSingleton (void)
{
 assert (m_pkSingleton);
 return m_pkSingleton;
}
```

And that's it, you finished your `mrInputManager` class. Now the only thing you need to do is create the three device classes.

mrKeyboard

Time to create your keyboard device. There are many steps from creating the device until you can get access to it and use it in your games.

To create a fully functional keyboard device, you need to complete the following steps:

1. Create the device.
2. Set the device data format.
3. Set the device cooperative level.
4. Acquire the device.

Okay, it isn't much, but it's a little troublesome. You will learn about all of these steps in a while. For now, here is the `mrKeyboard` class declaration:

```
 /* 'mrKeyboard.h' */

 /* Mirus base types header */
#include "mrDatatypes.h"
 /* Mirus error definitions header */
#include "mrError.h"
 /* Mirus Input Manager header file */
#include "mrInputManager.h"
 /* Windows header file */
#include <windows.h>
 /* Direct Input header file */
#include <dinput.h>
```

```
13:
14:  /* Include this file only once */
15: #pragma once
16:
17:  /* Mirus Keyboard class */
18: class mrKeyboard
19: {
20: protected:
21:    /* DirectInput objects */
22:  LPDIRECTINPUTDEVICE8 m_lpkDIDevice;
23:
24:    /* Our key buffer */
25:  mrUInt8              m_iKeyBuffer [256];
26:
27: public:
28:    /* Constructors / Destructor */
29:  mrKeyboard (void);
30:  ~mrKeyboard (void);
31:
32:    /* Keyboard manipulation routines */
33:  mrError32 Init (HWND hWindow);
34:  mrError32 Update (void);
35:
36:  mrBool32 IsButtonDown (mrUInt32 iButton);
37:  mrBool32 IsButtonUp (mrUInt32 iButton);
38: };
```

In this class you need to keep two members, a pointer to the `IDirectInputDevice8` interface (line 22), which will represent the keyboard, and the keyboard buffer (line 25). The keyboard buffer will hold the state for all the keys, storing whether they are pressed or not. You will see how this works in a minute, but for now, you need to implement your constructor:

```
 /* Default constructor */
mrKeyboard::mrKeyboard (void)
{
 m_lpkDIDevice = NULL;
 ZeroMemory (m_iKeyBuffer, sizeof (mrUInt8) * 256);
}
```

Which will only set the pointer to the interface to `NULL` and clear the key buffer to zero (so you don't get false keystrokes).

Next is the destructor:

```
13:  /* Default destructor */
14: mrKeyboard::~mrKeyboard (void)
15: {
16:  if (NULL != m_lpkDIDevice)
17:  {
18:   m_lpkDIDevice->Unacquire ();
19:   m_lpkDIDevice->Release ();
20:   m_lpkDIDevice = NULL;
21:  }
22: }
```

As always, in the destructor you need to release the device object as shown. Take note that you also `Unacquire` the device before releasing it. Not doing this may prevent other applications from getting access to the device. `Unacquire` is defined as:

```
HRESULT IDirectInputDevice8::Unacquire();
```

Next you need to initialize the keyboard. There are various steps to do this so let's go over them one at a time:

```
23:  /* Initializes the keyboard */
24: mrError32 mrKeyboard::Init (HWND hWindow)
25: {
26:   /* Create keyboard device */
27:  if (FAILED(mrInputManager::GetSingleton ()->GetInput ()->CreateDevice(
28:               GUID_SysKeyboard, &m_lpkDIDevice, NULL)) )
29:  {
30:   return mrErrorKeyboardCreateDevice;
31:  }
```

What you do here is get the pointer to the `IDirectInput8` interface of `mrInputManager` by the use of a Singleton to be able to call its `CreateDevice` method (line 27). `CreateDevice` is the method you use to create, obviously, the devices. It is defined as:

```
HRESULT IDirectInput8::CreateDevice (
 REFGUID rguid,
 LPDIRECTINPUTDEVICE * lplpDirectInputDevice,
 LPUNKNOWN pUnkOuter);
```

The first parameter is a reference to a device GUID you want to create. Fortunately for you, DirectX offers you two globally defined GUIDs that will always use the default primary keyboard (`GUID_SysKeyboard`) and mouse (`GUID_SysMouse`). Supplying these

GUIDs enables you to use these primary devices without worrying about their GUIDs. In this case, you will use GUID_SysKeyboard because you want to use the keyboard.

The second parameter is a pointer to a pointer to the IDirectInputDevice8 interface you want to create.

As before, the last parameter is a COM-specific parameter and you will pass NULL to it.

> **NOTE**
>
> In case you have forgotten, a GUID is a Globally Unique Identifier to a COM object.

Next you need to set the device data format:

```
  /* Set keyboard data format */
 if (FAILED (m_lpkDIDevice->SetDataFormat (&c_dfDIKeyboard)) )
 {
  return mrErrorKeyboardSetDataFormat;
 }
```

Setting the device format is pretty simple, eh? Well, it is for the keyboard (and mouse) because you can use a DirectX predefined structure to do it. This globally defined structure enables you to set a default format for the data using SetDataFormat defined as:

```
HRESULT IDirectInputDevice8::SetDataFormat (
 LPCDIDATAFORMAT lpdf);
```

Where the only parameter is a pointer to a DIDATAFORMAT structure. In Mirus you will use c_dfDIKeyboard because it sets up the data format like you want it, but just in case you want to use something different, here is the definition of DIDATAFORMAT:

```
typedef struct _DIDATAFORMAT {
 DWORD dwSize;
 DWORD dwObjSize;
 DWORD dwFlags;
 DWORD dwDataSize;
 DWORD dwNumObjs;
 LPDIOBJECTDATAFORMAT rgodf;
} DIDATAFORMAT;
```

The first parameter of this structure is the structure size and following is the size of the DIOBJECTDATAFORMAT structure (the last parameter of the structure).

Following are the flags, which can be either DIDF_ABSAXIS or DIDF_RELAXIS. The first one is used when you want to use absolute mode for the device and the second one is for relative mode.

The difference between the two modes is simple. Suppose your DirectInput application is a drawing application, so in this case you need to know the exact position of the mouse. Using the absolute mode, you could retrieve the position of the mouse from the start of the application. Supposing that the mouse started at position (0,0), the values returned by DirectInput for the mouse would be the current position of the mouse to position (0,0), as shown in Figure 14.2.

This is how Windows, without DirectX, works with the mouse.

While absolute mode is good for applications, most times it isn't good for games. In games you usually need to know how much the mouse moved since the last frame; this is how relative mode works. It returns the movement made since the last call to retrieve the position, as shown in Figure 14.3.

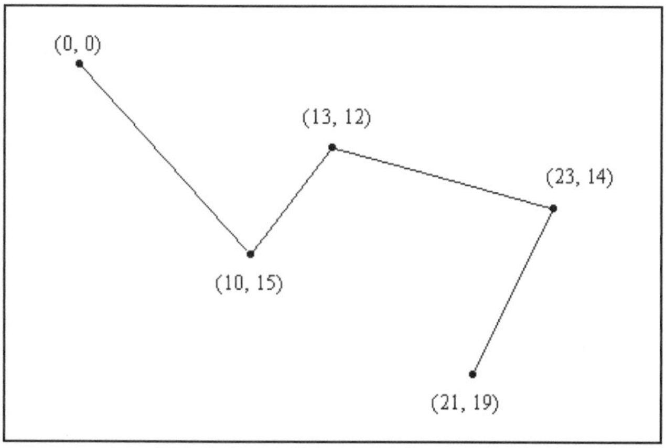

Figure 14.2

DirectInput absolute mode.

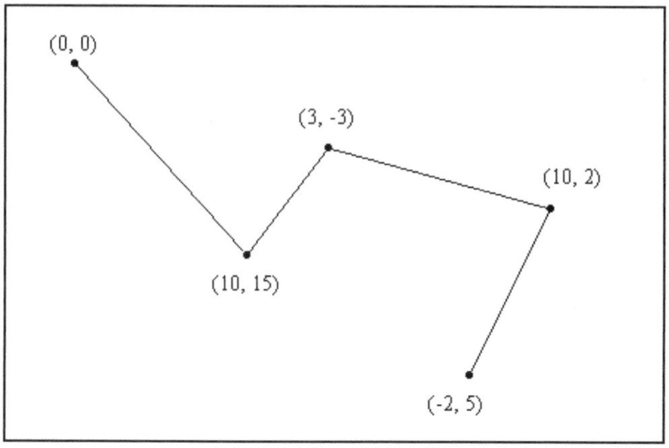

Figure 14.3

DirectInput relative mode.

While this is only important for devices that have axes (like the mouse or the joystick) it is good to know.

Okay, back to your structure. Following you have the size of the data packet that DirectInput retrieves, or the size of the structure DirectInput retrieves when you query the device state.

Next is the number of objects in the object data format array (the last parameter).

The last parameter is an array of DIOBJECTDATAFORMAT structures that define how an object data should be reported by DirectInput.

In almost every case you will want to use the predefined structures given to you by DirectX, but if you feel that they just don't work for you, don't hesitate to create your own.

After you set the device's data format, you need to set the device's cooperate level:

```
  /* Set keyboard cooperative level */
 if (FAILED (m_lpkDIDevice->SetCooperativeLevel (hWindow,
                DISCL_NONEXCLUSIVE | DISCL_FOREGROUND)) )
 {
  return mrErrorKeyboardSetCooperativeLevel;
 }
```

Setting the cooperative level is simple, you just call the SetCooperativeLevel method of IDirectInputDevice8 with the appropriate parameters and you're set. SetCooperativeLevel is defined as:

```
HRESULT IDirectInputDevice8::SetCooperativeLevel (
 HWND hwnd,
 DWORD dwFlags);
```

Where the first parameter is the handle to the window, which controls the device, and the last parameters are the flags specifying how you want to set the cooperative level. The available flags are shown in Table 14.1.

Finally you need to acquire the keyboard:

```
  /* Acquire keyboard */
 m_lpkDIDevice->Acquire ();

 return mrNoError;
}
```

Table 14.1 SetCooperativeLevel Flags

Flag	Description
DISCL_BACKGROUND	The application requires background access. This allows the application to acquire the device even if the application is not active.
DISCL_EXCLUSIVE	The application requires exclusive access. This doesn't allow any application other than this to obtain exclusive access to the device.
DISCL_FOREGROUND	The application requires foreground access. The device is automatically unacquired when the application is not active.
DISCL_NONEXCLUSIVE	The application requires nonexclusive access. Access to the device doesn't interfere with other applications.
DISCL_NOWINKEY	Disable the Windows logo key.

Which is done by calling `Acquire`, which gets access to the device and is defined as:

```
HRESULT IDirectInputDevice8::Acquire (void);
```

And you have your device ready to be used.

The next method you must implement is `Update`. `Update` will update the keyboard buffer in the `mrKeyboard` class with the current state of the device. `Update` should be called every frame when input is expected:

```
 /* Updates the keyboard status */
mrError32 mrKeyboard::Update (void)
{
  /* Get device data */
 HRESULT hRet = m_lpkDIDevice->GetDeviceState (sizeof (mrUInt8) * 256,
                                              (LPVOID) &m_iKeyBuffer);

 if ((FAILED (hRet)) && (hRet == DIERR_INPUTLOST))
 {
```

```
     /* Try to acquire keyboard */
   if (FAILED (m_lpkDIDevice->Acquire ()) )
   {
    return mrErrorKeyboardAcquire;
   }
  }
  else
  {
   return mrErrorKeyboardGetDeviceData;
  }
  return mrNoError;
}
```

You start by getting the device state with `GetDeviceState`. `GetDeviceState` retrieves the current state of the device. `GetDeviceState` is usually used for unbuffered mode and is defined as:

```
HRESULT IDirectInputDevice8::GetDeviceState (
 DWORD cbData,
 LPVOID lpvData);
```

Where the first parameter is the size of the buffer of the data (the second parameter), and the last parameter is a pointer to the data buffer.

Remember the keyboard buffer from the class definition? Well, you use it here to keep the state of each of the key combinations. You will see how to get the state in a bit.

Instead of usually returning an error if the DirectInput method fails, you will also check to see whether the device was lost by checking whether the return code is `DIERR_ INPUTLOST`, which occurs when the application loses focus. When this happens, you can try to get the device again by acquiring it with `Acquire` so you can use it in the next call to `Update`. If the return error isn't `DIERR_ INPUTLOST`, then something really wrong transpired and you should return a normal error code.

Now you simply need the methods to check whether the keys are pressed or not:

```
 /* Returns if a button is down */
mrBool32 mrKeyboard::IsButtonDown (mrUInt32 iButton)
{
  /* Check if button is pressed */
```

```
  if (m_iKeyBuffer [iButton] & (1<<7))
  {
   return mrTrue;
  }
  else
  {
   return mrFalse;
  }
}

  /* Returns if a button is up */
mrBool32 mrKeyboard::IsButtonUp (mrUInt32 iButton)
{
   /* Check if button isn't pressed */
  if (!(m_iKeyBuffer [iButton] & (1<<7)))
  {
   return mrTrue;
  }
  else
  {
   return mrFalse;
  }
}
```

These two methods work the same way, so let's go over `IsButtonDown`. There are two things you need to pay special attention to here. First is the fact that you use a normal `mrUInt32` to define a key. This is because the DirectInput uses a scan code for each key, which means that each key is represented by a number. While this is good to know, knowing the exact scan code for each key you want to use is a pain, so DirectInput has defined each of the key codes to a constant that you can plug right in. The available constants are shown in Table 14.2.

So, when you have the buffer index of the key you want to check the state of, what you need to do is determine whether the highest bit of the array element is set. Because you have used the globally defined data format for the keyboard, DirectInput returns the state of the key by setting the highest bit if it is pressed, or by not setting it if it isn't. Knowing this, you need to determine whether the highest bit is set, which is done by using the `&` (and) bit operator.

TABLE 14.2 DirectInput Keyboard Constants

Flag	Description
DIK_0 ... DIK_9	Numbers from zero through nine on the main keyboard
DIK_A ... DIK_Z	Letters from A through Z on the main keyboard
DIK_F1 ... DIK_F15	Keys F1 through F15
DIK_NUMPAD0 ... DIK_NUMPAD9	Numbers from zero through nine on the numeric keypad
DIK_ADD	Plus sign on the numeric keypad
DIK_SUBTRACT	Subtract sign on the numeric keypad
DIK_MULTIPLY	Multiply sign (*) on the numeric keypad
DIK_DIVIDE	Divide sign (/) on the numeric keypad
DIK_DECIMAL	Period on the numeric keypad
DIK_NUMPADENTER	Enter on the numeric keypad
DIK_SCROLL	Scroll Lock key
DIK_CAPITAL	Caps Lock key
DIK_NUMLOCK	Num Lock key
DIK_PAUSE	Pause key
DIK_LCONTROL	Left Ctrl key
DIK_RCONTROL	Right Ctrl key
DIK_LMENU	Left Alt key
DIK_RMENU	Right Alt key
DIK_LSHIFT	Left Shift key
DIK_RSHIFT	Right Shift key
DIK_LWIN	Left Microsoft Windows logo key

TABLE 14.2 DirectInput Keyboard Constants *(continued)*

Flag	Description
DIK_RWIN	Right Microsoft Windows logo key
DIK_UP	Up arrow
DIK_DOWN	Down arrow
DIK_LEFT	Left arrow
DIK_RIGHT	Right arrow
DIK_HOME	Home key
DIK_END	End key
DIK_NEXT	Page down key
DIK_PRIOR	Page up key
DIK_INSERT	Insert key
DIK_DELETE	Delete key
DIK_ESCAPE	Escape key on the main keyboard
DIK_RETURN	Enter on the main keyboard
DIK_SPACE	Space key on the main keyboard
DIK_TAB	Tab key on the main keyboard
DIK_BACK	Backspace
DIK_PERIOD	Period on the main keyboard
DIK_COMMA	Comma
DIK_SEMICOLON	Semicolon on the main keyboard
DIK_EQUALS	Equals key on the main keyboard
DIK_MINUS	Minus key on the main keyboard
DIK_APOSTROPHE	Apostrophe on the main keyboard
DIK_SLASH	Forward slash on the main keyboard

Using the keyboard with Mirus is also easy. You just need to `init` the input manager and the keyboard, and you can start querying it like the following:

```
 /* '02 Main.cpp' */

 /* Mirus header */
#include "mirus.h"

 /* Input class */
class InputWindow : public mrWindow
{
  /* Input related classes */
 mrInputManager      m_kInputManager;
 mrKeyboard          m_kKeyboard;

  /* Mirus related classes */
 mrScreen            m_kScreen;
 mrABO               m_kABO;

public:
  /* Constructor / Destructor */
 InputWindow (void);
 ~InputWindow (void);

 void Init (HINSTANCE hInstance);

  /* Window manipulation functions */
 mrBool32 Frame (void);
};

InputWindow::InputWindow (void)
{
}

InputWindow::~InputWindow (void)
{
}
```

Notice how I declared the input manager and the device (lines 10 and 11).

```
36: void InputWindow::Init (HINSTANCE hInstance)
37: {
38:   /* Initialize the screen and the ABO (a smily) */
39:  m_kScreen.Init (m_hWindow);
40:  m_kScreen.SetMode (false, 640, 480, 32, true);
41:  m_kABO.LoadFromFile ("smile.txt");
42:  m_kABO.SetSize (60, 60);
43:  m_kABO.SetPosition (320, 240);
44:  m_kABO.SetColor (255,255,255,255);
45:
46:   /* Initialize the input manager and device */
47:  m_kInputManager.Init (hInstance);
48:  m_kKeyboard.Init (m_hWindow);
49: }
```

Here I initialized the screen and the smiley (lines 38 through 44) and the devices (lines 47 and 48).

```
50:
51:  /* Render frame */
52: mrBool32 InputWindow::Frame(void)
53: {
54:   /* Start rendering */
55:  m_kScreen.Clear (0, 0, 0, 0);
56:  m_kScreen.StartFrame ();
57:
58:   /* Render */
59:  m_kABO.Render ();
60:
61:   /* Get the input and move the smily */
62:  m_kKeyboard.Update ();
63:  int iX = m_kABO.GetXPosition ();
64:  int iY = m_kABO.GetYPosition ();
65:
66:  if (m_kKeyboard.IsButtonDown (DIK_UP))
67:  {
```

```
68:     iY -= 1;
69:   }
70:   if (m_kKeyboard.IsButtonDown (DIK_DOWN))
71:   {
72:     iY += 1;
73:   }
74:   if (m_kKeyboard.IsButtonDown (DIK_RIGHT))
75:   {
76:     iX += 1;
77:   }
78:   if (m_kKeyboard.IsButtonDown (DIK_LEFT))
79:   {
80:     iX -= 1;
81:   }
82:   m_kABO.SetPosition (iX, iY);
83:
84:   m_kScreen.EndFrame ();
85:
86:   return mrTrue;
87: }
```

In this function, in the main part of the program, I just updated the device status (line 62) and checked if any of the keys were pressed (lines 66 through 81) and moved the smiley.

And the same `WinMain` code:

```
 89:   /* "WinMain Vs. main" */
 90: int WINAPI WinMain (HINSTANCE hInstance, HINSTANCE hPrevInst,
 91:                     LPSTR lpCmdLine, int nShowCmd)
 92: {
 93:    /* Our window */
 94:   InputWindow  kWindow;
 95:
 96:    /* Create window */
 97:   kWindow.Create (hInstance, "Keyboard");
 98:   kWindow.SetSize (640, 480);
 99:
100:   kWindow.Init (hInstance);
101:   kWindow.Run ();
102:
```

```
 return 0;
}
```

And you are done with the keyboard. It wasn't that hard, was it? Well, now you will see how you can use the mouse, which is a little trickier since it uses buffered data.

mrMouse

Setting up the mouse with DirectInput isn't difficult, it simply involves a few more steps than the keyboard, mostly due to the fact that you will be using buffered input so you have a more accurate description of the mouse movement. You will see the differences in a bit, but for now, let's take a look at the class definition:

```
 /* 'mrMouse.h' */

 /* Mirus base types header */
#include "mrDatatypes.h"
 /* Mirus error definitions header */
#include "mrError.h"
 /* Mirus Input Manager header file */
#include "mrInputManager.h"
 /* Windows header file */
#include <windows.h>
 /* Direct Input header file */
#include <dinput.h>

 /* Include this file only once */
#pragma once

 /* Mirus Mouse class */
class mrMouse
{
protected:
  /* DirectInput objects */
 LPDIRECTINPUTDEVICE8 m_lpkDIDevice;
 DIDEVICEOBJECTDATA   m_akDeviceData [8];

public:
  /* Constructors / Destructor */
 mrMouse (void);
```

```
~mrMouse (void);

  /* Mouse manipulation routines */
mrError32 Init (HWND hWindow);
mrError32 Update (void);

mrBool32 IsButtonDown (mrUInt32 iButton);
mrBool32 IsButtonUp (mrUInt32 iButton);
mrUInt32 GetXAxis (void);
mrUInt32 GetYAxis (void);

mrError32 Clear (void);
};
```

There are only a couple of differences from the keyboard definition, the most important being the `m_akDeviceData` array. This works like the keyboard buffer, but holds specific information for the mouse (and the joystick as you will see later). Apart from that, the differences are mostly due to the fact that the mouse has axes, so you need a few more methods to return the values for them and a `Clear` method to clear all the states from the device. You have this method since it is possible that you want to discard all the mouse movement because you are using buffered mode.

Okay, now to the implementation:

```
 /* Default constructor */
mrMouse::mrMouse (void)
{
 m_lpkDIDevice = NULL;
 ZeroMemory (&m_akDeviceData, sizeof (DIDEVICEOBJECTDATA) * 2);
}
```

Just like you did for the keyboard, you need to clear your data buffer in the constructor to prevent random data from being reported as a state. And as with the keyboard, you also need to release the `IDirectInputDevice8` object in the destructor:

```
 /* Default destructor */
mrMouse::~mrMouse (void)
{
 if (NULL != m_lpkDIDevice)
 {
  m_lpkDIDevice->Unacquire ();
  m_lpkDIDevice->Release ();
  m_lpkDIDevice = NULL;
```

```
  }
}
```

Which is exactly the same as when you did it for the keyboard. Following, you need to implement your Init method. The first part of this method is exactly like the keyboard, just passing a couple of different parameters, the second part is when you tell DirectInput to use buffered data for this device:

```
 /* Initializes the mouse */
mrError32 mrMouse::Init (HWND hWindow)
{
  /* Create mouse device */
 if (FAILED(mrInputManager::GetSingleton ()->GetInput ()->CreateDevice(
             GUID_SysMouse, &m_lpkDIDevice, NULL)) )
 {
  return mrErrorMouseCreateDevice;
 }

  /* Set mouse data format */
 if (FAILED (m_lpkDIDevice->SetDataFormat (&c_dfDIMouse)) )
 {
  return mrErrorMouseSetDataFormat;
 }

  /* Set mouse cooperative level */
 if (FAILED (m_lpkDIDevice->SetCooperativeLevel (hWindow,
              DISCL_EXCLUSIVE | DISCL_FOREGROUND)) )
 {
  return mrErrorMouseSetCooperativeLevel;
 }
```

As you can see, you have used exactly the same methods as you did before with the only differences being that for SetDataFormat you have used the globally defined structure c_dfDIMouse and in the SetCooperativeLevel method you have used the DISCL_EXCLUSIVE | DISCL_FOREGROUND combination of flags.

Next you have to tell DirectInput that you will be using buffered data with this device:

```
  /* Set buffered input (8 events) */
 DIPROPDWORD kDIProp;

 kDIProp.diph.dwSize       = sizeof(DIPROPDWORD);
 kDIProp.diph.dwHeaderSize = sizeof(DIPROPHEADER);
```

```
kDIProp.diph.dwObj         = 0;
kDIProp.diph.dwHow         = DIPH_DEVICE;
kDIProp.dwData              = 8;

if (FAILED (m_lpkDIDevice->SetProperty (DIPROP_BUFFERSIZE,
                                        &kDIProp.diph)) )
{
 return mrErrorMouseSetProperty;
}
```

A little interlude before proceeding. DirectInput enables you to change device properties on-the-fly. What this means is that you can change the way a device behaves by calling the `SetProperty` method of `IDirectInputDevice8` with the correct parameters. There are various properties that you can set, but for now, you will only take interest in one. You will see more when you start working with the joystick.

Back to your code. To set the buffer size you will need to call `SetProperty` with the appropriate parameters. Before seeing what they are, here is the `SetProperty` prototype:

```
HRESULT IDirectInputDevice8::SetProperty (
 REFGUID rguidProp,
 LPCDIPROPHEADER pdiph);
```

The first parameter is a GUID specifying the property you want to set, in your case it is `DIPROP_BUFFERSIZE`. There are various properties you can set, some of them are shown in Table 14.3.

TABLE 14.3 SetProperty Properties

GUID	Description
DIPROP_AUTOCENTER	Specifies whether the device should be self-centered
DIPROP_AXISMODE	Sets the axis movement mode
DIPROP_BUFFERSIZE	Sets the buffer size of a device
DIPROP_DEADZONE	Sets the value for the dead zone of the joystick
DIPROP_RANGE	Sets the range values of a device

You will see some of these properties when you work with the joystick.

The last parameter of `SetProperty` is a pointer to a `DIPROPHEADER` structure, shown in Figure 14.4. This is where you will set the property value, but there is a catch. The `DIPROPHEADER` doesn't have any value you can set in relation to your property. It describes how the property is going to be applied to the device and describes the parent structure which contains the property stuff.

As you can see from the figure, the parent structure will hold a `DIPROPHEADER` structure, which defines the parent structure. By passing only the `DIPROPHEADER` structure to the `SetProperty` method, DirectInput will know how to get the necessary data from the parent structure.

Take a look at the `DIPROPHEADER` structure declaration:

```
typedef struct _DIPROPHEADER
{
 DWORD dwSize;
 DWORD dwHeaderSize;
 DWORD dwObj;
 DWORD dwHow;
} DIPROPHEADER;
```

The first parameter is the size of the parent structure and the second one is the size of this structure (the header). Next you have the object for which the object property should be accessed and the last parameter is how it should be accessed.

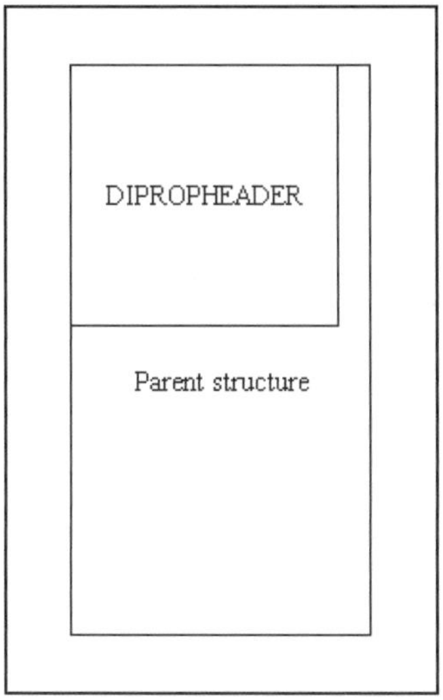

Figure 14.4

DIPROPHEADER and its parent structure.

Now, you will always want to set the property for the device you are working with so you can just use DIPH_BYOFFSET in this parameter and use the value of zero for dwObj.

Now that you have seen the header structure, you need to know the parent structure. There are various parent structures, depending on what property you want to set, and because you want to set the buffer size you must use the DIPROPDWORD structure that is defined as:

```
typedef struct _DIPROPDWORD
{
 DIPROPHEADER diph;
 DWORD dwData;
} DIPROPDWORD;
```

Where the first element is the header defining this structure and the last one is the data you want to set.

To recap with your code, you initialized the DIPROPHEADER member of DIPROPDWORD with the necessary parameters to let DirectInput know you will be using a DIPROPDWORD structure, and then you set the data member in DIPROPDWORD to 8, which is the size of the buffer you want to use.

And you finish by acquiring the mouse device as follows:

```
  /* Acquire mouse */
 m_lpkDIDevice->Acquire ();

 return mrNoError;
}
```

And that's it! It wasn't much different from the keyboard, was it? Now you need to update the mouse data buffer:

```
 /* Updates the mouse status */
mrError32 mrMouse::Update (void)
{
 mrUInt32 iElement;
ZeroMemory (m_akDeviceData, sizeof (DIDEVICEOBJECTDATA) * 8);
  /* Update each element */
 for (iElement = 0; iElement < 8; iElement ++)
 {
  mrUInt32 dwElements = 1;

```

```
    /* Get device data */
   HRESULT hRet = m_lpkDIDevice->GetDeviceData (
                                 sizeof(DIDEVICEOBJECTDATA),
                                 &m_akDeviceData [iElement],
                                 &dwElements, 0);
   if ((FAILED (hRet)) && (hRet == DIERR_INPUTLOST))
   {
     /* Try to acquire mouse and get device data */
    m_lpkDIDevice->Acquire ();
    if (FAILED (m_lpkDIDevice->GetDeviceData (
                                 sizeof(DIDEVICEOBJECTDATA),
                                 &m_akDeviceData [iElement],
                                 &dwElements, 0)) )
    {
     return mrErrorMouseGetDeviceData;
    }
   }
   else
   {
    return mrErrorMouseGetDeviceData;
   }
  }

  return mrNoError;
 }
```

As you can see, there is little difference from getting the keyboard state. What you need to do is store data according to the buffer element. You do this by using a loop to go through each element and get the corresponding state with `GetDeviceData` that is defined as:

```
HRESULT IDirectInputDevice8::GetDeviceData (
 DWORD cbObjectData,
 LPDIRECTDEVICEOBJECTDATA rgdod,
 LPDWORD pdwInOut,
 DWORD dwFlags);
```

The first parameter is the size of one single element of the second parameter, or the size of a `DIDEVICEOBJECTDATA` structure. The second parameter is an array of `DIDEVICEOBJECTDATA` structures that will keep each of the states of the mouse.

Following you have a pointer to the number of elements you want to retrieve and in the end you have the flags specifying how you want to get the data. There is only one possible flag for retrieving the data with `GetDeviceData`, which is `DIGDD_PEEK`. If you supply this flag, `GetDeviceData` will retrieve the data, but won't remove it from the buffer. If you supply this parameter to `GetDeviceData`, a following call to `GetDeviceData` will return the same buffer.

The array you pass as the second parameter is the one you declared in the class definition. You will see the declaration of `DIDEVICEOBJECTDATA` in the next section.

In your code, if a call to `GetDeviceData` failed because the device was lost, you try to acquire the device again so you don't lose any of the buffered data.

And that's about it. Now you have to do a few methods to allow you to query the mouse buffer you stored in the `Update` method to know what happened to the mouse.

The first method you will see is `IsButtonDown`:

```
 /* Returns if a button is down */
mrBool32 mrMouse::IsButtonDown (mrUInt32 iButton)
{
 mrUInt32 iElements;
 mrUInt32 iMouseButton;

 switch (iButton)
 {
  case 0:
   iMouseButton = DIMOFS_BUTTON0;
  break;
  case 1:
   iMouseButton = DIMOFS_BUTTON1;
  break;
  case 2:
   iMouseButton = DIMOFS_BUTTON2;
  break;
  case 3:
   iMouseButton = DIMOFS_BUTTON3;
  break;
  default:
   iMouseButton = DIMOFS_BUTTON0;
  break;
```

```
  }

   /* Check for all states to see if button was pressed */
  for (iElements = 0; iElements < 8; iElements ++)
  {
   if ((m_akDeviceData [iElements].dwOfs == iMouseButton) &&
       (m_akDeviceData [iElements].dwData & (1<<7)))
   {
    return mrTrue;
   }
  }
  return mrFalse;
 }
```

The first thing you must do in this method is to convert the button numbers zero, one, two, and three to the corresponding DirectInput values. This is easily done with a single `switch` statement where you correspond each number to `DIMOFS_BUTTONX`, where `X` is the corresponding button number. Next you need to go through each element in the buffer and see whether the corresponding buffer was pressed. To do this, you first check the `dwOfs member` for information about the button number, and then check the `dwData member` to see whether that button was pressed. Both these members are part of the `DIDEVICEOBJECTDATA` structure. `DIDEVICEOBJECTDATA` stores the information about a specific state of a device and is declared as follows:

```
typedef struct _DIDEVICEOBJECTDATA
{
 DWORD dwOfs;
 DWORD dwData;
 DWORD dwTimeStamp;
 DWORD dwSequence;
 UINT_PTR uAppData;
} DIDEVICEOBJECTDATA;
```

Where the first member is the offset into the data format. This member will tell you what happened to the device and whether it was a mouse button press or a movement in the Y-axis. The next member is the actual data describing what happened (if a button was pressed or how much the mouse moved).

The third parameter is the system time when the event occurred, and following is the sequence number, or action number for the state. The last parameter is related to DirectInput Action Mapping.

Now, to know whether a button was pressed, you need to check whether the dwOfs member is the same as the button constant you want to check (you got the correct constant in the switch statement). If the number is the same, then you have to check whether the last bit of dwData is set, just like you did with the keyboard.

If the button was pressed, the method returns mrTrue; if not, it returns mrFalse.

Now you need to do it the other way around, to determine whether a button was pressed. This is basically the same as checking to see if a button was up, except you return mrFalse if the button was pressed:

```
 /* Returns if a button is up */
mrBool32 mrMouse::IsButtonUp (mrUInt32 iButton)
{
 mrUInt32 iElements;
 mrUInt32 iMouseButton;

 switch (iButton)
 {
  case 0:
   iMouseButton = DIMOFS_BUTTON0;
  break;
  case 1:
   iMouseButton = DIMOFS_BUTTON1;
  break;
  case 2:
   iMouseButton = DIMOFS_BUTTON2;
  break;
  case 3:
   iMouseButton = DIMOFS_BUTTON3;
  break;
  default:
   iMouseButton = DIMOFS_BUTTON0;
  break;
 }

  /* Check for all states to see if button was released */
 for (iElements = 0; iElements < 8; iElements ++)
 {
  if ((m_akDeviceData [iElements].dwOfs == iMouseButton) &&
```

```
      (m_akDeviceData [iElements].dwData & (1<<7)))
   {
    return mrFalse;
   }
  }
  return mrTrue;
 }
```

It's as simple as that. You first get the correct mouse button constant, and then loop through every element in your buffer array to see whether that button was pressed, and return the according value.

Now you just need to do the movement method before you move to your last method. You will start with getting the movement along the X-axis, and then do it for the Y-axis, which is basically the same:

```
  /* Returns mouse horizontal axis */
 mrUInt32 mrMouse::GetXAxis (void)
 {
  mrUInt32 iElements;
  mrUInt32 iMovement;

  iMovement = 0;

   /* Sum all the relative X movement of the mouse in the last events */
  for (iElements = 0; iElements < 8; iElements ++)
  {
   if (DIMOFS_X == m_akDeviceData [iElements].dwOfs)
   {
    iMovement += m_akDeviceData [iElements].dwData;
   }
  }
  return iMovement;
 }
```

What you need to do here is check whether the `dwOfs` member of the `DIDEVICEOBJECTDATA` is set to mouse horizontal movement constant, `DIMOFS_X`, and if so, add the `dwData` member to the movement. Adding the movement for each element in the buffer will give you the relative movement of all the movements done. Confused? Take a look at Figure 14.5 to see what I mean.

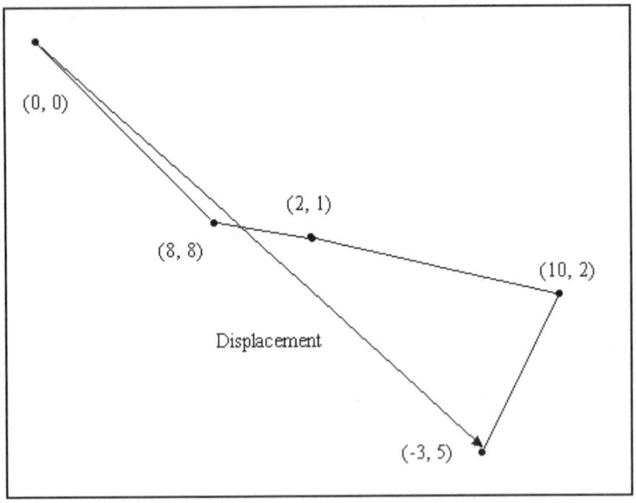

Figure 14.5

The displacement of the mouse.

If the user does the three movements described in Figure 14.5, you can do one of two things to handle them, you can either handle each of the movements independently or you can add them all together to get the total movement (or displacement). If the application depended on the exact movement to do something, like recognition of the movement to perform some action, you would handle it accordingly, but since most games only need the total movement, you will add it all together to get the displacement.

And for the Y-axis you do the same thing:

```
 /* Returns mouse vertical axis */
mrUInt32 mrMouse::GetYAxis (void)
{
 mrUInt32 iElements;
 mrUInt32 iMovement;

 iMovement = 0;

  /* Sum all the relative Y movement of the mouse in the last events */
 for (iElements = 0; iElements < 8; iElements ++)
 {
  if (DIMOFS_Y == m_akDeviceData [iElements].dwOfs)
  {
   iMovement += m_akDeviceData [iElements].dwData;
```

```
    }
  }
  return iMovement;
}
```

But this time checking if the dwOfs member is equal to DIMOFS_Y, which is the constant for mouse movement on the Y-axis.

To finish mrMouse, you will see how you can clear the device buffer:

```
  /* Clears the mouse buffer */
mrError32 mrMouse::Clear (void)
{
   /* Clear device buffer */
  ZeroMemory (m_akDeviceData, sizeof (DIDEVICEOBJECTDATA) * 8);

  mrUInt32 dwItems = INFINITE;
  if (FAILED (m_lpkDIDevice->GetDeviceData (sizeof(DIDEVICEOBJECTDATA),
                                             NULL, &dwItems, 0)) )
  {
   return mrErrorMouseGetDeviceData;
  }

  return mrNoError;
}
```

You start by resetting all the elements of your buffer to zero with ZeroMemory. This will ensure that if you query the mouse state before calling Update, you won't get any false movements. Next you have to clear the device buffer. This is done by supplying as the number of elements INFINITE, which is a DirectInput predefined value, and supplying NULL to the second parameter where the buffer to store the data would be. This will clear the device buffer, discarding any movement done until this call.

The next program is the same as the previous except for the Frame:

```
  /* Render frame */
mrBool32 InputWindow::Frame(void)
{
   /* Start rendering */
  m_kScreen.Clear (0, 0, 0, 0);
  m_kScreen.StartFrame ();

```

```
58:   m_kABO.Render ();
59:
60:   /* Get the input and move the smily */
61:   m_kMouse.Update ();
62:   int iX = m_kABO.GetXPosition ();
63:   int iY = m_kABO.GetYPosition ();
64:
65:   iX += m_kMouse.GetXAxis ();
66:   iY += m_kMouse.GetYAxis ();
67:
68:   m_kABO.SetPosition (iX, iY);
69:
70:   m_kScreen.EndFrame ();
71:
72:   return mrTrue;
73: }
```

Instead of checking for a key press, use the displacement of the mouse (lines 65 and 66) to move the smiley.

And that's it for the mouse. In the next section you will see how to use the joystick, which shares many similarities with the mouse.

mrJoystick

When you work with the joystick, probably the hardest part is getting it set up. There can be various joysticks plugged in, or none at all; you can't use a predefined GUID to identify the joystick like you did before. Now you need to get the GUID of the joysticks from DirectInput.

Before checking how you do this, take a look at the `mrJoystick` class definition:

```
 /* 'mrJoystick.h' */

 /* Mirus base types header */
#include "mrDatatypes.h"
 /* Mirus error definitions header */
#include "mrError.h"
 /* Mirus Input Manager header file */
#include "mrInputManager.h"
```

```
 /* Windows header file */
#include <windows.h>
 /* Direct Input header file */
#include <dinput.h>

 /* Include this file only once */
#pragma once

 /* Joystick enumeration callback */
BOOL CALLBACK EnumJoysticksCallback (
         const DIDEVICEINSTANCE * pdidInstance, VOID* pContext);

 /* Mirus Joystick class */
class mrJoystick
{
protected:
  /* DirectInput objects */
 LPDIRECTINPUTDEVICE8 m_lpkDIDevice;
 DIJOYSTATE2          m_kDeviceData;

public:
  /* Constructors / Destructor */
 mrJoystick (void);
 ~mrJoystick (void);

  /* Joystick manipulation methods */
 mrError32 Init (HWND hWindow, mrInt32 iMin, mrInt32 iMax,
                 mrInt32 iDeadZone);
 mrError32 Update (void);

 mrBool32 IsButtonDown (mrUInt32 iButton);
 mrBool32 IsButtonUp (mrUInt32 iButton);

 mrUInt32 GetXAxis (void);
 mrUInt32 GetYAxis (void);
};
```

Which looks very much like the mouse class, except this time you use only one state structure, DIJOYSTATE2 since you won't be using buffered data, and there is a global function, EnumJoysticksCallback. Before you start checking the class methods, let's take a look at EnumJoysticksCallback:

```
 6:  /* Enumeration function */
 7: BOOL CALLBACK EnumJoysticksCallback(
 8:             const DIDEVICEINSTANCE *pdidInstance, VOID* pContext)
 9: {
10:  LPDIRECTINPUTDEVICE8 * lpkDevice = (LPDIRECTINPUTDEVICE8 *) pContext;
11:
12:   /* Create joystick device */
13:  if (FAILED(mrInputManager::GetSingleton ()->GetInput ()->CreateDevice (
14:                 pdidInstance->guidInstance, lpkDevice, NULL)) )
15:  {
16:   return DIENUM_CONTINUE;
17:  }
18:  else
19:  {
20:   return DIENUM_STOP;
21:  }
22: }
```

This is your first callback function so go over it slowly. First of all, a callback function is a function that is called from another function. Looks just like any other function up until now, no? Well, there is a catch! This function isn't called directly. You pass the address of the function to another function, which will in turn call your first function a number of times. Seems a little weird, right? Don't worry, sounds weird to me, too.

What happens in DirectInput is that you don't know which devices are attached, and for the ones you know are attached, you don't know anything about them. DirectInput calls the callback function for each device you try to enumerate, and your function is responsible for checking whether you want to use the device or not, and if so, create it.

This is what happens in your function, DirectInput will call your function for every device you enumerate (you will see how to do this later) and send the according GUID as the first parameter and the address of the pointer to the device you want to create.

You then need to cast the pointer passed as the second parameter (pContext) to a pointer to LPDIRECTINPUTDEVICE8 so you can use it when you try to create the device (lines 13 and 14) with CreateDevice.

If you have created the device successfully, then you can quit the enumeration process, which is done by returning DIENUM_STOP, which will tell DirectInput to stop the enumeration. If any error occurred, you return DIENUM_CONTINUE, which will continue to call your function for other devices until either you create the device or you run out of devices.

In this callback function you could query the device for its name and properties to see whether it supported the features you wanted, and only then create it; but for now, you will leave it like so.

Now that you have seen the callback function, you can take a look at the constructor and the destructor, which don't do much besides initialize the device to NULL in the constructor and to release it in the destructor:

```
 /* Default constructor */
mrJoystick::mrJoystick (void)
{
 m_lpkDIDevice = NULL;
 ZeroMemory (&m_kDeviceData, sizeof (DIDEVICEOBJECTDATA));
}

 /* Default destructor */
mrJoystick::~mrJoystick (void)
{
 if (NULL != m_lpkDIDevice)
 {
  m_lpkDIDevice->Unacquire ();
  m_lpkDIDevice->Release ();
  m_lpkDIDevice = NULL;
 }
}
```

Nothing different from before. As usual, you have the Init method which initializes the device:

```
 /* Initializes the joystick */
mrError32 mrJoystick::Init (HWND hWindow, mrInt32 iMin, mrInt32 iMax,
                            mrInt32 iDeadZone)
{
  /* Find first available joystick */
 if (FAILED (mrInputManager::GetSingleton ()->GetInput ()->EnumDevices (
                DI8DEVCLASS_GAMECTRL, EnumJoysticksCallback, &m_lpkDIDevice,
```

```
                  DIEDFL_ATTACHEDONLY)) )
  {
   return mrErrorJoystickEnumDevices;
  }
```

Remember your callback function? Well, this is where you call it. By calling `EnumDevices`, using the address of your function (the name of the function represents its address) will call your function for each device. `EnumDevices` prototype is:

```
HRESULT IDirectInputDevice8::EnumDevices (
 DWORD dwDevType,
 LPDIENUMCALLBACK lpCallback,
 LPVOID pvRef,
 DWORD dwFlags);
```

The first parameter of `EnumDevices` specifies the type of devices you want to create. The available device types are shown in Table 14.4.

Because you are interested in enumerating the joystick devices, you will use `DI8DEVCLASS_GAMECTRL` as the first parameter to `EnumDevices`. The second parameter to `EnumDevices` is the address of the callback function. You will use the name of your function, which passes the address of your function to the function. Next you have the value you want to pass to the callback function as a parameter (`pContext` in `EnumJoysticksCallback`). Because you want to pass a pointer to the device you create, you will pass the address of the `lpkDIDevice` pointer. The last parameter specifies the scope of the enumeration, filtering only the desired devices. The values for this parameter can be found in Table 14.5.

TABLE 14.4 EnumDevices Device Filters

Flag	Description
`DI8DEVCLASS_ALL`	All devices
`DI8DEVCLASS_DEVICE`	All devices that don't fall to any other class
`DI8DEVCLASS_GAMECTRL`	All game controllers
`DI8DEVCLASS_KEYBOARD`	All keyboards
`DI8DEVCLASS_POINTER`	All pointer devices

Table 14.5 EnumDevices Device Scope

Flag	Description
DIEDFL_ALLDEVICES	All installed devices are enumerated
DIEDFL_ATTACHEDONLY	Only attached and installed devices are enumerated
DIEDFL_FORCEFEEDBACK	Only devices that support force feedback are enumerated
DIEDFL_INCLUDEALIASES	Includes devices that are aliases for other devices
DIEDFL_INCLUDEHIDDEN	Include hidden devices
DIEDFL_INCLUDEPHANTOMS	Include placeholder devices

Because you only want to create devices that are attached and installed, you will use `DIEDFL_ATTACHEDONLY`.

Now that the device was created in the callback function, you can resume your `Init` method by setting up the joystick:

```
  /* Set joystick data format */
 if (FAILED(m_lpkDIDevice->SetDataFormat (&c_dfDIJoystick2)))
 {
  return mrErrorJoystickSetDataFormat;
 }

  /* Set joystick cooperative level */
 if (FAILED(m_lpkDIDevice->SetCooperativeLevel (hWindow,
            DISCL_EXCLUSIVE | DISCL_FOREGROUND)))
 {
  return mrErrorJoystickSetCooperativeLevel;
 }
```

Except for using `c_dfDIJoystick2` as a parameter to `SetDataFormat`, the steps to set up the joystick are the same.

Now, like the mouse, there are some specific properties for the joystick. These properties enable you to use the joystick more efficiently.

The first property you will see is the joystick range:

```
 /* Set joystick axis ranges */
DIPROPRANGE kDIRange;

kDIRange.diph.dwSize       = sizeof(DIPROPRANGE);
kDIRange.diph.dwHeaderSize = sizeof(DIPROPHEADER);
kDIRange.diph.dwHow        = 0;
kDIRange.diph.dwObj        = DIPH_DEVICE;
kDIRange.lMin              = iMin;
kDIRange.lMax              = iMax;

if (FAILED(m_lpkDIDevice->SetProperty (DIPROP_RANGE, &kDIRange.diph)))
{
 return mrErrorJoystickSetProperty;
}
```

The range of the joystick is the minimum and maximum values the joystick will report for its minimum and maximum positions. To set up the range of a joystick you need to use the DIPROPRANGE structure, which is defined as follows:

```
typedef struct _DIPROPRANGE
{
 DIPROPHEADER diph;
 LONG lMin;
 LONG lMax;
} DIPROPRANGE;
```

Where the first member is a DIPROPHEADER structure defining this structure (it's the same thing you did for the mouse, but this time the second parameter must be the size of a DIPROPRANGE structure) and the next two members are the minimum and maximum range of the joystick.

In the end, you just need to call SetProperty with DIPROP_RANGE as the first parameter to specify you want to set the range property and pass the address of the diph member of the DIPROPRANGE structure and you are done.

Next mission, set the joystick dead zone:

```
 /* Set joystick dead zone */
DIPROPDWORD kDIDeadZone;

kDIDeadZone.diph.dwSize       = sizeof(DIPROPDWORD);
kDIDeadZone.diph.dwHeaderSize = sizeof(DIPROPHEADER);
```

```
kDIDeadZone.diph.dwHow          = 0;
kDIDeadZone.diph.dwObj          = DIPH_DEVICE;
kDIDeadZone.dwData               = iDeadZone * 100;

if (FAILED (m_lpkDIDevice->SetProperty (DIPROP_DEADZONE,
                                         &kDIDeadZone.diph)) )
{
 return mrErrorJoystickSetProperty;
}
```

The joystick dead zone is the amount of movement from the center (rest) for which the joystick will return that the joystick is at rest. This is extremely useful to use with those hard to calibrate old joysticks.

Figure 14.6 shows the joystick dead zone at work.

DirectInput sets the dead zone as a percentage—well, sort of. For the dead zone, DirectInput uses values between 0 and 10,000, (0 being no dead zone and 10,000 being the entire range of the dead zone). To make it easier to work with Mirus, the dead zone parameter to `Init` should be a percentage value (ranging from 0 to 100 percent), which will be multiplied by 100 to get the correct result.

You finish setting this up by calling `SetProperty` with the first parameter being `DIPROP_DEADZONE` and the second parameter being the address to the `diph` member, as usual.

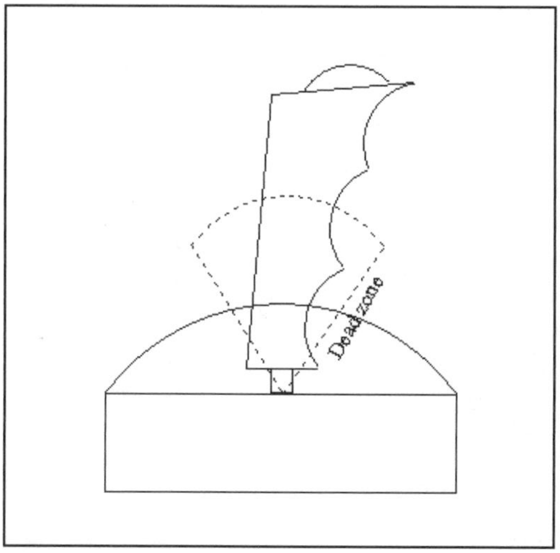

Figure 14.6

No movement is reported when the joystick is in the dead zone.

Now you need to poll the joystick and you are done with the initialization:

```
  /* Acquire joystick */
 HRESULT hRet = m_lpkDIDevice->Poll ();
 if (FAILED (hRet))
 {
  hRet = m_lpkDIDevice->Acquire ();

  while (hRet == DIERR_INPUTLOST)
  {
   hRet = m_lpkDIDevice->Acquire ();
  }
 }
 return mrNoError;
}
```

Before explaining the code, let me just make a side note. While some devices, like the mouse or the keyboard, don't need to be polled, most joystick devices do. Polling a device is like synchronizing it with DirectInput, sort of like what you do with DirectInput when you retrieve the device state. DirectInput sometimes needs to retrieve the device state, which is done by polling the device.

Okay, so to poll a device you need to call the `Poll` method that is defined as:

```
HRESULT IDirectInputDevice8::Poll (void);
```

Simple, no?

In your code, you try to poll the device first, and if it failed, you try acquiring it. If you couldn't acquire the device because the input was lost, you loop continually until you can.

And you have finished the joystick setup. Well, now you just need the `Update` and some methods to query the joystick state and you are done:

```
  /* Update joystick status */
mrError32 mrJoystick::Update (void)
{
   /* Poll the joystick */
  if (FAILED (m_lpkDIDevice->Poll ()) )
  {
    /* Acquire joystick */
   HRESULT hRet = m_lpkDIDevice->Acquire ();

```

```
  if ((FAILED (hRet)) && (hRet == DIERR_INPUTLOST))
  {
   m_lpkDIDevice->Acquire ();
  }
  else
  {
   return mrErrorJoystickAcquire;
  }
 }

  /* Get device data */
 if (FAILED (m_lpkDIDevice->GetDeviceState (sizeof (DIJOYSTATE2),
                                               &m_kDeviceData)) )
 {
  return mrErrorJoystickGetDeviceState;
 }
 return mrNoError;
}
```

To update the device you start by polling it, and if you can't, you then try to acquire it. In the end you call `GetDeviceState` to get the current state of the device. You will use the `DIJOYSTATE2` structure you declared in your class to store the joystick state. `DIJOYSTATE2` is defined as:

```
typedef struct _DIJOYSTATE2
{
 LONG lX;
 LONG lY;
  /* … */
 LONG rgbButtons [128];
  /* … */
} DIJOYSTATE2;
```

Although `DIJOYSTATE2` has many other members, you are interested only in these three. The first two members specify the movement along the X-axis and the Y-axis, respectively, while the `rgbButtons` array stores the state of each button.

You now need to implement some methods to see whether the button is down or not:

```
 /* Returns if a button is down */
mrBool32 mrJoystick::IsButtonDown (mrUInt32 iButton)
{
```

```
142:   /* Check if button is pressed */
143:  if (m_kDeviceData.rgbButtons [iButton] & (1<<7))
144:  {
145:   return mrTrue;
146:  }
147:  else
148:  {
149:   return mrFalse;
150:  }
151: }
```

As with the mouse and the keyboard, if a button is pressed, then it has its higher bit set. To check whether a joystick button is pressed, you need to check whether the rgbButtons corresponding element (rgbButtons [0] for button zero, rgbButtons [1] for button one, and so on) for the button has its high bit set, which is done in line 143.

To check whether a joystick button isn't pressed, you just do the same thing but return an inverse value:

```
153:  /* Returns if a button is up */
154: mrBool32 mrJoystick::IsButtonUp (mrUInt32 iButton)
155: {
156:   /* Check if button isn't pressed */
157:  if (m_kDeviceData.rgbButtons [iButton] & (1<<7))
158:  {
159:   return mrFalse;
160:  }
161:  else
162:  {
163:   return mrTrue;
164:  }
165: }
```

To get the X-axis and Y-axis movements, you just need to return the corresponding member of the DIJOYSTATE2 structure:

```
167:  /* Returns joystick horizontal axis */
168: mrUInt32 mrJoystick::GetXAxis (void)
169: {
170:  return m_kDeviceData.lX;
171: }
172:
```

```
/* Returns joystick vertical axis */
mrUInt32 mrJoystick::GetYAxis (void)
{
 return m_kDeviceData.lY;
}
```

And finally, the joystick demo will use the same code as before, but this time changing `Init`:

```
36: void InputWindow::Init (HINSTANCE hInstance)
37: {
38:   /* Initialize the screen and the ABO (a smily) */
39:  m_kScreen.Init (m_hWindow);
40:  m_kScreen.SetMode (false, 640, 480, 32, true);
41:  m_kABO.LoadFromFile ("smile.txt");
42:  m_kABO.SetSize (60, 60);
43:  m_kABO.SetPosition (320, 240);
44:  m_kABO.SetColor (255,255,255,255);
45:
46:   /* Initialize the input manager and device */
47:  m_kInputManager.Init (hInstance);
48:  m_kJoystick.Init (m_hWindow, -10, 10, 1);
49: }
```

This method initializes the screen (lines 38 through 44) and initializes the joystick (lines 47 and 48) but this time setting the ranges and the dead zone. And that's it! You finished the input component of Mirus. Now you can let the players use the input device they prefer.

> **NOTE**
> **For this component to work, you will need to include the `dxguid.lib` and `dinput.lib` libraries in your projects.**

Summary

In this chapter you covered most of the basic functionality of DirectInput. While DirectInput offers you many more features, such as Force Feedback or 3D input devices, the matter covered in this chapter is more than enough to get your games running smoothly.

By using Mirus to show how DirectInput worked, you not only covered the DirectInput API, but also how you can realistically use it in any game.

Questions and Answers

Q: Why should you use buffered data for the mouse?

A: The mouse movement is usually very precise and fast, so by using buffered data you will be able to get the correct mouse movement, in case of fast movements.

Q: Why do you need to poll the joystick but not poll the mouse and keyboard?

A: The mouse and keyboard send their information to the computer automatically; unfortunately, the joystick doesn't. You need to ask the joystick to send the data to the computer.

Exercises

1. What are the two DirectInput objects you used?
2. What is the bit that DirectX sets for any device if the button is pressed?
3. What is the difference between `GetDeviceData` and `GetDeviceState`?
4. What is the dead area of a joystick?

CHAPTER 15

DirectSound

To finish all this talk about DirectX and move on to what is really fun, game programming, I will cover the basics of DirectSound, and also create a small CD player. While most of the games nowadays use MP3 or another kind of encoding algorithm for music, using MP3s is sometimes costly (because the creators require money so you can use their algorithms in your games) or time-consuming and complicated due to the complexity of the files.

Using the code you will develop in this chapter, you can use waveform (.wav) files to make sound, or music if you can afford the space. Using the CD as music allows the players to play their favorite CDs while they play the game.

Sound Theory

Sound is waves moving around the air. The waves go around and around the place until they disappear (you will see what this means later). Sounds complicated? It is, but fortunately, you only need to care for a few details of sound.

The first thing I will talk about is amplitude. *Amplitude* is the amount of air a wave moves when it's traveling. The more air it moves, the louder the sound. I don't know whether you have been to a nightclub lately, but if you have, you probably have seen some of those giant speakers moving. If you are close to it, you will feel like the floor is moving (apart from the fact that you probably will become deaf). What the big speakers are doing is moving a very large amount of air to produce very loud sounds.

The next thing you need to know about sound is the frequency of the sound. The *frequency* is the number of cycles a wave makes per second. A *cycle* is the distance between the two high or low peaks of the wave. The frequency of the sound is how high (treble) or low (bass) a sound is. Figure 15.1 shows the most simple sound wave, the sine wave.

As you can see from Figure 15.1, the sine wave has a frequency of 1,000 Hertz (each cycle takes one millisecond).

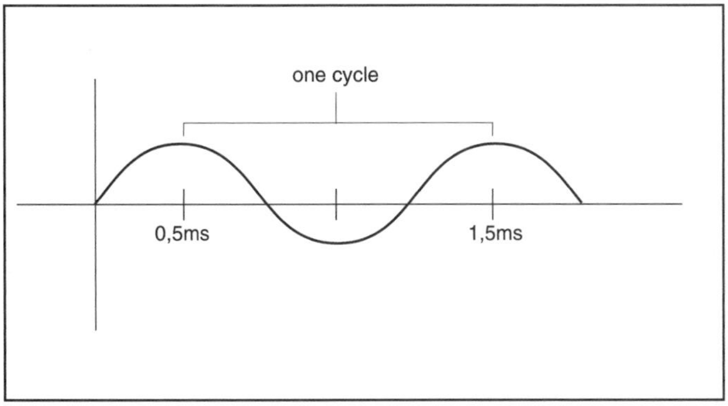

Figure 15.1

The sine wave.

The average human being can hear sounds on the 20-2,000 Hz frequencies.

The last term you need to understand about sound is waveforms. *Waveforms* describe how the shape of the sound wave changes over time. The number of different waveforms is proportional to your imagination! When you say a phrase, the waveform will have a different shape than if you say something else.

And that's about all you need to know about sound.

DirectSound Basics

DirectSound offers you two ways to produce sound in your computers, digital and synthesized. *Digital sounds* are waveforms that are usually prerecorded from some input hardware (like a microphone or line in) whereas *synthesized sound* is a mathematical representation of a sound usually based on some formula. If you think about it, you can mix sine, cosine, and other wave-like equations to form new waves, thus producing new sounds, which is exactly what the computer does.

Synthesized sound is almost nonexistent in today's games. Although you can do many nice things with synthesized sound, digital sound sounds a lot better, and with the current hardware and CD-ROM sizes, games just use digital sound of some sort.

Back to your program! DirectSound, like all components of DirectX, is based on the COM model, and as such, works by using several interfaces. While DirectX Audio (the audio component of DirectX) contains many interfaces (for 3D sounds, input, synthesized music, and others) you will only be interested in the DirectSound most basic object `IDirectSound8` and the `IDirectSoundBuffer8`, which is where you will store your waveform data.

You must follow several steps to make DirectSound work; it isn't difficult, it simply adds one step more than before:

1. Create an `IDirectSound8` object.
2. Set the `IDirectSound8` cooperative level.
3. Create an `IDirectSoundBuffer8` object.
4. Load the waveform data to the `IDirectSoundBuffer8` object.
5. Play the `IDirectSoundBuffer8` object.

And that's it. Not really different from DirectXGraphics or DirectInput, is it?

By using various `IDirectSoundBuffer8` objects, or just buffers, you can combine various sounds to one waveform to produce the final result, as shown in Figure 15.2.

You will see how to do all this next while you develop Mirus.

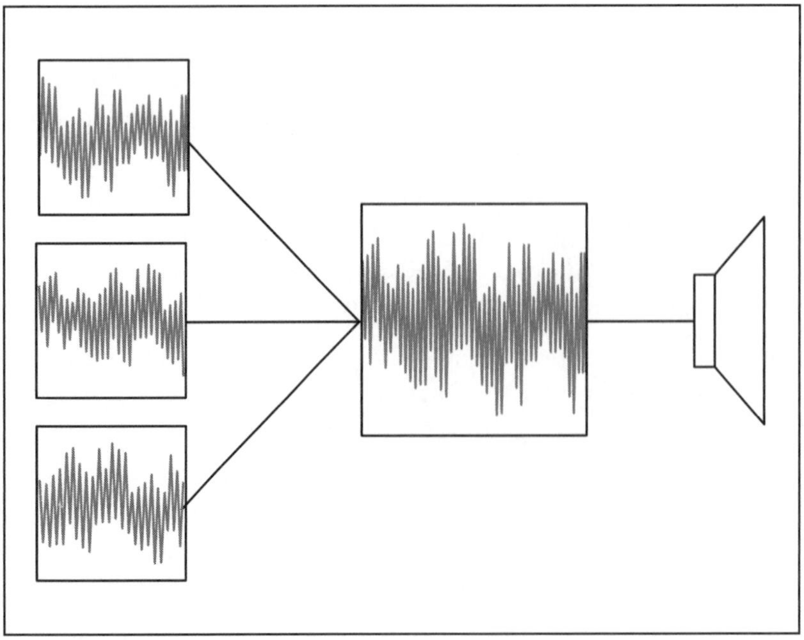

Figure 15.2

DirectSound converts various waveforms to one final output waveform.

mrSoundPlayer

The first class for your sound component is `mrSoundPlayer`. This is where you will keep the `IDirectSound8` object and set the cooperative level.

Your class definition is as follows:

```
 /* 'mrSoundPlayer.h' */

 /* Mirus base types header */
#include "mrDatatypes.h"
 /* Mirus error definitions header */
#include "mrError.h"
 /* Windows header file */
#include <windows.h>
 /* Direct Sound header file */
#include <dsound.h>
/* Assert header file */
#include <assert.h>

 /* Include this file only once */
#pragma once

 /* Mirus Sound Player class */
class mrSoundPlayer
{
protected:
  /* DirectSound objects */
 LPDIRECTSOUND8          m_lpkDSound;

  /* Singleton */
 static mrSoundPlayer * m_pkSingleton;

public:
  /* Constructors / Destructor */
 mrSoundPlayer (void);
 ~mrSoundPlayer (void);

  /* Sound player manipulation routines */
 mrError32 Init (HWND hWindow);
```

```

  /* Sound player maintenance routines */
 LPDIRECTSOUND8 GetSound (void);

  /* Singleton */
 static mrSoundPlayer * GetSingleton (void);
};
```

Pretty simple, no? If you pay close attention, you also made this class a Singleton, so you can create new sounds wherever you are by accessing the `IDirectSound8` object with `GetSound`.

Let's get to the implementation then.

The first things you will take into account are the constructor and the destructor:

```
 /* Default constructor */
mrSoundPlayer::mrSoundPlayer (void)
{
 m_lpkDSound = NULL;

 assert (!m_pkSingleton);
 m_pkSingleton = this;
}

 /* Default destructor */
mrSoundPlayer::~mrSoundPlayer (void)
{
 if (NULL != m_lpkDSound)
 {
  m_lpkDSound->Release ();
  m_lpkDSound = NULL;
 }

 assert (m_pkSingleton);
 m_pkSingleton = NULL;
}
```

Both the contructor and destructor are pretty simple. You handle the class as a Singleton class, so you need to set the pointers accordingly, and release the `IDirectSound8` object by using the `Release` method. The `Release` method is similar to the ones you have already seen for other DirectX objects.

Next you have the init method, which is where you will create your object and set the cooperative level:

```
31:  /* Initializes the sound player */
32: mrError32 mrSoundPlayer::Init (HWND hWindow)
33: {
34:   /* Create DirectSound object */
35:  DirectSoundCreate8 (NULL, &m_lpkDSound, NULL);
36:
37:  if (NULL == m_lpkDSound)
38:  {
39:   return mrErrorCreateSoundDevice;
40:  }
41:
42:   /* Set DirectSound cooperative level */
43:  if (FAILED (m_lpkDSound->SetCooperativeLevel (hWindow, DSSCL_NORMAL)) )
44:  {
45:   return mrErrorSetCooperativeLevel;
46:  }
47:  return mrNoError;
48: }
```

You start by creating the DirectSound object using the `DirectSoundCreate8` method (line 35) and its prototype is:

```
HRESULT DirectSoundCreate8 (
 LPCGUID lpcGuidDevice,
 LPDIRECTSOUND8 * ppDS8,
 LPUNKNOWN pUnkOuter);
```

Where the first parameter is a pointer to a GUID describing the type of object you want to create. By using `NULL` as a parameter, you specify that you will be using the default audio playback device. The available GUIDs are shown in Table 15.1.

The second parameter is a pointer to the address of an `IDirectSound8` object. The last parameter is a COM-specific argument that isn't supported in DirectSound, so you must supply `NULL`.

Now that you have your object created, you need to set the DirectSound cooperative level. Setting the cooperative level for the device will set the way in which you can access the device.

Table 15.1 DirectSoundCreate8 Audio GUIDs

Value	Description
DSDEVID_DefaultPlayback	System-wide default audio playback device. Same as NULL.
DSDEVID_DefaultVoicePlayback	Default voice playback device.

You set the cooperative level of a device by calling its SetCooperativeLevel method (line 43). SetCooperativeLevel is defined as:

```
HRESULT IDirectSound8::SetCooperativeLevel (
 HWND hwnd,
 DWORD dwLevel);
```

Where the first parameter is the handle to the window, which will serve as a parent to the device, and the second parameter is the cooperative level you want to set the device with. The available levels are defined in Table 15.2.

Table 15.2 DirectSoundCreate8 Levels

Levels	Description
DSSCL_EXCLUSIVE	The application that creates the device will be the only one that can be heard.
DSSCL_NORMAL	Sets the normal level for this device. It has the smoother multitasking level, but output is limited to 8-bit.
DSSCL_PRIORITY	Sets the priority level for this device. Allows calls to SetFormat and Compact.
DDSCL_WRITEPRIMARY	Sets the write-primary level. The application can write to the primary buffer, and no secondary buffers are available.

You will use the DSSCL_NORMAL level for your applications, because it is the simplest to work with.

And that's about it. You are ready to start creating some sound buffers with mrSound.

mrSound

The mrSound class is where you will keep your sound buffer, IDirectSoundBuffer8. You will also have some methods to load wave files and to play and stop the buffers, but for now, take a look at the class definition:

```
 /* 'mrSound.h' */

 /* Mirus base types header */
#include "mrDatatypes.h"
 /* Mirus error definitions header */
#include "mrError.h"
 /* Mirus sound player header file */
#include "mrSoundPlayer.h"
 /* Windows header file */
#include <windows.h>
 /* C++ file stream header file */
#include <fstream.h>
 /* Direct Sound header file */
#include <dsound.h>

 /* Include this file only once */
#pragma once

 /* Mirus Sound class */
class mrSound
{
protected:
  /* DirectSound objects */
 LPDIRECTSOUNDBUFFER          m_lpkSound;

public:
  /* Constructors / Destructor */
 mrSound (void);
 ~mrSound (void);

```

```
  /* Sound manipulation routines */
 mrError32 LoadFromFile (LPSTR lpszFilename);
 mrError32 SetVolume (mrUInt32 iVolume);
 mrError32 Play (mrUInt32 iLoop);
 mrError32 Stop (void);
};
```

> **NOTE**
> Remember to release your buffer object in the destructor.

Nothing too abnormal, right?

You will see how to implement each method next, starting with `LoadFromFile`, which will both load a wave file from a specified location and create the `IDirectSoundBuffer8`, but before that, let's see how a wave file is stored.

A wave file is comprised of a series of chunks, and each chunk contains various information that belongs to that chunk. This may sound a little complicated but think of it this way: your head has various parts, such as mouth, eyes, nose, and so on. And then each of these organs has several parts, such as the retina for the eyes, lips for the mouth, and so on. This is the same for wave files. The main wave file has several chunks, and then each chunk has data.

When you deal with wave files, you use three important chunks: the file type chunk, the format chunk, and the data chunk. The thing with wave files is that they are just a subset of several other files. What I mean is that while a .wav file can be a normal wave file like the ones you will be using, it can also have different formats and compression schemes.

You need to use the first 12 bytes to see which kind of file it is.

The three size 4 members of the file are described in Table 15.3.

TABLE 15.3 Wave File Identifier

Field	Size	Description
File identifier	4	File identifier, should be "RIFF"
File size	4	Wave file size
File type	4	File type identifier, should be "WAVE"

Now, if both the file identifier and file type match what you want ("RIFF" and "WAVE"), then you know this is a valid waveform file.

After the WAVE file identifier structure, you should get a 4-byte string telling you what would be the next chunk. Because this is a waveform file, you know that the next chunk is "fmt," so you can start to read the data for this chunk. The "fmt" or format chunk, is described in Table 15.4.

You don't really need to care about most of the information in this table, except for the channels and samples per second. The channels describe whether the waveform is in mono (one channel) or stereo (two channels) format. The samples per second describe the number of samples the waveform has per second; the higher the samples, the higher the quality of the waveform.

Following the format chunk you have the "data" format, which contains the size of the waveform data (4 bytes) and the actual waveform data.

Waveform files have been something people had problems working with, mostly due to the variety of formats they can have. Of course, if you can make some assumptions, like the ones here, which assumed that the wave file was a PCMwaveform file without compression, making a file loader is simple!

NOTE

PCM, or Pulse Code Modulation, is a way of digitalizing the ones and zeros in binary form (a file) to a desired audio output.

Table 15.4 Format Chunk

Field	Size	Description
Format tag	2	Waveform-audio format type.
Channels	2	Number of channels in the waveform-audio data.
Samples per second	4	Sample rate, in samples per second.
Average bytes per second	4	Required average data-transfer rate, in bytes per second.
Block alignment	2	Block alignment, in bytes.
Bits per sample	2	Bits per sample for the `wFormatTag` format type.

Let's see how this works:

```
22:  /* Load the wave from file */
23: mrError32 mrSound::LoadFromFile (LPSTR lpszFilename)
24: {
25:  fstream     kWave;
26:
27:   /* Open the wave file */
28:  kWave.open (lpszFilename, ios::in | ios::binary);
29:
30:  if (kWave.is_open ())
31:  {
32:   mrInt8 aiID [5];
33:    /* Read the string RIFF identifier */
34:   kWave.read (aiID, sizeof (mrInt8) * 4);
35:   aiID [4] = '\0';
36:    /* If not RIFF, it is not supported */
37:   if (0 != strcmp (aiID, "RIFF"))
38:   {
39:    return mrErrorWaveNotSupported;
40:   }
```

After you open the file successfully, you read the first four bytes of the file to check whether it is a valid file, so you compare it with the "RIFF" string (line 37). You have added the `NULL` terminator to the end of the string since the data saved in the file isn't `NULL` terminated.

Now you can start reading the rest of the file chunk:

```
42:   mrUInt32 iSize;
43:    /* Read the size of the wave */
44:   kWave.read ((mrInt8 *) &iSize, sizeof (mrUInt32));
45:
46:    /* Read the string WAVE identifier */
47:   kWave.read (aiID, sizeof (mrInt8) * 4);
48:   aiID [4] = '\0';
49:    /* If not WAVE, it is not supported */
50:   if (0 != strcmp (aiID, "WAVE"))
51:   {
52:    return mrErrorWaveNotSupported;
53:   }
```

Next you read the size of the wave file (line 44) and the "WAVE" string identifier (line 47). If the file type identifier isn't "WAVE", then you abort because this isn't a PCM Wave file (line 50).

```
54:    /* Ignore 'fmt ' string */
55:   kWave.seekg (4, ios::cur);
56:
57:    /* Read the 'fmt ' chunk length  */
58:   mrUInt32 iFormatLength;
59:   kWave.read ((mrInt8 *) &iFormatLength, sizeof (mrUInt32));
60:
61:    /* Read the WAVEFORMATEX structure */
62:   WAVEFORMATEX kWaveFormat;
63:
64:   kWave.read ((mrInt8 *) &kWaveFormat, sizeof (WAVEFORMATEX));
```

Since you are sure this is a wave file, you can ignore the format chunk identifier and simply read the format information. You do this by reading the information to a `WAVEFORMATEX` type. While the `WAVEFORMATEX` isn't exactly the same as the format chunk, it resembles it very much. It is defined as follows:

```
typedef struct
{
 WORD wFormatTag;
 WORD nChannels;
 DWORD nSamplesPerSec;
 DWORD nAvgBytesPerSec;
 WORD nBlockAlign;
 WORD wBitsPerSample;
 WORD cbSize;
} WAVEFORMATEX;
```

As you can see, this is the same as the format chunk except it has an extra field, `cbSize`, which is used to store some extra information about the waveform. This field won't be used.

Why do you use this structure since it doesn't match the format chunk exactly? Well, because the next data following the format chunk is the "data" identifier string, you can ignore this, so `cbSize` won't have any relevant information, and since you will need a `WAVEFORMATEX` structure correctly filled to create your sound buffer, you can use this one.

Now, take a look at code that reads the actual audio data:

```
65:    /* Ignore two bytes since we already read the first two of
66:       the 'data' chunk string since WAVEFORMATEX has an extra
67:       two bytes */
68:   kWave.seekg (2, ios::cur);
69:   kWaveFormat.cbSize = 0;
70:
71:    /* Read the size of the wave data */
72:   mrUInt32 iDataSize;
73:   kWave.read ((mrInt8 *) &iDataSize, sizeof (mrUInt32));
74:
75:    /* Read the sound data */
76:   mrUInt8 * pkSoundBuffer = new mrUInt8 [iDataSize];
77:   kWave.read ((mrInt8 *) pkSoundBuffer, iDataSize);
```

What you did first was to move two bytes. Remember that you have read an extra two bytes because of the `cbSize` field of the `WAVEFORMATEX` before? Well, now you need to ignore two more bytes, which produces the same result as if you had read the "data" identifier from the file.

Next you read the waveform buffer size (line 73), and allocate the needed memory to read the sound buffer (line 76), and obviously, read it (line 77).

Next you will create the DirectSound buffer and copy the waveform data to it:

```
 /* Fill DirectSound buffer description */
DSBUFFERDESC          kBufferDesc;

ZeroMemory (&kBufferDesc, sizeof (DSBUFFERDESC));
kBufferDesc.dwSize        = sizeof (DSBUFFERDESC);
kBufferDesc.dwBufferBytes = iDataSize;
kBufferDesc.lpwfxFormat   = &kWaveFormat;
kBufferDesc.dwFlags       = DSBCAPS_CTRLVOLUME;

 /* Create the sound buffer */
if (FAILED (mrSoundPlayer::GetSingleton()->GetSound ()->
            CreateSoundBuffer (&kBufferDesc, &m_lpkSound, NULL)) )
{
 return mrErrorCreateSoundBuffer;
}
```

The first thing you must do is fill the buffer description information (line 80) so you can create the buffer later. The DSBUFFERDESC structure is defined as follows:

```
typedef struct {
 DWORD dwSize;
 DWORD dwFlags;
 DWORD dwBufferBytes;
 DWORD dwReserved;
 LPWAVEFORMATEX lpwfxFormat;
 GUID guid3Dalgorithm;
} DSBUFFERDESC;
```

You are only interested in three of them, but even so, let's see which is which. The first one, dwSize, is the size of this structure, and the next is dwFlags, which specifies the flags this buffer has. You will only use DSBCAPS_CTRLVOLUME so you can control the volume, but for your games you may want a little more control, so check out the values in Table 15.5 for other flags.

If you are interested in using these flags, you should check out the DirectX SDK reference to see how they work.

The next member you are interested in is the dwBufferSize, which specifies the size of the buffer wave data. Finally, you also need to point lpwfxFormat to a valid LPWAVEFORMATEX structure, or in your case, the structure you used earlier to read from the file.

TABLE 15.5 DSBUFFERDESC Flags

Value	Description
DSBCAPS_CTRLFREQUENCY	The buffer can control the frequency of the sound.
DSBCAPS_CTRLPAN	The buffer can control the pan of the sound.
DSBCAPS_CTRL3D	The buffer has 3-D control capability.
DSBCAPS_CTRLFX	The buffer supports effects processing.

Next `dwReserved` is reserved and must be 0. Next is the `lpwfxFormat`, which is a structure that describes the sound buffer format.

The last one, `guid3DAlgorithm`, is the virtualization algorithm for a two-speaker set. You won't like it, so you must supply `NULL`.

In the end, you create the sound buffer using the `CreateSoundBuffer` method that is defined as follows:

```
HRESULT IDirectSoundBuffer8::CreateSoundBuffer (
 LPCDSBUFFERDESC pcDSBufferDesc,
 LPDIRECTSOUNDBUFFER * ppDSBuffer,
 LPUNKNOWN pUnkOuter);
```

The first parameter is a pointer to a `DSBUFFERDESC` structure, and the second parameter is a pointer to an `IDirectSoundBuffer8` object. The last parameter is a COM-specific parameter and must be `NULL`.

To finish this method you need to lock the buffer and copy the data you read from the file to it.

```
    /* Lock the sound buffer */
   LPVOID lpvAudio;
   DWORD  dwBytes;
   if (FAILED (m_lpkSound->Lock(0, 0,&lpvAudio, &dwBytes, NULL, NULL,
                                   DSBLOCK_ENTIREBUFFER)) )
   {
    return mrErrorSoundBufferLock;
   }

    /* Copy the wave data to the DirectSound buffer */ */
   memcpy (lpvAudio, pkSoundBuffer, dwBytes);
   m_lpkSound->Unlock(lpvAudio, dwBytes, NULL, 0);

    /* Delete the memory used by the wave data and close the file */
   delete [] pkSoundBuffer;
   kWave.close ();
  }

  return mrNoError;
}
```

You start by locking the buffer with a call to Lock, which is defined as:

```
HRESULT IDirectSoundBuffer8::Lock (
 DWORD dwOffset,
 DWORD dwBytes,
 LPVOID * ppvAudioPtr1,
 LPDWORD pdwAudioBytes1,
 LPVOID * ppvAudioPtr2,
 LPDWORD pdwAudioBytes2,
 DWORD dwFlags);
```

Where the first parameter is the offset from the start of the buffer you want to lock, and the second parameter is the number of bytes to lock. Next it is a pointer to the first audio block and the size of the audio block. Following is a pointer to the second audio block and the size of that block. In the end, there are the lock flags, which describe how DirectSound should lock the buffer and can be either DSBLOCK_FROMWRITECURSOR which only locks the specified position or DSBLOCK_ENTIREBUFFER which locks the entire buffer.

Now, a word about the two audio blocks. The second pointer is only valid if the locked segment you have supplied expands to the end of the buffer, in this case, the locked region will be wrapped, and the second pointer will point to the beginning of the buffer.

After you do this, you need to copy the file data to the buffer using memcpy (line 105), and unlock the buffer with Unlock, which is defined as follows:

```
HRESULT IDirectSoundBuffer8::Unlock (
 LPVOID pvAudioPtr1,
 DWORD dwAudioBytes1,
 LPVOID * ppvAudioPtr2,
 LPDWORD pdwAudioBytes2);
```

Where the parameters stand for the same thing as their correspondents in Lock.

Unlock will make sure that any data written to this pointer will be copied to the actual buffer.

Finally, you just need to release the allocated memory for the sound buffer (line 109) and close the file (line 110).

Now that wasn't so bad, was it? And now you have a buffer ready to be played whenever you want as you will see later. For now, you need to continue developing your library:

```
 /* Set the sound volume */
mrError32 mrSound::SetVolume (mrUInt32 iVolume)
{
 if (FAILED (m_lpkSound->SetVolume ((100-iVolume) * 100)) )
 {
  return mrErrorSoundSetVolume;
 }

 return mrNoError;
}
```

This method, `SetVolume`, sets the volume a sound should play, with the lowest volume 0 and the maximum 100. It calls the `SetVolume` method of `IDirectSoundBuffer8`, which is defined as follows:

```
HRESULT IDirectSoundBuffer8::SetVolume (
 LONG iVolume);
```

Where the first parameter is the volume in hundredths of decibels, where 0 is the highest volume, and –10000 is silent. This is why you do some calculations in Mirus, so a value of 100 represents 0, and a value of 0 represents –10000.

Next you need to know how to play the sound:

```
 /* Play the sound */
mrError32 mrSound::Play (mrUInt32 iLoop)
{
  /* Go to beginning of sound */
 m_lpkSound->SetCurrentPosition (0);
  /* Play sound */
 if (FAILED (m_lpkSound->Play (0, NULL,
             (iLoop != 0) ? DSBPLAY_LOOPING : 0)) )
 {
  return mrErrorPlay;
 }
 return mrNoError;
}
```

There are two important steps in this method, you first need to set the buffer's position to the initial position, which is done with `SetCurrentPosition`, and its prototype is:

```
HRESULT IDirectSoundBuffer8::SetCurrentPosition (
 DWORD dwNewPosition);
```

Which takes as the only argument the new position for the buffer, or in your case, 0, since you want the beginning of the buffer.

Next you need to play the sound with the `Play` method, which is defined as follows:

```
HRESULT IDirectSoundBuffer8::Play (
 DWORD dwReserved1,
 DWORD dwPriority,
 DWORD dwFlags);
```

Where the first parameter must be 0, and the second parameter is the priority of this buffer, but only if it is a voice buffer; since it isn't, it must be `NULL`. The last parameter can only be 0, or `DSBPLAY_LOOPING`, if you want to loop the sound. In Mirus, you only repeat the sound if the only parameter passed to `mrSound::Play` isn't 0 (or false).

Next you need to stop the sound:

```
 /* Stop playing the sound */
mrError32 mrSound::Stop (void)
{
 if (FAILED (m_lpkSound->Stop ()) )
 {
  return mrErrorStop;
 }
 return mrNoError;
}
```

Which is pretty simple, you call the `Stop` method, which is defined as follows:

```
HRESULT IDirectSoundBuffer8::Stop ();
```

Which takes no parameters.

Pretty simple, no? When you want to use Mirus to play sounds, you first need to initialize the sound player, and then create the sound object, load it from the file, and play it:

```
mrSoundPlayer kSoundPlayer;
 /* Initialize DirectSound */
kSoundPlayer.Init (hParentWindow);
mrSound kSoundOne;
mrSound kSoundTwo;
 /* Load the files from the disk */
kSoundOne.LoadFromFile ("SoundA.wav");
kSoundTwo.LoadFromFile ("SoundA.wav");
 /* Play first sound without repeating */
kSoundOne.Play (mrFalse),
 /* Play first sound with repeating */
kSoundTwo.Play (mrTrue),
 /* Stop playing the sounds */
kSoundOne.Stop ();
kSoundTwo.Stop ();
```

That's it, simple isn't it? And you are done with DirectSound. There are many other features you could tackle, such as DirectSound3D, DirectMusic, or paths, but that brings more advanced stuff to the game. If you are interested, check out the SDK documentation.

Media Control Interface

The media control interface, or MCI (shown in Figure 15.3), is a set of functions and structures that enable you to play and record multimedia devices. You will only be interested in playing multimedia, more accurately, the CD player.

There are two ways to use the MCI: command messages or command strings. The first consists of a set of structures and constants to define the commands and devices, while the second uses formatted strings to define the commands and devices. While it is easier to use command messages, understanding them is not easy. Using command strings is like directly telling the MCI what you want to do.

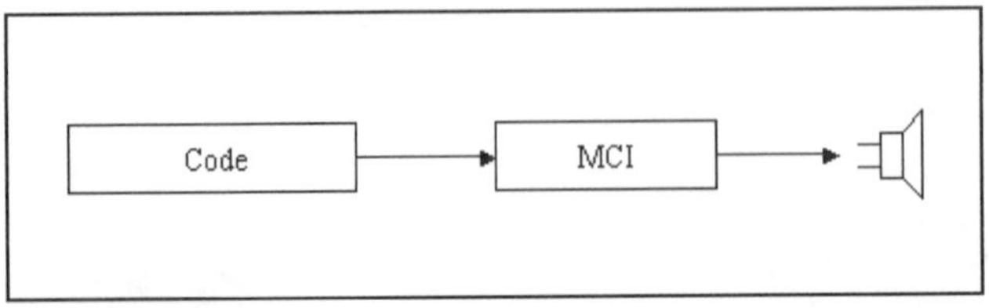

Figure 15.3

MCI and the computer.

For example, if you wanted to know the number of tracks on a CD, you would use the string: `"status cdaudio number of tracks"`. There are various status, commands, and devices, but you will only focus on the basics to be able to play a CD.

Sending a string to the MCI is as simple as calling `mciSendString` with a certain number of parameters. `mciSendString` is defined as follows:

```
MCIERROR mciSendString (
 LPCTSTR lpszCommand,
 LPTSTR lpszReturnString,
 UINT cchReturn,
 HANDLE hwndCallback);
```

Where the first argument is the string defining the command you want to send, and the second argument is a string with the return value. The third value is the size of the returned string, and the last one is a handle to the window callback, but this doesn't interest us.

To be able to use a device, you first need to open it, which is done with the string `"open device"` where `device` is the name of the device. You also need to close the device with the string `"close device"`.

Okay, now that you know the basics, let's make your CD player.

mrCDPlayer

Your CD player class is very simple, you will use it to have minimal control over the CD player and get basic information about the current CD. The Windows API allows many things to be done with the CD player, so if you are interested, check out MSDN or some nice book about Windows.

Your CD player class is defined as follows:

```
 /* 'mrCDPlayer.h' */

 /* Mirus base types header */
#include "mrDatatypes.h"
 /* Mirus error definitions header */
#include "mrError.h"
 /* Standard input/output header file */
#include <stdio.h>
 /* Windows header file */
#include <windows.h>
```

```
 /* Windows Multimedia header file */
#include <mmsystem.h>

 /* Include this file only once */
#pragma once

 /* Mirus CD Player class */
class mrCDPlayer
{
protected:
  /* CD information */
 mrUInt32         m_iNumberTracks;
 mrUInt32         m_iCurrentTrack;
 mrInt8           m_szLength [256];

public:
  /* Constructors / Destructor */
 mrCDPlayer (void);
 ~mrCDPlayer (void);

  /* CD player manipulation routines */
 void Eject (void);
 void Play (mrUInt32 iTrack);
 void Stop (void);
 void Update (void);

  /* CD player maintenance routines */
 mrUInt32 GetNumberOfTracks (void);
 mrInt8 * GetLength (void);
 mrUInt32 GetCurrentTrack (void);
 mrBool32 IsReady (void);
};
```

This is the main class from where you will control the CD player. It offers the basic functionality offered from simple CD players, which is what you need for your games.

You now need to start developing the class methods.

```
 /* Default constructor */
mrCDPlayer::mrCDPlayer (void)
{
```

```
  /* Open the cd device */
 mciSendString ("open cdaudio", NULL, 0, NULL);
}
```

In the constructor, you need to open the device for use. You do this by sending the message `"open cdaudio"` to MCI. `"cdaudio"` is the string identifier that defines the CD-ROM for audio.

```
 /* Default destructor */
mrCDPlayer::~mrCDPlayer (void)
{
  /* Stop playing */
 Stop ();
  /* Close the cd device */
 mciSendString ("close cdaudio", NULL, 0, NULL);
}
```

In the destructor you need to first stop the playback by calling the method `Stop` (which you will develop later) and by sending the `"close audio"` command to MCI.

```
 /* Eject the current CD */
void mrCDPlayer::Eject (void)
{
 mciSendString ("set cdaudio door open", NULL, 0, NULL);
}
```

To eject a CD, you need to send the `"set cdaudio door open"` string to the MCI. The `"set"` string sets some value of the MCI device, in this case it is to set the `"door"`, `"open"`.

```
 /* Play a track */
void mrCDPlayer::Play (mrUInt32 iTrack)
{
 mrInt8 szSendString [256];

  /* Play from iTrack to the final track */
 sprintf (szSendString, "play cdaudio from %d to %d", iTrack, m_iNumberTracks);
mciSendString (szSendString, NULL, 0, NULL);
}
```

In this method, you first need to create the string that you will send, because to play a track, you need to tell the MCI which track to start playing, and which track to stop playing. In this case, you will be playing all the tracks from the specified track to the last one. To do this you create a string like: `"play cdaudio from`

StartTrack to FinalTrack" where the StartTrack is the first track, and the FinalTrack is the last one (line 34). Then send that string to the MCI (line 35).

```
38:  /* Stop playing */
39: void mrCDPlayer::Stop (void)
40: {
41:  mciSendString ("stop cdaudio", NULL, 0, NULL);
42: }
```

To stop a device from playing you need to send the "stop device" string to the MCI, as shown for the "cdaudio".

```
44:  /* Update CD information */
45: void mrCDPlayer::Update (void)
46: {
47:  mrInt8 szReturnString [256];
48:
49:   /* Get number of tracks */
50:  mciSendString ("status cdaudio number of tracks", szReturnString, 255, NULL);
51:  m_iNumberTracks = atoi (szReturnString);
52:
53:   /* Get CD length */
54:  mciSendString ("status cdaudio length", m_szLength, 255, NULL);
55: }
```

In this method you want to know the number of tracks, and the CD length, so you need to make two calls to mciSendString. The first one using "status cdaudio number of tracks" which will return a string with the number of tracks (line 50), which you then need to convert to an integer using atoi (line 51). Next you need to send the "status cdaudio length" message to the MCI so it returns the CD length (line 54). The length of the CD is returned in the "HH:mm:ss" format.

```
75:  /* Returns if the CD is ready to be used */
76: mrBool32 mrCDPlayer::IsReady (void)
77: {
78:  mrInt8 szReturnString [256];
79:
80:  mciSendString ("status cdaudio ready", szReturnString, 255, NULL);
81:
82:  if (0 == strcmp (szReturnString, "true") )
83:  {
84:   return mrTrue;
```

```
  }
  else
  {
   return mrFalse;
  }
}
```

And your last method is used to determine whether the CD is ready to be used, and to do this, you send the `"status cdaudio ready"` string to the MCI, and it will return either `"true"` if it is ready, or `"false"` if it isn't.

> **TIP**
>
> **For this component to work, you will need to include the winmm.lib and dsound.lib libraries in your projects.**

And you are done. Making a CD player for games is pretty simple. I just wonder why most companies don't use CD audio for their music.

Just for fun, make a small program that plays a CD track and repeats a sound until the program closes:

```
 /* '02 Main.cpp' */

 /* Mirus header */
#include "mirus.h"

 /* Sound class */
class SoundWindow : public mrWindow
{
  /* Sound classes */
 mrSoundPlayer   m_kSoundPlayer;
 mrSound          m_kSound;
 mrCDPlayer      m_kCDPlayer;

public:
  /* Constructor / Destructor */
 SoundWindow (void);
 ~SoundWindow (void);

 void Init (HINSTANCE hInstance);

  /* Window manipulation functions */
```

```
22:  mrBool32 Frame (void);
23: };
```

This is the normal window class declaration. I just added the needed sound and CD player class for the program (lines 10 through 12).

Next is the constructor and destructor:

```
25: SoundWindow::SoundWindow (void)
26: {
27: }
28:
29: SoundWindow::~SoundWindow (void)
30: {
31:    /* Stop playback */
32:  m_kSound.Stop ();
33:  m_kCDPlayer.Stop ();
34: }
```

While the constructor does nothing, the destructor stops both the CD player and the sound (lines 32 and 33).

```
36: void SoundWindow::Init (HINSTANCE hInstance)
37: {
38:     /* Initialize DirectSound */
39:  m_kSoundPlayer.Init (m_hWindow);
40:    /* Load the files from the disk */
41:  m_kSound.LoadFromFile ("Sound.wav");
42:  m_kSound.Play (mrTrue);
43:    /* Play CD */
44:  m_kCDPlayer.Update ();
45:  m_kCDPlayer.Play (1);
46: }
```

Here you have to initialize the sound manager (line 39) and load the wave from a file (line 41). Next play the sound (line 42) repeatedly and update the CD info (line 44) and play the first track (line 45).

And the rest of the program is the usual `WinMain` and `Frame`:

```
48:  /* Render frame */
49: mrBool32 SoundWindow::Frame(void)
50: {
```

```
  return mrTrue;
}

  /* "WinMain Vs. main" */
int WINAPI WinMain (HINSTANCE hInstance, HINSTANCE hPrevInst,
                    LPSTR lpCmdLine, int nShowCmd)
{
   /* Our window */
  SoundWindow  kWindow;

   /* Create window */
  kWindow.Create (hInstance, "Sound Test");
  kWindow.SetSize (640, 480);

  kWindow.Init (hInstance);
  kWindow.Run ();

  return 0;
}
```

Summary

Not a long chapter, but you have learned enough to get started in sound. By learning the basics of DirectSound and windows multimedia, you are now able to play both music and sound effects in your games.

Questions and Answers

Q: How can you mathematically generate sounds?

A: By using a combination of formulas, you can create various sounds. You can also use already existing sounds and manipulate them to make new sounds.

Q: What is DirectMusic?

A: DirectMusic is a component of DirectXAudio that enables you to load various files and play them according to formulas or effects. This lets you change the volume, the speed, the frequency, and the amplitude of the sound being played in real time, depending on the state of the game.

Q: What are the advantages of using command messages over command strings when using the MCI?

A: Command messages are easier to work with because you can use constants to define commands. Also, working with return values with commands is easier because you don't need to convert from strings to numbers.

Exercises

1. What is the simplest sound wave?
2. What is the file identifier in wave files for a PCM uncompressed wave?
3. What happens if YOU try to lock over the size of the buffer?
4. What is the string command to open the CD-Rom?

PART THREE

Hardcore Game Programming

16 Introduction to Game Design

17 Data Structures and Algorithms

18 The Mathematical Side of Games

19 Introduction to Artificial Intelligence

20 Introduction to Physics Modeling

21 Building Breaking Through

22 Publishing Your Game

CHAPTER 16

Introduction to Game Design

Many years have passed since games were designed in a couple of hours at the family barbeque. Today, games are required to be fun, addictive but at the same time meaningful and intuitive. The latest games released by the big companies take months to design and that is with the help of various designers. On the contrary to popular belief, a game designer isn't the guy whose sole purpose is to think of an idea, and then give the idea to the programmers to make a game.

A designer must think of the game idea, elaborate it, illustrate it, define it, and describe just about everything from the time the CD is inserted into the CD-ROM drive to the time when the player quits the game. Figure 16.1 shows a storyboard.

This chapter is here to help you understand a little more about game design, as well as give you some tips about it and in the end show you a small game design document for a very popular game.

What Is Game Design?

So what exactly is game design? Game design is the ancient art of creating and defining games. Well, at least the short definition, that is.

Game design is the entire process of creating a game idea, from research to the graphical interface to the unit's capabilities. Having an idea for a game is easy, making a game from that idea is the hard part, and that is just the design part.

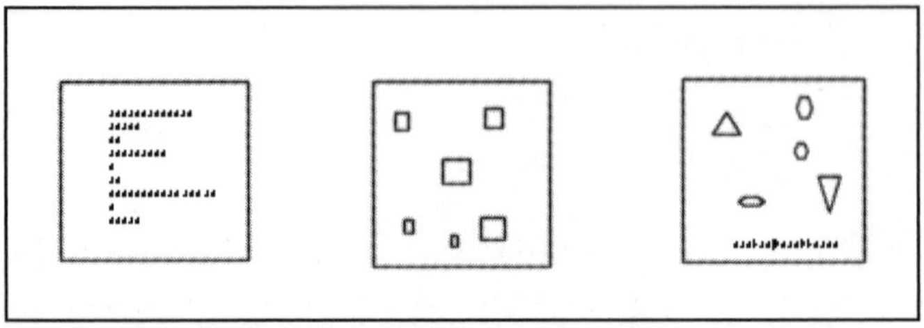

Figure 16.1

A sample storyboard.

Some of the jobs of a designer when creating a game are:

- Define the game idea
- Define all the screens and how they relate to each other and menus
- Explain how and why the interaction with the game is done
- Create a story that makes sense
- Define game goals
- Write dialogs and other specific game texts
- Analyze the balance of the game and modify it accordingly
- And much, much more . . .

The Dreadful Design Document

Now that you finally have decided what kind of game you are making and have almost everything planned out, it's time to prepare a design document.

For better understanding of what a design document should be, think of the movie industry.

When a movie is shot, the story isn't in anyone's head, it is completely described in the movie script. Actually, the movie script is usually written long before shooting starts. The author writes the script and then needs to take it to a big Hollywood company to get the necessary means to produce the movie, but this doesn't mean it is easy, it is a long process. After a company picks the movie, each team (actors, camera people, director) will get the copies of the script to do their job. When the wardrobe is done, the actors know the lines and emotion, the director is ready, so they start shooting the movie.

When dealing with game design, the process is sort of the same, in that the designer(s) do the design document, then they pitch the company that they work for to see if they have interest in the idea (no, trying to sell game designs to companies isn't a very nice future). When the company gives the go, probably after revising the design and for sure, messed it up, each team (artists, programmers, musicians) gets the design document and starts doing their jobs, when some progress is done by all the teams, the actual production starts (testing the code with the art, including the music).

One more thing before proceeding: just because some feature or menu is written in the design document, it doesn't mean it has to be that way no matter what. It's similar to the movies, in that the actors follow the script, but sometimes they improvise, which makes the movie even more captivating.

Why the "It's in My Head" Technique Isn't Good

Many young and beginning game programmers defend the idea of "The game is in my head" and refuse to do any kind of formal design. This is a bad approach for several reasons.

The first one is probably the most important if you are working with a team: If you are working with other people on the game, and you have the idea in your head, there are two options: your team members are psychic or you spend 90 percent of the time you should be developing your game explaining why the heck the player can't use the item picked in the first level to defeat the second boss, which is in no way fun.

Another valid reason to keep a formal design document is to keep focus, when you have the idea in your head, you will be working on it and modifying it even when you are finishing the programming part. This is bad because it will eventually force you to change code and lose time. I'm not saying that when you write something down, it is written in stone. All the aspects of the design document can and should be changing during development. The problem is that when you have some formal design, it's easy to keep focus and progress, whereas if you keep it in your head, it will be hard to progress due to the fact that you won't settle with something, because you will always be thinking of other stuff.

The last reason why you shouldn't keep the designs in your head is because you are human. We tend to forget stuff. Suppose you have the design in your head and are about 50 percent done programming the game, but for some reason you have to stop developing the game for three weeks (vacation, exams month, aliens invading). When you get back to developing the game, most of the stuff that was previously so clear will not be as obvious, thus making you lose time re-thinking it.

The Two Types of Designs

Even if there isn't an official distinction between design types, separating the design process into two types makes it easier to understand what techniques are more advantageous to the games you are developing.

Mini Design

The mini design is the sort of design you can do in about a week or so, that features a complete, but general, description of the game.

A mini design document should be enough for any team member to pick it, read it, get the same idea of the game as the designer but be allowed to include a little bit of her own ideas on the game (like the artist designing the main character or the programmer adding a couple of features like cloud movement or parallax scrolling).

Mini designs are useful when you are creating a small game or a game that is heavily based on another game or very known genre.

Some distinctive aspects of a mini design document are

General overview of the game
Game goals
Interaction of player and game
Basic menu layout and game options
Story
Overview of enemies
Image theme

Complete Design

The complete design document looks like the script from *Titanic.* It features every possible aspect of the game, from the menu button color to the number of hit points the barbarian can have. It is usually designed by various people, with help from external people like lead programmers or lead artists.

This kind of design is almost strict to it. It takes too much time to make, to be ignored or misinterpreted. Anyone reading it should see exactly the same game, the same colors and backgrounds as the designer(s).

This kind of designs are reserved for big companies that have much money to spare. Small teams or lone developers should stay away from this type of design since most of the time they don't have the resources to do it.

Some of the aspects a complete design should have are

General overview of the game
Game goals
Game story

Characters' story and attributes
NPCs attributes
Player/NPCs/Other rule charts
All the rules defined
Interaction of player and game
Menu layout and style and all game options
Music description
Sound description
Description of the levels and their themes and goals

A Fill In Design Document Template

Following is a sample design document that you can use for your own designs but remember these are just guidelines that you don't have to follow exactly. If you don't think a section applies to your game or it is missing something, don't think twice about changing it.

General Overview

This is usually a paragraph or two describing the game very generally. It should describe the game genre and basic theme, as well as the objective of the player briefly.

It is a summary of the game.

Target System and Requirements

This should include the target system—Windows, Macintosh, or any other system like consoles—and a list of requirements for the game.

Story

Come on, this isn't any mind breaker, it is the game story. What happened in the past (before the game starts), what is happening when the player is starting the game, and possibly what will happen while the game progresses.

Theme: Graphics and Sound

This section describes the overall theme of the game, if it is set in ancient time in a land of fantasy or two thousand years in the future on planet Neptune. It should also contain descriptions or at least hints of the scenery and sound to be used.

Menus

This section should contain a small description and objective of the main menus, like Start Game or the Options menu.

Playing a Game

This is probably the trickier section, it should describe what happens from the time the user starts the game to when it starts to play, what usually happens, and how it ends. It is like you were describing what you would be seeing on the screen if you were playing the game yourself.

> **NOTE**
>
> NPC stands for Not Player Characters or Non Player Controlled. I've seen both descriptions being used to describe what an NPC is, but they basically say the same thing, so just pick the one you prefer.

Characters and NPCs Description

This section should describe the characters and the NPCs as well as possible. Their names, backgrounds, attributes, special attacks, and so on.

Artificial Intelligence Overview

There are two options for this section, either give an all-around general description of the game artificial intelligence and let the programmers pick that and develop their own set of rules, or describe just about every possible reaction and action an NPC can have.

Conclusion

This is usually a small paragraph with, obviously, a conclusion to the game. It may feature the motivation to create the game or some explanation why the game is as it is done.

A Sample Game Design: Space Invaders

Presented in Figure 16.2 is a sample mini design document for a Space Invaders type of game. Space Invaders is a relatively old game that you are probably familiar with.

After reading this design document you should be able to develop it on your own using the Mirus framework you developed earlier.

General Overview

Space Invaders is a typical arcade shooter game. The objective of the game is to destroy all the enemy ships in each level.

The player controls a ship that can move horizontally in the bottom of the screen while it tries to avoid the bullets from the alien ships.

Target System and Requirements

Space Invaders is target to Windows 32-bit machines with DirectX 8.0 installed.

Being such a low-end game, the basic requirements are minimal, such as:

Pentium 200 processor or equivalent (for DirectX performance)
16/32 Megabytes of memory (depending on system)
5 Megabytes of free disk space
SVGA DirectX compatible video card

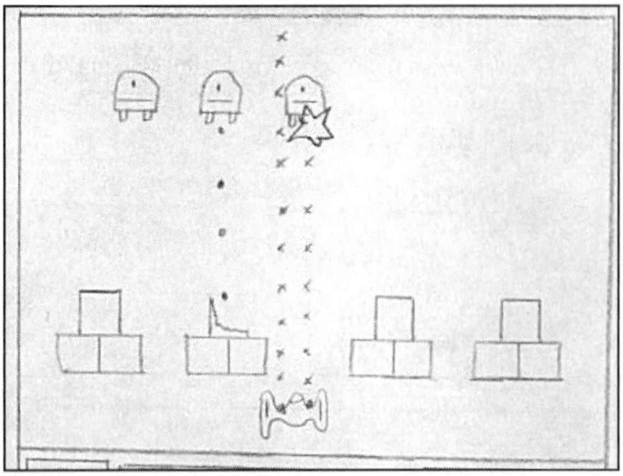

Figure 16.2

Space Invaders prototype.

Story

Around 2049 A.D., aliens arrived at our planet, and they were not peaceful. They have destroyed two of the major cities in the world and are now threatening to destroy more.

The United Defense Force has decided to send their special agent, Gui Piskounov (don't ask) to destroy the alien force with the new experimental ship: ZS 3020 Airborne.

You play the role of Piskounov. Your mission: To destroy all the alien scum.

Theme: Graphics and Sound

The whole game has a futuristic feeling to it. The main menus are heavily based on metallic walls and wire.

The game itself is played in space, and as such, most of the backgrounds are stars or small planets. The ships have a very futuristic look to them.

The game is ensconced in heavy trance techno music with a very fast beat. Sounds are basically based on metal beating, explosions, and firing bullets effects.

Menus

When the game starts, the user is presented with the main menu—in this menu he has five options.

Start New Game

This option starts a new game. The player is sent to the new game menu where he can enter his name and chose the game difficulty.

Continue Previously Saved Game

This option starts a game that was previously saved. The player is sent to the load game menu where he can choose a game from a list of previous saved games.

See Table of High Scores

This option shows the high scores table.

Options

This option shows the Options menu. The player is sent to the Options menu where he can change the graphics, sound, and control settings.

Exit

This option exits the game.

Playing a Game

When the game starts, a company splash screen is shown for three seconds. After the three seconds the screen fades to black and a splash screen starts to fade in. After four seconds the screen re-fades to black and the player is sent to the main menu.

When the player starts a new game, he is presented with a new menu screen where he can enter his name, and choose the game difficulty. After this is done, the user is sent to the game itself.

When each level starts, there is a three-seconds countdown for the game to start.

The player can move his ship to the left or right and shoot using the controls defined in the Options menu.

When all the enemies are destroyed, the player advances a level. When the player is shot by an alien, he loses a life. If the player loses all the lives, the game ends.

If the aliens reach the bottom of the screen, the game is also over.

If the player presses the Escape key while playing, the game is paused and a dialog appears asking what the user wants to do, and he can choose from the options:

Save game—Saves the game

Options—Shows the Options menu

Quit game—Returns to the main menu

Characters and NPCs Description

In this version of Space Invaders there are two versions of alien ships. The first, the normal ones that are constantly on the screen trying to destroy the player, and the second randomly appear and if shot gives bonus points to the player.

Normal Ships

Normal ships are the typical enemies of the player. They can have various images but their functionality is the same. They move left and right and randomly shoot bullets to the player vertically. When the ships reach a vertical margin, they move down a bit.

These ships are destroyed with a single shot and each ship destroyed gives one hundred points to the player.

As the levels progress, the faster the ships move.

Bonus Ships

Bonus ships show randomly on the top of the screen. They move horizontally and very quickly.

These ships exist only to give bonus points to the player and don't affect the gameplay since they don't shoot at the player and are not required to be destroyed.

When a bonus ship is destroyed, the game awards 500 points to the player.

Artificial Intelligence Overview

This game is very simple and requires almost no artificial intelligence. The ships move horizontally only until they reach one of the vertical margins where they move down.

They also randomly shoot a bullet down, in a vertical-only direction.

Conclusion

The decision to keep this game simple but addictive was done to appeal to both younger players but also to just about any age genre, especially, hardcore arcade gamers.

> **NOTE**
> Space Invaders is a very simple game, and as such, has a very simple design document.

Summary

A rather small chapter for such an important topic, but this is a book about programming mostly, not design.

If you have been paying attention, you should by now have a vague idea why designs are important, and also be able to pick some of the topics covered here and design your own games.

If you are having troubles, just pick the fill-in template design document provided and start designing.

Questions and Answers

Q: Why should I care for designing if I want to be a programmer?

A: Tough question. The first reason is probably because you will start developing your small games before moving to a big company and follow 200-page design documents where you don't have any word in it. Next, being able to at least understand the concept of designing games will make your life a lot easier if when you are called for a meeting with the lead designer, you will at least understand what is happening.

Q: What is the best way to get a position as a full-time game designer in some big game company?

A: First, chances of doing that are very thin, really. But the best way to try would be to start low and eventually climb the ladder. Start by working at the beta testing team, then maybe try to move to quality assurance or programming, and eventually, try to get a game design to your boss. Please be aware that there are many steps from beta testing to even be a guest designer for a section of a game; time, patience, and perseverance are very important.

Exercises

1. On your own, try to create a design document for a Tetris-like game.
2. Try to describe in a separate document the artificial intelligence of a racing game.

CHAPTER 17

Data Structures and Algorithms

Every computer program ever made can be split up into two parts: the data and the operations that are performed upon the data. How data is stored and accessed can make a great difference on whether your program runs quickly or slowly. I will take a look at some of the more common data structures and their purposes, as well as some sorting and compression algorithms.

The Importance of the Correct Data Structures and Algorithms

In the beginning, all programmers had for storage were tiny registers. These registers are small collections of circuits on the processor that contain data, often limited to storing only 4 or 8 integers at a time. You can see that the programmers had very little storage space to work with, and thus they could only make simple programs. With the invention of external data storage, most notably RAM, programmers were allowed to create entire arrays of data, which could be accessed easily by index. Slowly, as circuits grew smaller, RAM became cheaper and cheaper, and data structures grew to be more complex.

The data structures I will be examining here each have their own purpose. It is important to note that every data structure has its strengths and its weaknesses, and that no single data structure is better than the others.

Think of the data structures at your disposal as a toolbelt. Is a Phillips-head screwdriver any better than a flat-head screwdriver? Of course not! Each tool is used on a different type of screw. Just like carpentry tools, each data structure is used to solve a different type of problem.

Algorithms are very much like data structures, except that they operate on the data, rather than store the data.

> **CAUTION**
>
> **You must be careful to analyze the circumstances of the problem you are trying to solve, and make an intelligent decision on which tools you will use. If you choose a data structure/algorithm that has a weakness in the one area you need it to be efficient, it can lead to a disaster.**

A newly added feature of C++ is the Standard Template Library (STL). This library contains all sorts of data structures and algorithms, programmed by some of the best computer scientists in the world. This is great, of course, but it has some problems:

First of all, when you use someone else's code, you also use his quirks, his weaknesses, and his hacks. What worked well for them on one system might be undesirable for you on another system. The only data structures you can use are the ones in the library, and most of the time they could be optimized further to your own purposes. For example, STL's list structure is doubly-linked and circular (you'll learn what these terms mean when I explain lists). These are some traits that the user might not want in a list, but you have no choice but to use them.

Second, when people use other libraries, they tend to learn the interface, but not the inner workings. Of course, one of the tenets of object-oriented programming is abstraction; it is very easy to use a module without knowing how it works inside or how it was made, but some in-depth knowledge is required in order to use your tools correctly and efficiently. Look at it this way: Anyone can jump into a car and drive it. They all have similar features: the gas pedal, brakes, steering wheel. But each car has its own quirks, some cars may handle inclines better in rainy weather, some cars have rear-wheel drive, and the list goes on. Learning an interface to a data structure enables you to use its basic functionality, but in order to really use the data structure, you must know how it works, and how it is implemented.

Of course you can use STL's or other people's code, but you probably are reading this book to learn how to do it yourself and not use someone else's code, right?

Sometimes it is better to re-invent the wheel. Some software engineers will see that as a weakness, but often it is viewed as a strength. Many people learn better with a hands-on approach, and implementing your own data structures is a great way to learn all their little nuances. I'm not telling you to go crazy and make an entire STL on your own; that would be a waste of time. If you're in a really tight situation, and a data structure or algorithm you are using is too slow, try making your own.

The last point is that a data structure and algorithm library may not be documented well enough. The programmers may leave out small pieces of information that they think are insignificant, but might end up causing you endless troubles.

NOTE

Data structures and algorithms are highly specialized. One variant of a structure may work fine in one situation, but not in another. Be aware of the tiny differences between data structures of the same type.

Lists

Chances are good that you've worked on a project that requires you to store a large number of items somewhere, but you do not have any idea how many items you will need to store at any given time. Previously, you used arrays, which have worked fine until now. But arrays have an inherent weakness—resizing them takes a very long time, and making them too large wastes memory. Let's suppose that you currently have 500 items that need to be stored somewhere, but you might need to store up to 1,000 items in the future. Let's also suppose that the 1,000-item requirement is only needed on a very rare occasion; the average number of items you will need to store at any given time is much closer to 500. There are a few problems with using an array in this instance. If you created a 1,000 index array, half of the indexes will be wasted for most of the program's execution time. Your program, on average, will use much more memory than it should actually require. One possible solution is to keep the array at a smaller size most of the time, and then resize the array when more data is needed.

This method has its advantages, of course, mainly, you still get to access the items in a random fashion. This method has two major problems, however. Resizing a large array takes quite a bit of work. You must first allocate enough memory for the new array, all the while keeping the old array in memory at the same time (remember, the new array will have garbage data in it, so you need to keep the old data and copy it over). On low-memory systems this could become a problem. Resizing a 500-item array to a 1,000-item array will require 1,500 indexes total, and the system might not have that much space available. After both arrays have been allocated, you still need to copy over all the items in the old array, and depending on the size of the data, this could take a long time to complete.

Here is where the list comes to the rescue! The list (also known as a linked list) data structure was invented to make dynamically varying data sets easier to manage. Lists are called a sequential data structure, as opposed to arrays, which are called random-access. You'll see what this means later when you see how a list is accessed. The list's major strength is that the number of items that can be stored in it at any given time is variable. Unlike a static array, there are no wasted indexes. It is a simple structure to implement, and there are many variations, each with its own strengths and weaknesses. There are singly linked lists, doubly linked lists, singly linked circular lists, and so on.

Basic Structure

First, let's look at the singly linked variation, because that is the simplest variation. At the heart of a list lies the node. When you think of an array, the data is stored sequentially, each item stored in an element. A list node is similar to an element, but more complex. First of all, elements are just a concept, while nodes need to be implemented as a small structure or class of its own. The key to the list structure is that it is not stored sequentially in memory (keep in mind that the list is still conceptually a sequential structure, however), rather, the nodes in a list can be in any part of the memory at any given time. Each linked list node maintains a pointer to the next node in the list, and if the node is the last node in the list, it points to nothing.

You can think of this easily as a long building. If you walk into an arrayed building, and want to go to room five, you just walk past the first four rooms, and there you are. The linked building across the street is a bit more complex. In order to get to the fifth room in that building, you need to first go to the first room, and ask the guy who is sitting in there where room number two is. He'll tell you, of course (because he is a nice guy), and then you can walk over to room number two, and ask the guy sitting there where room number three is, and so on, until you reach room five.

Figure 17.1 shows how a list is structured. Conceptually, it is a linear structure, similar to an array. The actual list class points to one node, commonly called the `head`

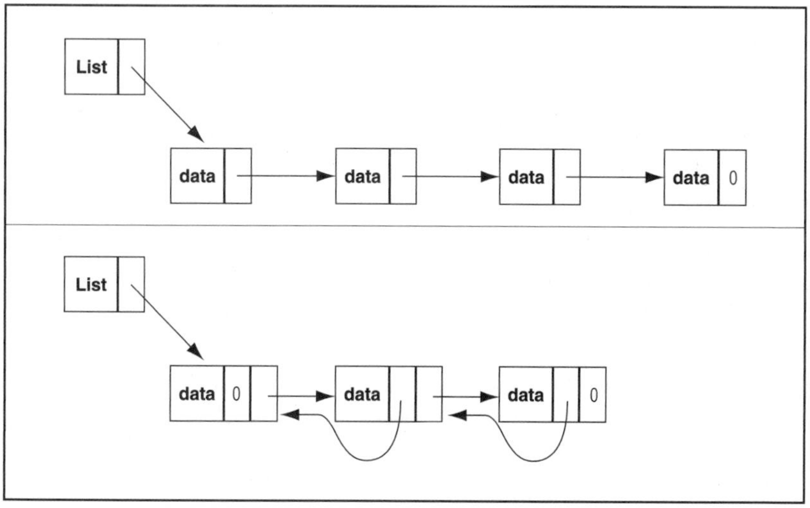

Figure 17.1

Singly (top) and doubly (bottom) linked lists.

node, and each node points to the next node in the sequence. Using this type of structure enables you to easily extend a sequence of data and insert or remove data from the list without significantly changing the structure. For your demo programs, you will be using a simple mrGamePlayer class to demonstrate the usage of the data structures.

Here is a listing of the mrGamePlayer class:

```
/* mrGamePlayer.h */
class mrGamePlayer
{
public:
  mrInt m_iLife;
  mrInt m_iLevel;
};
```

Now you will create a singly linked list node class that can hold GamePlayer.

```
/* mrListNodeGP.h */
#include "mrGamePlayer.h"
class mrListNodeGP
{
public:
   /* The GamePlayer stored In the node */
  mrGamePlayer m_kPlayer;
   /* A pointer to the next node in the list */
  mrListNodeGP* m_kNext;
};
```

If you didn't already guess, the GP appended to the name of the class stands for "GamePlayer" (it is read as "List node of type GamePlayer"). If you called the class List, then there would be a horrible mess when you tried to make another List class for a different data type.

So each node contains an mrGamePlayer object and a pointer to the next node in the list. Now for the mrListGP (similarly pronounced "List of GamePlayers") header, the class which will manage all the nodes:

```
class mrListGP
{
public:
  void StartIterator();
  void MoveForward();
```

```
  mrGamePlayer& GetCurrentItem();
  mrBool32 IsIteratorValid();
  void InsertItem( mrGamePlayer player );
  void RemoveCurrentItem();
  void AppendItem( mrGamePlayer player );
  mrInt GetCount();
private:
  mrListNode* m_kHead;
  mrListNode* m_kCurrent;
  mrInt m_iCount;
};
```

Let's just look at the private variables for the time being (all the functions will be explained a bit later in this chapter). It's pretty simple, as I said before. There is a count variable, which keeps track of how many items are stored in the list, and there is a pointer to the head node of the list. The `m_kCurrent` variable is called the iterator pointer. An iterator pointer is simply an easy way to keep track of a traversal through the list.

Iterators

Accessing the items in an array is easy. All you need to do is supply a number, and the compiler takes care of the multiplication and retrieves the required item for you. Lists do not have this advantage, however. To get to a specified item in the list, you must first follow the trail of pointers until you get to the correct item. (Remember the building analogy, you are required to visit each room and inquire where the next room is located.) This is why lists are called sequential. Another way to think of this is like an audio or videotape cassette. You cannot just tell the tape player to jump right to the middle or the end of the tape, you must first fastforward through everything before your desired destination. Because of this limitation, accessing items is a more complicated task. You cannot simply provide the list with a number and have it return to you with the requested item. This mandated the creation of a new concept, called iterators. An *iterator* is a conceptual structure, which is used to move or scan over the items in a list, allowing you to access, modify, and delete items in a list. Your implementation of the iterator concept is internal; the list itself keeps track of the "current" node. Some of the more complex iterator implementations are external, where a separate class keeps track of an item, but these types are usually not needed often. More times than not, an internal iterator will do the job you want to accomplish.

There are six iterator-related functions in your list class. The first four are simple routines that only require a few lines:

```
1:  /* Move the iterator to the beginning of the list */
2: void StartIterator()
3: {
4:  m_kCurrent = m_khead;
5: }
6:  /* Move the iterator forward to the next item */
7: void MoveForward()
8: {
9:  if( NULL != m_kCurrent )
10:  m_kCurrent = m_kCurrent->m_kNext;
11: }
12:  /* return a pointer to the item in the current node */
13: mrGamePlayer& GetCurrentItem()
14: {
15:  return &(m_kCurrent->m_kPlayer);
16: }
17:  /* determine whether the iterator is valid or not */
18: mrBool32 IsIteratorValid()
19: {
20:  if( NULL != m_kCurrent )
21:   return mrTrue;
22:  return mrFalse;
23: }
```

`StartIterator` (line 2) resets the position of the iterator so that it points to the head node of the list. This is like an instant-rewind function. If there are no items in the list, the iterator is still invalid.

`MoveForward` (line 7) moves the iterator to the next node in the list. If the next node doesn't exist, then the iterator becomes null. This routine first checks to see whether the iterator is valid. If it is not, this routine does nothing.

`GetCurrentItem` (line 13) returns a reference to the player stored in the current node. Be very careful, however. If the current iterator is invalid, then this will cause the program to crash, because the routine tries to dereference an item in a node that doesn't exist.

> **TIP**
>
> **You should make it a habit to check whether the iterator is valid before you attempt to retrieve an item.**

You can check to see whether the iterator is valid by using the `IsIteratorValid` (line 18) function. If the list is empty, the `IsIteratorValid` function will always return false. The way to determine whether the iterator is valid is to make sure it is not `NULL`.

Notice how the `GetCurrentItem` routine returns a reference. This enables you to modify the player in the current node without adding a special function in the list class to do this. Here is an example of a function, which will use the four basic iterator functions listed previously to cycle through a list and add a little life to each game player inside the list:

```
1: void AddLife( mrListGP& list, mrInt life )
2: {
3:   for( list.StartIterator(); list.IsIteratorValid(); list.MoveIteratorForward() )
4:     list.GetCurrentItem().m_iLife += life;
5: }
```

A reference to a list is passed in to the routine, so that you can operate on any list, and not worry about the destructor or copy constructor being called on the passed-in list. The initialization part of the `for` loop on line 3 is important to note, because it resets the internal iterator of the list to the beginning again. If any other routines elsewhere were using the iterator at the same time, they are out of luck!

CAUTION

Because you are using a simple internal iterator, don't count on your iterator being valid when you let another routine or function touch the list.

The iteration condition of the `for` loop uses the `IsValidIterator` routine to see whether the iterator is valid, then continues on with the loop if it is, or exits if it is not. The great thing about this is that it even works with an empty list. The `for` statement will see that the iterator is invalid (remember, if a list is empty, the iterator is always invalid) and immediately jump out, doing nothing.

The last part of line 3 is important. It moves the iterator forward to the next item after the body of the `for` loop is completed.

Line 4 retrieves the current game player, and modifies his life variable. Remember, you can do this because `GetCurrentItem` returns a reference, and since the reference acts like a pointer, the game player stored in the node is modified without the end user actually ever having to touch the node class at all! Pretty neat, huh?

The other two iteration routines are complex, and will be discussed next in their own sections.

Inserting into a List

The InsertItem routine inserts a player object into a new node, and then inserts the new node directly after the current node. If the current node is invalid, it reverts to the AppendItem routine to add the item at the end of the list. For a singly linked list, the operation looks like Figure 17.2.

Here's the code listing:

```
void mrListGP::InsertItem( mrGamePlayer player ) {
  mrListNodeGP* node;
  if( IsIteratorValid() ) {
    node = new mrListNodeGP;
    node->m_kPlayer = player;
    node->m_kNext = m_kCurrent->m_kNext;
    m_kCurrent->m_kNext = node;
  }
  else {
    AppendItem( player);
  }
}
```

There are two distinct cases when using this function: the iterator can be either invalid or valid. If the iterator is invalid, the routine calls the AppendItem routine and doesn't do anything else. You are interested in what happens when the iterator is valid.

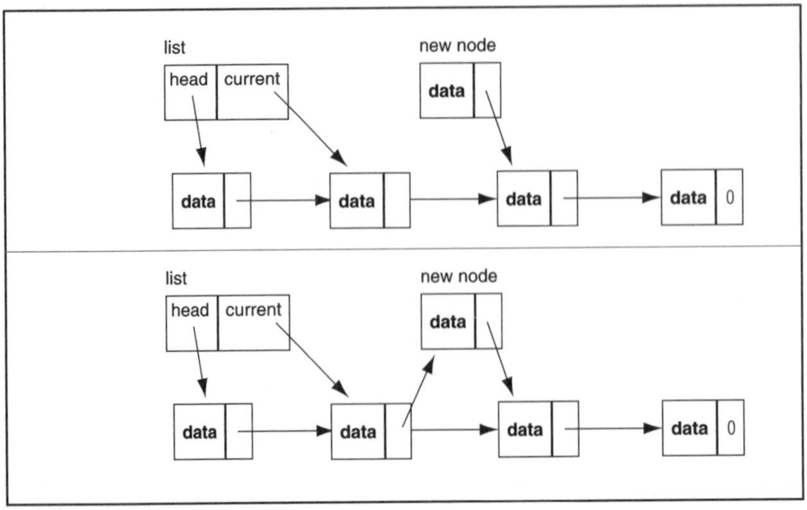

Figure 17.2

A list before and after an insertion.

At line 4, you create a new node, and put the player object into the node in line 5. Line 6 sets the new node's link pointer to point to the same thing that the current node's link is pointing to. Note that this routine handles the case where the current node is the last node in the list easily. Because the new node is inserted after the iterator, the new node will become the last node in the list, and because it copies the current node's link pointer, its pointer will be zero as well.

Line 7 tells the current node that it will now point to the new node.

Note that the iterator still points to the same item it did before the operation.

Appending Items to a List

Appending an item to the list is as easy as inserting an item into the middle of the list.

```
 1: void mrListGP::AppendItem( mrGamePlayer player ) {
 2:  mrListNodeGP* node = new mrListNodeGP;
 3:  node->m_kNext = NULL;
 4:  node->m_kPlayer = player;
 5:  mtListNodeGP* temp = m_kHead;
 6:  if( NULL != temp ) {
 7:   while( NULL != temp->m_kNext )
 8:    temp = temp->m_kNext;
 9:   temp->m_kNext = node;
10:  }
11:  else {
12:   m_kHead = node;
13:  }
14: }
```

As before, you first create a new node and set all of its info (lines 2 through 4), only this time, since you know that the new node will be the last node, its link pointer is automatically set to zero.

There are two cases in this routine as well: The list could be empty or the list could be non-empty. If the list is not empty, you need to find the last node in the list, using a `while` loop (lines 7 and 8). This loop runs through the list until it finds a node whose link pointer is `NULL` (which means that it is the last node in the list), and when it finds that node, it appends the new node after it (line 9).

If the list is empty, the routine sets the head node to point to the new node.

Like I said earlier, it's pretty simple.

Deleting a Node from a List

Deleting a node from a list is conceptually simple, but the speed at which it takes place depends on how the list is structured. Singly linked lists are much worse at removing nodes than doubly linked lists. See Figure 17.3.

The node before the node to be removed needs to be told to point to the node after the node to remove, and the iterator pointer is moved forward. Visually simple, there is, however, a major caveat in the singly linked list version. The algorithm needs to know what the previous node is, but singly linked lists do not maintain this information. I can hear some of you groaning right now. Yes, implementing a remove algorithm for a singly linked list requires a time-consuming loop.

```
 1: void mrListGP::RemoveCurrentItem() {
 2:  mrListNodeGP* previous;
 3:  if( NULL == m_kCurrent )
 4:   return;
 5:  if( m_kHead == m_kCurrent ) {
 6:   m_kCurrent = m_kHead->m_kNext;
 7:   delete m_kHead;
 8:   m_kHead = m_kCurrent;
 9:  }
10:  else {
11:   previous = m_kHead;
12:   while( previous->m_kNext != m_kCurrent )
13:    previous = previous->m_kNext;
14:   m_kCurrent = m_kCurrent->m_kNext;
15:   delete previous->m_kNext;
16:   previous->m_kNext = m_kCurrent;
17:  }
18: }
```

First off, you must make the routine do nothing when the iterator is invalid. So on line 3, you check whether the iterator is invalid, and if so, you exit out of the routine on line 4.

Now, there are two cases when removing a node. The first case is when the node to be removed is the head node of the list. This case is handled on lines 5 through 9. You move the iterator forward to the next item in the list on line 6, delete the node on line 7, and make the head pointer point to the current node, which is now the new head node of the list.

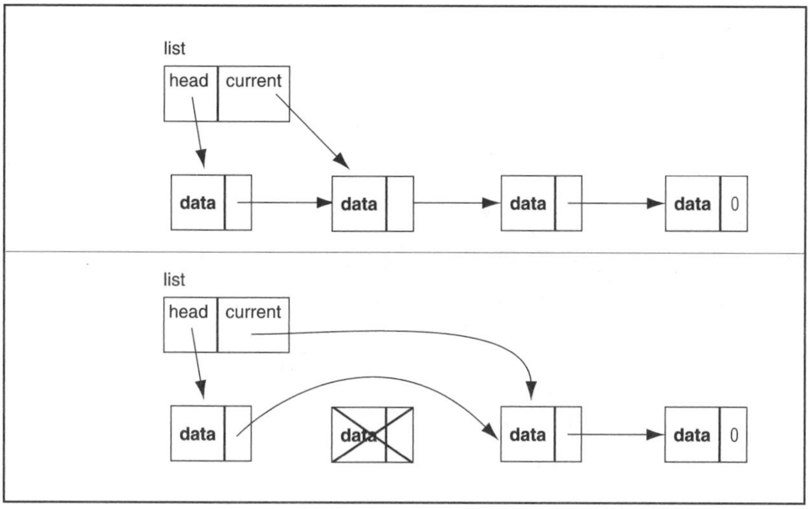

Figure 17.3

Removing a node from a list.

The second case happens when the node to be removed has a previous node. As I stated a minute ago, the node to be removed has no idea which node is its parent in a singly linked list, so you must search for it. This search is accomplished on lines 11 through 13. You start at the head node in the list (line 11), and loop through until you find the node that points to the current node. When that node is found, you can move the current pointer forward to the next node (line 14), delete `previous`'s next node (line 15), and then update `previous` so that its next node is now the current iterator.

Doubly Linked Lists

Now, I'm not going to spend as much time on doubly linked lists as I did with singly, because almost all of the algorithms and concepts on a doubly linked list are the same. A doubly linked list is essentially a singly linked list in which each node maintains a pointer to the previous node in addition to the next node. Depending on the size of the data you are storing in each node, this could potentially increase the size of each node by up to 50% (assuming that the size of the data in the node is at least the size of a pointer), because you are adding another pointer to each node. Usually, a doubly linked list class adds another iterator traversal routine:

```
void MoveIteratorBack()
```

Because each doubly linked list node has a pointer to the previous node, it is possible to move back and forth while iterating. This is the main advantage of using a doubly linked list as opposed to a singly linked list. Because you can move backward in a doubly linked list, most implementations also maintain a pointer to the last node in the list, allowing you to easily reverse-iterate through the list. Depending on your needs, you may or may not want a last-node pointer.

Modifying the Algorithms for Doubly Linked Lists

The only algorithms that need to be modified are the `InsertItem`, `RemoveCurrentItem`, and `AppendItem` routines. `InsertItem` and `AppendItem` only need to set the previous node pointer of the new node added, a simple addition. `RemoveCurrentItem` actually gets simplified. Remember how you needed to add a section of code that searches for the previous node? It's no longer needed.

Circular Lists

This popular variation of the list structure can be applied to both the singly linked lists and the doubly linked lists. Instead of the last node pointing to null, the last node instead points to the first node in the list (hence the name circular), and in doubly linked lists, the first node's `previous` pointer points to the last node in the list. This method may initially seem to create more work, but in actuality, it allows for some assumptions to be made when removing nodes, especially with doubly linked lists. Figure 17.4 shows how it simplifies the routine.

Node 'b' is the one you will try to remove. So, what happens when 'c' or 'a' doesn't actually exist in a non-circular list? Remember, when removing a node from a doubly linked list, both the previous and next node must be notified that an adjacent node has changed. However, since 'c' or 'a' might be null, an `if` statement must be added to check whether they exist or not, and then only after checking their existence, can the pointers be modified.

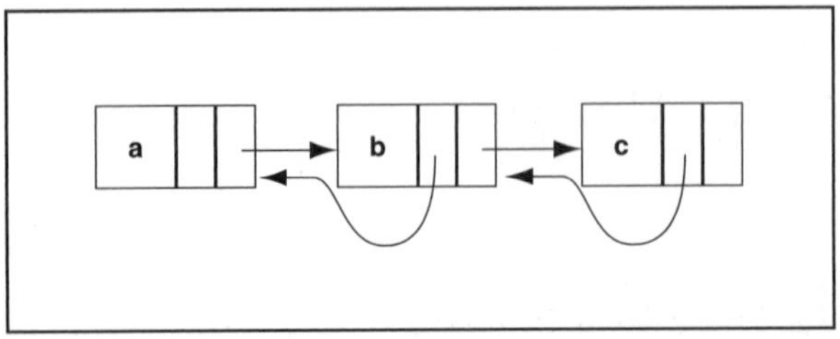

Figure 17.4

Circular doubly linked list.

In a circular list implementation, both of those nodes will always exist, and the `if` statement can be removed. You can always assume that both the previous and next nodes will be valid. In fact, the only special condition that needs to be considered in a circular list is when the node being removed is the head node, leaving only one `if` statement in the entire process, instead of four, as with the standard doubly linked list removal.

Note that circular doubly linked lists do not need to maintain a last-node pointer, because it would be redundant and would cause the routine to become more complex than it needs to be.

While it seems like a trivial gain in performance, you must remember that many `if()` statements on modern processors slow down the program immensely, especially on Pentium and Athlon processors. I won't go into the specifics here, because I just wanted you to know that these structures exist. In fact, the STL (Standard Template Library) implementation of lists uses a Circular Doubly Linked List data structure as its basis.

Advantages of Lists

Advantages of all linked lists:

- Fast insertions
- Virtually unlimited storage space

Singly linked list advantages:

- Smaller than doubly linked lists

Doubly linked list advantages:

- Two-way traversal
- Fast removals

Circular list advantages:

- Faster insertions and removals due to assumptions that can be made

Disadvantages of Lists

Disadvantages of all linked lists:

- Sequential access only.
- Use more memory than arrays because of the pointers.

Singly linked list disadvantages:

- Only one-way traversing.
- Slow removals.

Doubly linked list disadvantages:

- Uses more space than a singly linked list.

Circular linked list disadvantages:

- It is more difficult to tell when an iterator goes past the end of the list.

Trees

Trees are an interesting part of computer science. Because they are modeled on their real-world equivalent (that is, biological trees), they are somewhat simple to understand. When you look at a tree (from the ground up, just ignore everything underground), it has a single trunk, and off of that trunk come several branches. Off of each branch there are even more branches, and off of these branches there are twigs, and off of the twigs are leaves. If you break off a branch, it essentially becomes a mini-tree; the branch becomes the new trunk.

Because of this, trees are called recursive or fractal structures. A *recursive structure* basically repeats itself on many different levels, exactly like a tree does. Trees have many uses within the realm of computer programming, and some of the most important include program compilers, advanced artificial intelligence, and path finding routes for games. You'll be looking at two simple trees here: The general tree and the binary search tree (BST).

The basic underlying structure of a tree, just like a list, is the node. In this case, instead of each node pointing to the next node in a list, each node contains a pointer to each of its child nodes (branches in the tree). Figure 17.5 shows a sample tree.

The first thing you may notice is that the tree is upside-down. No, folks, that is not a mistake, but rather intentional. Computer trees are drawn with the roots on the top and the leaves on the bottom. It's a standard drawing convention that computer scientists have adopted, and rarely will you find trees drawn differently. You see, a tree is a hierarchical structure; therefore, the most important information in a tree is at the top. Think of a family tree, for example. Putting your great grandfather and great grandmother at the top makes sense.

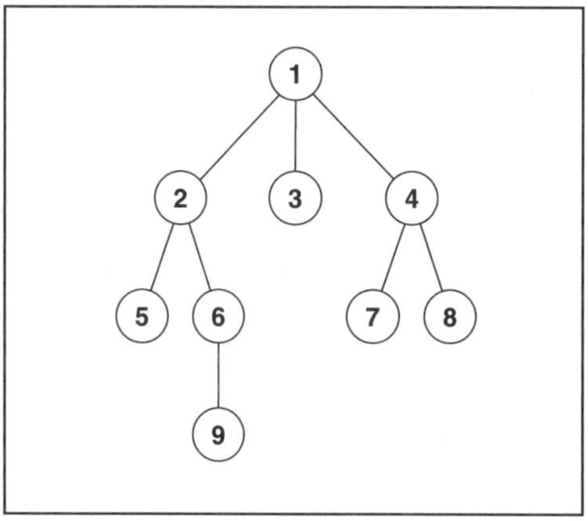

Figure 17.5

Example of a tree.

Now for some terminology: As I've said before, the root is at the top of the tree, and in your sample tree, node 1 is the root. Since a tree is hierarchical, the nodes all have a parent-child relationship with each other. Therefore, you can say that nodes 2, 3, and 4 are all child nodes to node 1, and that node 1 is their parent. Nodes that have the same parents as each other are called sibling nodes. For example, nodes 2, 3, and 4 are all siblings of each other. There is one other type of node in a tree: a leaf node. A leaf node is a node that has no children, so in your sample tree, 5, 9, 3, 7, and 8 are all child nodes.

General Trees

A general tree is a very flexible tree. General trees are also commonly known as linked trees. Basically, a general tree is a tree in which any node can have any number of children. Since each node has no idea how many children it might have at any given time, it is best to use a flexible and easily extendible container to store pointers to its children. Where have you heard these exact features listed before? That's right, lists! Each general tree node has a list of child pointers, looking something like Figure 17.6.

For your general tree implementation, you'll be using a simple singly linked list to store child node pointers. In Figure 17.6, the circles represent the actual tree nodes, and the boxes represent list nodes containing child pointers. While this may seem complex at first, you can easily think about it this way: Each node contains a singly linked list, and each node in the list points to a tree node. Let's

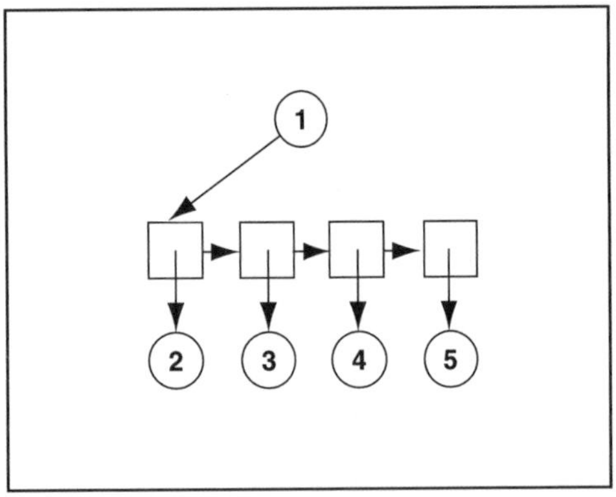

Figure 17.6

Innards of a simple general tree.

look at the structure of a node in C++ (you'll be using integers as the basis of your tree class):

```
class mrGenTreeNodeInt
{
 mrInt m_iValue;
 mrListNodeGenTreeInt* m_kFirstChild;
 mrListNodeGenTreeInt* m_kCurrent;
};
```

So you combine the features of a linked list and a tree into the node structure: the node acts like a linked list, pointing to a list node, but it also acts like a node itself, containing a single data element.

Now, you need to make the `mrListNodeGenTreeInt` (`List` node containing a pointer to a general tree of type `Int`) class, which is exactly like the list node class you developed for the singly linked list in the previous section:

```
class mrListNodeGenTreeInt
{
 mrGenTreeNodeInt* m_kNode;
 mrListNodeGenTreeInt* m_kNext;
};
```

These are simple structures, of course, but the concepts may be difficult to understand. The easiest way to think about it is to study Figure 17.6.

Now, remember when you made the linked list class, you had a separate class that contained a pointer to the first node in the list? You can do the same thing with a tree, and make a simple class that maintains a pointer to the root of the tree, but you aren't going to do that here. The main reason for making a simple container for the nodes was so that you can have an easy way to traverse, insert, and delete nodes from a list. An abstract container like that is not needed when dealing with trees, because a tree is recursive and its access mechanisms are much more complicated and may differ in each implementation. Each tree node is essentially a small tree of its own, so you build trees by inserting sub-trees into the child list of each node. There is no intuitive interface you could give to a general tree container.

The functions that will make up your general tree node are similar to those of a linked list:

```
void Start();
void MoveForward();
mrGenTreeNodeInt* GetChild();
mrBool32 IsChildValid();
void RemoveCurrentChild();
void AppendChild( mrGenTreeNodeInt* child );
```

I've removed the `InsertChild` routine for simplicity. Most of the time, there is no need to include advanced insertion options, like in a linked list, because sibling order relationships are not nearly as important in a tree as in a list. Instead, the hierarchical parent-child relationships are much more important. In the end, it all comes down to need. If you end up having a tree that needs to be able to insert children into the middle of its child list, you should program the routine using the singly linked list insertion algorithm from the last section. The following code listing is similar to a singly linked list:

```
 /* Move the child pointer to the first child */
void mrGenTreeNodeInt::Start()
{
 m_kCurrent = m_kFirstChild;
}
 /* Move the current child pointer to the next child */
void mrGenTreeNodeInt::MoveForward()
{
 if( NULL != m_kCurrent )
 m_kCurrent = m_kCurrent->m_kNext;
}
 /* return a pointer to the current child node */
mrGenTreeNodeInt* mrGenTreeNodeInt::GetChild()
```

```
{
 return m_kCurrent->m_kNode;
}
 /* determine whether the current child is valid or not */
mrBool32 mrGenTreeNodeInt::IsChildValid()
{
 if( NULL != m_kCurrent )
  return mrTrue;
 return mrFalse;
}
 /* remove the current node */
void mrGenTreeNodeInt::RemoveCurrentChild() {
 mrListNodeGenTreeInt* previous;
 if( NULL == m_kCurrent )
  return;
 if( m_kFirstChild == m_kCurrent ) {
  m_kCurrent = m_kFirstChild->m_kNext;
  delete m_kFirstChild;
  m_kFirstChild = m_kCurrent;
 }
 else {
  previous = m_kFirstChild;
  while( previous->m_kNext != m_kCurrent )
   previous = previous->m_kNext;
  m_kCurrent = m_kCurrent->m_kNext;
  delete previous->m_kNext;
  previous->m_kNext = m_kCurrent;
 }
}
 /* append a child node to the end of the list */
void mrGenTreeNodeInt::AppendChild( mrGenTreeNodeInt* child ) {
 mrListNodeGenTreeInt* node = new mrListNodeGenTreeInt;
 node->m_kNext = NULL;
 node->m_kNode = child;
 mrListNodeGenTreeInt* temp = m_kFirstChild;
 if( NULL != temp ) {
  while( NULL != temp->m_kNext )
   temp = temp->m_kNext;
  temp->m_kNext = node;
 }
```

```
else {
  m_kFirstChild = node;
 }
}
```

All the same rules apply to this code as with the singly linked list class, except for one important fact: when you delete a child node from a list using the `RemoveChild()` routine, you merely remove the child from the list, but the entire sub-tree still exists. If you forget to store a pointer to a child node before you remove it from a child list, you will end up with a potentially dangerous memory leak. You must remember to delete it manually, later.

Constructing a General Tree

Two methods are used to build a general tree, depending on what you are using it for. The most popular method is called the Top-Down approach. In this method, you build a tree by creating the topmost nodes first, and then adding children. Here is how you would build Figure 17.5 using the top-down approach:

```
 1: mrGenTreeNodeInt root( 1 );
 2: mrGenTreeNodeInt* temp = 0;
 3: root.AppendChild( new mrGenTreeNodeInt( 2 ) );
 4: root.AppendChild( new mrGenTreeNodeInt( 3 ) );
 5: root.AppendChild( new mrGenTreeNodeInt( 4 ) );
 6: root.Start();
 7: temp = root.GetChild();
 8: temp->AppendChild( new mrGenTreeNodeInt( 5 ) );
 9: temp->AppendChild( new mrGenTreeNodeInt( 6 ) );
10: temp->Start();
11: temp->MoveForward();
12: temp = temp->GetChild();
13: temp->AppendChild( new mrGenTreeNodeInt( 9 ) );
14: root.MoveForward();
15: root.MoveForward();
16: temp = root.GetChild();
17: temp->AppendChild( new mrGenTreeNodeInt( 7 ) );
18: temp->AppendChild( new mrGenTreeNodeInt( 8 ) );
```

At line 1, you create the root node with the value 1 in it, and keep track of it. You create a temporary variable (line 2) to be used for inserting child nodes into the tree which aren't directly connected to the root.

In lines 3 through 5, you simply append nodes 2, 3, and 4 to the root, making them children. Then, starting at line 6, you make the tree's child iterator begin at the first child (node 2), and make `temp` point to that node. In lines 8 and 9, you add the children of node 2, namely nodes 5 and 6. Again, you repeat the process, and use the iterator of node 2 to retrieve a pointer to node 6 (lines 10 through 12), then add node 9 as a child to node 6 (line 13). Now, since this branch is completely built, you can skip back up to the root node and move on to the next child. Note how the child pointer in the root node still points to node 2; this will become important later when you want to traverse the tree using the recursive tree traversal routines. So, at lines 14 and 15, you skip over node 3 because it has no children, and make `temp` point to node 4. Then you add nodes 7 and 8 to the child list of node 4, and you are done.

This method of construction is used most often, and makes the most sense when building trees. Think of it in terms of a family tree: You start out with a person (the root), and when that person has a child, you append it to his or her child list. Then you continue adding children in this fashion, and pretty soon the children of the root are having children of their own, and adding them to their child lists, and so on.

The other method of making a tree is to use the Bottom-Up approach: You build the sub-trees first, then add them to their parent node after the sub-tree is complete. I'm not going to show an example of this method, simply because it's messy to do in a normal routine like the preceding one. Mostly, bottom-up construction is used in recursive tree building algorithms (such as algebra compilers), where you make the leaves first and work your way up to the root.

Traversing a General Tree

There are two methods for traversing a tree so that you are guaranteed to reach every node in the tree. Both are recursive in nature, so their implementation is somewhat simple. However, if you do not have a firm grasp on recursion yet, then this might be a bit confusing at first.

The first method of traversal is called the Pre-Order traversal. The basic premise of this traversal is to process the item in the current node, and then process call the pre-order routine on each of its children. Here is the pre-order traversal code to print out the items in a tree:

```
void mrGenTreeNodeInt::PreOrder()
{
```

```
 cout << m_iValue << ", ";
 for( Start(); IsChildValid(); MoveForward() )
  GetChild()->PreOrder();
}
```

The routine, when called on the root node, proceeds to print out the value at the root node, and then iterates through each of its children, calling the same routine. When executed on the tree from Figure 17.5, it will give you the sequence: 1, 2, 5, 6, 9, 3, 4, 7, 8. Trace through the figure with your finger, and you'll see how recursion works. Essentially, the pre-order routine called on any sub-tree will give you a segment of the final sequence. For example, PreOrder called on node 2 will give you: 2, 5, 6, 9.

The Post-Order traversal is very similar to Pre-Order. The only difference lies in how the processing takes place:

```
void mrGenTreeNodeInt::PostOrder()
{
 for( Start(); IsChildValid(); MoveForward() )
   GetChild()->PostOrder();
 cout << m_iValue << ", ";
}
```

In this case, the child nodes are processed first, and the data at the current node is processed after the children. Using this traversal method on your sample tree gives you the sequence: 5, 9, 6, 2, 3, 7, 8, 4, 1.

You've only done simple traversals here to print out the items in a tree, but in reality, you can do any processing you'd like within these traversal methods. One thing you must note from these routines is that they reset the child pointer, and they rely on the child pointer for accurately traversing the tree. Think of it this way: When a PreOrder is called on node 1, its child pointer is reset to point to node 2, even if it was previously pointing to something else. This method totally resets every child pointer for every node in the entire tree. Also note that you should not modify the child pointers inside the algorithms unless you need to. If, while you are processing node 1, you move the child pointer forward by one child (maybe inadvertently by calling a subroutine which does so), you will end up skipping over an entire child branch during the processing, and that will surely mess things up. Even worse, you might inadvertently reset the child pointer to the first child node again, and in this case you will end up with an infinite loop that will never finish, thus causing your program to lock up. Creating a solution to this problem is somewhat simple; instead of using the built-in iterator routines, you may make your own temporary variable to keep track of which child node is being processed at each level. I'll leave this as a user exercise.

General Tree Destructor

Now, there will be times when you want to delete a tree and its entire sub-tree, as well. Lucky for you, when you delete a tree node, its defined behavior also recursively deletes all of its children, and all of its children's children, and so forth. This also means you must be careful, because if you delete a node, then all of its children will be deleted, even if you intend to save them for later use. Before deleting any tree node, you must be careful to remove any children you wish to keep first. Here is what the algorithm looks like:

```
1: mrGenTreeNodeInt::~mrGenTreeNodeInt()
2: {
3:  Start();
4:  while( IsChildValid() )
5:  {
6:    delete GetChild();
7:    RemoveCurrentChild();
8:  }
9: }
```

At line 3, you set the child pointer to the beginning. Since you are in the process of deleting the node, it does not matter if you modify the child pointer anyway. Now, you loop through each child node, deleting first the actual tree node and then the list node. Here's the clever part: Each time you delete a child tree node, it in turn deletes all of its children. Essentially, this routine deletes the nodes with a PostOrder algorithm. So keep in mind that when you delete a node, all of its child nodes are deleted as well.

Uses of General Trees

General trees are used for all kinds of applications. As I've said before, they can be used to represent family trees or other structures that are hierarchical in nature. They can be used in compilers and computer game AIs, or for storing level structures and maps. A general tree is just what its name implies: general. You can use it for whatever purpose you feel is appropriate. When you find something that needs to be stored in a hierarchy (maybe the pecking order of bad guys in a game?), chances are good that a general tree is your best bet!

Binary Search Trees

Binary trees are a type of tree that each branch (child) is divided in two, thus the name binary. This decreases the time needed for traversal.

A Primer on Binary Trees

Before you get into what a binary search tree (BST) is exactly, you need to understand what a binary tree is. A binary tree is similar to a general tree, except that a binary tree can only have up to two children at any given time, hence the name binary. Because a binary tree has a discrete number of children, you do not need to use a flexible container to store the children. Instead you can just use two pointers in each node. You have special names for those two pointers: the Left pointer and the Right pointer. Figure 17.7 shows a binary tree.

The basic naming concepts still apply: 1 is the root node; 2 and 3 are children of the root node; and 4, 5, 6, and 7 are all leaf nodes. Node 2 is a left child, 3 is a right child, and so on.

Here's what a binary tree node looks like in C++:

```
class mrBinaryTreeNodeInt
{
public:
 mrInt m_iValue;
 mrBinaryTreeNodeInt* m_kLeft;
 mrBinaryTreeNodeInt* m_kRight;
};
```

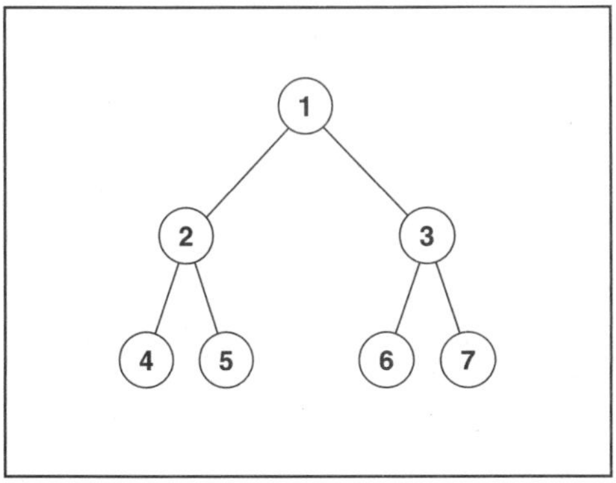

Figure 17.7

Sample binary tree.

Nothing really spectacular here. This node structure also stores an integer and has two discrete child pointers.

What Is a Binary Search Tree?

A binary search tree is used for what its name implies: searching. A BST arranges data in a manner that makes it more efficient to search through than a linear list or array.

Simply put, a Binary Search Tree is a binary tree, but it is not arranged in any sort of hierarchical manner, like trees typically are. Instead, a binary search tree has specific rules for inserting, searching for, and removing items. A BST attempts to split the data it will contain into halves so that when you try to find data within the tree, you can find it much faster than searching through each index in a sequential container.

There is one rule that must be followed at all times in a binary search tree: Every item in the left sub-tree of any given node in the tree must be less than the value in the node, and every item in the right sub-tree of any given node in the tree must be greater than the value in the node. Before you build a BST, check out Figure 17.8 to see what one looks like.

Starting at the root node, you'll notice that every item in the left part of the tree is less than 4, and every item to the right is greater than 4. The same applies to nodes 2 and 4, and if 1, 3, 5, or 7 had any children, they would also follow the BST rule.

Now, previously, you looked at lists and general trees. The list class you created had a separate container class that managed the nodes for you, making insertions, itera-

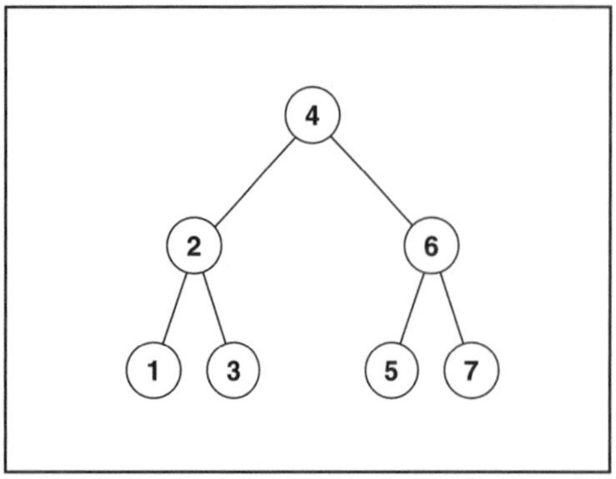

Figure 17.8

Sample binary search tree.

tions, and removals easier. Remember also that you decided that such a container class was not really necessary with general trees? A binary search tree, unlike the general tree, will have need for an abstracted container class, because the BST class has a specific method of access. Your BST class will contain a pointer to the root node and an item counter:

```
class mrBSTInt
{
private:
 mrBinaryTreeNodeInt* m_kRoot;
 mrInt m_iCount;
};
```

Again, a fairly simple class. Notice how you made the data items private in this class; this is because you want to hide the implementation of the class from users of the class. The users only care about using the provided interface:

```
 mrBool32 Insert( mrInt value );
 mrBool32 Search( mrInt value );
 mrBool32 Remove( mrInt value );
```

Routines will enable you to insert, search for, and remove data from the tree. Each item returns a boolean value, depending on whether the operation has failed or completed successfully. A return value of `mrTrue` means that the operation was completed successfully, and `mrFalse` means a failure.

Searching a Binary Search Tree

The recurring theme when dealing with trees and recursion is Divide and Conquer. Indeed, recursion and recursive structures aim to divide problems up into smaller problems. Say you want to search for the item 1 in your sample binary search tree. You would first start by examining the root node. Since you see that the value at the root is 4, and you know that everything in the left sub-tree is less than 4, you can safely assume that 1 is not contained within the right sub-tree of 4, effectively eliminating half of the entire tree in one comparison. So now that you know that 1 is less than 4, you travel down to the left, and again examine the node. This time, you see that the node is 2, and since 1 is less than 2, you can again, eliminate the entire right sub-tree of node 2. You go left one more level, and there you find the number 1! Out of a seven-item tree, you only needed to examine three items to find your desired item. You can plainly see how this algorithm divides the tree to shorten processing times, when compared to an ordinary list or array.

Three comparisons may not seem to be that many fewer than seven, but the beauty of a binary search tree appears later, when you construct huge trees with many levels. For example, if you were to create a balanced 4-level tree, you could store 15 items in it, but finding any single item would only take 4 comparisons. At level 5, you could store 31 items, and only need 5 comparisons. Better yet, in a 10-level tree, you could store 1,023 items, and only need to compare 10 items to find something!

So what happens when you try searching for an item that doesn't exist in the tree? Look for the number 8, for example. This time, 8 is greater than the root node, so you travel down to the right. 8 is also greater than 6, so you go right again. Finally, you compare 8 again and see that it is still greater than 7, so you go down to the right, but there is no right child! This means, of course, that the number 8 does not exist within the tree. Whenever the search algorithm reaches a `NULL` node, then it can exit and say that it has not found the node.

Let's take a look at the search algorithm:

```
 1: mrBool32 mrBSTInt::Search( mrInt value )
 2: {
 3:  mrBinaryTreeNodeInt* node = m_kRoot;
 4:  while( NULL != node )
 5:  {
 6:   if( value == node->m_iValue )
 7:    return mrTrue;
 8:   if( value < node->m_iValue )
 9:    node = node->m_kLeft;
10:   else
11:   node = node->m_kRight;
12:  }
13:  return mrFalse;
14: }
```

So, on line 3, you create a temporary node pointer and make it point to the root, because that is where you start searching. Then, on line 4, you start the `while` loop. Note that whenever a `NULL` node is reached, the algorithm exits and returns `mrFalse`. This takes care of the case where the tree is empty, so you don't need to add in any special-case code to take care of this occurrence.

Next, on line 6, you compare the value you are searching for and the value in the current node. If they are the same, you return true, because the algorithm is complete. If they are not equal, however, you compare the values again. If the value you are searching for is less than the value in the current node, you set the current node pointer to point to its left child, and if the value you are searching for is greater than the value in the current node, you set the current node pointer to point to its right child.

Inserting into a Binary Search Tree

Inserting an item into a BST is a simple and straightforward process. The insertion algorithm is similar to the search algorithm, except that when you find a NULL node, you create a new node and place it in that spot. Now, when the algorithm finds an item of the same value already in the tree, it exits, because binary search trees usually only allow one instance of an item in the tree.

```
mrBool32 mrBSTInt::Insert( mrInt value )
{
 mrBinaryTreeNodeInt* node = m_kRoot;
 if( NULL == m_kRoot )
  m_kRoot = new mrBinaryTreeNodeInt( value );
 else
 {
  while( NULL != node )
  {
   if( value == node->m_iValue )
    return mrFalse;
   else if( value < node->m_iValue )
   {
    if( NULL == node->m_kLeft )
    {
     node->m_kLeft = new mrBinaryTreeNodeInt( value );
     node = NULL;
    }
    else
     node = node->m_kLeft;
   }
   else
   {
    if( NULL == node->m_kRight )
    {
     node->m_kRight = new mrBinaryTreeNodeInt( value );
     node = NULL;
```

```
28:       }
29:       else
30:         node = node->m_kRight;
31:     }
32:   }
33: }
34: m_iCount++;
35: return mrTrue;
36: }
```

In this algorithm, you need to check whether the root node is NULL or not. If the root is null, then you need to create a new node (line 5) and make that the new root. If the root node already exists, then you do a search through the tree just like the search algorithm. This time, however, if you find that the value is already in the tree, you exit, returning mrFalse for failure (lines 10 and 11).

At line 12, you check to see whether the value you are inserting is less than the value in the current node. If so, you need to check to see whether its left child exists. When searching, you just went down one level, but this time, you need to check whether the children are NULL first. If so, you create a new node with the given value, and set that as the new left child, and set the current node to NULL so you can exit from the routine. If the left child is not NULL, then you set the current node pointer to point to its left child, just like the regular search routine (line 20). You repeat the same process if the value is greater than the current node on lines 24 through 30.

When the loop finally exits, it will go to line 24, and the item count is incremented by one, and mrTrue is returned to signify that the insertion routine was a success.

Removing a Value from a Binary Search Tree

Removing items is perhaps the most difficult part of making a binary search tree. Removing a leaf node or a node, which contains only one child, is no problem for the algorithm. The real problem occurs when you remove a node that has two children. Because you need to keep the BST property of the tree valid, you can't just pick any node within the two sub-trees to move up and take the place of the node to remove.

Removing a leaf node is a simple process: Find the node and remove it from its parents' child pointers. Because the node has no children, it can be deleted, and the operation is completed. Figure 17.9 is the same tree as Figure 17.8, but with node 7, a leaf node, removed.

Now, let's say you wanted to remove node 6 from Figure 17.9. It has one child, so instead of just deleting the node, you need to move up its child sub-tree one level, and then delete the node. In this case, you move 5 up to be the new right child of 4, and then delete 6, thus creating the tree in Figure 17.10.

Now comes the hard part. Removing a node that already has two child nodes is somewhat difficult. You cannot just move up one of the sub-trees, because either or both of them may also have two child trees of their own. Let's say you want to remove node 4 from Figure 17.11:

Notice that by removing node 4, you leave a huge gap within the tree. The question is, which node do you chose to move up to take 4's place? You cannot move up 2 or 6, because both of them have two children of their own, and you would need

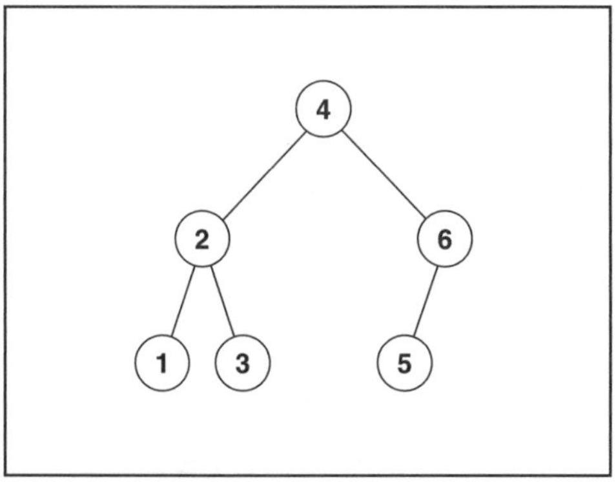

Figure 17.9

Removing a leaf node.

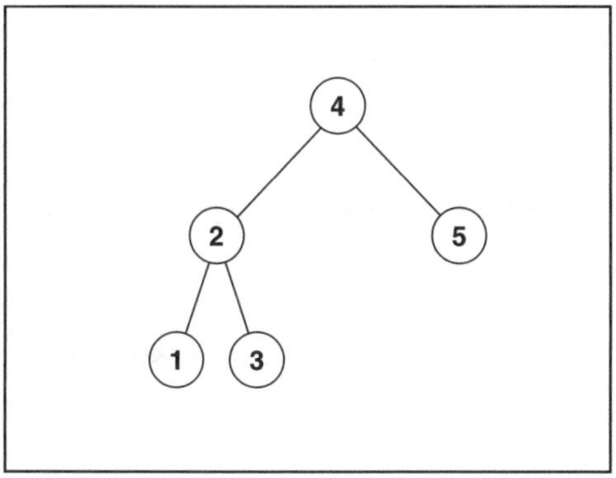

Figure 17.10

Removing a node with one child.

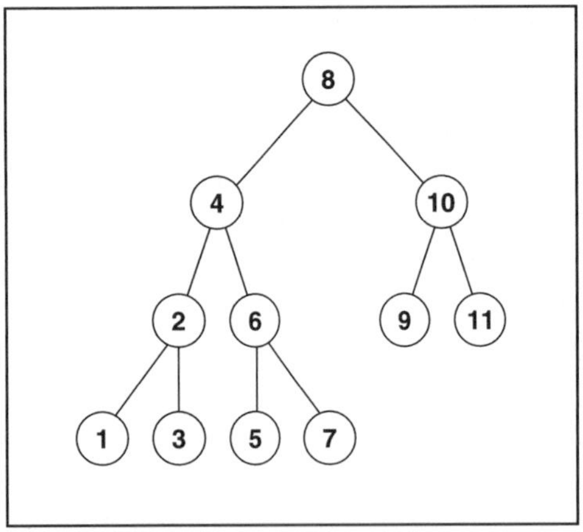

Figure 17.11

Larger binary search tree.

to find a place for the other node, which is a complex and time-consuming task. Considering that the rest of the binary search tree is designed to be simple and fast, this method simply will not do for your purposes.

You need to find a node in the sub-tree that can be moved up easily, thus this node should only have zero or one children. Luckily for you, several things can be assumed when using a binary search tree, thus making your search for a node, which can be moved up, easy and methodical. The rule that you will be taking advantage of is this: *The largest node in any given sub-tree is guaranteed to have at most one child.* Think about this for a moment. Due to the BST rules, the largest node in a sub-tree cannot have a right child, since any item in the right child would need to be larger than the data in the largest node. A contradiction occurs, and if the largest node in any given sub-tree has a right child, then it is an invalid BST.

So, using this information, you find the largest node in the left sub-tree of the node you are removing, remove that node, and move it up to take the place of the node you are removing. In your sample trees case, you will move up the largest node in 4's left sub-tree, which is 3.

The first thing you need to do is find the largest node. Knowing the rules of a BST, you can easily see that the largest node in a sub-tree is the right-most node of that tree. That is, you travel down to the right from the sub-tree's root until you hit the last node. Since 2 is the root of the sub-tree that you are searching, you travel down to the right until you reach the last node, which is 3. Now you need to move node 3 up in place of 4.

Again, you see that all you need to do is remove node 3 using the leaf-node removal algorithm, and replace 4.

Now let's look at the code required to accomplish all this. You'll split the removal algorithms into two algorithms: The algorithm that removes nodes with zero or one children, and the algorithm that removes nodes with two children. Both of these algorithms will take as parameters a pointer to the parent of the node to remove, and a Boolean which determines whether the child to remove is the left or right child. If `NULL` is passed in as the parent pointer, that means that the root node is to be removed.

Here is the general purpose remove routine, which will determine which of the two removal algorithms to call.

```
mrBool32 mrBSTInt::Remove( mrInt value )
{
 mrBinaryTreeNodeInt* parent = 0;
 mrBinaryTreeNodeInt* node = m_kRoot;
 mrBool32 done = mrFalse;
 mrBool32 isLeft = mrFalse;
 while( !done )
 {
  if( NULL == node )
   return mrFalse;
  if( value == node->m_iValue )
   done = mrTrue;
  else
  {
   parent = node;
   if( value < node->m_iValue )
    node = node->m_kLeft;
   else
    node = node->m_kRight;
  }
 }
 if( NULL != parent )
 {
  if( parent->m_kLeft == node )
   isLeft = mrTrue;
 }
 if( NULL != node->m_kLeft && NULL != node->m_kRight )
```

```
28:    Remove2( parent, isLeft );
29:   else
30;    Remove01( parent, isLeft );
31:   node->m_kLeft = 0;
32:   node->m_kRight = 0;
33:   delete node;
34:   m_iCount--;
35:   return mrTrue;
36: }
```

This routine does three things: First it finds the node to remove using the standard BST search algorithm. Then it determines which of the two removal algorithms to call, and finally it deletes the actual node.

Because your binary tree node class is simple, and does not maintain pointers to the parent node, this complicates things somewhat. You need to keep track of the parent of the node to remove as you move down in the tree. You'll notice that this is a similar approach to what you did with singly linked lists. Because the nodes do not know who their parents are, you need to keep track of those. So, the local variables `parent` (line 3) and `node` (line 4) keep track of the parent of the node to remove, and the node to remove, respectively. On line 5, you declare a Boolean that keeps track of whether or not you have found the node to remove yet, and another Boolean on line 6 is used to keep track of whether the node to remove is a left child or a right child of the parent.

On line 7, you begin the search algorithm, and continue looping until you either find the node to remove or reach a null node. If you reach a null node, you just exit out with a failure (lines 9 and 10), because you cannot remove a node if it does not exist.

Line 11 detects whether you have found the node to remove, and if so, it sets the `done` Boolean to true. If not, you reset the parent node to point to the current node, compare the value you are searching for at the current node, and move down to the left or right child depending on how they compare.

At line 22, you have found the node to be removed. So you determine whether that node is a left child or a right child. The special case is when the parent node is `NULL`; that means that the node to be removed is the root node, so it cannot be a left child or a right child.

On line 27, you check the node's children. If both children are not `NULL` (that is, both children exist), then you call the algorithm to remove a node with both children: `Remove2`. If not, the node either has one or no children, so you call `Remove01`.

Although the node has been removed, it has not been deleted yet. The two removal algorithms only remove the node from the tree, but do not delete it. You'll see why you chose this method later when I explain the `Remove2()` algorithm.

At line 31 you set both of the node's children to zero. This is because of the deletion routine for trees: When a tree node is deleted, all of its sub-trees are deleted, as well. And since the sub-trees of the node might still be valid, you clear them, then finally delete the node on line 33, and return success on line 34.

Now let's look at the individual removal algorithms, starting with the simplest one first:

```
mrBinaryTreeNodeInt* mrBSTInt::Remove01( mrBinaryTreeNodeInt* parent, mrBool32
   isLeft )
{
  mrBinaryTreeNodeInt* node = 0;
  mrBinaryTreeNodeInt* child = 0;
  if( NULL == parent )
   node = m_kRoot;
  else
  {
   if( isLeft )
    node = parent->m_kLeft;
   else
    node = parent->m_kRight;
  }
  if( NULL != node->m_kLeft )
   child = node->m_kLeft;
  else
   child = node->m_kRight;
  if( NULL == parent )
  {
    m_kRoot = child;
  }
  else
  {
   if( isLeft )
    parent->m_kLeft = child;
   else
    parent->m_kRight = child;
  }
  return node;
}
```

First, let's examine the parameters. You pass in the parent node because, as I have said before, the node you want to remove does not know who its parent is, and you'll need to modify the parent node to tell it who its new child will be. Then you pass in a Boolean which determines whether the node you are removing is a left node or a right node. Using this information you can successfully perform a removal operation. Last, you return a pointer to the node you just removed. Remember, since the routine only removes the node, but does not actually delete it, you need to return a pointer so that the caller can delete it if he wants, or do other things with it. The reason you did it this way will be explained along with the explanation for the `Remove2` algorithm.

Now, the local variable `node`, defined on line 3, will keep track of the node you are going to remove. The `child` variable will keep track of the one child of the node, if it has one. On lines 5 through 13, you determine which node you are supposed to remove using the parent pointer and the `isLeft` Boolean. Then, on lines 14 through 17, you determine which of the nodes' two children are valid, if any.

At line 18, you determine whether or not the node you are removing is the root node, and if so, you set the root pointer to point to the child pointer. If the node you are removing is a leaf, then the child pointer is null, and the root is set to null also, because you are removing the last node in the tree.

If the node you are removing is not the root node, you go on and modify the parents' child pointer to point to the child node on lines 22 through 28. After that, you just return a pointer to the node you just removed.

The beauty of this algorithm is that it works perfectly in both of the cases that are passed into it. Whether the node you are removing has one child or no children at all makes no difference. Many programming books that I have seen have split this algorithm into two parts, but that is a folly in my opinion.

Here is the second removal algorithm:

```
1: mrBinaryTreeNodeInt* mrBSTInt::Remove2( mrBinaryTreeNodeInt* parent, mrBool32
   isLeft )
2: {
3:  mrBinaryTreeNodeInt* largest = 0;
4:  mrBinaryTreeNodeInt* largestparent = 0;
5:  mrBinaryTreeNodeInt* node = 0;
6:  if( NULL == parent )
7:   node = m_kRoot;
8:  else
```

```
 9:   {
10:    if( isLeft )
11:     node = parent->m_kLeft;
12:    else
13:     node = parent->m_kRight;
14:   }
15:   if( NULL == node->m_kLeft->m_kRight )
16:    largest = Remove01( node, mrTrue );
17:   else
18:   {
19:    largestparent = node;
20:    largest = node->m_kLeft;
21:    while( NULL != largest->m_kRight )
22:    {
23:     largestparent = largest;
24:     largest = largest->m_kRight;
25:    }
26:    Remove01( largestparent, mrFalse );
27:   }
28:   largest->m_kLeft = node->m_kLeft;
29:   largest->m_kRight = node->m_kRight;
30:   if( NULL == parent )
31:   {
32:    m_kRoot = largest;
33:   }
34:   else
35:   {
36:    if( isLeft )
37:     parent->m_kLeft = largest;
38:    else
39:     parent->m_kRight = largest;
40:   }
41:   return node;
42: }
```

Again, the parameters follow the same rules as the previous function. This time, you might be searching for the largest node in a sub-tree, so you need two more node pointers: `largest` and `largestparent` (lines 3 and 4). Lines 6 through 14, just like the previous function, find the appropriate node to remove based on the information passed in through the parameters.

You will now attempt to find the largest node in the left sub-tree of the node you are removing. Now, there are two cases when finding the largest node: The largest node is the root of its own sub-tree, or the largest node is further down in the sub-tree. If the largest node is the root of its own sub-tree (determined on line 15, if the left node of the node you are removing has no right child then you know immediately that it is the largest node in the sub-tree), then it is a left child, and you call the `Remove01` algorithm on it right away on line 16. If not, you then loop through the left sub-tree and find the largest node, hidden deeper. The loop takes place on lines 19 though 25, and you also keep track of the parent of each node as you travel down. On line 26, you have found the largest node, so you call the `Remove01` algorithm on its parent.

Now, you can explain why the removal algorithms do not actually delete the node. Because you are essentially removing the largest node from the tree using the `Remove01` algorithm, there was no need to duplicate the code, so instead you re-used the algorithm to remove the node. Now that the largest node has been removed, you can replace it with the node that you actually want to delete from the tree. This process takes place on lines 30 through 40.

And there you have it.

Efficiency Considerations

Now, for all the examples I have given, I've used nicely created, balanced trees. This is somewhat unrealistic given the real-world circumstances in which you'll be using these trees. The first and foremost problem with BSTs lies in the order in which data is inserted into the BST. If data is inserted in a random fashion, usually you will get a decent-looking tree. But what happens when data is inserted into a BST in a somewhat ordered manner? Trace through the insertion algorithm using this sequence: 1, 2, 3, 4, 5. Notice what type of tree you get? See Figure 17.12.

It looks just like a list, doesn't it? This is a VERY inefficient binary search tree. It takes up 5 levels, and contains only 5 items, making it no better than a list for searching purposes. This is a problem with BSTs.

I won't go over how to solve this problem in this book, because it is a fairly large problem, but let me inform you that solutions do exist.

> **NOTE**
>
> **You must be very careful when inserting data into a normal BST because you may end up with an inefficient tree.**

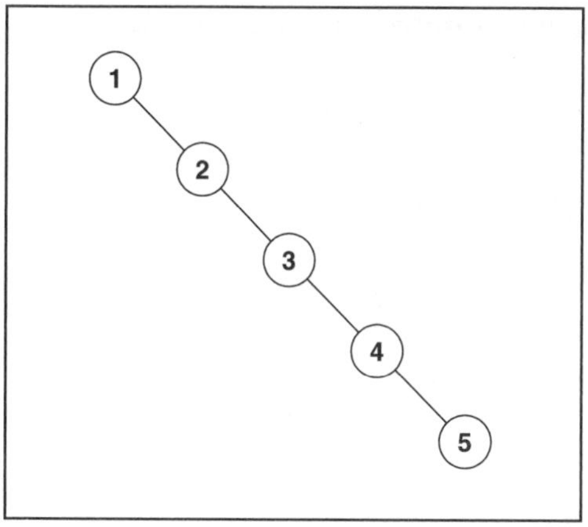

Figure 17.12

BST created using ordered data.

For example, one variation of a BST that solves this problem is the AVL tree. This type of tree uses dynamic node modifying algorithms to rotate nodes into their correct positions and maintain a height balance. These trees are named after their creators, Adelson-Velskii and Landis, and are an efficient alternative to BSTs.

Another variation of BSTs are called splay trees, which try to move the most frequently accessed data items to the top of the tree using a process called splaying.

The third most popular variation of a BST is a red-black tree, which does not keep its height levels as balanced as an AVL tree, but the algorithm used for balancing is a little simpler, and thus faster.

All of these algorithms can be found in almost any textbook dedicated specifically to data structures and algorithms, if they pique your interest. I would suggest looking into them if you need to make more efficient BSTs in the future. For now, I've given you enough to work with.

Uses of Binary Search Trees

Binary search trees are primarily used for searching to see whether data exists within a set. Quite often, the set problem occurs within game programming, where you need to find out quickly whether one thing exists within a set. For example, many multi-player game servers use BSTs to quickly search for players who are online if another player requests to talk with him or her. Other uses include game players inventory, when you want to search quickly to see whether a player has a certain item or not. The possibilities are practically endless, since a large part of computer programming is dedicated to searching for data.

One other use of BSTs lies in 3D graphics. DOOM was one of the first games to utilize this concept, using a very modified version of a BST called a Binary Space Partition (BSP). These BSPs use the same Divide and Conquer methodology that is frequently seen with trees to divide a 3D world into little pieces, speeding up drawing algorithms tremendously.

As with all data structures, BSTs have an infinite number of uses and can be used whenever you feel the time is right.

Sorting Data

Quite often in computing there arises a need to sort your data so that items are arranged in an array in a user-defined order. Let's take a look at two of these sorting algorithms: the bubble sort, and the quick sort.

Bubble Sort

The bubble sort is generally considered the simplest sort to implement. However, it is also considered the slowest sort. The bubble sort essentially bubbles up the highest value in an array in each iteration, until the array is sorted. See Figure 17.13.

So, you start off with five numbers, in this order: 0, 20, 50, 10, 30. You want to sort them so that they are eventually in the order: 0, 10, 20, 30, 50. The arrays before

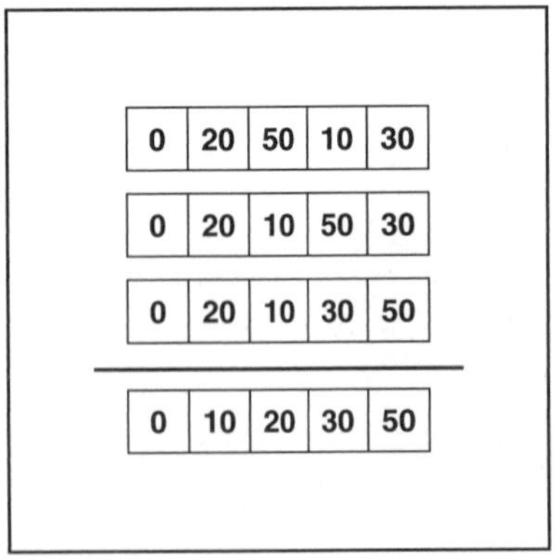

Figure 17.13

Two iterations of a bubble sort.

the line represent the first iteration, and the numbers below the line represent the second iteration. Here is the psuedocode for a bubble sort:

```
BubbleSort( array, size )
 integer temp
 for i = 0 to size-1
  for j = 0 to size-2
   if array[j] > array[j+1] then
    temp = array[j]
    array[j] = array[j+1]
    array[j+1] = temp
   end if
  end for
 end for
end BubbleSort
```

Simply put, the algorithm iterates through the list `size` times, then on each iteration it cycles through the list, and any time a number in an index has a value greater than the number in the next index, it swaps the two values. From Figure 17.13, you see that on the first iteration it swaps 10 and 50, and then swaps 50 and 30. Essentially, the 50 is bubbled up to the top of the list. On the second iteration, it swaps 10 and 20, and on the 3rd, 4th, and 5th iterations, no swaps are made.

Why do you make the outer iteration loop through the same number of times as there are items? Because if the list is in exact reverse order, it will take that many iterations to sort it into correct order with a bubble sort. Try it on paper. The bubble sort algorithm will require, at most, as many iterations as there are indexes.

Now, why did I show pseudocode instead of C++ code? Simply because no one in his right mind would actually implement a real bubble sort like that. The bubble sort you'll be using has several key enhancements, improving performance greatly.

Swap Counter Optimization

Notice how nothing is done in the 3rd, 4th, and 5th iterations of the preceding example. Indeed, the list is sorted after the end of the 2nd iteration. One method of making the bubble sort detect when it is completed is to include a swap counter. For example, when the algorithm goes through iteration 3 and detects that no swaps were made, the algorithm can exit safely, because the list was sorted before all the iterations were completed.

Declining Inner Iterations

Now, you know that in the first iteration the largest number is bubbled up to the last index, and the second largest number is bubbled up into the second-to-last index in the second iteration, and so on. Using this knowledge, it's possible to concoct a simple optimization: After the first iteration, there is no longer any need to see whether the last index needs to be swapped, and after the second iteration, there is no longer any need to see whether the last two indexes need to be swapped, and so on. On the first iteration, `size-1` comparisons need to be made, but the second iteration requires only `size-2`, and the third only requires `size-3`, and so on.

Combining the Optimizations

Now you are ready to concoct your optimized bubble sort algorithm:

```
 1: void BubbleSortInt( int* array, int size )
 2: {
 3:   int temp;
 4:   int swaps;
 5:   int maxindex = size-1;
 6:   int i;
 7:   do {
 8:     swaps = 0;
 9:     for( i = 0; i < maxindex; i++ ) {
10:     if( array[i] > array[i+1] ) {
11:        temp = array[i];
12:        array[i] = array[i+1];
13:        array[i+1] = temp;
14:        swaps++;
15:      }
16:    }
17:    maxindex--;
18:  } while( swaps != 0 );
19: }
```

Note how you changed the outer iteration from a `for` loop in the pseudocode to a `do...while` loop. This ensures that the sort will run through at least once, and if the `swap` variable is zero at the end of a loop, it exits because the array is sorted. Note that the swap variable is reset to zero at each iteration on line 8, and increased each time a number is swapped on line 14.

The second optimization is implemented on line 17, when the `maxindex` is decremented at the end of each iteration. There you have it!

The Quick Sort

Whoever named this sort, named it aptly. The quick sort really is the fastest of the general-purpose sorts (technically, the radix sort is faster most of the time, but it's not considered general purpose since it can only work on numbers and not any other kind of data). It's a simple recursive sort that uses a method of divide and conquer to sort the list. Essentially, instead of swapping variables all over the place like the bubble sort, the quick sort finds the correct place for a single number (the pivot) by moving everything smaller than the pivot below it, and everything larger than the pivot above it. It then splits the list into two parts divided by the pivot, then recursively calls the quick sort algorithm on each segment. If you understand how recursion works, this is not a difficult sort to understand.

Choosing a pivot value is important. Because the algorithm splits up the array into two parts at each iteration, the most efficient pivot node that could be chosen is the median of the array (the value that has exactly the same number of values above and below it in the sorted array). Unfortunately, the algorithm for finding the median is quite complex, and ends up making the sort less efficient in the end. Some simple implementations use the first or last values in the array for a median value, but you're going to use a simple optimization called *median of three pivot choosing*. You take the first value, the middle value (size/2, integer division), and the last value, and compare them. The median of these three is then used as the pivot. This optimization may not seem like much, but it has been proven to be an immense boost to performance on large arrays.

The first, middle, and last values of the array are compared, and the middle value is chosen as the pivot. In the example in Figure 17.14, the pivot will be 30, because it is between 50 and 0.

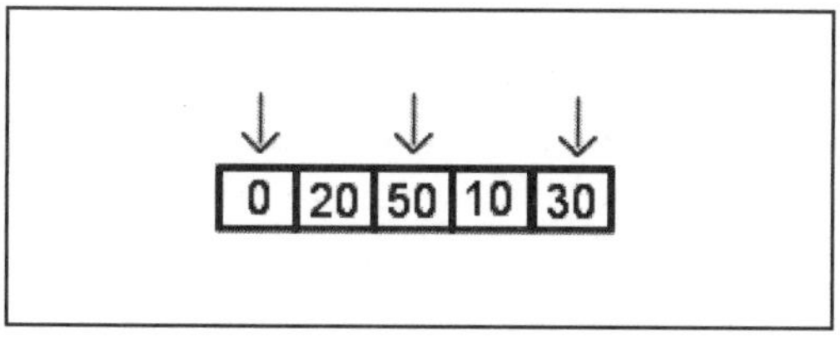

Figure 17.14

Selection of the pivot.

After you have chosen a pivot value, you make sure it's in the first index of the array. Once the pivot is there, you remove it, store it in a temporary variable, and treat the first index as if it were empty. Then you cycle through, starting at the last index and moving downward, and when you find the first value that is less than the pivot, it is swapped into the first index and the index is marked. After that, you cycle up from the second index until you find the first value that is greater than the pivot, and swap that into the index you marked in the last step. You then start again with the first step, cycling down, then the second step, and so on.

Eventually, when the algorithm cycles up or down and reaches the empty index without making any swaps, then you know that you have found the correct place for the pivot node. Figure 17.15 shows a diagram showing the steps of the process.

So, your possible pivot values are 40, 50, and 5. Since the median is 40, and it's already in the first index, you make it the pivot, without swapping anything else. Now in step 2, you scan from right to left and find the first value less than 40, which is 5. This is then swapped into the empty index, and you go on to step 3. Step 3 scans from left to right, finding the first value larger than 40, which is 50. 50 is moved into the empty index, and then you start scanning from right to left again in step 4. 30 is less than 40, so it's moved into the empty index, and you start scanning from left to right again. This time, you see nothing before the empty index that is below 40, so you know that you have found 40's position in the array. You place 40 into the empty spot, and then call the quick sort on the two halves of the array split by 40, indexes 0-4 and 6. Note how the second partition is just one index.

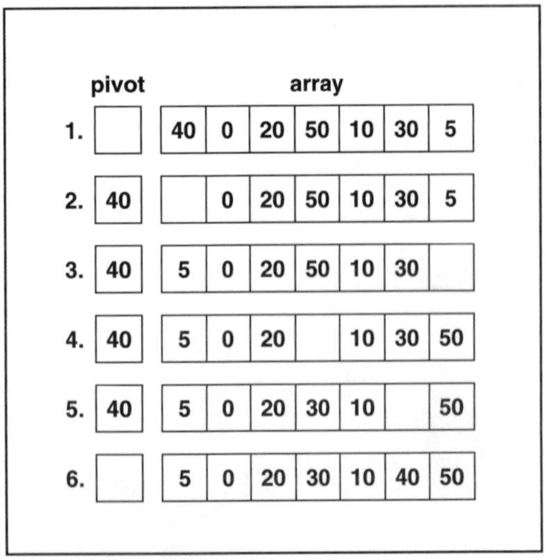

Figure 17.15

First step of a quick sort.

Notice that the pivot wasn't really optimal. There was only one index past 40. The optimal pivot node would have been 20. Using 20 as a pivot node would have split the array nicely into two equal parts, making the algorithm finish sooner.

Another Optimization

Notice that whenever you make a swap in the quick sort, you know that everything before the previous empty index is below the pivot, and everything after the previous empty index is above the pivot. This means you can safely ignore values below the previous empty index when comparing. For example, in step 3, when you're scanning upward, you don't need to bother comparing 5; in step 4, you don't need to compare 50; and in step 5, you don't need to compare 30 or anything below it. This drastically cuts down on the amount of comparisons required for a quick sort.

Source Listing

I've put the `FindMedianOfThree` function into a separate function so that the actual quick sort function is smaller and easier to understand. Basically, all it does is find the median of three values in the array and returns the index.

```
void QuickSortInt (int* array, int min, int size)
{
 int pivot;
 int last = min + size - 1;
 int lower = min;
 int higher = last;
 int mid;
 if ( size > 1) {
  mid = FindMedianOfThree (array, min, size);
  pivot = array [mid];
  array [mid] = array[min];
  while (lower < higher ) {
   while( pivot < array[higher] && lower < higher )
    higher--;
   if( higher != lower ) {
    array[lower] = array[higher];
    lower++;
   }
   while( pivot > array[lower] && lower < higher )
    lower++;
   if( higher != lower ) {
```

```
22:       array[higher] = array[lower];
23:       higher--;
24:     }
25:   }
26:   array[lower] = pivot;
27:   QuickSortInt( array, min, lower-min );
28:   QuickSortInt( array, lower+1, last-lower );
29:  }
30: }
```

The variables you have are the pivot, the higher and lower indexes, the number of the last index in the segment to be sorted, and the index of the median value . If the size of the array to be sorted is less than 2, don't bother sorting it because an array segment of size 1 is already sorted. So if you have 2 or more values in the array segment, you sort it.

Lines 9 through 11 find the pivot node and set it aside from the array. Then, at line 12, you loop through until the two index variables (lower and higher) meet at a single index, and this index is the place where the pivot goes.

Inside the loop, you follow the quick sort algorithm (like in the preceding example) by first scanning from the higher index downward until you find a value less than the pivot (lines 13 through 18), and move that into the lower index. Then you scan upward until you find a value greater than the pivot (lines 19 through 24), and move that into the higher index.

After the loop exits, you place the pivot in its correct place, and call quick sort on the two halves of the array, split by the pivot.

Here's a listing of the `FindMedianOfThree` function:

```
int FindMedianOfThree( int* array, int first, int size )
{
  int last = first+size-1;
  int mid = first+(size/2);
  if( array[first] < array[mid] && array[first] < array[last] ) {
    if( array[mid] < array[last] )
      return mid;
    else
      return last;
  }
  if( array[mid] < array[first] && array[mid] < array[last] ) {
    if( array[first] < array[last] )
      return first;
```

```
14:     else
15:       return last;
16:   }
17:   if( array[mid] < array[first] )
18:     return mid;
19:   else
20:     return first;
21: }
```

This compares the three values and returns the index of the item with the median value. Lines 3 and 4 pre-calculate the indexes of the three values to compare. There are basically six cases that you need to be prepared with, separated into three major cases: the first value is less than both the middle and the last values (line 5), the middle value is less than both the first and last values (line 11), and the last value is less than both the first and middle values (line 17). After you've determined the lowest of the three, you can compare the other two remaining values and return whichever is the lower of the two (since the higher of the two is the highest of all three, the lower is the median).

Note that when you get to line 17, there is no need to check whether the last value is the lowest. You can assume that it is the lowest of the three, because if it weren't, the algorithm would have already exited.

Comparisons of the Sorts

I don't really have time to get into the specifics of how sorting algorithms are rated for efficiency, but it is important to know a little bit. Generally speaking, the bubble sort is the slowest sort that exists, even with the optimizations you made. This is because the algorithm you made follows a basic worst case scenario that is inherent to the bubble sort algorithm, and no little tricks or optimizations are going to change it, because you use a double-nested `for` loop at the heart. Because of this, the worst case (at most, how many comparisons must be made during a bubble sort) of the bubble sort is considered to be n^2, where *n* represents the number of items in the array. The quick sort, on the other hand, uses a more efficient method of sorting. It attempts to find the correct position of every item in the array, and all the swaps made at each level move the numbers closer to their proper indexes than a bubble sort would do. Because the quick sort is a smarter sort, it does much less work than a bubble sort, and as the size of the data increases, the number of comparisons needed increases at a much slower rate than the bubble sort. In fact, a quick sort is rated at $n*\log_2(n)$. Table 17.1 shows how much work occurs in each of the sorts as the data set increases in size:

Table 17.1 Speed Comparison of Sorts

Data Size	Bubble Sort	Quick Sort
4	16	8
8	64	24
16	256	64
32	1024	160
256	65536	2048

As you can see, at low data sizes, the algorithms are similar, but when the data set increases in size, a great disparity between the two sorts arises. The quick sort is clearly superior.

Compression

Many times in computer programming you need to take a chunk of data and make it as small as possible. In the older days of computing, this was a very important concept, because storage space was very limited, and communications devices were slow. (Anyone remember 300 cps modems? No? Bah!) So if you wanted to distribute the newest patch for your program or the program itself, and didn't want to anger your customers, you needed to make the files as small as possible, so they would fit on the small diskettes or not take hours to download on that slow modem. Nowadays, with broadband technology becoming a de facto standard, compression is not as important as it used to be. Don't sell compression short, however! It is still quite an important concept. Most video cards these days use some sort of texture compression so that game designers can pack as many textures as possible in the limited video memory available to them, and with huge amounts of people flocking to the Internet daily, compression becomes important for large servers who distribute files and need to pay for every kilobyte sent. I'll discuss the simplest of the compression mechanisms here, just to give you an idea of how compression works.

RLE Compression

RLE stands for Run-Length Encoding. RLE is perhaps the simplest compression in existence. How well it compresses, however, greatly depends on the type of data you are compressing. Basically, this compression works on the concept that some chunk of data will have "runs" of repeating data items. For example, take the text string `aaaaaaa`. This is considered a run of "a"s. Instead of putting seven "a"s into the final data chunk, RLE compresses the run into a quantity and a value. In this case, the quantity is 7, and the value is "a." See Figure 17.16.

As you might guess, this is a lousy encoding method for English text. Look at the preceding paragraph. See how many runs occur in it? Not many at all. Run-length encoding is best used for data sets in which large numbers of items are repeated on a regular basis. My favorite example is bitmaps with transparency (usually bitmapped fonts are best). Because bitmaps are usually encoded horizontally, line by line, a bitmap with transparency will have large runs of the transparent color.

If you'll look at the letter "A" in Figure 17.16, you'll notice that the first 11 horizontal lines are all the same color. Since the width of the bitmap is 64 pixels, 11*64 = 704. There are 704 pixels in the first 11 lines, all the same color. On the next line, the first 28 pixels are also white. In a run-length encoded bitmap of this letter, the first run's quantity would be 732, and its value would be white. Depending on what color format you're using, white could be defined in any number of ways. Since this is just an abstract example, I won't specify any particular color encoding.

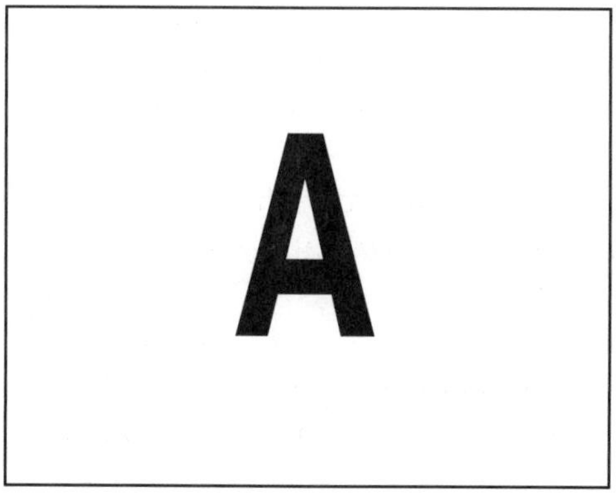

Figure 17.16

The letter "A."

How much space should be allocated to the quantity part of a run? It depends. On an old font system I created, I limited the letter width to 8 bits (256 pixels), and used an RLE modification where each horizontal line in a bitmap is encoded into RLE individually. Thus, in the previous example, the first 11 lines would be 11 runs of 64 pixels each. While this method is less storage-efficient, I chose to do it this way because some of the fonts had more than 2 colors on a single line, and letting each run use more than 8 bits for the quantity part was an even larger waste (another reason had to do with my rendering engine, but that is beside the point).

If your runs are going to be relatively small (less than 256), it is probably better to use only 8 bits for the quantity, but it's all up to your needs in the end. Usually, it's best to experiment with sample data to find out which is the best size to use. It's also a good idea to try to use byte-multiples for your quantity, unless you want to deal with all sorts of bit fiddling in your encoding and decoding algorithms.

RLE Compression Code

Basically, all you need to do to make an RLE compressed chunk of data is to count the number of repeated items in an uncompressed chunk of data. It looks something like this:

```
mrRLE RLECompressInt( mrInt* array, mrInt size )
{
 mrInt i;
 mrInt last = array[i];
 mrInt count = 1;
 mrRLE RLE;
 for( i = 0; i < size; i++ )
 {
  if( last != array[i] )
  {
   RLE.AddRun( count, last );
   last = array[i];
   count = 0;
  }
  count++;
 }
 RLE.AddRun( count, last );
 return RLE;
}
```

The variable `i` will keep track of the index as you loop through the integer array, and the variable `last` will keep track of the last integer in the current run. `count` will keep track of how many items are in the current run, and `RLE` is an abstract class that enables you to add runs to itself.

So, you will loop through the entire array, and whenever you find a new integer in the array, you store the current run in the RLE structure, reset the `last` variable, and reset the count. It's a very simple compression to implement.

The RLE class will probably use a linked list to store each run, since you have no idea how many runs you are going to have when you start out. After this routine is finished executing, you will probably want to convert the RLE list into a class which is a little more space efficient, such as an array, because the entire purpose of an RLE is to compress data, after all.

Summary

In this chapter, you've seen only a brief glimpse of the wonderful world of data structures and algorithms. I've hinted at the more complicated algorithms available from time to time, but I've only skimmed the surface. The truth of the matter is, an entire book could be written entirely about data structures and algorithms, their strengths, their weaknesses, and when to use them most efficiently.

Now that you have an idea of how important data structures and algorithms are to efficient programming, I hope that you are ready to take your programming to the next level.

Questions and Answers

Q: Why make your own implementation of the algorithms and not use STL's or another available library?

A: Using someone else's already available code is a good thing, but sometimes, they are just too generic and slow for your own use. When this happens, the only alternative you have is to develop your own code.

Q: What are the advantages of linked lists over normal arrays?

A: Linked lists are fast when you try to insert an element into it and don't have any limit in size (depends only on the available memory).

Q: Why use iterators?

A: Using iterators to access lists offers you the possibility to make the traversals faster while giving you enough room for optimization and modification.

Q: When should you use RLE compression?

A: As you can imagine, RLE compression isn't perfect. Sometimes RLE compression works very well and other times very badly. The best types of data for this compression algorithm are ones that are linear and repetitive. RLE usually works well for small images, which store text or vector type graphics. Extremely complicated data such as executables and already compressed files are not good candidates for RLE compression.

Exercises

1. What is a linked list?
2. What is an iterator?
3. What is a tree?
4. Why does a binary search tree REDUCE Search time in comparison to normal lists?
5. What is the basis of the RLE compression technique?
6. On your own: Try to modify the functions in this chapter to be as abstract as possible. (Hint: Use polymorphism and inheritance.)

CHAPTER 18

The Mathematical Side of Games

As you may already know, math is an extremely important subject in computer programming, especially in computer game programming.

Vectors, matrices, functions, and other math-related topics compose an indispensable section in any game-programming curriculum. In this chapter, I will go over basic linear algebra like vector operations and matrices and also probability and a bit of calculus when I deal with functions.

Trigonometry

Trigonometry is the study of angles and their relationships to shapes and various other geometries.

You will use some of the material covered here as support for some advanced operations you will build later.

Visual Representation and Laws

Before going into the details of trigonometry, let me introduce a new concept to the game—radians. A *radian* is a measurement of an angle, just like a degree. One radian is the angle formed in any circle where the length of the arc defined by the angle and the circle radius are of same length, as shown in Figure 18.1.

You will use radians as your measurement because it is the unit C++ math functions use for angles. Because you are probably accustomed to using degrees as your unit of measurement, you need to be able to convert from radians to degrees and vice-versa. As you may know, π radians is the angle that contains half a circle, as you can see in Figure 18.2. You also know that 180 degrees is also the angle that contains half a circle. Knowing this, you can convert any radian unit to degrees, as shown in Equation 18.1 and vice-versa using Equation 18.2.

Equation 18.1

$$Radians = \frac{Degrees * \pi}{180}$$

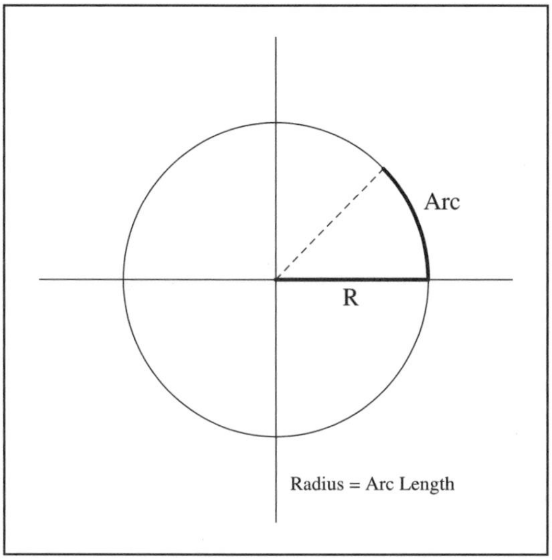

Figure 18.1

Relation of the arc length and radius of the circle.

Equation 18.2

$$Degrees = \frac{Radians * 180}{\pi}$$

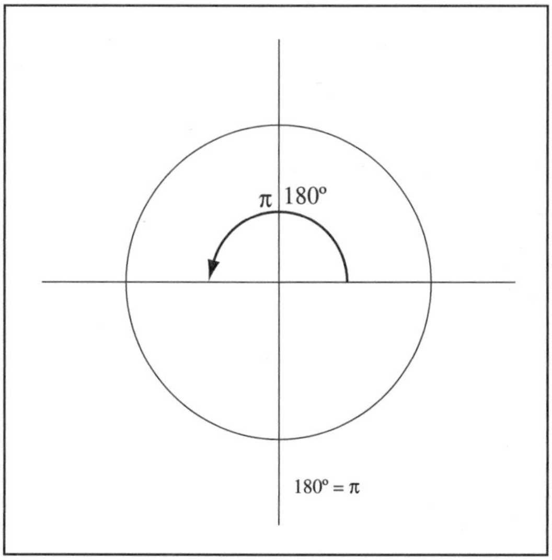

Figure 18.2

Half a circle denoted by radians and degrees.

```
mrReal32 DegreeToRadian (mrReal32 & rfDegree)
{
 return (rfDegree * PI / 180);
}
mrReal32 RadianToDegree (mrReal32 & rfRadian)
{
 return (rfRadian * 180 / PI);
}
```

Now that you know what a radian is, I'll explain how to use them. Take a look at Figure 18.3, from the angle and the circle radius you can get the triangle sides and angles.

If you examine that circle a little bit better, you will see that in any triangle that contains the center of the circle and the end of the arc as vertices, the hypotenuse of that same triangle is the line formed from the circle center to the end of the arc. Now you need to find the two other lines' lengths that form the triangle. You will find these using the cosine and sine functions.

Some mathematician a long time ago came up with three equations that relate the cosine, sine, and tangent with the triangle formula. See the cosine Equation 18.3, the sine Equation 18.4, and the tangent Equation 18.5.

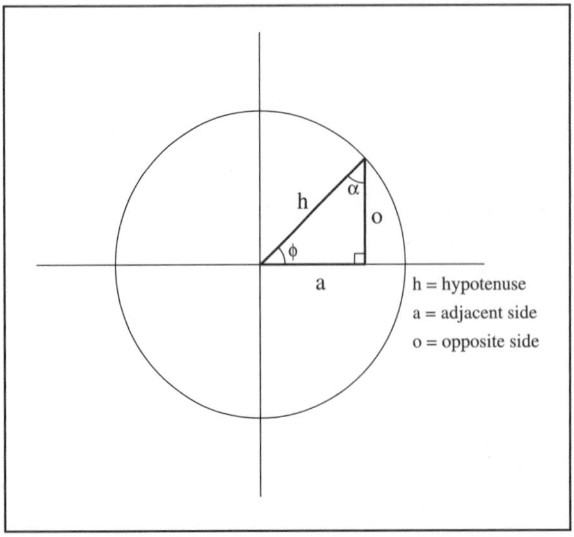

Figure 18.3

Triangle formed by a circle radius and an angle; π radians = 180 degrees.

Equation 18.3

$$\text{cosine}(\phi) = \frac{AdjacentSide}{Hypotenuse}$$

Equation 18.4

$$\text{sine}(\phi) = \frac{OppositeSide}{Hypotenuse}$$

Equation 18.5

$$\text{tangent}(\phi) = \frac{\sin(\phi)}{\cos(\phi)} = \frac{OppositeSide}{AdjacentSide}$$

These trigonometric operations can be calculated using the MacLaurin series but that is beyond the scope of this chapter or book.

So now you can determine the length of the adjacent side of the triangle on the circle by using the cosine, as shown in Equation 18.6.

Equation 18.6

$$\text{cosine}(\phi) = \frac{AdjacentSide}{Hypotenuse} \Leftrightarrow$$
$$AdjacentSide = CircleRadius * \text{cosine}(\phi)$$

And what if you want to know the angles at each side of the triangle? You will use exactly the same equations from before to get the sine or the cosine. When you have them you will use the inverse of those operations to get the angles. Taking the triangle in Figure 18.3 you will find both the angles. You don't need to find one of the angles since you already know that the triangle is a right angle triangle, and as such, the angle formed is 90 degrees, or half a π.

Equation 18.7

$$\text{cosine}(\phi) = \frac{AdjacentSide}{Hypotenuse} \Leftrightarrow$$
$$\phi = \text{cosine}^{-1}\left(\frac{AdjacentSide}{CircleRadius}\right)$$

Equation 18.8

$$\text{cosine}(\alpha) = \frac{OppositeSide}{Hypotenuse} \Leftrightarrow$$

$$\alpha = \text{cosine}^{-1}\left(\frac{OppositeSide}{CircleRadius}\right)$$

What is the difference between them? Well, if you look carefully, you are trying to get the angle α using the cosine and the opposite side, you do this because the opposite side of the angle α is actually the adjacent side in relation to that angle. So what does this mean? It means that the terms adjacent and opposite are relative to the angle they are referred to. So, in the second calculation the opposite side should actually be the adjacent side of that angle.

In Table 18.1 you can see the C++ functions for the trigonometric functions.

This may seem complicated, but it will become clearer when you start using all of this later.

Angle Relations

There are a couple of relations that can prove useful when you are dealing with angles and trigonometric functions. One of the most important relations is the trigonometric identity shown in Equation 18.9.

Table 18.1 C++ Trigonometric Functions

Trigonometric	C++ Function	C++ Function Inversed
cosine	cos	acos
sine	sin	asin
tangent	tan	atan/atan2

*These functions are all defined in `math.h`.

Equation 18.9

$$\text{sine}^2(\phi) + \text{cosine}^2(\phi) = 1$$

This equation is the base of all the other relations. To be honest, these relations are used only for problem-solving or optimizations. For that reason, I will not go over them in detail but just show them so you can use them at your discretion. The following equations are derived from Equation 18.9 and should be used to optimize your code.

Equation 18.10

$$\text{sine}(2\phi) = 2\,\text{sine}(\phi) * \text{cosine}(\phi)$$

Equation 18.11

$$\text{cosine}(2\phi) = \text{cosine}^2(\phi) - \text{sine}^2(\phi)$$

Equation 18.12

$$\text{tangent}(2\phi) = \frac{2\,\text{tangent}(\phi)}{1 - \text{tangent}^2(\phi)}$$

Now you are done with trigonometry. Trigonometry per se isn't very useful, but it will prove an indispensable tool later when you will be using it with other concepts like vectors or matrices.

Vectors

A vector is an n-tuple of ordered real values that can represent anything with more than one dimension. For example, a 2D or 3D Euclidean space, but basically vectors are nothing more than a set of components.

Equation 18.13

$$\vec{Vector} = \begin{pmatrix} V_1 \\ V_2 \\ V_3 \\ V_n \end{pmatrix} \in \Re^n$$

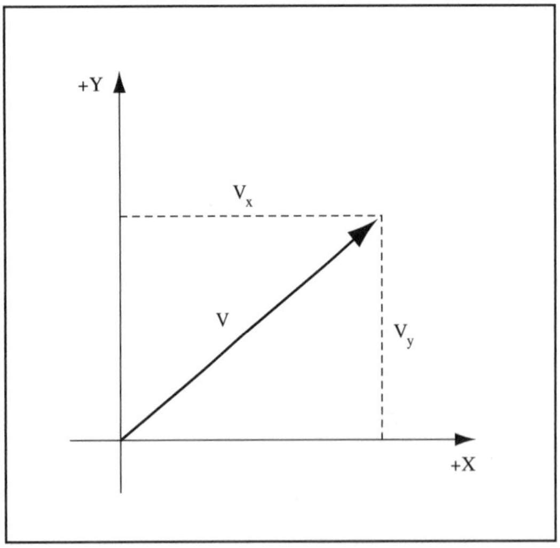

Figure 18.4

2D vector composed of two scalars defining the orientation.

Vectors describe both magnitude and direction. In the two-dimensional case, the x and y components represent the distance from the relative origin to the end of the vector as you can see in Figure 18.4.

Because you are using a 2D world, as stated before, you define vectors using two components, for convenience with a common known notation (x, y). You can also represent just one component of the vector by using a subscript either with the order of the element or with the component identification as shown in Equation 18.14.

Equation 18.14

$$\vec{Vector} = (V_1;V_2) = (V_x;V_y)$$

$$\vec{Vector} = (12;9)$$

You can perform several operations with vectors (I will go over them in a minute), but for now just declare the vector class.

```
 /* 'mrVector2D.h' */

 /* Mirus base types header */
#include "mrDatatypes.h"
 /* C++ math  header file */
#include <math.h>

```

```
 /* Include this file only once */
#pragma once

 /* Mirus vector 2D class */
class mrVector2D
{
protected:
 mrReal32   m_afComponents [2];

public:
  /* Constructors / Destructor */
 mrVector2D (void);
 mrVector2D (mrVector2D & rkVector);
 mrVector2D (mrReal32 fXComponent, mrReal32 fYComponent);
 ~mrVector2D (void);

  /* Operators */
 mrVector2D & operator = (mrVector2D & rkVector);
 mrVector2D & operator += (mrVector2D & rkVector);
 mrVector2D & operator -= (mrVector2D & rkVector);
 mrVector2D & operator *= (mrReal32 iMultiplier);
 mrVector2D & operator /= (mrReal32 iDivider);
 mrVector2D operator + (mrVector2D & rkVector);
 mrVector2D operator - (mrVector2D & rkVector);
 mrVector2D operator * (mrReal32 iMultiplier);
 mrVector2D operator / (mrReal32 iDivider);
 mrVector2D operator - (void);
 mrReal32 & operator [ ] (const mrInt IComponent);

  /* Linear algebra operations */
 mrReal32 Length (void);
 void Normalize (void);
 mrVector2D Perpendicular (void);
 mrReal32 DotProduct (mrVector2D & rkVector);
 mrReal32 Angle (mrVector2D & rkVector);
 mrReal32 PerpDotProduct (mrVector2D & rkVector);

  /* Manipulation operations */
 void Reset (void);
 void SetVector (mrVector2D & rkVector);
```

NOTE

This class needs the `mrDataTypes.h` header you built earlier and `math.h` that is the C++ math header file.

```
mrReal32 * GetVector (void);
};
```

As you can see, the vector is constituted by an array of two components, in your case, x (m_afComponents [0]) and y (m_afComponents [1]). The constructors aren't hard so just have a quick check on them:

```
/* 'mrVector2D.cpp' */
/* Complement header file */
#include "mrVector2D.h"
/* Default constructor */
mrVector2D::mrVector2D (void)
{
 Reset ();
}
mrVector2D::mrVector2D (mrVector2D & rkVector)
{
 m_afComponents [0] = rkVector [0];
 m_afComponents [1] = rkVector [1];
}
mrVector2D::mrVector2D (mrReal32 fXComponent, mrReal32 fYComponent)
{
 m_afComponents [0] = fXComponent;
 m_afComponents [1] = fYComponent;
}
mrVector2D::~mrVector2D (void)
{
 Reset ();
}
```

You will also implement an assignment operator to make it easier to use this class:

```
mrVector2D & mrVector2D::operator = (mrVector2D & rkVector)
{
 m_afComponents [0] = rkVector [0];
 m_afComponents [1] = rkVector [1];
```

```
34:  return *this;
35: }
```

You won't implement the assignment-operation operators, but feel free to implement them using the operators you will develop later.

From now on, all your vector operations will be in 2D space. I will cover the algebra specific operations next.

Addition and Subtraction

Vectors can be added or subtracted to form new vectors. You can see in Equation 18.15 that the addition of two vectors is completed component by component, this proves true for subtraction also.

Equation 18.15

$$\vec{AddedVector} = \vec{A} + \vec{B} \Leftrightarrow$$
$$\vec{AddedVector} = (A_x + B_x; A_y + B_y)$$

Equation 18.15 also shows that vector addition can be done in any order, but this isn't true for vector subtraction. If you take a look at Figure 18.5, you can see how the same vectors subtracted in different order produce a vector that is the same in length but different in orientation. But before moving on, let's just create your addition method.

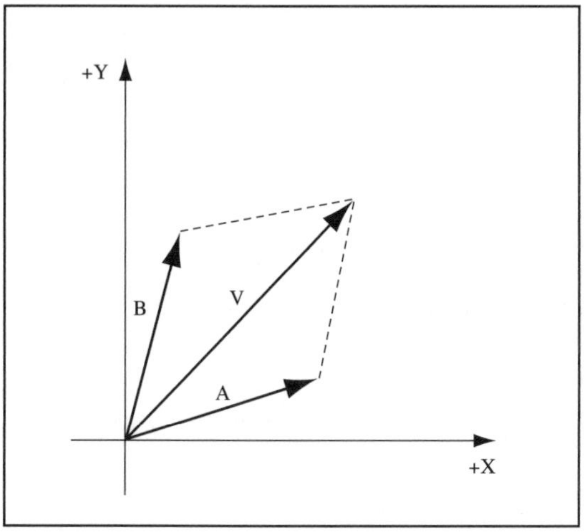

Figure 18.5

Addition of two vectors.

```
mrVector2D mrVector2D::operator + (mrVector2D & rkVector)
{
  return mrVector2D (m_afComponents [0] + rkVector [0],
   m_afComponents [1] + rkVector [1]);
}
```

As you can see by Figure 18.6, the subtraction of two vectors gives you the distance between them, but isn't commutative. If you subtract $\vec{A} - \vec{B}$ you get the distance from $\vec{A}$ to $\vec{B}$ where in $\vec{B} - \vec{A}$ you get the distance from $\vec{B}$ to $\vec{A}$. This is shown in Equation 18.16.

Equation 18.16

$$\vec{Substracted\ Vector} = \vec{A} + \vec{B} \Leftrightarrow$$
$$\vec{Substracted\ Vector} = (A_x + Bx; A_y + B_y)$$

> **CAUTION**
>
> **In Figure 18.6 you see that the product of the subtraction has its origin on the end of the first vector. This isn't true. Correctly, the vector origin should be the origin of the world.**

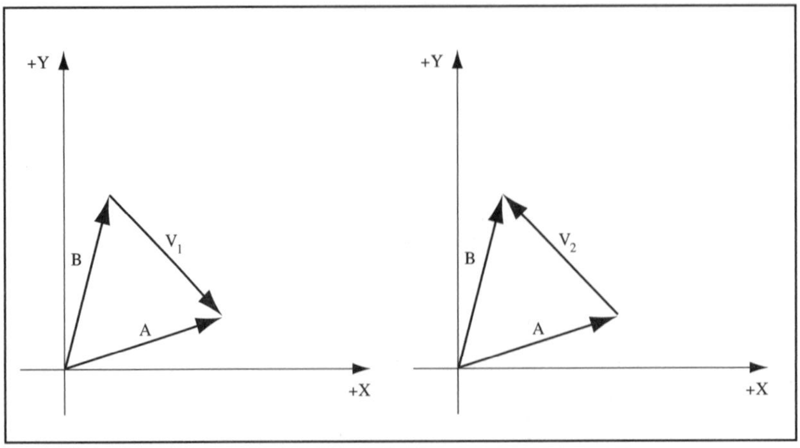

Figure 18.6

Subtraction of two vectors in different order.

a) $-\vec{V}_1 = \vec{A} - \vec{B}$

b) $\vec{V}_2 = \vec{B} - \vec{A}$

And to finalize this section you build the subtraction method for your vector class.

```
mrVector2D mrVector2D::operator - (mrVector2D & rkVector)
{
 return mrVector2D (m_afComponents [0] - rkVector [0],
  m_afComponents [1] - rkVector [1]);
}
```

Scalar Multiplication and Division

Vectors can be scaled by multiplying or dividing them by scalars, just like normal scalar to scalar operations. To do this, you multiply or divide each vector component by the scalar. You can see this in Equation 18.17 where you multiply each of the vector components by a scalar to produce a new vector.

Equation 18.17

$$\vec{MultipliedVector} = \left(V_x * Scalar ; V_y * Scalar\right)$$

In code you have:

```
mrVector2D mrVector2D::operator * (mrReal32 iMultiplier)
{
 return mrVector2D (m_afComponents [0] * iMultiplier,
  m_afComponents [1] * iMultiplier);
}
```

And you do the same for division, as you can see in Equation 18.18.

Equation 18.18

$$\vec{DividedVector} = \left(\frac{V_x ; V_y}{Scalar}\right)$$

And to end the normal operations you build your division method.

```
mrVector2D mrVector2D::operator / (mrReal32 iDivider)
{
 return mrVector2D (m_afComponents [0] / iDivider,
  m_afComponents [1] / iDivider);
}
```

Length

The length is the *size* of the vector. The length is used in several other vector operations and should be the first one to learn.

If you remember the Pythagorean theorem from school, you'll know that the square of the hypotenuse is equal to the sum of the square of each side. You will use the same theorem to get the length of the vector. You can see this in Equation 18.19.

Equation 18.19

$$\left\|\vec{Vector}\right\| = \sqrt{V_x^{2} + V_y^{2}}$$

As usual, you will build your class method to calculate the length of a vector.

```
mrReal32 mrVector2D::Length (void)
{
  return (mrReal32) sqrt (m_afComponents[0] * m_afComponents[0] +
   m_afComponents[1] * m_afComponents[1]);
}
```

Normalization

As you saw earlier, vectors have both an orientation and a length, also referred to as the norm. Some calculations you will use will need a vector of length 1.0. To force a vector to have length 1.0, you must normalize the vector, or in other words divide the components of the vector by its total length, as shown in Equation 18.20.

Equation 18.20

$$\vec{NormalizedVector} = \left(\frac{V_x ; V_y}{\left\|\vec{V}\right\|} \right)$$

And so, you build your normalize method.

```
void mrVector2D::Normalize (void)
{
  mrReal32 fLength;
  fLength = Length ();

```

```
  if (0 != fLength)
  {
   m_afComponents [0] /= fLength;
   m_afComponents [1] /= fLength;
  }
}
```

Perpendicular Operation

Finding the perpendicular of a vector is one of those operations you use once a year, but that time will arrive in the physics chapter so you better go through it here. A vector perpendicular to another is a vector that forms a 90-degree angle, or half π radians angle with the other. In Figure 18.7 you can see that vector $\vec{B}$ forms a 90-degree, counter-clockwise angle with vector $\vec{A}$.

Finding the perpendicular vector of a 2D vector is easy, you just need to negate the *y* component and swap it with the *x* component of the vector as shown in Equation 18.21.

Equation 18.21

$$\vec{PerpendicularVector}_{\perp} = (-V_y; V_x)$$

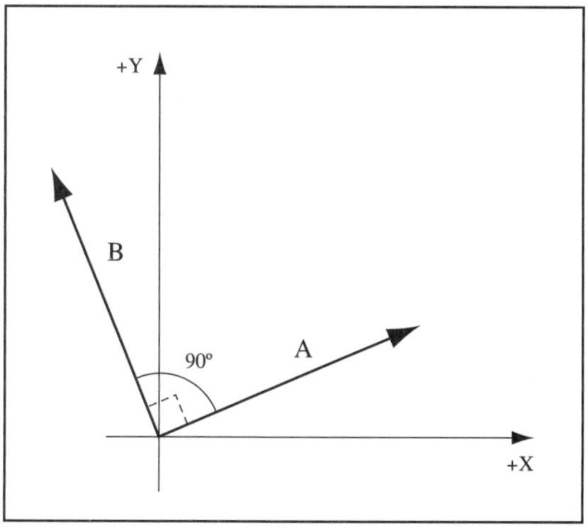

Figure 18.7

A perpendicular vector $\vec{B}$ forming a 90-degree, counter-clockwise angle with vector $\vec{A}$.

Just one little thing, you see that reversed T in Equation 18.21? That is the perpendicular symbol. Okay, code now, right?

```
mrVector2D mrVector2D::Perpendicular (void)
{
  return mrVector2D (-m_afComponents [1], m_afComponents [0]);
}
```

Dot Product

The dot product is probably the most used operation with vectors. It can be used to multiply two vectors using Equation 18.22.

Equation 18.22

$$\vec{A} \cdot \vec{B} = A_x * B_x + A_y * B_y$$

In code you have the following:

```
mrReal32 mrVector2D::DotProduct (mrVector2D & rkVector)
{
  return m_afComponents [0] * rkVector [0] +
           m_afComponents [1] * rkVector [1];
}
```

Equation 18.23 resulted in a scalar value, but what does that give to you? Well, much and almost nothing. Using the dot product per se isn't very informative, but the dot product can also be defined by Equation 18.21.

Equation 18.23

$$\vec{A} \cdot \vec{B} = \left\|\vec{A}\right\| * \left\|\vec{B}\right\| * \text{cosine}(\phi)$$

Now, this equation gives a little more information, don't you agree? In case you didn't know, ø is the smallest angle formed by the two vectors. With a little thought and by combining Equations 18.22 and 18.23, you can get the equation to find the smallest angle of two vectors. See Equation 18.24.

Equation 18.24

$$\text{cosine}(\phi) = \frac{\vec{A} \cdot \vec{B}}{\left\|\vec{A}\right\| * \left\|\vec{B}\right\|} \Leftrightarrow$$

$$\phi = \text{cosine}^{-1}\left(\frac{\vec{A} \cdot \vec{B}}{\left\|\vec{A}\right\| * \left\|\vec{B}\right\|}\right)$$

And so, you finally have some use for the dot product. If you calculate the arc cosine of the dot product of the two vectors divided by the product of their lengths you have the smallest angle between them.

So now you can build your angle method.

```
mrReal32 mrVector2D::Angle (mrVector2D & rkVector)
{
  return (mrReal32) acos (DotProduct (rkVector) /
   (Length() * rkVector.Length()));
}
```

Perp-dot Product

The perp-dot product is nothing new. It is the dot product of a calculated perpendicular vector. This operation is mostly used in physics, as you will see later. So, how do you find the perp-dot product? Easy, you find the perpendicular of a vector and calculate the dot product of that vector with another as shown in Equation 18.25.

Equation 18.25

$$\vec{PerpDot} = \vec{A}_{\perp} \cdot \vec{B}$$

Or in code:

```
mrReal32 mrVector2D::PerpDotProduct (mrVector2D & rkVector)
{
  return Perpendicular ().DotProduct (rkVector);
}
```

Matrices

In a simple way of defining a matrix, you can say that a matrix is a table of values.

Equation 18.26

$$Matrix_{pq} = \begin{bmatrix} m_{11} & m_{12} & \cdots & m_{1q} \\ m_{21} & m_{22} & \cdots & m_{2q} \\ \cdots & \cdots & \cdots & \cdots \\ m_{p1} & m_{p2} & \cdots & M_{pq} \end{bmatrix} \in \Re$$

You can see in Equation 18.26 that a matrix is defined by a set of rows and columns. The number of columns is given by *p* and the number of rows by *q*. You can also access any element of the matrix using the letter *i* for the row and the letter *j* for the column. This is shown in Equation 18.27.

Equation 18.27

$$m_{ij} = \begin{bmatrix} \cdots & \cdots & \cdots \\ \cdots & \cdots & m_{23} \\ \cdots & \cdots & \cdots \end{bmatrix}$$

$$i = 2; j = 3$$

From now on you will just use a matrix of size 2×2, or more correctly, M_{22}. And for now let's declare your matrix class.

```
/* 'mrMatrix22.h' */

/* Mirus base types header */
#include "mrDatatypes.h"
/* Mirus 2D vector header */
#include "mrVector2D.h"
/* C++ math  header file */
#include <math.h>

/* Include this file only once */
#pragma once

/* Mirus matrix 2x2 class */
```

```
class mrMatrix22
{
protected:
 mrReal32                  m_aafElements [2][2];

public:
  /* Constructors / destructor */
 mrMatrix22 (void);
 mrMatrix22 (mrMatrix22 & rkMatrix);
 mrMatrix22 (mrReal32 * pMatrix);
 ~mrMatrix22 (void);

  /* Operators */
 mrMatrix22 & operator = (mrMatrix22 & rkMatrix);
 mrMatrix22 & operator += (mrMatrix22 & rkMatrix);
 mrMatrix22 & operator -= (mrMatrix22 & rkMatrix);
 mrMatrix22 & operator *= (mrReal32 fMultiplier);
 mrMatrix22 & operator /= (mrReal32 fDivider);
 mrMatrix22 operator + (mrMatrix22 & rkMatrix);
 mrMatrix22 operator - (mrMatrix22 & rkMatrix);
 mrMatrix22 operator * (mrReal32 fMultiplier);
 mrMatrix22 operator / (mrReal32 fDivider);
 mrMatrix22 operator - (void);
 mrReal32 & operator [] (const mrInt iElement);

  /* Operations */
 void Zero (void);
 void Identity (void);
 void Transpose (void);
 mrMatrix22 Concatenate (mrMatrix22 & rkMatrix);
 void Transform (mrVector2D & rkVector);

  /* Manipulation operations */
 void SetMatrix (mrMatrix22 & rkMatrix);
 mrReal32 * Matrix (void);
};
```

This matrix class will be used in the 2D transformation chapter to produce various effects to your objects.

NOTE

This class needs the `mrDataTypes.h` and `mrCVector2.h` header files you built earlier and `math.h` that is the C++ math header file.

The constructors and destructor are pretty simple:

```
   /* 'mrMatrix22.cpp' */

   /* Complement header file */
#include "mrMatrix22.h"

   /* Default constructor */
mrMatrix22::mrMatrix22 (void)
{
 Identity ();
}

mrMatrix22::mrMatrix22 (mrMatrix22 & rkMatrix)
{
 *this = rkMatrix;
}

mrMatrix22::mrMatrix22 (mrReal32 * pMatrix)
{
 mrInt8  iI;
 mrInt8  iJ;

 for (iJ = 0; iJ < 2; iJ++)
 {
  for (iI = 0; iI < 2; iI++)
  {
   m_aafElements [iJ][iI] = pMatrix [iJ * 2 + iI];
  }
 }
}

mrMatrix22::~mrMatrix22 (void)
{
 Zero ();
}
```

And as the vector class, you will create the assignment operator:

```
mrMatrix22 & mrMatrix22::operator = (mrMatrix22 & rkMatrix)
{
```

```
  SetMatrix (rkMatrix);

  return *this;
}
```

Addition and Subtraction

Matrix addition and subtraction is done exactly the same way as the vector addition and subtraction. You will add, or subtract, each element of one matrix to, or from, the other to produce a third matrix, as shown in Equation 18.28 for the addition operation.

Equation 18.28

$$MatrixAdded_{ij} = Ai_j + B_{ij}$$

$$MatrixAdded = \begin{bmatrix} a & b \\ c & d \end{bmatrix} + \begin{bmatrix} 1 & 2 \\ 3 & 4 \end{bmatrix} \Leftrightarrow$$

$$MatrixAdded = \begin{bmatrix} a+1 & b+2 \\ c+3 & d+4 \end{bmatrix}$$

Or in code you have the following:

```
mrMatrix22 mrMatrix22::operator + (mrMatrix22 & rkMatrix)
{
 mrInt8  iI;
 mrInt8  iJ;
 mrMatrix22 kMatrix;

 for (iJ = 0; iJ < 2; iJ++)
 {
  for (iI = 0; iI < 2; iI++)
  {
   kMatrix [iJ * 2 + iI] = m_aafElements [iJ][iI] + rkMatrix [iJ * 2 + iI];
  }
 }
 return kMatrix;
}
```

As you can see, matrix addition is commutative (that is, independent of the order), but this isn't the case for subtraction as you can see in Equation 18.29.

Equation 18.29

$$MatrixSubstracted_{ij} = Ai_j - B_{ij}$$

$$MatrixSubstracted = \begin{bmatrix} a & b \\ c & d \end{bmatrix} - \begin{bmatrix} 1 & 2 \\ 3 & 4 \end{bmatrix} \Leftrightarrow$$

$$MatrixSubstracted = \begin{bmatrix} a-1 & b-2 \\ c-3 & d-4 \end{bmatrix}$$

Again in code:

```
mrMatrix22 mrMatrix22::operator - (mrMatrix22 & rkMatrix)
{
 mrInt8  iI;
 mrInt8  iJ;
 mrMatrix22 kMatrix;

 for (iJ = 0; iJ < 2; iJ++)
 {
  for (iI = 0; iI < 2; iI++)
  {
   kMatrix [iJ * 2 + iI] = m_aafElements [iJ][iI] - rkMatrix [iJ * 2 + iI];
  }
 }
 return kMatrix;
}
```

Scalar and Multiplication and Division

Again, to multiply or divide a matrix by a scalar, you multiply or divide each matrix element by the scalar, as shown in Equation 18.30 for multiplication and Equation 18.31 for division.

Equation 18.30

$$MatrixMultiplied_{ij} = A_{ij} * Scalar$$

$$MatrixMultiplied = \begin{bmatrix} a & b \\ c & d \end{bmatrix} * Scalar \Leftrightarrow$$

$$MatrixMultiplied = \begin{bmatrix} a * Scalar & b * Scalar \\ c * Scalar & d * Scalar \end{bmatrix}$$

And in code you have:

```
mrMatrix22 mrMatrix22::operator * (mrReal32 fMultiplier)
{
 mrInt8  iI;
 mrInt8  iJ;
 mrMatrix22 kMatrix;
 for (iJ = 0; iJ < 2; iJ++)
 {
  for (iI = 0; iI < 2; iI++)
  {
   kMatrix [iJ * 2 + iI] = m_aafElements [iJ][iI] * fMultiplier;
  }
 }
 return kMatrix;
}
```

This is exactly the same for the division process shown in Equation 18.31 and the following code.

Equation 18.31

$$MatrixDivided_{ij} = \frac{A_{ij}}{Scalar}$$

$$MatrixDivided = \frac{\begin{bmatrix} a & b \\ c & d \end{bmatrix}}{Scalar} \Leftrightarrow$$

$$MatrixDivided = \begin{bmatrix} \frac{a}{Scalar} & \frac{b}{Scalar} \\ \frac{c}{Scalar} & \frac{d}{Scalar} \end{bmatrix}$$

```
mrMatrix22 mrMatrix22::operator / (mrReal32 fDivider)
{
 mrInt8  iI;
 mrInt8  iJ;
 mrMatrix22 kMatrix;

 for (iJ = 0; iJ < 2; iJ++)
 {
  for (iI = 0; iI < 2; iI++)
  {
```

```
    kMatrix [iJ * 2 + iI] = m_aafElements [iJ][iI] / fDivider;
   }
  }
  return kMatrix;
}
```

Scalar operations in matrices are pretty easy, and usually, not very needed. Next I will go over the most useful matrix operations, so relax, grab a cup of coffee, and keep on reading.

Special Matrices

There are two special matrices I want to go over. The zero matrix and the identity matrix. First, the zero matrix. The zero matrix is a matrix that when added to any other matrix produces the matrix shown in Equation 18.32.

Equation 18.32

$$Matrix = ZeroMatrix + Matrix$$

$$ZeroMatrix = \begin{bmatrix} 0 & 0 \\ 0 & 0 \end{bmatrix}$$

No matter what M is, as long as it is a 2×2 matrix, the result of this operation is M.

And the code for this operation is the following:

```
void mrMatrix22::Zero (void)
{
  mrInt8  iI;
  mrInt8  iJ;
  for (iJ = 0; iJ < 2; iJ++)
  {
   for (iI = 0; iI < 2; iI++)
   {
    m_aafElements [iJ][iI] = 0;
   }
  }
}
```

Now, the identity matrix is the matrix that multiplied by any other matrix produces the same matrix as shown in Equation 18.33.

Equation 18.33

$$Matrix = IdentityMatrix * Matrix$$

$$IdentityMatrix = \begin{bmatrix} 1 & 0 \\ 0 & 1 \end{bmatrix}$$

Again, no matter what M is, as long as it is a 2×2 size matrix, the result of this operation is M.

In code you have the following:

```
void mrMatrix22::Identity (void)
{
 mrInt8  iIdentity;
 Zero ();
 for (iIdentity = 0; iIdentity < 2; iIdentity++)
 {
  m_aafElements [iIdentity][iIdentity];
 }
}
```

Transpose

A transposed matrix is a matrix where the matrix values are swapped with the other diagonal element, proving Equation 18.34 true.

Equation 18.34

$$MatrixTransposed_{ij} = M_{ji}$$

$$\begin{bmatrix} 1 & 2 \\ 3 & 4 \end{bmatrix} = \begin{bmatrix} 1 & 3 \\ 2 & 4 \end{bmatrix}$$

So, after this, let's build your method:

```
void mrMatrix22::Transpose (void)
{
 mrReal32   fTransposedValue;
 fTransposedValue = m_aafElements [0][1];

 m_aafElements [0][1] = m_aafElements [1][0];
 m_aafElements [1][0] = fTransposedValue;
}
```

This operation is usually used to change coordinate systems in 3D. In 2D you don't have much use for it other than creating some wicked effects as you will see later.

Matrix Concatenation

You have reached one of the most needed, and one of the most complicated, matrix operations: matrix multiplication, or more correctly concatenation. Concatenation is the real name for matrix multiplication. Concatenation comes from *joining* various matrices. This operation enables you to concatenate various matrices to produce various effects like rotating or shearing, which I will go over in the 2D chapter. Matrix multiplication can be defined by Equation 18.35.

Equation 18.35

$$MatrixConcatenated_{ij} = \sum_{u=1}^{2} A_{iu} * B_{uj}$$

Well, you have a new symbol in your game. Σ symbol, in English, the sum symbol. Look at the following math in Equation 18.36 and you will think of it as a programmer.

Equation 18.36

$$\sum_{i=0}^{n} mass_i$$

You have three things to explain: the symbol, the number above it, and the number below it. What you do with this bit of math is sum all the masses you have in the equation above `n`. So let's say that mass is an array of size for like `int mass [n]`, and you want to add every element of mass from `i = 0` to `n`, in code you have:

```
int iSumMass = 0;
for (int i=0; i<n; i++)
{
 iSumMass += mass [i];
}
```

It's easy if you think of it like a programmer, no? So, in review, the sum symbol means that you will add each element of an array from `i` to `n`.

In Equation 18.37, what you actually do is add all the products of the row of matrix A with the column of matrix B to get each element of the result matrix. It's easier to check this with the simple example you see next.

Equation 18.37

$$MatrixConcatenated = \begin{bmatrix} a & b \\ c & d \end{bmatrix} * \begin{bmatrix} 1 & 2 \\ 3 & 4 \end{bmatrix} \Leftrightarrow$$

$$MatrixConcatenated = \begin{bmatrix} a*1+b*3 & a*2+b*4 \\ c*1+d*3 & c*2+d*4 \end{bmatrix}$$

Let's go over how you actually came to these results. First, you will find $MatrixConcatenated_{11}$. If you resort to Equation 18.38, you know that $MatrixConcatenated_{11} = A_{1u} * B_{u1} + A_{1(u+1)} * B_{(u+1)1}$. Since u starts at 1 and ends at 2, you can say that $MatrixConcatenated_{11} = A_{11} * B_{11} + A_{12} * B_{21}$, or $MatrixConcatenated_{11} = a*1+b*3$. So, you do the same for each element as follows:

$MatrixConcatenated_{12} = A_{11} * B_{12} + A_{12} * B_{22} = a*2+b*4$

$MatrixConcatenated_{21} = A_{21} * B_{11} + A_{22} * B_{21} = c*1+d*3$

$MatrixConcatenated_{22} = A_{21} * B_{12} + A_{22} * B_{22} = c*2+d*4$

Equation 18.38

$$MatrixConcatenated_{ij} = \sum_{u=1}^{2} A_{iu} * B_{uj}$$

Now you will build a matrix multiplication method as such:

```
mrMatrix22 mrMatrix22::Concatenate (mrMatrix22 & rkMatrix)
{
 mrInt8  iI;
 mrInt8  iJ;
 mrMatrix22 kMatrix;
 for (iJ = 0; iJ < 2; iJ++)
 {
  for (iI = 0; iI < 2; iI++)
  {
   kMatrix [iJ * 2 + iI] = m_aafElements [0][iI] * rkMatrix [iJ * 2 + 0] +
                           m_aafElements [1][iI] * rkMatrix [iJ * 2 + 1];
  }
 }
 return kMatrix;
}
```

This code does exactly what Equation 18.33 does. Because `n= 2`, you optimize the code to save a couple of nested loops.

Vector Transformation

Being able to transform vectors by matrices is one of the fundamental tasks for 2D manipulation, but the concept behind it is very simple. If you treat a 2D vector as a matrix of size 1 × 2, you can multiply the *matrix vector* by another matrix the same way you would do it with two matrices, as shown in Equation 18.39.

Equation 18.39

$$\vec{VectorTransformed} = A * \vec{V}$$

$$\vec{VectorTransformed} = \begin{bmatrix} a & b \\ c & d \end{bmatrix} * \begin{bmatrix} 1 \\ 2 \end{bmatrix} \Leftrightarrow$$

$$\vec{VectorTransformed} = \begin{bmatrix} a*1+b*2 \\ c*1+d*2 \end{bmatrix}$$

Easy, no? You just treat the vector as a matrix and there you have it. Let's build your transformation method.

```
void mrMatrix22::Transform (mrVector2D & rkVector)
{
  mrVector2D  kVector;
  kVector [0] = kVector [0] * m_aafElements [0][0] + kVector [1] * m_aafElements [0][1];
  kVector [1] = kVector [0] * m_aafElements [1][0] + kVector [1] * m_aafElements [1][1];
}
```

Probability

Probability is a study of math that analyzes events and then tries to evaluate the odds of it happening. Let's go over a simple example.

From yesterday's weather forecast, there is a good probability of heavy wind and a 50% chance of rain.'

This forecast actually tells you the probability of heavy wind or rain happening. From the text you can say there is a good probability of heavy wind, so you can say heavy wind has about a 75–90% chance of happening, and as for rain, only 50%. What does this tell you? Well, if you had 100 days with the exact same forecast, you would probably end up with about 75-90 days with heavy wind, and 50 days with rain.

In case you didn't know, 50% is actually 0.5. The % symbol represents percent, in this case meaning 50 percent, or per hundred.

You will use probability mostly in artificial intelligence so I will cover the basic concepts now.

Sets

A *set* is an unordered collection of objects. The objects are what you evaluate when dealing with probability. They can be numbers, letters, real objects, or just about anything. A set is denoted by a capital letter and the objects contained in it are between curly braces, like `SetA = {2, 5, 12, 22}`. Sets are usually defined as a circle with the letter caption and the objects contained, as shown in Figure 18.8.

Union

The union operation creates a new set that combines both the sets. You can see this in Equation 18.40.

Equation 18.40

$$
\begin{aligned}
A &= \{1,3,6,9\} \\
B &= \{2,7,10\} \\
A \cup B &= \{1,3,6,9\} + \{2,7,10\} \Leftrightarrow \\
A \cup B &= \{1,2,3,6,7,9,10\}
\end{aligned}
$$

This is actually very easy, and you can see this visually in Figure 18.9.

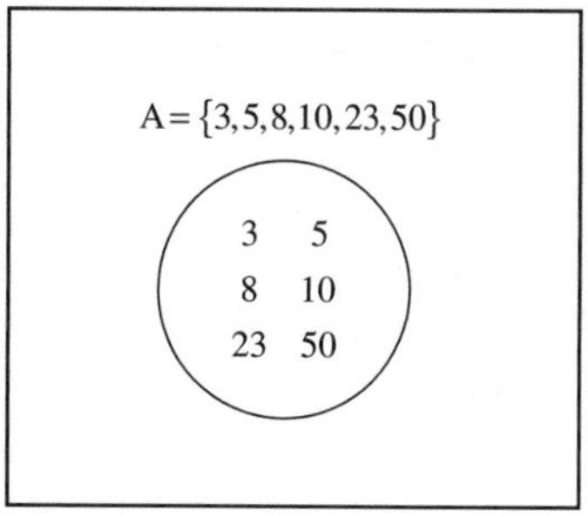

Figure 18.8

Graphical representation of sets.

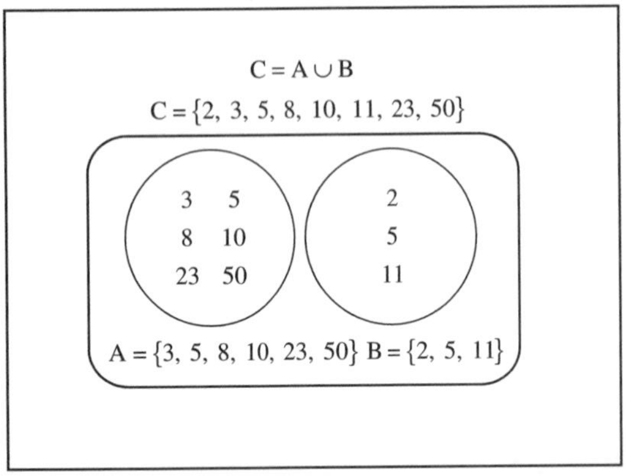

Figure 18.9

Union of two sets.

Or in code you would do the following:

```
List kUnionSet;
List kSetA;
List kSetB;
kUnionSet = kSetA;
For each element of kSetB
Begin
  If element exists in kSetA do nothing
  If element doesn't exists in kSetA, add it to the list kUnionSet
End
```

> **NOTE**
> We have supposed that the `List` class exists and has the used methods implemented.

Intersection

The intersection operation is straightforward. You compare each element of a set to another set. The elements that are contained in both sets are elements that show in the *intersected* set as shown in Equation 18.41 and Figure 18.10.

Equation 18.41

$$A = \{1,2,5,9\}$$
$$B = \{2,5,7,10\}$$
$$A \cap B = \{1,2,5,9\} - \{2,5,7,10\} \Leftrightarrow$$
$$A \cap B = \{2,5\}$$

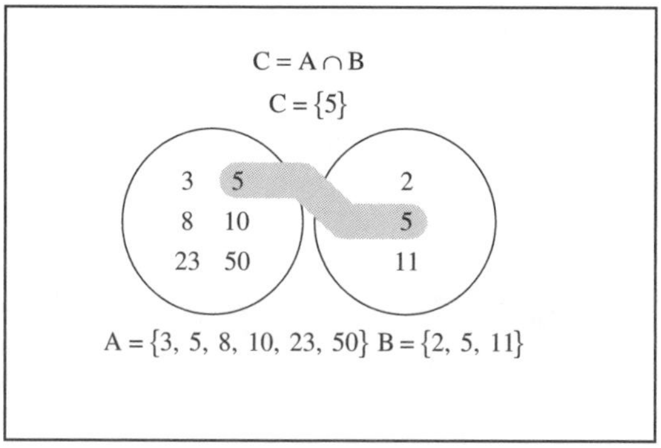

Figure 18.10
Intersection of two sets.

As usual, in code you have the following:

```
List kIntersectionSet;
List kListA;
List kListB;
For each element of kSetB
Begin
  If element exists in kSetA add It to kIntersectionSet
  If element doesn't exists in kListA do nothing
End
```

As you can see by the code, you will go over each element of the set, and see whether it exists in the other set. If it does, it is added to the final set; if it doesn't exist, it is ignored.

Functions

A function is really an equation, but since you used equation names for all the formulas before, you need to distinguish the two things. So, you will call this stuff functions. But what is this stuff? I think an example will help.

If every day I gain 0.22 lb, how much weight would I have gained after 15 days? You can multiply the 0.22 lb by 15 to get 3.31 lb. This is correct, but what if you want to know how much I will weigh after 23 days? And what about after 93 days? You can mathematically represent this as a function, as shown in Equation 18.42.

Equation 18.42

$$WeightGained(Days) = 100 * Days$$

And you can see this graphically in Figure 18.11.

Functions can be used to express various series, ideas, and so on. Functions are a nice tool to know and one that you will use frequently in Chapter 20, "Introduction to Physics Modeling."

Integration and Differentiation

Differentiation and integration are advanced calculus math topics. I will go over some basic theories related to physics, since you will need it later.

If you are driving a car, and you press the gas pedal, producing an acceleration of 11.16 mph, how do you get to the velocity and position functions? First, you need to define your acceleration function as Equation 18.43.

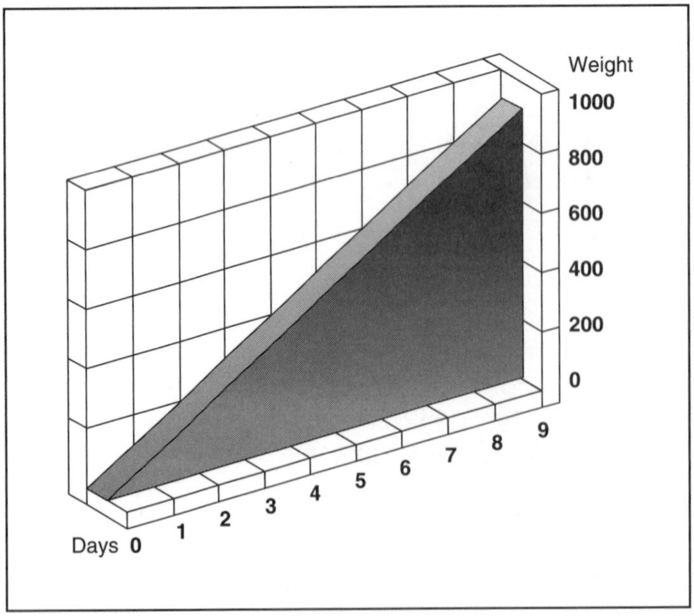

Figure 18.11

Graphical representation of a function.

Equation 18.43

$$Acceleration(time) = 5m/s^2$$

So, looking at Equation 18.43, how do you get the velocity function? You need to integrate this function. How? Well, this is a rather simple function so you can easily do it as shown in Equation 18.44.

Equation 18.44

$$\begin{aligned}
&Velocity(time) = \int Acceleration(time) * \Delta time \Leftrightarrow \\
&Velocity(time) = InitialVelocity + Acceleration * time \Leftrightarrow \\
&Velocity(time) = 5 * time
\end{aligned}$$

How do you know the integration is like this? You cheat. In Appendix E you will find a table of useful integration constants. And now that you have the velocity function, how about getting the position function? Take a look at Equation 18.45.

Equation 18.45

$$\begin{aligned}
&Position(time) = \int Velocity(time) * \Delta time \Leftrightarrow \\
&Position(time) = InitialPosition + InitialVelocity * time + \tfrac{1}{2} Acceleration * time^2 \Leftrightarrow \\
&Position(time) = 0 + 0 * time + \tfrac{1}{2} 5 * time^2 \Leftrightarrow \\
&Position(time) = \tfrac{1}{2} 5 * time^2
\end{aligned}$$

You also can cheat and use Appendix E to get to the final equation.

Differentiation

A function derivative gives you the slope of the function at any given position. Differentiating a function is the exact opposite of integrating. Using the example given in the integration section, you can get the acceleration from velocity and velocity from position as shown in Equations 18.46 and 18.47.

Equation 18.46

$$\begin{aligned}
&Velocity(time) = Position(time)' \Leftrightarrow \\
&Velocity(time) = (\tfrac{1}{2} 5 * time^2)' \Leftrightarrow \\
&Velocity(time) = (5 * time)
\end{aligned}$$

Equation 18.47

$$Acceleration(time) = Velocity(time)' \Leftrightarrow$$
$$Acceleration(time) = (5*time)' \Leftrightarrow$$
$$Acceleration(time) = 5$$

As in the integration process, you also can cheat and use Appendix E tables to get the derivatives.

Why am I not going through all of the integration and derivation processes? Honestly, because it would cover an entire chapter by itself. You hardly need this in games, but it can be useful to know the basics of physics. If you are brave, check the references and go over this on your own.

Summary

You have covered a lot of ground here. Math is one of the fundamental aspects of game programming. This chapter introduced you to the very basics needed to cover the rest of the book rather easily, but consider it only a starting point. There are many other mathematical concepts you will need to know during your game programming career so don't hesitate to check the references to learn some new cool stuff.

The classes you built in this chapter can be used in any 2D application and will be used throughout the rest of the book. So I if you haven't already, try to understand the code well.

Questions and Answers

Q: What is the relation of trigonometry with vectors and matrices?

A: As you will see in the 2D transformation chapter, trigonometry is used to produce rotations; and matrices are used to provide a way to do these rotations.

Q: Do vectors really have a starting point?

A: This is a disputed issue among mathematicians. Some defend that a vector doesn't have a starting point, or origin. Others defend that each vector has an origin, at the origin of the system it is referred to. All your vectors have origin in the center of your world, that is $\vec{V}=(0;0)$.

Q: Why do you represent *i* with row and *j* with column? Wouldn't it be more logical to do it the other way around, like *x* and *y* in the array?

A: Even for us programmers it would be easier to have *i* and *j* swapped, but the way *i* and *j* are used is mathematically correct.

Q: If I want more information on functions, in what kind of books should I look?

A: You should look for just about everything related to calculus. University calculus textbooks are your best choice, though.

Exercises

1. Being [Ø] the angle between the hypotenuse and the adjacent side 0,98 radians, and being the hypotenuse 12 centimetERs, calculate the adjacent and opposite side length.
2. If $\vec{a}$ =(12;3), $\vec{b}$=(24;3), and $\vec{C}$=(−2;–34), what is the result of the following operation: $\vec{A}$ + ($\vec{b}$−C)?
3. What is the perp-dot product of the vector $\vec{A}$=(4;2) and vector $\vec{b}$=(−2;3)?
4. Using the class vector that is built, what is the code to represent the operation in B?
5. What do the *I* and *J* letters after the matrix name represent?
6. Using the matrix class you built, what is the code to represent the following operation: A + B * Scalar * $\vec{C}$?
7. What is the result of multiplying a zero matrix by an entity matrix?
8. What is a set?
9. If a car is moving at a constant velocity of 89.46 miles per hour, where will it be after 21 seconds?
10. Derive the following equation: $f(x)=2x^2$.

CHAPTER 19

Introduction to Artificial Intelligence

Probably the thing I hate most about games is when the computer cheats. I'm playing my strategy game and I have to spend 10 minutes finding their units while they automatically know where mine are, which type, their energies, and so on. It's not the fact that they cheat to make the game harder, it's the fact that they cheat because the artificial intelligence is very weak. The computer adversary should know just about the same information as the player. If you look at a unit, you don't see their health, their weapons, and their bullets. You just see a unit and depending on your units, you respond to it. That's what the computer should do, that's what artificial intelligence is all about.

In this chapter you will first go through a quick overview about several types of artificial intelligence, and then pick one or two and see how you can apply them to games.

In this chapter, I'm going to do something I really hate in books, which is to explain the concepts with little snippets of code instead of complete programs. The reason I'm doing this is because each implementation of each field of artificial intelligence is first of all, very specific to what you are doing, and secondly, they wouldn't be very fun. Where is the fun in watching a graph giving you the percentage of the decisions, if you can't actually see the bad guy hiding and cornering you? For this reason I will go over several concrete artificial intelligence examples, giving only the theory, and some basic code for the implementation, and it is up to you to chose the best implementation for what you want to do.

The Various Fields of Artificial Intelligence

There are many fields of artificial intelligence, some more game-oriented and others more academic. While it is possible to use almost any of them in games, there is a set of them that stands out.

Expert Systems

Expert systems solve problems, which are usually solved by specialized humans. For example, if you go to a doctor, she will analyze you (either by asking you a set of questions or doing some analysis herself) and according to her knowledge, she gives you a diagnosis.

An expert system could be the doctor if it had a knowledge base broad enough. It would ask you a set of questions, and depending on your answers, it would consult its knowledge base, and give you a diagnosis.

The system checks each of your answers with the possible answers of its knowledge base, and depending on your answer, asks you other questions, until it could easily give you a diagnosis.

For a sample knowledge tree, take a look at Figure 19.1.

So, a few questions would be asked, and according to the answers, the system would descend the according tree branch until it reached a leaf.

A very simple expert system for a doctor could be:

```
Answer = AskQuestion ("Do you have a fever?");
if (Answer == YES)
{
 Answer = AskQuestion ("Is it a high fever (more than 105.8 F)?");
 if (Answer == YES)
 {
  Solution = "Go to a hospital now!";
}
```

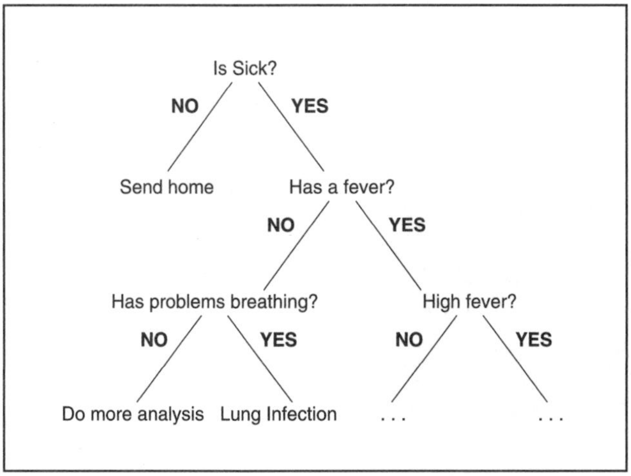

Figure 19.1

An expert system knowledge tree.

```
  else
  {
   Answer = AskQuestion ("Do you feel tired?");
   if (Answer == YES)
   {
    Solution = "You probably have a virus, rest a few days!";
   }
   else
   {
    Solution = "Knowledge base insufficient. Further diagnosis needed.";
   }
  }
}
else
{
 Answer = AskQuestion ("Do you have problems breathing?");
 if (Answer == YES)
 {
  Solution = "Probably a lung infection, need to do exams."
}
 else
 {
  Solution = "Knowledge base insufficient. Further diagnosis needed.";
 }
}
```

As you can see, the system follows a set of questions, and depending on the answer, either asks more questions or gives a solution.

You will use a system similar to this later for some game AI.

NOTE

For the rest of this chapter, it is assumed that the strings work exactly like other variables and you can use the operators like = and == to the same effect as in normal types.

Fuzzy Logic

Fuzzy logic expands on the concept of an expert system. While an expert system can give values of either true (1) or false (0) for the solution, a fuzzy logic system can give values in-between. For example, to know if a person is tall, an expert system would do the following:

```
Answer = AskQuestion ("Is the person's height more than 5' 7"?");
if (Answer == YES)
{
Solution = "The person is tall.";
}
else
{
 Solution = "The person is not tall.";
}
```

While a fuzzy set would appear like so:

```
Answer = AskQuestion ("What is the person's height?");
if (Answer >= 5' 7")
{
 Solution = "The person is tall.";
}
if ((Answer < 5' 7") && (Answer < 5' 3"))
{
 Solution = "The person is almost tall.";
}
if ((Answer < 5' 3") && (Answer < 4' 11"))
{
 Solution = "The person isn't very tall.";
}
else
{
Solution = "The person isn't tall.";
}
```

Where the result would be fuzzy. Usually a fuzzy set returns values from 0 (false) to 1 (true) representing the membership of the problem. In the last example, a more realistic fuzzy system would use the graph described in Figure 19.2 to return a result.

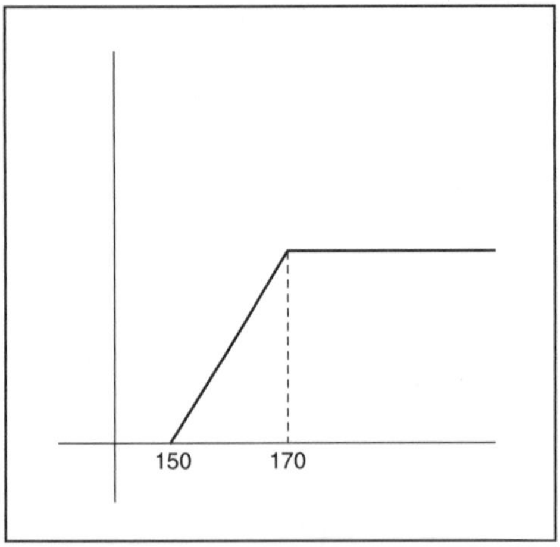

Figure 19.2

Fuzzy membership.

As you can see from the graph, for values greater than 5' 7", the function returns 1, for values less than 4' 11", the function returns 0, and for values in-between, it returns the corresponding value between 5' 7" and 4' 11". You could get this value by subtracting the height from 5' 7" (the true statement) and dividing by 20 (5' 7"–4' 11", which is the variance in the graph). In code this would be something like the following:

```
Answer = AskQuestion ("What is the person's height?");
if (Answer >= 5' 7")
{
 Solution = 1
}
if (Answer <= 4' 11")
{
 Solution = 0
}
else
{
 Solution = (Answer - 5' 7") / (5' 7"- 4' 11")
}
```

You may be wondering why you don't just use the equation only and discard the `if` clauses. The problem with doing so is that if the `Answer` is more than 5' 7" or less than 4' 11", it will give values outside the 0 to 1 range, thus making the result invalid.

Fuzzy logic is extremely useful when reasoning is needed in games. Later, you will see how you can apply fuzzy logic to games.

Genetic Algorithms

Genetic algorithms are a method of computing solutions to a problem that relies on the concepts of real genetic concepts (such as evolution and hereditary logic).

You may have had a biology class in high school that explained what heredity is, but in case you haven't, it is the field of biology that studies the evolution of subjects when they reproduce (okay, maybe there is a little more to it than this, but you are only interested in this much).

As you know, everyone has a blood type with the possible types being A, B, AB, and O, and each of these types can be either positive or negative. When two people have a child, their types of blood will influence the type of blood the child has.

Now, all that you are is written in your DNA. While the DNA is nothing more than a collection of bridges between four elements, it can hold all the information about you, such as blood type, eye color, skin type, and so on. The little "creatures" that hold this information are called genes.

What you may not know is that although you have only one type of blood, you have two genes specifying which blood type you have. So, how can it be? If you have two genes describing two types of blood, how can you have only one type of blood? Predominance! Certain genes' information is stronger (or more influential) than others, thus dictating the type of blood you have.

What if the two genes' information is equally strong? You get a hybrid of the two. For your blood type example, both type A and type B are equally strong, this makes the subject have a blood type AB.

Figure 19.3 shows all the possible combinations of the blood types.

You can get from this table that both the A type and B type are the predominant ones, and the O type isn't. You can also see that positive is the predominant type.

So, how does this apply to the computer? There are various implementations that range from solving mathematical equations to full generation of artificial creatures for scientific research. Genetic algorithms may also be used for learning, which uses the previous progenitors' information to form some kind of memory.

Parent 1	Parent 2	Offspring
A	A	A
A	O	A
A	B	AB
B	B	B
B	O	B
B	A	AB
O	O	O

Figure 19.3

Gene blood type table.

Implementing a simple genetics algorithm in the computer isn't difficult. The necessary steps are described here:

1. Pick up a population and set up initial information values.
2. Order each of the information values to a flat bit vector.
3. Calculate the fitness of each member of the population.
4. Keep only the two with the highest fitness.
5. Mate the two to form a child.

And you have a child that will be the product of the two best subjects in the population. Of course, to make a nice simulator, you wouldn't use only two of the subjects, but you would group various subjects in groups of two, and mate them to form various children, or offspring.

Now for the explanation of each of the steps:

You first need to use the initial population (all the subjects, this can be creatures, structures, or mathematical variables) and set them up with their initial values (these can be information universally known, previous experiences of the subject, or completely random).

Then, you need to order the information to a bit vector as shown in Figure 19.4.

While some researchers say that an implementation of a genetic algorithm must be done with bit vectors, others say that the bit vectors can be replaced by a function or

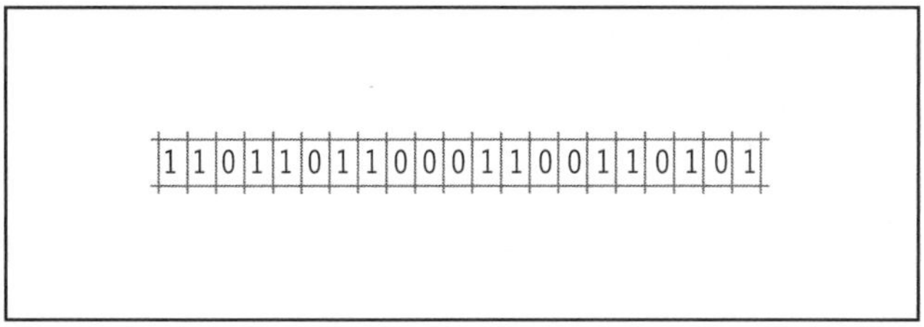

Figure 19.4

Bit vectors (or binary encoding) of information—the virtual DNA.

equation that will analyze each gene of the progenitors and generate the best one out of the two. To be coherent without DNA talk earlier, you will use bit vectors.

You would now have to calculate the fitness of each subject. The fitness is a value that indicates whether you have a good subject (for a creature, this could be if the creature was strong, smart, fast) or a bad subject. Calculating the fitness is completely dependent on the application, so you need to find some equation that will work for what you want to do.

After calculating the fitness, get the two with the highest fitness and mate them. You can do this various ways, either by randomly selecting which gene comes from which progenitor, or by intelligently selecting the best genes of each to form an even more perfect child. If you want to bring mutation to the game, after you get the final offspring you can switch a bit here and there. This entire process is shown in Figure 19.5.

And that's it, you have your artificial offspring ready to use.

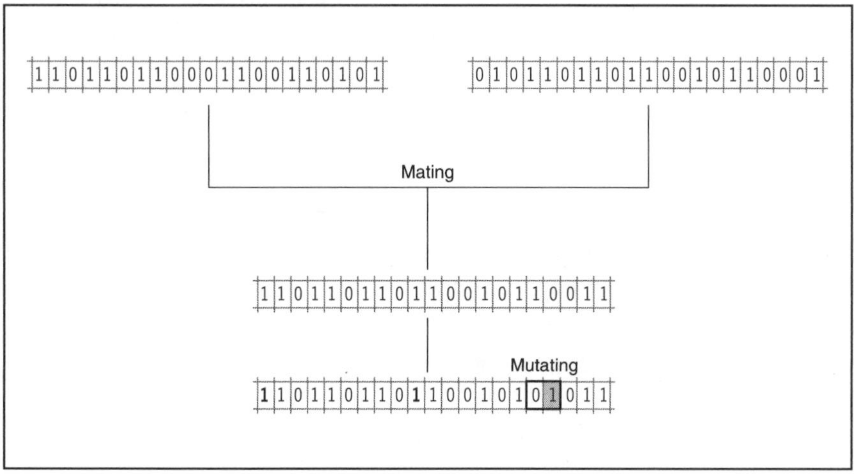

Figure 19.5

Mating and mutation of an offspring.

A good use of this technology in games is to simulate artificial environments. Instead of keeping the same elements of the environment over and over, you could make them evolve to stronger, smarter, and faster beings that would interact with the environment and us.

Neural Networks

Neural networks are an attempt to solve problems by imitating the workings of a brain. Researchers started by trying to mimic animal learning by using a collection of idealized neurons and applying stimuli to them to change their behavior.

Neural networks have evolved much in the past few years, mostly due to the discovery of various new learning algorithms, which made it possible to implement the idea of neural networks with success. Unfortunately, there still aren't major discoveries in this field to make it possible to simulate the human brain efficiently.

The human brain is made of around 50 billion neurons (give or take a few billion). Each neuron can compute or process information and send this information to other neurons. Trying to simulate 50 billion neurons in a computer would be disastrous. Each neuron takes various calculations to be simulated, which would lead to around 200 billion calculations. You can forget about modeling the brain fully, but you can use a limited set of neurons (the human brain only uses around 5-10% of its capacity) to mimic basic actions of humans.

In 1962, Rosenblatt created something called a perceptron, one of the earliest neural network models. A *perceptron* is an attempt to simulate a neuron by using a series of inputs, weighted by some factor, which would output a value of 1 if the sum of all the weighted inputs was bigger than a threshold, or 0 if it wasn't.

The idea of a perceptron, and its resemblance to a neuron, is shown in Figure 19.6.

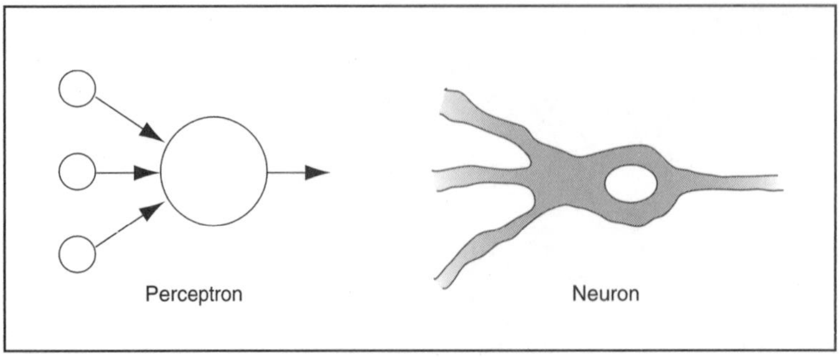

Figure 19.6

A perceptron and a neuron.

While a perceptron is a simple way to model a neuron, many other ideas evolved from this, such as the same values being used for various inputs, adding a bias or memory term, and mixing various perceptrons using the output of one as input for others. All of this together formed the current neural networks seen in research today.

There are several ways to apply neural networks to games, but probably the most predominant is the use of neural networks to simulate memory and learning.

This field of artificial intelligence is probably one of the most interesting parts of artificial intelligence, but unfortunately, too lengthy to give a proper explanation of it here. Fortunately, neural networks are becoming more and more popular these days and numerous publications are available about the subject.

Deterministic Algorithms

Deterministic algorithms are more of a game technique than an artificial intelligence concept. Deterministic algorithms are predetermined behaviors of objects in relation to the universe problem.

> **NOTE**
>
> **The universe, or universe problem, is the current state of the game that influences the subject when reasoning, and it can range from as simple as the subject's health, to the terrain slope, number of bullets, number of adversaries, and so on.**

You will consider three deterministic algorithms in this section: random motion, tracking, and patterns. While some defend that patterns aren't a deterministic algorithm, I've included them in this section because they are predefined behaviors.

Random Motion

The first, and probably simpler, deterministic algorithm is random motion. While random motion can't really be considered intelligence (it's random), there are a few things you can make to simulate some simple intelligence.

Let's pick an example, if you are driving on a road and you reach a fork, and you really don't know your way home, you usually take a random direction, unless you are superstitious and always take the right road. Now, this isn't very intelligent, but you can simulate this in your games like so:

```
NewDirection = rand ()% 2;
```

Which will give a random value that is either 0 or 1, which would be exactly the same thing as if it were you that was driving.

While this kind of algorithm can be used in your games, it isn't very fun. But there are things to improve here. Another example? Okay.

Suppose you are watching some guard patrolling an area, there are two things that may happen, he (or she) could be moving in a logical way, maybe a circle or straight line, but most of the time the guard will move randomly. He will move from point A to B, then to C, then go to B, then C again, then D, get back to A, and repeat this in a totally different form.

Take a look at Figure 19.7 to see this in action.

His movement can be described in code with something like:

```
mrVector2D kGuardVelocity;
mrVector2D kGuardPosition;
mrInt32 kGuardCycles;
 /* Initialize random velocity and cycles */
kGuardVelocity [0] = rand () % 10 - 5;
kGuardVelocity [1] = rand () % 10 - 5;
kGuardCycles = rand () % 20;
while (GameIsRunning)
{
  /* If we still have some cycles with the current movement */
 while (kGuardCycles-- > 0)
 {
```

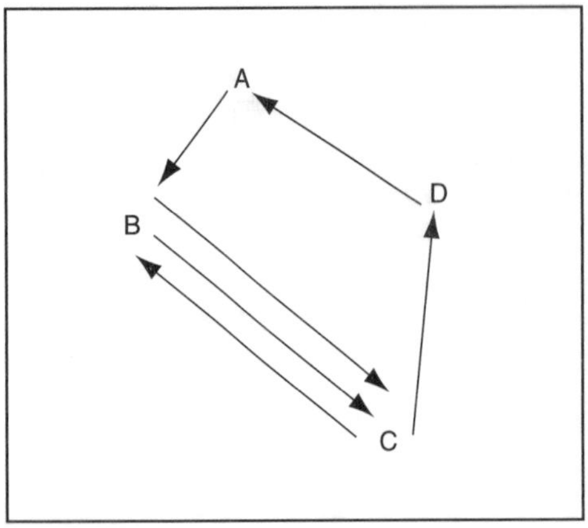

Figure 19.7

A very bad guard.

```
  kGuardPosition += kGuardVelocity;
 }
  /* Change velocity and cycles */
 kGuardVelocity [0] = rand () % 10 - 5;
 kGuardVelocity [1] = rand () % 10 - 5;
 kGuardCycles = rand () % 20;
}
```

And you have your guard. Now that you know what happened, you may think this isn't very intelligent, but if you were only playing the game, you would only see that the guard was patrolling the place, and you would think that he was being intelligent.

NOTE

You will be using the code you developed in Chapter 18, "The Mathematical Side of Games," to represent vectors. This way you can do the code, and explain the logic in a vector way, which is more correct.

Tracking

When you are trying to catch someone, there are a few things you must do. First, move faster than him, or else you will never catch him, and move in the direction he is from you. There is no logic in running south if he is north of you.

To solve this problem, and add a little more intelligence to your games, you will use a tracking algorithm.

Let's suppose that the guard has spotted an intruder. He would probably start running toward him. If you wanted to do this in your game, you would do the following:

```
mrVector2D kGuardVelocity;
mrVector2D kGuardPosition;
mrVector2D kIntruderPosition;
mrUInt32 iGuardSpeed;
 /* Intruder was spotted, run to him */
mrVector2D kDistance;
kDistance = kIntruderPosition - kGuardPosition;
kGuardVelocity = kDistance.Normalize ();
kGuardVelocity *= iGuardSpeed;
kGuardPosition += kGuardVelocity;
```

What this code does is get the direction from the intruder to the guard (the normalized distance) and move the guard to that direction by a speed factor.

Of course, there are several improvements to this algorithm such as taking into account the intruder's velocity, and maybe some reasoning about the best route to take.

The last thing to learn about tracking algorithms is anti-tracking algorithms. An anti-tracking algorithm uses the same concepts as the tracking algorithm, but instead of moving toward the target, it runs away from the target. In your previous guard example, if you wanted the intruder to run away from the guard, you could do something like the following:

```
mrVector2D kGuardVelocity;
mrVector2D kGuardPosition;
mrVector2D kIntruderPosition;
mrUInt32 iGuardSpeed;
 /* Guard has spotted the intruder, intruder run away from him*/
mrVector2D kDistance;
kDistance = kGuardPosition - kIntruderPosition;
kGuardVelocity = -kDistance.Normalize ();
kGuardVelocity *= iGuardSpeed;
kGuardPosition += kGuardVelocity;
```

As you can see, the only thing you need to do is negate the distance to the target (distance from the guard to the intruder). You could also use the distance from the intruder to the guard, and not negate it, because it would produce the same final direction.

Patterns

A pattern, as the name indicates, is a collection of actions. When those actions are performed in a determined sequence, a pattern (repetition) can be found.

Let's look at, for example, my rice-cooking pattern (rice . . . yummy). There are several steps I take for cooking rice:

1. Take the ingredients out of the ingredients case.
2. Get the cooking pan from under the sink (hey, it's a good place to keep it).
3. Add about two liters of water to the pan.
4. Boil the water.
5. Add 250 grams of rice, a pinch of salt, and a little lemon juice.
6. Let the rice cook for 15 minutes.

And presto, I have rice ready to be eaten (you don't mind if I eat while I write, do you?). Whenever I want to cook rice, I usually follow these steps, or this pattern.

In games, a pattern can be as simple as making an object move in a circle, to as complicated as executing orders like attacking, defending, harvesting food, and so on.

So, how is it possible to implement a pattern in a game? Well, you first need to decide how a pattern is defined, for your small implementation, you will use a simple combination of two values: the action description and the action operator. The action description defines what the action does, and the action operator defines how it does it. The action operator can express the time to execute the action, how to execute it, or the target for the action, depending on what the action is.

Of course, your game may need a few more arguments to an action than only these two, so, if you need to, just add the needed parameters.

Let's resume your guard example. Remember that there were two things he may be doing if he was patrolling the area, moving either randomly (as you saw before) or in a logical way. For this example, let's say the guard is moving in a logical way, that he is performing a square-styled movement as shown in Figure 19.8.

As you can see, the guard moves around the area in a square-like pattern, which is more realistic than moving randomly as before.

Now, doing this in code isn't difficult, but to do so, you first need to define how an action is represented. For simple systems like yours, you can define an action with a description and an operator. The description field describes the action (well . . . duh!), but the operator can have various meanings. It can be the time the action should be performed, the number of shoots that should be shot in that action, if

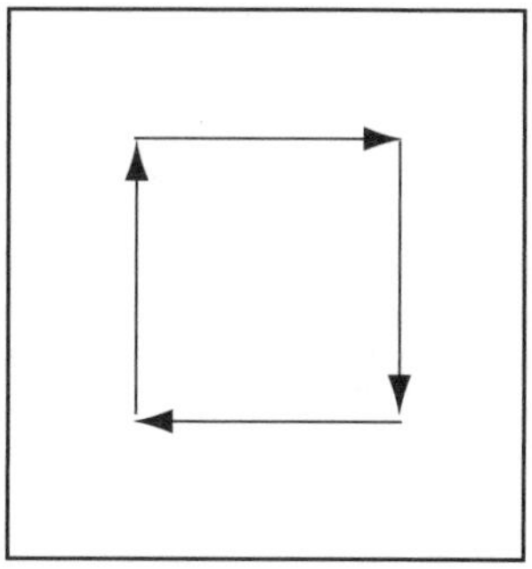

Figure 19.8

A good guard patrolling the area.

the action was to attack something, or anything else that relates to the action. For your guard example, the operator would be the number of feet to move.

While this system works for many actions, you may want to introduce more data to the pattern. Doing so is easy; you simply need to include more operators in the action definition.

A simple example could be:

```
class Action
{
public:
 string Description;
 string Operator;
};
```

To make your guard pattern, you could do something like:

```
Action GuardPattern [4];
GuardPattern [0].Description = "MoveUp";
GuardPattern [0].Operator = "10";
GuardPattern [1].Description = "MoveRight";
GuardPattern [1].Operator = "10";
GuardPattern [2].Description = "MoveDown";
GuardPattern [2].Operator = "10";
GuardPattern [3].Description = "MoveLeft";
GuardPattern [3].Operator = "10";
```

And your guard pattern would be defined. The last thing you need to do is the pattern processor. This isn't hard, you just need to check the actual pattern description, and depending on it, do the action like so:

```
mrUInt32 iNumberOfActions = 4;
mrUInt32 iCurrentAction;
for (iCurrentAction = 0; iCurrentAction < iNumberOfActions;
      iCurrentAction++)
{
 if (GuardPattern [iCurrentAction].Description == "MoveUp";
 {
  kGuardPosition [1] += GuardPattern [iCurrentAction].Operator;
 }
 if (GuardPattern [iCurrentAction].Description == "MoveRight";
```

```
  {
   kGuardPosition [0] += GuardPattern [iCurrentAction].Operator;
  }
  if (GuardPattern [iCurrentAction].Description == "MoveDown";
  {
   kGuardPosition [1] -= GuardPattern [iCurrentAction].Operator;
  }
 if (GuardPattern [iCurrentAction].Description == "MoveUp";
  {
   kGuardPosition [0] -= GuardPattern [iCurrentAction].Operator;
  }
 }
```

Which would execute the pattern to make the guard move in a square. Of course, you may want to change this to only execute one action per frame, or execute only part of the action per frame, but that's another story.

Finite State Machines

Random logic, tracking, and patterns should be enough to enable you to create some intelligent characters for your game, but they don't depend on the actual state of the problem to decide what to do. If, for some reason, a pattern tells the subject to fire the weapon, and there isn't any enemy near, then the pattern doesn't seem very intelligent, does it? That's where finite state machines (or software) enter.

A finite state machine is a machine that has a finite number of states as simple as a light switch, that can be either on or off, or as complicated as a VCR which can be either idle, playing, pausing, recording, and more depending on how many bucks you spend on it. A finite state software application is an application that has a finite number of states.

These states can be represented as the state of the playing world. Of course, you won't create a state for each difference in an object's health (if the object had a health ranging from 0 to 1,000, and you had ten objects, that would mean 1000^{10} different states, and I don't even want to think about that case), but you can use ranges, like whether an object's health is below a number or not, and only use the object's health for objects that are near the problem you are considering. This would reduce the states from 1000^{10} to about four or five.

Let's resume your guard example. If an intruder were approaching the area, until now you would only make your guard run to him. But what if the intruder is too far? Or too near? And if the guard had no bullets in his gun? You may want to make the guard act differently. For example, consider the following cases:

1. Intruder is in a range of 1000 feet: just pay attention to the intruder.
2. Intruder is in a range of 500 feet: run to him.
3. Intruder is in a range of 250 feet: tell him to stop.
4. Intruder is in a range of 100 feet and has bullets: shoot first, ask questions later.
5. Intruder is in a range of 100 feet and doesn't have bullets: sound the alarm.

So, you have five scenarios, or more accurately, states. You could include more factors on the decision such as whether there are any other guards in the vicinity, or more complicated, using the guard's personality to decide. If the guard is too much of a coward, you probably never shoot, but just run away.

The previous steps can be described in code like the following:

```
 /* State 1 */
if ( (DistanceToIntruder () > 500) && (DistanceToIntruder () < 1000) )
{
 Guard.TakeAttention ();
}
 /* State 2 */
if ( (DistanceToIntruder () > 250) && (DistanceToIntruder () < 500) )
{
 Guard.RunToIntruder ();
}
 /* State 3 */
if ( (DistanceToIntruder () > 100) && (DistanceToIntruder () < 250) )
{
 Guard.WarnIntruder ();
}
if (DistanceToIntruder () < 100)
{
  /* State 4 */
 if (Guard.HasBullets ())
 {
  Guard.ShootIntruder ();
 }
```

```
  /* State 5 */
 else
 {
  Guard.SoundAlarm ();
 }
}
```

Not hard, was it? If you combine this with the deterministic algorithms you saw previously, you can make a very robust artificial intelligence system for your games.

Fuzzy Logic

You have already covered the basics of fuzzy logic, but this time you will go in-depth with several of the fuzzy logic techniques, and how to apply them to games.

Fuzzy Logic Basics

Fuzzy logic uses some mathematical sets theory, called fuzzy set theory, to work. If you're rusty with sets, check the mathematics chapter and come back here.

Fuzzy logic is based on the membership property of things. For example, while all drinks are included in the liquids group, they aren't the only ones in the group (some detergents are liquids too, and you don't want to drink them do you?). The same way as drinks are a sub group, or more accurately, a sub set of the liquids group, some drinks may also be sub sets of other groups, like alcoholic and non-alcoholic drinks. Then in the alcoholic groups there are the considered white drinks (usually having a alcohol rate higher than 40%) and soft drinks, like beer and wine. Then, there are non-alcoholic drinks, like non-alcoholic beer that even if it has a very small rate of alcohol (usually around 0.3%) it isn't a subset of the alcoholic group. This is because the membership of this kind of beer is very small to the alcoholic group and high in the non-alcoholic group.

Now, all this talk about alcoholic and non-alcoholic drinks was for demonstration purposes only, so don't go out and drink alcohol just to see if I'm right. Alcohol damages your brain and your capacity to code, so stay away from it as much as possible (drugs too).

Okay, let's stop being so paternalist and get back to fuzzy logic. Grab a glass and fill it with some water (as much as you want). Now, the glass can have various states, it can be empty, half full, or full (or anywhere in between). So, how do you know which state the glass is in? Take a look at Figure 19.9.

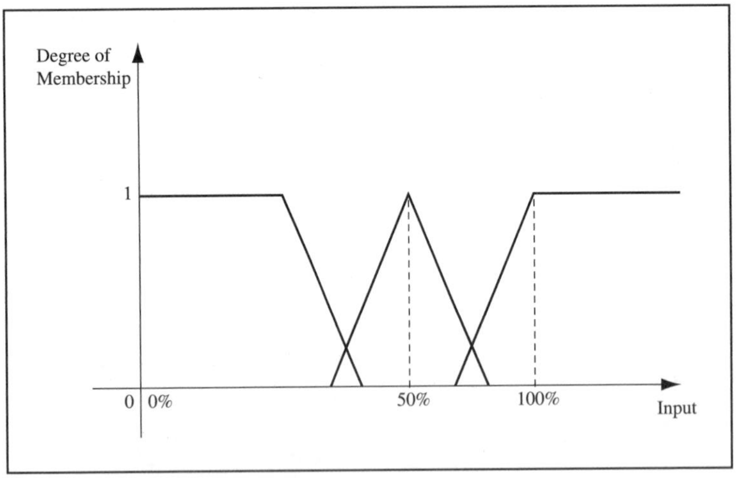

Figure 19.9

Group membership for a glass of water.

As you can see, when the glass has 0% of water, it is totally empty, when it has 50% of water is half full (or half empty if you want) and when it has 100% of its size with water, then it is full. Now, what if you only poured 30% of the water? Or 10%? Or 99%? Well, as you can see from the graph, the glass will have a membership value for each group.

If you want to know the membership values of whatever percentage of water you have, you will have to see where the input (the percentage) meets the memberships graphs, to get the degree of membership of each as shown in Figure 19.10.

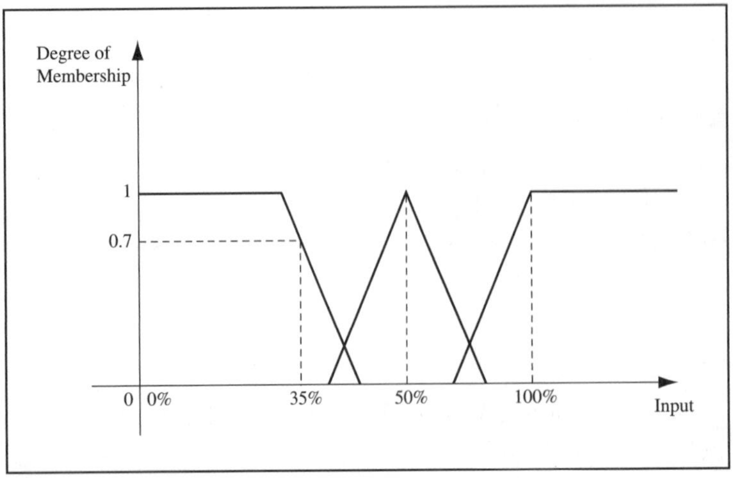

Figure 19.10

Group membership for a glass of water for various values.

Memberships graphs can be as simple as the ones in Figure 19.10, to trapezoids, exponential or other equation derived function. For the rest of this section you will only use normal triangle shapes to define memberships.

As you can check in Figure 19.10, you can see that the same percentage of water can be part of two or more groups, where the greater membership value will determine the value final membership.

You can also see that the final group memberships will range from zero to one. This is one of the requirements for a consistent system.

To calculate the membership value on a triangle membership function, assuming that the value is inside the membership value (if it isn't, the membership is just zero) you can use the following code:

```
mrReal32 fCenterOfTriangle = (fMaximumRange - fMinimumRange) / 2;
 /* Value is in the center of the range */
if (fValue == fCenterTriangle)
{
 fDegreeOfMembership = 1.0;
}
 /* Value is in the first half of the range */
if (fValue < fCenterTriangle)
{
 fDegreeOfMembership = (fValue - fMinimumRange) /
                        (fCenterTriangle - fMinimumRange);
}
/* Value is in the second half of the range */
if (fValue > fCenterTriangle)
{
 fDegreeOfMembership = ((fMaximumRange  - fCenterTriangle) - (fValue -
fCenterTriangle)) /
                        (fMaximumRange  - fCenterTriangle);
}
```

And you have the degree of membership. If you played close attention, what you did was to use the appropriate line slope to check for the vertical intersection of `fValue` with the triangle.

Fuzzy Matrices

The last topic about fuzzy logic you should cover is fuzzy matrices. This is what really makes you add intelligence to your games.

First, pick a game example to demonstrate this concept. Anyone like soccer? Well, I'm from Europe so no American football, and since the World Cup is near, soccer is a good sport to demonstrate this concept. More concretely, what a player should do in various situations.

There are three states of the game you will be defining:

1. Player has the ball
2. Player team has the ball
3. Opposite team has the ball

While there are many other states, you will only be focusing on these three. Now, for each of these states, there is a problem state for the player, you will be considering the following:

1. Player is clear
2. Player is near adversary
3. Player is open for goal

Now, using this three states, and the previous three ones, you can define a matrix that will let you know which action the player should take when the two states overlap.

The action matrix can be seen in Figure 19.11.

Using this matrix would make the player react like normal players do, if he is clear and doesn't have the ball, try to get a favorable position for goal. If he at shooting position and has the ball, try to score, and so on.

But how do you calculate which state is active? Easy, you use the group membership of each state, for both inputs, and multiply the input row with the column row to get the final result for each cell (its not matrix multiplication, you just multiply each row position by the column position to get the row column value).

	Player has ball	Player team has ball	Adversaries have ball
Player is clear	Run for goal	Try to get a good position	Run to nearest adversary
Player is near adversary	Pass the ball	Try to get clear	Try to tackle the adversary
Player is open for goal	Shoot	Get a good position to shoot	Run to nearest adversary

Figure 19.11

Action matrix for a soccer player.

This will give you the best values to chose from, for example, if one cell has a value of 0.34 and the other 0.50 then the best choice is probably to do what the cell with 0.50 says. While this isn't an exact action, it is the best you can take.

There are several ways to improve this matrix, such as using randomness, evaluation of the matrix with another matrix (such as personality of the player) and many more.

A Simple Method for Memory

Although programming a realistic model for memory and learning is hard, there is a method I personally think it's pretty simple to implement—to store game states as memory patterns.

This method will save the game state for each decision it makes (or for each few, depending on the complexity of the game) and the outcome of that decision, and store the decision result in a value from zero to one (being zero a very bad result, and one a very good result).

Take, for example, a fighting game. After every move the subject makes, it logs the result of it (if it hit the target, missed the target, provoked much damage or if the subject was hurt after the attack).

By storing this information, other decisions the subject had to make, you could make him look at his database, and chose the more efficient attack, and do it. Then calculate the result, and adjust the memory result for that attack.

This would make the computer learn what is good or not against a certain player, especially if a player is one of those players that likes to follow the same techniques over and over again.

This method can be used for just about any game, from tic-tac-toe, where you would store the players plays and decide which would be the best play to do using the current state of the game and the memory, to racing games where you would store the movement of the cars from point to point, and depending of the result, it would chose a new way to get to the path or not.

The possibilities are infinite, of course, this only simulates memory, and using only memory isn't the best thing to do, but it is usually best to act based on memory than just pure logic.

Artificial Intelligence and Games

While there are various fields of artificial intelligence, some are getting more advanced each day. The use of neural networks and genetic algorithms for learning is pretty normal in today's games.

Even if all these techniques are being applied to games nowadays, all the hype is out, it doesn't mean you need to use it in your own games. If you just need to model a fly, just make it move randomly. There is no need to apply the latest techniques in genetic algorithms to make the fly sound like a fly, random movement will do just as good, or better than any other algorithm.

There are a few rules I like to follow when developing the artificial intelligence for a game:

1. If it looks intelligent, then your job is done.
2. Put yourself in the place of the subject, and code what you think you would do.
3. Sometimes the simpler technique is the needed one.
4. Always pre-design the artificial intelligence. Don't expect that some tries in coding will make the subject intelligent, design!
5. When nothing else works, just use random logic.

Summary

This has been a small introduction to artificial intelligence since such a broad topic could easily take a few sets of books to be explained, and even so, many details would have to be left of.

The use of artificial intelligence depends much on the type of game you are developing, and because of that it is usually also very application specific. While 3D engines can be used over and over again, it is less than likely that artificial intelligence code can.

While this chapter covered some of the basics of artificial intelligence, this is just a small subset of what you may use, so don't be afraid an experiment around.

Questions and Answers

Q: What are the three deterministic algorithms you covered?

A: Random logic, tracking and patterns.

Q: What is the best method to create a finite state software?

A: Finding out which are the possible states is the hardest task when doing a finite state software. After the possible states are known, finding which actions to take is as simple as asking yourself: "If I was the computer, what would I do in this situation?" and you have your answer.

Q: Can fuzzy matrices be used without multiplying the input memberships?

A: Yes, some people actually prefer to use AND and OR operators, and then randomly select the active cells action.

Exercises

1 What are the main differences between expert system shells and fuzzy logic?
2. What are genetic algorithms based on?
3. How can genetic algorithms be used to solve mathematical problems?
4. What is a deterministic algorithm?
5. What is a finite state machine?

CHAPTER 20

Introduction to Physics Modeling

Making an advanced physics system that can handle practically every variable of a car running, or just creating some realistic falling objects, will differentiate your games from the others.

Up until a few years ago, few games employed realistic physics in them, this usually led to a boring, or limited gameplay. Today, you are seeing games that totally depend on physics engines to fully explore the gameplay.

In the end, I will also talk about particle systems, even though they are mostly a graphics effect, they are based on physics to be done, so I will cover them here.

During the rest of this chapter I will discuss some of the basic physics from which all the other more advanced stuff derives.

Introduction to Physics

There are several fields of physics, from quantum physics, to fluid mechanics. For your games, you will be using part of a specialized field, kinetics, or more accurately, Classic Mechanics. Sir Isaac Newton was one of the philosophers who most contributed to this field. Sometimes also referred to as Newtonian physics, the ideas and mathematics behind this field represent the reality extremely well for the motion of objects that don't approach the speed of light (an object becomes weightless by approaching the speed of light, making many of the following equations unusable).

Physics is heavily based on mathematics, but the good thing is that each equation you learn can be used to make a cool effect, but you should have understood Chapter 18, "The Mathematical Side of Games," well before continuing. If you still have problems with the dot product of two vectors re-read the math chapter and come back to this part.

You will also be using the International System to represent quantities. This is the system the scientific community uses, and it's helpful because people all over the world understand it whether they are from China, France, or Saudi Arabia.

Building a Physics Engine

Building a physics engine isn't as hard as it looks. Of course, if you are planning to support springs, cloth, deformable objects, liquids, and other stuff, it sure is, but you aren't interested in that stuff, you are interested in kinetics, and a physics engine that only incorporates kinetics isn't hard. You don't believe me? You will see when you finish the chapter.

Why Make a Physics Engine?

Physically modeling objects is, even in the most trivial games, one of the aspects that remains the same. Gravity is gravity no matter whether it is a car game or a platform game. Collisions occur both in first-person shooters and with spaceships. Re-writing the same algorithms over and over again is a tedious, unneeded, and money-consuming (time is money) task. As discussed in Chapter 9, modular and re-usable code is one of the fundamental laws of trying to achieve software perfection. There is no better way than making a small physics engine for your task.

Designing the Engine

You need an engine that is flexible, to be able to support various kinds of games; that is robust, to get accurate effects; and that is simple, so any programmer on your team is able to use it. You need to be able to plug it into any project you are doing or have already done to avoid wasting a week's time trying to integrate it without compiler or runtime errors.

You will be working with only one class for your little engine. This class holds all the information about an object, including its physical attributes and physics variables, and allows you to apply forces, handle collisions, and so on.

You could create an entity manager, but doing so would limit the possibilities of the engine, because you couldn't use different constants for different objects (sometimes it is handy to use different gravities to achieve some cool effects).

Using only one class, `mrEntity`, you can do just about anything you can imagine, as you will see.

mrEntity

mrEntity is your physics class. It describes a physics object with the necessary attributes and methods to realistically simulate the movement of objects. Here is the class definition:

```
 /* 'mrEntity.h' */

 /* Mirus base types header */
#include "mrDatatypes.h"
 /* Mirus 2D vector header */
#include "mrVector2D.h"

 /* Include this file only once */
#pragma once

 /* Mirus Entity class */
class mrEntity
{
protected:
  /* Physical attributes */
 mrVector2D     m_kCenterOfMass;
 mrReal32       m_fMass;
 mrReal32       m_fInertia;
 mrReal32       m_fStaticFrictionCoefficient;
 mrReal32       m_fKineticFrictionCoefficient;
 mrReal32       m_fCoefficientOfRestitution;

  /* Physics variables */
 mrVector2D     m_kPosition;
 mrVector2D     m_kLinearVelocity;
 mrReal32       m_fOrientation;
 mrReal32       m_fAngularVelocity;

 mrVector2D     m_kTotalForce;
 mrReal32       m_fTotalTorque;
 mrVector2D     m_kFrictionForce;
 mrReal32       m_fTotalImpulse;

public:
```

```
  /* Constructor / Destructor */
mrEntity (void);
~mrEntity (void);

void Simulate (mrReal32 fStep);

void ApplyLinearForce (mrVector2D & rkForce);
void ApplyTorque (mrReal32 fTorque);
void ApplyForce (mrVector2D & rkForce, mrVector2D & rkPointOfContact);
void ApplyFriction (mrReal32 fGravity);

void HandleCollision (mrEntity & rkOtherEntity,
                        mrVector2D & rkCollisionNormal);

 /* Entity maintenance methods */
void SetPosition (mrVector2D & rkPosition);
void SetOrientation (mrReal32 fOrientation);
void SetLinearVelocity (mrVector2D & rkLinearVelocity);
void SetAngularVelocity (mrReal32 fAngularVelocity);
void SetMass (mrReal32 fMass);
void SetCenterOfMass (mrVector2D & rkCenterOfMass);
void SetInertia (mrReal32 fInertia);
void SetStaticFriction (mrReal32 fStaticFrictionCoefficient);
void SetKineticFriction (mrReal32 fKineticFrictionCoefficient);
void SetCoefficientOfRestitution (mrReal32 fCoefficientOfRestitution);

mrVector2D GetPosition (void);
mrReal32 GetOrientation (void);
mrVector2D GetLinearVelocity (void);
mrReal32 GetAngularVelocity (void);
mrReal32 GetMass (void);
mrVector2D GetCenterOfMass (void);
mrReal32 GetInertia (void);
mrReal32 GetStaticFriction (void);
mrReal32 GetKineticFriction (void);
mrReal32 GetCoefficientOfRestitution (void);
};
```

As you can see, this class uses the previously developed `mrVector2D` class all over, so if you skipped the math chapter, you may have some problems grasping the code.

I will leave the explanation of each variable and method to the appropriate time, and since I will cover them all in the chapter, there is no need to worry. Just remember, as always, to create the default constructor and destructor setting all the members to zero or to a zero vector.

Basic Physics Concepts

Even though most of the topics you will cover in this section you probably know, there are some distinctions from the common world to the physics world—well, not really, the problem is that in the real world people usually use incorrect terms when referring to the physics terms.

Mass

The first concept you should understand is mass. If you haven't heard of mass before, I have some advice for you, shut down your computer, turn off the TV, and go outside because you have been living in your room for way too long.

Every known (and unknown) object has mass (please, no Quantum theories). Even a single atom has some mass. Mass is the measurement of how much matter an object has. The physics and chemistry principles behind mass calculation are well beyond the scope of this book (and honestly, probably human intelligence). If you are really curious, drive to the local library and check out some books on the subject, but don't tell me I didn't warn you.

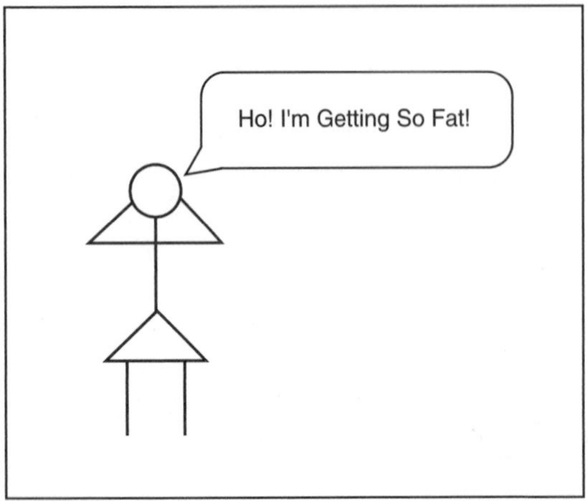

Figure 20.1

Who hasn't heard this from his girlfriend?

Before I go further, I want to clarify one thing that most people still confuse. *Mass* is the measurement of how much matter an object has, and doesn't change depending on what planet you are on. Mass always remains the same. On the other hand, *weight* is the representation of the mass in the current gravitational field. You all know an elephant weighs less on the moon than down here on Earth, right? Its mass remains the same but its weight (which is a force, by the way) will change.

I talk about this when I talk about gravitational fields.

The international system unit for mass is the kilogram (kg).

Time

I could try to describe time in ten, no twenty, no maybe one hundred pages. I could spend hours and hours thinking about it, but in the end, I still couldn't define what time is.

Time is one of those concepts one learns not by reading a book but by experiencing. We all know what time is, but how can we define it? How can we say what it is? My honest opinion is that we can't. We, humans, created the concept of time. We never saw it, we never felt it, we just assumed it was there. Things move, and when they move, we know something has passed or happened, we just don't know what or why, but something changed. During that period of time, something happened, we're just not sure what (not the actual movement, but what happened in terms of, well, time).

I will assume that we all know what time is, and you can use it without being confused by it.

The international system unit for measuring time is the second (s).

Position

Every object has a position. You stand there, I stand here, he stands on the other side of the planet, but we all have a position. You can express the position by using angles (latitude and longitude), a Cartesian plane (x and y values), or any other method you like.

There is just one thing to remember about positions: they are all relative. It is the distance of one object to another. You can say that an object is in location (23, 54) in the Cartesian plane, and you would mean that the object is at a distance of 23 units horizontally and 54 units vertically away from the referential center, usually (0, 0).

Take a look at Figure 20.2.

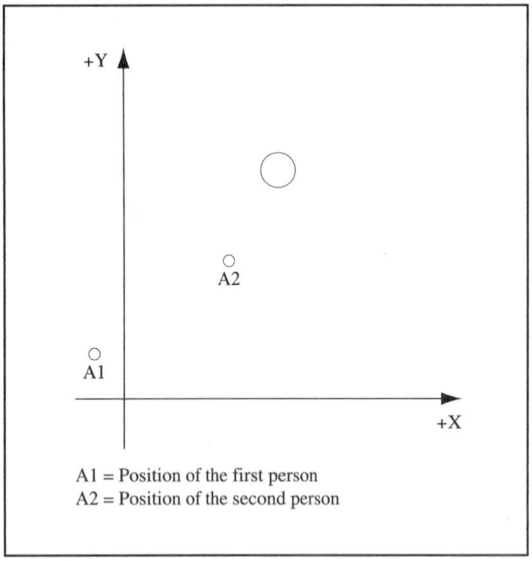

Figure 20.2

The ball is in the same position relative to the origin, but it still can have various positions relative to the other objects.

As you can see, the ball is at position (10, 7) relative to the origin. When a position is the distance to the center of the world, or the origin, you will say it is its world space position.

The other two objects are in different positions, so, in this case, you can say that the ball has three relative positions, one to the origin of the space, another to one object, and another to the other object. If you want to see how you can get the relative position of the ball to all objects, take a look at the following:

$$\vec{Ball} = (10, 7)$$
$$\vec{ObjectOne} = (-4, 2)$$
$$\vec{ObjectTwo} = (5, 5)$$
$$\vec{BallToObjectOne} = \vec{Ball} - \vec{ObjectOne}$$
$$\vec{BallToObjectTwo} = \vec{Ball} - \vec{ObjectTwo}$$
$$\vec{BallToObjectOne} = (14,5)$$
$$\vec{BallToObjectTwo} = (5,2)$$

Easy, isn't it? Well, your position in `mrEntity` is always relative to the center of the world; that is (0, 0). This way, you can easily calculate the relative positions of different objects using the equation shown in Equation 20.1.

Equation 20.1

$$\vec{PositionAToB} = \vec{PositionB} - \vec{PositionA}$$

Velocity

Velocity is another concept that is so badly used in the real world that Newton probably rolls over in his grave. Velocity is not the same thing as speed. People usually confuse the two, but they are totally different things, and are represented differently, as you will see.

Linear Velocity

Linear velocity is the change of position of an object during a period of time. It is represented as vectors, which tell you how many units (depending on the measurement you are using) you move per unit of time. For example, 40 kilometers per hour means that in each hour you move 40 kilometers. Of course, since velocity is a vector, you would need to specify in which direction. You could be moving 40 kilometers along the y-axis, or the x-axis, or both axes (even though, if you would be traveling 40 kilometers per hour on each axis, you would actually be traveling faster than 40 kilometers per hour, but you will learn about this in a little while).

So, how do you define the velocity? *Velocity* is basically the change in position during a period of time, and can be expressed as shown in Equation 20.2.

Equation 20.2

$$\vec{V}\text{elocity (time)} = \vec{P}\text{osition' (time)}$$

Remember from the preceding chapter that a ' after an equation means you are using its derivative.

Or if you aren't interested in an equation, but rather a way to instantaneously calculate the velocity, you can use the formula shown in Equation 20.3.

Equation 20.3

$$\vec{V}\text{elocity} = (\vec{C}\text{urrentPosition} - \vec{L}\text{astPosition}) \; / \; (\text{CurrentTime} - \text{LastTime})$$

Which would give you the velocity in that period of time. If you can make `CurrentTime` very close to `LastTime`, you can almost know the exact velocity an object has.

Like the position, velocity is also relative to another object or system. For your purposes, you will do as you did for the position, and assume the velocity is always relative to the world origin.

Velocity is measured in meters per second (m/s).

Speed

Now you have speed. But if you have velocity, what do you need speed for? While the velocity gives you the direction and quantity of movement on each axis, speed only gives you the quantity of movement. If you want to implement a car game, and you need to show the speed the car is going, you won't show it as a vector will you? Normally you show the movement without caring for the direction, which is obviously done with speed.

To get the speed out of a velocity vector, you need to calculate the norm of the vector, as shown in Equation 20.4.

Equation 20.4

$$\text{Speed} = \text{Norm}\ (\vec{\text{Velocity}})$$

Angular Velocity

So, I have talked about linear velocity and speed, so what the heck is angular velocity? *Angular velocity* is the change in orientation an object has in a period of time. For example, if you have a beach disc, and you throw it to a friend, it will rotate right (if not, then you must learn how to throw it). So, the disc has linear velocity and rotates, thus having angular velocity.

Angular velocity is the change of rotation of the object during a period of time, simple really.

You can calculate angular velocity using Equation 20.5.

Equation 20.5

$$\text{AngularVelocity} = (\text{CurrentOrientation} - \text{LastOrientation})\ /\ (\text{CurrentTime} - \text{LastTime})$$

Angular velocity is a scalar value because orientation in 2D is stored as an angle. If this were a 3D book, the angular velocity would be stored as an asset of three angles.

Angular velocity is measured in radians per second (r/s).

Acceleration

You have now arrived at acceleration. Acceleration is an important concept to know because you will use it to actually move your objects after you apply forces to them. As with the velocity, there are two types of acceleration: linear and angular.

Linear Acceleration

Linear acceleration is the change of linear velocity in a period of time, similar to linear velocity. If you accelerate a car by ten meters in a second, you will change the car's velocity from the current velocity to the current velocity plus ten after one second.

You can calculate the acceleration by using the methods shown in Equations 20.6 and 20.7.

Equation 20.6

$$\vec{\text{Acceleration}}\ (\text{time}) = \vec{\text{Velocity}}\,'\ (\text{time})$$

Or:

Equation 20.7

$$\vec{\text{Acceleration}} = (\vec{\text{CurrentVelocity}} - \vec{\text{LastVelocity}}) \ / \ (\text{CurrentTime} - \text{LastTime})$$

Very simple, really.

Angular Acceleration

The angular acceleration is the change of angular velocity during a period of time. It's the same thing as the linear acceleration but for the rotational component of velocity, angular velocity.

To determine angular acceleration, use Equation 20.8.

Equation 20.8

$$\text{AngularAcceleration} = (\text{CurrentAngularVelocity} - \text{LastAngularVelocity}) \ / \ (\text{CurrentTime} - \text{LastTime})$$

And that's it.

> **NOTE**
>
> Like for linear acceleration and linear velocity, angular acceleration and angular velocity can also be described as equations in function of time. It is basically the same thing as for the linear parts, but taking in account the angular components.

Center of Mass

The last thing I should talk about is the center of mass. In a catch phrase, the center of mass is the point of an object from where all mass distribution is equal, frequently called the center of gravity. If there are no external forces, no wind (not the tiniest wind), and you can find the exact, perfect center of mass of an object, you can balance any object on the tip of a pin, really! Of course, if you try to put a 20-kilogram object over a pin, I can't guarantee the pin will resist, but if it does, and all the conditions are met, then the object, no matter what, will balance itself.

Equation 20.9 will calculate the center of mass.

Equation 20.9

$$\vec{CenterOfMass} = \Sigma(\vec{Position}\ i * mass\ i)\ /\ \Sigma mass\ I$$

This means you will sum all the masses of all the points of an object multiplied by their positions, and then divide the total by the sum of all the masses, or the total mass. Unless you are doing some life or death experiments, you usually pick some distinct points of the object and use those points with approximate masses to find the center of mass. (Finding the exact center of mass involves a few integrations and weird calculations.)

Take a look at Figure 20.3, you will calculate the center of mass of that set in a bit.

As I said before, you won't use every exact point of the object. You assume that your object is divided into a smaller set of objects (the cubes) that have a distinct

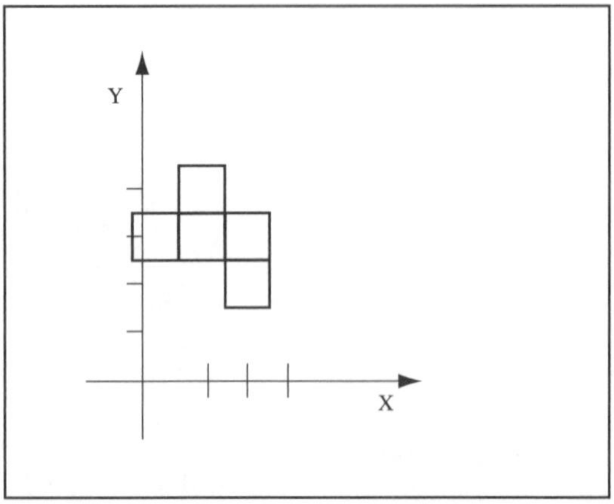

Figure 20.3

A simple set of play cubes.

mass (the mass of each cube is always the same) and position (you will consider the exact center of the cube, a Cartesian coordinate) to get the center of mass.

So, in Figure 20.3 you have 5 cubes, each with a mass of one kilogram. You can find the center of mass using Equation 20.9 as:

$$CenterOfMassX=(1*1+1*2+1*2+1*3+1*3)\ /\ (1+1+1+1+1) = 2.2$$

$$CenterOfMassY=(1*4+1*4+1*5+1*4+1*3)\ /\ (1+1+1+1+1) = 4$$

$$\vec{C}enterOfMass = (CenterOfMassX, CenterOfMassY)$$

$$\vec{C}enterOfMass\ (2.2, 4)$$

You first calculate the x-coordinate of the center of mass, and then you do the same for the y-axis. After this, you create a vector with these two positions to get the final center of mass.

Forces

The base for most concepts in physics is a force. Forces come in various shapes and sizes, big or small, simple or composed, causing movement or not, red or blue. Okay, I jumped over the wagon with the color stuff but the other things are true. Let's do a little exercise. Use your hand to pick up your mouse. Do you know how many forces you exerted on the mouse and how many external forces were exerted on the mouse? No? Take a look at Figure 20.4 to get the answer.

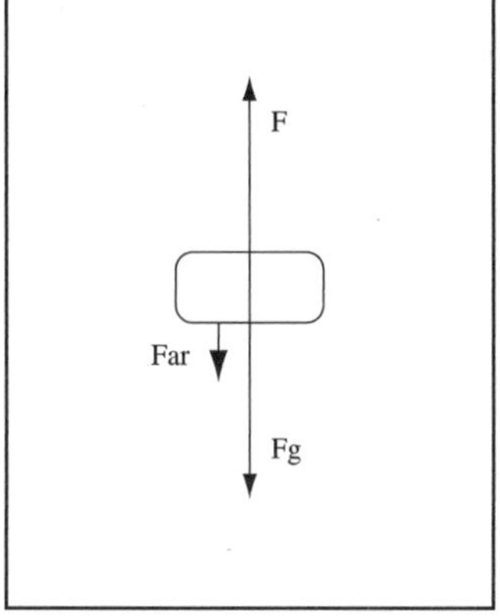

Figure 20.4

Forces exerted on lifting a mouse.

To move the mouse up, you need to produce a force that is greater than the external resistant forces. As you can see by Figure 20.4, you produce a force $\vec{F}$ that is bigger than the other two forces together. I will get into gravity in a minute, before that I just want to explain what $\vec{Far}$ is. $\vec{Far}$ is the force produced by the air resistance when you are moving the object. Unless you are prototyping some system where you need a really accurate simulation, like an airplane simulation, for example, where there are lives at stake, you can usually discard this force from your system.

Now, forces applied to objects resolve to two different kinds of forces: linear and angular forces. You usually call the linear forces, forces, and you call angular forces torque. You can calculate the results of forces separately. Let's go over the linear part of the force, then the angular, and then wrap it all together.

Linear Force

A *linear force* is a force that affects the center of mass of an object. When a force is applied to an object, it exerts a linear effect to the object usually resulting in acceleration of the object, and thus a change of velocity.

If you can remember from high school, Newton's second law tells you that:

The acceleration of a particle is proportional to the force acting on the particle and in a colinear direction with the net force.

This law is illustrated in a mathematical way in Equation 20.10.

Equation 20.10

$$\vec{Force} = Mass * \vec{Acceleration}$$

Forces are usually measured in Newton (N). Some books still prefer to use the unit kg*m/s², which is the same as a Newton. Let's see, if you use Equation 20.10, you get:

$$\vec{Force} = Mass\ \vec{Acceleration} \Leftrightarrow$$

$$\vec{Force}\ (N) = Mass\ (kg) * \vec{Acceleration}\ (m/s^2) \Leftrightarrow$$

$$N = kg * m/s^2$$

Which is exactly the same thing.

So you can see the direct relationship of forces and acceleration. You can get the velocity of the object by integrating the acceleration to get Equation 20.11.

Equation 20.11

$$\vec{Velocity} = \int \vec{Acceleration} <=>$$
$$\vec{Velocity} = \vec{InitialVelocity} + \vec{Acceleration} * Time$$

And you can get the position by integrating the velocity to get Equation 20.12.

Equation 20.12

$$\vec{Position} = \int\int Acceleration * Time$$
$$\vec{Position} = \int (\vec{InitialVelocity} + \vec{Acceleration} * Time)TimeConstant$$
$$\vec{Position} = \vec{InitialPosition} + (\vec{InitialVelocity} * Time) + \frac{1}{2} * (\vec{Acceleration} * Time^2)$$

And you can have the acceleration out of the velocity, and the velocity out of the position by deriving them as shown in Equation 20.13.

Equation 20.13

$$\vec{Acceleration} = \vec{Velocity}' = \vec{Position}''$$

As you can see, you just reverse the integration process.

Forces are vectors, and you treat each component independently. That is, the x component is independent of the y component, and the y component is independent of the horizontal component. Take a look at Figure 20.5 and you will see what I mean.

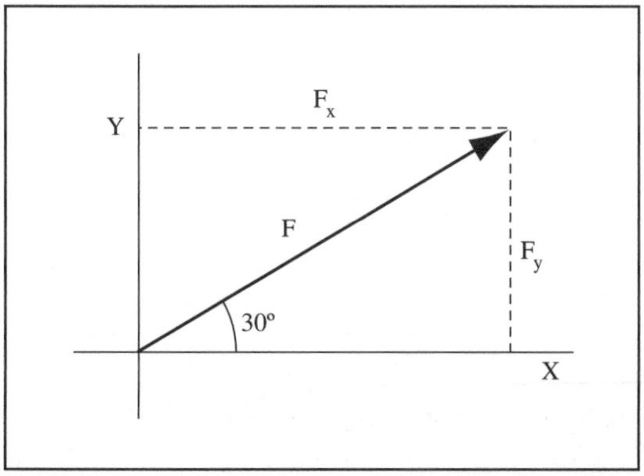

Figure 20.5

Force decomposed to the x-axis and the y-axis.

You can see that a force applied to an object at a 30-degree angle on the x-axis produces a force on both the x-axis and the y-axis. Using the trigonometry you covered in the math chapter, you can see that

$$\vec{Forcex} = \vec{Force} * \text{Cosine } (30)$$
$$\vec{Forcey} = \vec{Force} * \text{Sine } (30)$$

And voilá, you have your force separated into x and y components.

One more thing before you begin with the practical example. The force you used in Equation 20.10 is the resulting force on the object; that is, the sum of all linear forces applied to the object.

To prove all the blabbering above, let's apply it to a simplified real situation. You have a small toy car of mass two kilograms that you apply a constant force of 50 Newton parallel to the x-axis of the world and you want to know the position of the car after ten seconds.

First you need to calculate the acceleration of the car. From Equation 20.10 you know that:

$$\vec{Acceleration} = \vec{Force} \;/\; \text{Mass} \Leftrightarrow$$
$$\vec{Acceleration} = 50 \;/\; 2 \Leftrightarrow$$
$$\vec{Acceleration} = 2.5 \text{ m/s}$$

Now that you have the acceleration you can choose Equation 20.12 and fill up the variables. Since both the initial position and initial velocity are zero, you get the following:

$$\vec{Position} \text{ (time)} = 0 + 0 + 1/2 * \vec{Acceleration} * \text{time}$$

Which gives you:

$$\vec{Position} \text{ (10)} = 0 + 0 + 1/2 * 2.5 * 10 \Leftrightarrow$$
$$\vec{Position} \text{ (10)} = 12.5 \text{ m} \Leftrightarrow$$

Now, that was easy! Knowing this will let you know what to do with your code later.

NOTE

Even if this example was in one dimension, you are still using vectors, so don't forget the vector symbol.

So, in your code, you will add the linear force to the total forces of the entity like so:

```
 /* Apply a linear force to the entity */
void mrEntity::ApplyLinearForce (mrVector2D & rkForce)
{
 m_kTotalForce += rkForce;
}
```

Torque

The next thing you need to know about forces is torque. *Torque* is the angular result of a force. Not all forces produce torque, as you will see in a bit.

When you apply a force to an object, it results in both a linear force (as you saw earlier) and in an angular force. An angular force is a force that only makes the object rotate, never move. This type of force is called torque.

How can you calculate this force? The first thing to find is the distance from the point you apply the force to the center of mass of the object. This is called the arm of the force.

After that you will use the perp-dot product of the arm with the force to find the final torque. This is shown in Equation 20.14.

Equation 20.14

$$\vec{Arm} = \vec{PointOfContact} - \vec{CenterOfMass}$$

$$\vec{Torque} = \vec{Arm} \;|.\; \vec{Force}$$

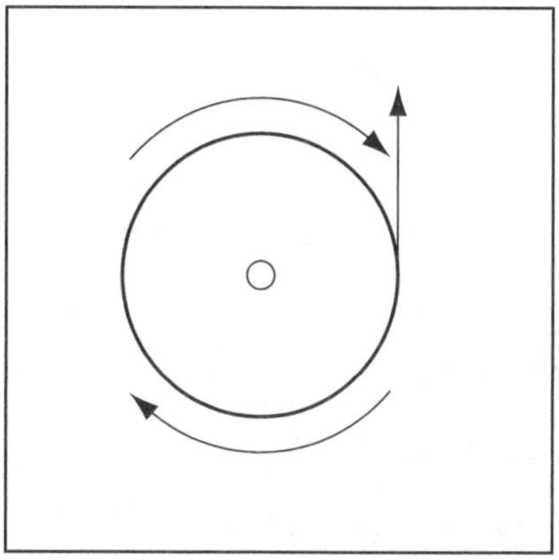

Figure 20.6

Pushing a globe will only make it rotate.

And your code for applying torque is:

```
/* Apply torque to the entity */
void mrEntity::ApplyTorque (mrReal32 fTorque)
{
 m_fTotalTorque += fTorque;
}
```

Now, to get the angular acceleration out of torque, you need to bring a new concept to the game—inertia.

So, what is inertia? According to Newton, *inertia* is the resistance an object has to changing movement.

An object at rest or motion tends to stay in that state unless an external force is applied to it.

Why do you care for inertia anyway? Well, it is with inertia that you get the angular acceleration out of torque, sort of like Equation 20.10 but for rotations now.

And the equation you all were waiting for is shown in Equation 20.15.

Equation 20.15

$$\text{Torque} = \text{AngularAcceleration} * \text{Inertia}$$

As you can see, inertia is sort of like mass, shown in Equation 20.10.

The Resulted Force

So, what happens when you apply a force to an object? Will it only move? Will it only rotate? Nothing will happen? Or both things will happen?

The answer is: Depends!

Depends on the object, where the force is applied, and if the object can freely move and rotate, or not.

Usually, a force produces both linear and angular movements. There isn't a linear movement if there is an external force acting on the object preventing it from moving (the object is nailed down or against a wall).

About the angular movement, there are two cases, either there is an external force that prevents the object from spinning, or the angle between the force and the arm of the force is 180. In this case, the resulting torque will be 0.

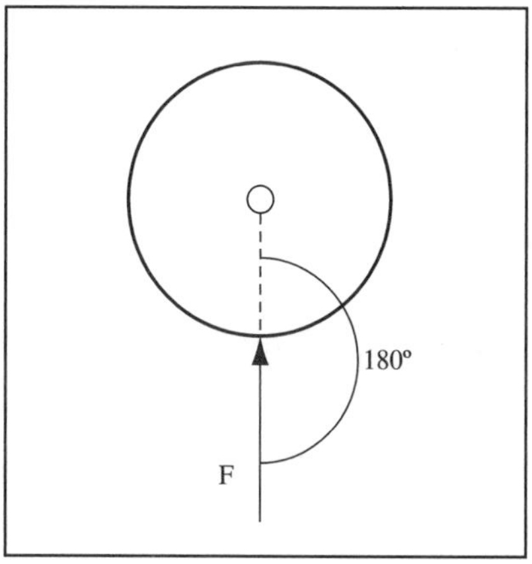

Figure 20.7

Why an object doesn't rotate when the angle of the arm of the force and the force is 180.

So, a general method to apply any force is:

```
 /* Apply a force to the entity */
void mrEntity::ApplyForce (mrVector2D & rkForce,
                           mrVector2D & rkPointOfContact)
{
 m_kTotalForce += rkForce;

 mrVector2D rkArm;

  /* Calculate arm of force */
 rkArm = rkPointOfContact - m_kCenterOfMass;

 m_fTotalTorque += rkArm.PerpDotProduct (rkForce);
}
```

Where you first add the linear component of the force to the total linear force, then use Equation 20.14 to first get the arm of the force, then the perp-dot product of the arm and the force to get the produced torque, and add it to the total torque.

Gravitational Interaction

When you consider two objects in space, apart from other forces (like air resistance and frictions), you also have to deal with gravity. Gravity is just a representation of a high concept, narrowed down to a planet. What really happens is something called gravitational interaction, or in other words, the interaction of the fields created by the objects. No, you usually can't see these fields so you can stop staring at your mouse.

Law of Universal Gravitation

The Law of Universal Gravitation tells you that any two objects in a field exert attracting forces between them. For example, take a look at Figure 20.8.

As you can see, both the objects exert an attracting force, which can be expressed as shown in Equation 20.16.

Equation 20.16

$$\text{GravitationalForce} = \text{GravitationalConstant} * (\text{MassA} * \text{MassB}) \; / \; (\text{DistanceAtoB})^2$$

Which gives you the magnitude of the gravitational force. If you wanted to know the exact direction, you would have to take the distance vector from A to B (or vice versa, depending on which of the forces you are calculating) and transform that vector by the magnitude, and in case you have forgotten, the steps would be:

1. Get the distance vector
2. Normalize the distance vector
3. Multiply the normalized vector by the magnitude

And you would have your force!

There is just one more thing about Equation 20.16 that I haven't talked about yet, the gravitational constant. This constant is the gravitational constant of your universe (I don't know if there are others, but just in case), which is equal to

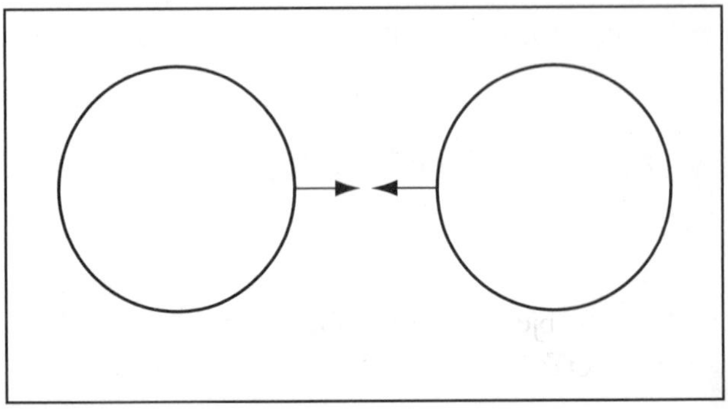

Figure 20.8

Two objects exert attracting forces (in magnitude) between each other.

$6.67*10^{-11}$ $N*m^2*kg^{-2}$. You really don't need to worry about the units, as long as you use mass kilograms, and distance as meters, the equation will give you Newton as result.

To prove this, and give you a little lesson in life, let's do a little practical example.

Let's suppose you weigh 80 kilograms, and the girl you like weighs 60 kilograms. Ask her to stand very near to you (about 5 centimeters), and then kiss her. Go on; don't be shy.

Now, two things may have happened, you have been slapped, or she asks you what the heck happened. Let's hope it was the second, this way you can excuse yourself with the fact that you didn't really kiss her, but rather the fields between you both, attracted you (and her) for the kiss. Let's see this in numbers:

From Equation 20.16:

$$\text{Force} = G * 80 * 60 / 0.05^2 \Leftrightarrow$$

$$\text{Force} = 6.67 * 10^{-11} * 80 * 60 / 0.05^2 \Leftrightarrow$$

$$\text{Force} = 0.0012 \text{ N}$$

Of course, this translated to acceleration is about the same as nothing, but hopefully she doesn't know that the gravitational constant is $6.67 * 10^{-1}$, so just tell her it's something like $6.67 * 10^{-4}$, which gives 128 Newtons of force, which translates to roughly an acceleration of 1.6 m/s^2. Hopefully she will buy it and you will get a kiss; of course, the slap is also a possibility.

NOTE
The gravitational force is a linear force only and should never cause any rotation on an object.

Gravity on Earth and Other Planets

You probably have heard that gravity on Earth is 9.8 m/s^2. Well, this is only partly true, but before I explain why it is only partly true, let's see why it is this value.

If you wanted to use Equation 20.16 to get the force that a planet exerts on an object, you would do:

$$\text{Force} = 6.67*10^{-11} * \text{MassOfObject} * \text{MassOfPlanet} / (\text{DistanceObjectToPlanet})^2$$

One little thing, when you use the distance of the object to the planet, you use the distance from the center of mass of each. So, the `DistanceObjectToPlanet` would be the distance from the object's center of mass to the planet's center of mass. Now, since you are using very large values for the radius of the planets, and usually you use small objects near the planets, you can use the radius of the planet only for the distance. For example:

$$\text{RadiusPlanet} = 6.35 * 10^6 \text{ m}$$

$$\text{RadiusObject} = 2 \text{ m}$$

$$\text{DistanceObjectToPlanet} = 6.35 * 10^6 - 2 \sim = 6.35 * 10^6$$

So you can just use the planet's radius to make things simpler. Of course, if you are using large objects, or objects that are very far away from the planet, it's better to use the real values.

If you use the preceding equation for calculations on planet Earth, you would notice that the result would be an object of mass equal to one kilogram.

$$\text{Force} = 6.67*10^{-11} * 1 * 5.98*10^{24} / (6.38*10^6)^2$$

$$\text{Force} = 9.799 \text{ N}$$

Which would give a force of 9.799, or 9.8 N. If you remember from Equation 20.10, you can get the acceleration by dividing the force by the mass as:

$$\text{Acceleration} = 9.8 / 1 = 9.8 \text{ m/s}^2$$

And that's how you reach the conclusion that the acceleration down here on Earth is 9.8 m/s^2.

Now, why isn't this completely correct? Earth doesn't have a perfect sphere shape, it's more like a light oval. If you change the radius a little bit, you get values between 9.7 and 9.9 N in extreme parts of the planet. For practical purposes, assume that the gravity acceleration where you are is 9.8 m/s^2, but if you want, just find the exact distance between your longitude and latitude position to the center of the Earth to calculate the distance from where you are.

Having proved this, you can get the gravity force on Earth by multiplying the object's mass by the gravity acceleration as shown in Equation 20.17.

Equation 20.17

$$\text{GravityForce} = \text{Mass} * 9.8$$

About the force on the planet, well, due to the fact that it results in such a small acceleration, something in the 0.0000000000000000001 order, it is usually discarded, as you can see in Figure 20.9.

You don't have a method to apply gravity in your engine but if you want to simulate gravity you can just do:

```
mrEntity kEntity;
kEntity.SetMass (10);
mrVector2D kGravity;
kGravity [0] = 0;
kGravity [1] = 9.8 * kEntity.GetMass ();
Entity.ApplyLinearForce (kGravity);
```

In the previous example, you are supposing that gravity has only a vertical component. While this is true most of the time, it depends on the referential system you have chosen for your game.

Simulating Projectiles

The last topic with relation to gravity I should explain is projectiles. For the rest of this section I will refer to a projectile as a particle or an object that has a mass, which had a force exerted at the beginning of the simulation, and the only force applied to the object is gravity. Even though there are several forces and effects you could model when dealing with trajectories, such as drag and the Magnus effect, those would take a whole book to be explained.

Before proceeding, take a look at Figure 20.10.

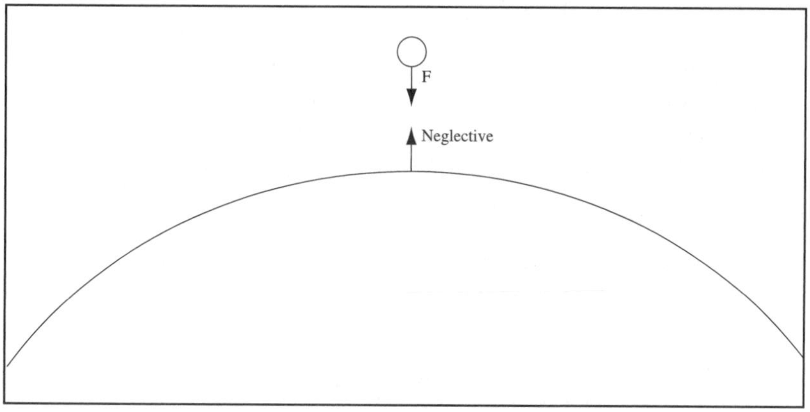

Figure 20.9

An object in a planet's field neglects the movement of the planet.

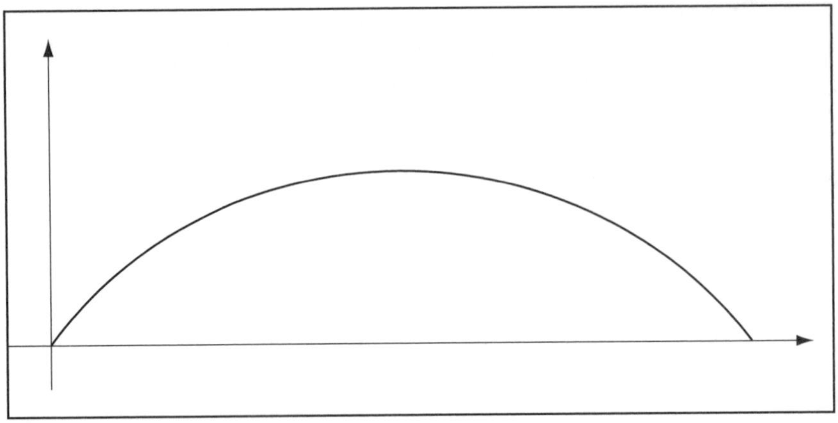

Figure 20.10

A simple trajectory.

This is usually what happens when you deal with projectiles. Of course, the object can be a little higher or lower than the end position, but those are only special cases of this general one.

As you can see from Figure 20.10, there are several things you can assume:

The trajectory is a parabola.

The velocity at the end is the same as the velocity when launched.

The vertical component of velocity at the apex (higher point) of the trajectory is zero.

The horizontal component of velocity is constant (horizontal acceleration is zero).

The time to reach the apex is the same time it takes to go from the apex to the ground (apex time = total time / 2).

Okay, now that those are known, you want formulas, right? Let's start, then.

The first thing you need to do regarding this problem is to get the horizontal and vertical components of the initial velocity. You should already know that this is accomplished by multiplying the cosine of the angle by the initial velocity to get the horizontal component and multiplying the sine of the angle by the initial velocity for the vertical component, like so:

$$\text{InitialVelocityx} = \text{InitialVelocity} * \text{Cosine}\ (\theta)$$

$$\text{InitialVelocityy} = \text{InitialVelocity} * \text{Sine}\ (\theta)$$

You know from Equation 20.11 that the velocity equation is:

$$\text{Velocity}_y\ (\text{time}) = \text{InitialVelocity}_y + \text{Acceleration}_y * \text{time} \Leftrightarrow$$

$$\text{Velocity}_y\ (\text{time}) = \text{InitialVelocity} * \text{Sine}\ (\theta) + (-9.8) * \text{time}$$

Now you know how to get the velocity at any time of the projectile's trajectory. By integrating this, you can get the position as:

NOTE

You are assuming that gravity is a vector that has only a vertical component, and is negative since its direction is in the negative direction of the axis.

$$\text{Position}_y\ (\text{time}) = \text{InitialPosition}_y + \text{InitialVelocity} * \text{Sine}\ (\theta) * \text{time} + 1/2 * (-9.8) * \text{time}^2$$

Now you know how to get the position and the velocity at any time during the projectile's trajectory. This is enough to do your simulation, but just in case you are also studying for a physics exam, there are a few other things that are good to know.

Probably the first thing that comes in handy when solving some problems is the time it takes to reach the final position. Since you know that at the apex, the vertical component of the velocity is zero, you can use this to your advantage. If you solve the velocity equation for the final velocity being zero, you can get the time it takes to reach the apex:

$$0 = \text{InitialVelocity}_y * \text{Acceleration}_y * \text{time} \Leftrightarrow$$

$$0 = \text{InitialVelocity} * \sin\ (\theta) + (-9.8) * \text{time} \Leftrightarrow$$

$$\text{time} = \text{InitialVelocity} * \sin\ (\theta)\ /\ 9.8$$

And you would have the time it takes to reach the apex. You know that the time it takes to reach the apex is the same it takes to do the other half of the parabola, so you can multiply it by two to get the total time of the trajectory:

$$\text{TotalTime} = 2 * \text{InitialVelocity} * \text{Sine}\ (\theta)\ /\ (-9.8)$$

Since you know that the maximum height a projectile can reach is when it is at the apex, you can get this value by using the vertical position equation with time being the time the projectile reaches the apex like:

$$\text{Positiony (time)} = \text{InitialPositiony} + (\text{InitialVelocityy} * (\text{InitialVelocityy} / 9.8) + 1/2 * (-9.8) * (\text{InitialVelocityy} / 9.8)^2$$

And after a lot of simplification (this is your homework) you get:

$$\text{MaximumHeight} = \text{InitialPositiony} + \text{InitialVelocityy}^2 / 2*9.8$$

The only thing left is to get the maximum distance on the horizontal axis, this is also done by using the position equation, and swapping time by the `TotalTime`, you get the maximum distance like:

$$\text{Positionx (time)} = \text{InitialPositionx} + \text{InitialVelocityx} * \text{time} \Leftrightarrow$$

$$\text{Distance} = \text{InitialPositionx} + (\text{InitialVelocityx} * \text{TotalTime})$$

Pretty simple, as long as you know the base equations of movement and velocity, projectiles are easy.

Now, I just hope you ace your next physics exam!

Friction

One of the most dreaded aspects of physics is probably friction. Not because it's hard, actually, on paper it's pretty simple to calculate physics forces. The only problem is that doing it on the computer usually takes a lot of patience to work correctly, mostly due to the restrictions imposed.

Friction Concept

Generally, friction is the resistance an object has to moving when in contact with others (or fluid) to motion. It's caused by electrical, mechanical, and thermal losses. There are some rules when using friction in games:

- The friction force can never cause movement on its own.
- The friction force always has the inverse direction of the object.

- The magnitude of the frictional force is proportional to the object's weight.
- There are two equations and constants when using physics, one for static friction and the other for kinetic friction.

I will go over each of these during the rest of this section.

Decomposing Friction

Working with friction means being able to use either static or kinetic friction in the correct direction. This is easy on paper, but not so easy on a computer. You will see how to calculate friction as it is usually done on paper, then I will explain the computer method.

The Normal Force

The first thing you must know to work with friction is the normal force. The normal force of an object in relation to a surface is the force that prevents the object from intersecting the surface. Your monitor is still on your desk, right? Well, even though a gravity force is being exerted on it, it doesn't go below the surface of the desk, does it? This is due to the normal force. See Figure 20.11.

The normal force has the same magnitude as the gravity force, but it is always in the opposite direction of it.

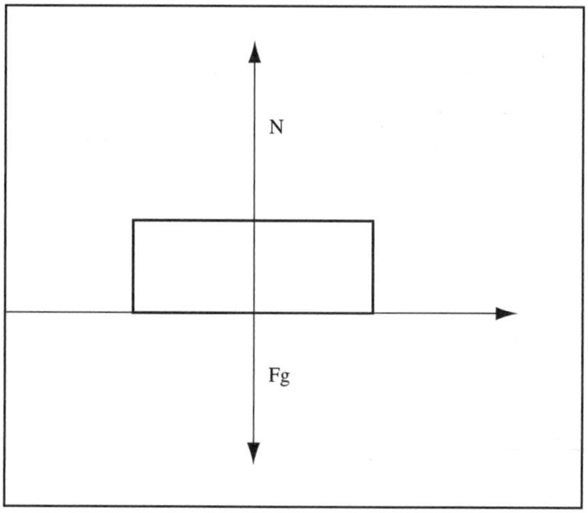

Figure 20.11

The normal reaction force.

So, you can get the normal force by just negating the gravity force:

Equation 20.18

$$\text{NormalForce} = -\text{GravityForce}$$

Nothing hard, but what if the object is on a sloped surface? Take a look at Figure 20.12 to see what I mean.

As you can see, the normal force doesn't equal the gravity force but the proportional part of the gravity force perpendicular to the surface, or:

$$\text{NormalForcey} = \text{GravityForce} * \text{Cosine }(\theta)$$

You do this by using a relative set of axes for the object, and then use the angle between the vertical axis of the object and the real axis to get the normal force. The rest of the force, the part proportional to the gravity force parallel to the surface is:

$$\text{NormalForcex} = \text{GravityForce} * \text{Sine }(\theta)$$

This is the part of the force that makes the object slide down the surface (if friction is not big enough).

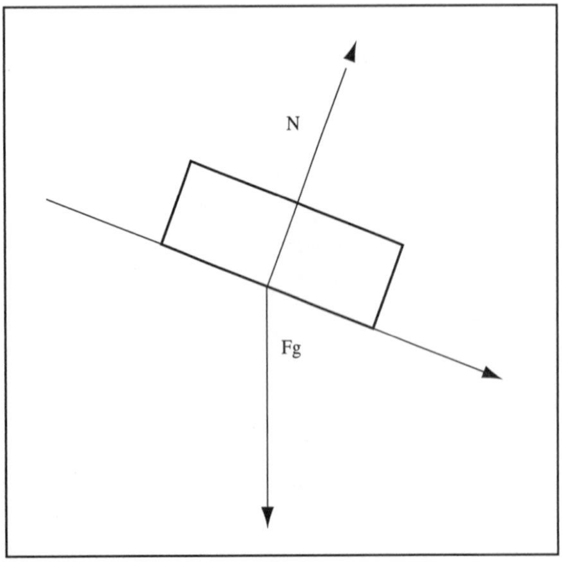

Figure 20.12

The normal reaction force on a sloped surface.

> **NOTE**
>
> When it is said that the normal force equals the gravity force, it is meant that its magnitude is the same, but the direction opposite.

Static Friction

Now that you have the lowdown about the normal reaction, let's start talking about friction. The first kind of friction I will talk about is static friction. *Static friction* is the friction force exerted on an object when it is still (velocity is 0). Take a look at Figure 20.13.

When a force is applied to a still object, static friction occurs, making the movement of the object a little harder. See Equation 20.19.

Equation 20.19

$$\text{StaticFriction} = \text{NormalForce} * \mu_s$$

Where μ_s is the coefficient of static friction and must be comprehended between 0 and 1.

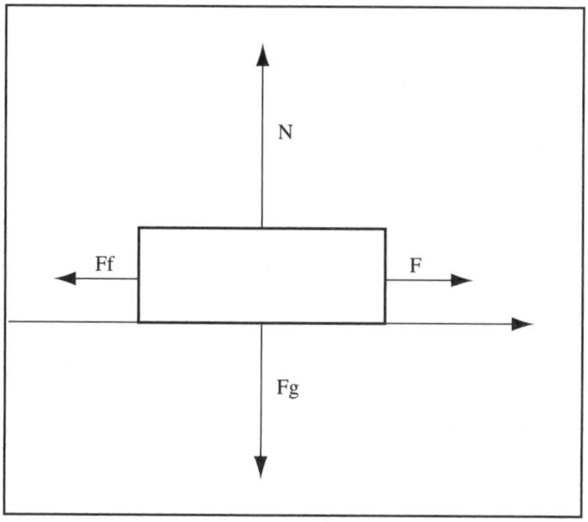

Figure 20.13

Static friction in action.

You can get the value of μ_s by either performing some experiments and calculating μ_s, or you can pick up some physics book and check it out.

And there you have it, the value of the static friction force. Now you just have to apply it to the inverse direction of the force.

After you push an object, and beat static friction, an object is easier to push, but still has some force making the movement hard. This is due to kinetic friction.

Kinetic Friction

Kinetic friction is the friction force exerted on an object when it is already moving (velocity is not 0).

Kinetic friction is similar to static friction but it is applied to the inverse direction of the velocity of the object and is given by the formula shown in Equation 20.20.

Equation 20.20

$$\text{KineticFriction} = \text{NormalForce} * \mu_k$$

Where μ_s is the coefficient of kinetic friction and must be comprehended between 0 and 1 and be smaller than μ_s.

Friction on a Sloped Surface

The last thing I will discuss about friction before moving to programming is how friction is used on a sloped surface. Take a look at Figure 20.14.

You can see that `GravityForcey` and `NormalForcey` both nullify leaving the only forces active being the `GravityForcex` and the friction force.

For this reason you will use the `NormalForcex` only when calculating friction, so in Equations 20.19 and 20.20, you can replace `NormalForce` with `NormalForcex` and get the correct friction force:

$$\text{StaticFriction} = \text{NormalForcex} * \mu_s$$

$$\text{KineticFriction} = \text{NormalForcex} * \mu_k$$

And that's about it. You now need to know how to apply this to your games.

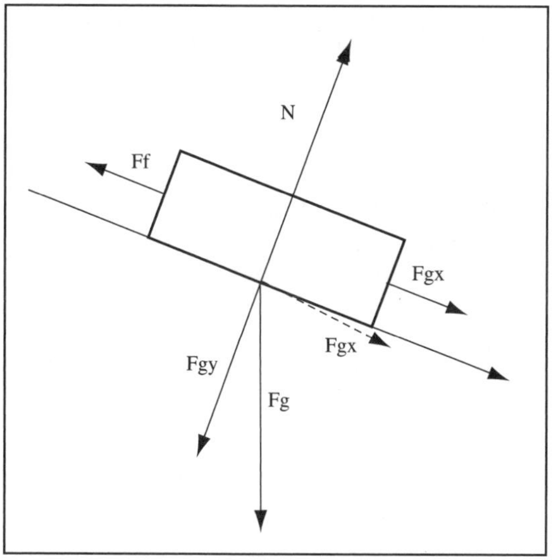

Figure 20.14

Friction on a sloped surface.

The Computer Method

You have seen how to use friction, but using the previous methods is hard when you want to make them work in your programs. For this reason, a few different formulas are used.

Remembering the first friction rule:

The friction force can never cause movement on its own.

This means that when an object is static, the friction force can only be as big as the sum of all the forces in the object. So if the friction force given by Equations 20.19 and 20.20 is greater than all the forces of the object, you need to make the friction force the same size as the sum of the forces.

You also know that friction must be in the opposite direction of the sum of forces, so to find the friction vector you would do the following steps:

1. Calculate the sum of all forces.
2. Normalize the sum of all forces.
3. Negate the normalized sum of all forces.
4. Multiply the negated normalized sum of all forces by the gravity, the mass, and the coefficient of static friction.

Or as shown in Equation 20.21.

Equation 20.21

$$\text{StaticFriction} = -\ \text{Normalize (AllForce)} * \text{Gravity} * \text{Mass} * \mu_s$$

And you would have the static friction vector. You still need to make sure that no movement is caused due to friction, so if any of the friction components was bigger than the sum of the forces component, you would need to equal them.

To get the kinetic friction, you would do the same as for the static friction, but instead of using the sum of all the forces, you would use the velocity of the object:

Equation 20.22

$$\text{KineticFriction} = -\ \text{Normalize (AllForce)} * \text{Gravity} * \text{Mass} * \mu_k$$

And that's about it. If you want the code, check out the following:

```
 /* Apply a friction force to the entity */
void mrEntity::ApplyFriction (mrReal32 fGravity)
{
 mrVector2D kFrictionVector;

  /* If velocity is too small, use static friction, otherwise,
     use kinetic */
 if (m_kLinearVelocity.Length () < 1)
 {
   /* Calculate friction vector */
  kFrictionVector = m_kTotalForce;
  kFrictionVector.Normalize ();

  kFrictionVector *= -(fGravity * m_fMass) *
                      m_fStaticFrictionCoefficient;
 }
 else
 {
   /* Calculate friction vector */
  kFrictionVector = m_kLinearVelocity;
  kFrictionVector.Normalize ();

  kFrictionVector *= -(fGravity * m_fMass) *
                      m_fKineticFrictionCoefficient;
```

```
    }
    m_kFrictionForce += kFrictionVector;
}
```

Which does exactly what I described earlier. You still need to check whether friction would cause movement, but you will do this in the `Simulate` method of `mrEntity`.

Handling Collisions

The last thing you need to learn about is collisions. Having a physics engine where the objects go through one another isn't very good, so you need to use some kind of system to prevent this.

Maintaining the Momentum

The momentum of an object is like the inertia an object has when moving. Momentum of an object can be calculated using the formula shown in Equation 20.23.

Equation 20.23

$$\vec{\text{Momentum}} = \text{Mass} * \vec{\text{Velocity}}$$

And as you can imagine, the units to use are kg * m/s.

Momentum as just an attribute isn't useful for us. Usually you use the momentum for collisions of objects or the conservation of the momentum.

Conservation of Momentum

The conservation of the momentum of a system states that within a collision, the momentum of the system before the collision must be the same as the momentum after the collision. The only caveat is that it isn't! This is only true on a perfectly elastic collision; that is, when two objects collide, the heat dispersed from the collision and any other energy loss proprieties are 0, the energy of the system remains the same. For solving elastic collisions (when you take into account heat dispersion) you will use Newton's impulse method, but for now, let's continue with perfectly elastic collisions.

> **NOTE**
>
> **A *system* is a collection or group of objects you are analyzing.**

So, the conservation of the momentum would tell you that for a perfectly elastic collision, the formula shown in Equation 20.24 is true.

Equation 20.24

MassA * InitialVelocityA + MassB * InitialVelocityB =
MassA * FinalVelocityA + MassB * FinalVelocityB

You can solve this equation directly if you know three of the velocities, which usually isn't the case. What usually happens is that you only know the initial velocities and need the final ones. You need to talk about kinetic energy and then solve a system of two unknown variables, which is quite troublesome, really. Since you are mostly interested in inelastic collisions, the final formulas for the final velocities of each object are shown in Equation 20.25.

Equation 20.25

FinalVelocityA = (2 * MassB * InitialVelocityB + InitialVelocityA * (MassA–MassB)) / (MassA + MassB)

FinalVelocityB = (2 * MassA * InitialVelocityA – InitialVelocityB * (MassA–MassB)) / (MassA + MassB)

And you can get the final velocities only knowing the mass of the objects and their initial velocities.

The Impulse Method

Newton's impulse method for handling collisions is probably the best method to simulate collisions. There are some restrictions (such as ignoring the friction between the bodies at collision) but those are minor things that you aren't interested in for now. Newton's impulse method also brings a new quantity to your simulation, the impulse. The impulse is a quantity, which allows you to change the velocity directly. Remember from the first equations that the velocity could only change with some acceleration, and was a continuous process? With impulse, you can change the velocities of bodies directly. Thus, you can prevent objects from penetrating each other.

Impulse can be compared to a very big force applied over a really short period of time (ideally, approaching zero), thus changing the velocity almost instantaneously, but in your case, it will only be a scalar value describing how you change the velocity.

To respond to collisions, you need to apply the impulses at the time of the collision to prevent your objects from interpenetrating.

Calculating the impulse caused by a collision isn't hard, but there are a few things that you need to know beforehand.

The first thing you should take into account with Figure 20.15 is there is a plane for collision, having its normal pointing toward the object A (by convention). This is the normal of the collision.

Getting the normal of the collision depends on the type of collision detection you use; for irregular polygons, you need to find which vertex collided with which line, and use the line as the plane and then get the normal. For spheres, you use the perpendicular vector of the distance of object A to B to get the plane normal and then use normal of the plane, or more directly, you just use the distance vector from A to B, since it is the same as the normal of the plane.

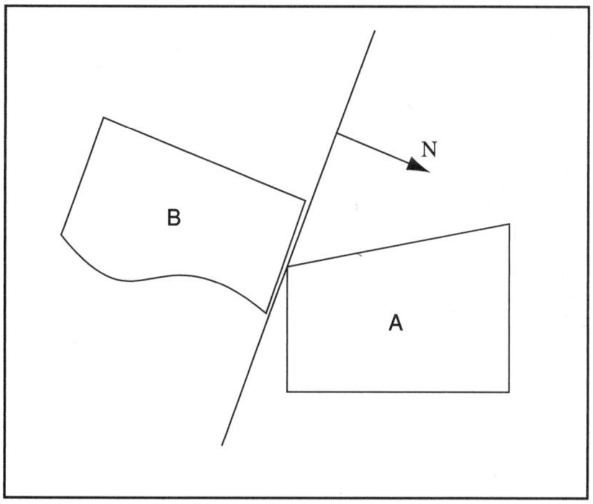

Figure 20.15

A collision between two irregular objects.

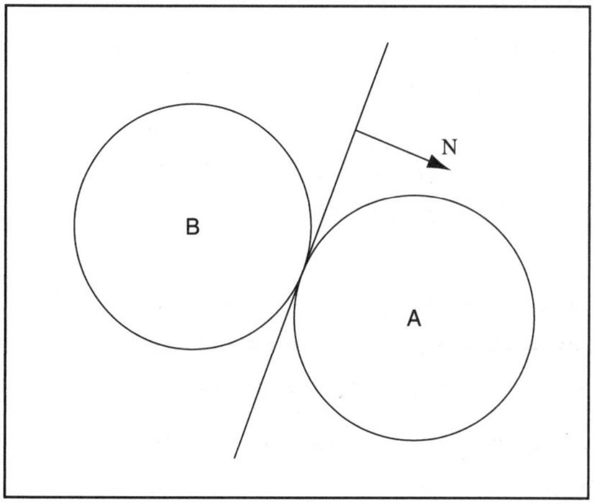

Figure 20.16

A collision between two spheres.

Detecting when a collision occurs and the plane of the collision is the job of the application, not the physics simulator, so for your collision method, you will assume that a collision really happened and that you know the plane of collision.

Back to the physics, you need to introduce another quantity (don't worry, I promise it's the last one), the coefficient of restitution, or ε. The coefficient of restitution describes the relationship between the final and the initial velocities of two objects upon a collision. See Equation 20.26.

Equation 20.26

$$\varepsilon = (\text{FinalVelocityB} - \text{FinalVelocityA}) \,/\, (\text{InitialVelocityB} - \text{InitialVelocityA})$$

Finding the coefficient of restitution can be done experimentally, or you can just look it up in a book. Different objects have different coefficients, but usually a magic number is good enough for your simulator.

Now, you just need to get your impulse scalar and change the velocities.

Getting the impulse scalar is simpler than it appears; take a look at Equation 20.27.

Equation 20.27

$$\text{Impulse} = (-(1 + \varepsilon) * \text{InitialVelocityAtoB} \,.\, \text{CollisionNormal}) \,/\, (\text{CollisionNormal}.\ \text{CollisionNormal}\ (1/\ \text{MassA} + 1/\text{MassB}))$$

Even if this looks kind of complicated, it really isn't. First, you need to know the relative initial velocity of object A to B, which can be calculated the same way as the relative position, by subtracting the velocity of B from A like:

$$\text{VelocityAtoB} = \text{VelocityA} - \text{VelocityB}$$

Now, knowing this, and since the `CollisionNormal` is given, you can replace the values of each variable.

And you have the impulse scalar, now you just have to change the velocities of the objects and you are done. This is done with Equation 20.28.

TIP

There are a few dot products using the `CollisionNormal` so that `CollisionNormal` can be a non-unit vector. If you will always use a normalized vector, you can avoid some of them.

Equation 20.28

FinalVelocityA = InitialVelocityA + (Impulse / MassA) CollisionNormal

FinalVelocityB = InitialVelocityB – (Impulse / MassB) CollisionNormal

And you will have the final velocities for each of the objects after the collision. Neat, huh?

Now, before moving into code, there is one catch in this method. If, for example, you have four objects in your game (A, B, C, D), you can't handle the collisions for all of them. Therefore, if you handle the collision of objects A and C, you can't handle the collision of objects C and A, since this would cause two collisions, which would nullify themselves. What you need to do is use a tree-like collision handler like in Figure 20.17.

This would ensure that two objects are only handled once. If you are worrying how you can do this in code, look at the following:

```
int Objects [TotalObjects];
int ObjectA;
int ObjectB;
For (ObjectA = 0; ObjectA < TotalObjects; ObjectA++)
{
 for (ObjectB = ObjectA; ObjectB < TotalObjects; ObjectB++)
 {
  HandleCollision (Objects [ObjectA], Objects [ObjectB]);
 }
}
```

Which would call `HandleCollision` the same way it is described in Figure 20.17.

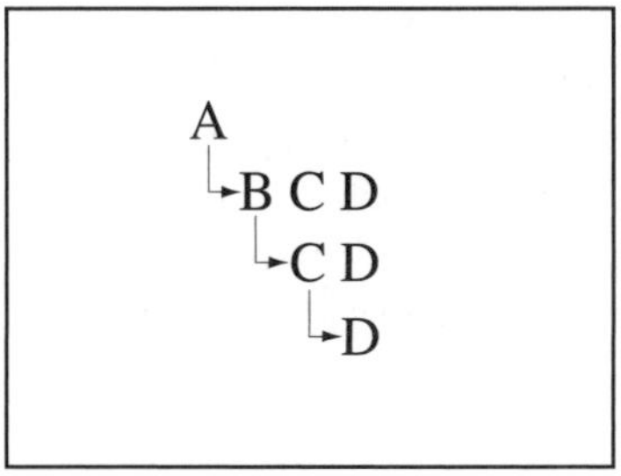

Figure 20.17

Possible tree to handle collisions.

You want the code for handling the collisions? No problem:

```
 92:  /* Handle collisions between two objects */
 93: void mrEntity::HandleCollision (mrEntity & rkOtherEntity,
 94:                                  mrVector2D & rkCollisionNormal)
 95: {
 96:  mrReal32 fImpulse;
 97:  mrVector2D kRelativeVelocity;
 98:
 99:   /* Normalize collision normal */
100:  rkCollisionNormal.Normalize ();
101:
102:   /* Get relative velocities */
103:  kRelativeVelocity = (m_kLinearVelocity -
104:                        rkOtherEntity.GetLinearVelocity ());
105:  kRelativeVelocity *= - (1 + m_fCoefficientOfRestitution);
106:
107:   /* Calculate sum of inverse of entities mass */
108:  mrReal32 fInverseMassSum;
109:  fInverseMassSum = (1 / m_fMass) + (1 / rkOtherEntity.GetMass ());
110:
111:   /* Calculate impulse */
112:  fImpulse = (kRelativeVelocity.DotProduct (rkCollisionNormal)) /
113:    rkCollisionNormal.DotProduct (rkCollisionNormal * fInverseMassSum);
114:
115:   /* Get object velocity */
116:  m_kLinearVelocity = m_kLinearVelocity +
117:                       rkCollisionNormal * (fImpulse / m_fMass);
118:
119:   /* Get other object velocity */
120:  mrVector2D kOtherVelocity;
121:  rkOtherEntity.SetLinearVelocity (rkOtherEntity.GetLinearVelocity () -
122:             rkCollisionNormal * (fImpulse / rkOtherEntity.GetMass ()));
123: }
```

You start by normalizing the collision plane (line 100) and calculating the relative velocities of the two objects (lines 103 and 104). Then you calculate the impulse scalar using Equation 20.27 (lines 105 through 112) and change the final velocities of the objects using Equation 20.28 (lines 116 through 122).

NOTE

It was said earlier that if the collision normal was normalized, you could avoid some dot products in Equation 20.27. Well, this is true on paper, but on the computer it isn't, because there are floating-point errors when storing the numbers. If you normalize the velocity beforehand, you introduce a very small error, while if you don't, you still introduce a small error, but being a little bigger than if you didn't normalize the normal.

Simulating

Now you just need to integrate the quantities, ensure that friction doesn't move the object, apply some damping, and reset the forces.

Take a look at the code for your `Simulate` method:

```
 /* Simulate (integrate) the entity */
void mrEntity::Simulate (mrReal32 fStep)
{
  /* Use Euler integration */
 m_kLinearVelocity  += (m_kTotalForce / m_fMass) * fStep;
 m_kPosition        +=  m_kLinearVelocity * fStep;

 m_fAngularVelocity += (m_fTotalTorque / m_fInertia) * fStep;
 m_fOrientation     +=  m_fAngularVelocity * fStep;

  /* Only apply friction if it doesn't cause movement */
  /* Use separate vector components */
 if (fabs (m_kLinearVelocity [0]) >=
      fabs ((m_kFrictionForce [0] / m_fMass) * fStep))
 {
  m_kLinearVelocity [0] += (m_kFrictionForce [0] / m_fMass) * fStep;
 }
 else
 {
```

NOTE

Damping is the term used when you want to either make a value zero if the value is very near the zero value (something like 0.04) or multiply a value by a factor between zero and one to make it smaller, proportionally direct to the value (for example, 6 * 0.995 would result in 5.97, and successive calls to this would bring the object near zero.

Damping is not correct in a physics simulator, but you usually do it since you don't simulate all the necessary forces to stop a particle.

```
 m_kLinearVelocity [0] = 0;
}
if (fabs (m_kLinearVelocity [1]) >=
    fabs ((m_kFrictionForce [1] / m_fMass) * fStep))
{
 m_kLinearVelocity [1] += (m_kFrictionForce [1] / m_fMass) * fStep;
}
else
{
 m_kLinearVelocity [1] = 0;
}

 /* Apply some damping to solve problems of floating accuracy */
if (fabs (m_kLinearVelocity [0]) <= 0.1f)
{
 m_kLinearVelocity [0] = 0;
}
if (fabs (m_kLinearVelocity [1]) <= 0.1f)
{
 m_kLinearVelocity [1] = 0;
}
 /* Applies damping since we don't apply any friction to angular
    velocity */
m_fAngularVelocity *= 0.995f;

 /* Reset forces */
```

```
170:   m_fTotalTorque                = 0;
171:   m_fTotalImpulse               = 0;
172:   m_kTotalForce                 = mrVector2D (0, 0);
173:   m_kFrictionForce              = mrVector2D (0, 0);
174: }
```

The first thing you do is integrate the quantities by the step (lines 129 through 133). After that you need to check whether the friction force creates any change in velocity that is bigger than the actual velocity; if so, set the velocity to zero, if not, add the change of velocity to the actual velocity. (Remember that the friction force is always contrary to movement, so adding the "friction velocity" will always reduce the actual velocity.) Then you do some damping to the linear velocity if the value is too small, to prevent nasty things from happening in the integration, and also apply some damping to the angular velocity since you didn't use anything to change it (lines 157 through 167).

In the end, you reset all your forces (lines 170 through 173) since you don't want any force applied in this step to be applied in others.

Now, what is the step? You will see this next.

Getting the Step

The last thing you need to know to simulate the application is the step. The step is the time in seconds it takes to draw a frame. You can limit the frame rate and have a constant step for your games, but this is rather dull. What is the purpose of spending 400 bucks on a GeForce 3 if you get 25 frames per second in games?

The easier way to get the time a frame takes to render is to divide one (second) by the number of frames drawn per second. This is simply logic like:

If in one second it draws X frames,

Then it takes 1/X seconds to draw a frame.

And since Mirus offers a method to get the frames per second, you could simulate your entities like:

```
mrReal32 fStep;
fStep = 1 / (mrReal32)mrScreen::GetSingleton ()->GetFPS ();
Entity.Simulate (fStep);
```

Don't forget you need to caste the frames per second to a floating-point type, if you don't, the final result will be an integer, which will cause errors.

And that's it! You have your physics simulator up and running. Using it is as simple as setting the initial properties of the entities, and then applying some forces and simulating. Don't forget to check for collisions and handle them.

The following program allows you to play with physics a little. Take a look at the class declaration for now:

```
 1: /* '02 Main.cpp' */
 2:
 3: /* Mirus window framework header */
 4: #include "mirus.h"
 5:
 6: /* Custom derived class */
 7: class CustomWindow : public mrWindow
 8: {
 9: public:
10:  /* Mirus related classes */
11:  mrInputManager       m_kInputManager;
12:  mrKeyboard           m_kKeyboard;
13:  mrScreen             m_kScreen;
14:
15:  /* Our balls */
16:  mrEntity             m_akBalls [4];
17:  mrABO                m_akBallsABO [4];
18:
19:  /* Constructor / Destructor */
20:  CustomWindow (void) {};
21:  ~CustomWindow (void) {};
22:
23:  void Init (HINSTANCE hInstance);
24:
25:  /* Window manipulation functions */
26:  mrBool32 Frame (void);
27: };
```

The only difference of this class from others you created is that you create an array of four `mrEntity` classes (line 16).

Next you need to init your members. This is as simple as going for each class member and calling the appropriate methods to set up the stuff. Take a look at the following (feel free to change the values of the physics constants if you prefer):

```
29: void CustomWindow::Init (HINSTANCE hInstance)
30: {
```

```
/* Initialize the screen and the ABO (a smily) */
m_kScreen.Init (m_hWindow);
m_kScreen.SetMode (false, 640, 480, 32, true);

/* Load the ball ABO */
m_akBallsABO [0].LoadFromFile ("ball.txt");
m_akBallsABO [0].SetSize (32, 32);
m_akBallsABO [0].SetRadius (16);
m_akBallsABO [0].SetColor (255,255,255,255);

m_akBallsABO [1].LoadFromFile ("ball.txt");
m_akBallsABO [1].SetSize (32, 32);
m_akBallsABO [1].SetRadius (16);
m_akBallsABO [1].SetColor (255,255,255,255);

m_akBallsABO [2].LoadFromFile ("ball.txt");
m_akBallsABO [2].SetSize (32, 32);
m_akBallsABO [2].SetRadius (16);
m_akBallsABO [2].SetColor (255,255,255,255);

m_akBallsABO [3].LoadFromFile ("ball.txt");
m_akBallsABO [3].SetSize (32, 32);
m_akBallsABO [3].SetRadius (16);
m_akBallsABO [3].SetColor (255,255,255,255);

/* Set each balls physics properties */
m_akBalls [0].SetMass (10);
m_akBalls [0].SetPosition (mrVector2D (300, 100));
m_akBalls [0].SetStaticFriction (0.7f);
m_akBalls [0].SetStaticFriction (0.6f);
m_akBalls [0].SetCoefficientOfRestitution (0.4f);

m_akBalls [1].SetMass (10);
m_akBalls [1].SetPosition (mrVector2D (300, 300));
m_akBalls [1].SetStaticFriction (0.7f);
m_akBalls [1].SetStaticFriction (0.6f);
m_akBalls [1].SetCoefficientOfRestitution (0.4f);

m_akBalls [2].SetMass (10);
m_akBalls [2].SetPosition (mrVector2D (200, 300));
m_akBalls [2].SetStaticFriction (0.7f);
```

```
  m_akBalls [2].SetStaticFriction (0.6f);
  m_akBalls [2].SetCoefficientOfRestitution (0.4f);

  m_akBalls [3].SetMass (10);
  m_akBalls [3].SetPosition (mrVector2D (400, 300));
  m_akBalls [3].SetStaticFriction (0.7f);
  m_akBalls [3].SetStaticFriction (0.6f);
  m_akBalls [3].SetCoefficientOfRestitution (0.4f);

  /* Initialize the input manager and device */
  m_kInputManager.Init (hInstance);
  m_kKeyboard.Init (m_hWindow);
}
```

Long, but simple. You could have made initialization in a loop, but because you want different positions for the balls, you just set them up all manually!

Next is the Frame method, which is where the main part of the physics engine starts to work:

```
/* Render frame */
mrBool32 CustomWindow::Frame(void)
{
  mrVector2D  kTempPosition;
  /* Start rendering */
  m_kScreen.Clear (0, 0, 0, 0);
  m_kScreen.StartFrame ();

  /* Simulate according to elapsed time */
  if (m_kScreen.GetFPS () != 0)
  {
   /* Move main ball */
   kTempPosition = m_akBalls [0].GetPosition ();
   m_kKeyboard.Update ();
   if (m_kKeyboard.IsButtonDown (DIK_UP))
   {
    kTempPosition [1] -= 1;
   }
   if (m_kKeyboard.IsButtonDown (DIK_DOWN))
   {
    kTempPosition [1] += 1;
   }
```

```
if (m_kKeyboard.IsButtonDown (DIK_LEFT))
{
 kTempPosition [0] -= 1;
}
if (m_kKeyboard.IsButtonDown (DIK_RIGHT))
{
 kTempPosition [0] += 1;
}
m_akBalls [0].SetPosition (kTempPosition);
/* Apply main force */
if (m_kKeyboard.IsButtonDown (DIK_SPACE))
{
 m_akBalls [0].ApplyLinearForce (mrVector2D (0, 15000));
}
/* Apply friction */
m_akBalls [0].ApplyFriction (9.8f);
m_akBalls [1].ApplyFriction (9.8f);
m_akBalls [2].ApplyFriction (9.8f);
m_akBalls [3].ApplyFriction (9.8f);
```

Up to this point, you are checking whether any of the cursor keys are pressed, and if so, moving the first ball. Also, if you press the spacebar, you will apply a force of 15000 Newtons to the ball and you end up applying the friction to all the balls.

Okay, let's continue:

```
/* Simulate first ball */
if (m_akBallsABO [0].Collide (m_akBallsABO [1], true))
{
 m_akBalls [0].HandleCollision (m_akBalls [1],
  (m_akBalls [1].GetPosition () - m_akBalls [0].GetPosition ()));
}
if (m_akBallsABO [0].Collide (m_akBallsABO [2], true))
{
 m_akBalls [0].HandleCollision (m_akBalls [2],
  (m_akBalls [2].GetPosition () - m_akBalls [0].GetPosition ()));
}
if (m_akBallsABO [0].Collide (m_akBallsABO [3], true))
{
 m_akBalls [0].HandleCollision (m_akBalls [3],
  (m_akBalls [3].GetPosition () - m_akBalls [0].GetPosition ()));
}
```

```
  /* Simulate second ball */
  if (m_akBallsABO [1].Collide (m_akBallsABO [2], true))
  {
   m_akBalls [1].HandleCollision (m_akBalls [2],
     -m_akBalls [1].GetPosition () - m_akBalls [1].GetPosition ());
  }
  if (m_akBallsABO [1].Collide (m_akBallsABO [3], true))
  {
   m_akBalls [1].HandleCollision (m_akBalls [3],
     -m_akBalls [1].GetPosition () - m_akBalls [1].GetPosition ());
  }
  /* Simulate third ball */
  if (m_akBallsABO [2].Collide (m_akBallsABO [3], true))
  {
   m_akBalls [2].HandleCollision (m_akBalls [3],
     -m_akBalls [2].GetPosition () - m_akBalls [2].GetPosition ());
  }
  /* Simulate fourth ball */
  m_akBalls [0].Simulate (1/(mrReal32)m_kScreen.GetFPS ());
  m_akBalls [1].Simulate (1/(mrReal32)m_kScreen.GetFPS ());
  m_akBalls [2].Simulate (1/(mrReal32)m_kScreen.GetFPS ());
  m_akBalls [3].Simulate (1/(mrReal32)m_kScreen.GetFPS ());
 }
```

This looks difficult, but it isn't. You are checking whether any of the balls collided, and if so, handling the collision (with the `HandleCollision` method). If you don't understand why the order of collisions is done this way, go a few pages back to review why this is happening. After you handled the collisions, you just need to call the `Simulate` method of each ball to integrate the equations.

Here is the final part of the method:

```
/* Modify the ABO's so they use the same position as the entities */
kTempPosition = m_akBalls [0].GetPosition ();
m_akBallsABO [0].SetPosition ((mrUInt32)kTempPosition [0],
 (mrUInt32)kTempPosition [1]);
kTempPosition = m_akBalls [1].GetPosition ();
m_akBallsABO [1].SetPosition ((mrUInt32)kTempPosition [0],
 (mrUInt32)kTempPosition [1]);
kTempPosition = m_akBalls [2].GetPosition ();
m_akBallsABO [2].SetPosition ((mrUInt32)kTempPosition [0],
```

```
   (mrUInt32)kTempPosition [1]);
  kTempPosition = m_akBalls [3].GetPosition ();
  m_akBallsABO [3].SetPosition ((mrUInt32)kTempPosition [0],
   (mrUInt32)kTempPosition [1]);

  /* Render balls */
  m_akBallsABO [0].Render ();
  m_akBallsABO [1].Render ();
  m_akBallsABO [2].Render ();
  m_akBallsABO [3].Render ();
  m_kScreen.EndFrame ();

  return mrTrue;
 }
```

Which only synchronizes the entities' positions and ABO's positions, and renders the ABOs. Easy, huh? Okay, just take a look at `WinMain` for reference:

```
/* "WinMain Vs. main" */
int WINAPI WinMain (HINSTANCE hInstance, HINSTANCE hPrevInst,
                    LPSTR lpCmdLine, int nShowCmd)
{
 /* Our window */
 CustomWindow  kWindow;

 /* Create window */
 kWindow.Create (hInstance, "02 Physics Demo");
 kWindow.SetSize (640, 480);

 kWindow.m_kScreen.Init (kWindow.GetHandle ());
 kWindow.m_kScreen.SetMode (false, 640,480,32,true);

 kWindow.Init (hInstance);

 kWindow.Run ();
 return 0;
}
```

It looked harder than it was, right? Well, try it by moving the main ball with the cursor keys and press space to apply a force to the ball. You will see the effects of friction, forces, and collisions.

> **NOTE**
> If you try the program, you will see a small bug, which makes objects get stuck to each other sometimes. Well, this isn't really a bug, but just a feature that prevents actual interpenetration of the objects. There are some accurate physics models to do this, but they are complicated. A good workaround is to move the objects back if there is a collision. I challenge you to try it!

Particle Systems

You have heard of them, you have seen them in the latest games, you have received communications from outer space saying they were here to stay, but you still don't know how to create one. Don't worry, I'm going to play the role of Saint Nick and give you a little present, a few pages about particle systems. Now, where are my milk and cookies?

Particle Systems 101

What is a particle system, you ask? A particle system is nothing more than a collection of particles that have a modular or programmed behavior.

In the old days, particles were nothing more than a small pixel or with luck a solid polygon. Nowadays, with the current computers and video cards, you can have textured, alpha-blended polygons with special effects to create the most realistic kind of particle systems ever.

Designing a Particle System

For now, I will only define the data structures needed for your particle system, and how it works generally. Since you will also create a Mirus particle system class, I will leave the implementation of some effects to that section.

Particle Systems' Data Structures

There are two main classes you need to have to create a particle system. A particle class and a particle system class which contains an array of particles.

A particle, like any particle in the real world, has some basic attributes, such as position, velocity, size, and age (even if these are everyday concepts, if the word physics is unknown to you, you probably should take a look at the physics chapter in Part 3). These basic attributes are enough to create a basic particle system. But you want to be one step ahead of the basics, right? So I will throw in color, previous velocity, and effect, making it possible to create just about any effect imaginable.

So, how do you define the particle? Well, you will need to have just about every attribute such as position, velocity, color, size, and so on. Without further ado, here is your particle class:

```
 /* 'mrParticle.h' */

 /* Mirus base types header */
#include "mrDatatypes.h"
 /* Mirus 2D vector header */
#include "mrVector2D.h"
 /* Mirus screen header */
#include "mrScreen.h"

 /* Include this file only once */
#pragma once

 /* Mirus Particle System setup class */
class mrParticleSystemParams
{
public:
 mrVector2D      m_kPosition;
 mrVector2D      m_kInitialVelocity;

 mrReal32        m_fSize;
 mrReal32        m_fFinalSize;

 mrUInt32        m_iColor;
 mrUInt32        m_iFinalColor;

 mrReal32        m_fLifetime;

 mrReal32        m_fDispersion;
 mrReal32        m_fSpeed;
};
```

```

 /* Mirus Particle class */
class mrParticle
{
protected:
 mrVector2D     m_kPosition;
 mrVector2D     m_kOldPosition;

 mrVector2D     m_kVelocity;

 mrReal32       m_fSize;
 mrReal32       m_fFinalSize;

 mrReal32       m_fLife;
 mrReal32       m_fLifetime;

 mrUInt32       m_iColor;
 mrUInt32       m_iFinalColor;

  /* Effects attributes */
 mrReal32       m_fDispersion;
 mrReal32       m_fSpeed;

public:
   /* Constructor / Destructor */
 mrParticle (void);
 ~mrParticle (void);

 void Simulate (mrReal32 fStep);
 mrError32 Render (mrVector2D & rkPosition);

  /* Particle maintenance methods */
 void Create (mrParticleSystemParams & rkParams);
 mrReal32 GetLife (void);
};
```

This isn't one but two classes. Let me explain. The first class, `mrParticleSystemParams` is just a container class; that is, its only purpose is to contain the information about the particle system. There are no methods or logic. If you pay close attention, you will see that the `mrParticle` class has all the data `mrParticleSystemParams` has. This class was designed to make it easier to create new particles. Instead of passing various attributes of the particle, you just pass the class. It is not only easier, but faster, too.

Some members like `m_kVelocity` and `m_kColor` are pretty obvious, but others aren't. Don't worry, though, in a bit you will be extremely proficient with all of this.

Particles usually have some start attributes, but they end differently (like starting with a blue color and changing to green or starting really small and ending up big). Well, that's why you have both a color and a final color, and a size and a final size. This allows you to set how the particle starts and ends.

Next is `m_fLife`. This variable will hold the life of the particle. When `m_fLife` has a value of zero, it means that the particle was just created; when it has a life of one or more, it means it is dead; values between zero and one are its age. You can get its real age by multiplying `m_fLife` by `m_fLifetime`, but it was done like this to avoid many divisions later on. I guess you just figured what `m_fLifetime` is then, the final life (when it transitions from alive to dead) of the particle.

The next two variables, `m_fDispersion` and `m_fSpeed`, are used to set up the initial velocity, but you will see this in a bit.

You will only have the `GetLife` maintenance method since this is the only method you need outside the particle class. I will go over the other methods in a bit.

> **NOTE**
>
> You won't be using `m_kOldPosition` in this particle system, but it is extremely useful to have if you want to draw sparks or rain or any line based particle system so you know from where to draw.

Now it's time for the particle system class:

```
 /* 'mrParticleSystem.h' */

 /* Mirus base types header */
#include "mrDatatypes.h"
 /* Mirus 2D vector header */
#include "mrVector2D.h"
 /* Mirus particle header */
#include "mrParticle.h"
 /* Mirus texture header */
#include "mrTexture.h"
 /* Mirus screen header */
#include "mrScreen.h"
```

```

 /* Include this file only once */
#pragma once

 /* Mirus Particle System class */
class mrParticleSystem
{
protected:
 mrParticleSystemParams m_kParameters;

 mrUInt32                m_iParticlesActive;
 mrParticle *            m_pkParticles;
 mrUInt32                m_iMaxParticles;
 mrTexture *             m_pkTexture;

  /* Creation manipulation */
 mrUInt32                m_iParticlePerSecond;
 mrReal32                m_fResidue;
 mrBool32                m_bDontCreate;

public:

 mrParticleSystem (void);
 ~mrParticleSystem (void);

  /* Particle maintenance methods */
 void Create (mrParticleSystemParams & rkParameters,
              mrUInt32 iMaxParticles, mrUInt32 iParticlePerSecond,
              mrTexture * pkTexture);
 void Simulate (mrReal32 fStep);
 void Render (void);

 void SetPosition (mrVector2D & rkPosition);
 void SetDontCreate (mrBool32 iDontCreate);
 mrVector2D GetPosition (void);
};
```

In this class you keep a copy of an mrParticleSystemParams class so you know how to create the particles. You also have an array (which you will allocate later) of particles, the number of particles the particle system can have, and the maximum particles per step that can be created.

I will talk about the particle system related methods next; for now, you just need to implement the constructors and the maintenance methods.

Making It Work

Making a particle system work isn't hard, you just have to create the necessary methods for each class and you are done.

mrParticle

Simulating a particle system is as easy as pie. You just need to integrate the quantities and that's it. Really! Take a look at your `Simulate` method:

```
 /* Simulate (integrate) the particle */
void mrParticle::Simulate (mrReal32 fStep)
{
  /* Integrate variables */
 m_kOldPosition = m_kPosition;
 m_kPosition    += m_kVelocity * fStep;
 m_fLife        += fStep / m_fLifetime;
}
```

You first store the old position, and then integrate the velocity to get the new position. In the end you age your particle.

You probably are a little confused on how you age the particle; don't worry, I'll explain it. Remember that `m_fLife` must be in the range of zero to one, right? So, what you want to do is get the fraction of lifetime represented by `fStep` in the range of zero to one. You know that `m_fLifeTime` is the value for which `m_fLife` takes the value of one, so, the value you want to increase `m_fLife` is:

```
LifeIncrease / 1 = fStep / m_fLifeTime
```

So, if `fStep` is 0.23 seconds and `m_fLifeTime` is 20 seconds, the value to increase `m_fLife` would be:

$$0.23 \ / \ 20 = 0.0115$$

Meaning that 0.23 seconds is the same as 0.0115 of the particle's life.

Now you must know how to render the particle. Rendering a particle has two distinctive parts—the interpolation and the rendering:

```
 /* Render the particle */
mrError32 mrParticle::Render (mrVector2D & rkPosition)
```

```
{
  mrUInt32 iColor;
  mrReal32 fSize;

  mrUInt8 fRed;
  mrUInt8 fGreen;
  mrUInt8 fBlue;
  mrUInt8 fAlpha;

   /* Get the new color of each component */
  fAlpha = (mrUInt8) (((m_iColor & 0xFF000000) >> 24) +
           ((mrReal32) ((m_iFinalColor & 0xFF000000) >> 24) -
            (mrReal32) ((m_iColor & 0xFF000000) >> 24)) * m_fLife);

  fRed   = (mrUInt8) (((m_iColor & 0x00FF0000) >> 16) +
           ((mrReal32) ((m_iFinalColor & 0x00FF0000) >> 16) -
            (mrReal32) ((m_iColor & 0x00FF0000) >> 16)) * m_fLife);

  fGreen = (mrUInt8) (((m_iColor & 0x0000FF00) >> 8) +
           ((mrReal32) ((m_iFinalColor & 0x0000FF00) >> 8) -
            (mrReal32) ((m_iColor & 0x0000FF00) >> 8)) * m_fLife);

  fBlue  = (mrUInt8) ((m_iColor & 0x000000FF) +
           ((mrReal32) (m_iFinalColor & 0x000000FF) -
            (mrReal32) (m_iColor & 0x000000FF)) * m_fLife);

  iColor = D3DCOLOR_RGBA (fRed, fGreen, fBlue, fAlpha);
   /* Get the new size */
  fSize = m_fSize + ((m_fFinalSize - m_fSize) * m_fLife);
```

I call this phase the interpolation. You probably have no idea what interpolation is, so let me explain.

An interpolation is a method to calculate a value between two other values by a factor. For example, if I wanted to know the position I was, if I knew I was in the middle of a street that is exactly 100 meters long, I could easily say I was at 50 meters from either side. But how can I describe this mathematically?

> **NOTE**
>
> **Colors in `mrParticle` are in Direct3D format; that is, ARGB, not the usual format RGBA. This makes it easier to create the color for rendering.**

Well, you know that the street is 100 meters long, so you know that the difference between the start of the street and the end is 100. Then you know you are exactly in the middle of the street, so you know you have a factor of 0.5. Putting this together you get

$$0 + (100 - 0) * 0.5 = 50$$

What you do is add the difference of the two positions by the factor to the initial position. Generally speaking:

$$\text{Interpolated} = \text{Start} + (\text{Final} - \text{Start}) * \text{Factor}$$

Using a factor of zero will give you the `Start` result, and using a factor of one will give you the `Final` result, and anything between will give you the respective value.

So, what is the use for this when you are working with particles? By using interpolation between the final size and color, and the starting size and color, by the factor of `m_fLife` (remember that `m_fLife` only has values between zero and one, that's why you did those weird calculations earlier), you can get the size and color of the particle at the current age.

What you do in the code is get each of the final and start color components, interpolate them by `m_fLife` to create the color corresponding to the particle age (lines 58 through 72), and do the same for the particle size (line 76).

Now that you have the size and color of the particle at its current age, you can render it:

```
78:   /* Move to absolute position */
79:  mrReal32 fX = m_kPosition [0] + rkPosition [0];
80:  mrReal32 fY = m_kPosition [1] + rkPosition [1];
81:
82:  mrVertex kVertices [] =
83:  {  /* x, y, z, w, color, texture coordinates (u,v) */
84:   {fX - fSize, fY - fSize, 0, 1.0f, iColor, 0, 0},
85:   {fX + fSize, fY - fSize, 0, 1.0f, iColor, 1, 0},
86:   {fX + fSize, fY + fSize, 0, 1.0f, iColor, 1, 1},
87:   {fX - fSize, fY + fSize, 0, 1.0f, iColor, 0, 1},
88:  };
89:   /* Render particle */
90:  if (FAILED (mrScreen::GetSingleton ()->GetDevice ()->DrawPrimitiveUP (
91:                                         D3DPT_TRIANGLEFAN, 2,
```

```
                                           kVertices, sizeof (mrVertex))) )
 {
  return mrErrorDrawPrimitive;
 }

 return mrNoError;
}
```

You first move the particle to the absolute position. This is the position of the particle system. Okay, you're confused. When a particle is in a particle system, its position is relative to the particle system, not to the world, but when you want to render it, you want to make it appear in the right place, so you need to add the particle system position to the relative position of the particle to get the final position. You pass the particle system position as an argument to Render.

Next you fill in the vertices and render the particle, nothing you haven't done before.

Now is the really neat stuff of your particle system, creating new particles. If all the particles you created had the same velocity, the particle system would be dull, so what you do is create all the particles with the same color, size, and other attributes, but make each particle have a random velocity (not totally random as you will see).

```
 /* Create the particle */
void mrParticle::Create (mrParticleSystemParams & rkParams)
{
  /* Create the particle with the given parameters*/
 m_kPosition       = mrVector2D (0,0);
 m_kOldPosition    = mrVector2D (0,0);
 m_fSize           = rkParams.m_fSize;
 m_fFinalSize      = rkParams.m_fFinalSize;
 m_fLife           = 0;
 m_fLifetime       = rkParams.m_fLifetime;

 m_iColor          = rkParams.m_iColor;
 m_iFinalColor     = rkParams.m_iFinalColor;

 m_fDispersion     = rkParams.m_fDispersion;
 m_fSpeed          = rkParams.m_fSpeed;
```

You start by setting the particle's attributes, which were supplied as an argument. This will ensure that all the particles are created the same. Next you need to create the particle's velocity, the fun part.

```
117:    /* Set the particle direction depending on the dispersion
118:       If dispersion is one, then a full circle is used, if
119:       dispersion is zero, particles will be sent straight down */
120:
121:    /* Get circle of dispersion */
122:   mrReal32 fDispersion;
123:   mrReal32 fAngle;
124:
125:   fDispersion = (1 - (2 * ((mrReal32)rand () / (mrReal32)RAND_MAX))) *
126:                 (180 * 0.0174f);
127:   fAngle = (3.14159f / 2.0f) + fDispersion * m_fDispersion;
128:
129:    /* Calculate the directions */
130:   m_kVelocity [0] = (mrReal32)cos (fAngle);
131:   m_kVelocity [1] = (mrReal32)sin (fAngle);
132:
133:    /* Now we set the particle speed */
134:   mrReal32 fNewSpeed;
135:   fNewSpeed = m_fSpeed * 100 + (rand () / RAND_MAX) * m_fSpeed * 100;
136:   m_kVelocity *= fNewSpeed;
137: }
```

What you do here is create particles with a random velocity, but that adhere to some rules.

You start by calculating a random dispersion (line 125) for the velocity. You get a random value between $-\pi$ and π. You do this by using the following formula:

```
1 - (2 * ((mrReal32)rand () / (mrReal32)RAND_MAX))
```

Which will return a value between –1 and 1. Think about it, if you divide a random number between zero and `RAND_MAX`, you will always get a value between zero and one. After that, you multiply that value to get a value between zero and two. After that, you subtract one from that value and you get a random value between –1 and 1.

Okay, so you get a random value between –1 and 1 and then you multiply it by 180 * 0.0174f, and if you haven't skipped any of the previous chapters, you should know that this is the value for half a circle in radians or π. So by multiplying a random number between –1 and 1 by π you get a random number between $-\pi$ and π. This will make a full circle. So if you wanted to create particles that went in any direction randomly, you would leave it like this, but since you want to be able to limit it, you multiply this value by `m_fDispersion`. Now, which values can `m_fDispersion` take? Any value between zero and one; if you use zero, all the particles will be sent in a straight line, and if you use one, all the particles will be sent in a full circle randomly. What you are doing is limiting the random number you created earlier to m_fDispersion.

Next you add half π to the recipe. Why do you do this? Well, I wanted to send my particles up if dispersion was zero, and since half π is straight up, that's the value I've used. If you wanted to send it straight to the left, you could use π or to the right you could have used zero.

This may sound a little confusing, but don't worry, my advice is to try the code; change the m_fDispersion and see what happens. Things will become clear.

Next, you pick the random angle created and calculate the x and y coordinates using the cosine and sine of the angle (check the math chapter if you don't know what is happening).

In the end, you scale the velocity by m_fSpeed and some randomness. There are two multiplications by 100. This was done so you don't have to supply huge values for m_fSpeed in the mrParticleSystemParams.

And you are done with mrParticle. It wasn't that hard, was it? And when you see the results, trust me, you will say it was well worth it.

mrParticleSystem

Now it's time for the particle system class. This class is responsible for creating and managing the particles.

The first thing to do is probably the Create method.

```
 /* Create the particle system */
void mrParticleSystem::Create (mrParticleSystemParams & rkParameters,
                               mrUInt32 iMaxParticles,
                               mrUInt32 iParticlePerSecond,
                               mrTexture * pkTexture)
{
  /* Create the particle system with the required attributes */
 memcpy (&m_kParameters, &rkParameters, sizeof(mrParticleSystemParams));
 m_pkParticles        = new mrParticle [iMaxParticles];
 m_iMaxParticles      = iMaxParticles;
 m_iParticlePerSecond = iParticlePerSecond;
 m_pkTexture          = pkTexture;
}
```

This method creates an array for the particles and sets up the particle system's particle information.

Next you have Simulate, which is also pretty simple:

```
/* Simulate the particle system */
void mrParticleSystem::Simulate (mrReal32 fStep)
{
 mrUInt32 iParticle;
 mrInt32  iParticlesToCreate;

 iParticlesToCreate = 0;

  /* Check how many particles we need to create */
 iParticlesToCreate = mrUInt32(m_iParticlePerSecond * fStep + m_fResidue);
  /* Store residue of particles (partial particles) */
 m_fResidue = (m_iParticlesPerSecond * fStep + m_fResidue) - iParticlesToCreate;

 for (iParticle = 0; iParticle < m_iMaxParticles; iParticle++)
 {
   /* Simulate the particle */
  if (m_pkParticles [iParticle].GetLife () < 1.0f)
  {
   m_pkParticles [iParticle].Simulate (fStep);
  }
   /* If particle is dead, try to recreate it */
  else
  {
   if (mrFalse == m_bDontCreate)
   {
     /* Only create the particle if we haven't reached the limit */
    if (iParticlesToCreate > 0)
    {
     m_pkParticles [iParticle].Create (m_kParameters);
     iParticlesToCreate --;
    }
   }
  }
 }
}
```

You go through every particle, and if it is alive, simulate that particle by calling the particle's Simulate method. If it is dead, you try to re-create it.

You get the number of particles to create this step, by multiplying the maximum allowed particles to be created per second by the frame step to get the maximum particles per frame and adding the residue from last frame. The *residue* is the number of particles, or more accurately, the partial of particles you should have created in the last frame.

For example, if the step was 0.004, and the maximum particles created per second was three, you would always have to create 0.012 particles. There were two possible solutions, you would have to make your time step bigger, or you would have to create the particles. If you use the residue, which is the partial particle that you didn't create, you will only be creating the particle if all the partial particles' sum is one or more.

You also check with m_fDontCreate to see whether the particle system should create the particles or not (the particle system may be deactivated).

Finally, you have Render. This is tricky because it involves Direct3D render states so you get a nice effect:

```
 /* Render particle system */
void mrParticleSystem::Render (void)
{
 mrUInt32   iParticle;
  /* Set as active texture */
 m_pkTexture->SetActiveTexture ();

  /* Set alpha blending to particle mode */
 mrScreen::GetSingleton ()->GetDevice ()->SetRenderState (
                             D3DRS_SRCBLEND, D3DBLEND_SRCALPHA);
 mrScreen::GetSingleton ()->GetDevice ()->SetRenderState (
                             D3DRS_DESTBLEND, D3DBLEND_ONE);

  /* Draw the particles */
 mrScreen::GetSingleton ()->GetDevice ()->SetVertexShader (
                                         D3DFVF_MIRUSVERTEX);

  /* Render each particle */
 for (iParticle = 0; iParticle < m_iMaxParticles; iParticle++)
```

```
{
  if (m_pkParticles [iParticle].GetLife () < 1.0f)
  {
   m_pkParticles [iParticle].Render (m_kParameters.m_kPosition);
  }
 }

   /* Set alpha blending to normal mode */
 mrScreen::GetSingleton ()->GetDevice ()->SetRenderState (
                                D3DRS_SRCBLEND, D3DBLEND_SRCALPHA);
 mrScreen::GetSingleton ()->GetDevice ()->SetRenderState (
                                D3DRS_DESTBLEND, D3DBLEND_INVSRCALPHA);
}
```

What you do here is set the destination blend mode to D3DBLEND_ONE. How is this going to affect your program? Well, instead of picking the texture's alpha channel, it will use the white intensity for alpha. What this means is that a black picture will not be drawn, and a white one will be fully drawn. Of course, shades of gray get more or less drawn depending on the amount of white.

Why do you set these render states instead of using the alpha channel? There is one simple explanation: it's easier to create particle textures this way. In particles you can't set color keys, so you would need a paint program that supports alpha channels, which may leave you out of the group already, but even if you have a nice program, most don't allow you to do shades in the alpha channel, you can either choose if a pixel is visible or not, and this is what you don't want. You need smooth transition gradients like in Figure 20.18, and doing these in alpha channels is difficult.

Figure 20.18

A radial gradient.

Rendering the image with these render states allows you not to use the alpha channel but to use shades of gray to set alpha. Since the color of the particle will be calculated with the particle system, you don't need to worry about losing the green or red of the texture. Now tell me, isn't Direct3D nice?

```
  /* Draw the particles */
 mrScreen::GetSingleton ()->GetDevice ()->SetVertexShader (
                                            D3DFVF_MIRUSVERTEX);

  /* Render each particle */
 for (iParticle = 0; iParticle < m_iMaxParticles; iParticle++)
 {
  if (m_pkParticles [iParticle].GetLife () < 1.0f)
  {
   m_pkParticles [iParticle].Render (m_kParameters.m_kPosition);
  }
 }
```

After setting the render states, you render each particle, but only if it is alive. Remember, a particle is dead if its life is one or more.

```
   /* Set alpha blending to normal mode */
 mrScreen::GetSingleton ()->GetDevice ()->SetRenderState (
                              D3DRS_SRCBLEND, D3DBLEND_SRCALPHA);
 mrScreen::GetSingleton ()->GetDevice ()->SetRenderState (
                              D3DRS_DESTBLEND, D3DBLEND_INVSRCALPHA);
}
```

Finally you set the render states back to normal and you are done. Your own particle system! Go try it, come on!

Particle Demo

To finish the chapter and the talk about particle systems, let's create a demo that shows you how to create a realistic flame:

```
 /* '01 Main.cpp' */

 /* Mirus window framework header */
#include <mirus.h>

```

```
 /* Custom derived class */
class CustomWindow : public mrWindow
{
public:
 mrScreen             m_kScreen;

  /* Our particle system */
 mrParticleSystem    m_kParticleSystem;

  /* Constructor / Destructor */
 CustomWindow (void) {};
 ~CustomWindow (void) {};

  /* Window manipulation functions */
 mrBool32 Frame (void);

};

 /* Render frame */
mrBool32 CustomWindow::Frame(void)
{
  /* Start rendering */
 m_kScreen.Clear (0, 0, 0, 0);
 m_kScreen.StartFrame ();

  /* Simulate according to elapsed time */
 if (0 != m_kScreen.GetFPS ())
 {
  m_kParticleSystem.Simulate (1 / (mrReal32)m_kScreen.GetFPS ());
 }

  /* Render particle system and end frame */
 m_kParticleSystem.Render ();
 m_kScreen.EndFrame ();

 return mrTrue;
}

 /* "WinMain Vs. main" */
```

```
int WINAPI WinMain (HINSTANCE hInstance, HINSTANCE hPrevInst,
                    LPSTR lpCmdLine, int nShowCmd)
{
  /* Our window */
 CustomWindow  kWindow;

  /* Create window */
 kWindow.Create (hInstance, "Flame Example");
 kWindow.SetSize (640, 480);

 kWindow.m_kScreen.Init (kWindow.GetHandle ());
 kWindow.m_kScreen.SetMode (false, 640,480,32,true);

  /* We need a texture for our particle system */
 mrRGBAImage rkImage;
 rkImage.LoadFromBitmap ("gradientcircle.bmp");

 mrTexture kTexture;
 kTexture.Create (&rkImage);

  /* Our system parameters */
 mrParticleSystemParams kParameters;

 kParameters.m_fSize        = 20;
 kParameters.m_fLifetime    = 0.3f;
 kParameters.m_iColor       = D3DCOLOR_RGBA (255, 208, 51, 136);
 kParameters.m_iFinalColor = D3DCOLOR_RGBA (255, 0, 0, 0);
 kParameters.m_kPosition    = mrVector2D (310,230);
 kParameters.m_fFinalSize   = 30;
 kParameters.m_fSpeed       = -4;
 kParameters.m_fDispersion = 0.02f;

  /* Create the particle system */
 kWindow.m_kParticleSystem.Create (kParameters, 200, 75, &kTexture);

 kWindow.Run ();
 return 0;
}
```

This program is pretty simple, you set up the particle system parameters as you want, create the particle system with 200 particles, and then you simulate and render it in `Frame`. See Figure 20.19.

If you don't like the fire, play around with the parameters. By only messing with the parameters, I was able to get the star field effect shown in Figure 20.20.

Figure 20.19

Your particle system at work

Figure 20.20

Changing the parameters gives a completely different result.

Summary

One of the most interesting topics of games is physics. Adding realism to your games is one of the fundamental aspects of game programming, and will enhance your games a lot.

In this chapter you made both a general purpose physics engine and a particle system that can be used in your games without having to worry about the details.

Questions and Answers

Q: Is the relative position of an object A to B the same as for the object B to A?

A: No, while the magnitude of the distances is the same, the direction of the vector would be the opposite.

Q: Is inertia an angular property only?

A: No, inertia also exists for linear movement, since it is the resistance an object has to change its movement. You usually only use the inertia for the rotation since you can get the linear velocity using only the mass.

Q: Why is the normal reaction used when solving physics problems but not on the computer?

A: Use the normal reaction when you have the data needed (such as the angle of the surface) and when you can change the coordinate systems makes it easier to solve the problems, but if you are programming, you usually don't have this, so you need to resort to other methods such as the ones presented.

Q: Why shouldn't you call the `HandleCollision` method for each object, instead of calculating both the objects' velocities?

A: If you would use two calls to `HandleCollision`, the second call would be incorrect since you had changed the velocity of the first object in the first call.

Q: Why do you apply damping to the angular velocity?

A: If you didn't, the object would spin forever until something made it stop, and since you don't have any way of stopping it (unless applying another force), the object would spin out.

Exercises

1. What are the five rules of projectiles?
2. If an object on the Moon weighs exactly half what it weighs on Earth, what is the gravity acceleration on the Moon?
3. Would a projectile that is launched at a height of 100 meters reach the floor (0 meters) with the same horizontal velocity as it was launched?
4. What is the international system unit for mass?
5. What is kinetic friction?
6. Make the potential tree for the calls to `HandleCollision` for the following list of objects: A, B, D, E, Y, Z, C.
7. What is the step of a frame, if the program is running at 403 frames per second?
8. Try to change the particle system parameters so the effect matches the one in Figure 20.21.

CHAPTER 21

Building Breaking Through

It is now time for your final game. You will develop a clone of a well-known game, Breakout or Arkanoid (depending how old you are), but with a little more eye-candy and a little different gameplay as you will see.

I've chosen this game because it is well known, so understanding the base concepts behind it isn't hard, and also since it's a game you don't need thousands of lines of code.

Designing Breaking Through

The Breaking Through concept isn't anything new. Anyone who has played computer games has played the game, or at least seen someone play it, which will make your task of creating the game simpler since the concept is well known.

General Overview

The general concept of Breaking Through is a game where the user controls a paddle and tries to prevent the ball from touching the bottom of the screen while destroying all the blocks of each level.

When the ball touches a block, the block is destroyed. When all the blocks are destroyed, the level is complete and the player advances to the next level.

Target System and Requirements

Breaking Through doesn't require much processing power, but since it uses some Direct3D functionality and nice graphics, a decent video card is required.

Breaking Through is targeted to run in all Windows platforms that fully support DirectX 8.0.

The minimum requirements for playing Breaking Through are:

- 333MHz PentiumII
- 64MB of RAM
- 100% DirectX 8.0 compatible video card with at least 8 MB of memory
- 100% DirectX 8.0 compatible sound card

Story

In the year 2043, the leaders of the three most powerful factions of the universe converge to decide how rebellions and terrorist attacks could be stopped.

Being that the people are the biggest supporter of the terrorist acts, the three factions have concluded that the only way to control the people would be to cut the terrorist support, and thus, discarding any menace.

The solution to the problem was not simple, but it was decided that to control the people, a new sport would be created.

This new sport would offer the chance to any team to try to survive through all the arenas, and if successful, to be rewarded with a big cash prize. Many tried to conquer the available four arenas, but up til now, no team has gotten out alive from the tournaments.

It is your time to try!

Rules

Playing this game is very simple. The player is given three balls (sphere capsules), each of which contains a team element that controls the paddle. By controlling the paddle, the player must prevent the ball from falling into the bottom of the arena, which will destroy the ball, and thus, one of the team elements.

Controlling the paddle (main ship) is done by applying force to it. By applying a stronger force, the paddle will move faster, but it will also be harder to control.

Each time the ball touches a block, the block is destroyed. Destroying all the blocks in an arena will allow the team to progress to the next arena.

When all the arenas are conquered, the game ends with victory.

When there are no more team elements, the game ends with defeat.

Theme: Graphics

The graphics of Breaking Through have a futuristic look; that is, metallic looking. The paddle is made of two sections, the actual metal paddle and two surrounding borders.

The design of the paddle is shown in Figure 21.1.

The paddle is divided into two sections, the sides are bumpers so the paddle bounces off the wall borders.

The blocks can have various colors but share all the same 3D design like shown in Figure 21.2.

The main game borders are made of shiny metal and the background is a seamless pattern.

A sample of the border can be found in Figure 21.3 and the pattern in Figure 21.4.

There is also lighting at the bottom of the screen, and when the ball touches the lighting, it is destroyed with a particle explosion.

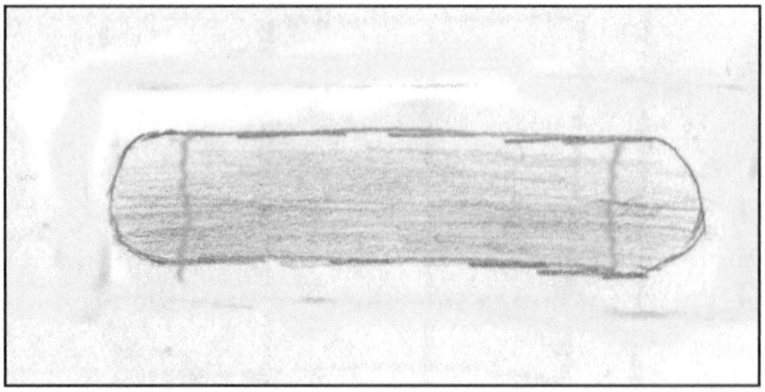

Figure 21.1

The paddle prototype.

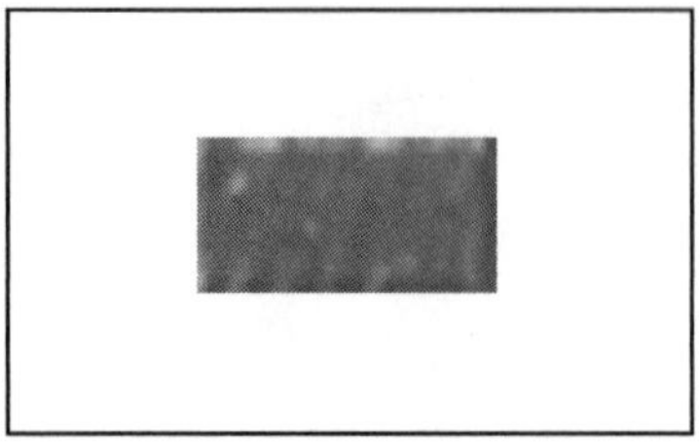

Figure 21.2

A game block.

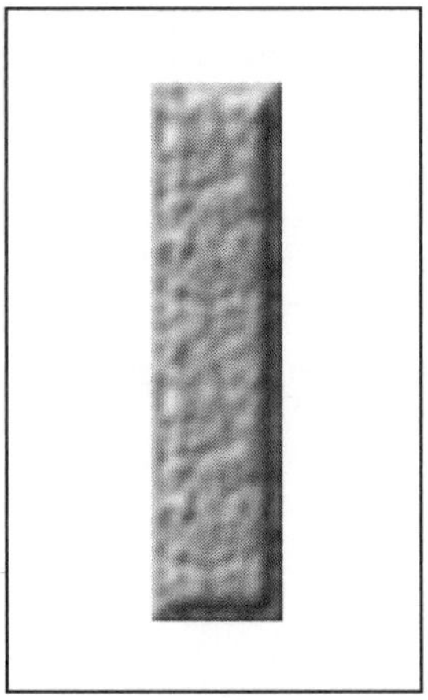

Figure 21.3

A possible border.

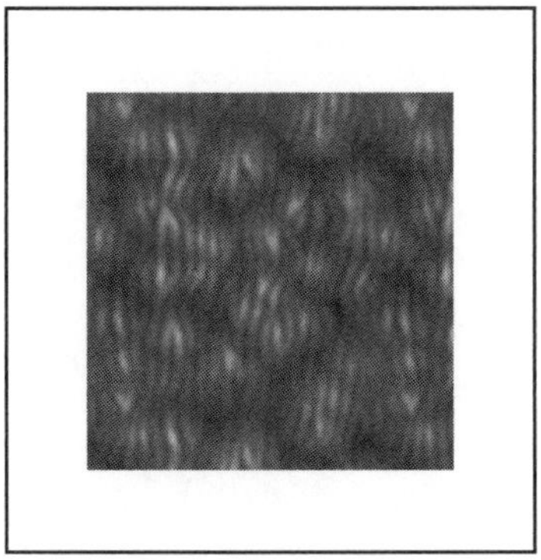

Figure 21.4

A sample pattern.

Menus

There is only one menu in the game, the main menu. In this menu, the player is allowed to choose from three options:

- **New game.** The player will start a new game from the beginning, with three balls and no score.
- **Load game.** The player will start a new game from the start of the level when the game was saved with the previous score and balls.
- **Quit game.** The player will be brought back to Windows.

Playing a Game

Playing a game is simple. The player is first presented with a welcome screen for the game, a sample mock-up of this screen can be found in Figure 21.5.

Next the user is presented with the main menu where he can press `N` for a new game, `L` to load a previous game, and `Q` to quit the game. Suppose the player wants to start a new game. The image behind the menu is the same as the start screen, which can be seen in Figure 21.6.

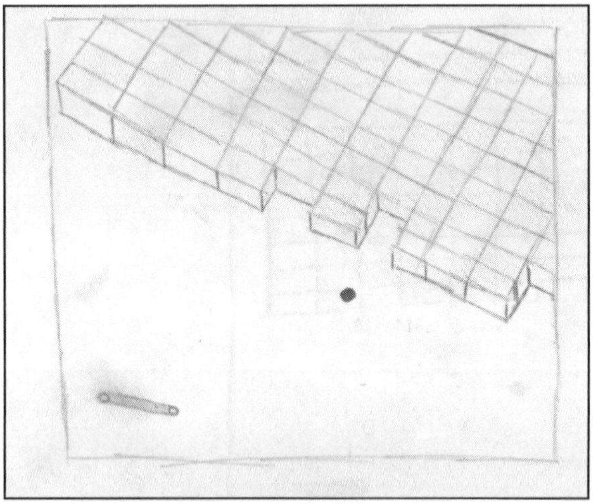

Figure 21.5

Mock-up of the start screen.

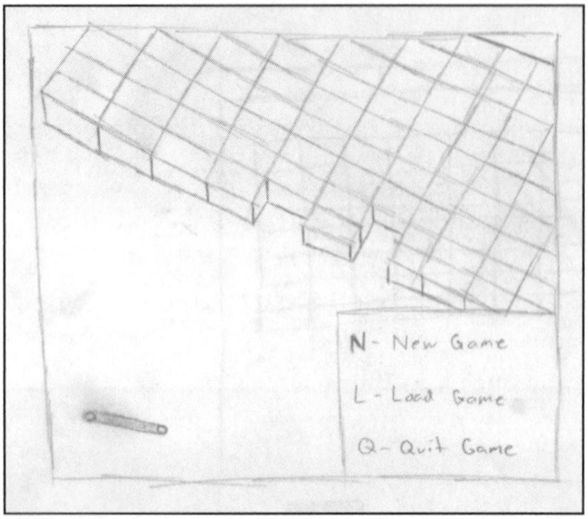

Figure 21.6

Mock-up of the main menu.

When the player starts the game, the words Ready and Go are presented just before the ball starts moving. There is a bolt at the bottom of the screen, and just above it, the paddle. A little under the top of the screen are the blocks.

The screen is also covered with three borders from where the ball will ricochet. The score of the player is shown in the top right corner while the lives are shown as balls in the top left corner.

This is shown in Figure 21.7.

When the user presses either the right or left arrows, the paddle is accelerated to that side, but if it bumps into a border, it will bounce back.

If the ball hits any of the borders, blocks, or the paddle, it will bump, sometimes back, other times not (this was done to increase the difficulty).

When a ball hits the block, the block is destroyed.

When the ball hits the lighting on the bottom, the ball is destroyed with an explosion.

If the ball hits the border, blocks, or paddles, a small "blink" sound is played, and if the ball is destroyed, a "boom" sound is played.

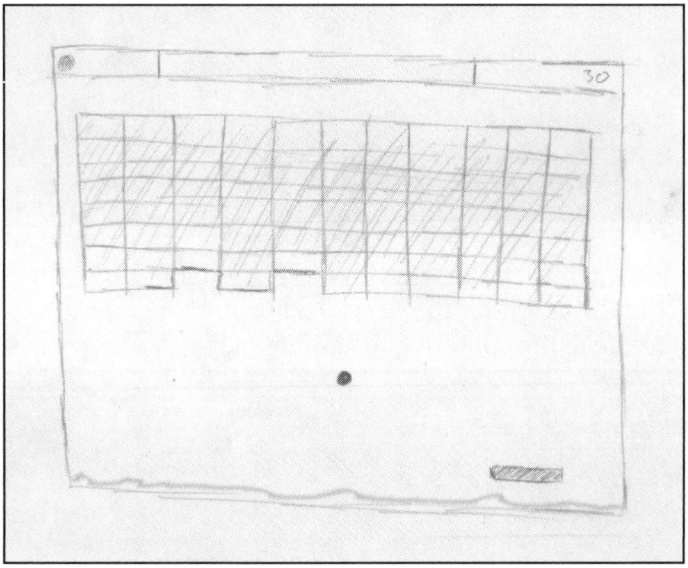

Figure 21.7

Mock-up of the main game.

Code Design

To make the code object-oriented, you will treat each object in the game as a separate class, and then join them all together in a game class.

You will start with the simple classes and move to the more complicated ones, so first, let's see how the block class should be.

btBlock

The `btBlock` class describes a block in the game. This class will store an entity object, for collisions, the block size and color, and the block ABO. The class's primary methods are:

- `Create`
- `Destroy`

btPaddle

The `btPaddle` will hold the information about the paddle. This class contains the main paddle and both the side bumpers' information.

Its main methods are:

- `Create`
- `Render`
- `Synchronize`
- `Update`

btBall

The next class you will have is for the ball. This call will hold the ball position and size. This class is a little more complicated than the previous two in that you will use a particle system with it to create the explosion effect when the ball is destroyed.

The main methods of this class are:

- `Create`
- `Destroy`
- `Render`
- `Synchronize`
- `Update`

btGame

This class is the most important class in the game. This class will be responsible for just about everything related to the game, from loading levels, to rendering the object, and handling collisions.

The main methods of `btGame` are:

- `Start`
- `LoadLevel`
- `Render`
- `RenderXXX`
- `HandleCollisions`
- `HandleCollisionXXX`
- `Process`
- `ProcessXXX`
- `LoadGame`
- `SaveGame`

(The methods with `XXX` are those methods that do what their name indicates, but for the state or object. For example, `RenderMenu` will render the game main menu, and so on.)

BreakThroughWindow

The `BreakThroughWindow` class is used for controlling the Windows aspect of the game; that is, to create the window, set up DirectX, handle messages, and so on.

The class main methods are:

- `Frame`
- `Init`

Building Breaking Through

As seen before, the Breaking Through game is comprised of four classes for the gameplay and another class for the window creation and DirectX setup.

You will see each of these classes next.

btBlock

As you saw before, the btBlock class is simple. Take a look at the class definition:

```
/* 'btBlock.h' */

/* Mirus window framework header */
#include "Mirus\Mirus.h"

/* Include this file only once */
#pragma once

/* Break Through ball class */
class btBlock
{
protected:
  /* Physics object */
 mrEntity           m_kObject;

  /* Real size of block */
 mrUInt32           m_iWidth;
 mrUInt32           m_iHeight;

  /* Is block alive */
 mrBool32           m_bIsAlive;

  /* Block ABO ID */
 mrUInt32           m_iABO;

  /* Block colors */
 mrUInt8            m_iRed;
 mrUInt8            m_iGreen;
 mrUInt8            m_iBlue;
 mrUInt8            m_iAlpha;

public:
  /* Constructor / Destructor */
 btBlock (void);
 ~btBlock (void);

  /* Block manipulation routines */
```

```
void Create (mrUInt32 iABO, mrVector2D kPosition, mrUInt8 iRed,
             mrUInt8 iGreen, mrUInt8 iBlue, mrUInt8 iAlpha);
void Destroy (void);

 /* Block maintenance routines */
void SetSize (mrUInt32 iWidth, mrUInt32 iHeight);
mrUInt32 GetABO (void);

mrUInt8 GetRed (void);
mrUInt8 GetGreen (void);
mrUInt8 GetBlue (void);
mrUInt8 GetAlpha (void);

mrUInt32 GetWidth (void);
mrUInt32 GetHeight (void);
mrEntity * GetObject (void);
mrBool32 GetIsAlive (void);
};
```

Apart from the many accessor methods, all the other important methods will be covered. For now, check out the constructor and the destructor:

```
 /* 'btBlock.cpp' */

 /* Complement header file */
#include "btBlock.h"

btBlock::btBlock (void)
{
 m_iWidth    = 0;
 m_iHeight   = 0;
 m_bIsAlive = mrFalse;
 m_iABO      = 0;
 m_iRed      = 0;
 m_iGreen    = 0;
 m_iBlue     = 0;
 m_iAlpha    = 0;
}

btBlock::~btBlock (void)
{
```

```
20:  m_iWidth   = 0;
21:  m_iHeight  = 0;
22:  m_bIsAlive = mrFalse;
23:  m_iABO     = 0;
24:  m_iRed     = 0;
25:  m_iGreen   = 0;
26:  m_iBlue    = 0;
27:  m_iAlpha   = 0;
28: }
```

Because there isn't any allocation of memory, the only thing you need to do in both methods is to set all the members to 0 or `mrFalse`.

```
30: void btBlock::Create (mrUInt32 iABO, mrVector2D kPosition,
31:                       mrUInt8 iRed, mrUInt8 iGreen,
32:                       mrUInt8 iBlue, mrUInt8 iAlpha)
33: {
34:   /* Setup the ABO */
35:  m_iABO = iABO;
36:
37:   /* Setup the color */
38:  m_iRed   = iRed;
39:  m_iGreen = iGreen;
40:  m_iBlue  = iBlue;
41:  m_iAlpha = iAlpha;
42:
43:   /* Setup the initial paddle size */
44:  SetSize (32, 16);
45:
46:  m_bIsAlive = mrTrue;
47:
48:   /* Setup the entity */
49:  m_kObject.SetMass (10000000000);
50:  m_kObject.SetStaticFriction (0);
51:  m_kObject.SetCoefficientOfRestitution(1);
52:  m_kObject.SetKineticFriction (1);
53:  m_kObject.SetPosition (kPosition);
54: }
```

Setting up a block is pretty easy also, you just set the ABO ID (line 35), which you will learn about later, and the color components (lines 38 through 41). Next you set the block size (line 44) and make it alive (line 46).

You just have to initialize the entity class with the necessary values (lines 49 through 53). If you remember from Chapter 20, "Introduction to Physics Modelling", when two objects collide, usually they both change velocities unless one of the objects has a very high mass. This is why we supply such a high value for the block mass.

The next method you need to develop is `Destroy`:

```
56: void btBlock::Destroy (void)
57: {
58:  SetSize (0, 0);
59:  m_bIsAlive = mrFalse;
60: }
```

In this method, you set the ABO size to 0, 0, so the ABO isn't rendered, and you set the `m_bIsAlive` to `mrFalse`.

Next are the accessor methods:

```
62: void btBlock::SetSize (mrUInt32 iWidth, mrUInt32 iHeight)
63: {
64:  m_iWidth  = iWidth;
65:  m_iHeight = iHeight;
66: }
67:
68: mrUInt32 btBlock::GetABO (void)
69: {
70:  return m_iABO;
71: }
72:
73: mrUInt8 btBlock::GetRed (void)
74: {
75:  return m_iRed;
76: }
77:
78: mrUInt8 btBlock::GetGreen (void)
79: {
80:  return m_iGreen;
81: }
82:
83: mrUInt8 btBlock::GetBlue (void)
84: {
85:  return m_iBlue;
```

```
}

mrUInt8 btBlock::GetAlpha (void)
{
 return m_iAlpha;
}

mrUInt32 btBlock::GetWidth (void)
{
 return m_iWidth;
}

mrUInt32 btBlock::GetHeight (void)
{
 return m_iHeight;
}

mrEntity * btBlock::GetObject (void)
{
 return &m_kObject;
}

mrBool32 btBlock::GetIsAlive (void)
{
 return m_bIsAlive;
}
```

This was the simplest class of the game. You will use this class later in btGame.

btPaddle

Except for the fact that the paddle is made of the main part and the side bumpers, the btPaddle isn't hard at all.

Take a look at the class definition:

```
 /* 'btPaddle.h' */

 /* Mirus window framework header */
#include "Mirus\Mirus.h"

 /* Include this file only once */
```

```
#pragma once

 /* Break Through paddle class */
class btPaddle
{
protected:
  /* Paddle is made up of three parts */
 mrABO          m_kMainPaddle;
 mrABO          m_akSidePaddles [2];

  /* Physics object */
 mrEntity       m_kObject;

  /* Real size (all parts) of the paddle */
 mrUInt32       m_iWidth;
 mrUInt32       m_iHeight;


public:
  /* Constructor / Destructor */
 btPaddle (void);
 ~btPaddle (void);

  /* Paddle manipulation routines */
 void Create (void);
 void Render (void);
 void Synchronize (void);
 void Update (mrReal32 fStep);

  /* Paddle maintenance routines */
 void SetSize (mrUInt32 iWidth, mrUInt32 iHeight);
 mrUInt32 GetWidth (void);
 mrUInt32 GetHeight (void);
 mrEntity * GetObject (void);
};
```

As usual, let's check the constructor and the destructor first:

```
 /* 'btPaddle.cpp' */

 /* Complement header file */
#include "btPaddle.h"
```

```
 5:
 6:  /* Default constructor */
 7: btPaddle::btPaddle (void)
 8: {
 9:  m_iWidth  = 0;
10:  m_iHeight = 0;
11: }
12:
13:  /* Default destructor */
14: btPaddle::~btPaddle (void)
15: {
16:  m_iWidth  = 0;
17:  m_iHeight = 0;
18: }
```

And again, you just set the members to 0.

The next method involves a little more work (which is good, right?):

```
20:  /* Create the paddle */
21: void btPaddle::Create (void)
22: {
23:   /* Setup the ABOs */
24:  m_akSidePaddles [0].LoadFromFile ("data/paddleside.txt");
25:  m_akSidePaddles [0].SetColor (255,255,255,255);
26:  m_akSidePaddles [1].LoadFromFile ("data/paddleside.txt");
27:  m_akSidePaddles [1].SetColor (255,255,255,255);
28:
29:  m_kMainPaddle.LoadFromFile ("data/paddle.txt");
30:  m_kMainPaddle.SetColor (255,255,255,255);
```

You start by loading each of the side bumps from file and setting their color (lines 24 through 30) and then loading the main paddle part and setting its color (lines 29 and 30).

```
32:   /* Setup the initial paddle size */
33:  SetSize (75, 10);
34:
35:   /* Setup the entity */
36:  m_kObject.SetMass (10000);
37:  m_kObject.SetLinearVelocity (mrVector2D (0,0));
38:  m_kObject.SetCoefficientOfRestitution (1);
39:  m_kObject.SetStaticFriction (0.62f);
```

```
40:  m_kObject.SetKineticFriction (0.51f);
41:  m_kObject.SetPosition (mrVector2D (316, 433));
42:
43:  Synchronize ();
44: }
```

Next, you need to set the paddle size. If you prefer a large or bigger paddle, you will change the values (line 33). You also set the entity properties with some values that work well for your simulation (lines 36 through 41).

In the end, you synchronize the paddle with `Synchronize` (line 43), which you will see later.

The next method will render the paddle:

```
46:  /* Render the paddle */
47: void btPaddle::Render (void)
48: {
49:   /* Render each part of the paddle */
50:  m_akSidePaddles [0].Render ();
51:  m_akSidePaddles [1].Render ();
52:  m_kMainPaddle.Render ();
53: }
```

This method calls the `Render` method of each paddle ABO.

The next method you need to implement is `Synchronize`. `Synchronize` is used to make the ABO the correct size and position since the size can change (if you want) and the position is controlled by the entity object:

```
55:  /* Synchronizes the entity and the ABO positions */
56: void btPaddle::Synchronize (void)
57: {
58:  mrVector2D kPosition;
59:
60:   /* Set correct size for the ABOs */
61:  m_kMainPaddle.SetSize (m_iWidth - m_akSidePaddles [0].GetWidth (),
62:                         m_iHeight);
63:  m_akSidePaddles [0].SetSize (m_iHeight, m_iHeight);
64:  m_akSidePaddles [1].SetSize (m_iHeight, m_iHeight);
65:
66:   /* Set correct position for the ABOs */
67:  kPosition = m_kObject.GetPosition ();
68:
```

```
69:  m_kMainPaddle.SetPosition ((mrUInt32)kPosition [0],
70:                              (mrUInt32)kPosition [1]);
71:  m_akSidePaddles [0].SetPosition ((mrUInt32)kPosition [0] - m_iWidth/2
72:                                    + m_akSidePaddles [0].GetWidth ()/2,
73:                                     (mrUInt32)kPosition [1]);
74:  m_akSidePaddles [1].SetPosition ((mrUInt32)kPosition [0] + m_iWidth/2
75:                                    - m_akSidePaddles [0].GetWidth ()/2,
76:                                     (mrUInt32)kPosition [1]);
77: }
```

You start by setting the size of each ABO (lines 61 through 64). After this is done, you get the position from the entity (line 67) and set the correct ABO position for each part of the paddle (lines 69 through 76).

The last method you will take a look at is `Update`, which simulates the ball:

```
78:  /* Update the paddle */
79: void btPaddle::Update (mrReal32 fStep)
80: {
81:   /* Apply friction, simulate and synchronize the positions */
82:  m_kObject.ApplyFriction (59.8f);
83:  m_kObject.Simulate (fStep);
84:
85:  m_kMainPaddle.Update ();
86:
87:  Synchronize ();
88: }
```

You start this method by applying friction to the entity and simulating it (lines 82 and 83). You then `Update` the main paddle ABO (line 85) and synchronize the paddle (line 88).

Next are the acessor methods:

```
90:  /* Sets the paddle size */
91: void btPaddle::SetSize (mrUInt32 iWidth, mrUInt32 iHeight)
92: {
93:  if (iWidth > 200)
94:  {
95:   iWidth = 200;
96:  }
97:  if (iWidth < 30)
98:  {
```

```
    iWidth = 30;
  }
  m_iWidth  = iWidth;
  m_iHeight = iHeight;
}

 /* Returns the paddle width */
mrUInt32 btPaddle::GetWidth (void)
{
  return m_iWidth;
}

 /* Returns the paddle height */
mrUInt32 btPaddle::GetHeight (void)
{
  return m_iHeight;
}

 /* Returns the paddle entity */
mrEntity * btPaddle::GetObject (void)
{
  return &m_kObject;
}
```

And that's about it. You will use this class in the btGame class later.

btBall

Before you move to the main class of Breaking Through, let's take a look at the ball class. The ball class, in addition to being a container for all the information related to the ball (position, color), also contains a particle system you will use to show the explosion of the ball.

Take a look at the class definition:

```
 /* 'btBall.h' */

 /* Mirus window framework header */
#include "Mirus\Mirus.h"

 /* Include this file only once */
```

```
#pragma once

 /* Break Through ball class */
class btBall
{
protected:
  /* Ball ABO */
 mrABO              m_kBall;

  /* Physics object */
 mrEntity           m_kObject;
 mrReal32           m_fSpeed;

  /* Real size of the ball */
 mrUInt32           m_iRadius;

  /* Particle system */
 mrParticleSystem  m_kParticleSystem;
 mrTimer            m_kTimer;
 mrReal32           m_fTimerCount;
 mrTexture          m_kParticleTexture;

 mrBool32           m_bIsAlive;

public:
  /* Constructor / Destructor */
 btBall (void);
 ~btBall (void);

  /* Ball manipulation routines */
 void Create (void);
 void Destroy (void);
 void Render (void);
 void Synchronize (void);
 void Update (mrReal32 fStep);

  /* Ball maintenance routines */
 void SetSpeed (mrReal32 fSpeed);
 void SetSize (mrUInt32 iRadius);
 mrReal32 GetSpeed (void);
```

```
mrUInt32 GetSize (void);
mrEntity * GetObject (void);
mrBool32 GetIsAlive (void);
};
```

Again, this class doesn't look much different from the others. By giving the same name to functions that do the same thing, or at least are used to do something related, you can easily identify which set of functions is for what, and use them correctly.

Okay, back to the code. Let's take a look at the constructor and the destructor:

```
 /* 'btBall.cpp' */

 /* Complement header file */
#include "btBall.h"

 /* Default constructor */
btBall::btBall (void)
{
 m_fTimerCount = 0;
 m_iRadius     = 0;
 m_bIsAlive    = mrFalse;
}

 /* Default destructor */
btBall::~btBall (void)
{
 m_fTimerCount = 0;
 m_iRadius     = 0;
 m_bIsAlive    = mrFalse;
}
```

Like the previous classes, these methods don't do anything more than set the class members to 0.

Next you have the `Create` method:

```
 /* Create the ball */
void btBall::Create (void)
{
  /* Setup the ABO */
 m_kBall.LoadFromFile ("data/ball.txt");
```

```
27:  m_kBall.SetColor (255,255,255,255);
28:
29:   /* Setup the initial ball size */
30:  m_iRadius = 10;
31:
32:   /* Setup the entity */
33:  m_kObject.SetInertia (1);
34:  m_kObject.SetMass (1);
35:  m_kObject.SetPosition (mrVector2D (316, 400));
36:  m_kObject.SetCoefficientOfRestitution (1);
37:
38:   /* Setup ball attributes */
39:  m_bIsAlive     = mrTrue;
40:  m_fTimerCount = 0;
```

You start by loading the ball ABO from a file (line 26) and set its color (line 27) and radius (line 30). You then set the physical attributes of the ball (lines 33 through 36). In the end you just set the ball to be alive and set the timer to 0 (lines 39 and 40).

Next you will need to get a random velocity for the ball:

```
42:   /* Setup ball direction */
43:  mrVector2D kVelocity;
44:  mrReal32 fAngle;
45:  fAngle = 0;
46:
47:   /* Randomize */
48:  srand (GetTickCount ());
49:
50:   /* To prevent the ball from going almost straight up, we get a random
51:      angle until it suits what we want */
52:  while ((fAngle < 0.15f) && (fAngle > -0.15f))
53:  {
54:   fAngle = (1 - (2 * ((mrReal32)rand () / (mrReal32)RAND_MAX))) *
55:            (40 * 0.0174f);
56:  }
57:  fAngle -= (90 * 0.0174f);
58:
59:   /* Calculate the direction */
60:  kVelocity [0] = (mrReal32)cos (fAngle);
61:  kVelocity [1] = (mrReal32)sin (fAngle);
```

```
62:
63:  m_kObject.SetLinearVelocity (kVelocity);
64:  SetSpeed (250);
```

To get a random velocity, you start by randomizing the system with `srand` (line 48). You want the velocity to have its vertical component a bit bigger than the horizonal one (or else the game would be easy). To do this, you will set the parameter that until the angle is between –0.15 and 0.15, you repeat the whole process for getting a random angle (line 52).

To get a random angle you will first get a random value between –1 and 1, and multiply it by the arc angle you want to use (the arc angle is the dispersion you want the ball to have, the smaller the value, the smaller the horizontal velocity of the ball). You do this by multiplying by `40 * 0.0174f`, which is the same as a 40-degree arc converted to radians (lines 54 and 55).

After that, you need to add 90 to the angle (line 57) so the ball goes up, and not to the right.

Then you use the cosine and sine with the above to get the velocity direction (lines 60 and 61).

In the end, you set the ball's speed (line 64).

The next thing on the `Create` list is to create the particle system:

```
66:   /* Setup the particle system */
67:  if (m_kParticleTexture.GetID ()==0)
68:  {
69:    /* Load the texture */
70:   mrRGBAImage rkImage;
71:   rkImage.LoadFromBitmap ("Graphics/flare.bmp");
72:
73:   m_kParticleTexture.Create (&rkImage);
74:
75:    /* Setup particle system parameters */
76:   mrParticleSystemParams kParameters;
77:
78:   kParameters.m_fSize        = 6;
79:   kParameters.m_fLifetime    = 0.40f;
80:   kParameters.m_iColor       = D3DCOLOR_RGBA (255, 208, 51, 255);
81:   kParameters.m_iFinalColor = D3DCOLOR_RGBA (255, 0, 0, 0);
82:   kParameters.m_kPosition    = mrVector2D (310,230);
83:   kParameters.m_fFinalSize   = 9;
```

```
84:    kParameters.m_fSpeed        = 0.25f;
85:    kParameters.m_fDispersion = 1;
86:
87:     /* Create the particle system */
88:    m_kParticleSystem.Create (kParameters, 50, 100, &m_kParticleTexture);
89:    m_kParticleSystem.SetDontCreate (mrTrue);
90:   }
91:   Synchronize ();
92: }
```

Creating the particle system is easy. You first check to see whether the particle was already created (line 67). If it hasn't been created, you need to load the particle texture from a file (lines 71 and 73) and then set the particle system parameters (lines 78 through 85). The way to get the values is by experimenting to see which ones look more like an explosion and which ones don't.

The next step is to create the particle system (line 88), set the particle to not active (line 89), and `Synchronize` the ball.

Next you need to destroy the ball:

```
 95:  /* Destroy the ball */
 96: void btBall::Destroy (void)
 97: {
 98:    /* Setup necessary variables to destroy the ball */
 99:   m_bIsAlive     = mrFalse;
100:   m_fTimerCount = 0;
101:   SetSpeed (0);
102:   SetSize (0);
103:
104:    /* Move ball to correct position so it doesn't disapear */
105:   mrVector2D kPosition;
106:   kPosition      = m_kObject.GetPosition ();
107:   kPosition [1] = 443;
108:
109:    /* Modify particle system */
110:   m_kParticleSystem.SetDontCreate (mrFalse);
111:   m_kParticleSystem.SetPosition (kPosition);
112: }
```

You start by setting the ball to `dead`, and the other members to 0. Then you to set the ball position so it doesn't disappear (lines 106 and 107).

After that, you just set the particle system state and positions (lines 110 and 111).

```
114:  /* Render the ball */
115: void btBall::Render (void)
116: {
117:  m_kBall.Render ();
118:  m_kParticleSystem.Render ();
119: }
```

Rendering a ball is as simple as calling the `Render` methods of each ABO.

Next you need to synchronize the ball:

```
121:  /* Synchronizes the entity and the ABO position */
122: void btBall::Synchronize (void)
123: {
124:  mrVector2D kPosition;
125:
126:   /* Set correct size for the ABO */
127:  m_kBall.SetSize (m_iRadius, m_iRadius);
128:
129:   /* Set correct position for the ABO */
130:  kPosition = m_kObject.GetPosition ();
131:  m_kBall.SetPosition ((mrUInt32)kPosition [0],
132:                       (mrUInt32)kPosition [1]);
133: }
```

This sets the ball's correct size (line 127) and sets the ball's position (lines 131 and 132).

```
134:
135:  /* Update the ball */
136: void btBall::Update (mrReal32 fStep)
137: {
138:   /* Simulate and synchornize */
139:  m_kObject.Simulate (fStep);
140:  Synchronize ();
141:
142:   /* Update timer and stop particle system if needed */
143:  m_fTimerCount += fStep;
144:
145:  if (m_fTimerCount >= 0.25f)
146:  {
```

```
147:    m_kParticleSystem.SetDontCreate (mrTrue);
148:   }
149:   m_kParticleSystem.Simulate (fStep);
150: }
```

What you did up to here is simulate and synchronize the ball (lines 139 and 140), and update the internal timer with the elapsed time (line 143). If the elapsed time is more than 0.25 (one-quarter of one second) (line 145), you will deactivate the particle system since you don't want any more particles to be created (line 147). In the last line you call `Simulate` to simulate the particles system.

```
152:  /* Sets the ball speed */
153: void btBall::SetSpeed (mrReal32 fSpeed)
154: {
155:  m_fSpeed = fSpeed;
156:   /* Get the direction of the ball and scale it by the speed */
157:  mrVector2D kVelocity;
158:  kVelocity = m_kObject.GetLinearVelocity ();
159:  kVelocity.Normalize ();
160:  kVelocity *= m_fSpeed;
161:  m_kObject.SetLinearVelocity (kVelocity);
162: }
163:
164:  /* Sets the ball size */
165: void btBall::SetSize (mrUInt32 iRadius)
166: {
167:  m_iRadius = iRadius;
168: }
```

The rest are accessor methods:

```
169:
170:  /* Returns the ball speed */
171: mrReal32 btBall::GetSpeed (void)
172: {
173:  return m_fSpeed;
174: }
175:
176:  /* Returns the ball size */
177: mrUInt32 btBall::GetSize (void)
178: {
179:  return m_iRadius;
```

```
}

 /* Returns the ball entity */
mrEntity * btBall::GetObject (void)
{
 return &m_kObject;
}

 /* Returns if the ball is alive */
mrBool32 btBall::GetIsAlive (void)
{
 return m_bIsAlive;
}
```

And that's it. You have made your ball class. You will see how to use this class next.

btGame

btGame is the main controller of your game. It will take care of initializing the sound and input, handle collisions, render the screen, and so on.

Take a look at the class definition:

```
 /* 'btGame.h' */

 /* Mirus window framework header */
#include "Mirus\Mirus.h"

 /* Breaking Through header files */
#include "btPaddle.h"
#include "btBall.h"
#include "btBlock.h"

 /* Include this file only once */
#pragma once

 /* Break Through game states */
enum btGameState
{
 btGameRunning              = 1,
 btGameLostBall             = 2,
```

```
  btGameLost               = 3,
  btGameSplash             = 4,
  btGameMenu               = 5,
  btGameLevelStarting      = 6,
  btGameLevelComplete      = 7,
  btGameComplete           = 8,
  btGameQuit               = 9,

  btGameStateForceDWord    = 0xFFFFFFFF
};
```

The btGameState enumeration describes the possible nine states the game can be in. Depending on the state of the game, you will call the appropriate methods to process and render the game.

Back to the class:

```
 /* Break Through game class */
class btGame
{
protected:
  /* Game information */
 btGameState          m_eGameState;
 mrUInt32             m_iBalls;
 mrUInt32             m_iScore;
 mrReal32             m_fTimer;

  /* Game objects */
 btBlock *            m_pkBlocks;
 mrABO *              m_pkBlocksABO;
 mrUInt32             m_iBlocks;
 btPaddle             m_kPaddle;
 btBall               m_kBall;

  /* Paddle controlled by keyboard */
 mrInputManager      m_kInputManager;
 mrKeyboard           m_kKeyboard;

  /* Levels information */
 mrInt8               m_aszLevels [10][256];
 mrUInt32             m_iLevels;
```

```
mrUInt32              m_iCurrentLevel;

  /* Score and ball ABOs */
mrABO                  m_kBallABO;
mrABO                  m_kScore;

  /* Sound members */
mrSoundPlayer        m_kSoundPlayer;
mrSound               m_kSoundDie;
mrSound               m_kSoundBlink;

  /* Background and particle information */
mrTexture             m_kLightningTexture;
mrSurface             m_kBackground;
mrSurface             m_kSplash;
mrSurface             m_kGameComplete;
mrSurface             m_kMainMenu;
mrEntity              m_kBorder;
mrABO                  m_kReadyGo;

public:
  /* Constructor / Destructor */
btGame (void);
~btGame (void);

void Start (HINSTANCE hInstance, HWND hWindow);
void LoadLevel (LPSTR lpszFilename);

  /* Render methods */
void Render (void);
void RenderFrame (void);
void RenderLostBall (void);
void RenderSplash (void);
void RenderMenu (void);
void RenderLevelStarting (void);
void RenderComplete (void);

  /* Render support methods */
void RenderBolt (mrUInt32 iRandomness);
void RenderBlocks ();
```

```
void RenderScoreBalls ();

 /* Handle collisions methods */
void HandleCollisions (void);
void HandleCollisionsBlocks (void);
void HandleCollisionsPaddle (void);
void HandleCollisionsBorder (void);

 /* Process methods */
mrBool32 Process (mrReal32 fStep);
void ProcessFrame (mrReal32 fStep);
void ProcessLostBall (mrReal32 fStep);
void ProcessLostGame (mrReal32 fStep);
void ProcessSplash (mrReal32 fStep);
void ProcessMenu (mrReal32 fStep);
void ProcessLevelStarting (mrReal32 fStep);
void ProcessLevelComplete (mrReal32 fStep);
void ProcessComplete (mrReal32 fStep);

 /* Game loading methods */
void LoadGame (void);
void SaveGame (void);
};
```

You probably are a little scared with the size of this class. . . . Well, even though you do many things in this class, the inner workings of each method shouldn't be anything new to you, as you will see as you develop them.

Let's start with the constructor and the destructor:

```
 /* 'btGame.cpp' */

 /* Complement header file */
#include "btGame.h"

 /* Default constructor */
btGame::btGame (void)
{
 m_eGameState  = btGameSplash;
 m_fTimer      = 0;
 m_pkBlocks    = NULL;
```

```
  m_pkBlocksABO = NULL;
}

 /* Default destructor */
btGame::~btGame (void)
{
 if (m_pkBlocks)
 {
  delete [] m_pkBlocks;
  m_pkBlocks    = NULL;
 }
 if (m_pkBlocksABO)
 {
  delete [] m_pkBlocksABO;
 m_pkBlocksABO = NULL;
 }
 m_eGameState  = btGameSplash;
 m_fTimer      = 0;
}
```

In the constructor you do nothing but set the the variables to 0 or NULL, whereas in the destructor you do the same, but this time releasing any memory used by the class.

The next method in the lineup is Start:

```
33:  /* Start the game */
34: void btGame::Start (HINSTANCE hInstance, HWND hWindow)
35: {
36:   /* Create the objects */
37:  m_kPaddle.Create ();
38:  m_kBall.Create ();
39:
40:   /* Setup the keyboard for the paddle */
41:  m_kInputManager.Init (hInstance);
42:  m_kKeyboard.Init (hWindow);
```

Start starts by calling the appropriate Create methods of m_kBall and m_kPaddle (lines 37 and 38).

You then need to initialize the input manager and the keyboard (lines 41 and 42) so you can use the keyboard in the game.

Next you will load other support images that aren't directly related to any of the previous objects:

```
44:   /* Load support images */
45:  mrRGBAImage kTempImage;
46:  kTempImage.LoadFromBitmap ("Graphics/splash.bmp");
47:  m_kReadyGo.LoadFromFile ("data/readygo.txt");
48:  m_kReadyGo.SetPosition (320,200);
49:  m_kReadyGo.SetSize (0,0);
50:  m_kReadyGo.SetColor (255,255,255,255);
51:  m_kScore.LoadFromFile ("data/numbers.txt");
52:  m_kSplash.Create (&kTempImage);
53:  kTempImage.LoadFromBitmap ("Graphics/complete.bmp");
54:  m_kGameComplete.Create (&kTempImage);
55:  kTempImage.LoadFromBitmap ("Graphics/menu.bmp");
56:  m_kMainMenu.Create (&kTempImage);
57:  m_kBallABO.LoadFromFile ("data/ball.txt");
58:  m_kBallABO.SetColor (255,255,255,255);
59:  m_kBallABO.SetSize (10, 10);
```

What you do here is load the splash screen bitmap (line 46) and the `Ready` and `Go` animations (lines 47 through 50). Then you load the numbers from the disk (line 51) and also load the game complete image (line 53), and then load the main menu image (line 55). In the end, you load the ball ABO from file and set the ball size and color (lines 57 through 59).

Next you need to `init` the sound stuff:

```
61:   /* Init sound */
62:  m_kSoundPlayer.Init (hWindow);
63:  m_kSoundDie.LoadFromFile ("sounds/die.wav");
64:  m_kSoundBlink.LoadFromFile ("sounds/blink.wav");
```

This is done by first calling `Init` from `m_kSoundPlayer` (line 62) and then loading each wave file from the drive (lines 63 and 64).

To finish this method, you will load the levels information. The levels information is in the following format:

```
NumberOfLevels
LevelFileName [0]
LevelFileName [1]
...
LevelFileName [NumberOfLevels-1]
```

Where each level file name is just the file name of the level file, which you will store and use later.

The code to load the levels is shown here:

```
66:   /* Load levels */
67:  fstream kLevels;
68:  kLevels.open ("data/levels.txt", ios::in);
69:
70:  if (kLevels.is_open ())
71:  {
72:    /* Load number of levels */
73:   kLevels >> m_iLevels;
74:   mrUInt32 iLevel;
75:
76:    /* Load each level name */
77:   for (iLevel=0;iLevel<m_iLevels;iLevel++)
78:   {
79:    kLevels >> m_aszLevels [iLevel] ;
80:   }
81:   m_iCurrentLevel=0;
82:  }
83:  kLevels.close ();
84: };
```

You start by opening a file for input in text mode (line 68), and read the number of levels (line 73). Then for each level in the file you will loop through it and read it (lines 77 through 81). You finish this method by setting the current level to 0 (line 81), and closing the file (line 83).

And you have another problem! You want to load a level file but you still don't have a level format. To maintain the same text format as you did earlier, each level can be described as:

```
BackgroundFilename BackgroungImageType
NumberOfDifferentABOs
ABOFilename [0]
ABOFilename [1]
...
ABOFilename [NumberOfDifferentABOs - 1]
NumberOfBlocks
Block [0]
Block [1]
```

```
...
Block [NumberOfBlocks - 1]
```

And each block can be described as:

```
ABOID Red Green Blue Alpha Xposition Yposition Width Height
```

Where the first parameter is the ID of the ABO this block uses. This number must be between 0 and `NumberOfDifferentABOs`. Next are the color components, the position, and the block size.

It isn't hard, is it? Of course not, so let's see how to load this file in code with `LoadLevel`:

```
 /* Load a level from a file */
void btGame::LoadLevel (LPSTR lpszFilename)
{
 fstream       kLevel;

 kLevel.open (lpszFilename, ios::in);

 if (kLevel.is_open ())
 {
  m_kBorder.SetMass (10000000000);

   /* Get background name and type */
  mrInt8 aBackgroundName [256];
  kLevel >> aBackgroundName;

  mrUInt32 iBackgroundType;
  kLevel >> iBackgroundType;

   /* Load the texture image */
  mrRGBAImage kTempImage;

  if (1 == iBackgroundType)
  {
   kTempImage.LoadFromBitmap (aBackgroundName);
  }
  if (2 == iBackgroundType)
  {
   kTempImage.LoadFromTarga (aBackgroundName);
  }
```

```
115:
116:     /* Create the surface */
117:    m_kBackground.Create (&kTempImage);
```

You start by opening the file for input (line 93), after this is done you set the border mass to a very high number (to prevent the border from moving if the ball hits it). Next you read the background filename and type (lines 99 and 102). Depending on the type of the background, you call the appropriate method to load the image (lines 107 through 114), and after the image is loaded, you just need to create the background surface with `Create` (line 117).

Next you will start to read the block's ABO information:

```
119:     /* Read number of block ABOs */
120:    mrUInt32 iBlockABOS;
121:    kLevel >> iBlockABOS;
122:
123:    m_pkBlocksABO = new mrABO [iBlockABOS];
124:
125:     /* For each block, read the block ABO name and load it */
126:    mrUInt32 iABO;
127:    for (iABO = 0; iABO < iBlockABOS; iABO++)
128:    {
129:     mrInt8 aAboName [256];
130:     kLevel >> aAboName;
131:     m_pkBlocksABO [iABO].LoadFromFile (aAboName);
132:    }
```

Here you start by reading the number of ABOs there are for this level (line 121) and then allocate a big enough array to hold them (line 123). Then you read each of the ABOs' filenames (line 130) and load it (line 131).

Next you will read the actual block data:

```
134:    /* Read number of blocks */
135:    kLevel >> m_iBlocks;
136:
137:    m_pkBlocks = new btBlock [m_iBlocks];
138:
139:    mrUInt32 iBlock;
140:
141:     /* For each block, read the block properties */
142:    for (iBlock = 0; iBlock < m_iBlocks; iBlock++)
```

```
    {
      /* Read ABO ID */
     mrUInt32 iABO;
     kLevel >> iABO;

      /* Read block color */
     mrUInt32 iRed;
     kLevel >> iRed;
     mrUInt32 iGreen;
     kLevel >> iGreen;
     mrUInt32 iBlue;
     kLevel >> iBlue;
     mrUInt32 iAlpha;
     kLevel >> iAlpha;

      /* Read block position */
     mrReal32 fXPosition;
     kLevel >> fXPosition;
     mrReal32 fYPosition;
     kLevel >> fYPosition;

      /* Read block size */
     mrUInt32 iWidth;
     kLevel >> iWidth;
     mrUInt32 iHeight;
     kLevel >> iHeight;

      /* Create the block */
      /* Set block position */
     mrVector2D kPosition;
     kPosition [0] = fXPosition;
     kPosition [1] = fYPosition;
     m_pkBlocks [iBlock].SetSize (iWidth, iHeight);

     m_pkBlocks [iBlock].Create (iABO, kPosition, (mrUInt8)iRed,
      (mrUInt8)iGreen, (mrUInt8)iBlue,
      (mrUInt8)iAlpha);
    }
   kLevel.close ();
  }
}
```

You start by reading the number of blocks (line 135) and allocating the memory to store them (line 137). Next you will go through each of the blocks (line 142) and read all the information about each block (lines 144 through 175) and then create the ABO (lines 177 through 179).

You finish this method by closing the file (line 181).

The next call you will see is Render:

```
 /* Render the game */
void btGame::Render (void)
{
  /* Render appropriate state */
 switch (m_eGameState)
 {
 case btGameRunning:
  RenderFrame ();
  break;
 case btGameLostBall:
  RenderLostBall ();
  break;
 case btGameSplash:
  RenderSplash ();
  break;
 case btGameMenu:
  RenderMenu ();
  break;
 case btGameLevelStarting:
  RenderLevelStarting ();
  break;
 case btGameComplete:
  RenderComplete ();
  break;
 }
}
```

This method is nothing more than a placeholder so you call the appropriate method each frame, depending on the game state. You will see each of the render methods next:

```
 /* Render the frame */
void btGame::RenderFrame (void)
{
```

```
 m_kBackground.Render (NULL);
 RenderBlocks ();
 RenderBolt (10);
 RenderScoreBalls ();
 m_kPaddle.Render ();
 m_kBall.Render ();
}
```

This method will call the Render method of each of the objects to render, the same as the next one:

```
 /* Render a lost ball */
void btGame::RenderLostBall (void)
{
 m_kBackground.Render (NULL);
 RenderBlocks ();
 RenderBolt (10);
 RenderScoreBalls ();
 m_kPaddle.Render ();
 m_kBall.Render ();
 m_kReadyGo.Render ();
}
```

The next method will render the splash screen:

```
 /* Render the splash screen */
void btGame::RenderSplash (void)
{
 m_kSplash.Render (NULL);
}
```

The following method will render the menu:

```
 /* Render the menu */
void btGame::RenderMenu (void)
{
 m_kMainMenu.Render (NULL);
}
```

The next method shows the start of a level:

```
 /* Render the start of a level */
void btGame::RenderLevelStarting (void)
{
```

```
 m_kBackground.Render (NULL);
 RenderBlocks ();
 RenderBolt (10);
 RenderScoreBalls ();
 m_kPaddle.Render ();
 m_kBall.Render ();
 m_kReadyGo.Render ();
}
```

And the last Render method will show the winning image:

```
 /* Render game complete */
void btGame::RenderComplete (void)
{
 m_kGameComplete.Render (NULL);
}
```

After you have implemented each of the render methods, you will develop the necessary help methods to render the game, such as RenderBolt:

```
 /* Renders the bolt on the bottom of the screen */
void btGame::RenderBolt (mrUInt32 iRandomness)
{
 m_kLightningTexture.SetActiveTexture ();
 mrVector2D kBoltLines [100];

  /* Setup start and final positions */
 kBoltLines [0] [0] = 8;
 kBoltLines [0] [1] = 447;
 kBoltLines [100-1] [0] = 624;
 kBoltLines [100-1] [1] = 447;

 mrReal32 fDone;
  /* Percentage done */
 fDone = (kBoltLines [100-1] [0] - kBoltLines [0] [0]) * 1/100;

  /* Get a bigger displacement for the first end bolt */
 kBoltLines [1] [0] = kBoltLines [0] [0] + fDone;
 kBoltLines [1] [1] = kBoltLines [0] [1] + iRandomness/2 -
  (rand () % (iRandomness));

  /* Draw first bolt */
```

```
287:  mrScreen::GetSingleton ()->DrawLine (kBoltLines [0][0],
288:                                        kBoltLines [0][1],
289:                                        kBoltLines [1][0],
290:                                        kBoltLines [1][1],
291:                                        60, 180, 255, 150);
```

Up to here, what you do is set the first and last bolt positions to the ones you want (lines 272 and 275). Then you need to calculate the percentage done (line 279), and calculate the position of the second bolt (line 282). Getting the second bolt was included here rather than in the loop because you want the first bolt to have a bigger displacement.

Getting the new horizontal position is easy since you just need to add `fDone`, which is the number of bolts you have already drawn. Getting the new vertical position is what you want to do.

If you think about it, to get a new vertical position you need to select a random value between –1 and 1 and multiply it by some randomness factor and add it to the last bolt's vertical position to produce some random displacement on the new bolt. And that's it. Looked a lot more complicated, didn't it? Well, for this first bolt you didn't do this since you want to limit the vertical position, but you will use this idea in a little while.

In the end you draw the line with `mrScreen::DrawLine` (lines 287 through 291).

Now you need to create and render each of the bolts:

```
293:  mrUInt32 iCurrentBolt;
294:  iCurrentBolt = 2;
295:
296:  while (iCurrentBolt < 100-1)
297:  {
298:    /* Percentage done */
299:   fDone = (kBoltLines [100-1]-kBoltLines [0])[0] * iCurrentBolt / 100;
300:
301:    /* Get a random displacement, and increase the x position by the
302:       percentage done */
303:   kBoltLines [iCurrentBolt] [0] = kBoltLines [0][0] + fDone;
304:   kBoltLines [iCurrentBolt] [1] = kBoltLines [iCurrentBolt - 1] [1]
305:          + (1 - (2 * ((mrReal32)rand () / (mrReal32)RAND_MAX))) *
306:          0.1f * iRandomness;
307:
308:    /* If too big, clamp it */
309:   if (fabs (kBoltLines [iCurrentBolt] [1] - kBoltLines [0] [1]) >
```

```
310:        iRandomness /2)
311:    {
312:     kBoltLines [iCurrentBolt] [1] += -(kBoltLines [iCurrentBolt] [1]
313:      - kBoltLines [0] [1]) / 2;
314:    }
315:
316:    /* Draw bolt */
317:    mrScreen::GetSingleton ()->DrawLine (kBoltLines [iCurrentBolt-1][0],
318:                                         kBoltLines [iCurrentBolt-1][1],
319:                                         kBoltLines [iCurrentBolt][0],
320:                                         kBoltLines [iCurrentBolt][1],
321:                                         60, 180, 255, 150);
322:    iCurrentBolt ++;
323:   }
324:
325:   /* Draw last bolt */
326:   mrScreen::GetSingleton ()->DrawLine (kBoltLines [iCurrentBolt-1][0],
327:                                        kBoltLines [iCurrentBolt-1][1],
328:                                        kBoltLines [100-1][0],
329:                                        kBoltLines [100-1][1],
330:                                        60, 180, 255, 150);
331: }
```

You will loop through every bolt (line 296) to create the bolt from one point of the screen to another. For each bolt, you start by calculating the new bolt position using the idea presented earlier (lines 303 through 306). After this, you see if the vertical displacement is too big, and if so, reduce it (lines 309 through 314) this will assure that the bolt is leveled. Next you just need to draw the bolt (lines 317 through 321).

Now, you need to render the last bolt and you are done with this (lines 326 through 330).

The next method will render all the blocks:

```
333:   /* Render the blocks */
334: void btGame::RenderBlocks ()
335: {
336:    /* Render each block */
337:   mrEntity *  pkBlock;
338:   mrUInt32    iWidth;
339:   mrUInt32    iHeight;
340:   mrVector2D  kPosition;
341:   mrUInt32    iBlock;
```

```
342:
343:   for (iBlock=0; iBlock < m_iBlocks; iBlock++)
344:   {
345:     /* Get block properties */
346:    iWidth    = m_pkBlocks [iBlock].GetWidth ();
347:    iHeight   = m_pkBlocks [iBlock].GetHeight ();
348:    pkBlock   = m_pkBlocks [iBlock].GetObject ();
349:    kPosition = pkBlock->GetPosition ();
350:
351:     /* Setup the ABO */
352:    m_pkBlocksABO [m_pkBlocks [iBlock].GetABO()].SetColor (
353:     m_pkBlocks [iBlock].GetAlpha (), m_pkBlocks [iBlock].GetRed (),
354:     m_pkBlocks [iBlock].GetGreen (), m_pkBlocks [iBlock].GetBlue ());
355:    m_pkBlocksABO [m_pkBlocks [iBlock].GetABO ()].SetSize (iWidth, iHeight);
356:    m_pkBlocksABO [m_pkBlocks [iBlock].GetABO ()].SetPosition (
357:     (mrUInt32)kPosition[0], (mrUInt32)kPosition[1]);
358:
359:     /* Render the ABO */
360:    m_pkBlocksABO [m_pkBlocks [iBlock].GetABO ()].Render ();
361:   }
362: }
```

What you do here is circle through each block (line 343), and render it. You have seen before that if a block is destroyed, its size is set to 0, 0, so you don't need to worry about destroyed blocks appearing.

There is a lot of code to just render the blocks since you need to get the position and size of each block.

The last render method will be used to render the score and the balls/lives left:

```
364:  /* Render the score and balls */
365: void btGame::RenderScoreBalls (void)
366: {
367:  mrInt8 szScore [15];
368:  mrUInt32 iStart;
369:
370:   /* Convert integer to string */
371:  itoa (m_iScore, szScore, 10);
372:
373:   /* Render each digit */
374:  mrUInt32 iDigit;
375:  m_kScore.SetSize (8,12);
```

```
376:  for (iDigit=0; iDigit < strlen (szScore); iDigit++)
377:  {
378:   iStart = 624 - strlen (szScore) * 8;
379:   m_kScore.SetColor (255,255,225,225);
380:   m_kScore.SetCurrentAnimation (szScore [iDigit] - 48);
381:   m_kScore.SetPosition (iStart + iDigit * 8, 8);
382:   m_kScore.Render ();
383:  }
```

What you do here is to first convert the integer score to a string (line 371) with `itoa`. Now you have a string that holds your score, since you know that the character numbers from zero to nine are stored as numbers in ASCII, and they are stored as 48 to 57, you can use the ASCII code minus 48 to get the correct number character. With this done, you just need to set the current animation to that character (line 380) and the position of the character, depending on which digit is being rendered (line 382).

And you have your score rendered, now you need to render the number of lives:

```
385:   /* Render each ball */
386:  mrUInt32 iBall;
387:  for (iBall=0; iBall < m_iBalls; iBall++)
388:  {
389:   iStart = 15;
390:   m_kBallABO.SetColor (255,255,225,225);
391:   m_kBallABO.SetPosition (iStart + iBall * 12, 8);
392:   m_kBallABO.Render ();
393:  }
394: }
```

Rendering each ball to represent each life isn't hard, what you will do is perform a loop for the number of lives the player has (line 387), and each time the loop is increased, the position is also (line 391) and the ball is rendered (line 392).

And that's it! You are done with the render methods. Now it's time to handle some collisions:

```
396:  /* Handle all collisions */
397: void btGame::HandleCollisions (void)
398: {
399:  HandleCollisionsBorder ();
400:  HandleCollisionsBlocks ();
401:  HandleCollisionsPaddle ();
402: }
```

This method is also a container for all the `HandleCollisions` methods, which you will see next:

```
 /* Handle collision of ball and blocks */
void btGame::HandleCollisionsBlocks (void)
{
 mrEntity * pkBlockEntity;
 mrEntity * pkBallEntity;

 mrUInt32   iBlockWidth;
 mrUInt32   iBlockHeight;
 mrUInt32   iBallRadius;

 mrVector2D kBlockPosition;
 mrVector2D kBallPosition;

  /* Get ball information */
 iBallRadius   = m_kBall.GetSize ();
 pkBallEntity  = m_kBall.GetObject ();
 kBallPosition = pkBallEntity->GetPosition ();
```

What you did up to here is just declare the needed variables and get the ball size, entity, and position.

Next you will check if the ball has collided with the block:

```
 mrUInt32 iBlock;
 for (iBlock=0; iBlock < m_iBlocks; iBlock++)
 {
   /* If block is active */
  if (m_pkBlocks [iBlock].GetIsAlive () == mrTrue)
  {
    /* Get block properties */
   iBlockWidth    = m_pkBlocks [iBlock].GetWidth ();
   iBlockHeight   = m_pkBlocks [iBlock].GetHeight ();
   pkBlockEntity  = m_pkBlocks [iBlock].GetObject ();
   kBlockPosition = pkBlockEntity->GetPosition ();

    /* Test to see if the ball touched the block and if so,
       destroy the block, add points and play sound */
   if ((kBallPosition [0] >= kBlockPosition [0] - iBlockWidth/2) &&
       (kBallPosition [0] <= kBlockPosition [0] + iBlockWidth/2) &&
       (kBallPosition [1] >= kBlockPosition [1] - iBlockHeight/2) &&
```

```
439:         (kBallPosition [1] <= kBlockPosition [1] + iBlockHeight/2) )
440:     {
```

What you do is go through all the blocks that are alive (lines 422 through 426) and check if it collides with the ball (lines 436 through 439). If it doesn't, you will just move to the next block, if it does collide, you must handle it:

```
441:      m_pkBlocks [iBlock].Destroy ();
442:      m_iScore += 10;
443:      m_kSoundBlink.Play (mrFalse);
444:
445:       /* Get distance from ball to the all the block sides */
446:      mrReal32 iX1;
447:      mrReal32 iY1;
448:      mrReal32 iX2;
449:      mrReal32 iY2;
450:
451:      iX1 = kBlockPosition [0] + iBlockWidth/2 -
452:             (kBallPosition [0]-iBallRadius);
453:      iX2 = kBlockPosition [0] - iBlockWidth/2 -
454:              (kBallPosition [0]+iBallRadius);
455:      iY1 = kBlockPosition [1] + iBlockHeight/2 -
456:              (kBallPosition [1]-iBallRadius);
457:      iY2 = kBlockPosition [1] - iBlockHeight/2 -
458:              (kBallPosition [1]+iBallRadius);
459:       /* Depending on which side of the block the ball hit,
460:           handle the collision */
461:          with the appropriate collision plane normal */
462:      if ( (fabs(iX1) < fabs(iX2)) &&
463:           (fabs(iX1) < fabs(iY1)) &&
464:           (fabs(iX1) < fabs(iY2)) )
465:      {
466:       pkBallEntity->HandleCollision (*pkBlockEntity, mrVector2D (-1,0));
467:      }
468:      if ( (fabs(iX2) < fabs(iY1)) &&
469:           (fabs(iX2) < fabs(iY2)) )
470:      {
471:       pkBallEntity->HandleCollision (*pkBlockEntity, mrVector2D (1,0));
472:      }
473:      else if ( fabs(iY1) < fabs(iY2) )
474:      {
475:       pkBallEntity->HandleCollision (*pkBlockEntity, mrVector2D (0,-1));
```

```
476:       }
477:       else
478:       {
479:        pkBallEntity->HandleCollision (*pkBlockEntity, mrVector2D (0,1));
480:       }
481:      }
482:     }
483:   }
484: }
```

If a collision did occur, then you must destroy the block, increase the score, and play a sound (lines 441 through 443). Next you need to know in which side of the block the ball hit. This is very important so you can supply a valid collision normal to HandleCollision. What you will do is check the distances from the ball edges to each of the block sides (lines 451 through 458), and then when you determine which distance is smaller is where the collision occurred, and you need to give a collision normal pointing out of the block (lines 462 through 484).

Now you need to develop the HandleCollisionsPaddle that will check for the collisions of the paddle and the borders and of the paddle and the ball.

```
  /* Handle collisions of paddle with border and paddle with ball */
void btGame::HandleCollisionsPaddle (void)
{
 mrVector2D   kPaddlePosition;
 mrEntity *   kPaddleEntity;
 mrUInt32     iPaddleWidth;
 mrUInt32     iPaddleHeight;

 mrEntity *   pkBallEntity;
 mrVector2D   kBallPosition ;
 mrUInt32     iBallRadius;

  /* Get paddle and ball information */
 iBallRadius      = m_kBall.GetSize ();
 pkBallEntity     = m_kBall.GetObject ();
 kBallPosition    = pkBallEntity->GetPosition ();
 kPaddleEntity    = m_kPaddle.GetObject ();
 kPaddlePosition = kPaddleEntity->GetPosition ();
 iPaddleHeight    = m_kPaddle.GetHeight ();
 iPaddleWidth     = m_kPaddle.GetWidth ()-iPaddleHeight;
```

What you did up to this point is get the paddle positions and size. You will use these values to check for collisions:

```
502:   /* Handle collision of ball with paddle */
503:  if ((kBallPosition [0] + iBallRadius >
504:        kPaddlePosition [0] - iPaddleWidth / 2) &&
505:       (kBallPosition [0] - iBallRadius <
506:        kPaddlePosition [0] + iPaddleWidth / 2) &&
507:       (kBallPosition [1] + iBallRadius >
508:        kPaddlePosition [1] - iPaddleHeight / 2) &&
509:       (kBallPosition [1] + iBallRadius <
510:        kPaddlePosition [1] + iPaddleHeight / 2) )
511:  {
512:   pkBallEntity->SetPosition (mrVector2D(kBallPosition [0],
513:      (kPaddlePosition [1] - iPaddleHeight / 2) - iBallRadius));
514:   pkBallEntity->HandleCollision (*kPaddleEntity, mrVector2D (0, -1));
515:   m_kSoundBlink.Play (mrFalse);
516:  }
```

If the ball collided with the paddle (lines 503 through 510), then prevent the ball from getting stuck inside the paddle (lines 512 and 513), and handle the collision (line 514). You will also play a small blink sound (line 515).

Next, you need to handle the collisions of the paddle and borders:

```
518:   /* Handle collisions of paddle and borders */
519:  if (kPaddlePosition [0] - m_kPaddle.GetWidth() / 2 < 8)
520:  {
521:   kPaddleEntity->SetPosition (mrVector2D (
522:      (mrReal32)(8 + m_kPaddle.GetWidth()/2),kPaddlePosition [1]));
523:   kPaddleEntity->HandleCollision (m_kBorder, mrVector2D (1, 0));
524:  }
525:  if (kPaddlePosition [0] + m_kPaddle.GetWidth()/2 > 624)
526:  {
527:   kPaddleEntity->SetPosition (mrVector2D (
528:      (mrReal32)(624 - m_kPaddle.GetWidth()/2),kPaddlePosition [1]));
529:   kPaddleEntity->HandleCollision (m_kBorder, mrVector2D (-1, 0));
530:  }
531: }
```

What you do here is to check whether the paddle has hit any of the sides (lines 519 and 525) and if so, prevent from getting the paddle stuck inside the wall (lines 521 and 522 and lines 527 and 528), and handle the collisions (lines 523 and 529).

The last collision method you need to implement is for collisions between the ball and the borders:

```
533:  /* Handle collisions of ball and border */
534: void btGame::HandleCollisionsBorder (void)
535: {
536:  mrEntity *    pkBallEntity;
537:  mrVector2D    kBallPosition;
538:  mrUInt32      iBallRadius;
539:
540:   /* Get ball information */
541:  iBallRadius      = m_kBall.GetSize ();
542:  pkBallEntity     = m_kBall.GetObject ();
543:  kBallPosition    = pkBallEntity->GetPosition ();
544:
545:   /* Check if ball hit any of the borders */
546:  if (kBallPosition [0] + iBallRadius > 624)
547:  {
548:   pkBallEntity->SetPosition (mrVector2D ((mrReal32)(624 - iBallRadius),
549:                                          kBallPosition [1]));
550:   pkBallEntity->HandleCollision (m_kBorder, mrVector2D (1, 0));
551:   m_kSoundBlink.Play (mrFalse);
552:  }
553:  if (kBallPosition [0] - iBallRadius < 8)
554:  {
555:   pkBallEntity->SetPosition (mrVector2D ((mrReal32)(8 + iBallRadius),
556:                                          kBallPosition [1]));
557:   pkBallEntity->HandleCollision (m_kBorder, mrVector2D (1, 0));
558:   m_kSoundBlink.Play (mrFalse);
559:  }
560:  if (kBallPosition [1] - iBallRadius < 16)
561:  {
562:   pkBallEntity->SetPosition (mrVector2D (kBallPosition [0],
563:                                          (mrReal32)(16 + iBallRadius)));
564:   pkBallEntity->HandleCollision (m_kBorder, mrVector2D (0, 1));
565:   m_kSoundBlink.Play (mrFalse);
566:  }
567: }
```

What you do in this method is the same thing you did in the previous method. You check to see whether the ball hit any of the borders (lines 546, 553, and 560), and if it did, prevent from getting the ball stuck inside a border (lines 548 and 549, lines 555 and 556, and lines 562 and 563), handle the collisions (lines 550, 557, and 564), and play a blink sound (lines 551, 558, and 565).

The next method is `Process`, which is called each frame, and depending on the game state, will call the appropriate method:

```
569:  /* Process the game */
570: mrBool32 btGame::Process (mrReal32 fStep)
571: {
572:   /* Process appropriate state */
573:  switch (m_eGameState)
574:  {
575:  case btGameRunning:
576:   ProcessFrame (fStep);
577:   break;
578:  case btGameLostBall:
579:   ProcessLostBall (fStep);
580:   break;
581:  case btGameLost:
582:   ProcessLostGame (fStep);
583:   break;
584:  case btGameSplash:
585:   ProcessSplash (fStep);
586:   break;
587:  case btGameMenu:
588:   ProcessMenu (fStep);
589:   break;
590:  case btGameLevelStarting:
591:   ProcessLevelStarting (fStep);
592:   break;
593:  case btGameLevelComplete:
594:   ProcessLevelComplete (fStep);
595:   break;
596:  case btGameComplete:
597:   ProcessComplete (fStep);
598:   break;
599:  case btGameQuit:
600:   return mrFalse;
601:   break;
602:  }
603:  return mrTrue;
604: }
```

The following method, `ProcessFrame`, is where most of the game logic is implemented, or called, so pay attention to it:

```
606:  /* Process the current frame */
607: void btGame::ProcessFrame (mrReal32 fStep)
608: {
609:
610:  /* Check if the ball hit the bottom of the screen */
611:  if ((m_kBall.GetObject ()->GetPosition () [1] >= 443) &&
612:       (m_kBall.GetIsAlive ()))
613:  {
614:   m_kBall.Destroy ();
615:   m_eGameState = btGameLostBall;
616:   m_fTimer = 0;
617:   m_kSoundDie.Play (mrFalse);
618:  }
```

If the ball hit the bottom of the screen (lines 611 and 612), then destroy the ball (line 614) and play a die sound (line 617).

After that you will check to see whether all the blocks were destroyed:

```
620:   /* Check the number of blocks that are alive */
621:  mrUInt32 iBlock;
622:  mrUInt32 iBlocksAlive;
623:  iBlocksAlive = 0;
624:  for (iBlock=0; iBlock < m_iBlocks; iBlock++)
625:  {
626:   if (m_pkBlocks [iBlock].GetIsAlive () == mrTrue)
627:   {
628:    iBlocksAlive ++;
629:   }
630:  }
631:   /* If no blocks are alive, level is complete */
632:  if (iBlocksAlive == 0)
633:  {
634:   m_eGameState = btGameLevelComplete;
635:  }
```

What you do is go through every block of the game, and for each block that is alive (line 626), it will increase a counter (line 628). If the counter is zero, then the level was complete (lines 632 through 635).

Next you need to handle keyboard input:

```
637:  mrEntity * pkPaddleEntity;
638:
639:  pkPaddleEntity = m_kPaddle.GetObject ();
640:   /* Update the keyboard and see if there are any keys pressed,
641:      if so, apply the corresponding force to the paddle */
642:  m_kKeyboard.Update ();
643:  if (m_kKeyboard.IsButtonDown (DIK_RIGHT))
644:  {
645:   pkPaddleEntity->ApplyLinearForce (mrVector2D (4500000, 0));
646:  }
647:  if (m_kKeyboard.IsButtonDown (DIK_LEFT))
648:  {
649:   pkPaddleEntity->ApplyLinearForce (mrVector2D (-4500000, 0));
650:  }
651:   /* Save game */
652:  if (m_kKeyboard.IsButtonDown (DIK_S))
653:  {
654:   SaveGame ();
655:  }
```

You first update the keyboard state (line 642) to get up-to-date information. Next you check to see whether the player pressed the right cursor (line 643) or the left cursor (line 647). If any of these keys was pressed, then a force is applied to that direction (lines 645 and 649).

If the player pressed the `S` key (line 652), then you just save the game (line 654).

```
656:   /* Update all the game members */
657:  HandleCollisions ();
658:  m_kPaddle.Update (fStep);
659:  m_kBall.Update (fStep);
660: }
```

To finish, you call `HandleCollisions` (line 657) and update both the paddle and the ball (lines 658 and 659).

The next method will be called when the user loses a ball:

```
662:  /* Process lost ball */
663: void btGame::ProcessLostBall (mrReal32 fStep)
664: {
```

```
665:  m_fTimer += fStep;
666:  m_kBall.Update (fStep);
667:   /* If no more balls, game over */
668:  if (m_iBalls == 0)
669:  {
670:     /* Wait a little for ball explosion */
671:    if (m_fTimer > 1)
672:    {
673:     m_eGameState = btGameLost;
674:    }
675:  }
```

Up to this point you check to see whether the number of balls available is equal to zero (line 668), if so wait one second and set the game state to btGameLost (lines 671 through 674).

Now, if you have any balls left, you need to restart playing, but you must take care of some things first:

```
676:    /* Restart playing */
677:  else
678:  {
679:     /* If only one second has passed, show ready */
680:    if ( (m_fTimer > 1) && (m_fTimer <= 2) )
681:    {
682:     m_kReadyGo.SetSize (254, 126);
683:     m_kReadyGo.SetCurrentAnimation (0);
684:    }
```

If one second has passed since the player lost the ball, the Ready word will appear on the screen, which is the first animation of m_kReadyGo.

```
685:     /* If only two seconds has passed, show go */
686:    if ( (m_fTimer > 2) && (m_fTimer <= 3) )
687:    {
688:     m_kReadyGo.SetSize (254, 126);
689:     m_kReadyGo.SetCurrentAnimation (1);
690:    }
```

If two seconds have passed since the player lost the ball, the Go word will appear on the screen, which is the second animation of m_kReadyGo.

```
691:     /* If three seconds has passed, restart game */
692:    if (m_fTimer > 3)
```

```
    {
     m_kReadyGo.SetSize (0, 0);
     m_kBall.Create ();
     m_kPaddle.Create ();
     m_eGameState = btGameRunning;
     m_fTimer      = 0;
     m_iBalls--;
    }
  }
}
```

Finally, if three seconds have passed, you need to restart playing. You do this by reducing the number of available balls and set up the ball and paddle to their initial positions and hide the `Ready` and `Go` words.

```
 /* Process lost game */
void btGame::ProcessLostGame (mrReal32 fStep)
{
 m_eGameState = btGameMenu;
 m_fTimer      = 0;
}
```

If the player has lost the game, he will only be sent to the main menu without much hassle.

```
 /* Process splash screen */
void btGame::ProcessSplash (mrReal32 fStep)
{
  /* Wait three seconds then switch to the main menu */
 m_fTimer += fStep;
 if (m_fTimer <= 3)
 {
 }
 else
 {
  m_eGameState = btGameMenu;
  m_fTimer      = 0;
 }
}
```

The `ProcessSplashScreen` waits three seconds and then moves the game to main menu.

Next is the ProcessMenu method:

```
 /* Process menu */
void btGame::ProcessMenu (mrReal32 fStep)
{
 m_kKeyboard.Update ();
  /* If 'N' key was pressed, start a new game */
 if (m_kKeyboard.IsButtonDown (DIK_N))
 {
  m_iCurrentLevel=0;
  LoadLevel (m_aszLevels[m_iCurrentLevel]);
  m_eGameState = btGameLevelStarting;
  m_fTimer     = 0;
  m_iBalls     = 2;
  m_iScore     = 0;
  m_kBall.Create ();
  m_kPaddle.Create ();
 }
```

If the player pressed the N key, a new game will start. If you want to change the number of lives the player starts with, you can do it here.

```
  /* If 'L' key was pressed, load a game */
 if (m_kKeyboard.IsButtonDown (DIK_L))
 {
  LoadGame ();
  LoadLevel (m_aszLevels[m_iCurrentLevel]);
  m_eGameState = btGameLevelStarting;
  m_fTimer     = 0;
  m_kBall.Create ();
  m_kPaddle.Create ();
 }
```

If the letter L was pressed, the game will resume from the last saved position.

```
  /* If 'Q' key was pressed, quit the game */
 if (m_kKeyboard.IsButtonDown (DIK_Q))
 {
  m_eGameState = btGameQuit;
 }
}
```

If the letter Q was pressed, the game will quit.

The next method is ProcessLevelStarting:

```
/* Process level starting */
void btGame::ProcessLevelStarting (mrReal32 fStep)
{
 m_fTimer += fStep;

  /* If only one second has passed, show ready */
 if ( (m_fTimer > 1) && (m_fTimer <= 2) )
 {
  m_kReadyGo.SetSize (254, 126);
  m_kReadyGo.SetCurrentAnimation (0);
 }
```

If only one second has passed, show the Ready word.

```
  /* If only two seconds has passed, show go */
 if ( (m_fTimer > 2) && (m_fTimer <= 3) )
 {
  m_kReadyGo.SetSize (254, 126);
  m_kReadyGo.SetCurrentAnimation (1);
 }
```

If two seconds have passed, show the Go word.

```
  /* If three seconds has passed, restart game */
 if (m_fTimer > 3)
 {
  m_kReadyGo.SetSize (0, 0);
  m_eGameState = btGameRunning;
  m_fTimer     = 0;
 }
}
```

If three second have passed, the game will start. The next method will be called when the user has finished a level.

```
/* Process level complete */
void btGame::ProcessLevelComplete (mrReal32 fStep)
{
 m_iCurrentLevel ++;
  /* Level complete */
 if (m_iCurrentLevel >= m_iLevels)
 {
```

```
792:    m_eGameState = btGameComplete;
793:   }
794:    /* Load new level */
795:   else
796:   {
797:    LoadLevel (m_aszLevels [m_iCurrentLevel]);
798:    m_kBall.Create ();
799:    m_kPaddle.Create ();
800:    m_eGameState = btGameLevelStarting;
801:    m_fTimer = 0;
802:   }
803: }
```

This code increases the current level (line 788) and checks whether the player finished the game (lines 790 through 793), and if so, changes the game state to `btGameComplete`. If not, then you load a new level and restart playing (lines 796 through 802).

The next method will be executed when the player has finished the game:

```
805:  /* Process game complete */
806: void btGame::ProcessComplete (mrReal32 fStep)
807: {
808:   /* Wait five seconds then switch to the main menu */
809:  m_fTimer += fStep;
810:  if (m_fTimer <= 5)
811:  {
812:  }
813:  else
814:  {
815:   m_eGameState = btGameMenu;
816:   m_fTimer = 0;
817:  }
818: }
```

This method will wait five seconds and then will return to the game menu.

```
820:  /* Load a game from file */
821: void btGame::LoadGame (void)
822: {
823:  fstream kGame;
```

```
824:  kGame.open ("game.sav", ios::in);
825:
826:  if (kGame.is_open ())
827:  {
828:    /* Read game data */
829:   kGame >> m_iBalls;
830:   kGame >> m_iScore;
831:   kGame >> m_iCurrentLevel;
832:  }
833:  kGame.close ();
834: }
```

Loading a game is simple, you just open the file for input (line 824) and read the needed data from the file (lines 829 through 831). Since you are using text mode for everything you do, you have also used text mode to save your games, which is shown next:

```
836:  /* Save a game to a file */
837: void btGame::SaveGame (void)
838: {
839:  fstream kGame;
840:  kGame.open ("game.sav", ios::out);
841:
842:  if (kGame.is_open ())
843:  {
844:    /* Save game data */
845:   kGame << m_iBalls << " ";
846:   kGame << m_iScore << " ";
847:   kGame << m_iCurrentLevel << " ";
848:  }
849:  kGame.close ();
850: }
```

You start by opening a file for output (line 840) and then you write the data to the file (lines 845 through 847). You have included a whitespace after the value you save so you can load the game with the normal input functions.

And that's it for this class, and you are very close to finishing this game, just one class left.

BreakThroughWindow

This is your last class, and it doesn't even need much explanation since you have been using this class throughout the rest of the book.

Here is the class definition:

```
 /* 'BreakThrough.cpp' */

 /* Mirus header */
#include "Mirus\mirus.h"

 /* */
#include "btGame.h"

 /* BreakThrough class */
class BreakThroughWindow : public mrWindow
{
  /* Game related classes */
 btGame               m_kGame;

  /* Mirus related classes */
 mrScreen             m_kScreen;

public:


  /* Constructor / Destructor */
 BreakThroughWindow (void);
 ~BreakThroughWindow (void);

 void Init (HINSTANCE hInstance);

  /* Window manipulation functions */
 mrBool32 Frame (void);

};
```

The only difference between this class and others you have been using is that you have a btGame in it, and an extra method, Init:

```
void BreakThroughWindow::Init (HINSTANCE hInstance)
```

```
41: {
42:  m_kScreen.Init (m_hWindow);
43:  m_kScreen.SetMode (false, 640, 480, 16, true);
44:  m_kGame.Start (hInstance, m_hWindow);
45: }
```

This method will set up Direct3D for rendering (lines 42 and 43) and then start the game (line 44). If you want to change the resolution of the game, you can do it here.

The last method you will see is `Frame`:

```
47:  /* Render frame */
48: mrBool32 BreakThroughWindow::Frame(void)
49: {
50:   /* Start rendering */
51:  m_kScreen.Clear (0, 0, 0, 0);
52:  m_kScreen.StartFrame ();
53:
54:   /* Process and render game */
55:  if (m_kScreen.GetFPS () != 0)
56:  {
57:   if (mrFalse == m_kGame.Process (1 / (mrReal32)m_kScreen.GetFPS ()))
58:   {
59:    return mrFalse;
60:   }
61:   m_kGame.Render ();
62:  }
63:
64:   /* Render particle system and end frame */
65:  m_kScreen.EndFrame ();
66:
67:  return mrTrue;
68: }
```

In this method, you do the usual setup of Direct3D for rendering, and you also process (line 57) and render (line 61) the game.

Next is the main program:

```
70:  /* "WinMain Vs. main" */
71: int WINAPI WinMain (HINSTANCE hInstance, HINSTANCE hPrevInst,
72:                     LPSTR lpCmdLine, int nShowCmd)
```

```
73: {
74:    /* Our window */
75:   BreakThroughWindow  kWindow;
76:
77:    /* Create window */
78:   kWindow.Create (hInstance, "Break Through 1.0");
79:   kWindow.SetSize (640, 480);
80:
81:   kWindow.Init (hInstance);
82:   kWindow.Run ();
83:
84:   return 0;
85: }
```

The only difference between the previous code you have been using is a call to `Init` (line 81) to initialize your game.

And that's it, you have developed Breaking Through. You still need the graphics, data, and the sound files, but you can find these on the CD-ROM.

Conclusion

And you have developed your first game. It may not seem like much, but if you understood what the code does and why, you are on your way to game development Vahalla!

You might be wondering, "Who would buy a game like this?". Well, I've just visited the local computer store and they have a breakout clone much uglier and jerkier than this being sold for $10. So get your gear together and start developing!

CHAPTER 22

Publishing Your Game

You have finally made it. You have finished your game and you want to publish it. Read the following sections for some advice on how you can do it.

Is Your Game Worth Publishing?

The first step you must complete is to evaluate your game. Be truthful to yourself, and also ask friends, family, and the guy down the street to play your games and give you some feedback.

Put yourself in the position of the buyer—would you buy your own game if you saw it in the stores? And if so, how much would you pay for it? These are very important questions to ask yourself when thinking about approaching a publisher.

Let's go over a few steps you can follow to see whether your game is worth publishing. Please note these aren't strict rules.

Probably the most important thing to evaluate in your game is whether it is graphically attractive. Don't get me wrong; I play my old Spectrum games (the good old days) more often than the new 3D perspective mumbo-jumbo out there. But unfortunately, only a small group of people does so. Users want their $250 video cards to be stretched to the last polygon. They want to see an infinite number of lights, models, huge maps, and unfortunately, games of that size require much time from many people.

Don't despair, there is still room for the 2D games out there, but they must be very good to beat the new 3D ones. A nice user interface, friendly graphics, and some tricks can do the job, but understand this is difficult to do. So, your game is fascinating? Has nice graphics and animations and even plays smoothly? Great, move on to the next topic.

Not so important but still a picker is the sound. Does the sound match the actions? Is it immersive? One good way to test this would be to play the game and have a friend sit with his back to the computer and try to describe what the sounds depict to him. If he says that it sounds like a machine gun when you have exploded a mine, it isn't a good sign. You should also pay extra attention to the music. Music should immerse the player into the game not make him deaf. Make sure the music is nice to the ears but still contains the mood of the game. An example of a bad soundtrack would be if you were doing a horror game and your soundtrack was the Bee Gees and the Spice Girls. The music shouldn't force the user to turn it off but rather make him feel he is in the game itself.

One thing to be critical about when evaluating your game is: does it have a beginning, a middle, and an end? Does the player progress through various parts of the game feeling he achieved something? Nowadays you can't just throw a game to the player and expect him to play if you don't reward him for accomplishing something or if you don't explain why he should do things. Don't overlook this part of the game because it's ten times more important than to have cool alpha blend effects. The time of games that consisted of putting a player in a dungeon with a pistol and just letting him play are long gone, my friend.

Another aspect of the game you should be concerned with is, whether it pulls the player back to play. Is it attractive? Will it make the player be late to his job because he just had the desire to kill the boss in level seven? If he does, then you have probably done your job, and well.

The last topic you can analyze to see whether your game is worth publishing is to determine whether it fits into any hardcore genre; for example, if your game isn't very pretty or doesn't have nice sound but it has a million and one options to run an army, it will probably be interesting to a small hardcore group that is interested in that. The people in these groups tend to buy the game that fits their genre even if it isn't very good graphically or musically, but it's excellent in what they look for. There are many games groups like these. Some examples are war games, strategy games, puzzle games, and more.

Whose Door to Knock On

This depends much on the type of game and the game's quality. You can't expect CodeMasters to pick your Pac-Man clone. Nor should you expect a company that is strictly into the strategy genres to pick your shooter. Knowing what type of game genres publishers are more interested in could help you deeply.

If you have no previous game published, it may be hard to find a publisher even if you have a very good game. You should start at the bottom and build up. Do some small games and sell them online or through budget publishers. Then start to do a bit more complex games and try to have some small publisher take it. As you build a name for yourself or for your company, make a lot of contacts along the way, and you will see that it will be easier to get to publishers and work out some deals.

Another suggestion is to attend conferences like E3, the Game Developers Conference, Xtreme Game Developers Conference, ECTS, and others, and try to get the latest scope about what publishers are looking for and even make some contacts and exchange business cards with some of them.

Learn to Knock Correctly

One of the worst errors new developers make is to get too excited about their games and bombard just about every publisher 20 times about their game. Learning to go through the correct channels to submit a game can help you much.

First, check the publisher's Web site and try to find information on how to submit games to them. If you can't find any information, such as a phone number or e-mail address, then e-mail the Webmaster and politely ask for who to contact to talk about publishing opportunities. This usually works. If you know a publisher's phone number, you can call to get this information and take a chance to do some scouting.

Now that you have your contact, it's time to let her know you have a game. Send an e-mail to them and say you have a game of a certain genre, give a two- to three-line description of the game, and explain that you would be interested in working some deal with them, and if it exists, a URL for the game's demo and/or screenshots. If the publisher is interested in your game, she will probably send a Non-disclosure Agreement (NDA) and give you the guidelines to submit the game.

Now, it's up to you to convince them that your game is worth publishing and they should be the ones publishing it.

Don't ever disrespect or attack the publisher even if they refuse your game. They may not want this game but may want the following, and if you do anything to make them angry, you can forget about trying to go to that publisher again with another game.

Contracts

The most important advice I can give you when you start dealing with a contract is . . . Get a lawyer. Get a good lawyer. If possible, try to find a lawyer who has experience negotiating publishing contracts, and the ideal one is, of course, one who has experience in the game industry.

Getting a lawyer to analyze the contract for you, checking any loopholes, seeing whether it is profitable for you is a must if you plan to publish your games. Don't count on common sense only when you are reading a contract. There are many paragraphs we (law impaired) think we understand, but we don't. Again, get a good lawyer.

Also, make sure you put all things in writing. Don't count on oral agreements. If they promise you something, make sure it is documented in writing.

> **NOTE**
>
> "A picture is worth a thousand words." Especially if the picture is the signature of the publisher.

Now that I gave you my advice, here's an overview of the types of papers you will need to sign.

Non-disclosure Agreement

The Non-disclosure Agreement, or NDA for short, is probably the first thing the publisher will ask you to sign even before any negotiation is made.

This legally bound paper works as a protection for both you and the publisher. Some people think the NDA is sort of a joke, beware, it isn't. A breach of any paragraph in the NDA can, and probably will, get you in trouble. NDAs are usually safe to sign without much hassle, but still check with a lawyer or someone with expertise in the field just to be safe.

The main objective of the NDA is to protect the confidentiality of all talks, papers, files, or other information shared between the publisher and the developer. Some NDAs also include some legal protection (mostly for the publisher) about future disputes that may arise from working together.

Some topics the typical NDA covers are:

- Confidentiality
- Protection of material submitted by either party
- All materials submitted by either party will not breach any existing law
- Damage liability
- Time of execution

The Actual Publishing Contract

The actual publishing contract is what you are looking for. The NDA doesn't give you any assurance on the part of the publisher of even taking your game for review, but the actual contract assures that the publisher (and you) has to execute all the paragraphs implied. There isn't much general information I can give you on this one since these contracts change from publisher, game type, and game budget.

My main advice is to run the contract through a lawyer, because he will be able to help you more than I will. Just be sure to analyze dates and numbers yourself because your lawyer doesn't know how much time you need and how much money you want.

Some of the typical topics a normal agreement covers are the following:

- Distribution rights
- Modifications to the original game
- Schedule for milestones
- Royalties
- Confidentiality
- Dates for publishing

Milestones

So, you finally got the contract signed, time to lay back and expect the money to pour into your pocket, right? Wrong! You are now at the publisher's mercy. You have to make all the changes in your game you have agreed to in the contract, you have to fix bugs that for some reason don't occur on your computer but happen on others, you have to include the publisher's messages, include the publisher's splash images including their logos, build demos, and just about everything stated in the contract. A painful task for sure.

Bug Report

So, you thought you were finished with debugging and bug fixing until the publisher sent you a list with 50+ bugs? Don't worry; it's natural!

When you get a bug report from the publisher, there are usually three types of bugs: critical, normal, and minimal (by order of importance). Some publishers require that you fix all the bugs, others just force you to fix the first two and neglect the last. My advice is to fix them all! If it becomes public that your game has bugs, it will be a disaster!

Release Day

You made it to release day! Congratulations, not many do. Time to start thinking of your next game. Start designing, program, do art so you can have your second game on the shelves as soon as possible!

No Publisher, Now What?

You couldn't get any publisher to take your game? Don't despair, because it isn't over yet. You can still sell the game yourself. Start a Web site, find a host that can handle credit card purchases or pay for a service, do a lot of advertising, and you may still have a chance to profit from your game.

Interviews

Nothing better than a little insider input from the ones in the business, is there? The following people: André LaMothe from Xtreme Games LLC and Niels Bauer from NIELS BAUER SOFTWARE DESIGN were kind enough to answer the following questions.

Niels Bauer: NIELS BAUER SOFTWARE DESIGN

Niels Bauer has been programming since he was 10 years old. He currently owns NIELS BAUER SOFTWARE DESIGN and is studying law at the University of Freiburg in Germany.

Q: You founded NIELS BAUER SOFTWARE DESIGN in 1999. Was it hard for a single person to develop the games alone?

NIELS: In two years, I finished three games. Unfortunately they weren't very successful. In spring of 2001, I wanted to leave the game business and do something else. Finally, I decided to make only one more game, Smugglers, and just for myself and nobody else. So I decided to use Delphi, because I wanted to concentrate 100% on the gameplay. I wanted a game that I would really like to play myself, even after weeks of development. When the game was finished, after about one month, I showed it to some friends and they immediately became addicted. Suddenly I became aware of the potential of the game and decided to release it. As you can see from this little story the most difficult part of working alone is keeping yourself motivated until you have the first hit. I am working with five other very talented people and have left this field. Smugglers 2 is the last game where I have written most of the code myself. In the future, I will concentrate more on the business and design part.

Q: I've noticed that Smugglers has been a cover mount on some computer magazines. How easy, or difficult, was it to achieve this?

NIELS: I would say it was very difficult and pure luck that I got the necessary contacts. I sent e-mails to many magazines, but from most I didn't even get a reply. The main problem for this could have been that Smugglers 1 didn't have cool graphics and you needed to play the game to become addicted. Those editors became addicted and so they made a very good offer that I couldn't turn down, but unfortunately, from the feedback I got this is very uncommon.

Q: What do you think made Smugglers so popular?

NIELS: Well, this is a difficult question. There are a lot of elite-like games out there. Unfortunately most are too complex to be understood [by] the casual player. Even [I], as an experienced player, have problems with most. Smugglers on the other hand, is very easy to learn and play. With the short interactive tutorial, you can really start off immediately. On the other hand, it could have been so successful because it provided the player with a lot of freedom while still keeping the complexity low. For example, he can be a trader, a smuggler, a pirate, or even fight for the military. Or, for example, you can fly capital ships and attack planets. These are a lot of options. What I especially liked myself was the opportunity to receive ranks and medals depending on [your] own success. The last time I saw something like this was in Wing Commander 1, and this was a while back.

Q: You have released Smuggler 2 recently. Any projects for the future?

NIELS: Yes, definitely. The team already began to work on an online version. This time we say goodbye to the menu system used in previous Smugglers titles and use a very nice top-down view of the universe. I am very excited about the possibility of such a game. By the time this book is released it might already be available.

Q: [From] a developer's perspective, what do you think of the game industry at this moment?

NIELS: I feel very sorry for it. Where [have] all the cool games like Pirates, Wing Commander 1, Civilization, Ultima 7, and Elite gone to? I can tell you. They all landed in the trashcan because they don't have high-tech graphics. Only those games with the best graphics get bought these days in huge masses, and unfortunately these are the games with the lowest fun and the most bugs. I can't imagine a single game—except Counterstrike and that was a mod—that I really liked to play for longer than a couple of hours. I don't believe I can change this with Smugglers, but maybe I can provide a safe haven for some people who feel like [I do]. Considering the attention I got for Smugglers it might not be a few.

Q: Any final advice to the starting game developer?

NIELS: Concentrate on the gameplay. I needed two years to understand that it's not C++ and DirectX that makes a game cool. There are thousands of those games out there. What makes a game really good is two important factors:

1. Extremely easy to learn (your mother needs to be able to play it right off).
2. You need to like it, to play it yourself all day long.

Someone said in a book, which I unfortunately don't remember [the name of] now, that you most likely need to make 10 crappy games before you will finally make a good game. This is definitely true.

*Niels Bauer Software Design (**http://www.nbsd.de**) located in Germany has concentrated on complex, but still easy to learn, games. Their latest product, Smugglers 2, which you can find at http://www.smugglers2.com is an elite-like game from a strategic point of view. It features a lot of new ideas, like crew management, boarding enemy ships, attacking planets, treasure hunting, smuggling, and a lot more.*

If you want to make a game in the Smugglers universe under the loose guidance of this company, give them a call. You can reach them by the Web sites above or using the e-mail address: contact@nbsd.de.

André LaMothe: Xtreme Games LLC

André LaMothe has been in the computing industry for more than 24 years. He has worked in just about every field of computing and even worked for NASA. He currently owns Xtreme Games LLC, a computer games publishing company.

Q: At this time, with gamers wanting 3D environments with cube mapping and realistic particle systems, what game type do you think a small developer would have more luck with?

André: That's really hard to say. Even if a small developer makes a game better than Quake Arena, it really doesn't matter since it's nearly impossible to get distribution these days, and publishers [screw] developers at percentage rates of 5-10% being common. So my advice is, "simply make what you want to play."

Q: Being Xtreme Games LLC, a publisher, what are the minimum requirements for publishing a game with you?

André: That the game be of professional quality, bug-free, and competitive with other value games on the market.

Q: With the new growth of Xtreme Games LCC, what kind of games would you be more interested in seeing?

André: Value sports games, 3D games leveraging the Genesis engine, etc., and quality Palm and PocketPC games.

Q: What steps are involved? And [what is] the process from the point that a developer gives you a complete game to retail distribution?"

André:

1. The game is tested until all bugs are removed.
2. The packaging of the product is created.
3. Buyers at chains make purchase orders for the product.
4. The product is manufactured and units are shipped to distribution points and warehouses.
5. The product is shelved.
6. The money for the product is paid (3–6 months it takes).
7. Royalties are dispersed.

Q: From a developer's perspective, what do you think of the current state of the industry at this time?

André: Very bad I'm sorry to say, corporate America has got into it really deep now, and completely taken the fun out of game development. Programmers work 100+ hours a week trying to meet impossible schedules dictated by marketing, distribution, and manufacturing that aren't even "real," and in the end 99% of all games don't even break even. On top of that, game programmers are not paid well, their average pay is less than programmers that are nowhere near as technically skilled, but work in more mainstream software endeavors like Internet, database, etc. The problem with the entire game development industry is that the people running it still to this day don't understand it. If the developers ran it, we would all be a lot happier. Just because we are nerds doesn't mean we aren't smarter than MBAs when it comes to business. They better not ever let us in charge, instead of a business that is replete with failure, huge losses, and dismal earnings to gross revenues. We would ACTUALLY make money!

Q: Do you have any final advice to the small developer that wants to try to get in this challenging industry?

ANDRÉ: Don't think about how to make "them" happy, just do what makes you happy, stay focused, and finish what you start, keep this up and sooner or later something good has to happen.

Xtreme Games LLC was founded 5 years ago and develops and publishes games for the PC, Palm, and PocketPC platforms. Xtreme Games is always looking for good products to license. If you're interested, contact us at:

Xtreme Games LLC
fax: 208.485.9762
http://www.xgames3d.com
info@xgames3d.com

Summary

You have been through a crash course in software publishing and this was just the tip of the iceberg. There are many options, many contracts, many publishers you need to check, and that's just the beginning.

As you start to get more experienced, you will start to easily check what are the good and bad contracts, which publishers are good, and which aren't.

So what are you waiting for? Finish the game and start looking!

References

Below are some URLs of publishing companies. Please note that neither I nor Premier Press recommend any over another.

CodeMasters: **http://www.codemasters.com/**

Crystal Interactive, Inc.: **http://www.crystal-interactive.com/**

eGames: **http://www.egames.com/**

GarageDeveloper International: **http://www.garagedeveloper.com/garagedevframeset.html**

HeadGames Publishing: **http://www.headgames.net/**

MonkeyByte Games: **http://www.mbyte.com**

On Deck Interactive: **http://www.odigames.com/**

RealGames: **http://realguide.real.com/games/**

Xtreme Games LLC: **http://www.xgames3d.com/**

E3: **http://www.e3expo.com**

Game Developers Conference: **http://www.gdconf.com**

Game Developers Conference Europe: **http://www.gdc-europe.com**

Xtreme Games Conference: **http://www.xgdc.com**

ECTS: **http://www.ects.com**

Conclusion

Is this the end? Well, it is for me, but not for you.

It is now time for you to sit in your dark room with a few liters of coffee and some Chinese food, and come out a few months from now with a final game. Well, okay, you can discard all the above and sit in a well-lit room with nutritious food and program your game, but it isn't as fun.

More seriously, this book was just the tip of the iceberg. There are hundreds of other good books, and thousands of sites on the Internet, so you can build from this book to help you become a complete game programmer.

Appendix H, "More Resources," gives you a starting point to various books and sites that I recommend you visit.

And it is farewell. When you finish your games, I hope you will send me a copy!

Have fun!

PART FOUR

Appendixes

A What's on the CD-ROM

B Debugging Using Microsoft Visual C++

C Binary, Hexadecimal, and Decimal System

D A C Primer

E Answers to the Exercises

F C++ Keywords

G Useful Tables

H More Resources

APPENDIX A

What's on the CD-ROM

The *Game Programming All in One* companion CD-ROM contains a great deal of information to enrich and ease your game-programming endeavors.

When you first insert the CD-ROM, it launches automatically and presents you with the Premier Press license agreement. You must agree to the terms in order to use the CD-ROM content legally.

NOTE

The Premier Press Game Development CD-ROM interface uses dynamic HTML, which was designed to work with recent versions of Microsoft Internet Explorer. If Netscape Navigator (or another browser) is your default Web browser, you should perform the following steps:

1. Launch Internet Explorer.
2. Open the File menu.
3. Select Open.
4. Browse to the CD-ROM drive.
5. Double-click on the start_here.html file.

This will ensure that the interface will look and behave as intended.

Once past the agreement, the CD-ROM interface window pops up. It's a simple and intuitive system where you click on a category button to the left to display the contents in the right panel. When you click on an item in the right display panel, one of three things happens:

a. You are prompted to download the file to your local drive. From there you can extract it and access the contents.

b. You are presented with textual information.

c. An installation routine begins.

Most often, you will be prompted to download a file. With this approach, you have total control of which files you download and where they are stored on your drive. You need a basic understanding of how to handle files and folders as well as a standard extraction utility such as WinZip.

Source

All the source code for the programs listed on the book can be found under the Source button. Each chapter is organized in its own workspace, which contains all the projects for the chapter. Each chapter contains both the source code and a ready-to-run executable. Each collection of files in a chapter is compressed into a single zip file that contains the correct directory structure. Download the files to a location of your choice on your local drive and then extract the contents. Be sure to maintain the directory structure.

Microsoft DirectX 8.0 SDK

You have used the DirectX 8.0 SDK all throughout the book. It wouldn't make much sense if I told you to go and download 160 MBs, now would it?

The entire DirectX SDK can be found on the CD-ROM. Because of the large size of the DirectX 8 file, when you click on the link there may be a pause while it is processing the information. After this pause, you will be prompted to download the zip file to your hard drive. After that is done, extract the contents with the directory structure intact. Finally, launch the Install.exe file and the Microsoft SDK installation interface will start.

Programs

Making games isn't all programming. You also need to make graphics and sound, and there is no better way to get a professional look from your game than using the tools the professionals use.

Jasc Paint Shop Pro 7

With numerous features, an easy-to-use interface, and simplicity, this program has it all. If you even need to do anything in 2D, this is the program to use.

A 30-day trial version is available on the CD-ROM. This program begins the installation procedure directly from the CD-ROM interface.

Syntrillium Cool Edit 2000

Cool Edit 2000 is the next best thing next to a full studio you will have on your computer. This program can do anything you imagine, and most likely, many things you don't even imagine.

By providing an easy-to-use interface with a professional look, you can convert a skimpy voice to your main hero voice in a few steps.

A 30-day trial version is available on the CD-ROM. This program begins the installation procedure directly from the CD-ROM interface.

Caligari TrueSpace 5

TrueSpace 5 is a simple to use, powerful 3-D modeler. Probably one of the most used modelers available, this low-cost program has just about everything you will ever need to create models for your games.

A 14-day no-save trial version is available on the CD-ROM. This program needs to be downloaded and extracted. Once extracted, you can read the QuickStart tutorial (quickstart.doc), watch the QuickStart movie (tS5quickstart.wmv), install the interface guide (tSInterfaceGuide.exe), or install TrueSpace 5 itself (tsetupt51.exe).

Games

All work and no play make anyone a dull boy (or girl). Because of that, you will find a small set of games available on the CD-ROM.

Gemdrop

Gemdrop was developed solely by Keith Weatherby II as one of his first games. The game resembles Tetris but adds a bunch of new stuff like new levels.

Go ahead and try it. This program must be downloaded from the CD-ROM and extracted.

Smiley

Smiley was also developed by Keith Weatherby II. With an addictive gameplay and a rare idea, Smiley is a game that will make your eyes burn from playing it too much. (This program must be downloaded from the CD-ROM and extracted.)

Smugglers 2

SMUGGLERS 2 is the sequel to the first version of this popular game. It enables you to be a smuggler, a pirate, a sly trader, or a soldier with more than 13 solar systems to visit and 20 planets to explore. This program begins the installation procedure directly from the CD-ROM interface.

Loads of cool things, right? So what are you waiting for? Just put the CD in the drive and enjoy!

APPENDIX B

Debugging Using Microsoft Visual C++

Debugging is an important part of the development cycle. Being able to check variable types, change values, stop execution, and many other debugging steps are very important to master.

> **NOTE**
>
> All the steps discussed here can only be accomplished when using the debug version of the executables.

Breakpoints and Controlling Execution

The most important aspect of debugging is being able to stop the program where you want, and resume it from where you want—being able to stop the program at a single line or every few lines, or even run the program line by line.

Breakpoints

You can stop the program several ways, but the first way I will talk about is using breakpoints.

Breakpoints are points in the code where the program stops execution when doing a debug run. Lines with breakpoints are identified with a red circle to the left of them, as shown in Figure B.1.

You can create breakpoints by either right-clicking the line you want to include the breakpoint and selecting Insert, Remove Breakpoint from the drop-down menu, or moving the text cursor to that line and pressing F9. If you want to remove a breakpoint, you can do exactly the same thing you did for adding a breakpoint because if that breakpoint exists, it will be removed.

If you want to keep a breakpoint, but want to try a debug run without stopping the program at that point, you can disable it by right-clicking the line in which the

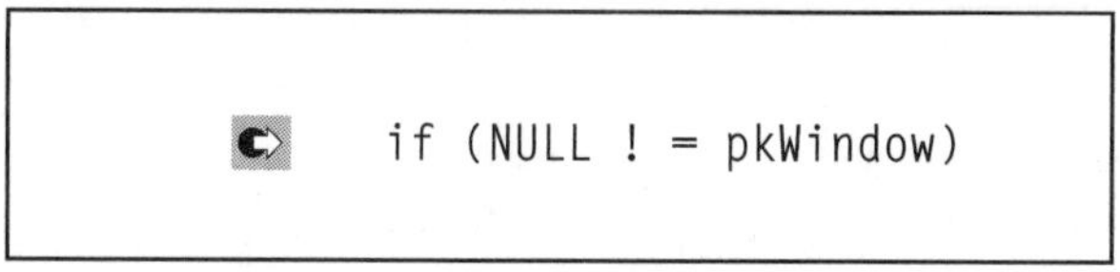

Figure B.1

Breakpoints are used during a debug run.

breakpoint exists and choosing Disable Breakpoint. You can enable it again by doing the same for a line with a disabled breakpoint.

You can now do a debug run by either pressing F5 or by going to Build, Start Debug and selecting Go.

You will notice that the program will stop and show you a couple of windows in Visual C++. I will explain those in a little while.

Controlling the Execution

You can control the execution of your program two other ways. You can go over each single line of the program by either pressing F11 or selecting Step Into from the Build, Start Debug menu.

You will notice that execution stops every line, but this isn't limited to only your files; it goes over every line of the files you are calling functions from.

The other way to control the execution is to run the program to a specific line, which works similarly to a breakpoint but runs the program to the position where the cursor is. You can do this by selecting Run to Cursor from the Build, Start Debug menu or pressing Ctrl+F10.

Modifying Variables During Runtime

When the execution of a program stops because of a breakpoint, you probably are presented with a screen similar to what is shown in Figure B.2.

The debug mode is divided into four main sections. The primary one is the code section, which normally takes half the Visual C++ window. At the bottom is the output window, and between these two, you have on the left, the variables window and on the right, the watch window. Let's focus on the variables window now.

The variables window is also divided into three parts: the variable names on the left, their values on the right, and the variables scope in the bottom.

From Figure B.2 you can see that you have four variables in the Local scope of the breakpoint. This means that, in the scope of the code block where the breakpoint is, there are four variables you can mess with. The `Auto` scope lets Visual C++ evaluate which variables are more important to that breakpoint and the `this` scope shows the scope of the `this` pointer, usually used when dealing with classes.

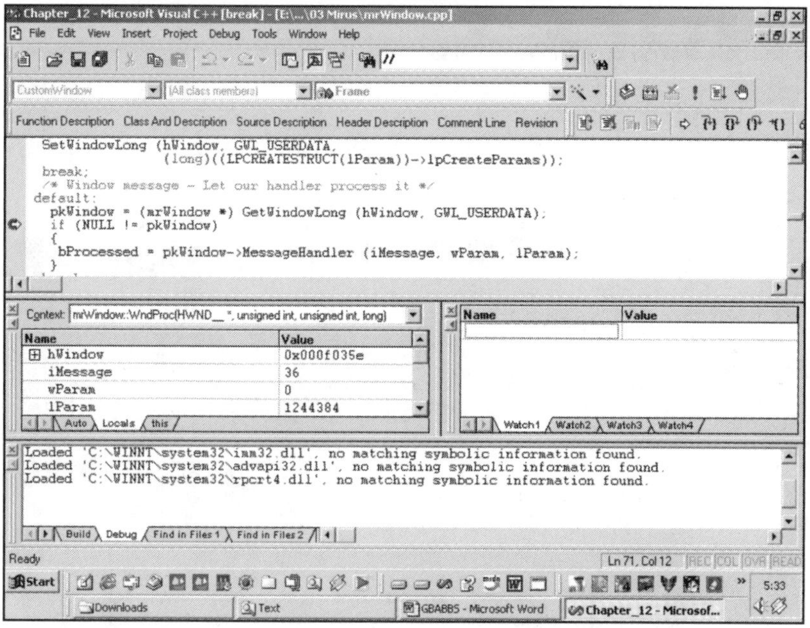

Figure B.2

Visual C++ debug mode.

If you wanted to modify any of the values of the variables, you would double-click the right part of them and write the new value.

When you are dealing with classes or structures, there is a plus sign to the left of the variable name that lets you expand the class members so you can change them individually.

Watching Variables

The final topic I want to explain about debugging is watching variables. This works similarly to the changing variables section, but lets you specify the name of the variable on it, and watches it at every breakpoint. You can also change like you did before in the variables window.

This is extremely useful if you know that a certain variable is jacking up your program and you want to watch its value every time instead of going through every variable in the scope list.

You can watch a variable by typing its name on the left part of the Watch window and after that, that section of the window will behave exactly like it was one of the Variable window variables.

APPENDIX C

Binary, Hexadecimal, and Decimal System

Binary, hexadecimal, and decimal are the most used systems in computer terminology. The computer stores all the information in the binary system but you usually use the decimal system. Let's go over each of them, shall we?

Binary

The binary system is a base 2 (binary means dual, two) system where the numbers are represented by either a one (1) or a zero (0). This is the system the computer uses to store all the data in memory. Each digit in the number represents a power of two.

The number 10101110 can be decomposed as:

(1 -> 1 * 2^7 = 128) +
(0 -> 0 * 2^6 = 0) +
(1 -> 1 * 2^5 = 32) +
(0 -> 0 * 2^4 = 0) +
(1 -> 1 * 2^3 = 8) +
(1 -> 1 * 2^2 = 4) +
(1 -> 1 * 2^1 = 2) +
(0 -> 0 * 2^0 = 0)
= 176

Expressing numbers in binary form is a pain; look at how the number 2316548 is in binary form—1000110101100100000100. Scary, isn't it? Even if this is the system computers use to store numbers due to the design of computer chips and memory, you can use the hexadecimal or decimal system in C++.

Hexadecimal

Another system you can use is hexadecimal. This system is of base 16, since you formerly used the numbers 0 through 9, letters had to be introduced to represent values from 10 through 15 in a single digit, namely A for 10 to F for 15.

This system works similarly to the binary one using powers of 16. The number F5 can be decomposed to:

```
(F -> 15 * 16^1 = 240) +
(5 -> 5 * 16^0 = 5) +
= 245
```

Decimal

You have probably been using the decimal system since first grade (or even earlier). This is a base 10 system that is expressed as powers of 10.

For example, the number 892 is natural to you. You know what it means and why, but do you know how it means—eight hundred ninety two? The decimal system has 10 digits (thus the name decimal) that go from zero (0) to nine (9). Because each number in 892 represents a value to the power of 10, you can decompose it as:

```
(8 -> 8 * 10^2 = 800) +
(9 -> 9 * 10^1 = 90) +
(2 -> 2 * 10^0 =2) =
392
```

Any number in the decimal system can be decomposed to the preceding format.

APPENDIX D

A C Primer

C and C++ share many functions and headers, but they don't work exactly the same. Here are some of the differences you should pay more attention to if you want to develop C-only code.

Standard Input and Output

In C, to be able to process input and output from the user, you need to use two C functions, namely `scanf` and `printf`.

Take a look at the sample program that follows:

```
 1:  /* 01 Main.cpp */
 2:
 3:  /* Standard Input/Output */
 4: #include <stdio.h>
 5:
 6:
 7: void main ()
 8: {
 9:  short Age;
10:
11:   /* Print message */
12:  printf ("How old are you?");
13:   /* Get input from the user */
14:  scanf ("%d", &Age);
15:   /* Print the age */
16:  printf ("You are %d years old.\n", Age);
17: }
```

This might seem a little awkward at first, but it is pretty simple actually. The first thing to do is include the standard C input and output header file, as shown in line 4. In C++ you used the `iostream` as the input/output stream, but in C it's `stdio.h`.

In line 12, you print a message to the screen using `printf ("How old are you? ");`, which prints the message `How old are you?` to the screen.

`printf` is like the `cout` you used for console output in C++.

The printf function outputs a string to the output stream, which is by default the screen.

Line 14 shows a message and retrieves a value from the user using scanf. The scanf function outputs any character in the string until reaching a format specification.

A format specification is a character (percent sign %) which indicates that a value from the argument list should be printed or retrieved from the stream. The letter(s) following the % specifies the type it should get or send.

For each format specifier you need to have an extra argument in the function. Format specifiers are bound to the arguments in exact order. For example:

```
printf (Name: %s    Age: %d    Blood type: %c, Name, Age, Blood);
```

Would print:

```
Name: Jules Mano   Age: 34   Blood type: A;
```

If, of course, those were the values of the variables.

printf does the same thing as scanf—it outputs a string until reaching a format specification—but instead of retrieving the value, it outputs the value of the corresponding argument.

> **NOTE**
>
> **When using scanf with format specifiers, you need to always pass the variable address to scanf rather than the variable, but when using printf, you need to pass the variable rather than the address of it.**

File Input and Output

Working with files in C is similar to using the input and output functions mentioned previously, with the exception that you need to open and close the files and also supply the stream (file) from where to read or write the functions.

Take a look at the following example which is similar to the previous one but saves the age to file and then loads it from the file you created.

```
/* 02 Main.cpp */

/* Standard Input/Output */
#include <stdio.h>


void main ()
```

```
 8: {
 9:   short Age;
10:
11:    /* File */
12:   FILE *File;
13:
14:    /* Print message */
15:   printf ("How old are you?");
16:    /* Get input from the user */
17:   scanf ("%d", &Age);
18:
19:    /* Open file for writing in text mode */
20:   File = fopen ("file.txt", "wt");
21:
22:    /* Write information to file */
23:   fprintf (File, "%d", Age);
24:
25:    /* Close the file */
26:   fclose (File);
27:
28:    /* Open file for writing in text mode */
29:   File = fopen ("file.txt", "rt");
30:
31:    /* Read information from file */
32:   fscanf (File, "%d", &Age);
33:
34:    /* Close the file */
35:   fclose (File);
36:
37:    /* Print the age from read file */
38:   printf ("You are %d years old.\n", Age);
39: }
```

Let's go over the differences between this program and the previous one. The first thing to note is probably line 12. Here you declare a pointer to a `FILE` type. This will be your actual pointer to the file. `FILE` is the C type for streams.

The second thing to notice is line 20. You open the file using `fopen`. `fopen` returns a pointer to the opened file and takes as first parameter the filename and as second parameter the open mode. The open mode is a string with a combination of

Table D.1 File Open Modes

Open Mode	Description
r	reading
a	appending
w	writing
r+	reading and writing
t	text
b	binary

characters that specifies how the file is opened. In this case, `wt` would mean writing and text. Check Table D.1 for some of the most used modes.

You retrieve the age from the user the same way you did before, but this time, instead of outputting it directly to the screen, you write it to the file. You do this with the `fprintf` function, which works almost exactly like `printf` but instead of using the default output stream, it takes as first parameter the stream you want to output, in this case `File` since it was the actual stream you opened. In line 26, you close the file using `fclose`.

> **NOTE**
> I know I could use more original names but I'm running out of ideas so please bare with me, okay?

The next step is to read the data from the file, for this you have to open the file in read mode. So in line 29, you open the file `file.txt` using `rt` for reading in text mode.

You then use `fscanf` to read from the file in line 32 the same way you used `scanf` for reading from the default input stream in the previous example, but supplying the file stream as the first parameter. To finalize the program, you close the file in line 35 and output the variable value in line 38.

Check out Table D.2 for some of the other input and output functions in C++ and then check MSDN to learn how to use them.

Table D.2 C File Input and Output Functions

Function	Description
`fputc`	Outputs a character to file
`fgetc`	Gets a character from file
`fread`	Reads an amount of data from a binary file
`fwrite`	Writes an amount of data to a binary file
`fseek`	Changes the file pointer position
`puts`	Outputs a string to file
`gets`	Gets a string from file

Structures: Say Bye-Bye to Classes

I have already discussed classes and structures, but C structures are different from C++ structures. While a C++ structure was treated like a class that by default had all members public, C structures will only be able to hold data and they have all the members exclusively public also.

Apart from this, there isn't much of a difference between C++ structures and C structures.

Dynamic Memory

To be able to work with dynamic memory in C you will have to use at least two functions, `malloc` and `free`. These functions work similarly to `new` and `delete` from C++.

> **NOTE**
> `malloc` and `free` are defined in the `stdlib.h` header file.

NOTE

Don't free a pointer that was allocated with `new` with `free` or vice versa. Even though they both allocate and deallocate similarly, the way they are stored in memory is different, and mixing the two types of dynamic memory allocation and deallocation can cause severe damage to the program's heap.

`malloc` takes as parameter the size of the memory block to allocate and returns a pointer to void (`void *`) that needs to be cast to the appropriate type pointer. `free` takes the allocated pointer as the only argument and deallocates it.

Here is a simple example:

```
 /* 03 Main.cpp */

 /* Standard Input/Output */
#include <stdio.h>
 /* Standard library */
#include <stdlib.h>


void main ()
{
 short CurrentValue;
 short *Values;

  /* Allocate memory */
 Values = (short *) malloc (sizeof (short) * 5);

  /* Enter some values to the array */
 for (CurrentValue = 0; CurrentValue < 5; CurrentValue++)
 {
  Values [CurrentValue] = CurrentValue * CurrentValue;
 }

  /* Go through every element and output it */
```

```
24:  for (CurrentValue = 0; CurrentValue < 5; CurrentValue++)
25:  {
26:   printf ("%d\n", Values [CurrentValue]);
27:  }
28:
29:   /* Free allocated memory */
30:  free (Values);
31: }
```

This is a simple program. It first allocates five `short`s in line 15 using:

```
Values = (short *) malloc (sizeof (short) * 5);
```

`malloc` allocates a block of memory the size of its first argument, in this case, the size of a `short`, multiplied by five. Since you want five elements, `malloc` returns a pointer to a `void` that you then have to convert to a pointer to a `short` using type casting.

The rest of the program fills the array you created with values and prints them on the screen. This code shouldn't be anything new to you.

In the end, you release the memory allocated using `free` in line 30. The only parameter you pass to `free` is the pointer you want to release—`Values`.

APPENDIX E

Answers to the Exercises

Chapter 1

1. When you create a new project, you specify the D:\Book\Hello directory in the directory project box.
2. The iostream header contains all the necessary functions, classes, and namespaces to do console input and output.
3. There is a " missing at the end of the string.
4.

```
Line 1
Line 2
Line 3
```

5. Normal error, fatal error, and linking error.
6.

```
#include <iostream>
int main (void)
{
 cout < "What is wrong with this ?";
}
```

7. `iostream`.
8. There isn't a ; terminating the line.
9. A linking error is an error that occurs during the linking stage of compilation.
10. MSDN.

Chapter 2

1. First byte 9, second byte 17.
2. `int` is a 32-bit value for 32-bit operating systems (Windows 95+, Linux, and so on) and 16-bit for 16-bit operating systems (DOS).
3. `Short` must be lowercase.
4. A variable name can't start with a number.
5. –471.

6. Postfix operators.
7. To reduce code size.
8. `Result` hasn't been initialized.
9. 11.

Chapter 3

1. The function prototype and function body.
2. There shouldn't be a semicolon at the end of the first line.
3. A local variable is available only to the code block it was declared in whereas a global variable is available to the entire file where it was declared.
4. Since the `a` isn't increased, the loop will run forever.
5. They are usually used for (by order) initialization, loop control, and loop progress.

Chapter 4

3. The code between the preprocessor directives is only compiled if `_FILE_H` is defined.
4. The `_FILE_H` was never defined, so the header code will not be included in the compile.

Chapter 5

1. An array is a collection of variables of the same type that share the same name and are identified by an index.
2. The access to the array will be out of bounds when `i` is equal to 123.
3. Creates a five element array and initializes it to: 10, 23, 123, 3433, 43.
4. A pointer is a variable that holds the address of another variable.
5. Dynamically allocate a block of memory.
6. The call to `delete` is incorrect because the array was allocated with `new []`, so it needs to be free with `delete []`.
7. To the fifth.
8. It represents the end of a string.
9. `"Happy birtHello you"`.

Chapter 6

1. A class is a collection of functions and data in a single handy namespace.
2. public, protected, and private.
3. It misses the semicolon at the end of the class definition.
4. Inheritance is the ability of a class to inherit the methods and data from a parent class.
5. Polymorphism is the ability of a class to change its type from one class to another.
6. A texture manager and an enemy manager.
7. Polymorphism is a way (or the possibility) of traveling class hierarchies by converting or casting derived classes to base classes.

Chapter 7

This chapter didn't warrant exercises.

Chapter 8

1. A stream is a sequence of bytes.
2. A normal string is a sequence of bytes while a file stream is a sequence of bytes that is connected to some physical hardware device.
4. You are trying to open an already opened file.

Chapter 9

1. A top-down approach starts by thinking of the problem as a big problem, and slowly dividing it into smaller problems.
2. A bottom-up approach starts by thinking of each small problem, and slowly starts to connect the problems to form a bigger problem.
3. You should create modules for their re-use properties and code independency.
4. `iTime`

   ```
   cName;
   pPointer;
   msgWindowMessage;
   hApp
   ```

Chapter 10

This chapter didn't warrant exercises.

Chapter 11

1. Post a `WM_QUIT` message to the window.
2. By making a real-time loop, you will only process the message if there are any pending, thus saving processor time.
3. `PeekMessage` will check the queue to see whether there is a message while `GetMessage` waits for the message.
4. You need to create a static method because to create a function you need to supply a static function as the message handler. The non-static method is called from the static one.

Chapter 12

1. Support on various Windows machines, full hardware support, and if there isn't a hardware function, DirectX emulates it.
2. DirectX is heavily based on COM.
3. A virtual table is a table that holds the address of functions of a class.
4. Component reuse and a structured method of distribution.

Chapter 13

1. Surfaces can't have an alpha channel and can't be clipped or color keyed while textures can.
2. The number red:31, green:57, and blue:17.
3. Only the last fourth of the texture would be shown (it would look scaled).
4. A template set is a collection of images organized in a grid for easier access.
5. Since you want the rectangles to be closed, you can either use the first vertex again or use a new one, which is what was done.

Chapter 14

1. `IDirectInput8` and `IDirectInputDevice8`.
2. The highest bit.

3. GetDeviceData is used to retrieve data from buffered mode while GetDeviceState is used to get the current state of the device.
4. The dead area of the joystick is the range for which the joystick returns as if there is no movement.

Chapter 15

1. The Sine wave.
2. The "WAVE" string.
3. The ppvAudioPtr2 parameter of Lock will point to the beginning of the sound buffer.
4. "close cdaudio".

Chapter 16

These exercises don't have answers; they are more like challenges to the reader.

Chapter 17

1. The primary advantage of a linked list over an array is that a linked list is essentially an infinite container, constrained only by the size of available memory. Extending a linked list to contain more items is much faster than resizing an array.
2. For one, a linked list will take up more memory than an array, because it must maintain extra pointers. Also, a linked list is not indexable like an array, so to get to the nth item in a list, you must traverse every node in front of it. For those of you who are intimate with how a computer works, you may also realize that linked lists do not have any locality-of-reference properties, like arrays do.
3. 2, 3.
4. Because they potentially split the search space in half for every item they compare, thus giving a logarithmic algorithm complexity.
5.

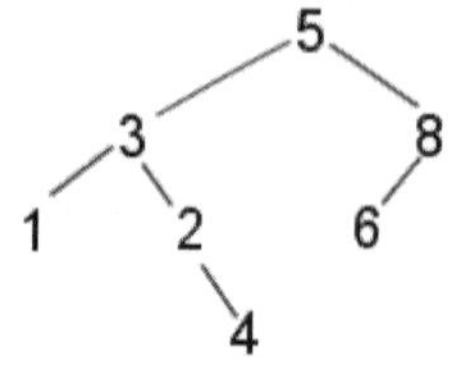

4,1,2.

6. 5,3,4,2,8,1,4,9

   3,4,2,5,1,4,8,9

   3,2,4,1,4,5,8,9

Notice how the largest number is "bubbled" up to the top on each pass.

Chapter 18

1. Adjacent size = cos (0.98) * 12 = 6.68 and Opposite size = sin (0.98) * 12 = 6.96
2. (38. 40)
3. (38, 40)
4. kVectorA + kVectorB – kVectorC
5. They represent the size of the matrix.
6. kMatrixA + kMatrixB * Scalar * kMatrixC
7. The zero matrix.
8. A set is nothing more than a collection of objects.
10. f'(x)= 4x

Chapter 19

1. Expert system shells give results of true (1) or false (0) while fuzzy logic gives results in a range of true (1) and false (0)
2. In genetic biology.
3. By generating a random solution, the genetic algorithm can approximate the result to its final solution by adapting its child.
4. Deterministic algorithms are predefined algorithms to simulate artificial intelligence.
5. A finite state machine is a machine (or program) that has a finite number of states describing the state of the machine.

Chapter 20

1. The trajectory is a parabola. The velocity at the end is the same as the velocity when launched. The vertical component of velocity at the apex (higher point) of the trajectory is zero. The horizontal component of velocity is constant (horizontal acceleration is zero). The time to reach the apex is the same time it takes to go from the apex to the ground (apex time = total time / 2).

2. Half the one of on Earth, 4.9 m/s.
3. Yes if you neglect any force caused by window or air resistance.
4. Kilogram (Kg).
5. Kinetic friction is the resistance to movement of an object when it is already moving.
6. 0.00248.
7.

```
A
└►BDEYZC
   └►DEYZC
      └►EYZC
         └►YZC
            └►ZC
               └►C
```

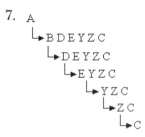

APPENDIX F

C++ Keywords

Some basic C++ keywords exist in the C++ language without the inclusion of any header files. They are a part of C++. Microsoft also gave us an expanded set of keywords to better use Visual C++. Table F.1 lists the C++ keywords and Table F.2 lists the Visual C++ specific keywords.

Table F.1 C++ Keywords

auto	bool	break	case
cast	catch	char	class
const	const_cast	continue	default
delete	do	double	dynamic_cast
else	enum	explicit	extern
false	float	for	friend
goto	if	inline	int
long	mutable	namespace	new
operator	private	protected	public
register	reinterpret_cast	return	short signed
sizeof	static	static_cast	struct
switch	template	this	throw
true	try	typedef	typeid
typename	union	unsigned	using
virtual	void	volatile	while

Table F.2 Visual C++ Specific Keywords

__asm	__assume	__based	__cdecl
__declspec	dllexport	dllimport	__except
__fastcall	__forceinline	__finally	__inline
__int8	__int16	__int32	__int64
__leave	__multiple_ inheritance	__single_inheritance	__virtual_ _inheritance
naked	noreturn	__stdcall	thread
__try	uuid	__uuidof	

APPENDIX G

Useful Tables

ASCII Table

Dec	Hex	ASCII	Dec	Hex	ASCII
000	00	null	032	20	space
001	01	☺	033	21	!
002	02	☻	034	22	“
003	03	♥	035	23	#
004	04	◆	036	24	$
005	05	♣	037	25	%
006	06	♠	038	26	&
007	07	•	039	27	‘
008	08	◘	040	28	(
009	09	○	041	29	)
010	0A	◙	042	2A	*
011	0B	♂	043	2B	+
012	0C	♀	044	2C	’
013	0D	♪	045	2D	-
014	0E	♫	046	2E	.
015	0F	☼	047	2F	/
016	10	►	048	30	0
017	11	◄	049	31	1
018	12	↕	050	32	2
019	13	‼	051	33	3
020	14	¶	052	34	4
021	15	§	053	35	5
022	16	–	054	36	6
023	17	↨	055	37	7
024	18	↑	056	38	8
025	19	↓	057	39	9
026	1A	→	058	3A	:
027	1B	←	059	3B	;
028	1C	∟	060	3C	<
029	1D	↔	061	3D	=
030	1E	▲	062	3E	>
031	1F	▼	063	3F	?

Dec	Hex	ASCII	Dec	Hex	ASCII
064	40	@	096	60	`
065	41	A	097	61	a
066	42	B	098	62	b
067	43	C	099	63	c
068	44	D	100	64	d
069	45	E	101	65	e
070	46	F	102	66	f
071	47	G	103	67	g
072	48	H	104	68	h
073	49	I	105	69	i
074	4A	J	106	6A	j
075	4B	K	107	6B	k
076	4C	L	108	6C	l
077	4D	M	109	6D	m
078	4E	N	110	6E	n
079	4F	O	111	6F	o
080	50	P	112	70	p
081	51	Q	113	71	q
082	52	R	114	72	r
083	53	S	115	73	s
084	54	T	116	74	t
085	55	U	117	75	u
086	56	V	118	76	v
087	57	W	119	77	w
088	58	X	120	78	x
089	59	Y	121	79	y
090	5A	Z	122	7A	z
091	5B	[	123	7B	{
092	5C	\	124	7C	¦
093	5D	]	125	7D	}
094	5E	^	126	7E	~
095	5F	–	127	7F	Δ

Dec	Hex	ASCII	Dec	Hex	ASCII
128	80	Ç	160	A0	á
129	81	ü	161	A1	í
130	82	é	162	A2	ó
131	83	â	163	A3	ú
132	84	ä	164	A4	ñ
133	85	à	165	A5	Ñ
134	86	å	166	A6	ª
135	87	ç	167	A7	º
136	88	ê	168	A8	¿
137	89	ë	169	A9	⌐
138	8A	è	170	AA	¬
139	8B	ï	171	AB	½
140	8C	î	172	AC	¼
141	8D	ì	173	AD	¡
142	8E	Ä	174	AE	«
143	8F	Å	175	AF	»
144	90	É	176	B0	█
145	91	æ	177	B1	█
146	92	Æ	178	B2	█
147	93	ô	179	B3	│
148	94	ö	180	B4	┤
149	95	ò	181	B5	╡
150	96	û	182	B6	╢
151	97	ù	183	B7	╖
152	98	ÿ	184	B8	╕
153	99	Ö	185	B9	╣
154	9A	Ü	186	BA	║
155	9B	¢	187	BB	╗
156	9C	£	188	BC	╝
157	9D	¥	189	BD	╜
158	9E	₧	190	BE	╛
159	9F	ƒ	191	BF	┐

Dec	Hex	ASCII	Dec	Hex	ASCII
192	C0	└	224	E0	α
193	C1	┴	225	E1	β
194	C2	┬	226	E2	Γ
195	C3	├	227	E3	π
196	C4	─	228	E4	Σ
197	C5	+	229	E5	σ
198	C6	╞	230	E6	μ
199	C7	╟	231	E7	γ
200	C8	╚	232	E8	Φ
201	C9	╔	233	E9	Θ
202	CA	╦	234	EA	Ω
203	CB	╦	235	EB	δ
204	CC	╠	236	EC	∞
205	CD	═	237	ED	Ø
206	CE	╬	238	EE	∈
207	CF	╧	239	EF	∩
208	D0	╨	240	F0	≡
209	D1	╤	241	F1	±
210	D2	╥	242	F2	≥
211	D3	╙	243	F3	≤
212	D4	╘	244	F4	⌠
213	D5	╒	245	F5	⌡
214	D6	╓	246	F6	±
215	D7	╫	247	F7	≈
216	D8	╪	248	F8	°
217	D9	┌	249	F9	•
218	DA	┌	250	FA	·
219	DB	█	251	FB	√
220	DC	▄	252	FC	^{n}
221	DD	▌	253	FD	^{2}
222	DE	▐	254	FE	■
223	DF	▀	255	FF	

Integral Table

$\int x^n dx = \frac{x^{(n+1)}}{n+1} + C$
$\int \frac{1}{x} dx = \ln\lvert x\rvert + C$
$\int e^x dx = e^x + C$
$\int b^x dx = \frac{b^{(x+1)}}{\ln(b)} + C$
$\int \ln(x) dx = x\ln(x) - x + C$
$\int \sin(x) dx = -\cos(x) + C$
$\int \cos(x) dx = \sin(x) + C$
$\int \tan(x) dx = -\ln\lvert\cos(x)\rvert + C$
$\int \arcsin(x) dx = x\arcsin(x)x + \sqrt{1 - x^2} + C$
$\int \arccos(x) dx = x\arccos(x)x - \sqrt{1 - x^2} + C$
$\int \arctan(x) dx = x\arctan(x)x - \frac{1}{2}\ln(1 + x^2) + C$

Derivatives Table

$(u^x)' = xu^{x-1}$
$(e^x)' = x'e^x$
$\ln(u)' = \frac{u'}{u}$
$\sin(u)' = u'\cos(u)$
$\cos(u)' = -u'sen(u)$
$\tan(u)' = \frac{u'}{\cos^2(u)}$

Inertia Equations Table

Object	Inertia Equations
Solid cylinder (horizontal axis)	$I = \frac{1}{2}mr^2$
Solid cylinder (vertical axis)	$I = \frac{1}{4}mr^2 + \frac{1}{12}ml^2$
Ring (horizontal axis)	$I = mr^2$
Ring (vertical axis)	$I = \frac{1}{2}mr^2 + \frac{1}{12}ml^2$
Empty Sphere	$I = \frac{2}{3}mr^2$
Solid Sphere	$I = \frac{2}{5}mr^2$
Cone	$I = \frac{3}{10}mr^2$

APPENDIX H

More Resources

With the click of a button (okay, and some keystrokes) you can find just about everything on the Internet, from how to cook Chinese food to implementing the latest 3D technology in your games. To make it a just a little easier for you, here is a collection of sites I greatly recommend if you are interested in game development (of course you are, why else would you have bought this book) to computing in general, and my favorite, computer humor.

Have fun on the Net.

Game Development and Programming

There are hundreds, if not thousands, of game development sites over the Internet. Some are good, some bad, but in my personal opinion, all in the following list are in the first category:

GameDev LCC: **http://www.gamedev.net**

FlipCode: **http://www.flipcode.com/**

MSDN DirectX: **http://msdn.microsoft.com/directx**

MSDN Visual C++: **http://msdn.microsoft.com/visualc**

Game Developers Search Engine: **http://www.gdse.com/**

CFXWeb: **http://www.cfxweb.net/**

CodeGuru: **http://www.codeguru.com**

Programmers Heaven: **http://www.programmersheaven.com**

AngelCode.com: **http://www.angelcode.com**

OpenGL: **http://www.opengl.org**

IsoHex: **http://www.isohex.net/**

NeHe Productions: **http://nehe.gamedev.net/**

NeXe: **http://nexe.gamedev.net/**

Game Institute: **http://www.gameinstitute.com**

Game Developer: **http://www.gamedeveloper.net/**

Wotsit's Format: **http://www.wotsit.org/**

News, Reviews, and Download Sites

Keeping up with all that is happening is, to say the least, a daunting task. New things happen every minute all over the world, and hopefully, the next set of links will help you keep up-to-date with it all:

Games Domain: **http://www.gamesdomain.com**

Blue's News: **http://www.bluesnews.com**

Happy Puppy: **http://www.happypuppy.com**

Download.com: **http://www.download.com**

Tucows: **http://www.tucows.com**

Slashdot: **http://slashdot.org**

Engines

Sometimes it is not worth reinventing the wheel. There are several good engines, both 2D and 3D out there.

Below are some of the engines I have had the pleasure (or pain) to work with that I want to recommend to you. Some are expensive, but then again, some are free, see which is best for you and start developing:

LithTech: **http://www.lithtech.com**

CDX: **http://www.cdx.sk/**

Jet3D: **http://www.jet3d.com**

Genesis3D: **http://www.genesis3d.com**

RenderWare: **http://www.renderware.com**

Crystal Space: **http://crystal.linuxgames.com/**

Independent Game Developers

You know, almost everyone started as you are starting, by reading books and magazines or getting code listings from friends or relatives. Some of the developers listed next struggled hard to be where they are now, some are still struggling.

Visit them, give them your support, and who knows, in the next book, it may be your site listed here:

Longbow Digital Arts: **http://www.longbowdigitalarts.com/**

Spin Studios: **http://www.spin-studios.com/**

Positech Computing Ltd: **http://www.positech.co.uk/**

Samu Games: **http://www.samugames.com/**

QUANTA Entertainment: **http://www.quanta-entertainment.com/**

Satellite Moon: **http://www.satellitemoon.com/**

Myopic Rhino Games: **http://www.myopicrhino.com/**

Industry

If you want to be in the business, you need to know the business. Reading magazines and visiting association meetings will help you for sure.

The following list contains links to both physical and online magazines, trade associations, conferences, and developers associations:

Game Development Magazine (GDMag): **http://www.gdmag.com**

GamaSutra: **http://www.gamasutra.com**

International Game Developers Association: **http://www.igda.com**

Game Developers Conference: **http://www.gdconf.com**

Game Developers Conference Europe: **http://www.gdc-europe.com/**

Xtreme Game Developers Conference: **http://www.xgdc.com**

Association of Shareware Professionals: **http://www.asp-shareware.org/**

RealGames: **http://www.real.com/games**

Computer Humor

Forget about Garfield or Calvin, check out the following (please, don't point the finger at me when you're at work and you fall off your chair laughing, and yes, it did happen to me):

User Friendly: **http://www.userfriendly.org**

Geeks!: **http://www.happychaos.com/geeks/**

Off the Mark: **http://www.offthemark.com/computers.htm**

Player Versus Player: **http://www.pvponline.com**

Books

Books are probably the best tool a programmer can have. Unfortunately, they aren't as cheap as a local call to your Internet provider.

Following is a list of the books I strongly recommend if you want to be a proficient programmer. Of course, you don't need all of them—just pick a few of each topic and you should be set:

C++: The Complete Reference by Herbert Schildt; Osborne/McGraw-Hill, 1998

Code Complete by Steve McConnell; Microsoft Press, 1993

The C++ Programming Language by BjarneStroustrup; Addison Wesley Longman, 2000

Thinking in C++, Volume I: Introduction to Standard C++, Second Edition by Bruce Eckel; Prentice Hall, 2000

Learning to Program in C++ by Steve Heller; Prentice Hall, 2000

C++ from the Ground Up by Herbert Schildt; Osborne/McGraw-Hill, 1998

Teach Yourself C++ by Herbert Schildt; Osborne/McGraw-Hill, 1997

Beginning Direct3D Game Programming by Wolfgang Engel and Amir Geva; Premier Press, 2001

Programming Applications for Microsoft Windows by Jeffrey M. Richter; Microsoft Press, 1999

Windows 98 Programming from the Ground Up by Herbert Schildt; Osborne McGraw-Hill, 1997

Learn Computer Game Programming with DirectX 7.0 by Ian Parberry; Wordware Publishing, 2000

Programming Windows, Fifth Edition by Charles Petzold; Microsoft Press, 1998

Tricks of the Windows Game Programming Gurus by André LaMothe; Sams, 1999

Developing Games That Learn by Lornard Dorfman and Narendra Ghosh; Manning, 1996

Game Programming Gems edited by Mark DeLoura; Charles River Media, 2000

Game Programming Gems 2; edited by Mark DeLoura; Charles River Media, 2001

Isometric Game Programming with DirectX 7.0 by Ernest Pazera, Premier Press, 2000

AI for Games and Animation: A Cognitive Modeling Approach by John Funge; A K Peters, 1999

Game Architecture and Design by Andrew Rollings and Dave Morris; Coriolis Group, 1999

Index

Symbols

' ' (ASCII conversion characters), 210
! (NOT operator), 45
"" (quotation marks), 10
& (address-of operator), 117
&& (AND operator), 44-45
*** (indirection operator),** 117-119
/* (comment delimiter), 16
; (line-ending token), 12
{} (braces), 11
|| (OR operator), 45
<< (insertion operator), 11, 252-253
= (assignment operator), 37
>> (extraction operator), 251
\0 (NULL-terminating character), 131-132
16-bit mode, 378-380
32-bit mode, 378-380

A

absolute mode, 530-532
acceleration
  mathematical functions, 693
  physics, 732
    angular, 733
    linear, 733
accessing
  classes, 158-161, 174
  mrABO class, 516-517
acos function, 666
Acquire function, 532-533, 546
acquiring
  mrKeyboard class, 532-533
  mrMouse class, 546
adapters (Direct3D), 380
Add to Project command (Project menu), 8
adding
  matrices, 681-682
  vectors, 671-673
AddLife function, 617
address-of operator (&), 117
Adelson-Velskii, 647
AI (artificial intelligence), 698
  deterministic algorithms
    patterns, 710-713
    random motion, 707-709
    tracking, 709-710
    universe problem, 707
  expert systems, 698-700
  finite state machines, 713-715
  fuzzy logic, 701-703
    fuzzy matrices, 717-719
    membership values, 715-717
    state, 715
    triangles, 717
  genetic algorithms, 703-706
  knowledge trees, 699
  memory model, 719-720
  neural networks, 706-707
  overview, 720
algorithms
  Bresenham, 435
  deterministic
    patterns, 710-713
    random motion, 707-709
    tracking, 709-710
    universe problem, 707
  doubly linked lists, 622
  genetic, 703-706
  lines, 433-437
    Cartesian plane, 435
    deltas, 437
  overview, 610-611
  STL, 611

allocating memory, 505
alpha blending, 417-418
- loading, 421-422
- structure, 420-421

alpha pixels, 416
American Standard Code for Information Interchange (ASCII), 151
- character conversion, 210

amplitude (sound), 568
AND (&&) operator, 44-45
angles
- radians, 662-664
- relations, 666-667
- triangles, 665-666
- vectors, 676

angular acceleration, 733
angular velocity, 732
animation. *See also* images; objects; physics; polygons; primitives
- defining, 305
- Direct3D
  - constructor, 495-496
  - defining, 494-495
  - destructor, 495-496
  - developing, 493-501
  - rendering, 496-500
  - rotating polygons, 497-498
- mrABO class
  - accessing, 516-517
  - allocating memory, 505
  - collision detection, 512-516
  - color keys, 508-509
  - constructor, 503-504
  - creating, 504
  - defining, 501-503
  - destructor, 503-504
  - formats, 505-506
  - libraries, 519
  - loader, 505-511
  - loading animations, 509-510
  - members, 506-507
  - properties, 505-506
  - rendering, 511
  - rotating, 517-518
  - template sets, 509
  - textures, 508-509
- template sets, 422-424

APIs (Application Programming Interfaces), 322
- comparison, 360-361
- Windows, 322

AppendChild function, 628
appending nodes, 619
AppendItem function, 618-619, 622
Application Programming Interfaces. *See* APIs
applications. *See* programs
ApplyForce function, 741
ApplyFriction function, 753-755
ApplyLinearForce function, 739
ApplyTorque function, 740
Area function, 56
arguments
- command-line, 327
- functions, 248
- parameters, 57
- strings, 145-147, 327

Arkanoid, 792
arrays, 108
- bubble sorts, 648-651
  - declining iterations, 650
  - swap counters, 649
- copying, 129-130
- declaring, 109
- implementing, 109-112
- initializing, 112
- lists comparison, 612
- memory, 122-126
- multidimensional, 112-116
- pointers, 119-122
  - functions, 120-122
- quick sorts, 651-655
- size, 109, 122-126, 151
- sorting comparison, 655-656
- strings, 131-132

artificial intelligence. *See* AI
ASCII (American Standard Code for Information Interchange), 151
- character conversion, 210

asin function, 666

assert function, 187
assert.h header, 187
assignment operator (=), 37
  compound assignment operators, 41
  game design, 283
  mrRGBAImage class, 460-461
atan function, 666
atof function, 145
atoi function, 143-144
atol function, 145
audio. *See* sound
audio blocks (mrSound class), 583
auto keyword, 63
automatic variables, 63
AVL (Adelson-Velskii and Landis)trees, 647

B

back buffering, 338-339. *See also* buffers
  full-screen mode, 519
  mrScreen class, 447-448
  surfaces, 396
background
  color, 201-207
  windows, 330-331
backward compatibility
  DirectX, 362
  Windows, 319
balls (Breaking Through game), 809-817
Basic Input Output System, (BIOS), 26
Bauer, Niels, 857-859
BeginScene function, 385
binary mathematical operators, 39-41
binary search trees. *See* BSTs
binary streams, 246-247
  markers, 268-269
  reading, 267-268
  writing, 264-267
binary trees, 633
BIOS (Basic Input Output System), 26
bitdepth (mrScreen class), 456-457
bitmaps
  loading, 413-414
  structure, 411-413
bits, defined, 27
bitwise shift operators, 41-42
black box model, 362-363
blending, alpha. *See* alpha blending
blocks. *See* code
body, functions, 56-58
bool keyword, 29
Boolean values, 210
bottom up game design, 282
bounding circles, 425-426
bounding rectangles, 426-427
bounding volumes, 424-425
braces ({}), 11
break statement, 75, 80
breaking loops, 75
Breaking Through game
  balls, 809-817
  blocks, 800-804
  building, 799
  class overview, 798-799
  code design, 798-799
  game controller, 817-847
  gameplay, 796-797
  graphics, 794-795
  menus, 795
  paddles, 804-809
  rules, 793
  story, 793
  system requirements, 792-793
  windows, 848-850
Breakout, 792
BreakThroughWindow class, 848-850
Bresenham's algorithm, 435
BSTs (binary search trees), 624
  advanced, 646-647
  deleting nodes, 638-646
  inserting nodes, 637-638
  overview, 634-635
  searching nodes, 635-637
  using, 647-648
btBall class, 809-817
btBlock class, 800-804
btGame class, 817-847
btPaddle class, 804-809

bubble sorts, 648-651
declining iterations, 650
swap counters, 649
BubbleSort function, 649
BubbleSortInt function, 650
buffers, 388
back buffering, 338-339
full-screen mode, 519
mrScreen class, 447-448
surfaces, 396
clearing, 384-385
copying, 129-130
data, 523-524
mrMouse class, 543-548
mrSound class, 580-582
vertex, 371
bug, millennium, 30
bug reports, 856-857
Build menu command, Set Active Configuration, 15
building
applications, 323-326
headers, 326
instances, 326
window state, 327
Breaking Through game, 799
classes, 155-157
general trees, 629-630
matrices, 678-681
Monster game, 215
classes, 216-221
description, 216
design, 216-221
objective, 215
rules, 215-216
mrEntity class, 725-728
particle systems, 773-774, 780-784
particles, 770-773
physics engines, 725-728
windows, 323-326
background, 330-331
class names, 331
CreateWindow function, 332-334
cursors, 329-330
handles, 332
headers, 326
instances, 326-328
menus, 330
message handlers, 328
state, 327
styles, 328
title bar icons, 329
WNDCLASS, 328-331
bytes, 26-27

C

C prefix, 165
C++
overview, 4
STL, 611
CalculateIVA function, 58-59
calculus
acceleration, 693
differentiation, 693-694
integration, 692-693
overview, 691-692
velocity, 693
callback functions, 556-559
career ladder, 608
Cartesian plane, 435, 729-730
case-sensitivity, preprocessor definitions, 101
casting classes, 179
const, 180
dynamic, 181
reinterpreting, 180
static, 180-181
cbClsExtra field, 328
cbWndExtra field, 328
CDs (mrCDPlayer class), 306-307
developing, 588-593
MCI, 586-587
cells, flashing, 492
center of mass (physics), 734-735
CGame class, 218-221
char keyword, 29
characters
ASCII conversion, 210
\n (new string), 11

NULL-terminating (\0), 131-132
variables, 28
CheckCollisions function, 221, 238-240
Checkers, 113-114
Chess, 113-114
circles
bounding, 425-426
drawing, 438
radians, 662-664
circular lists, 622-623
class keyword, 156-157
classes
accessing, 158-161, 174
Breaking Through game, 798-799
BreakThroughWindow, 848-850
btBall, 809-817
btBlock, 800-804
btGame, 817-847
btPaddle, 804-809
building, 155-157
C prefix, 165
casting, 179
const, 180
dynamic, 181
reinterpreting, 180
static, 180-181
CGame, 218-221
ConLib
constructor, 202-203
defining, 199-202
destructor, 200-203
header, 199-202
implementing, 202-215
overview, 198
constants (enum keyword), 182-183
constructors, 161-163
copy, 162-163
parameters, 162
copying, 162-163
CPlayer, 216-218
CString
constructors, 167-168
declaring, 167
destructors, 168
headers, 166-167
operators, 167-171
using, 171-172
CustomWindow, 351
declaring, 156-157
defining, 96, 156-157
derived, 159-160, 173-174, 179
virtual functions, 174-178
designing, 155-156
destructors, 163-164
images, 316
implementing, 157
inheritance, 172-178
virtual functions, 174-178
istream, 247-251
List, 614
m prefix, 165
MFC, 7
modes, 158-161
Monster game, 216-221
mrABO, 305
accessing, 516-517
allocating memory, 505
animations, 504
collision detection, 512-516
color keys, 508-509
constructor, 503-504
defining, 501-503
destructor, 503-504
formats, 505-506
libraries, 519
loader, 505-511
loading animations, 509-510
members, 506-507
properties, 505-506
rendering, 511
rotating, 517-518
template sets, 509
textures, 508-509
mrAnimation, 305, 480
constructor, 495-496
defining, 494-495
destructor, 495-496
developing, 493-501
rendering, 496-500
rotating polygons, 497-498

classes *(continued)*
- mrBinaryTreeNodeInt, 633
- mrBSTInt, 635
  - deleting nodes, 638-646
  - inserting nodes, 637-638
  - searching nodes, 635-637
- mrCDPlayer, 306-307
  - developing, 588-593
  - MCI, 586-587
- mrEntity
  - building, 725-728
  - collisions, 759-763
  - forces, 739-741
  - frame rates, 763-764
  - friction, 753-755
  - physics techniques, 764-770
- mrGamePlayer lists, 614
- mrGenTreeNodeInt, 626-630
  - destructors, 632
- mrInputManager
  - developing, 524-527
- mrJoystick, 308
  - callback functions, 556-559
  - constructor, 557
  - dead zone, 561
  - defining, 554-556
  - destructor, 557
  - developing, 554-565
  - initializing, 557-562
  - libraries, 565
  - polling, 562-563, 566
  - properties, 560-561
  - state, 563-565
- mrKeyboard, 307
  - acquiring, 532-533
  - constructor, 528
  - cooperative levels, 532
  - declaring, 527-528
  - destructor, 529
  - developing, 528-541
  - formats, 530-532
  - initializing, 529-530
  - polling, 566
  - state, 534-537
  - using, 538-541
- mrListGP lists, 614-615
- mrListNodeGenTreeInt, 626-627
- mrMatrix22
  - adding, 681-682
  - building, 678-681
  - concatenating, 686-687
  - dividing, 682-684
  - identity matrices, 684-685
  - multiplying, 682-684
  - subtracting, 681-682
  - transforming vectors, 688
  - transposing, 685-686
  - zero matrices, 684
- mrMouse, 307
  - acquiring, 546
  - constructor, 542-543
  - cooperative levels, 543
  - data buffering, 543-548
  - defining, 541-542
  - destructor, 542-543
  - developing, 541-554
  - formats, 543
  - implementing, 542
  - initializing, 543
  - movement, 551-553
  - polling, 566
  - properties, 544-546
  - state, 548-551
- mrParticle, 770-773
  - interpolation, 776-777
  - rendering, 775-778
  - simulating, 775
  - velocity, 778-780
- mrParticleSystem, 773-774
  - building, 780-784
  - flames, 784-787
  - rendering, 782-784
  - simulating, 781-782
- mrParticleSystemParams, 770-773
- mrReal32, 664
- mrRGBAImage, 303-304
  - assignment operator, 460-461
  - constructor, 460

copying images, 463-464
destructor, 460
developing, 458-472
flipping images, 464
loading images, 461-465
Targa files, 465-472
mrRLE, 658-659
mrScreen, 303
backbuffering, 447-448
bitdepth, 456-457
constructor, 442
cursors, 456
destructor, 443
developing, 439-458
drawing, 450-453
formats, 446-447
frames, 448-449
initializing, 442-443
render states, 447-448
screen modes, 444-445, 454-455
mrSound
audio blocks, 583
buffers, 580-582
defining, 575-576
developing, 575-586
implementing, 576-579
locking, 582-583
playing, 584-585
volume, 584
mrSoundPlayer, 306
cooperative levels, 574
defining, 571-572
developing, 571-575
implementing, 572
initializing, 573
mrSprite, 303
mrSurface, 304
constructor, 473-474
defining, 472-473
destructor, 473-474
developing, 472-479
filling, 476-477
locking surfaces, 475
pointers, 475-476
rendering, 478
mrTemplateSet, 304-305, 480
developing, 488-493
mrTexture, 304
constructor, 481-482
defining, 480-481
destructor, 481-482
developing, 480-488
mrTimer, 301, 309-314
mrVector2D, 668-671
adding, 671-673
dividing, 673
dot products, 676-677
multiplying, 673
normalizing, 674-675
perp-dot products, 677
perpendicular, 675-676
size, 674
subtracting, 671-673
mrWindow, 302
header, 342-344
hiding, 355
message handling, 346-349
naming, 345
position, 351-353
size, 345, 354
titles, 345-346
using, 350-351
variables, 345
object factories, 190-195
operators, overloading, 164-166
ostream, 251-253
overview, 154-155
polymorphism, 178-181
private, 159
game design, 285-288
protected, 159-160
public, 159
game design, 285-288
singletons, 186-189
advantages, 303, 316
static members, 185

classes *(continued)*
strings
constructors, 167-168
declaring, 167
destructors, 168
headers, 166-167
operators, 167-171
using, 171-172
troubleshooting (debug mode), 186
using, 158
variables (union keyword), 183-184
virtual, 343
window names, 331, 345
classic mechanics, 724
Clear function, 200-201, 208-210, 307, 384-385, 448
clearing
buffers, 384-385
screens, 201, 208-210, 372-376
surfaces, 384-385
windows, 384-385
close function, 255-258
closing streams, 253, 255-258
code
blocks
audio (mrSound class), 583
Breaking Through game, 800-804
creating, 11
functions, 52
game design, 284
statements, 66-67
Breaking Through game design, 798-799
commenting, 16
Craps game, 85-92
error handling, 17-19
fatal errors, 19
linking errors, 19
executing, 66
notation, 292-294
source, 14
Collide function, 305, 512
collisions
detection, 424
bounding circles, 425-426
bounding rectangles, 426-427
bounding volumes, 424-425
mrABO class, 512-516
elastic, 755
handling
conserving momentum, 755-756
impulse method, 756-761
maintaining momentum, 755
simulating, 756-763
color
alpha blending, 417-418
background, 201-207
keys, 419-420
pixels (alpha), 416
surfaces, 394
text, 201-207
theory, 416-418
color keys (mrABO class), 508-509
columns (matrices), 678
COM (Component Object Model), 363
DirectX, 363-365
objects, 365-366
command-line arguments, strings, 327
commands
Build menu, Set Active Configuration, 15
File menu, New, 5
Project menu, Add to Project, 8
comment delimiters (/*), 16
commenting programs, 16
comparing
strings, 138-143, 169-170
variables, 77-80
compatibility, backward
DirectX, 362
Windows, 319
compiling files, 14
Component Object Model. *See* COM
components
DirectX, 361-362
Mirus, 301
Graphics, 302-305
Helper, 301, 308-315
Input, 307-308
Sound, 306-307
Window, 302

compound assignment mathematical operators, 41
compression
overview, 656
RLE, 657-659
Concatenate function, 686-687
concatenating
matrices, 686-687
strings, 136-138
conditional operators, 43-44
conditional statements, 67-70
switch, 78-79
ConLib class
constructor, 202-203
defining, 199-202
destructor, 202-203
header, 199-202
implementing, 202-215
overview, 198
ConLib.h header, 199-202
console libraries. *See* ConLib class
consoles. *See* screens
const casting, 180
const keyword, 33-35
constants
enum keyword, 182-183
variables, 33-35
constructors
classes, 161-163
copy, 162-163
parameters, 162
ConLib class, 202-203
CString class, 167-168
mrABO class, 503-504
mrAnimation class, 495-496
mrJoystick class, 557
mrKeyboard class, 528
mrMouse class, 542-543
mrRGBAImage class, 460
mrScreen class, 442
mrSurface class, 473-474
mrTexture class, 481-482
ContainsPoint function, 305, 514-515
continue statement, 76-77
continuing loops, 76-77
contracts, 854-856
converting
characters (ASCII), 210
strings
floating-point numbers, 145
integers, 143-144
long values, 145
convex polygons, 437
cooperative levels
mrKeyboard class, 532
mrMouse class, 543
mrSoundPlayer class, 574
COORD variable, 208-209
coordinates
circles, 438
lines, 433-437
Cartesian plane, 435
deltas, 437
players, 216-218
polygons, 437-438
screens, 208-209
textures, 399-400
vertices, 401
copy constructor, 162-163
copying
arrays, 129-130
buffers, 129-130
classes, 162-163
images, 463-464
memory, 129-130
strings, 133-135, 169
CopyRects function, 396, 478-479
cos function, 666
cosines
angle relations, 666-667
look-up tables, 114-116
triangles, 664-666
counters, swap, 649
CPlayer class, 216-218
Craps game
code, 85-92
design, 84-85
objective, 83
rules, 84

crashes, 109
Create function, 302-305, 343, 474, 482, 509-511, 806
CreateDevice function, 382-383, 446-447, 529-530
CreateImageSurface function, 391
CreateSoundBuffer function, 582
CreateTexture function, 403
CreateWindow function, 332-334, 345
creating
  projects, 322-323
  windows, 302
cross-compatibility, languages, 365
cross-platform compatibility, 22
CString class
  constructors, 167-168
  declaring, 167
  destructors, 168
  headers, 166-167
  operators, 167-171
  using, 171-172
cursors
  mrScreen class, 456
  setting, 201, 210-211
  windows, 329-330
CustomWindow class, 351
cycles, sound, 568

D

D3DCOLOR ARGB macro, 394
D3DCOLOR XRGB macro, 394
D3DPRESENT PARAMETERS structure, 381-382
damping, 762, 788
data
  buffering
    DirectInput, 523-524
    mrMouse class, 543-548
  compression
    overview, 656
    RLE, 657-659
  sorting
    bubble sorts, 648-651
    comparison, 655-656
    declining iterations, 650
    quick sorts, 651-655
    swap counters, 649
data structures
  lists
    advantages, 623
    appending nodes, 619
    array comparison, 612
    circular, 622-623
    deleting nodes, 620-621
    disadvantages, 623-624
    doubly linked, 613, 621-622
    inserting nodes, 618-619
    iterators, 615-617
    nodes, 613-615
    overview, 612
    singly linked, 613-615
    structure, 613-615
  overview, 610-611
  random-access, 612
  sequential, 612
  STL, 611
data types, 27-30
date (strings), 147-150
dead zone (mrJoystick class), 561
debugging
  debug executable, 15
  troubleshooting classes, 186
declaring
  arrays, 109
  classes, 156-157
  CString class, 167
  functions, 55-58
  mrKeyboard class, 527-528
  pointers, 117
  variables, 30-31
declining iterations, 650
default directories, 10
default parameters, 58-59, 66
#define directive, 100-103
defining
  animations, 305
  classes, 96, 156-157
  ConLib.h, 199-201
  functions, 55-58, 96

global variables, 96
mrABO class, 501-503
mrAnimation class, 494-495
mrJoystick class, 554-556
mrMouse class, 541-542
mrSound class, 575-576
mrSoundPlayer class, 571-572
mrSurface class, 472-473
mrTexture class, 480-481
preprocessors, 100-101
types, 96
variables, 36
DefWindowProc function, 336
DegreeToRadian function, 664
delete operator, 123-126
deleting nodes, 620-621
BSTs, 638-646
Delta function, 301
deltas, 437
derived classes, 159-160, 173-174, 179
virtual functions, 174-178
design
classes, 155-156
games. *See also* AI
assignment operator, 283
bottom up, 282
Breaking Through game code, 798-799
code blocks, 284
Craps game, 84-85
design document, 599-600
detail, 601-602
example, 604-607
template, 602-603
difficulty, 220-221
equality operator, 283
I/O, 219-221
inline functions, 284-285
macros, 284-285
modules, 288-289
naming conventions, 289-292
overview, 280, 598-599
players, 216-218
private classes, 285-288
public classes, 285-288
screens, 217
statements, 284
status, 220-221
top down, 281-282
troubleshooting, 70
Monster game, 216-221
Destroy function, 803
destructors
classes, 163-164
ConLib class, 202-203
CString class, 168
general trees, 632
mrABO class, 503-504
mrAnimation class, 495-496
mrGenTreeNodeInt class, 632
mrJoystick class, 557
mrKeyboard class, 529
mrMouse class, 542-543
mrRGBAImage class, 460
mrScreen class, 443
mrSurface class, 473-474
mrTexture class, 481-482
deterministic algorithms
patterns, 710-713
random motion, 707-709
tracking, 709-710
universe problem, 707
developing
mrAnimation class, 493-501
mrCDPlayer class, 588-593
mrInputManager class, 524-527
mrJoystick class, 554-565
mrKeyboard class, 527-541
mrMouse class, 541-554
mrRGBAImage class, 458-472
mrScreen class, 439-458
mrSound class, 575-586
mrSoundPlayer class, 571-575
mrSurface class, 472-479
mrTemplateSet class, 488-493
mrTexture class, 480-488
programs, 12-14

devices
absolute mode, 530-532
joysticks. *See* mrJoystick class
keyboards. *See* mrKeyboard class
mouses. *See* mrMouse class
relative mode, 530-532
state, 523-524
dialog boxes
New
Files tab, 8
Projects tab, 6
Workspaces tab, 5
Set Active Project Configuration, 15
Win32 Console Application, 7
DIDATAFORMAT structure, 530
differentiation, 693-694
difficulty (game levels), 220-221
digital sound, 569
DIJOYSTATE2 function, 563
DIOBJECTDATAFORMAT structure, 530-532
DIPROPHEADER function, 560
DIPROPHEADER structure, 545-546
DIPROPWORD structure, 546
Direct3D
adapters, 380
alpha blending, 417-418
animation
constructor, 495-496
defining, 494-495
destructor, 495-496
developing, 493-501
rendering, 496-500
rotating polygons, 497-498
template sets, 422-424
bitmaps
loading, 413-414
structure, 411-413
buffers, 388
color keys, 419-420
enumerated types, 380-381
formats, 380-381
full screen mode, 379-380
functions, 384
images
assignment operator, 460-461
constructor, 460
copying images, 463-464
destructor, 460
developing, 458-472
flipping images, 464
loading images, 461-465
rotating, 430-433
scaling, 429-430
size, 429-430
Targa files, 465-472
translating, 428-429
initializing, 372-376
interfaces, 370-371
killing, 377, 384
mrABO class
accessing, 516-517
allocating memory, 505
animations, 504
collision detection, 512-516
color keys, 508-509
constructor, 503-504
defining, 501-503
destructor, 503-504
formats, 505-506
libraries, 519
loader, 505-511
loading animations, 509-510
members, 506-507
properties, 505-506
rendering, 511
rotating, 517-518
template sets, 509
textures, 508-509
objects, releasing, 386-387
polygons
coordinates, 399-401
render states, 406
rendering, 401-410
textures, 398-400
vertices, 397-398, 401, 405
screens
backbuffering, 447-448
bitdepth, 456-457
clearing, 372-376
color, 378-379

constructor, 442
cursors, 456
destructor, 443
developing, 439-458
drawing, 450-453
formats, 446-447
frames, 448-449
initializing, 442-443
render states, 447-448
resolution, 378-379
screen modes, 444-445, 454-455
setting up, 377-384
surfaces, 387-388
back buffering, 396
color, 394
constructor, 473-474
defining, 472-473
destructor, 473-474
developing, 472-479
filling, 476-477
locking, 391-392, 475
pitch, 392-393
pointers, 393-394, 475-476
rendering, 389-396, 478
size, 392-393
swap chains, 388-389
Targa files
loading, 421-422
structure, 420-421
template sets, 488-493
textures
constructor, 481-482
defining, 480-481
destructor, 481-482
developing, 480-488
locking, 404
rendering, 401-410
size, 403
video cards, 380
windowed mode, 379-380
windows
creating, 372-387
rendering, 385
troubleshooting, 345

DirectInput
data buffering, 523-524
device state, 523-524
interfaces, 522
mrInputManager class, 524-527
mrJoystick class
callback functions, 556-559
constructor, 557
dead zone, 561
defining, 554-556
destructor, 557
developing, 554-565
initializing, 557-562
libraries, 565
polling, 562-563, 566
properties, 560-561
state, 563-565
mrKeyboard class
acquiring, 532-533
constructor, 528
cooperative levels, 532
declaring, 527-528
destructor, 529
developing, 527-541
formats, 530-532
initializing, 529-530
polling, 566
state, 534-537
using, 538-541
mrMouse class
acquiring, 546
constructor, 542-543
cooperative levels, 543
data buffering, 543-548
defining, 541-542
destructor, 542-543
developing, 541-554
formats, 543
implementing, 542
initializing, 543
movement, 551-553
polling, 566
properties, 544-546
state, 548-551
setting up, 523

DirectInput8Create function, 526
directives
- #define, 100-103
- #elif, 105
- #else, 105
- #endif, 102-103
- #error, 105
- files, 99-101
- #ifdef, 102-103
- #ifndef, 105
- #import, 105
- #include, 10, 97-99
  - troubleshooting, 101
- #line, 105
- #pragma, 20-21, 101-102, 105-106
- #undef, 105

DirectMusic, 594
directories, 10
DirectSound
- MCI, 586-587
- mrCDPlayer class, 588-593
- mrSound class
  - audio blocks, 583
  - buffers, 580-582
  - defining, 575-576
  - developing, 575-586
  - implementing, 576-579
  - locking, 582-583
  - playing, 584-585
  - volume, 584
- mrSoundPlayer class
  - cooperative levels, 574
  - defining, 571-572
  - developing, 571-575
  - implementing, 572
  - initializing, 573
- overview, 569-570

DirectSoundCreate8 function, 573
DirectX
- backward compatibility, 362
- COM, 363-365
- components, 361-362
- DLLs, 362
- error handling, 377
- HAL, 362-363
- history, 359
- interfaces, pointers, 376
- Mirus. *See also* Mirus
  - components, 301
  - Graphics component, 302-305
  - Helper component, 301, 308-315
  - Input component, 307-308
  - overview, 300
  - Sound component, 306-307
  - Window component, 302
- objects, 365-366
- OpenGL comparison, 360-361
- overview, 358
- virtual tables, 365
- Visual C++ interaction, 366-367

DirectX Graphics. *See* Direct3D
disabling warnings, 20-22
DispatchMessage function, 335, 339
displaying I/O, 88
dividing
- matrices, 682-684
- vectors, 673

DLLs (Dynamic Link Libraries)
- DirectX, 362
- MFC, 7

do...while loops, 72-73
DOS applications, 7
dot products (vectors), 676-677
DotProduct function, 676-677
double keyword, 29
doubly linked lists, 613, 621-622
DrawCircle function, 303, 452-453
drawing. *See also* rendering
- circles, 438
- lines, 433-437
  - Bresenham's algorithm, 435
  - Cartesian plane, 435
  - deltas, 437
  - slope, 433
- mrScreen class, 450-453
- polygons, 437-438

DrawLine function, 303, 450, 830
DrawPrimitiveUP function, 371, 408-409, 452

DrawRectangle function, 303, 451
DSBUFFERDESC structure, 580-582
DWORD variable, 208-209
dynamic casting, 181
Dynamic Link Libraries. *See* DLLs

E

Eject function, 307
elastic collisions, 755
#elif directive, 105
#else directive, 105
else statement, 70
employment, 608
encapsulating DirectX. *See* Mirus
End of File (EOF), 250
EndFrame function, 303, 449
EndGame function, 221, 240
#endif directive, 102-103
engines, physics, 725-728
enum keyword, 182-183
EnumAdapterModes function, 454
EnumDevices function, 558
enumerated types, 380-381
enumerations, classes, 182-183
EnumJoystickCallback function, 556-557
EOF (End of File), 250
equal sign (assignment operator), 37
equality operator, 283
error checking, 389
#error directive, 105
error handling, 17-19
  DirectX, 377
  fatal errors, 19
  linking errors, 19
Esc key, 238
Euclidean space, 667
events, 201, 212-215
example, design document, 604-607
executables
  debug, 15
  MFC, 7
  Notepad, 22
  release, 15
executing code, 66
expert systems, 698-700
  knowledge trees, 699
Exponential function, 64-65
exponents, 28
extraction operator (>>), 151, 251

F

factories (object), 190-195
false value, 48
fans, 409-410
fatal errors, 19
fields (WNDCLASS) structure
  cbClsExtra, 328
  cbWndExtra, 328
  hbrBackGround, 330-331
  hCursor, 329-330
  hIcon, 329
  hInstance, 328
  lpfnWndProc, 328
  lpszClassName, 331
  lpszMenuName, 330
  style, 328
File menu command, New, 5
file streams, 253
filename extension (.h), 10
files
  compiling, 14
  creating, 8
  directives, 99-101
  headers, 10, 96-99
    assert.h, 187
    ConLib.h, 199-202
    CString class, 166-167
    functions, 55-56
    Mirus.h, 316
    mrDataTypes.h, 308-309
    mrError.h, 301, 315
    mrWindow.h, 342-344
    preventing multiple, 101-102
    stdlib.h, 83
    time.h, 83
    windows.h, 200, 326

files *(continued)*
include, 10, 97-99
troubleshooting, 101
interrelating, 97-99
iostream, 10
macros, 104-105
mrError.h, 301
naming, 8-9
preprocessors, 100-101
setting up, 8-9
source, 96-99
Targa
loading, 421-422
mrRGBAImage class, 465-472
structure, 420-421
Files tab (New dialog box), 8
FillConsoleOutputAttribute function, 209-210
FillConsoleOutputCharacter function, 209-210
filling, mrSurface class, 476-477
FindMedianOfThreefunction, 653-655
finite state machines, 713-715
fire, 784-787
flashing cells, 492
flipping images, 464
floating keyword, 29
floating-point numbers, 28, 145
flush function, 252
for loops, 73-75
for statements, 73-75
force
kinetic friction, 752
normal, 749-751
static friction, 751-752
forces
gravitational, 741
Law of Universal Gravitation, 742-743
planets, 743-745
projectiles, 745-748
physics, 735-736
linear, 736-739
resulted, 740-741
torque, 739-740
formats
Direct3D, 380-381
mrABO class, 505-506
mrKeyboard class, 530-532
mrMouse class, 543
mrScreen class, 446-447
fractal structures, 624
Frame function, 302, 349, 377, 384, 395-396, 766
frames
mrScreen class, 448-449
rates, 763-764
frequency (sound), 568
friction (physics), 748-749
inclines, 752
kinetic friction, 752
normal force, 749-751
static friction, 751-752
using, 753-755
fstream, 253
full screen mode, 379-380, 414-416, 519
functionality
DirectX. *See* Mirus
images, 303
screens, 303
sound, 306
functions
acos, 666
Acquire, 532-533, 546
AddLife, 617
AppendChild, 628
AppendItem, 618-619, 622
ApplyForce, 741
ApplyFriction, 753-755
ApplyLinearForce, 739
ApplyTorque, 740
Area, 56
arguments, 57, 248
arrays, passing, 120-122
asin, 666
assert, 187
atan, 666
atof, 145
atoi, 143-144
atol, 145
BeginScene, 385
body, 56-58
Boolean values, 210
BubbleSort, 649

BubbleSortInt, 650
CalculateIVA, 58-59
callback functions, 556-559
CheckCollisions, 221, 238-240
Clear, 200-201, 208-210, 307, 384-385, 448
close, 255-258
code blocks, 52
Collide, 305, 512
Concatenate, 686-687
constructors
- classes, 161-163
- ConLib class, 202-203
- CString class, 167-168
- mrABO class, 503-504
- mrAnimation class, 495-496
- mrJoystick class, 557
- mrKeyboard class, 528
- mrMouse class, 542-543
- mrRGBAImage class, 460
- mrScreen class, 442
- mrSurface class, 473-474
- mrTexture class, 481-482

ContainsPoint, 305, 514-515
CopyRects, 396, 478-479
cos, 666
Create, 302-305, 343, 474, 482, 509-511, 806
CreateDevice, 382-383, 446-447, 529-530
CreateImageSurface, 391
CreateSoundBuffer, 582
CreateTexture, 403
CreateWindow, 332-334, 345
declaring, 55-58
defining, 55-58, 96
DefWindowProc, 336
DegreeToRadian, 664
Delta, 301
Destroy, 803
destructors
- classes, 163-164
- ConLib class, 202-203
- CString class, 168
- general trees, 632
- mrABO class, 503-504
- mrAnimation class, 495-496
- mrGenTreeNodeInt class, 632
- mrJoystick class, 557
- mrKeyboard class, 529
- mrMouse class, 542-543
- mrRGBAImage class, 460
- mrScreen class, 443
- mrSurface class, 473-474
- mrTexture class, 481-482

Direct3D, 384
DirectInput8Create, 526
DirectSoundCreate8, 573
DispatchMessage, 335, 339
DotProduct, 676-677
DrawCircle, 303, 452-453
DrawLine, 303, 450, 830
DrawPrimitiveUP, 371, 408-409, 452
DrawRectangle, 303, 451
Eject, 307
EndFrame, 303, 449
EndGame, 221, 240
EnumAdapterModes, 454
EnumDevices, 558
EnumJoystickCallback, 556-557
error checking, 389
Exponential, 64-65
FillConsoleOutputAttribute, 209-210
FillConsoleOutputCharacter, 209-210
FindMedianOfThree, 653-655
flush, 252
Frame, 302, 349, 377, 384, 395-396, 766
get, 248-249
GetAction, 221, 233-234
GetAdapterDisplayMode, 380
GetAdapterModeCount, 454
GetBackBuffer, 396, 478
GetBitdepth, 456-457
GetChild, 627
GetColor, 518
GetCurrentAnimation, 512
GetCurrentFrame, 501
GetCurrentItem, 616-617
GetDelta, 311, 313, 449
GetDeviceData, 547-548
GetDeviceState, 534-537, 563

functions *(continued)*
GetDirection, 518
GetHeight, 517
GetKey, 200-201, 212-215
GetLength, 171
GetLife, 773
getline, 249-250
GetMessage, 334
GetPosition, 352-353
GetRadius, 518
GetSingleton, 187-189, 527
GetSize, 354
GetSound, 572
GetStatus, 221
GetStdHandle, 202-203
GetStockObject, 330
GetString, 171
GetType, 193-195
GetUV, 305, 496
GetWidth, 517
GetWindowLong, 347-348
GetWindowRect, 353-354
GetXAxis, 307-308, 551-552
GetXPosition, 517
GetYAxis, 307-308, 552-553
GetYPosition, 517
global, 66
HandleCollision, 759-761, 768, 788, 834
headers, 55-56
Identity, 684-685
ignore, 250
implementing, 96
Init, 303, 307-308, 529-530, 557-562, 573
inline (game design), 284-285
Insert, 635, 637-638
InsertChild, 627
InsertItem, 618, 622
is open, 256-258
IsButtonDown, 307-308, 534-535, 548-550
IsButtonUp, 307-308, 550-551
IsChildValid, 628
IsIteratorValid, 616-617
IsModeSupported, 303
KillDirect3D, 377, 384, 386-387, 395
Load, 274-275
LoadFromBitmap, 304, 414, 461
LoadFromFile, 305-306, 507-508, 576-579
LoadFromTarga, 304, 465
LoadIcon, 329
LoadLevel, 824
LocationOnLockedImage, 393
Lock, 582-583
LockRect, 391-392, 475
macros, 104-105
main, 11, 52, 326
mathematical
acceleration, 693
differentiation, 693-694
integration, 692-693
overview, 691-692
velocity, 693
mciSendString, 587-591
memcpy, 129-130
memset, 130-131
MessageHandler, 302, 346-349
Move, 218
MoveForward, 616, 627
MoveIteratorBack, 621-622
MoveIteratorForward, 617
MoveMonsters, 221, 234-235, 238-240
naming, 55, 66, 289-290
Normalize, 674-675
open, 254-255, 257-258, 461-462
operator, 304
OutputString, 200-201, 211
overloading, 59
overview, 52-54
parameters, 56-57
default, 58-59, 66
PeekMessage, 337-339
PerpDotProduct, 677
Perpendicular, 675-676
Play, 306-307, 584-585
Poll, 562-563, 566
PostOrder, 631
PostQuitMessage, 336
PreOrder, 630-631
Present, 385

Process, 221, 242-243, 839
ProcessGame, 236-238
ProcessLost, 242
ProcessLostLife, 241
ProcessMenu, 235-236
ProcessSplash, 235
put, 251-252
QueryPerformanceCounter, 313-314
QueryPerformanceFrequency, 311-312
QuickSortInt, 653
rand, 80-83
RandomLeap, 218
read, 267-268, 461-462
Read, 200-201, 212
ReadConsole, 212
recursive, 64-66
RegisterClass, 331
Release, 572
Remove, 635, 638-646
RemoveChild, 629
RemoveCurrentChild, 628
RemoveCurrentItem, 620-622
Render, 304-305, 478, 496-497, 511, 775-778, 782-784
return types, 55
RLECompressInt, 658-659
root, 629
Rotate, 305, 517
Run, 302, 343
Save, 274
SaveGame, 847
Search, 635-637
seekg, 268-269, 461-463
seekp, 269
SetActiveTexture, 305, 488
SetBackgroundColor, 200-201, 204-207
SetColor, 516
SetColorKey, 508-509
SetConsole, 221
SetConsoleCursorPosition, 211
SetConsoleTextAttribute, 205-207
SetConsoleTitle, 208
SetCooperativeLevel, 532, 543, 574
SetCurrentAnimation, 511
SetCurrentFrame, 501
SetDataFormat, 530-532, 543
SetImageBuffer, 461
SetMode, 444-445
SetModeClear, 303
SetPosition, 200-201, 210-211, 272-273, 351-352, 516
SetProperty, 544-546, 560-561
SetRadius, 516
SetRawImage, 474
SetRenderState, 406, 447-448
SetSize, 354, 516, 802
SetTextColor, 200-201, 207
SetTexture, 408
SetTextureState, 406-407
SetTitle, 200-201, 208
SetupDirect3D, 377-384
SetVolume, 306, 584
SetWindowLong, 347-348
SetWindowPos, 351-352, 354
SetWindowText, 345-346
Show, 221, 231-232, 355
ShowCursor, 303, 456
ShowExit, 230-231
ShowGame, 227-228
ShowHelp, 70
ShowLost, 230
ShowLostLife, 229-230
ShowWindow, 345, 355
ShowWon, 229
Simulate, 761-763, 768, 775, 781-782
sin, 666
size, 134
sprintf, 145-147
Square, 55
srand, 83
Start, 627
StartFrame, 303, 448-449
StartIterator, 616
StartNewGame, 221, 232-233
Stop, 306-307, 585
strcat, 136-138
strchr, 140-142
strcmp, 169-170

functions *(continued)*
- strcomp, 138-140
- strcpy, 133-134, 169
- strftime, 147-150
- strlen, 135-136, 171
- strncat, 138
- strncomp, 140
- strncpy, 134-135
- strstr, 142-143
- Synchronize, 807
- tan, 77, 666
- tellg, 269
- tellp, 269
- time, 83
- Transform, 688
- TranslateMessage, 335, 339
- Transpose, 685-686
- troubleshooting, 66
- Unacquire, 529
- Unlock, 583
- UnlockRect, 395
- Update, 301, 304-305, 307-308, 311, 448-449, 474, 483, 496, 511-512, 533, 808
- values, returning, 12
- variables
  - automatic, 63
  - global, 61-62
  - local, 61
  - scope, 60-63
  - static, 62-63
- virtual, 174-178
- void SetColorKey, 304
- WinMain, 326
- WndProc, 302
- write, 264-267, 277
- WriteConsole, 211
- Zero, 684
- ZeroMemory, 382

fuzzy logic, 701-703
- fuzzy matrices, 717-719
- membership values, 715-717
- state, 715
- triangles, 717

fuzzy matrices, 717-719

G

games
- Arkanoid, 792
- Breaking Through
  - balls, 809-817
  - blocks, 800-804
  - building, 799
  - class overview, 798-799
  - code design, 798-799
  - game controller, 817-847
  - gameplay, 796-797
  - graphics, 794-795
  - menus, 795
  - paddles, 804-809
  - rules, 793
  - story, 793
  - system requirements, 792-793
  - windows, 848-850
- Breakout, 792
- Checkers, 113-114
- Chess, 113-114
- Craps
  - code, 85-92
  - design, 84-85
  - objective, 83
  - rules, 84
- design. *See also* AI
  - assignment operator, 283
  - bottom up, 282
  - code blocks, 284
  - design document, 599-600
    - detail, 601-602
    - example, 604-607
    - template, 602-603
  - difficulty, 220-221
  - equality operator, 283
  - inline functions, 284-285
  - macros, 284-285
  - modules, 288-289
  - naming conventions, 289-292
  - overview, 280, 598-599
  - player, 216-218
  - private classes, 285-288

public classes, 285-288
screens, 217
statements, 284
status, 220-221
top down, 281-282
troubleshooting, 70
I/O, 218-221
libraries. *See* Mirus
loading, 270-277
troubleshooting, 276
Monster
building, 215-221
classes, 216-221
description, 216
design, 216-221
implementing, 221-244
loading, 270-277
objective, 215
rules, 215-216
saving, 270-277
players
coordinates, 216-218
lives, 216-218
scores, 216-218
publishing
bug reports, 856-857
contracts, 854-856
marketability, 852-853
milestones, 856-857
NDAs, 855
publishers, 853-854
references, 861
royalties, 856
self-publishing, 857
saving, 270-277
Smugglers, 857-859
state (universe problem), 707
general trees, 624
building, 629-630
destructors, 632
implementing, 625-629
nodes, 626
traversing, 630-632
using, 632
genetic algorithms, 703-706
get function, 248-249
GetAction function, 221, 233-234
GetAdapterDisplayMode function, 380
GetAdapterModeCount function, 454
GetBackBuffer function, 396, 478
GetBitdepth function, 456-457
GetChild function, 627
GetColor function, 518
GetCurrentAnimation function, 512
GetCurrentFrame function, 501
GetCurrentItem function, 616-617
GetDelta function, 311, 313, 449
GetDeviceData function, 547-548
GetDeviceState function, 534-537, 563
GetDirection function, 518
GetHeight function, 517
GetKey function, 200-201, 212-215
GetLength function, 171
GetLife function, 773
getline function, 249-250
GetMessage function, 334
GetPosition function, 352-353
GetRadius function, 518
GetSingleton function, 187-189, 527
GetSize function, 354
GetSound function, 572
GetStatus function, 221
GetStdHandle function, 202-203
GetStockObject function, 330
GetString function, 171
GetType function, 193-195
GetUV function, 305, 496
GetWidth function, 517
GetWindowLong function, 347-348
GetWindowRect function, 353-354
GetXAxis function, 307-308, 551-552
GetXPosition function, 517
GetYAxis function, 307-308, 552-553
GetYPosition function, 517
global functions, 66
global variables, 61-62
defining, 96
graphics. *See* images

Graphics component, Mirus, 302-305
gravity, 741
Law of Universal Gravitation, 742-743
planets, 743-745
projectiles, 745-748
grids, 113-114

H

.h filename extension, 10
HAL (Hardware Abstraction Layer), 362-363
HandleCollision function, 759-761, 768, 788, 834
handlers, message
pointers, 328
windows, 335-336, 346-349
handles
hWindow, 332
I/O, 202-203
keyboard, 200
pointers, 326
screen, 200
screens, 202-203
handling collisions
conserving momentum, 755-756
impulse method, 756-761
maintaining momentum, 755
simulating, 756-763
Hardware Abstraction Layer (HAL), 362-363
hbrBackGround field, 330-331
hCursor field, 329-330
headers, 10, 96-99
assert.h, 187
ConLib.h, 199-202
CString class, 166-167
functions, 55-56
Mirus.h, 316
mrDataTypes.h, 308-309
mrError.h, 301, 315
mrWindow.h, 342-344
preventing multiple, 101-102
stdlib.h, 83
time.h, 83
windows.h, 200, 326
Height parameter, 56
Hello World program, 9-12
Helper component (Mirus), 301, 308-315
hexadecimal notation, 27
hIcon field, 329
hiding windows, 355
hInstance field, 328
HINSTANCE parameter, 326
history
DirectX, 359
Windows, 318-319
HRESULT type, 377
Hungarian notation, 291
hWindow handle, 332

I

icons (title bars), 329
Identity function, 684-685
identity matrices, 684-685
IDirect3D8 interface, 370
IDirect3DDevice8 interface, 370
IDirect3DSurface8 interface, 371
IDirect3DTexture8 interface, 371
IDirect3DVertexBuffer8 interface, 371
IDirectInput8 interface, 522
IDirectInputDevice8 interface, 522
IDirectSound8 object, 571
IDirectsoundBuffer8, 575
if statements, 67-70
compared to switch, 78-79
#ifdef directive, 102-103
#ifndef directive, 105
ifstream, 253
ignore function, 250
images. *See also* animation; objects; physics; polygons; primitives
alpha blending, 417-418
animation, template sets, 422-424
Breaking Through game, 794-795
buffers, 388
classes (Mirus), 316
collision detection, 424
bounding circles, 425-426
bounding rectangles, 426-427
bounding volumes, 424-425

Direct3D
assignment operator, 460-461
constructor, 460
copying images, 463-464
destructor, 460
developing, 458-472
flipping images, 464
loading images, 461-465
Targa files, 465-472
fire, 784-787
functionality, 303
interfaces, 370-371
rotating, 430-433
scaling, 429-430
size, 429-430
surfaces. *See* surfaces
swap chains, 388-389
Targa files
loading, 421-422
structure, 420-421
textures, 304-305, 371, 398-400
coordinates, 399-400
translating, 428-429
iMessage parameter, 336
implementing
arrays, 109-112
classes, 157
functions, 96
general trees, 625-629
nodes, 626
Monster game, 221-244
mrMouse class, 542
mrSound class, 576-579
mrSoundPlayer class, 572
pointers, 117-119
#import directive, 105
impulse method (collisions), 756-761
inclines (physics), 752
#include directive, 10, 97-99
troubleshooting, 101
include files, 10, 97-99
troubleshooting, 101
indirection operator (*), 117-119
inertia, 788
inheritance, classes, 172-178
virtual functions, 174-178
Init function, 303, 307-308, 529-530, 557-562, 573
initializing
arrays, 112
Direct3D, 372-376
mrJoystick class, 557-562
mrKeyboard class, 529-530
mrMouse class, 543
mrScreen class, 442-443
mrSoundPlayer class, 573
pointers, 117
variables, 32-33
inline functions, 284-285
input. *See* I/O
Input component (Mirus), 307-308
INPUT RECORD structure, 212-215
Insert function, 635, 637-638
InsertChild function, 627
inserting nodes, 618-619
BSTs, 637-638
insertion operator (<<), 11, 252-253
InsertItem function, 618, 622
instances
applications, 326
singletons, 186-189
windows, 328
int keyword, 29
int type, 326
integers
strings, 143-144
variables, 28
integration (mathematical functions), 692-693
interfaces
DirectInput, 522
DirectX, pointers, 376
graphics, 370-371
IDirect3D8, 370
IDirect3DDevice8, 370
IDirect3DSurface8, 371
IDirect3DTexture8, 371
IDirect3DVertexBuffer8, 371
IDirectInput8, 522
IDirectInputDevice8, 522
MCI, 586-587

international system, 724
interpolation, particles, 776-777
intersecting sets, 690-691
interviews
Bauer, Niels, 857-859
LaMothe, Andre, 859-861
I/O
BIOS, 26
defined, 10-11
DirectInput. *See* DirectInput
displaying, 88
games, 218-221
handles, 202-203
joysticks. *See* mrJoystick class
keyboards. *See also* mrKeyboard class
handles, 200-201
mouses. *See* mrMouse class
mrInputManager class, 524-527
mrJoystick class
callback functions, 556-559
constructor, 557
dead zone, 561
defining, 554-556
destructor, 557
developing, 554-565
initializing, 557-562
libraries, 565
polling, 562-563, 566
properties, 560-561
state, 563-565
mrKeyboard class
acquiring, 532-533
constructor, 528
cooperative levels, 532
declaring, 527-528
destructor, 529
developing, 527-541
formats, 530-532
initializing, 529-530
polling, 566
state, 534-537
using, 538-541
mrMouse class
acquiring, 546
constructor, 542-543
cooperative levels, 543
data buffering, 543-548
defining, 541-542
destructor, 542-543
developing, 541-554
formats, 543
implementing, 542
initializing, 543
movement, 551-553
polling, 566
properties, 544-546
state, 548-551
screens, 200-201
streams, 247-253
input, 247-251
output, 251-253
strings, 132-133, 201, 211-212
SwapEffect keyword, 382
text (ConLib class)
constructor, 202-203
defining, 199-202
destructor, 202-203
header, 199-202
implementing, 202-215
overview, 198
variables, 31-32
iostream file, 10
is open function, 256-258
IsButtonDown function, 307-308, 534-535, 548-550
IsButtonUp function, 307-308, 550-551
IsChildValid function, 628
IsIteratorValid function, 616-617
IsModeSupported function, 303
istream class, 247-251
iterations, declining, 650
iterators
doubly linked lists, 621-622
lists, 615-617
nodes
appending, 619
deleting, 620-621
inserting, 618-619

J

joysticks. *See* mrJoystick class

K

k.message, 338
KB (kilobytes), 26
keyboards. *See also* events; mrKeyboard class
  Esc key, 238
  handles, 200-201
keys (color), 419-420
keywords
  auto, 63
  bool, 29
  char, 29
  class, 156-157
  const, 33-35
  double, 29
  enum, 182-183
  floating, 29
  int, 29
  long, 29
  operator, 165
  private, 159
  protected, 159-160
  public, 159
  register, 35-36
  short, 28-29
  signed, 28-29
  static, 185
  SwapEffect, 382
  union, 183-184
  unsigned, 28-29
  unsigned char, 28-29
  unsigned int, 29
  unsigned long, 29
  unsigned short, 29
  WINAPI, 326
KillDirect3D function, 377, 384, 386-387, 395
killing Direct3D, 377, 384
kilobytes (KB), 26
kinetic friction, 752
kinetics, 724
knowledge trees, 699

L

LaMothe, André, 859-861
Landis, 647
Law of Universal Gravitation, 742-743
legacy support (Windows), 319
length, triangle lines, 664-665
levels
  cooperative
    mrKeyboard class, 532
    mrMouse class, 543
    mrSoundPlayer class, 574
  game difficulty, 220-221
  operator precedence, 45-47
libraries
  console
    constructor, 202-203
    defining, 199-202
    destructor, 202-203
    header, 199-202
    implementing, 202-215
    overview, 198
  DLL
    DirectX, 362
    MFC, 7
  games. *See* Mirus
  mrABO class, 519
  mrJoystick class, 565
  static, 7
  STL, 611
#line directive, 105
linear acceleration, 733
linear forces, 736-739
linear velocity, 731-732
lines. *See also* vertices
  drawing, 433-437
    Bresenham's algorithm, 435
    Cartesian plane, 435
    deltas, 437
    slope, 433
  triangles, 664-665
linked lists. *See* lists
linked trees, 625
linking errors, 19
linking objects, 14-15, 19

Linux/Visual C++ compatibility, 22
List class, 614
lists
advantages, 623
arrays comparison, 612
circular, 622-623
disadvantages, 623-624
doubly linked, 613, 621-622
iterators, 615-617
nodes, 613-615
appending, 619
deleting, 620-621
inserting, 618-619
overview, 612
primitives, 409-410
singly linked, 613-615
structure, 613-615
lives, player, 28, 216-218
Load function, 274-275
loader (mrABO class), 505-511
LoadFromBitmap function, 304, 414, 461
LoadFromFile function, 305-306, 507-508, 576-579
LoadFromTarga function, 304, 465
LoadIcon function, 329
loading
animations (mrABO class), 509-510
bitmaps, 413-414
games, 270-277
troubleshooting, 276
images (mrRGBAImage class), 461-465
Targa files, 421-422
LoadLevel function, 824
local variables, 61
LocationOnLockedImage function, 393
Lock function, 582-583
locking
mrSound class, 582-583
surfaces, 391-392
mrSurface class, 475
textures, 404
LockRect function, 391-392, 475
logic, fuzzy, 701-703
fuzzy matrices, 717-719
membership values, 715-717
state, 715
triangles, 717
logical operators, 44-45
long keyword, 29
long values, converting, 145
look-up tables, 114-116
loops
breaking, 75
continuing, 76-77
do…while, 72-73
for, 73-75
message, 334-335
message handling, 346-349
real-time loops, 336-341
while, 70-72
LPCREATESTRUCT structure, 347
LPDIRECT3D8 object, 376
LPDIRECT3DDEVICE8 object, 376
lpfnWndProc field, 328
LPSTR lpCmdLine parameter, 327
lpszClassName field, 331
lpszMenuName field, 330
LPWAVEFORMATEX structure, 581

M

m prefix, 165
MacLaurin series, 665
macros, 104-105
D3DCOLOR ARGB, 394
D3DCOLOR XRGB, 394
error handling, 377
game design, 284-285
magic numbers, 182
main function, 11, 52, 326
managers
memory, 123
sound, 186
mantissas, 28
markers (binary streams), 268-269
marketability, games, 852-853
mass (physics), 728-729
center, 734-735

mathematical functions
acceleration, 693
differentiation, 693-694
integration, 692-693
overview, 691-692
velocity, 693
mathematical operators, 37, 395
binary, 39-41
compound assignment, 41
unary, 38-39
mathematics. *See* algorithms; calculus; trigonometry
matrices
adding, 681-682
building, 678-681
columns, 678
concatenating, 686-687
dividing, 682-684
fuzzy, 717-719
identity, 684-685
multiplying, 682-684
rows, 678
subtracting, 681-682
swapping, 685-686
tables, 678
transforming vectors, 688
transposing, 685-686
values, 678
zero, 684
MB (megabytes), 26
MCI (media control interface), 586-587
mciSendString function, 587-591
measures, international system, 724
megabytes (MB), 26
members
mrABO class, 506-507
static classes, 185
membership values (fuzzy logic), 715-717
memcpy function, 129-130
memory
AI model, 719-720
allocating (mrABO class), 505
arrays, 122-126
bits, 27
buffers, setting, 130-131
bytes, 26-27
copying, 129-130
hexadecimal notation, 27
KB, 26
managers, 123
MB, 26
RAM, 26
ROM, 26
streams, 278
variables, 27
size, 48
memset function, 130-131
menus
Breaking Through game, 795
windows, 330
MessageHandler function, 302, 346-349
messages
handlers
pointers, 328
windows, 335-336, 346-349
k.message, 338
loop, 334-335
queues, 322
WM NCCREATE, 345
methods. *See* functions
MFC (Microsoft Foundation Classes), 7
MFC AppWizard projects, 7
Microsoft Web site, 345
milestones, 856-857
millennium bug, 30
Mirus
components, 301
Graphics, 302-305
Helper, 301, 308-315
Input, 307-308
Sound, 306-307
Window, 302
DirectInput
data buffering, 523-524
device state, 523-524
interfaces, 522
setting up, 523

Mirus *(continued)*
DirectSound overview, 569-570
images, classes, 316
mrABO class
accessing, 516-517
allocating memory, 505
animations, 504
collision detection, 512-516
color keys, 508-509
constructor, 503-504
defining, 501-503
destructor, 503-504
formats, 505-506
libraries, 519
loader, 505-511
loading animations, 509-510
members, 506-507
properties, 505-506
rendering, 511
rotating, 517-518
template sets, 509
textures, 508-509
mrAnimation class, 480
constructor, 495-496
defining, 494-495
destructor, 495-496
developing, 493-501
rendering, 496-500
rotating polygons, 497-498
mrBinaryTreeNodeInt class, 633
mrBSTInt class, 635
deleting nodes, 638-646
inserting nodes, 637-638
searching nodes, 635-637
mrCDPlayer class
developing, 588-593
MCI, 586-587
mrEntity class
building, 725-728
collisions, 759-763
forces, 739-741
frame rates, 763-764
friction, 753-755
physics techniques, 764-770
mrGamePlayer class lists, 614
mrGenTreeNodeInt class, 626, 630
destructors, 632
mrInputManager class, 524-527
mrJoystick class
callback functions, 556-559
constructor, 557
dead zone, 561
defining, 554-556
destructor, 557
developing, 554-565
initializing, 557-562
libraries, 565
polling, 562-563, 566
properties, 560-561
state, 563-565
mrKeyboard class
acquiring, 532-533
constructor, 528
cooperative levels, 532
declaring, 527-528
destructor, 529
developing, 527-541
formats, 530-532
initializing, 529-530
polling, 566
state, 534-537
using, 538-541
mrListGP class lists, 614-615
mrListNodeGenTreeInt class, 626-627
mrMatrix22 class
adding, 681-682
building, 678-681
concatenating, 686-687
dividing, 682-684
identity matrices, 684-685
multiplying, 682-684
subtracting, 681-682
transforming vectors, 688
transposing, 685-686
zero matrices, 684
mrMouse class
acquiring, 546
constructor, 542-543

cooperative levels, 543
data buffering, 543-548
defining, 541-542
destructor, 542-543
developing, 541-554
formats, 543
implementing, 542
initializing, 543
movement, 551-553
polling, 566
properties, 544-546
state, 548-551
mrParticle class, 770-773
interpolation, 776-777
rendering, 775-778
simulating, 775
velocity, 778-780
mrParticleSystem class, 773-774
building, 780-784
flames, 784-787
rendering, 782-784
simulating, 781-782
mrParticleSystemParams class, 770-773
mrReal32 class, 664
mrRGBAImage class
assignment operator, 460-461
constructor, 460
copying images, 463-464
destructor, 460
developing, 458-472
flipping images, 464
loading images, 461-465
Targa files, 465-472
mrRLE class, 658-659
mrScreen class
backbuffering, 447-448
bitdepth, 456-457
constructor, 442
cursors, 456
destructor, 443
developing, 439-458
drawing, 450-453
formats, 446-447
frames, 448-449
initializing, 442-443
render states, 447-448
screen modes, 444-445, 454-455
mrSound class
audio blocks, 583
buffers, 580-582
defining, 575-576
developing, 575-586
implementing, 576-579
locking, 582-583
playing, 584-585
volume, 584
mrSoundPlayer class
cooperative levels, 574
defining, 571-572
developing, 571-575
implementing, 572
initializing, 573
mrSurface class
constructor, 473-474
defining, 472-473
destructor, 473-474
developing, 472-479
filling, 476-477
locking surfaces, 475
pointers, 475-476
rendering, 478
mrTemplateSet class, 480
developing, 488-493
mrTexture class
constructor, 481-482
defining, 480-481
destructor, 481-482
developing, 480-488
mrVector2D class, 668-671
adding, 671-673
dividing, 673
dot products, 676-677
multiplying, 673
normalizing, 674-675
perp-dot products, 677
perpendicular, 675-676
size, 674
subtracting, 671-673

Mirus *(continued)*
- overview, 300
- using, 316
- windows
  - header, 342-344
  - hiding, 355
  - message handling, 346-349
  - naming, 345
  - position, 351-353
  - size, 345-354
  - titles, 345-346
  - using, 350-351
  - variables, 345

Mirus.h header, 316

modes
- 16-bit, 378-380
- 32-bit, 378-380
- absolute, 530-532
- classes, 158-161, 186
- debug, 186
- full screen, 379-380, 414-416
  - backbuffers, 519
- relative, 530-532
- windowed, 379-380

modules, game design, 288-289

momentum, 755-756

Monster game
- building, 215
  - classes, 216-221
  - description, 216
  - design, 216-221
  - objective, 215
  - rules, 215-216
- implementing, 221-244
- loading, 270-277
- saving, 270-277

mouses. *See* mrMouse class

Move function, 218

MoveForward function, 616, 627

MoveIteratorBack function, 621-622

MoveIteratorForward function, 617

movement (mrMouse class), 551-553

MoveMonsters function, 221, 234-235, 238-240

moving. *See* AI; physics

mrABO class, 305
- accessing, 516-517
- allocating memory, 505
- animations, 504
- collision detection, 512-516
- color keys, 508-509
- constructor, 503-504
- defining, 501-503
- destructor, 503-504
- formats, 505-506
- libraries, 519
- loader, 505-511
- loading animations, 509-510
- members, 506-507
- properties, 505-506
- rendering, 511
- rotating, 517-518
- template sets, 509
- textures, 508-509

mrAnimation class, 305, 480
- constructor, 495-496
- defining, 494-495
- destructor, 495-496
- developing, 493-501
- rendering, 496-500
- rotating polygons, 497-498

mrBinaryTreeNodeInt class, 633

mrBSTInt class, 635
- deleting nodes, 638-646
- inserting nodes, 637-638
- searching nodes, 635-637

mrCDPlayer class, 306-307
- developing, 588-593
- MCI, 586-587

mrDataTypes.h header, 308-309

mrEntity class
- building, 725-728
- collisions, 759-763
- forces, 739-741
- frame rates, 763-764
- friction, 753-755
- physics techniques, 764-770

mrError.h header, 301, 315

mrGamePlayer class lists, 614

mrGenTreeNodeInt class, 626, 630
- destructors, 632

mrInputManager class, 524-527
mrJoystick class, 308
- callback functions, 556-559
- constructor, 557
- dead zone, 561
- defining, 554-556
- destructor, 557
- developing, 554-565
- initializing, 557-562
- libraries, 565
- polling, 562-563, 566
- properties, 560-561
- state, 563-565

mrKeyboard class, 307
- acquiring, 532-533
- constructor, 528
- cooperative levels, 532
- declaring, 527-528
- destructor, 529
- developing, 527-541
- formats, 530-532
- initializing, 529-530
- polling, 566
- state, 534-537
- using, 538-541

mrListGP class lists, 614-615
mrListNodeGenTreeInt class, 626-627
mrMatrix22 class
- adding, 681-682
- building, 678-681
- concatenating, 686-687
- dividing, 682-684
- identity matrices, 684-685
- multiplying, 682-684
- subtracting, 681-682
- transforming vectors, 688
- transposing, 685-686
- zero matrices, 684

mrMouse class, 307
- acquiring, 546
- constructor, 542-543
- cooperative levels, 543
- data buffering, 543-548
- defining, 541-542
- destructor, 542-543
- developing, 541-554
- formats, 543
- implementing, 542
- initializing, 543
- movement, 551-553
- polling, 566
- properties, 544-546
- state, 548-551

mrParticle class, 770-773
- interpolation, 776-777
- rendering, 775-778
- simulating, 775
- velocity, 778-780

mrParticleSystem class, 773-774
- building, 780-784
- flames, 784-787
- rendering, 782-784
- simulating, 781-782

mrParticleSystemParams class, 770-773
mrReal32 class, 664
mrRGBAImage class, 303-304
- assignment operator, 460-461
- constructor, 460
- copying images, 463-464
- destructor, 460
- developing, 458-472
- flipping images, 464
- loading images, 461-465
- Targa files, 465-472

mrRLE class, 658-659
mrScreen class, 303
- backbuffering, 447-448
- bitdepth, 456-457
- constructor, 442
- cursors, 456
- destructor, 443
- developing, 439-458
- drawing, 450-453
- formats, 446-447
- frames, 448-449
- initializing, 442-443
- render states, 447-448
- screen modes, 444-445, 454-455

mrSound class
audio blocks, 583
buffers, 580-582
defining, 575-576
developing, 575-586
implementing, 576-579
locking, 582-583
playing, 584-585
volume, 584
mrSoundPlayer class, 306
cooperative levels, 574
defining, 571-572
developing, 571-575
implementing, 572
initializing, 573
mrSprite class, 303
mrSurface class, 304
constructor, 473-474
defining, 472-473
destructor, 473-474
developing, 472-479
filling, 476-477
locking surfaces, 475
pointers, 475-476
rendering, 478
mrTemplateSet class, 304-305, 480
developing, 488-493
mrTexture class, 304
constructor, 481-482
defining, 480-481
destructor, 481-482
developing, 480-488
mrTimer class, 301, 309-314
mrVector2D class, 668-671
adding, 671-673
dividing, 673
dot products, 676-677
multiplying, 673
normalizing, 674-675
perp-dot products, 677
perpendicular, 675-676
size, 674
subtracting, 671-673
mrWindow class, 302
header, 342-344
hiding, 355
message handling, 346-349
naming, 345
position, 351-353
size, 345-354
titles, 345-346
using, 350-351
variables, 345
mrWindow.h header, 342-344
MSG structure, 335-338
multidimensional arrays, 112-116
multimedia, 586-587
multiplying
matrices, 682-684
vectors, 673
multitasking (Windows), 321
music, 586-587

N

\n new string character, 11
namespaces, std, 11
naming
classes, 165
conventions, game design, 289-292
files, 8-9
functions, 55, 66, 289-290
variables, 36, 60, 290-291
window classes, 331, 345
windows, 208
NDAs (non-disclosure agreements), 855
neural networks, 706-707
New command (File menu), 5
New dialog box
Files tab, 8
Projects tab, 6
Workspaces tab, 5
new operator, 123-126
new string character (\n), 11
Newton, Sir Isaac, 724
Niels Bauer Software Design, 857-859

nodes, 624
- appending, 619
- BSTs
  - inserting, 637-638
  - searching, 635-637
- deleting, 620-621
- general trees, 626
- inserting, 618-619
- lists, 613-615

non-disclosure agreements (NDAs), 855
normal force (friction), 749-751
Normalize function, 674-675
normalizing vectors, 674-675
NOT (!) operator, 45
notation
- code, 292-294
- Hungarian, 291

Notepad executables, 22
n-tuples, 667
NULL-terminating character (\0), 131-132
numbers
- constants, 182-183
- exponents, 28
- floating-point, 28, 145
- integers, 143-144
- long values, 145
- magic, 182
- mantissas, 28
- randomizing, 80-83
- seeds, 83
- variables, 183-184

O

objective
- Craps game, 83
- Monster game, 215

object-oriented programming, (OOP), 4
objects. *See also* animation; images; physics; polygons; primitives
- collisions. *See* collisions
- DirectX, 365-366
- factories, 190-195
- gravity. *See* gravity
- handles, 201
- IDirectSound8, 571
- IDirectSoundBuffer8, 575
- linking, 14-15
  - errors, 19
- LPDIRECT3D8, 376
- LPDIRECT3DDEVICE8, 376
- moving. *See* AI
- releasing, 386-387
- rotating, 430-433
- scaling, 429-430
- size, 429-430
- translating, 428-429

ofstream, 253
OOP (object-oriented programming), 4
open function, 254-255, 257-258, 461-462
OpenGL/DirectX comparison, 360-361
opening streams, 253-255, 257-258
operands, 37
operator function, 304
operator keyword, 165
operators
- ! (NOT), 45
- && (AND), 44-45
- || (OR), 45
- << (insertion), 11
- address-of (&), 117
- assignment (=), 37
  - game design, 283
  - mrRGBAImage class, 460-461
- conditional, 43-44
- CString class, 167-171
- delete, 123-126
- equality, 283
- extraction (>>), 151
  - streams, 251
- indirection (*), 117-119
- insertion (<<), 252-253
- logical, 44-45
- mathematical, 37, 395
  - binary, 39-41
  - compound assignment, 41
  - unary, 38-39

operators *(continued)*
new, 123-126
operands, 37
overloading, 164-166
pointers, 126-129
precedence, 45-47
relational, 42-43
shift, 41-42
sizeof, 48
ternary, 43
OR (||) operator, 45
orientation, vectors, 668
ostream class, 251-253
output. *See* I/O
output window, 17
OutputString function, 200-201, 211
overloading
functions, 59
operators, 164-166

P

paddles (Breaking Through game), 804-809
pAge pointer, 127-128
parameters
arguments, 57
constructors, 162
default, 58-59, 66
functions, 56
Height, 56
HINSTANCE, 326
iMessage, 336
LPSTR lpCmdLine, 327
size t, 134
unsigned short, 205
void, 56
Width, 56
WORD, 205
parent-child relationship, 625
particle systems
building, 773-774, 780-784
flames, 784-787
rendering, 782-784
simulating, 781- 782
particles
building, 770-773
interpolation, 776-777
rendering, 775-778
simulating, 775
velocity, 778-780
passing arrays, 120-122
patterns algorithm, 710-713
PCM (Pulse Code Modulation), 577
PDL (Program Design Language), 12-14
PeekMessage function, 337-339
perceptrons, 706
perp-dot products (vectors), 677
PerpDotProduct function, 677
perpendicular vectors, 675-676
Perpendicular function, 675-676
physics
acceleration, 732
angular, 733
linear, 733
advanced techniques, 764-770
Cartesian plane, 729-730
classic mechanics, 724
collisions
conserving momentum, 755-756
impulse method, 756-761
maintaining momentum, 755
simulating, 756-763
damping, 762
engines, 725-728
forces, 735-736
linear, 736-739
resulted, 740-741
torque, 739-740
frame rates, 763-764
friction, 748-749
inclines, 752
kinetic friction, 752
normal force, 749-751
static friction, 751-752
using, 753-755
gravity, 741
Law of Universal Gravitation, 742-743
planets, 743-745
projectiles, 745-748

international system, 724
kinetics, 724
mass, 728-729
center, 734-735
Newtonian, 724
particle systems
building, 773-774, 780-784
flames, 784-787
rendering, 782-784
simulating, 781-782
particles
building, 770-773
interpolation, 776-777
rendering, 775-778
simulating, 775
velocity, 778-780
position, 729-730
time, 729
velocity, 731-732
angular, 732
linear, 731-732
speed, 732
weight, 729
pInterest pointer, 127-128
pitch, surfaces, 392-393
pixels
blending, 417-418
color (alpha), 416
planes, Cartesian, 435, 729-730
planets, gravity, 743-745
Play function, 306-307, 584-585
players
coordinates, 216-218
creating, 216-218
lives, 28, 216-218
scores, 216-218
playing
Breaking Through game, 796-797
mrSound class, 584-585
POINT structure, 353
pointers
arrays, 119-122
functions, 120-122
buffers, 130-131
declaring, 117
handles, 326
implementing, 117-119
initializing, 117
interfaces, 376
message handlers, 328
mrSurface class, 475-476
operators, 126-129
pAge, 127-128
pInterest, 127-128
strings, 132
surfaces, 393-394
this, 166
variables, 116
PointerValues variable, 128-129
Poll function, 562-563, 566
polling
mrJoystick class, 562-563, 566
mrKeyboard class, 566
mrMouse class, 566
polygons. *See also* animation; images; objects; physics; primitives
convex, 437
drawing, 437-438
primitives
circles, 438
lines, 433-437
polygons, 437-438
types, 409-410
render states, 406
rendering, 401-410
rotating, 430-433
mrAnimation class, 497-498
scaling, 429-430
size, 429-430
textures, 371, 398-400
coordinates, 399-400
translating, 428-429
vertex buffers, 371
vertices, 397-398, 405
coordinates, 401
polymorphism, 178-181
position
grids, 113-114
physics, 729-730
relative, 788
windows, 351-353

PostOrder function, 631
PostQuitMessage function, 336
#pragma directive, 20-21, 101-102, 105-106
precedence, operators, 45-47
prefixes, 165
PreOrder function, 630-631
preprocessors
- defining, 100-101
- directives. *See* directives
- macros, 104-105
- preventing multiple headers, 101-102

Present function, 385
primitives. *See also* animation; images; objects; physics; polygons
- circles, 438
- lines
  - Cartesian plane, 435
  - deltas, 437
  - drawing, 433-437
  - slope, 433
- polygons, 437-438
- types, 409-410

private classes, 159, 285-288
private keyword, 159
probability
- overview, 688-689
- sets, 689
  - intersecting, 690-691
- unions, 689-690

Process function, 221, 242-243, 839
ProcessGame function, 236-238
ProcessLost function, 242
ProcessLostLife function, 241
ProcessMenu function, 235-236
ProcessSplash function, 235
Program Design Language (PDL), 12-14
programs
- building, 323-326
  - headers, 326
  - instances, 326
  - window state, 327
- code blocks, 11
- commenting, 16
- creating, 9-12, 322-323
- developing, 12-14
- DOS, 7
- executing, 66
- files, compiling, 14
- finite state machines, 713-715
- header files, 10
- Hello World, 9-12
- include files, 10
- input/output, 10-11
- namespaces, std, 11
- objects, linking, 14-15
- PDL, 12-14
- pseudocode, 12-14
- source code, 14
- streams, 10-11
- tokens, 12
- UNIX, 7
- Windows
  - creating, 7
  - Visual C++, 322-323

Project menu command, Add to Project, 8
projectiles, gravity, 745-748
projects
- creating, 322-323
- files, 8
- MFC AppWizard (dll), 7
- MFC AppWizard (exe), 7
- setting up, 6-8
- tools, 7
- Win32 API, 322
- Win32 Application, 7
- Win32 Console Application, 7
- Win32 Dynamic-Link Library, 7
- Win32 Static Library, 7

Projects tab (New dialog box), 6
properties
- mrABO class, 505-506
- mrJoystick class, 560-561
- mrMouse class, 544-546

protected classes, 159-160
protected keyword, 159-160
pseudocode, 12-14

public classes, 159, 285-288
public keyword, 159
publishers, 853-854
publishing games
  bug reports, 856-857
  contracts, 854-856
  marketability, 852-853
  milestones, 856-857
  NDAs, 855
  publishers, 853-854
  references, 861
  royalties, 856
  self-publishing, 857
Pulse Code Modulation (PCM), 577
put function, 251-252

Q

QueryPerformanceCounter function, 313-314
QueryPerformanceFrequency function, 311-312
queues, messages, 322
quick sorts, 651-655
QuickSortInt function, 653
quotation marks (""), 10

R

radians
  angles, 662-664
  circles, 662-664
RAM (random access memory), 26
rand function, 80-83
random motion algorithm, 707-709
random-access data structures, 612
randomizing numbers, 80-83
RandomLeap function, 218
rasterizing lines, 433-437
  Cartesian plane, 435
  deltas, 437
read function, 267-268, 461-462
Read function, 200-201, 212
ReadConsole function, 212
reading binary streams, 267-268
read-only memory (ROM), 26
real-time loops, 336-341
rectangles (collision detection), 426-427
recursive functions, 64-66
recursive structures, 624
Red Bull, 519
red-black trees, 647
references, games, 861
register keyword, 35-36
RegisterClass function, 331
registers (variables), 35-36
reinterpret casting, 180
relational operators, 42-43
relative mode, 530-532
relative positions, 788
release executables, 15
Release function, 572
releasing objects, 386-387
Remove function, 635, 638-646
RemoveChild function, 629
RemoveCurrentChild function, 628
RemoveCurrentItem function, 620-622
Render function, 304-305, 478, 496-497, 511, 775-778, 782-784
rendering. *See also* drawing
  mrABO class, 511
  mrAnimation class, 496-500
  mrSurface class, 478
  particle systems, 782-784
  particles, 775-778
  polygons, 401-410
  render states
    mrScreen class, 447-448
    polygons, 406
  surfaces, 389-396
  textures, 401-410
  windows, 385
resolution, 378-379
resulted forces (physics), 740-741
returning values, 12
RLE (Run-Length Encoding), 657-659
RLECompressIng function, 658-659
ROM (read-only memory), 26
root function, 629
Rotate function, 305, 517

rotating
- images, 430-433
- mrABO class, 517-518
- polygons, 497-498

rows (matrices), 678
royalties, 856
rules
- Breaking Through game, 793
- Craps game, 84
- Monster game, 215-216

Run function, 302, 343
Run-Length Encoding (RLE), 657-659

S

Save function, 274
SaveGame function, 847
saving games, 270-277
scalars, 668, 673
scaling images, 429-430
scope, variables, 60-63
scores, player, 216-218
screens
- clearing, 201, 208-210
- coordinates, 208-209
- Direct3D
  - backbuffering, 447-448
  - bitdepth, 456-457
  - clearing, 372-376
  - color, 378-379
  - constructor, 442
  - cursors, 456
  - destructor, 443
  - developing, 439-458
  - drawing, 450-453
  - formats, 446-447
  - frames, 448-449
  - initializing, 442-443
  - render states, 447-448
  - resolution, 378-379
  - screen modes, 444-445, 454-455
- full screen mode, 379-380
- functionality, 303
- game design, 217
- handles, 200, 202-203
- output, 11
- windowed mode, 379-380

Search function, 635-637
searching nodes, 635-637
seeds (numbers), 83
seekg function, 268-269, 461-463
seekp function, 269
self-publishing games, 857
semicolon (line-ending token), 12
sequential data structures, 612
service packs (Visual C++), 345
Set Active Configuration command (Build menu), 15
Set Active Project Configuration dialog box, 15
SetActiveTexture function, 305, 488
SetBackgroundColor function, 200-201, 204-207
SetColor function, 516
SetColorKey function, 508-509
SetConsole function, 221
SetConsoleCursorPosition function, 211
SetConsoleTextAttribute function, 205-207
SetConsoleTitle function, 208
SetCooperativeLevel function, 532, 543, 574
SetCurrentAnimation function, 511
SetCurrentFrame function, 501
SetDataFormat function, 530-532, 543
SetImageBuffer function, 461
SetMode function, 444-445
SetModeClear function, 303
SetPosition function, 200-201, 210-211, 272-273, 351-352, 516
SetProperty function, 544-546, 560-561
SetRadius function, 516
SetRawImage function, 474
SetRenderState function, 406, 447-448
sets
- intersecting, 690-691
- probability, 689

SetSize function, 354, 516, 802
SetTextColor function, 200-201, 207
SetTexture function, 408

SetTextureState function, 406-407
setting
  buffers, 130-131
  cursors, 201, 210-211
setting up
  Direct3D, 377-384
  DirectInput, 523
  Visual C++, 5
    files, 8-9
    projects, 6-8
    workspaces, 5-6
SetTitle function, 200-201, 208
SetupDirect3D function, 377-384
SetVolume function, 306, 584
SetWindowLong function, 347-348
SetWindowPos function, 351-352, 354
SetWindowText function, 345-346
shift operators, 41-42
short keyword, 28-29
Show function, 221, 231-232, 355
ShowCursor function, 303, 456
ShowExit function, 230-231
ShowGame function, 227-228
ShowHelp function, 70
ShowLost function, 230
ShowLostLife function, 229-230
ShowWindow function, 345, 355
ShowWon function, 229
signed keyword, 28-29
signed variables, 28
Simonyi, Charles, 291
Simulate function, 761-763, 768, 775, 781-782
simulating
  collisions, 756-763
  particle systems, 781-782
  particles, 775
sin function, 666
sines
  angle relations, 666-667
  look-up tables, 114-116
  triangles, 664-666
single quotes (ASCII conversion characters), 210
singletons, 186-189
  advantages, 303, 316
singly linked lists, 613-615
size
  arrays, 109, 122-126, 151
  functions, 134
  images, 429-430
  streams, 278
  strings, 135-136, 171
  surfaces, 392-393
  textures, 403
  variables, 30, 48
  vectors, 674, 676
  windows, 345, 354
size t parameter, 134
size of operator, 48
slope
  lines, 433
  physics, 752
Smugglers game, 857-859
sorting data
  bubble sorts, 648-651
  comparison, 655-656
  declining iterations, 650
  quick sorts, 651-655
  swap counters, 649
sound
  amplitude, 568
  CD players, 306-307
  cycles, 568
  digital, 569
  DirectSound, 569-570
  frequency, 568
  functionality, 306
  managers, 186
  MCI, 586-587
  mrCDPlayer class, 588-593
  mrSound class
    audio blocks, 583
    buffers, 580-582
    defining, 575-576
    developing, 575-586
    implementing, 576-579
    locking, 582-583
    playing, 584-585
    volume, 584

sound *(continued)*
mrSoundPlayer class
cooperative levels, 574
defining, 571-572
developing, 571-575
implementing, 572
initializing, 573
PCM, 577
synthesized, 569
theory, 568-569
waveforms, 569
waves, 568
Sound component (Mirus), 306-307
source code, 14
source files, 96-99
speed (physics), 732
splay trees, 647
sprintf function, 145-147
Square function, 55
srand function, 83
Standard Template Library (STL), 611
Start function, 627
StartFrame function, 303, 448-449
starting points, vectors, 694
StartIterator function, 616
StartNewGame function, 221, 232-233
state
devices, 523-524
fuzzy logic, 715
games (universe problem), 707
mrJoystick class, 563-565
mrKeyboard class, 534-537
mrMouse class, 548-551
windows, 327
statements
break, 75, 80
code blocks, 66-67
conditional, 67-70
switch, 78-79
continue, 76-77
do…while, 72-73
else, 70
for, 73-75
game design, 284
if, 67-70
compared to switch, 78-79
switch, 77-80, 336
while, 70-72
states
finite state machines, 713-715
render. *See* render states
static casting, 180-181
static friction, 751-752
static keyword, 185
static libraries, 7
static members, 185
static variables, 62-63
status
games, 220-221
streams, 256-258
std namespace, 11
stdlib.h header file, 83
STL (Standard Template Library), 611
Stop function, 306-307, 585
storing variables, 27
strcat function, 136-138
strchr function, 140-142
strcmp function, 169-170
strcomp function, 138-140
strcpy function, 133-134, 169
streams
binary, 246-247
markers, 268-269
reading, 267-268
writing, 264-267
closing, 253, 255-258
defined, 10-11
EOF, 250
extraction operator (>>), 251
file streams, 253
I/O, 247-253
input, 247-251
output, 251-253
insertion operator (<<), 252-253
memory, 278
opening, 253-255, 257-258
overview, 246
size, 278

status, 256-258
text, 246-247, 259-264
strftime function, 147-150
strings
arguments, 145-147
arrays, 131-132
classes
constructors, 167-168
declaring, 167
destructors, 168
headers, 166-167
operators, 167-171
using, 171-172
command-line arguments, 327
comparing, 138-143, 169-170
concatenating, 136-138
converting
floating-point numbers, 145
integers, 143-144
long values, 145
copying, 133-135, 169
extraction operator, 151
I/O, 132-133, 201, 211-212
new character (\n), 11
NULL-terminating character (\0), 131-132
pointers, 132
size, 135-136, 171
time, 147-150
strips (primitives), 409-410
strlen function, 135-136, 171
strncat function, 138
strncomp function, 140
strncpy function, 134-135
strstr function, 142-143
structures
D3DPRESENT PARAMETERS, 381-382
DIDDATAFORMAT, 530
DIOBJECTDATAFORMAT, 530-532
DIPROPHEADER, 545-546, 560
DIPROPWORD, 546
DSBUFFERDESC, 580-582
fractal, 624
INPUT RECORD, 212-215
LPCREATESTRUCT, 347
LPWAVEFORMATEX, 581
MSG, 335, 338
POINT, 353
recursive, 624
SIJOYSTATE2, 563
tm, 148, 313
WAVEFORMATEX, 579-580
WNDCLASS, 328-331
cbClsExtra field, 328
cbWndExtra field, 328
hbrBackGround field, 330-331
hCursor field, 329-330
hIcon field, 329
hInstance field, 328
lpfnWndProc field, 328
lpszClassName field, 331
lpszMenuName field, 330
style field, 328
styles (windows), 328
subtracting
matrices, 681-682
vectors, 671-673
support, legacy, 319
surfaces, 387-388
back buffering, 396
clearing, 384-385
color, 394
Direct3D
constructor, 473-474
defining, 472-473
destructor, 473-474
developing, 472-479
filling, 476-477
locking, 475
pointers, 475-476
rendering, 478
images, 304
locking, 391-392
pitch, 392-393
pointers, 393-394
rendering, 389-396
size, 392-393

swap chains, 388-389
swap counters, 649
SwapEffect keyword, 382
swapping matrices, 685-686
switch statement, 77-80, 336
Synchronize function, 807
syntax. *See* code
synthesized sound, 569
systems
crashes, 109
expert, 698-700
knowledge trees, 699
requirements, 792-793

T

tables
look-up, 114-116
matrices, 678
virtual, 365
tan function, 77, 666
tangents, 77, 664-667
angle relations, 666-667
look-up tables, 114-116
triangles, 664-666
Targa files
loading, 421-422
mrRGBAImage class, 465-472
structure, 420-421
tellg function, 269
tellp function, 269
template sets
animation, 422-424
developing, 488-493
mrABO class, 509
templates
design document, 602-603
STL, 611
template sets
animation, 422-424
developing, 488-493
mrABO class, 509
textures, 304-305
ternary operators, 43
text
characters
ASCII conversion, 210
variables, 28
color, 201-207
I/O (ConLib class)
constructor, 202-203
defining, 199-202
destructor, 202-203
header, 199-202
implementing, 202-215
overview, 198
streams, 246-247, 259-264
textures, 398-400
coordinates, 399-400
Direct3D
constructor, 481-482
defining, 480-481
destructor, 481-482
developing, 480-488
images, 304-305, 371
locking, 404
mrABO class, 508-509
rendering, 401-410
size, 403
theory
color, 416-418
sound, 568-569
this pointer, 166
time
physics, 729
strings, 147-150
time function, 83
time.h header file, 83
title bars, 329
titles (windows), 345-346
tm structure, 148, 313
tools, 7
top down game design, 281-282
torque (physics), 739-740
tracking algorithm, 709-710
Transform function, 688
transformed vertices, 519
transforming vectors, 688

TranslateMessage function, 335, 339
translating images, 428-429
Transpose function, 685-686
transposing matrices, 685-686
traversing general trees, 630-632
trees
AVL, 647
binary, 633
BSTs, 624
advanced, 646-647
deleting nodes, 638-646
inserting nodes, 637-638
overview, 634-635
searching nodes, 635-637
using, 647-648
fractal structures, 624
general, 624
building, 629-630
destructors, 632
implementing, 625-629
nodes, 626
traversing, 630-632
using, 632
knowledge, 699
linked trees, 625
nodes, 624
overview, 624-625
parent-child relationship, 625
recursive structures, 624
red-black, 647
splay, 647
triangles
angle relations, 666-667
angles, 665-666
cosines, 664-667
fuzzy logic, 717
line length, 664-665
sines, 664-667
tangents, 664-667
trigonometry
angles, 662-664
circles, 662-664
cosines, 664-667
MacLaurin series, 665
overview, 662-664
radians, 662-664
sines, 664-667
tangents, 77, 664-667
angle relations, 666-667
look-up tables, 114-116
triangles, 664-666
troubleshooting
cells, flashing, 492
classes (debug mode), 186
code notation, 292-294
crashes, 109
DirectX, 377
error handling, 17-19
fatal errors, 19
executables (Notepad), 22
functions, 66
game design
assignment operator, 283
code blocks, 284
equality operator, 283
inline functions, 284-285
macros, 284-285
modules, 288-289
naming conventions, 289-292
private classes, 285-288
public classes, 285-288
statements, 284
games, loading, 276
#include directive, 101
memory managers, 123
variables, 60
warnings, 20-22
windows, 345
true value, 48
types
data, 27-30
defining, 96
enumerated, 380-381
HRESULT, 377
int, 326
primitives, 409-410
return types, 55
variables, redefining, 36

U

Unacquire function, 529
unary mathematical operators, 38-39
unbuffered data, 523-524
#undef directive, 105
union keyword, 183-184
unions
classes, 183-184
probability, 689-690
universe problem, 707
UNIX applications, 7
Unlock function, 583
UnlockRect function, 395
unsigned char keyword, 28-29
unsigned int keyword, 29
unsigned keyword, 28-29
unsigned long keyword, 29
unsigned short keyword, 29
unsigned short parameter, 205
unsigned variables, 28
Update function, 301, 304-305, 307-308, 311, 474, 483, 496, 511-512, 533, 808
user events, 201, 212-215
using
BSTs, 647-648
classes, 158
CString class, 171-172
friction, 753-755
general trees, 632
Mirus, 316
mrKeyboard class, 538-541
windows, 350-351

V

values
Boolean, 210
damping, 762
false, 48
long, 145
matrices, 678
membership (fuzzy logic), 715-717
returning, 12
true, 48
variables, 77-80
vectors, 667
variables
arrays, 108
declaring, 109
functions, 120-122
implementing, 109-112
initializing, 112
memory, 122-126
multidimensional, 112-116
size, 109, 122-126, 151
automatic, 63
characters, 28
constants, 33-35
COORD, 208-209
data types, 27-30
declaring, 30-31
DWORD, 208-209
exponents, 28
floating-point numbers, 28
global, 61-62
defining, 96
handles, 201
I/O, 31-32
initializing, 32-33
integers, 28
local, 61
mantissas, 28
memory, 27
naming, 36, 60, 290-291
pointers, 116
arrays, 119-122
declaring, 117
implementing, 117-119
initializing, 117
operators, 126-129
PointerValues, 128-129
registers, 35-36
scope, 60-63
signed, 28

size, 30, 48
static, 62-63
storing, 27
troubleshooting, 60
types, redefining, 36
union keyword, 183-184
unsigned, 28
values, 77-80
windows, 345

vectors
adding, 671-673
angles, 676
dividing, 673
dot products, 676-677
Euclidean space, 667
multiplying, 673
normalizing, 674-675
n-tuples, 667
orientation, 668
overview, 667-671
perp-dot products, 677
perpendicular, 675-676
scalars, 668
size, 674
starting points, 694
subtracting, 671-673
transforming, 688
values, 667

velocity
mathematical functions, 693
particles, 778-780
physics, 731-732
angular, 732
linear, 731-732
speed, 732

vertex buffers, 371
vertices, 397-398. *See also* lines
coordinates, 401
polygons, 405
transformed, 519

video cards, 380
viewing windows, 355
virtual classes, 343
virtual functions, 174-178
virtual tables, 365
Visual C++
DirectX interaction, 366-367
Linux compatibility, 22
service packs, 345
setting up, 5
files, 8-9
projects, 6-8
workspaces, 5-6
Windows applications, 322-323

void parameter, 56
void SetColorKey function, 304
volume (mrSound class), 584
volumes, bounding, 424-425

W

warnings, 20-22
WAVEFORMATEX structure, 579-580
waveforms, 569
waves, 568
Web sites
Microsoft, 345
Niels Bauer Software Design, 859
Smugglers 2, 859
Xtreme Games LLC, 859

weight (physics), 729
while loops, 70-72
while statements, 70-72
Width parameter, 56
Win32 API projects, 322
Win32 Application projects, 7
Win32 Console Application dialog box, 7
Win32 Console Application projects, 7
Win32 Dynamic-Link Library projects, 7
Win32 Static Library projects, 7
WINAPI keyword, 326
Window component (Mirus), 302
window procedure. *See* message handler
windowed mode, 379-380

windows
Breaking Through game, 848-850
building, 323-326
background, 330-331
class names, 331, 345
CreateWindow function, 332-334
cursors, 329-330
handles, 332
headers, 326
instances, 326, 328
menus, 330
message handlers, 328
state, 327
styles, 328
title bar icons, 329
WNDCLASS, 328-331
clearing, 384-385
creating, 302
Direct3D
creating, 372-387
rendering, 385
full screen mode, 379-380
message handlers, 335-336
message loops, 334-335
Mirus
header, 342-344
hiding, 355
message handling, 346-349
naming, 345
position, 351-353
size, 345, 354
titles, 345-346
using, 350-351
variables, 345
naming, 208
output, 17
real-time loops, 336-341
troubleshooting, 345
windowed mode, 379-380
Windows, 319-320
Windows
API, 322
applications. *See* programs
bitmaps
loading, 413-414
structure, 411-413
history, 318-319
legacy support, 319
message queues, 322
multitasking, 321
windows, 319-320
Windows API/DirectX comparison, 360-361
windows.h header, 200, 326
WinMain function, 326
WM NCCREATE message, 345
WNDCLASS structure, 328-331
cbClsExtra field, 328
cbWndExtra field, 328
hbrBackGround field, 330-331
hCursor field, 329-330
hIcon field, 329
hInstance field, 328
lpfnWndProc field, 328
lpszClassName field, 331
lpszMenuName field, 330
style field, 328
WndProc function, 302
WORD parameter, 205
workspaces, 5-6
Workspaces tab (New dialog box), 5
write function, 264-267, 277
WriteConsole function, 211
writing binary streams, 264-267

X

Xtreme Games LLC, 859-861

Z

Zero function, 684
zero matrices, 684
ZeroMemory function, 382

License Agreement/Notice of Limited Warranty

By opening the sealed disc container in this book, you agree to the following terms and conditions. If, upon reading the following license agreement and notice of limited warranty, you cannot agree to the terms and conditions set forth, return the unused book with unopened disc to the place where you purchased it for a refund.

License:

The enclosed software is copyrighted by the copyright holder(s) indicated on the software disc. You are licensed to copy the software onto a single computer for use by a single user and to a backup disc. You may not reproduce, make copies, or distribute copies or rent or lease the software in whole or in part, except with written permission of the copyright holder(s). You may transfer the enclosed disc only together with this license, and only if you destroy all other copies of the software and the transferee agrees to the terms of the license. You may not decompile, reverse assemble, or reverse engineer the software.

Notice of Limited Warranty:

The enclosed disc is warranted by Premier Press, Inc. to be free of physical defects in materials and workmanship for a period of sixty (60) days from end user's purchase of the book/disc combination. During the sixty-day term of the limited warranty, Premier Press will provide a replacement disc upon the return of a defective disc.

Limited Liability:

THE SOLE REMEDY FOR BREACH OF THIS LIMITED WARRANTY SHALL CONSIST ENTIRELY OF REPLACEMENT OF THE DEFECTIVE DISC. IN NO EVENT SHALL PREMIER PRESS OR THE AUTHORS BE LIABLE FOR ANY OTHER DAMAGES, INCLUDING LOSS OR CORRUPTION OF DATA, CHANGES IN THE FUNCTIONAL CHARACTERISTICS OF THE HARDWARE OR OPERATING SYSTEM, DELETERIOUS INTERACTION WITH OTHER SOFTWARE, OR ANY OTHER SPECIAL, INCIDENTAL, OR CONSEQUENTIAL DAMAGES THAT MAY ARISE, EVEN IF PREMIER AND/OR THE AUTHORS HAVE PREVIOUSLY BEEN NOTIFIED THAT THE POSSIBILITY OF SUCH DAMAGES EXISTS.

Disclaimer of Warranties:

PREMIER AND THE AUTHORS SPECIFICALLY DISCLAIM ANY AND ALL OTHER WARRANTIES, EITHER EXPRESS OR IMPLIED, INCLUDING WARRANTIES OF MERCHANTABILITY, SUITABILITY TO A PARTICULAR TASK OR PURPOSE, OR FREEDOM FROM ERRORS. SOME STATES DO NOT ALLOW FOR EXCLUSION OF IMPLIED WARRANTIES OR LIMITATION OF INCIDENTAL OR CONSEQUENTIAL DAMAGES, SO THESE LIMITATIONS MIGHT NOT APPLY TO YOU.

Other:

This Agreement is governed by the laws of the State of Indiana without regard to choice of law principles. The United Convention of Contracts for the International Sale of Goods is specifically disclaimed. This Agreement constitutes the entire agreement between you and Premier Press regarding use of the software.